THE BOLSHEVIK REVOLUTION
1917–1923

A HISTORY OF SOVIET RUSSIA
by Edward Hallett Carr
in Norton Paperback Editions

The Bolshevik Revolution, 1917–1923 (I)

The Bolshevik Revolution, 1917–1923 (II)

The Bolshevik Revolution, 1917–1923 (III)

THE BOLSHEVIK REVOLUTION
1917-1923

BY

EDWARD HALLETT CARR

★

VOLUME THREE

W. W. NORTON & COMPANY
New York · London

Printed in the United States of America

First published as a Norton paperback 1985
by arrangement with The Macmillan Company, New York

W. W. Norton & Company, Inc., 500 Fifth Avenue,
New York, N.Y. 10110
W. W. Norton & Company Ltd., 37 Great Russell Street,
London WC1B 3NU

ISBN 0-393-30199-0

1 2 3 4 5 6 7 8 9 0

PREFACE

THE publication of this volume completes the first instalment of my study of the history of Soviet Russia. The three volumes together purport to describe the essential elements of the Bolshevik revolution down to the first consolidation of its power in the winter of 1922–1923. By this time the first wave of economic recovery following the introduction of NEP in 1921 and the excellent harvest of 1922 had reached its height; new agrarian, labour and civil codes promised legal stability; substantial progress had been made towards the establishment of diplomatic and commercial relations with foreign countries; and the Communist International no longer occupied the centre of the stage. The régime had come to stay. For the first time since 1917 a sense of security had begun to dawn. And it was at the moment when the worst obstacles seemed to have been finally surmounted that Lenin was laid low. His withdrawal from the scene marks an appropriate, almost a dramatic, stopping-place. The hazards that lay ahead belong to a fresh period.

The main difficulty of arrangement which I have encountered in writing this third volume has been to keep simultaneously in view the many-coloured but interconnected strands of Soviet Russia's relations with the outside world. Neatness can be achieved by treating Soviet relations with Europe and Soviet relations with Asia in water-tight compartments, or by making a sharp division between the activities of Narkomindel and of Comintern. But it is achieved at the cost of sacrificing the complexity and confusion of the authentic picture and at the risk of encouraging dogmatic opinions about the primary importance of this or that aspect of Soviet policy. I have therefore tried so far as possible to arrange my material in such a way as to interweave the different strands and to make clear the inner connexions between them. By way of exception to the general plan, I have reserved Soviet relations with the Far East for the last two chapters of the volume, since, owing to the civil war and the persistence of Japanese military intervention in Siberia, the Far East entered into the general stream of Soviet policy at a considerably later date than Europe, or than the rest of Asia. As in the two previous volumes, the exact point in time at which I have brought the narrative to a close has varied according to the exigencies of the subject-matter. Relations with European countries have, as a rule, not been carried beyond the end of 1922, since the French occupation of the Ruhr in January 1923 started a new train of events throughout Europe. On the other hand, the proceedings of the Lausanne conference have been followed down to their conclusion in the summer of 1923 ; and the natural terminus for the Far Eastern chapters was the end of the Joffe mission and the arrival of Karakhan in August 1923.

The collection of the copious but scattered material for the volume has been in itself a major task, and there are doubtless valuable sources which I have overlooked or failed to find. The archives and libraries of the Soviet Union being still virtually closed to independent research, the richest store of available material for Soviet history is to be found in the United States. In 1951 I paid a further visit to the United States at the kind invitation of the Johns Hopkins University, Baltimore, where I delivered a series of lectures on German-Soviet relations between 1919 and 1939. I was also able on this occasion to consult Soviet material in the Library of Congress, in the New York Public Library, and in the library of Columbia University. Unfortunately time did not allow me to revisit the richest and most comprehensive of all collections of Soviet material outside Soviet Russia — the Hoover Institute and Library at Stanford ; I am, however, under a special debt to Mrs. O. H. Gankin of the Hoover Library for the unfailing generosity and patience with which she has answered my numerous enquiries, and for her mastery of the vast stores of material collected there.

I have also particular obligations to a number of writers, scholars and research workers in the United States, some of them personal friends, others not known to me personally, who have most generously given me access to material or information in their possession and helped me to fill important gaps in my knowledge. Mr. Gustav Hilger, for many years counsellor of the German Embassy in Moscow and now resident in Washington, drew on his personal recollections for many significant items in the history of German-Soviet relations ; his memoirs, already announced for publication, will be an indispensable source for future historians. Mr. G. W. F. Hallgarten allowed me to read his notes of documents found in the captured German military archives now in Washington. Professor Owen Lattimore of the Johns Hopkins University put at my disposal published and unpublished Mongolian material in English translation, and gave me the benefit of his unique knowledge of Mongol affairs. Mr. Rodger Swearingen and Mr. Paul Langer communicated to me a large amount of material from Japanese sources on the history of Japanese communism which may now be found in their book, *Red Flag in Japan: International Communism in Action, 1919-1951*, published in the United States since the present volume went to press. Mr. A. S. Whiting of Northwestern University showed me the manuscript of his thesis on Soviet-Chinese relations between 1917 and 1922 which will shortly be published, and also drew my attention to the discrepancies in the records of the second congress of Comintern noted on page 252 (notes 3 and 4). Mr. George Kahin of Cornell University gave me valuable information drawn from local sources about the early development of communism in Indonesia. A friend who wishes to remain anonymous made available to me the unpublished German-Soviet diplomatic correspondence quoted on pages 94 (note 4), 95 (note 1), and 325 (notes 1 and 3). Finally, Mr. William Appleman Williams of the University of Oregon came to my aid at a late stage in my work by sending me illuminating extracts from the unpublished papers of Raymond Robins and Alex Gumberg, as well as notes taken by him from the National Archives of the United States, together with a part of the manuscript of his book *American-Russian Relations 1781–1947*, which has been published in the United States during the present autumn. But for the help so widely and so generously accorded, the volume would have lacked even that imperfect degree of balance and comprehensiveness to which it may now pretend. Many of those whose names I have cited, and to whom I tender this inadequate expression of my thanks, would differ widely from me and from one another in their interpretation of the events under discussion ; that mutual aid is not hampered by such divergences is an encouraging symptom of the independence which true scholarship always seeks to preserve and uphold.

I have once more received valuable assistance from nearly all those in this country whose help was gratefully acknowledged in the prefaces to the two previous volumes ; and to their names should be added those of Professor V. Minorsky, who helped me with expert advice on Central Asian matters in both the first and the third volumes ; of Mr. V. Wolpert who kindly let me see the unfinished manuscript of his study on the World Federation of Trade Unions, to be published under the auspices of the Royal Institute of International Affairs, and read the parts of my manuscript relating to the foundation of Profintern ; and of Mr. F. L. Carsten, who lent me a number of rare pamphlets and periodicals throwing light on the history of German communism. Mr. Isaac Deutscher again read a substantial part of my manuscript and made penetrating criticisms ; and Mrs. Jane Degras, who had already placed me in her debt by her ready and expert help in my constant search for material, undertook to read the whole text in proof and thus saved me from many errors and misprints. I have once more been under a heavy obligation to the devoted and efficient staffs of the libraries of the London School of Economics and of the Royal Institute of International Affairs.   Mindful of my own difficulties in running my sources to earth, I have endeavoured to increase the practical utility of a necessarily incomplete and selective bibliography by indicating where the volumes there listed can be found, if they are not in the British Museum ; Mr. J. C. W. Horne of the British Museum was good enough to check the bibliography for me with the Museum catalogue.   Last (for obvious reasons), but by no means least, Dr. Ilya Neustadt of University College, Leicester, has earned my very warm thanks by undertaking the arduous task of compiling the index for the three volumes.

The completion of *The Bolshevik Revolution 1917–1923* has naturally led me to survey the prospects of the larger work for which it is intended to be the prelude.   Though I am perhaps in a better position than ever before to appreciate the strength of the now popular argument in favour of collective enterprise in the writing of modern history, I am not without hope, if I can count on the same support from so many helpers as I have hitherto found, of being able to carry on my independent task.   I have already done much research, and some writing, for the next instalment, and hope that I may complete a further volume next year, though I have not yet reached a final conclusion about its scope, arrangement and title.

E. H. CARR

October 20, 1952

CONTENTS

PART V

SOVIET RUSSIA AND THE WORLD

PART V

SOVIET RUSSIA AND THE WORLD

FROM OCTOBER TO BREST-LITOVSK

" THE social-democratic movement ", wrote Lenin at the beginning of his career, " is international in its very essence." [1] It was international in two senses. The French revolution had introduced and popularized the view of revolution as a phenomenon which defied frontiers, so that it was both the right and the duty of revolutionaries to carry to other countries the torch of liberation which they had kindled in their own ; this was the origin of the conception of the revolutionary war. The revolution of 1848 had not been limited to one country, but had spread by process of contagion all over Europe as far as the boundaries of Russia. It was taken for granted that the socialist revolution would follow this pattern and, having achieved victory in one country, would quickly spread, partly by process of contagion and partly through the deliberate action of the revolutionaries themselves, all over Europe and, eventually, all over the world. But social-democracy was international also in another sense. " National differences and antagonisms between peoples ", declared the *Communist Manifesto*, " are daily vanishing more and more. . . . The supremacy of the proletariat will cause them to vanish still faster." The battle-cry of the social-democratic movement was " Workers of all countries, unite ! " Its programme was to break down national barriers " in order to open the way for division of a different kind, division by classes ".[2] Allegiance to class must, as Lenin insisted, always take precedence over allegiance to nation.[3] In virtue of this principle Lenin in 1914 unequivocally proclaimed " the transformation of the present imperialist war into a civil war ". As early as October 1915 he contemplated the possibility that the proletarian revolution might

---

[1] Lenin, *Sochineniya*, iv, 380.   [2] Stalin, *Sochineniya*, ii, 362.
[3] For specific assertions of this principle by Lenin see Vol. 1, p. 426.

break out first in backward Russia. In that event, a Russian proletarian government would have the task of completing the bourgeois democratic revolution at home, of raising the slogan of a democratic peace (which the bourgeois democratic governments of Europe would be unable to accept), and of stirring up national revolutions in Asia against the imperialist Powers. Thus the way would be prepared for the socialist revolution not only in Europe, but in Russia as well.[1]

When Lenin reached Petrograd on April 3, 1917, the question of war and peace was already acute. The overthrow of the Tsar and the establishment of a democratic government was regarded both by the Provisional Government and by the SR and Menshevik majority in the Petrograd Soviet as a justification for support of the war effort in the name of the defence of the revolution. The majority of the Soviet differed from the first Provisional Government, in which Milyukov was Minister for Foreign Affairs, only in insisting on an active campaign for a " democratic " peace " without annexations or indemnities ". Most of the Bolsheviks in Petrograd took the same line ; Kamenev had come out openly for national defence.[2] Lenin devoted the first of his ten " April theses " to the subject. He began by emphasizing that the Provisional Government was a capitalist government, and that its advent to power had not changed the character of the war on the part of Russia as " a robber imperialist war " : no concession to " revolutionary defencism " was therefore permissible. But the positive recommendations were cautious : a campaign to convince the still deluded masses of " the indissoluble link between capital and the imperialist war ", organization of propaganda in the army, and " fraternization ".[3] Ten days later at the Petrograd party conference he proposed a long and detailed resolution on the war, which reiterated the attack on " revolutionary defencism ", but contained passages obviously designed to placate critics and waverers. It admitted that " it would be completely senseless to suppose that the war can be ended by a unilateral refusal of the soldiers of *any one* country to continue the war, by a unilateral cessation of military action, a simple ' sticking of bayonets into

---

[1] Marx's views on war and Lenin's subsequent development of them before 1917 are discussed in Note E : " The Marxist Attitude to War ".

[2] See Vol. I, p. 75.   [3] Lenin, *Sochineniya*, xx, 87-88.

the ground ' ". The draft resolution invited the conference to
" protest yet again and again against the base slander spread by
the capitalists against our party that we are in favour of a separate
peace with Germany ". The German emperor was just as much
a " crowned robber " as Nicholas II or any of the allied monarchs.
A declaration in the party journal *Sotsial-Demokrat* of October
1915 was quoted to show that the party, if it obtained power,
intended at once to propose a democratic peace " to Germany
and *all the nations together* ". The draft resolution endorsed this
declaration, and added that " until the majority of the people . . .
understand the indissoluble link between the present war and the
interests of the capitalists, there is only one way to hasten the
cessation of the slaughter of peoples ". This way was fraternization at the front, and the purpose of such fraternization was to
bring about a complete transfer of state power, both in Germany
and in Russia, into the hands of Soviets of Workers' and Soldiers'
Deputies.[1] The draft resolution seems to have been shelved by
the conference, and was re-submitted by Lenin to the all-Russian
party conference (the so-called " April conference ") at the end
of the same month.

Before this conference met, the situation had been further
complicated by the visit to Petrograd during the second half of
April 1917 of a Danish socialist named Borgbjerg, who brought
an invitation to the executive committee of the Petrograd Soviet
to send representatives to an international socialist conference at
Stockholm to discuss peace terms. Two patriotic German
social-democrats, Scheidemann and Ebert, saw Borgbjerg, with
the approval of the German Government, before he left Copenhagen ; and the terms which they were prepared to support were
reported to include the evacuation by Germany of territories
occupied by her, a frontier rectification in Lorraine and cultural
autonomy for German Poland. The SR and Menshevik majority
in the Soviet, as well as some Bolsheviks, were ready to welcome
these overtures. At the Bolshevik " April conference " Lenin
treated the German proposals as showing that the situation in
Germany was desperate, and denounced Borgbjerg as an agent of
the German bourgeoisie and the proposed Stockholm conference

[1] *Ibid.* xx, 186-190 ; for the declaration of October 1915 see p. 563
below.

as a comedy.[1] Having thus disposed of the imputation of favouring separate negotiations with Germany, Lenin returned to
the question of the war, presenting a slightly amended version
of his draft resolution which had been worked out in a commission
of the conference. The resolution, which was adopted by the
conference unanimously with 7 abstentions, began by emphasizing
the capitalist character of the imperialist war and demanding " the
publication and abrogation of all secret robber treaties ". Its
second section denounced " revolutionary defencism ". Its third
section proclaimed that " this war can be ended with a democratic
peace *only* by means of a transfer of all state power in at least
several of the belligerent countries into the hands of the proletarians and semi-proletarians ". It repeated the programme
originally sketched out by Lenin in 1915, i.e. the immediate offer
to all the belligerents of a " democratic peace ". But it avoided
the overt proclamation of defeatism by taking it for granted, in so
many words, that " these measures and the public offer of peace
would bring about complete confidence of the workers of the
belligerent countries in one another and inevitably lead to risings
of the proletariat against those imperialist governments which
were opposed to the proffered peace ". Thus revolutionary
propaganda and fraternization at the front were contemplated as
necessary only till such time as " the revolutionary class in Russia
should take all state power into its hands " ; for this act would be
automatically followed by the transfer of power to the proletariat
in other countries.[2] A conference of Bolshevik organizations in
the army meeting in July 1917 to protest against the July offensive
on the Galician front recorded the same view in almost identical
language : the passing of power to the Soviets would be followed
by an offer of peace to all the belligerents and this offer " would
inevitably lead to a rising of the proletariat against all imperialist
governments which opposed such a peace ".[3]

   Thus, throughout the period from April to October 1917, it was

---

[1] Lenin, *Sochineniya*, xx, 254-265 ; Lenin quoted the alleged German terms
from the Menshevik journal *Rabochaya Gazeta*. The resolution to reject
Borgbjerg's overture was carried by 140 votes with 8 abstentions (*VKP(B) v
Rezolyutsiyakh* (1941), i, 230-232).

[2] *VKP(B) v Rezolyutsiyakh* (1941), i, 227-228.

[3] *Ibid.* i, 242 ; as late as August 1917 Kamenev spoke in VTsIK in favour
of the Stockholm conference, and was severely censured by Lenin (Lenin,
Sochineniya, xxi, 78-79).

the spoken or unspoken assumption in the Bolshevik camp that the Bolshevik revolution in Russia, the ending of the war with a " democratic " peace, and the proletarian revolution in Europe were parts of a single process and in practice inseparable from one another. In an article in the party journal at the end of September 1917 Lenin faced for a moment a less favourable alternative :

> If the least probable should occur, i.e. if no belligerent state accepts even an armistice, then the war on our side will become a really necessary, really just and defensive war. The mere fact that the proletariat and the poorest peasantry will be conscious of this will make Russia many times stronger in the military respect, especially after a complete break with the capitalists who rob the people, not to mention that then the war on our side will be, not in words, but in fact, a war in alliance with the oppressed classes of all countries, a war in alliance with the oppressed peoples of the whole world.[1]

But even in this event Lenin certainly assumed that the declaration of such a war would by itself lead to an immediate revolution in the capitalist countries. This was the picture in Lenin's mind when he continued to court the possibility of " revolutionary war ". His inherent optimism and faith in the revolution prevented him from facing the contingency that the capitalist Powers might reject a " democratic " peace, and still be capable of turning their military strength against the forces of the revolution.

Propaganda for a democratic peace without annexations or indemnities proved highly embarrassing to the Provisional Government, which from May 1917 onwards included SRs and Mensheviks, and began to press the western allies more and more insistently for a definition of war aims. The immediate effect in Great Britain of the February revolution was to strengthen all the forces of the Left which the war had driven into temporary eclipse and, in particular, to stimulate the demand for a definition of " democratic " war aims.[2] The first serious debate on war

---

[1] *Ibid.* xxi, 224.

[2] British reactions are described by a careful American critic in these terms : " The western stalemate and the lack of success on other fronts postponed indefinitely any hope of victory, while the recent exchanges between the statesmen, however barren of immediate results, established an atmosphere favourable to peace discussions. Against this background the Russian revolution, recognized at the time as an event of primary historical importance, stimulated all forms of Left-wing activity and, indeed, ultimately helped to bring the trade

aims took place in the House of Commons on May 16, 1917, on
a motion of Snowden, then a spokesman of the Independent
Labour Party, calling for a declaration of aims on the lines of the
Russian formula of self-determination, no annexations and no
indemnities; and the motion secured 32 votes — a noteworthy
minority demonstration. The impact of the February revolution
on American opinion was no less striking. Though there is
nothing to suggest that it hastened the entry of the United States
into the war, it removed one of the serious obstacles which the
sponsors of this act would have had to face; [1] and it stimulated
the demand for a declaration of peace aims more precise and far
more " democratic " than the other allies had hitherto judged
expedient. The reluctance of the allies to accede to this demand,
and the refusal of the British and French Governments to allow
British or French socialists to attend the proposed peace conference at Stockholm (which fell through as a result of this refusal),
was damaging to the Provisonal Government and made it
highly vulnerable to Bolshevik attack. In the autumn of 1917
the international as well as the domestic omens seemed to Lenin
increasingly propitious. The decision of the party central committee to seize power, which was reached on October 10, 1917,
against the dissenting votes of Zinoviev and Kamenev, opened
with a reference to " the international situation of the Russian
revolution " as one of the factors which " put armed insurrection
on the agenda ". The " international situation " comprised both
" the insurrection in the German fleet as an extreme example of
the growth of the world socialist revolution all over Europe ",
and " the threat of peace between the imperialists in order to
stifle that revolution in Russia ".[2] At the further meeting of

unionists over to views hitherto monopolized by the socialist societies. For this
favourable reaction to the revolution nothing was more responsible than its
slogan of immediate peace on the basis of no annexations, no indemnities, and
the right of every people to control its own destinies " (Carl F. Brand, *British
Labor's Rise to Power* (Stanford, 1941), p. 90).

[1] Lansing thought that it " removed the last obstacle to viewing the war as
one for democracy and against absolutism " (S. F. Bemis, *American Secretaries
of State*, x (N.Y., 1928), 97); and H. Notter, *The Origins of the Foreign Policy
of Woodrow Wilson* (Baltimore, 1937), p. 639, cites references to numerous
statements by congressmen in this sense.

[2] *VKP(B) v Rezolyutsiyakh* (1941), i, 273 ; the record of the meeting of
October 10, 1917, is in *Protokoly Tsentral'nogo Komiteta RSDRP* (1929), pp. 98-
101.

October 16, 1917, Lenin referred once more to the mutiny in the German fleet and argued that " the international situation gives us a series of objective grounds for believing that if we come out now, we shall have all proletarian Europe on our side "; and it was Stalin who at the same meeting argued for " more faith " in the international situation, and formulated more clearly than anyone else the issue between Lenin on the one side and Kamenev and Zinoviev on the other :

> There are two lines : one sets the course for the victory of the revolution and relies on Europe, the second does not believe in the revolution and counts only on being an opposition.[1]

Reliance on Europe was a major premise of the victory of socialism in Russia. Lenin remained faithful to the two conditions, the one domestic, the other international, which he had laid down as early as 1905 for the transition to the socialist revolution : the alliance with the Russian peasantry and the support of a proletarian revolution in Europe. Nor in October 1917 did he seriously believe that the victorious revolution could survive in Russia unless both these conditions were quickly fulfilled. The two first acts of the Bolsheviks on their seizure of power — the land decree and the peace decree — were attempts to bring about their fulfilment.

The famous " decree on peace " — in reality, an appeal to the governments and peoples of the belligerent countries for the conclusion of a democratic peace — was the first act of foreign policy of the " provisional workers' and peasants' government ", adopted by the second All-Russian Congress of Soviets on October 26/ November 8, 1917, the day after the victorious revolution. The motive force behind it was in part domestic. In one sense the peace decree was as much an appeal to the peasant — the peasant in uniform — as the land decree itself. The régime was at this critical moment dependent on the support of the peasant masses, especially the mobilized peasant masses, whose outlook remained, in Marxist terminology, " petty bourgeois "; and, so long as this

---

[1] Lenin, *Sochineniya*, xxi, 331-332 ; Stalin, *Sochineniya*, iii, 381 ; the whole discussion is in *Protokoly Tsentral'nogo Komiteta RSDRP* (1929), pp. 111-124.

was so, the revolution could not throw off its bourgeois-democratic trappings. The masses, as Lenin wrote later, " worn out and tortured by a four years' war, wanted only peace and were not in a condition to put the question, ' Why war ? ' ".[1] Nor was Lenin thinking solely of the peasants. Before the end of the nineteenth century bourgeois radical pacifism had begun to tinge much of social-democratic thinking about war and peace, especially in Germany. Russian social-democrats had not escaped the contagion ; even many Bolsheviks, as the experience of April 1917 had shown, found it easier to think in these terms rather than in terms of peace through national defeat and social revolution. At the crucial moment of the seizure of power when the survival of the régime still hung by a thread, Lenin was bound to speak in terms which would rally the most, and shock the fewest, of his potential supporters. The peace decree was, however, primarily an act of foreign policy, and certainly contained an element of calculated appeal to American opinion and to such radical opinion in other countries as might be sympathetic to it. Lenin had predicted two years earlier that " neither Germany nor England nor France " could accept peace on the terms which the Bolsheviks would offer. But it was good policy to offer terms reasonable enough to make rejection embarrassing and compromising ; and the temptation was obvious to draft them in language as close as possible to that issuing from the other side of the Atlantic. The Soviet Government had inherited from the Provisional Government the tradition of a common interest between the United States and revolutionary Russia in the campaign for a democratic peace.

It thus came about that the peace decree approved by the second All-Russian Congress of Soviets on the morrow of the revolution was far more Wilsonian than Marxist in language and inspiration, and deserves to be regarded not as some remote descendant of the *Communist Manifesto*, but rather as the immediate precursor of the fourteen points issued just two months later ; indeed the part indirectly played by the declaration in inspiring Wilson's fourteen points speech is well attested.[2] It

[1] Lenin, *Sochineniya*, xxiii, 237.
[2] According to House, it was " because the American mission failed to secure from the inter-allied conference the manifesto on war aims that might serve to hold Russia in the war " that Wilson began on December 18, 1917 to consider " a comprehensive address by himself " (C. Seymour, *The Intimate Papers of*

was a proposal for the immediate conclusion of peace, addressed
" to all the belligerent peoples and their governments " and
broadcast throughout the world.   It demanded not a socialist,
but a " just, democratic " peace — a peace without annexations
or indemnities, a peace based on the right of self-determination
for all nations by " a free vote ".   It declared secret diplomacy
abolished, and announced the intention of the government to
publish the secret treaties of the past and conduct all future
negotiations " completely openly before the whole people ".
Nothing was said of capitalism as the cause of war or of socialism
as its cure.   The one faint hint of world revolution occurred in its
concluding sentence in which the workers of England, France and
Germany were invited to assist their Russian comrades " to bring
to a successful conclusion the work of peace and also the work of
liberating the labouring and exploited masses of the population
from every kind of slavery and exploitation ".   A resolution of the
second All-Russian Congress of Peasants' Deputies passed on
December 3/16, 1917, on the occasion of the armistice negotiations
with the central Powers did not even go so far.   It appealed to
" the peasants, workers and soldiers of Germany and Austria "
merely to " oppose an uncompromising resistance to the imperialist
demands of their governments and in this way to guarantee the most
rapid conclusion of a people's peace ".[1]   An eye-witness of the first
weeks of the revolution has vividly depicted the prevailing mood :

> From the balcony of the Foreign Office a great red banner
> was flying in the winter wind.   On it were inscribed the words,
> " Long Live Peace ! "   The whole atmosphere of the place
> gave the impression that the Russian revolutionaries had

Col. House, iii (1928), 324-325).   On January 3, 1918, Wilson received a telegram
from the American Ambassador in Petrograd urging a restatement of war aims
as a possible means of keeping Russia in the war.   The form of the fourteen
points was suggested by a telegram of January 3, 1918, from Sisson, representative of the American Public Relations Committee in Petrograd, who advised
Wilson to " re-state anti-imperialistic war aims and requisites of America, 1000
words or less, short almost placard paragraphs " (E. Sisson, *One Hundred Red
Days* (Yale, 1931), p. 205 ; G. Creel, *Rebel at Large* (N.Y., 1947), p. 168).

[1] Trotsky, *Sochineniya*, iii, ii, 204 ; the resolution was presumably drafted
by Trotsky since it is included in his collected works.   A few days later VTsIK
issued a further appeal " to the toiling masses of all countries " for " a peace of
the peoples, a peace of democracy, a just peace " ; but it added that " we shall
get such a peace only if the peoples of all countries dictate its terms by a revolutionary struggle " (*Protokoly Zasedanii VTsIK 2 Sozyva* (1918), p. 133).

seriously entered upon a struggle for peace. The phraseology of the class war had, temporarily at least, disappeared from Trotsky's vocabulary and had been replaced by the words: " International peace of peoples ".[1]

And Radek, in an official commemorative article five years later, could describe the aim of Soviet policy in these first moments in terms which made no mention at all of class or of revolution: " to arouse the popular masses in the allied countries in order that the governments, under pressure from the masses, might sit round the table with us for peace negotiations and thus lead to a general peace which would be more favourable to us ".[2]

Besides the offer of a democratic peace to all the belligerent nations, the only other item of foreign policy announced by the Bolsheviks in advance of their seizure of power was the abrogation and publication of the secret treaties. This pledge was repeated in the peace decree. The publication of the treaties in which the belligerent allies had agreed on the division of the future spoils of victory was regarded as a major task and achievement of Soviet diplomacy. Secret diplomacy had long been a favourite target for the attacks both of social-democrats and of bourgeois radicals. It had been condemned at the Copenhagen congress of the Second International in 1910; in Great Britain an influential radical group with pacifist leanings had created during the war a Union of Democratic Control, whose main plank was the suppression of secret diplomacy and popular control of foreign policy; in the United States the constitution was so framed as to preclude the acceptance of any international engagements not publicly ratified by the Senate. Thus the publication of the treaties, like the peace decree, was in one respect an appeal to American opinion and to radical opinion in allied countries over the heads of the allied governments, whose sinister bargains with one another and with the dethroned Tsarist régime were thus revealed to the world. Publication of the treaties concluded between 1914 and 1917 [3]

---

[1] M. Philips Price, *My Reminiscences of the Russian Revolution* (1921), p. 183.

[2] *Za Pyat' Let* (1922), p. 60 : this was a collection of articles issued by the central committee of the party to celebrate the fifth anniversary of the revolution.

[3] As Trotsky explained to VTsIK, these were not in fact " treaties written on parchment " but " diplomatic correspondence and coded telegrams exchanged between governments " (*Protokoly Zasedanii VTsIK 2 Sozvya* (1918), p. 42). The first and most sensational of the agreements published was the Anglo-

began in *Izvestiya* on November 10/23, 1917, and the documents were reprinted in pamphlets, seven of which were issued in rapid succession from December 1917 to February 1918. Thereafter many secret documents of the pre-revolutionary period of Russian diplomacy were also published. The first publication in English in the *Manchester Guardian* of December 12, 1917, stimulated the demand in British radical circles for a definition of peace aims. It created a sensation in the United States, and certainly influenced Wilson in the framing of the fourteen points on which he began to work a few days later. It was no accident that the first of the points registered the demand of the young American democracy and the still younger Russian democracy in revolt against the traditional practices of the older Powers :

> Open covenants of peace, openly arrived at, after which there shall be no private international understandings of any kind, but diplomacy shall proceed always frankly and in the public view.

The appeal to enlightened radical opinion in the United States and elsewhere did not, however, exhaust the significance of the publication of the secret treaties. The democratic campaign against secret diplomacy had rested on that radical belief in the efficacy and in the rightness of public opinion which was so deeply rooted in ninteenth century democratic doctrine. The appeal from wicked governments to enlightened peoples had been a commonplace of Wilson's political utterances and of the propaganda of such bourgeois radical organizations as the Union of Democratic Control, and had found widespread and uncritical acceptance.[1] Here was a weapon ready to the hands of the Bolsheviks, who had merely to make the scarcely perceptible transition from the bourgeois democratic idealization of the people to the Marxist idealization of the proletariat, and to direct their shafts against bourgeois capitalism as a whole rather than

Franco-Russian exchange of telegrams in March 1915, under which Russia received the promise of Constantinople, Great Britain of the former neutral zone in Persia and France of Russian support for her territorial demands in western Europe.

[1] " If the bosses held back, he had only to appeal to the people. . . . The people wanted the high things, the right things, the true things " (R. S. Baker, *Woodrow Wilson: Life and Letters*, iii (1932), 173) ; the issue is discussed at length in E. H. Carr, *The Twenty Years' Crisis* (2nd ed., 1946), pp. 31-36.

specifically against capitalist governments. When in April 1917
Lenin declared that the secret treaties " revealed the contradictions
between the interests of the capitalists and the will of the people
in their most conspicuous form ", the transition was half made.[1]
The publication of the first treaties in *Izvestiya* was preceded by
a brief note over Trotsky's signature. In the opening paragraphs
he was content to strike the " democratic " note :

> The struggle against imperialism, which has bled the peoples
> of Europe white and destroyed them, means also a struggle
> against capitalist diplomacy which has reasons enough to fear
> the light of day. The Russian people and, with it, the peoples
> of Europe and the whole world ought to know the proven
> truth about the plans forged in secret by the financiers and
> industrialists together with their parliamentary and diplomatic
> agents. . . . The abolition of secret diplomacy is the primary
> condition of an honourable, popular, really democratic foreign
> policy.

But the concluding paragraph shifted cautiously to different
ground :

> Our programme formulates the burning aspirations of
> millions of workers, soldiers and peasants. We desire the
> speediest peace on principles of the honourable co-existence
> and cooperation of peoples. We desire the speediest overthrow
> of the domination of capital. Laying bare to the whole world
> the work of the ruling classes as expressed in the secret docu-
> ments of diplomacy, we turn to the toilers with the challenge
> which constitutes the unchangeable basis of our foreign policy :
> Workers of all countries, unite ![2]

A month later at a session of VTsIK he made a more uncompromising declaration of principle :

> There exists for us only one unwritten but sacred treaty,
> the treaty of the international solidarity of the proletariat.[3]

It would indeed be an error to treat the peace decree and the
publication of the secret treaties merely as passing idiosyncrasies
or useful expedients. An appreciation of the essentially international outlook inculcated by the Bolshevik ideology is necessary
to an understanding of the prevalent mood of the first few months

---

[1] Lenin, *Sochineniya*, xx, 259.
[2] Trotsky, *Sochineniya*, iii, ii, 164-165.
[3] *Protokoly Zi...danii VTsIK 2 Sozyva* (1918), p. 154.

of the Revolution. In the so-called pre-parliament on the eve of the October revolution Milyukov had mockingly caricatured the " formula " of " revolutionary democracy " :

No foreign politics, no diplomatic secrets, but an immediate so-called democratic peace ; and in order to achieve it all we need is to compel our allies to adopt the points of view of Lenin and Trotsky and say with them : " We wish nothing, we have nothing to fight for ". Then our enemies will repeat the same thing and the brotherhood of nations will become an accomplished fact.[1]

It was in this mood that the new revolutionary government was content to call itself a " provisional workers' and peasants' government ". To give it a geographical designation or assign territorial limits to its sovereignty would have seemed difficult, since no one could say at this stage which of the peoples of the former Tsarist empire would adhere to it ; and in any case whatever unit was formed was destined to be merged almost at once in some European or world republic or federation of republics — if the régime was to survive at all. But this was more than a question of necessity or convenience. The revolution had discarded the old divisions of nationality as obsolete and substituted those of class. To be a worker or a peasant, not to be a Russian, was the new badge of loyalty.

This conception had practical consequences. A decree of the French National Assembly of April 20, 1792, committed the French nation to " adopt in advance all foreigners who, by abjuring the cause of its enemies, shall range themselves under its banners and consecrate their efforts to the defence of liberty ". The Paris commune frequently referred to itself in its proclamations as the " universal republic " ; and, after the elections to the commune, it was ruled that, " considering the flag of the commune to be that of the universal republic ", the election of foreigners was valid.[2] In pursuance of these precedents, the citizenship of the Soviet republic was offered to all prisoners of war who were prepared to profess ideological loyalty to the régime ; and the constitution of the RSFSR conferred rights of citizenship " without any irksome formalities " on " foreigners working within the

[1] Quoted in Bunyan and Fisher, *The Bolshevik Revolution, 1917–1918* (Stanford, 1934), p. 43.
[2] P. Vesinier, *History of the Commune of Paris* (Engl. transl., 1872), p. 178.

territory of the Russian republic, provided that they belong to the working class or to the peasantry working without hired labour ".[1] The Red Army was not in origin and conception exclusively national. Simultaneously with its creation an appeal signed by three Americans appeared in *Pravda* of February 24, 1918, for recruits to an " international detachment of the Red Army " whose language was to be English; the appeal itself is said to have been distributed in five languages.[2] Conversely, the ready admission of foreigners to the revolutionary fold meant that the Bolshevik could feel himself a citizen of the world. As Radek, himself the type of an international revolutionary without defined national status, wrote at this time in an underground German publication, " we are no longer Muscovites or citizens of Sovdepia, but the advance guard of world revolution ".[3] Petrograd was not so much the capital of a national state as the staff headquarters of the revolutionary proletariat.

The same mood generated a haughty contempt for the ordinary conceptions and procedures of foreign policy. Trotsky, the newly appointed People's Commissar for Foreign Affairs, describing his attitude as one of " active internationalism ", announced his functions in an epigram recorded in his autobiography :

> I will issue a few revolutionary proclamations to the peoples of the world and then shut up shop.[4]

Nor was this an empty jest. During his tenure of office as People's Commissar for Foreign Affairs, he seems to have paid only one visit to the former Ministry of Foreign Affairs — an occasion on

---

[1] According to G. S. Gurvich, *Istoriya Sovetskoi Konstitutsii* (1923), p. 91, this article was inserted at the last moment on instructions from the party central committee.

[2] A. Rhys Williams, *Through the Russian Revolution* (1923), pp. 185-187.

[3] Quoted in E. Drahn and S. Leonhard, *Unterirdische Literatur in Revolutionären Deutschland* (1919), p. 150.

[4] L. D. Trotsky, *Moya Zhizn'* (Berlin, 1930), ii, 64 ; this is confirmed by Pestkovsky, who quotes Trotsky as saying : "I have accepted the post of Commissar of Foreign Affairs just because I wanted to have more leisure for party affairs. My job is a small one : to publish the secret documents and to close the shop " (*Proletarskaya Revolyutsiya*, No. 10, 1922, p. 99). The statement in Max Eastman, *Since Lenin Died* (1925), p. 16, that Trotsky " was appointed to the Commissariat of Foreign Affairs because that is by general acceptance second position in any government, and because at that particular moment in the international revolution it was the position which required the most reliable audacity and most comprehensive planning ", is unfounded.

which he assembled such members of the staff as chose to attend and told them " in two or three words " that anyone who was prepared to serve the new régime loyally could remain. But there was in fact nothing to be done, except to publish the secret treaties and sell the contents of the diplomatic bags which arrived from abroad full of presents for members of the staff. These functions were entrusted to a half-literate sailor named Markin, and a half-drunken student of doubtful political affiliations named Polivanov, with a reliable party member named Zalkind as general factotum.[1] Such diplomatic correspondence as there was — notes arranging for the passage of couriers or for the exchange of Bolsheviks held abroad (Chicherin in London was the most prominent of them) for foreigners in Russian territory — was conducted by Trotsky himself from Smolny in the intervals of weightier business. " The victorious revolution ", declared Sovnarkom in one of its broadcast appeals at this time, " does not require recognition from the professional representatives of capitalist diplomacy : "[2] and Trotsky a little later added in an interview that the Soviet authorities were " absolutely indifferent to this detail of diplomatic ritual ", and considered " diplomatic intercourse necessary not only with governments, but also with revolutionary socialist parties bent on the overthrow of the existing governments ".[3] Among the few documents of Trotsky's tenure of office as People's Commissar for Foreign Affairs was a decree published in *Pravda* of November 27/December 10, 1917, dismissing most of the leading Russian diplomats abroad, including the ambassadors in London, Washington and Rome, " in view of the non-receipt of answers to telegrams and radiotelegrams " sent to them.[4]

Contempt for traditional foreign policy and an ingrained internationalism were a logical outcome of the view commonly taken at this time of the prospects of the régime. Trotsky had expressed it emphatically on the morrow of the revolution :

If the peoples of Europe do not arise and crush imperialism, we shall be crushed — that is beyond doubt. Either the Russian

[1] Trotsky, *Sochineniya*, iii, ii, 97-99.
[2] Klyuchnikov i Sabanin, *Mezhdunarodnaya Politika*, ii (1926), 92.
[3] *Izvestiya*, December 16, 1917.
[4] Trotsky, *Sochineniya*, iii, ii, 123.

revolution will raise the whirlwind of struggle in the west, or the capitalists of all countries will stifle our struggle.[1]

Since European or world revolution was the acknowledged condition of the building of socialism in Russia and of the very survival of the régime, the fundamental aim of foreign policy must be to promote and further it. The methods of pursuing this aim were direct and simple. Among the early decrees of Sovnarkom was one which appeared in *Pravda* of December 13/26, 1917, over the signatures of Lenin as president and Trotsky as People's Commissar for Foreign Affairs, resolving " to place at the disposal of the representatives abroad of the Commissariat of Foreign Affairs for the needs of the revolutionary movement two million rubles ".[2] Within a few weeks of the revolution the People's Commissariat of Foreign Affairs (Narkomindel) had established a " section for international propaganda " under Radek, whose principal function was to produce a daily paper in German, *Die Fackel*, for circulation among German and Austrian prisoners of war and German troops on the eastern front.[3] On December 19, 1917/January 1, 1918, the bureau was transferred from Narkomindel to VTsIK and *Die Fackel* became *Der Völkerfriede*, described on its front page as appearing " daily under the editorship of Karl Radek for free distribution among our German brothers ". What is perhaps most surprising about these journals is the intellectual character of their appeal ; some familiarity with the basic tenets of Marxism is assumed in the reader. Similar publications appeared in Magyar, Rumanian, Serb, Czech and Turkish.[4] Emissaries were sent out to prisoner-of-war camps throughout Russia ; and 10,000 German and Austrian prisoners were organized and trained for revolutionary work among their compatriots. The rapid success of the work was

[1] *Vtoroi Vserossiiskii S"ezd Sovetov* (1928), pp. 86-87.

[2] *Sobranie Uzakonenii, 1917-1918*, No. 8, art. 112 ; its appearance in Trotsky, *Sochineniya*, iii, ii, 151 indicates Trotsky's authorship.

[3] According to a report in *Vos'moi S"ezd RKP(B)* (1933), pp. 434-435, the section was staffed by German and Austro-Hungarian prisoners of war.

[4] John Reed in *The Liberator* (N.Y.), January 1919, pp. 17-23, reproducing facsimiles of the front pages of *Die Fackel* and *Der Völkerfriede* ; *Revolyutsiya 1917 goda*, vi (ed. I. N. Lyubimov, 1930), 256. Thirteen numbers of *Der Völkerfriede* appeared down to January 10/23, 1918 (the last in the British Museum file) ; its career was ended by the Brest-Litovsk treaty.

attested by Trotsky's announcement on December 9/22, 1917, that revolutionary Austro-Hungarian prisoners of war had offered their services against German imperialism in the event of a resumption of hostilities.[1] A fortnight later *Pravda* published an " appeal to the proletariat of the Austro-Hungarian Monarchy and the German Empire " signed by the " Social-Democratic Organization of Prisoners of War in Russia ".[2]

While the main initial weight of revolutionary propaganda was directed against the enemy Powers, the western countries soon began to receive attention. Chicherin, just released from an English gaol, told the Third All-Russian Congress of Soviets in January 1918 that " the cause of English imperialism is near to bankruptcy ", that " in the very nearest future the fire of revolution will seize the English people also ", and that " this revolution will be the socialist revolution ".[3] The first three diplomatic appointments of the régime were Vorovsky in Stockholm, Karpinsky in Geneva and Litvinov in London.[4] Litvinov's public activity was mainly along the " democratic " lines of the peace declaration. In January 1918 he issued an appeal " to the workers of Great Britain " to support the demand for " an immediate, just, democratic peace on the principle of no annexations, no indemnities ", which would " spell the downfall of militarism in all countries ".[5] This made a favourable impression in Left circles ; and when Litvinov addressed the Labour Party conference at Nottingham on January 22, 1918, and explained that the Russian workers were " fighting an unequal fight against the imperialists of all the world for democratic principles honestly applied ", he received an ovation.[6] But his functions did not exclude more direct incitement to revolution. At the time when Radek had been put in charge of the German section, another section for international revolutionary propaganda had been set up by Narkomindel

[1] Trotsky, *Sochineniya*, iii, ii, 150-151.

[2] *Pravda*, December 22, 1917/January 4, 1918.

[3] *Tretii Vserossiiskii S"ezd Sovetov* (1918), p. 9 ; Petrov, of the British Socialist Party, who had been released with Chicherin, spoke after him in more guarded and general terms.

[4] Trotsky, *Sochineniya*, iii, ii, 133, 152-153.

[5] *The Call*, January 10, 1918.

[6] The speech was not included in the records of the conference, but was briefly reported in the *Labour Leader*, January 24, 1918 ; its concluding words were : " Speed up your peace ".

under an American citizen of Russian origin, Boris Reinstein. Reinstein was soon responsible for a copious output of revolutionary literature in English; and since the British Government, in order to secure the immunity of its diplomatic correspondence with Petrograd, had to concede reciprocal facilities to Litvinov in London, this literature quickly reached British shores in the diplomatic bag.[1] It infuriated the British Government against Litvinov and the Bolsheviks, but had no other visible result.

The failure of the peace decree to evoke any response from the western allies and the pressing need, in spite of this failure, to end the war with Germany first forced on the Soviet leaders the conception of a policy directed to meet national interests and national requirements. From this point onwards, a certain duality appeared in Soviet foreign policy. It was always theoretically possible to ask whether, in any given issue of policy, priority should be given — or, in retrospect, whether it had been given — to Soviet national interest or to the international interest of world revolution; and this could, in the heat of political controversy, be depicted as a choice between principle and expediency. But, since it was difficult, at any period now in question, to diagnose any fundamental incompatibility between the two interests, the question remained largely unreal, or reduced itself to a question of tactics. Lenin had long ago contemplated the possibility that a proletarian revolution in a single country — even perhaps in backward Russia — would find itself temporarily isolated in a capitalist world,[2] and was perhaps better prepared than most of his followers to take a realistic view of the resulting situation. After the triumph of the revolution, the illusion that foreign

---

[1] *Kommunisticheskii Internatsional*, No. 9-10 (187-188), 1929, p. 189. The British Government informed the American Government of this traffic in January 1918 (*Foreign Relations of the United States, 1918: Russia*, i (1931), 723); Litvinov, on the other hand, afterwards claimed that " everything issued by him [in England] was printed in England ", adding that " this the Foreign Office which seized all his papers can confirm " (*Foreign Relations of the United States, 1919: Russia* (1937), p. 16). An English journalist in 1919 described Reinstein as " head of the quite futile department which prints cwt. upon cwt. of propaganda in English, none of which by any chance reaches these shores " (A. Ransome, *6 Weeks in Russia in 1919* (1919), p. 24).

[2] See p. 563 below.

policy and diplomacy were no more than an evil legacy of capitalism, and that the headquarters of the proletarian dictatorship
would be the general staff of a militant movement rather than the
capital of an established state, was automatically and almost
unconsciously dissipated. On the day after the revolution Sovnarkom assumed responsibility for the public affairs of a territory
which, though lacking precise frontiers and even an official name,
none the less formed a unit in a world divided into states. From
the international standpoint the Soviet republic became a state in
virtue of this fact and independently of any deliberate act of its
new rulers. The instinct of self-preservation did the rest. The
Bolsheviks had a sound motive to uphold and maintain the
authority of the state against the encroachments of other states
until such time as their dream of revolution in Europe should
come true; and this meant, in the troubled conditions of the
autumn of 1917, that they had, in spite of themselves, to have a
foreign policy to bridge the interval. More specifically they had
at all costs to take Russia out of the war; for the peasants who
formed the rank and file of the army would only support a régime
which gave them peace. But it took two to make peace as Lenin,
unlike Trotsky, saw from the first; and this meant that, pending
the coming of world revolution, it was necessary to win a respite
from the warring capitalist countries. Thus a dual, and in some
respects self-contradictory, foreign policy was imposed on the
Bolsheviks by the situation in which they found themselves : to
attempt to hasten the downfall of the capitalist governments and
to attempt to negotiate with them.

Revolutionary doctrine presupposed an equally basic hostility
on the part of the Soviet power to all capitalist governments; and
it was assumed at first that this uniform disapproval would govern
day-to-day relations with the rest of the world. This impartiality
seemed to be justified by the experience of the first weeks of the
revolution. The boycott of the new régime by the embassies of
the allied Powers in Petrograd was absolute. The first allied
official who at this time attempted to establish friendly relations
with the new government, and expressed belief in the sincerity of
the Bolshevik leaders and in the durability of the régime, was an
eccentric radical captain in the French military mission, Sadoul
by name. His visits to Lenin and Trotsky were tolerated by his

chiefs, doubtless for the sake of the information he could obtain. But, when on November 17/30, 1917, he sought permission to send a telegram in his own name to his socialist friends in the French ministry, Albert Thomas and Loucheur, arguing against the continued boycott of the Soviet Government, it was refused.[1] Higher hopes were at first entertained of American sympathy. Raymond Robins, of the American Red Cross Commission in Petrograd, who was at first primarily concerned with the safety of Red Cross stores, but was quickly impressed with the strength and resilience of the new régime, secured an interview with Trotsky three or four days after the seizure of power,[2] and thereafter not only maintained contact with Trotsky, but became a strong advocate in American official circles of a favourable attitude towards the Soviet Government. His first convert was the military attaché, Judson. On November 18/December 1, 1917, after failing to enlist the cooperation of his British and French colleagues, but with the consent of the American Ambassador, Judson visited Trotsky and had a long and friendly interview.[3] Trotsky was prepared to admit that Russia had " a certain obligation to her allies "; and Judson urged him, in the event of an armistice, " to protect other fronts and prevent transfer thereto of German troops now confronting the Russian army " and also to prevent the liberation of German and Austrian prisoners of war. Trotsky replied that he " had thought of such provisos " and that " the armistice commission would be given instructions accordingly ".[4] He also assured Judson that the Allies would be

[1] J. Sadoul, *Notes sur la Révolution Bolchevique* (1919), pp. 125-126.

[2] The interview was arranged through Alex Gumberg, an American of Russian origin who had known Trotsky in New York, and now became Robins's secretary and interpreter ; information from the unpublished papers of Robins and Gumberg has been communicated to me by Mr. W. A. Williams, and will appear in his forthcoming book on Russian-American relations.

[3] Information from the unpublished papers of William Voorhees Judson in the Newberry Library, Chicago, communicated by Mr. W. A. Williams ; brief records of the interview are in *Foreign Relations of the United States, 1918 : Russia*, i (1931), 279 and in Trotsky, *Sochineniya*, iii, ii, 185.

[4] These instructions were carried out. Kamenev later explained that the Soviet delegates had not asked for an exchange of prisoners because " we risk supplying German imperialism with millions of soldiers ", adding : " If Liebknecht were ruling Germany we should have let the prisoners go " (*Protokoly Zasedanii VTsIK 2 Sozyva* (1918), p. 91) ; Sadoul claims to have been the first to suggest the proviso about the transfer of German troops (*Notes sur la Révolution Bolchevique* (1919), p. 120).

given an opportunity to " examine " the proposed terms and " make suggestions " on them. But by this time opinion in Washington was crystallizing fast against the Bolsheviks.[1] Judson was promptly disowned by his ambassador and recalled in disgrace to Washington ; and the State Department issued an intimation that " the President desires American representatives to withhold all direct communication with the Bolshevik government ".[2]

Equally indirect and unsatisfactory overtures were received by the Bolsheviks from the camp of the Central Powers. The ubiquitous Parvus, once Trotsky's associate,[3] but now a patriotic German social-democrat and supporter of the German cause, introduced various members of the German Social-Democratic Party, including Scheidemann, to Vorovsky, the Soviet emissary in Stockholm, during November and December 1917. Rietzler, the counsellor of the German legation in Stockholm, was also in touch with Vorovsky ; and Radek had a meeting with Scheidemann.[4] But these obscure discussions led to no result. A secret Bolshevik emissary sent to Germany apparently failed altogether to establish any contact with the German authorities.[5] The prospect seemed therefore fully to justify the Bolshevik conviction of a fundamental community of interests, more deep-seated than any passing conflicts and contradictions, between the belligerent Powers in opposing Bolshevism. In the winter of 1917–1918 both Lenin and Trotsky were firmly convinced that Germany and Great Britain, each now persuaded of the impossibility of winning the war outright, were likely to reach a settlement in which both would recoup themselves at the expense of Russia.[6]

[1] Lansing, prompted by officials of the State Department, seems to have been primarily responsible for this development ; see his memorandum of December 4, 1917, in *War Memoirs of Robert Lansing* (N.Y., 1935), pp. 339-345, and letter to Wilson in *Foreign Relations of the United States : The Lansing Papers (1914-1920)*, ii (1940), 343-345.

[2] *Foreign Relations of the United States, 1918: Russia*, i (1931), 289.

[3] See Vol. 1, p. 61, note 4 ; his real name was Helphand or, in its Russian form, Gelfand.

[4] P. Scheidemann, *Memoirs of a Social-Democrat* (Engl. transl., 1929), ii, 431-433, 435, 442-443.

[5] A confused account of this venture is in M. Philips Price, *My Reminiscences of the Russian Revolution* (1921), pp. 176-177 : it must have been given to the writer by the Soviet authorities.

[6] Lenin's view is recorded in J. Sadoul, *Notes sur la Révolution Bolchevique* (1919), p. 191. Trotsky told the third All-Russian Congress of Soviets that

On this hypothesis the opposition of the Soviet régime to capitalist governments was absolute, and could have no gradations. Trotsky continued to repel with acrimony the charge that the Soviet Government was more favourable to Germany than to the western

Germany's policy at Brest-Litovsk " is, according to our profound belief, silently approved in London ", and went on : " English imperialism clearly realizes that it is in no position to defeat Germany, and it is at the cost of Russia that compensation is offered to German imperialism in order to make it more malleable in its negotiations with its British and French counterpart. . . . Wilson, Kühlmann, Lloyd George and Clemenceau all have the same aims " (*Tretii Vserossiiskii S"ezd Sovetov* (1918), pp. 54-55). The belief that Germany and the allies would come to terms at the expense of Russia may have been inspired in part by the *a priori* argument that this was the natural step for capitalist Powers to take when confronted with a proletarian revolution. But it had strong empirical support in certain facts which were fairly well known at the time, but afterwards forgotten when events took a different turn. During the winter of 1917–1918 the internal situation in Germany became grave ; French military losses and British shipping losses seriously shook informed opinion in both countries ; American support, whose quantity and quality could only be guessed, could not be expected before July 1918. Leaders in all the European countries began to consider a compromise peace. Meanwhile it was increasingly clear after the summer of 1917 that Russia was no longer an effective ally ; and the October revolution and the Brest-Litovsk treaty dealt the *coup de grâce* to the eastern front. Kühlmann, who had been appointed German Minister for Foreign Affairs in August 1917, approached Briand (not then in office) through Belgian intermediaries in the following month ; and Briand was personally favourable to terms which would give France satisfaction in the west. The British Foreign Office at this time denied knowledge of an alleged meeting of allied " bankers " in Switzerland who were planning a peace with Germany at Russia's expense (*The Times*, September 15, 1917). Wickham Steed, foreign editor of *The Times*, who was aware of the approach to Briand and in touch with many currents of European opinion, wrote in a private letter of October 28, 1917 : " The most serious danger is that in France and here the politicians and the public may bite their teeth too deeply into Alsace-Lorraine and Belgium. That is what Kühlmann wants because he is an ' easterner ' in German politics, and would willingly sacrifice a good deal of the west in order to purchase for himself a free hand in regard to Russia and the east " (*The History of The Times*, iv (1952), i, 335 ; an account of these negotiations, which broke down on German intransigence on Alsace-Lorraine, is in D. Lloyd George, *War Memoirs*, iv (1934), 2081-2107). On November 29, 1917, when the Bolshevik revolution was three weeks old, the *Daily Telegraph* published Lansdowne's famous letter advocating a compromise peace ; and this, though criticized in *The Times* and the *Morning Post*, received widespread support. On December 28, 1917, Lloyd George informed C. P. Scott, the editor of the *Manchester Guardian*, that he was " in a very pacifist temper " and that " there is a good deal of feeling in the war cabinet towards peace " ; he gave Scott the impression that he was " inclining to the plan of compensating Germany in the east for concessions in the west " (J. L. Hammond, *C. P. Scott of the Manchester Guardian* (1934), pp. 219-220, 232). On January 5, 1918, he made his statement of war aims to the trade union congress, in which a rather

allies.[1] It was unthinkable at this time that the new régime should seek to favour one capitalist government, or group of governments, against another. The peace declaration, like most of the first pronouncements of the Soviet Government, was addressed to the world at large — to " all the belligerent peoples and their governments ".

The peace declaration had, however, been ignored everywhere ; and, with the Russian armies progressively disintegrating, something had to be done to clear up the position at the front. On November 8/21, 1917, Sovnarkom sent orders to Dukhonin, the commander-in-chief in the field, to propose to the enemy command immediate armistice negotiations.[2] This was, however, carefully balanced by a note from Trotsky to the allied ambassadors in Petrograd officially drawing their attention to the peace declaration and requesting them to " regard the said document as a formal

cryptic passage, after referring to the Bolsheviks' " separate negotiations with the common enemy ", reached the conclusion that " Russia can only be saved by her own people ". Three days later came Wilson's " fourteen points ", and monopolized attention for some time to come. But early in April 1918, after the German March offensive, there is a report of further discussions between Milner, Haldane, Lloyd George and the Webbs on a " negotiated peace with Germany at Russia's expense " (*The History of the Times,* iv (1952), i, 360 ; the information comes from Clifford Sharp who had it from the Webbs, and adds that it had been mentioned by them to Huysmans, the Belgian socialist, but denounced by him as " too infamous even for Scheidemann "). The change of fortunes on the western front in the summer of 1918 finally consigned these projects to oblivion. But some of them were certainly known, and others guessed, by the Soviet leaders. The wife of Litvinov, the Soviet envoy in London at the time, was a niece of Sidney Low, a publicist in close touch with Milner, who was the most active advocate in the war cabinet of a compromise peace : Low recorded Milner's views as early as March 1917, and on November 12, 1917, reported a highly pessimistic conversation in which Milner foresaw that Germany would demand a " free hand in Poland and Russia " as well as the " restoration of her African colonies " (D. Chapman-Houston, *The Lost Historian* (1936), pp. 268-269, 278). There is, however, no evidence that information percolated to Petrograd through this channel.

¹ Thus, when the Germans in a propaganda sheet designed for the Russian troops compared British imperialism with the imperialism of the Tsars, Trotsky replied in an article called *A Half-Truth,* that the comparison was just, but, that " German imperialism does not differ a jot from them " ; and, when the secret treaties with the allies were published, he was careful to point out that, when the German proletariat made its revolution, it would discover not less damning documents in the German archives (Trotsky, *Sochineniya,* iii, ii, 148-149, 164-165).

² Bunyan and Fisher, *The Bolshevik Revolution, 1917–1918* (Stanford, 1934), p. 233.

proposal for an immediate armistice on all fronts and an immediate opening of peace negotiations ".[1] Dukhonin's refusal to carry out the order led to his immediate dismissal. Krylenko, People's Commissar for War, was appointed commander-in-chief, and a proclamation was issued over the signatures of Lenin and Krylenko to all soldiers' and sailors' committees advising them to put the " counter-revolutionary generals " under guard and themselves elect representatives to open armistice negotiations.[2] This injunction remained, not surprisingly, a dead letter until Krylenko himself arrived at the front, and sent delegates across the German lines to request an armistice. On the following day, November 14/27, 1917, the German high command agreed to armistice negotiations to begin on November 19/December 2.[3] Trotsky at once informed the allied ambassadors in Petrograd and invited the allied governments to be represented at the negotiations.[4] A similar intimation was broadcast by radio to " the peoples of the belligerent countries ", concluding with a plain ultimatum :

> On November 18 we shall begin peace negotiations. If the allied nations do not send their representatives, we shall conduct negotiations alone with the Germans. We want a general peace, but if the bourgeois in the allied countries force us to conclude a separate peace the entire responsibility will be theirs.[5]

At the same time Trotsky explained in a speech to the Petrograd Soviet how the Soviet plenipotentiaries would conceive the work of peace-making :

> Sitting at one table with them, we shall ask them explicit questions which do not allow of any evasion, and the entire course of the negotiations, every word that they or we utter, will be taken down and reported by radiotelegraph to all peoples, who will be the judges of our discussions. Under the influence of the masses, the German and Austrian Governments have already agreed to put themselves in the dock. You may be sure, comrades, that the prosecutor, in the person of the

---

[1] Trotsky, *Sochineniya*, iii, ii, 157.
[2] Bunyan and Fisher, *The Bolshevik Revolution, 1917-1918* (Stanford, 1934), p. 236.
[3] *Ibid.* pp. 255-258.
[4] Trotsky, *Sochineniya*, iii, ii, 175-176.
[5] Klyuchnikov i Sabanin, *Mezhdunarodnaya Politika*, ii (1926), 92-94.

Russian revolutionary delegation, will be in his place and will in due time make a thundering speech for the prosecution about the diplomacy of all imperialists.[1]

A correspondent of *The Times*, who interviewed Trotsky in Petrograd on the day when the armistice negotiations began in Brest-Litovsk, reported that his attitude " indicates an illusion of the near approach of a sudden and simultaneous outburst of pacifism before which all thrones, principalities and powers must yield ".[2]

It was in these conditions that the Soviet armistice delegation, led by Joffe, Kamenev and Sokolnikov and comprising, besides military experts, a worker and a peasant, found itself at Brest-Litovsk alone and face to face with an imposing German delegation under General Hoffmann.[3] Joffe at once made an appeal to all other belligerent countries to send delegates. Hoffmann replied that he had no authority to negotiate with anyone but the Russians or on any but military questions. The situation was full of embarrassment for the Soviet delegates. Not only were they compelled to negotiate separately with one group of capitalist Powers (Austria-Hungary, Bulgaria and Turkey soon joined in the proceedings at Brest-Litovsk), but they were faced by what seemed a crucial question of principle — whether to seek peace by disintegrating the German front through revolutionary propaganda and hastening a proletarian revolution against the German Government, or by outwardly amicable negotiations with that government : to evade this difficult choice and to combine both methods was already the essential task of Soviet policy. Things did not turn out so badly as might have been feared. The Soviet delegates were not deeply interested in the military demands which were the prime consideration of the German general staff ; the Soviet desiderata about fraternization and the non-transfer of German units to the western front seemed to the German military delegation childish and incomprehensible, but not seriously

[1] Trotsky, *Sochineniya*, iii, ii, 178.
[2] *The Times*, December 7, 1917.
[3] A full and reasonably objective account of the armistice and peace negotiations from the German side is in *Die Aufzeichnungen des Generalmajors Max Hoffmann* (1929), ii, 197-218 (this incorporates Max Hoffmann, *Der Krieg der Versäumten Gelegenheiten*, originally published in 1923). The memoirs of one of the Soviet military experts, Fokke, in *Arkhiv Russkoi Revolyutsii* (Berlin), xx (1930), 5-207, contain many picturesque details.

harmful. Joffe secured a week's adjournment, with a continued suspension of hostilities, to consult the authorities in Petrograd. The report to VTsIK on the negotiations was made by Kamenev, who once more sought to exculpate the Soviet Government from the charge of seeking a separate peace and defined the aim of its policy :

> For a separate peace Germany's limit of concessions is quite wide. But we did not go to Brest for that ; we went to Brest because we are convinced that our words will reach the German people over the heads of the German generals, that our words will strike from the hands of the German generals the weapons with which they fool their people.[1]

Trotsky once again appealed to the allies, pointing out that they had now had more than a month to make up their minds : [2] this time he provoked, not indeed an official reply, but a formal *communiqué* from the British Embassy to the effect that the armistice negotiations were a violation of the allied agreement of September 5, 1914, not to conclude a separate peace. Joffe returned to Brest-Litovsk ; and there at length the armistice was signed between Russia and the central Powers on December 2/15, 1917. It left the German armies in occupation of all the Russian territory held by them, including the Moon Sound islands : in this respect it contained nothing unusual. Two non-military clauses made it, however, a unique document in military history. The German high command agreed not to take advantage of the cessation of hostilities to transfer troops to the western front other than those already under orders to move : this appeased Soviet scruples about concluding an agreement which might assist one capitalist group against the other.[3] The other extraordinary provision related to fraternization. Lenin in his April theses eight months earlier had demanded " the organization of wide-

---

[1] *Protokoly Zasedanii VTsIK 2 Sozyva* (1918), p. 82.

[2] Trotsky, *Sochineniya*, iii, ii, 192-194.

[3] Hoffmann (*Die Aufzeichnungen des Generalmajors Max Hoffmann* (1929), ii, 192) regarded this clause as particularly absurd, pointing out that the exception in favour of troops already under orders completely nullified its effect ; he was obviously puzzled by Soviet insistence on it. This provision was imitated in the armistice concluded on December 5/18, 1917, on the Russo-Turkish front, in which the parties bound themselves not to transfer troops from the Caucasus to the Mesopotamian front (*Dokumenty i Materialy po Vneshnei Politike Zakavkaz'ya i Gruzii* (Tiflis, 1919), pp. 11-12, 18-23).

spread propaganda . . . in the army on active service " and " fraternization " as a means of ending the imperialist war.[1] Hoffmann refused to agree to the unlimited importation of Bolshevik literature into Germany, but thought that by limiting its entry to specified points he could " exercise a certain control " over it.[2] The armistice agreement included an article permitting " organized intercourse between the troops " in the interest of " the development and strengthening of friendly relations between the peoples of the contracting parties ". Such intercourse was limited to parties of twenty-five men on either side at a time, but the exchange of news, newspapers, open letters and goods of everyday use was specifically allowed. The armistice was concluded for twenty-eight days : during that time negotiations for a peace treaty could begin.[3]

Paradoxical as the claim appeared, the Bolsheviks were able to treat the Brest-Litovsk armistice as a victory. The occupation of Russian territory by the German armies was a *fait accompli.* Its recognition in the armistice agreement cost nothing; and all this would be undone by the impending German revolution. The non-transfer of German troops to the west was the proof of Bolshevik sincerity, freedom of propaganda the guarantee of Bolshevik victory. Both these had been secured : these, said Trotsky afterwards, were the two vital points on which the delegates had instructions not to yield.[4] Through the fraternization points Bolshevik ideas and Bolshevik literature seeped into the German army, spreading the seeds of disintegration through Germany's eastern front. The armistice was celebrated by a proclamation from Trotsky's pen addressed " to the toiling peoples of Europe, oppressed and bled white ".

We conceal from nobody [it read] that we do not consider the present capitalist governments capable of a democratic peace. Only the revolutionary struggle of the working masses

[1] Lenin, *Sochineniya*, xx, 87-88 ; for the background of the idea, see p. 563, note 1, below.
[2] *Die Aufzeichnungen des Generalmajors Max Hoffmann* (1929), ii, 192.
[3] The Russian text of the armistice is in *Protokoly Zasedanii VTsIK 2 Sozyva* (1918), pp. 171-173 (the version in Klyuchnikov i Sabanin, *Mezhdunarodnaya Politika*, ii (1926), 97-98 is much abbreviated) ; an Engl. transl. is in *United States State Department, 1918: Texts of the Russian " Peace "*, pp. 1-10, and in J. W. Wheeler-Bennett, *Brest-Litovsk: The Forgotten Peace* (1939), pp. 379-384.   [4] Trotsky, *Sochineniya*, iii, ii, 197.

against their governments can bring Europe near to such a peace. Its full realization will be assured only by a victorious proletarian revolution in all capitalist countries.

Trotsky admitted that " we are compelled to undertake negotiations with those governments which still exist at the present moment ", but claimed that " in entering into negotiations with the present governments, saturated on both sides with imperialist tendencies, the Council of People's Commissars does not for a moment deviate from the path of social revolution ". He went on to define the " dual task " of Soviet foreign policy :

> In the peace negotiations the Soviet power sets itself a dual task : in the first place, to secure the quickest possible cessation of the shameful and criminal slaughter which is destroying Europe, secondly, to help the working class of all countries by every means available to us to overthrow the domination of capital and to seize state power in the interests of a democratic peace and of a socialist transformation of Europe and of all mankind.

And the manifesto ended with an exhortation to the proletarians of all countries to join in " a common struggle for the immediate cessation of the war on all fronts ", and to close their ranks " under the banner of peace and social revolution ".[1] The verbal contradiction in the concluding words aptly summed up the compromise inherent in the Soviet policy of the first weeks of the revolution.

The formal negotiations for a treaty of peace opened at Brest-Litovsk on December 9/22, 1917. Joffe once more led the Soviet delegation ; on the German side Kühlmann, Minister for Foreign Affairs, was in charge, Austria-Hungary, Bulgaria and Turkey also being represented.[2] After some preliminary skirmishing on the questions of publicity and national self-determination, in the course of which the German delegation showed its hand by demanding that Lithuania and Courland, together with parts of Livonia and Estonia should be detached from Russia, the proceedings were once more adjourned for ten days on the proposal of the Soviet delegation, in order to give the other belligerents the opportunity

---

[1] Klyuchnikov i Sabanin, *Mezhdunarodnaya Politika,* ii (1926), 100-102 ; Trotsky, *Sochineniya,* iii, ii, 206-209.
[2] The stenographic records of the conference were published by Narkomindel under the title *Mirnye Peregovory v Brest-Litovske,* i (1920).

to appear in response to the numerous appeals showered on them from Petrograd. The boycott of the allied Powers was, however, still unbroken when the conference resumed on December 22, 1917/January 9, 1918. The world was ringing with Wilson's proclamation on the previous day of his fourteen points. But these changed nothing at Brest-Litovsk. The only novelties there were the presence of a delegation appointed by the Ukrainian Rada and the appearance of Trotsky at the head of the Soviet delegation.

Serious sparring at once began. When Hoffmann, the German commander-in-chief, intervening for the first time, complained of radiotelegrams and proclamations, some of them " of a revolutionary character addressed to our armies ", Trotsky quite openly reserved the dual function of Soviet diplomacy ; the delegation had come to conclude a treaty with the German Government, but " neither the conditions of the armistice nor the character of the peace negotiations limit in any respect or in any direction the freedom of the press or freedom of speech of any of the contracting countries ".[1] The hope that underlay Trotsky's tactics during the ensuing days was transparently clear. It was time to assume the rôle, which he had announced five weeks earlier to the Petrograd Soviet, of " prosecutor " in the indictment of imperialist diplomacy, and to call on " all peoples ", who would be able to listen to broadcast reports of every word spoken, to sit as " the judges of our discussions ".[2] If he could sufficiently show up the insincerity of German professions, and if he could drag out the proceedings long enough, the eagerly awaited revolution might break out in Germany before any critical decision had to be taken by the Soviet Government. Nothing suited Trotsky better than to engage in protracted debates with Kühlmann on the principle of national self-determination and no annexations, and on the obligation to withdraw troops from contested areas whose fate would be settled by plebiscites. It was not till January 5/18, 1918, that the blunt but intelligent soldier Hoffmann cut short the talk by placing a map on the table. It showed a blue line behind which the German armies had no intention of withdrawing until Russian demobilization was complete. The line virtually left the whole of Polish,

---

[1] *Mirnye Peregovory v Brest-Litovske*, i (1920), p. 55.
[2] See p. 26 above.

Lithuanian and White Russian territory on the German side and divided Latvia into two; it also kept the islands of the Moon Sound in German hands. Further south, Hoffmann refused to disclose his hand : that was a matter for discussion with the delegation of the Ukrainian Rada. Faced with something like an ultimatum which gave no scope for further discussion, Trotsky demanded and obtained another ten days' adjournment in order to return to Petrograd for instructions.[1] The day chosen by Hoffmann for his declaration in Brest-Litovsk was the day on which the Constituent Assembly had begun and ended its career in Petrograd; its dissolution was still the talk of the capital when Trotsky arrived on January 7/20, 1918.

Trotsky's return to Petrograd opened a famous and momentous debate which marked the first serious crisis in relations between Soviet Russia and the outside world. It had hitherto been assumed that, in the event of Germany insisting on unacceptable terms, the Bolsheviks would wage against her a so-called " revolutionary war ", and that the German soldiers, apprised of the imperialist ambitions of their government, would mutiny rather than shoot down their revolutionary Russian brothers. That this view should have been taken and this assumption made was not altogether surprising. The Bolsheviks were still flushed with the enthusiasm and optimism of their victory in October; they had learned from Lenin to believe that boldness paid; and it had been a major premise of Bolshevik thought that the victory of the Russian proletariat would light the torch of revolution in Europe. Lenin when he proposed to seek an armistice had eloquently denied that he would accept a shameful peace : " we do not trust the German generals one jot, but we trust the German people ".[2] At a special gathering held in Petrograd early in December 1917 to celebrate the conclusion of the armistice, Trotsky had been still more explicit :

> If they propose terms unacceptable for us and for all countries, terms contradictory to the principles of our revolution, we shall submit these terms to the Constituent Assembly and say : " Decide ". If the Constituent Assembly agrees to these terms, then the Bolshevik party will retire and say : " Find

[1] *Mirnye Peregovory v Brest-Litovske*, i (1920), 126-127, 130-131.
[2] Lenin, *Sochineniya*, xxii, 76-77.

another party which will sign these terms ; we, the party of the Bolsheviks and, I hope, the Left SR's, will summon all to a holy war against the militarists of all countries ".[1]

Kamenev, in the speech to VTsIK already quoted, had expressed on the eve of the signing of the armistice the conviction " that our words will reach the German people over the heads of the German generals, that our words will strike from the hands of the German generals the weapon with which they fool their people " ; [2] and after the armistice had been signed and the peace negotiations were already in progress, he spoke again in a mood of unshaken optimism :

> There is no doubt that, if Germany dares now to lead her armies against revolutionary Russia, this would be done with the aim of finally trampling under foot the freedom of Poland, of Lithuania and of a series of other nations, and this will be the spark which in the end will cause the explosion and finally sweep away the whole edifice of German imperialism. We are convinced that Germany will not dare to make such an attempt, since, if that happens, we shall all the same, notwithstanding all obstacles, obtain peace in the end, though we shall then be conducting negotiations not with the representatives of German imperialism, but with the socialists whose efforts will overthrow the German Government.[3]

When Trotsky reached Petrograd from Brest-Litovsk, the third All-Russian Congress of Soviets had just reiterated, in a telegram to " proletarian organizations " throughout the world, the conviction that " the working classes of other countries will in the near future rise in victorious revolution against their bourgeoisie, and that there will be no force in the world capable of standing against the force of the working masses in revolt ".[4]

The leading Bolsheviks, including some of the provincial delegates who were in Petrograd for the third All-Russian Congress of Soviets, met for an informal discussion of the issue on the day after Trotsky's arrival. Lenin now for the first time — and even now Lenin almost alone — squarely faced a situation which disappointed the hopes and frustrated the confident calculations on

---

[1] *Protokoly Zasedanii VTsIK 2 Sozyva* (1918), p. 128.
[2] *Ibid.* p. 82.   [3] *Ibid.* p. 164.
[4] *S"ezdy Sovetov RSFSR v Postanovleniyakh* (1939), p. 57.

which Bolshevik policy had hitherto been based. The German Government, like the allies, had rejected all proposals for a " just, democratic peace "; and the German soldiers, far from rising against their masters to consummate the proletarian revolution, were preparing to march obediently against revolutionary Russia. Lenin, following his usual practice, expounded his views in advance of the meeting in a set of theses — the *Theses on the Question of the Immediate Conclusion of a Separate and Annexationist Peace* — which showed how rapidly and how radically he had abandoned the optimistic assumptions of the past six weeks. Here he laid down the argument which was to govern the whole debate :

> The state of affairs with the socialist revolution in Russia must form the basis of any definition of the international task of our Soviet power. The international situation in the fourth year of the war is such that the probable moment of the outbreak of revolution and of the overthrow of any one of the European imperialist governments (including the German Government) is completely incalculable. There is no doubt that the socialist revolution in Europe is bound to happen, and will happen. All our hopes of the *final* victory of socialism are founded on this conviction and on this scientific prediction. Our propaganda activity in general and the organization of fraternization in particular must be strengthened and developed. But it would be a mistake to build the tactics of the socialist government on attempts to determine whether the European, and in particular the German, socialist revolution will happen in the next half year (or some such short time) or will not happen.

Or in a later passage of the same theses :

> From the time of the victory of the socialist government in any one country questions must be settled not from the point of view of the preferability of one or the other imperialism, but exclusively from the point of view of the best conditions for the development and reinforcement of the socialist revolution which has already begun.

Finally, to make peace at whatever cost would in the long run be the best advertisement for world revolution :

> The example of a socialist Soviet republic in Russia will stand as a living model for the peoples of all countries, and the

propagandist, revolutionary effect of this model will be immense. On one side, the bourgeois order and a naked out-and-out war of annexation between the two groups of robbers : on the other, peace and the socialist republic of Soviets.[1]

The meeting of January 8/21, 1918, revealed the three broad lines along which party opinion continued to split throughout the debate till the final ratification of the treaty in March.[2] Of the 63 leading Bolsheviks who attended the meeting, 32 were not to be shaken from the uncritical mood of confidence which had prevailed throughout the party in November and December. These were dubbed by Lenin the " Muscovites ", since it was the Moscow regional bureau of the party which most stubbornly defended this view; [3] and they in turn claimed to " stand on Lenin's old position ". All Lenin's prestige and powers of persuasion could rally only 15 of those present in favour of his new policy of peace at any price. The remaining 16 supported the view of Trotsky who argued that, though war must not be resumed, it was wrong and unnecessary to conclude peace on the German terms. He did not share the belief of the first group in the practicability of a revolutionary war, but none the less thought that revolution in Europe was coming and hoped that the interval could be got over by manœuvring with words. He had a less real sense than Lenin of the limitations of verbal agility as a defence against Hoffmann's mailed fist. He was still prepared for a gamble : to risk a less favourable peace later on for the chance of hastening a European revolution which would make such a peace unnecessary.[4] In order to give effect to this plan, he proposed, in the event of the German delegation continuing to insist on un-

---

[1] Lenin, *Sochineniya*, xxii, 193-199 ; the theses were published for the first time in *Pravda* of February 24, 1918 — the day after Lenin's view had been finally accepted by the party central committee — with a brief preface by Lenin explaining their origin (*ibid.* xxii, 289).

[2] No record of the meeting has survived. The fullest accounts are in an unfinished memorandum by Lenin written at the time and not published till after his death (*Sochineniya*, xxx, 369-370) and in his manuscript notes taken while the meeting was in progress (*Leninskii Sbornik*, xi (1929), 42-44) ; the figures of the voting were obtained from the party archives by the editors of Lenin's works (*Sochineniya*, xxii, 600, note 88).

[3] The meeting had been summoned on the demand of a group of Moscow delegates (*Protokoly Tsentral'nogo Komiteta RSDRP* (1929), p. 287).

[4] According to Lenin's notes, Trotsky put the chances of a German advance at 25 per cent (*Leninskii Sbornik*, xi (1929), 43).

acceptable terms, to proclaim the war at an end, but refuse to sign a treaty of peace.

The formal decision on the instructions to Trotsky rested with the central committee at its meeting three days later, on January 11/24, 1918. Before this meeting, according to Trotsky's story, he had a conversation with Lenin and promised not to support the thesis of a revolutionary war. Lenin replied that in that case Trotsky's own plan would " probably not be so dangerous ", though it would no doubt result in the loss of Livonia and Estonia; he added jestingly that these would be well lost " for the sake of a good peace with Trotsky ".[1] Lenin restated in the committee his case for an immediate peace and was supported emphatically by Stalin and more dubiously by Zinoviev. But the only formal motion proposed by Lenin was the question-begging instruction to drag out the negotiations as long as possible : this was carried by 12 votes to one. The motion in favour of a revolutionary war found only two supporters, evidently Bukharin and Dzerzhinsky. The real vote was then taken on Trotsky's motion " to stop the war, not to conclude peace, to demobilize the army ". This was carried by the narrow margin of nine to seven ; the way in which individual members of the committee voted can no longer be established.[2]

Armed with this authority, Trotsky left once more for Brest-Litovsk on January 15/28, 1918. Externally the situation of the Soviet republic had further deteriorated since the adjournment ten days ago. After a period of anarchy and confusion, Bessarabia had been seized and occupied by Rumanian troops — an act which induced the Soviet Government to break off relations with Rumania and impound the Rumanian gold reserve deposited in Moscow for safe keeping during the war.[3] But the eyes of the

---

[1] L. Trotsky, *Moya Zhizn'* (Berlin, 1930), ii, 111 ; Lenin in the committee remarked that Trotsky's plan would mean the surrender of Estonia to the Germans (*Protokoly Tsentral'nogo Komiteta RSDRP* (1929), p. 201).

[2] *Ibid.* pp. 199-207.

[3] *Sobranie Uzakonenii, 1917-1918*, No. 16, art. 233. Three days later a statement was issued by the allied representatives in Bukharest declaring the Rumanian occupation of Bessarabia to be " a purely military operation without any political character whatever undertaken in full agreement with the allies " (*L'Ukraine Soviétiste* (Berlin, 1922), p. 51) ; the annexation of Bessarabia by Rumania was announced in April 1918 (for the Soviet protest see Klyuchnikov i Sabanin, *Mezhdunarodnaya Politika*, ii (1926), 138), and later formally recognized by the allies (see p. 346 below).

Bolsheviks were still fixed on central Europe. A wave of strikes in Budapest and Vienna had only just died down.[1] Now, while Trotsky was *en route* from Petrograd, mass strikes organized by a group of " revolutionary shop stewards " without declared political affiliations, and accompanied for the first time by open demonstrations against the war, broke out in Berlin and spread to other German centres ;[2] it seemed for a moment as if Bolshevik optimism and Trotsky's policy of procrastination were to be justified by the event. It was in these conditions that the conference at Brest-Litovsk was resumed on January 17/30, 1918. The Ukrainian Rada having now been dispossessed over the greater part of the Ukraine by the Ukrainian Soviet Government, two rival Ukrainian delegations appeared to take part in the negotiations, one being recognized by the Germans, the other by the Russians. Wrangling between them prolonged the proceedings for several days. The old phrases about self-determination, annexation and occupation were bandied about once more. Bobinsky and Radek, describing themselves as " Polish members of the all-Russian delegation " and " representatives of the Social-Democracy of Poland and Lithuania ",[3] read a declaration claiming the right of self-determination for Poland and condemning the occupation of Poland by German forces as a " veiled annexation ".[4] But the disturbances in Germany, which were the hidden force in the background of the negotiations, petered out ; and the outbreak of revolution in Finland and further Soviet successes in the Ukraine did not compensate for the failure of the German proletariat to rise. On January 26/February 8, 1918 the central Powers signed a treaty of

[1] For the Austrian disturbances of January 1918 see O. Czernin, *Im Weltkriege* (1919), pp. 322-323.

[2] The Reichstag committee of inquiry into the causes of the German collapse some years later collected opinions about " the great strike of January 1918 " ; many observers connected it generally with the Russian revolution or specifically with the Brest-Litovsk negotiations (R. H. Lutz, *The Causes of the German Collapse in 1918* (Stanford, 1934), pp. 99-135). Radek, at the seventh congress of the Russian Communist Party in March 1918, claimed that " the demonstrative policy at Brest provoked a general strike in Germany which was the first awakening of the European proletariat throughout the whole war " (*Sed'moi S"ezd Rossiiskoi Kommunisticheskoi Partii* (1923), p. 71).

[3] The official name of the Polish socialist party of the Left, opposed to the patriotic " Polish Socialist Party ", was the " Social-Democracy of the Kingdom of Poland and Lithuania ".

[4] *Mirnye Peregovory v Brest-Litovske*, i (1920), 173-175.

peace with the delegation of the Ukrainian Rada. At last, on January 28/February 10, 1918, everyone's patience was exhausted : and, as the Germans were preparing their ultimatum, Trotsky unexpectedly intervened with a long tirade against German designs, concluding with the announcement that " Russia, while refusing to sign an annexationist peace, for her part declares the state of war with Germany, Austria-Hungary, Turkey and Bulgaria at an end ".[1] The Soviet delegates left Brest-Litovsk for Petrograd the same evening. Judging by the state of bewilderment and annoyance in which they left their adversaries, they seemed to themselves to have scored a considerable victory.

The German civil authorities, had the matter rested with them, would have bowed to this unusual form of ending hostilities. But the general staff had other ideas.[2] It was decided to treat the breakdown of negotiations as an ending of the armistice ; and seven days later, on February 17, 1918, Hoffmann notified the Russians that military operations would be resumed on the next day. This at last raised in an inescapable form the real issue which Lenin had foreseen and Trotsky had tried to evade. The German advance was resumed on February 18 ; and the next week was the most critical in Petrograd since the revolution. The central committee of the party was in almost continuous session, and a series of votes showed how evenly opinion was divided. No one any longer openly supported a revolutionary war. But to accept a German peace was still too bitter a pill. When the notice of the resumption of hostilities was received on February 17, Lenin at once proposed to send an offer to the Germans to resume negotiations, but, though supported by Stalin, Sverdlov, Sokolnikov and Smilga, was voted down by a bare majority consisting of Trotsky, Bukharin, Lomov, Joffe, Uritsky and Krestinsky. A proposal " to delay the renewal of peace negotiations until the German offensive is sufficiently apparent and until its influence on the

---

[1] *Mirnye Peregovory v Brest-Litovske*, i (1920), 208.
[2] Max Hoffman (*Die Aufzeichnungen des Generalmajors Max Hoffmann* (1929), ii, 214-215) records that he insisted, in opposition to Kühlmann, on refusing to accept the Trotsky formula. R. von Kühlmann, *Erinnerungen* (Heidelberg, 1948), p. 545, confirms that he was in favour of accepting the formula and withdrawing all available troops to the west, his reason being the opposition of Austria to " a reopening of the eastern war " ; the Chancellor failed, however, to support him (*ibid.* p. 549). Trotsky's gesture apparently came nearer to success than was known at the time.

workers' movement is revealed " was carried by the same majority of six to five.   Lenin then put the final question whether, if the German army advanced and no revolution occurred in Germany and Austria, peace should be made.   At this point Trotsky wavered and went over to Lenin, who thus registered a majority of six, against one " no " (Joffe) and four abstentions.[1]   On the next day, when Zinoviev had joined Lenin's group and Dzerzhinsky the opposition, the same variations were repeated.   At the morning session Trotsky reiterated the argument that " it is indispensable to wait and see what impression all this makes on the German people ", and voted against an immediate offer to Germany, making the voting seven to six against.[2]   But in the evening, when the news arrived that the Germans were advancing, had taken Dvinsk and were moving into the Ukraine, Trotsky once more hesitatingly came over to Lenin's side, and the motion to approach the Germans with a statement of willingness to sign the original German terms and a request for fresh negotiations was carried by seven votes to five.[3]   The proposal was formally submitted to Sovnarkom the same night.   The Bolshevik commissars, bound by the decision of the central committee, voted solidly for it ; of seven Left SRs present, four voted with the Bolsheviks, though their action was afterwards disavowed by their party.[4]   The telegram of acceptance was immediately despatched to Brest-Litovsk.

This time, however, Hoffmann was in no hurry.   It was not till the morning of February 23, 1918, that the German terms at length reached Moscow.   They were harsher than the earlier terms, notably in the demands that the Soviet Government should withdraw its army from the Ukraine and make peace with the Ukrainian Rada, and that Livonia and Estonia should be evacuated by the

---

[1] The records of these votes are in *Protokoly Tsentral'nogo Komiteta RSDRP* (1929), pp. 228-239 ; no minutes of the meeting are extant.   According to Bunyan and Fisher, *The Bolshevik Revolution, 1917-1918* (Stanford, 1934), p. 514, an appendix to the 1928 edition of the records of the seventh party congress shows Trotsky as abstaining from the last vote ; but the authenticity of the official record of the voting, which was once again reprinted in Lenin, *Sochineniya*, xxii, 557, is beyond doubt.   The narrative of these events in L. Trotsky, *Moya Zhizn'* (Berlin, 1930), ii, 110-116, so far as it can be checked from other sources, is scrupulously accurate.

[2] *Ibid.* pp. 231-232.   [3] *Ibid.* pp. 233-240.
[4] I. Steinberg, *Als ich Volkskommissar war* (Munich, 1929), pp. 211-212.

Russians and occupied by German forces until such time as order had been restored there. The battle in the central committee was renewed on the same day. Lenin for the first and last time issued an ultimatum on his own account. If " the policy of revolutionary phrase-making " continued, he would resign from the government and from VTsIK. The hard choice had to be faced. He brushed aside an attempt by Stalin to suggest that it could once again be postponed by reopening negotiations with the Germans :

> Stalin is wrong when he says that it is possible not to sign. These conditions must be signed. If you do not sign them, you will sign the death warrant of the Soviet power within three weeks. . . . The German revolution is not yet ripe. That will take months. The terms must be accepted.[1]

Trotsky once more stated his objections. Resistance would have been possible if the party had been united. To sign peace meant " to lose support among the leading elements of the proletariat ". Unconvinced though he was, he did not wish to stand in the way of the unity of the party ; but he could not in the new conditions " remain and carry the personal responsibility for foreign affairs ". When the crucial vote was taken Trotsky, Joffe, Krestinsky and Dzershinsky abstained, thus allowing Lenin's motion to accept the German terms to be carried by seven votes (Lenin, Zinoviev, Sverdlov, Stalin, Sokolnikov, Smilga, Stasova) against four (Bukharin, Lomov, Bubnov and Uritsky).[2] On the same evening the same proposal came before VTsIK, and, at 4.30 on the morning of February 24, after an effective speech by Lenin, was carried by 116 votes to 84 ; even this comparatively favourable result was only secured through the abstention of most of the Bolshevik opponents of the proposal, who could not make common cause with the Right and Left SRs and Mensheviks against the decision of their party.[3] A telegram accepting the German terms was at once despatched to German headquarters.[4] The delegation,

---

[1] Lenin, *Sochineniya*, xxii, 277 ; the ultimatum was repeated in the same terms in the same day's issue of *Pravda* (*ibid*. xxii, 276).

[2] *Protokoly Tsentral'nogo Komiteta RSDRP* (1929), pp. 247-252.

[3] Lenin, *Sochineniya*, xxii, 608. No official record of this session of VTsIK was ever published ; the text of Lenin's speech is in *ibid.*, xxii, 280-283, a graphic account of the meeting in M. Philips Price, *My Reminiscences of the Russian Revolution* (1921), pp. 247-249.

[4] *Mirnye Peregovory v Brest-Litovske*, i (1920), 208.

headed this time by Sokolnikov and Chicherin — since neither
Trotsky nor Joffe was prepared to sustain the final humiliation —
left the same day for Brest-Litovsk with instructions to sign
without argument or discussion.[1]

A final concession was required. The Turkish delegation,
which had arrived late on the scene, demanded and obtained the
three frontier districts of Kars, Ardahan and Batum, which had
been taken from Turkey forty years earlier. Then on March 3,
1918, after a formal protest by Sokolnikov against an act of *force
majeure*, the Brest-Litovsk treaty was signed. Under this treaty
Russia renounced all rights over the city of Riga and its hinterland,
the whole of Courland and Lithuania and a part of White Russia,
the destiny of which was to be decided by Germany and Austria-
Hungary " in agreement with their population "; recognized the
German occupation of Livonia and Estonia until " proper national
institutions " had been established there; agreed to make peace
with the Ukrainian Rada; and ceded Kars, Ardahan and Batum,
whose population would " reorganize " these districts in agreement
with Turkey. Diplomatic intercourse between Soviet Russia and
the central Powers was to be resumed on the ratification of the
treaty. The financial clauses were less drastic, and there was a
mutual waiver of indemnities and other claims. But the provision
that each party should be responsible for payment for the maintenance of its nationals who had been prisoners of war put what
was in fact an immense financial burden on Soviet Russia. These
details, however, counted for little compared with the vast and
fertile territories which Russia was called on to abandon to the
will of the enemy.

In Moscow the formalities of ratification had still to be
approved and carried out. The seventh party congress, meeting
on March 6, 1918,[2] repeated the old arguments on both sides.
Lenin made one of his finest speeches: the " triumphal procession " of the first weeks of the revolution was over, and it was time
to face harsh realities by arming and working. Trotsky for the

---

[1] A pamphlet by Sokolnikov (*Brestskii Mir* (1920)) contains picturesque
details of an eventful journey.

[2] The decision to hold a party congress had been taken, in view of the
divisions in the central committee, on January 19/February 1, 1918 (*Protokoly
Tsentral'nogo Komiteta RSDRP* (1929), p. 216); the formal notice convening it
for March 5 appeared in *Pravda* of February 5/18, 1918.

last time stated his dissent from Lenin, but refused to vote against him. The result was a foregone conclusion. The motion proposed by Lenin approving ratification was carried by 28 votes to 9. Then on March 16, 1918, the fourth All-Russian Congress of Soviets, after two days of stormy debate during which no less than six opposition groups put forward resolutions, passed the government motion to ratify by a majority of 784 to 261. The long debate was closed at last. Neither it nor the German advance was ever reopened. German military power, which conditioned them both, was strained to its last convulsive effort in the great western offensive launched ten days after the final vote of ratification, and never recovered its freedom of action in the east.

In the last stages of the Brest-Litovsk discussions a new factor emerged which was destined to be of great importance in Soviet foreign policy. The dogmatic absolutism which assumed that the Soviet régime must maintain an attitude of equal and unqualified hostility to all capitalist governments (and they to it), and objected on this ground even to the conclusion of a separate peace, was not seriously tenable. According to any reasonable estimate, it was the split in the capitalist world which had enabled the Soviet Government to establish itself and was the best insurance for its survival. As Radek wrote some years later, it was the " fundamental fact " which " stood at the cradle " of Soviet foreign policy.[1] Lenin cautiously recognized this in his *Theses on the Question of the Immediate Conclusion of a Separate and Annexationist Peace* :

> By concluding a separate peace, we are freeing ourselves in the largest measure *possible at the present moment* from both warring imperialist groups ; by utilizing their mutual enmity we utilize the war, which makes a bargain between them against us difficult.[2]

From this recognition of the pragmatic value of the division in the enemy camp it was only a short step to the conscious exploitation of it as an asset of Soviet foreign policy, and to the abandonment of any doctrinal assumption of the uniform and unvarying hostility of the capitalist world.

[1] K. Radek, *Die Auswärtige Politik Sowjet-Russlands* (Hamburg, 1921), pp. 80-81.   [2] Lenin, *Sochineniya*, xxii, 198.

On the allied side the dilemma was also piquant. Were the allied capitalist Powers to seek the cooperation of a revolutionary socialist government against a capitalist foe ? They, too, like the Bolsheviks, were at first inhibited by what some called principles and others prejudices. Sadoul's eccentricities were barely tolerated by his superiors ; and Judson's initial approach to Trotsky had earned him a snub from Washington. But the idea was too fruitful to be lightly discarded. The official American ban on dealings with the Bolsheviks lent increased importance to Raymond Robins, who had quasi-official status, but was not bound by the orders of the State Department. During the early stages of the negotiations at Brest-Litovsk both Robins and Sadoul were in constant touch with Trotsky, putting forward pleas in favour of resistance to Germany. Since these pleas had no governmental backing, they can scarcely have carried much weight.[1] The two enthusiasts did, however, make some impression, however transitory, on their respective ambassadors. On December 5/18, 1917, Sadoul persuaded the French Ambassador, Noulens, to receive a visit from Trotsky, and Trotsky to make the visit — a remarkable feat, though unproductive of any useful result.[2] On December 20, 1917/January 2, 1918, after the first adjournment of the Brest-Litovsk peace negotiations, Robins persuaded the American Ambassador, Francis, to draft a telegram for eventual despatch to the State Department, recommending the American Government, in case of an imminent resumption of hostilities by the Bolsheviks against Germany, " to render all aid and assistance possible ", and an equally tentative note to the " Commissaire for Foreign Affairs ", to be used simultaneously with the telegram, informing him of this recommendation. Copies of these drafts were given to Robins, no doubt to show to Trotsky.[3] Up to this point the initiative had rested with Sadoul and Robins. But after Trotsky's first return from Brest-Litovsk, and while he was

---

[1] J. Sadoul, *Notes sur la Révolution Bolchevique* (1919), containing a series of almost daily letters to Albert Thomas, fully documents his activities at this time. Robins's personal papers have been preserved, and may shortly be made available ; W. Hard, *Raymond Robins' Own Story* (N.Y., 1920), is disappointingly vague in facts and dates, and adds little to other sources.

[2] J. Sadoul, *Notes sur la Révolution Bolchevique* (1919), p. 158.

[3] *Russian-American Relations*, ed. C. K. Cummings and W. Pettit (N.Y., 1920), pp. 66-67.

fighting the battle of his " no war, no peace " formula in the party central committee, he made an approach to both of them. To Sadoul he showed Hoffmann's map on which the frontier demanded by the German delegation was marked, and made a more or less formal statement :

> We do not want to sign this peace, but what is to be done ? A holy war ? Yes, we shall proclaim it, but what will be the result ? The moment has come for the allies to decide.

To Robins he must have spoken in the same sense, though the only recorded part of this conversation was Trotsky's enquiry about the prospects of recognition of the Soviet régime by the American Government and Robins's non-committal answer.[1] Neither of these approaches produced any effect in the allied camp. Kamenev, whose amiable disposition and manners seemed to fit him for a mission of propitiation, was despatched to London and Paris to seek help from the western allies against Germany. He landed at Aberdeen on February 23, 1918, and, having been relieved by the immigration authorities of his papers, was allowed to proceed to London, where he saw a few M.P.s and other public men. But he was not officially received and, when it was ascertained that the French Government refused to admit him, was unceremoniously deported.[2]

The crucial moment in these strange and halting negotiations came with the breakdown of the Brest-Litovsk negotiations after the " no war, no peace " declaration of January 28/February 10, 1918, and Trotsky's second return to the capital. Trotsky, having renounced the revolutionary war, yet still struggling against acceptance of a German peace, was now keenly eager to explore the forlorn hope of western help in resisting German menace. Kamenev's departure from Petrograd on his abortive journey

---

[1] J. Sadoul, *Notes sur la Révolution Bolchevique* (1919), p. 204 ; *Papers Relating to the Foreign Relations of the United States, 1918 : Russia*, i (1931), 358. The Sadoul conversation was reported on January 11/24, 1917 ; the Robins conversation took place on that day ; it was on the same day, no doubt after the conversations, that the " no war, no peace " formula was endorsed by the central committee.

[2] This episode is described, partly from oral sources, in J. W. Wheeler-Bennett, *Brest-Litovsk : The Forgotten Peace* (1939), pp. 284-286 ; the subject was twice raised by Ramsay MacDonald in the House of Commons (*House of Commons: 5th Series*, ciii, 1478-1479, 1494 ; 1606-1607, 1626).

coincided with the arrival in Petrograd of Bruce Lockhart as unofficial British agent. Lockhart's first interview with Trotsky on February 15, 1918, ended with Trotsky's words: " Now is the big opportunity for the allied governments ".[1] Thereafter Lockhart joined Sadoul and Robins as an active advocate of allied assistance to the Bolsheviks against the Germans. The German denunciation of the armistice and renewal of military operations on February 18 increased the urgency of the Soviet demand and stung the hitherto apathetic French Ambassador into an offer of assistance.[2] On February 22, 1918, the American Ambassador was able to telegraph to Washington that " five allied ambassadors agreed to support resistance if offered, and French and British through their engineer officers are assisting Red Guard destroying railway to prevent German advance ".[3]

It was on the same day that the proposal to accept French and British aid came up for full-dress debate in the central committee of the party. It was the moment when the revised German terms had been received in Petrograd, while the final decision to accept them still hung in the balance, and Trotsky was still clutching at straws in order to avoid acceptance. It was an instructive debate, revealing a straight cleavage between " realists ", who believed that the régime in its present plight, and whatever its attitude to the German terms, could not reject aid from whatever source, and " Leftists ", whose revolutionary principles still forbade any partnership with capitalist Powers. Compared with recent divisions in the party there was some cross-voting. Joffe, a fervent advocate of rejection of the German terms, now argued that it was " necessary to accept everything that aids our resistance "; on the other hand, Sverdlov, who had always voted with Lenin for acceptance of the German terms, now opposed Trotsky's proposal to accept allied aid, not, as he carefully explained, on grounds of principle, but because the English and French were " discredited in the eyes of the broad masses of Russia ". In

---

[1] R. H. Bruce Lockhart, *Memoirs of a British Agent* (1932), p. 228.

[2] J. Noulens, *Mon Ambassade en Russie Soviétique*, i (1933), p. 223 ; Sadoul, writing on February 20, 1918, attributes the initiative to himself (*Notes sur la Révolution Bolchevique* (1919), p. 241) ; but the instructions of the Quai d'Orsay to Noulens are confirmed in *Foreign Relations of the United States, 1918: Russia*, i (1931), 383.

[3] *Ibid.* i, 386.

general, however, it was those who had voted on principle for the
revolutionary war who now voted, equally on principle, for
rejecting aid from the capitalist Powers. Bukharin, once again
the leader of the Leftists, not only accused the allies of having a
plan to make Russia into their " colonies ", but thought it " inadmissible to enjoy the support of any kind of imperialism " :
he concluded with the formal proposal " to enter into no kind of
understandings with the French, English and American missions
respecting the purchase of arms or the employment of the services
of officers and engineers ". Uritsky lamented that " having seized
power, we have forgotten about world revolution " ; the majority
was thinking in military terms instead of contemplating " urgent
action on the German proletariat ". Bubnov complained that
" our internationalism is being bartered away ". Trotsky's motion
to accept from any source, even from capitalist governments,
though without entering into any political obligations, everything
needed to " arm and equip our revolutionary army with all essential
requirements ", was carried by six votes to five. Lenin was not
present at the meeting. The minutes contain a note from him in
the following terms :

> I request you to add my vote in favour of taking potatoes
> and ammunition from the Anglo-French imperialist robbers.

It is uncertain whether the note was read at the meeting or whether
it was added afterwards. At the conclusion of the meeting
Bukharin resigned his membership of the central committee and
his editorship of *Pravda* : he felt still more keenly about voluntary
acceptance of aid from one group of capitalists than about forced
submission to the terms of the other. This was the occasion on
which, according to Trotsky, Bukharin wept on his shoulder and
exclaimed : " They are turning the party into a dung-heap ".[1]

Except as a noteworthy opportunity for declarations of principle and policy, this debate remained without effect. The decision
to bow to the German ultimatum was taken in the central committee twenty-four hours later. Until the treaty was signed and
ratified, however, the issue remained ; and a small group of allied
representatives, notably Robins and Lockhart, continued to work

---

[1] *Protokoly Tsentral'nogo Komiteta RSDRP* (1929), pp. 243-246 ; L.
Trotsky, *Moya Zhizn'* (Berlin, 1930), ii, 118.

for aid to the Soviet Government in the event of renewed resistance to Germany, though their efforts were hampered by indifference in London and Washington and the now evidently impending Japanese moves in the Far East. On March 1, 1918, before the actual signature at Brest-Litovsk, at a moment when the German armies were still advancing on Petrograd and it had been decided to move the capital to Moscow, Lockhart had his first interview with Lenin, who appraised the situation coldly and critically. The " scandalous " peace terms would be signed. But " how long would the peace hold "? The Bolsheviks regarded Anglo-American capitalism " as almost as hateful as German militarism "; but for the moment German militarism was the immediate menace. Lenin continued :

> Our ways . . . are not your ways. We can afford to compromise temporarily with capital. It is even necessary, for, if capital were to unite, we should be crushed at this stage of our development. Fortunately for us, it is in the nature of capital that it cannot unite. So long, therefore, as the German danger exists, I am prepared to risk a cooperation with the allies, which should be temporarily advantageous to both of us. In the event of German aggression, I am even willing to accept military support. At the same time I am quite convinced that your government will never see things in this light. It is a reactionary government. It will cooperate with the Russian reactionaries.[1]

Two days later the treaty was signed at Brest-Litovsk, and the German advance stayed. But Trotsky, still unreconciled and less realistic than Lenin in his estimate of the allied attitude, tried yet another throw. On March 5, 1918, the day on which the delegation returned from Brest-Litovsk, he once more saw Robins, who asked him for a statement in writing to send to Washington. The statement, drafted by Trotsky and confirmed by Lenin, put three questions, contingent on the non-ratification of the treaty and the renewal of hostilities with Germany :

1. Can the Soviet Government rely on the support of the United States of America, Great Britain and France in its struggle against Germany ?
2. What kind of support could be furnished in the nearest

---

[1] R. H. Bruce Lockhart, *Memoirs of a British Agent* (1932), p. 239.

future, and on what conditions — military equipment, transportation supplies, living necessities ?

3. What kind of support would be furnished particularly and especially by the United States ?

Two supplementary and more specific questions were put in less formal terms. If Japan seized Vladivostok, what action would be taken by the allies, and in particular by the United States ? What prospect was there of British aid through Murmansk and Archangel ? The questions were put on the explicit assumptions " that the internal and foreign policies of the Soviet Government will continue to be directed in accord with the principles of international socialism, and that the Soviet Government retains its complete independence of all non-socialist governments ". On the same day Trotsky put the same questions, orally and in a less precise form, to Lockhart, who telegraphed them to London.[1] In order to allow time for the consideration of these overtures in Washington and London, Lenin agreed, at Robins's urgent request to postpone from March 12 to March 14 the opening of the session of the All-Russian Congress of Soviets which was to ratify the treaty.[2]

Before Trotsky's statement had been received in Washington,[3] President Wilson had despatched to the fourth All-Russian Congress of Soviets on March 11, 1918, a telegram of greeting whose fulsome language did not attenuate its central message that " the government of the United States is unhappily not now in a position to render the direct and effective aid it would wish to

[1] Trotsky's statement to Robins and Lockhart's report of his conversation with Trotsky are in *Russian-American Relations*, ed. C. K. Cumming and W. Pettit (N.Y., 1920), pp. 81-84. This version of Trotsky's statement is quoted from the Congressional Record ; a different translation is preserved in National Archives of the United States, Record Group 84 : United States Embassy, Moscow 1918, Correspondence. No Russian original has been found.

[2] Robins's testimony is in *United States Senate: Sub-Committee on the Judiciary, Brewing and Liquor Interests and German and Bolshevik Propaganda* (1919), iii, 805.

[3] Robins delivered it to the American Ambassador, Francis, at Vologda on March 8 (W. Hard, *Raymond Robins' Own Story* (N.Y., 1920), pp. 142-143). On March 9 Francis mentioned Robins's conversation with Trotsky in a telegram to the State Department but reported only that Trotsky had protested against " the threatened Japanese invasion of Siberia " ; only on March 12, on receipt of Wilson's message of the previous day, did Francis telegraph a summary of Trotsky's statement to Robins of March 5 (National Archives of the United States, Record Group 59 : 861.00/1262, 1302).

render ".[1] Official circles in Washington were content to treat this message as a sufficient reply to Trotsky's embarrassing approach. Lockhart equally failed to obtain any useful answer from the Foreign Office; and Balfour, in a wilfully obtuse speech in the House of Commons on March 14, 1918, by anticipation defended Japanese — and allied — intervention as designed " to help Russia ". Two days later the ratification of the treaty was voted by the fourth All-Russian Congress of Soviets. The story is told that, before Lenin delivered the speech which swayed the congress to ratify, he beckoned Robins to the rostrum and asked him, first, whether he had any reply from Washington, and then, whether Lockhart had heard from London. The reply to both questions was negative; and the treaty was ratified by a large majority.[2] Even this did not finally close the door. Sadoul relates how on March 20, 1918, he persuaded Trotsky to ask for 40 French officers to furnish technical advice and assistance in the reorganization of the army.[3] It was the moment when Trotsky was first seeking to attract former Tsarist officers into the Red Army as specialists and commanders. In this delicate task French help and French influence might have counted for much. On the next day Trotsky had an interview with Robins and a member of the American military mission, and made the request, which he confirmed in writing in the name of Sovnarkom to the head of the mission, for the assistance of an American officer " for the study of military questions and for connexions with you ", and of " units of railroad specialists " to work in Moscow, in European Russia and in Siberia.[4] Nothing came of this request. Three or four French officers were actually assigned; but, when Japanese intervention began in the first days of April, these " visibly disinterested themselves in the task for which they had been invited ".[5] The revolutionary war, as the *ultima ratio* of the policy of fomenting world revolution at all costs, had been rejected

---

[1] *Foreign Relations of the United States, 1918 : Russia*, i (1931), 395-396.

[2] W. Hard, *Raymond Robins' Own Story*, (N.Y., 1920), pp. 151-152.

[3] J. Sadoul, *Notes sur la Révolution Bolchevique* (1919), p. 274.

[4] Trotsky's letter is in National Archives of the United States, Record Group 84 : United States Embassy, Moscow, 1918, Correspondence.

[5] J. Sadoul, *Notes sur la Révolution Bolchevique* (1919), p. 386; later, Sadoul summed up by saying that, " since Brest, Trotsky and Lenin have multiplied their efforts to bring the Entente Powers into close and loyal collaboration for the economic and military reorganization of Russia " (*ibid.* p. 22).

as impracticable. Now the attempt to resort to more conventional diplomacy by playing off one group of hostile Powers against another had ended in failure. Every avenue appeared to have been closed.

The Brest-Litovsk crisis, wrote Lenin in *Pravda* in an article entitled *A Hard but Necessary Lesson*, would " appear as one of the greatest historical turning-points in the history of the Russian — and international — revolution ".[1] It was a significant eminence from which it was possible to look back on the past and forward to the future. The Brest-Litovsk crisis brought to a head the unresolved dilemma of the relations of Soviet Russia to the world, the dilemma of an authority which aspired to act at one and the same time as the driving-force of world revolution and as the sovereign power of a state in a world of states ; and it was at this time that the durable foundations of Soviet foreign policy were laid. The fundamental debate was between the advocates of a policy of rejecting the German terms and waging a revolutionary war — at first a large majority of the party — among whom Bukharin, Joffe, Dzerzhinsky and Radek were the most conspicuous, and Lenin's immediate followers including Zinoviev, Stalin and Sokolnikov, who, numerically weak at the outset, derived increasing strength from Lenin's persuasive persistence and from the harsh realities of the situation. Trotsky, brilliant, original and resourceful, sometimes wilful and misguided, always difficult to fit into any category or group, occupied an eccentric and shifting position which tended to blur the main issue. All this recalled the Trotsky of the period after 1903 ; what was new in his attitude was a profound personal regard for Lenin which coloured and often determined his final decisions.

That the survival of the revolution in Russia depended on its prompt extension to central and western Europe was so unquestioningly assumed that it was natural for the Bolsheviks to believe both that revolution in Europe was imminent and that their primary task was to hasten and promote it. These beliefs, held with all the revolutionary enthusiasm of the October victory, would not lightly be abandoned. The acceptance of Brest-Litovsk

[1] Lenin, *Sochineniya*, xxii, 290.

seemed an assault on both these articles of faith.   The existing position in Europe, exclaimed Bukharin at the seventh party congress, could only be described as " the collapse, the dissolution of the old capitalist relations " under the stress of war.   He cited the strikes and the setting up of Soviets in Vienna and Budapest in January 1918, and the strikes in Germany later in the same month, as proof that revolution in Europe was well on the way. This was the moment which Lenin chose to introduce a policy of peaceful cohabitation between Soviet Russia and the capitalist Powers.   To accept the treaty was to saw away the first plank of Soviet policy — the promotion and encouragement of world revolution.

> We said and we say [Bukharin went on bitterly] that in the end everything depends on whether the international revolution conquers or does not conquer.   In the end, the international revolution — and that alone — is our salvation. . . . Renouncing international propaganda, we renounce the keenest-edged weapon that we had.[1]

Bukharin and his followers held firmly to the view that to wage " revolutionary war " against capitalist governments was the prime function of the Soviet power, and one which could not be abandoned because the immediate prospects were forbidding. It was a view which continued to enjoy more sympathy in the party than the final votes on the treaty showed.

Lenin's approach to the problem was more complex.   Since 1905 he had never wavered for a moment in the firm conviction that the support of the European proletariat was a condition of a victorious socialist revolution in Russia, and had explicitly foreseen at the first All-Russian Congress of Soviets in June 1917 that, after the seizure of power, " circumstances may force us into the position of a revolutionary war ", though he had added with light-hearted optimism :

> It will be enough for you to declare that you are not pacifists, that you will defend your republic, the workers' proletarian democracy, against German and French and other capitalists — that will be enough to make peace secure.[2]

---

[1] Sed'moi S"ezd Rossiiskoi Kommunisticheskoi Partii (1923), pp. 34-35, 40-41.
[2] Lenin, Sochineniya, xx, 487.

But Lenin had also clung just as firmly, ever since 1905, to the other essential prerequisite of the Russian revolution — the alliance of the proletariat with the peasantry; and at the critical moment in October 1917 it was the peasants, clothed in the guise of a demoralized army clamouring for peace and land, who were Lenin's main preoccupation. The decrees on the land and on peace — the latter apparently attaching so much importance to peace and so little to world revolution — were the product of these anxieties. The revolutionary alliance was cemented after the all-Russian peasant congress of November 1917, when the Left SRs entered the Soviet Government. " At present ", said Lenin, arguing the necessity of accepting the " shameful " peace, " we rely for support not only on the proletariat, but on the poorest peasantry which will abandon us if the war continues." [1] In the Brest-Litovsk debate at the seventh party congress Bubnov, one of Bukharin's followers, not unaptly described the October revolution as " a simultaneous wager on international revolution and on the peasant ".[2] It was left to Ryazanov, learned Marxist and *enfant terrible* of the party, to blurt out at the congress that the proletarian party " was bound to be confronted with a dilemma at the moment when it seized power, and would have to decide the question whether to rely on the peasant masses or on the proletariat of western Europe ".[3]

Lenin steadfastly refused to admit the question in this form. In his mind no incompatibility could exist between the two essential conditions of the victory of socialism in Russia. In his January theses on the conclusion of peace he had asked for no more than " a certain interval of time, not less than a few months, during which the socialist government must have its hands completely free to overcome the bourgeoisie first of all in its own country ".[4] In the debates of the central committee Stalin and Zinoviev offered him heavy-handed support: Stalin declared that " there is no revolutionary movement in the west, no facts, only a potentiality ", and Zinoviev argued that, though " by making peace we shall strengthen chauvinism in Germany and for a certain time weaken the movement everywhere in the west ", this was at least

---

[1] Lenin, *Sochineniya*, xxii, 200.
[2] *Sed'moi S"ezd Rossiiskoi Kommunisticheskoi Partii* (1923), p. 63.
[3] *Ibid.* p. 87.   [4] Lenin, *Sochineniya*, xxii, 194.

better than " the ruin of the socialist republic ". Lenin rejected
support based on either of these arguments. There *was* " a mass
movement in the west " though the revolution had not yet begun ;
and, if the Bolsheviks changed their tactics on that account, they
would be " traitors to international socialism ". On the other
hand, if Zinoviev was right, and if " the German movement is
capable of developing at once in the event of a rupture of peace
negotiations ", then " we ought to sacrifice ourselves, since the
German revolution will be far more powerful than ours ".[1] In
his speech at the seventh party congress Lenin repeated in categorical terms what he had said many times before and was to say
many times again :

> It is not open to the slightest doubt that the final victory of
> our revolution, if it were to remain alone, if there were no
> revolutionary movement in other countries, would be hopeless.
> . . . Our salvation from all these difficulties, I repeat, is an all-
> European revolution.[2]

Little more than a month afterwards, in his polemic against the
Left opposition, he once more established the position of principle :

> In the question of foreign policy two fundamental lines
> confront us — the proletarian line which says that the socialist
> revolution is dearer than anything else and above anything else,
> and that we must take into account whether it is likely to arise
> quickly in the west or not, and the other line, the bourgeois line,
> which says that for me the status of a great Power and national
> independence are dearer than anything else and above anything
> else.[3]

And again :

> He is no socialist who has not proved *by deeds* his readiness
> for the greatest sacrifices on the part of " his own " country,
> if only the cause of the socialist revolution can be really
> advanced.[4]

These were not the words of a man who believed that, by accepting
the Brest-Litovsk peace, he had sacrificed the cause of revolution
in Europe. And when eight months later Germany was on the

[1] *Protokoly Tsentral'nogo Komiteta RSDRP* (1929), pp. 204-205 ; Lenin,
Sochineniya, xxii, 202.   [2] *Ibid.* xxii, 319.
[3] *Ibid.* xxii, 481.   [4] *Ibid.* xxiii, 181.

verge of military defeat, and revolution seemed imminent over
half the continent, Lenin could without much difficulty persuade
himself that this was the reward and the consequence of the
Brest-Litovsk policy :

> Now even the blindest of the workers of the different
> countries will see how right the Bolsheviks were in basing all
> their tactics on support of a world-wide workers' revolution and
> in not fearing to make various most heavy sacrifices.[1]

Lenin turned the tables on the advocates of the " revolutionary
war " by attempting to prove that what had really been done at
Brest-Litovsk was to sacrifice short-sighted national pride to the
long-term cause of world revolution.

Lenin's disagreements with Trotsky over Brest-Litovsk were
less profound than those which separated him from the followers
of Bukharin. Trotsky's strong personality and his dramatic rôle
in the Brest-Litovsk story gave them a greater practical importance
and a greater prominence in the eyes both of contemporaries and
of posterity. But the popular picture of Trotsky, the advocate of
world revolution, clashing with Lenin, the champion of national
security or socialism in one country, is so distorted as to be almost
entirely false. Trotsky's agility of mind and flamboyance of
manner constantly led him to assert in its most extreme and dogmatic form any position which he happened at a given moment to
occupy. If Trotsky, in his capacity as People's Commissar for
Foreign Affairs, treated it as his main function to raise the banner
of world revolution, he was also assiduous and eloquent in asserting
national interests. The revolution was a fortnight old when
Trotsky taunted " the ruling classes of Europe " with failing to
realize that the peace decree was " a proposal emanating from a
state which represented many millions of people ".[2] A few days
later he proudly announced that " every Russian citizen, be he
even a political emigrant or a revolutionary soldier in France, now
finds himself under the protection of the governmental authority

---

[1] Lenin, *Sochineniya*, xxiii, 215. Another speech a few weeks later is still
more explicit : " At the time of the Brest peace we had to go in the face of
patriotism. We said : If you are a socialist, you must sacrifice your patriotic
feelings in the name of the international revolution, which is coming, which has
not yet come, but in which you must believe if you are an internationalist " (*ibid.*
xxiii, 313).

[2] *Protokoly Zasedanii VTsIK 2 Sozyva* (1918), p. 40.

of the Russian revolution "; [1] and it was about the same time that the Serbian Minister in Petrograd complained that the Bolsheviks were " the most out-and-out imperialists " and that " in foreign policy there is really no difference between Sazonov and Trotsky ".[2] In the Brest-Litovsk controversy, though Trotsky was the most eloquent and ingenious advocate of world revolution, he was also the champion of the policy of playing off one group of capitalists against the other; he was at the opposite pole to those who stood on the ground of pure revolutionary principle unsullied by compromise or expediency. " Facts intersect ", as Trotsky said in the central committee, " and therefore there can be a middle position ".[3] It was this capacity to bestride two extreme positions which had made Lenin reproach Trotsky in the past with lack of principle : " It is impossible to argue with Trotsky on the substance," he had written bitterly in 1911, " since he has no opinions." [4] The mutual confidence between the two men which had developed since the summer of 1917 did not alter this difference of intellectual approach.

What therefore ultimately resulted from the long debates over Brest-Litovsk was not the dramatic defeat of one principle by another, but the slow hammering out of a synthesis which was to shape Soviet relations with the world for several years to come. The process of argument as well as the pressure of events gradually narrowed the rift between Lenin and Trotsky, even when the Leftists remained irreconcilable. Trotsky's initial emphasis on world revolution was based on a serious exaggeration of revolutionary prospects in Germany. At the outset his optimism had been shared by Lenin and the whole party; and the strikes in Austria and Germany in January 1918 seemed for a moment to revive flagging hopes. Where Trotsky erred was in clinging to this optimism long after Lenin had abandoned it. When he announced his " no war, no peace " formula to the astonished German delegation at Brest-Litovsk, he expressed the firm conviction that " the German people and the peoples of Austria-Hungary will not allow " a resumption of hostilities.[5] Even after the Germans had

---

[1] Trotsky, *Sochineniya*, iii, ii, 178.
[2] I. Maisky, *Vneshnyaya Politika RSFSR, 1917-1922* (1922), p. 24.
[3] *Protokoly Tsentral'nogo Komiteta RSDRP* (1929), p. 251.
[4] Lenin, *Sochineniya*, xv, 303.
[5] *Mirnye Peregovory v Brest-Litovske*, i (1920), 209.

announced the resumption of hostilities on February 18, 1918, he still thought it " indispensable to wait and see what impression this will produce on the German people " and " how this influences the German workers ".[1] His objection to acceptance of the German ultimatum was the likelihood that it would merely open " the possibility of further ultimatums ".[2] Thus Trotsky gradually moved over into a position where he contested only the accuracy of Lenin's diagnosis, not the rightness of Lenin's policy if the diagnosis were correct. On the other hand, Lenin, while insisting on the needs of national defence, was so far from abandoning world revolution that he constantly stressed it as the supreme goal of his policy. What was necessary was a breathing space to complete the overthrow of the bourgeoisie and to organize at home ; having made peace " we shall free both our hands, and then we shall be able to wage a revolutionary war with international imperialism ".[3]

> To assume that there will be no breathing space and that there will be constant ultimatums [said Stalin answering Trotsky] is to believe that there is no movement at all in the west. We assume that the Germans cannot do everything. We also put our stake on the revolution, but you reckon in weeks and we in months.[4]

Sokolnikov added that they would " sign the terms as a limited postponement in order to prepare for revolutionary war ", Lenin confirming that he too thought it " indispensable to prepare for revolutionary war ".[5] And a party manifesto afterwards issued to explain the decision to accept the German terms concluded with an argument based on the interests of world revolution :

> By upholding Soviet power we render the best and most powerful support to the proletariat of all countries in its unprecedentedly difficult and onerous struggle against its own bourgeoisie. There could be no greater blow now to the cause of socialism than the collapse of Soviet power in Russia.[6]

[1] *Protokoly Tsentral'nogo Komiteta RSDRP* (1929), pp. 231, 241.
[2] *Ibid.* p. 248.   [3] *Ibid.* p. 201.
[4] *Ibid.* p. 250 ; with one exception (Stalin, *Sochineniya*, iv, 27) Stalin's interventions in these debates in the central committee are not reprinted in his collected works.
[5] *Protokoly Tsentral'nogo Komiteta RSDRP* (1929), p. 251.
[6] *Ibid.* (1929), p. 292.

This was national defence, but national defence with a difference :

> We are " defencists "; since October 25, 1917, we have won the right to defend the fatherland. We are not defending the secret treaties, we have torn them up; we have revealed them to the whole world; we are defending the fatherland against the imperialists. We defend, we shall conquer. We do not stand for the state, we do not defend the status of a great Power : of Russia nothing is left save Great Russia. These are not national interests; we affirm that the interests of socialism, the interests of world socialism, are higher than national interests, higher than the interests of the state. We are " defencists " of the socialist fatherland.[1]

Thus the final precipitate of the Brest-Litovsk crisis was a foreign policy which was designed equally to promote world revolution and the national security of the Soviet republic, and denied any inconsistency between these two essential aims. World revolution was the sole guarantee of national security; but national security was also a condition of the successful promotion of world revolution. Scarcely had the immediate pressure of German intervention been removed from the Soviet republic when the intervention of the opposing capitalist group began with the Japanese landing at Vladivostok on April 4, 1918. Thereafter, for two and a half years with one short intermission, Soviet Russia was in a state of undeclared war against the allied Powers. In conditions of war no incompatibility could in any case occur between the two facets of Soviet foreign policy. Military weakness made revolutionary propaganda among the peoples of the hostile Powers the most effective defensive weapon in the Soviet armoury.

> The facts of world history [wrote Lenin in November 1918] have proved to those Russian patriots who will hear of nothing but the immediate interests of their country, conceived in the old style, that the transformation of our Russian revolution into a socialist revolution was not an adventure but a necessity since *there was no other choice* : Anglo-French and American imperialism will *inevitably* strangle the independence and freedom of Russia *unless* world-wide socialist revolution, world-wide Bolshevism triumphs.[2]

But the motive of national defence against the foreign invader and his agents could also be directly invoked, and invested Soviet

---

[1] Lenin, *Sochineniya*, xxii, 13-14.   [2] *Ibid.* xxiii, 291.

policy, especially towards the end of this period, with an aura of Russian patriotism. It was only when the civil war ended, and the establishment of peaceful relations with the capitalist Powers was once more placed on the agenda in the early months of 1921, that the controversies and embarrassments of the dual policy once more reared their head, as they had done in the more dramatic days of peace-making at Brest-Litovsk. In the meanwhile the two facets of Soviet foreign policy — the encouragement of world revolution and the pursuit of national security — were merely different instruments of a single consistent and integrated purpose.

CHAPTER 22

THE DUAL POLICY

Two harsh and disconcerting realities had been revealed in the flashlight of the Brest-Litovsk crisis. The first was the abject military helplessness of the Soviet republic, whose territory lay wide open to the enemy on all sides. Little more than a month separated the cessation of the German offensive in White Russia and on the Baltic from the first Japanese landing in the Far East; and the extension and consolidation of the German occupation of the Ukraine proceeded unchecked throughout this period. The second was the postponement of the European revolution, on which the confident calculations, not merely of a few optimists but of every Bolshevik of any account, had been based. The January strikes in Vienna and Berlin had been crushed; the German Government had been so successful in plastering over the cracks that even the Bolsheviks forgot that they had ever been visible, and began, by process of reaction, to overestimate Germany's powers of resistance. The moral was clear. Whatever the future might hold, the Soviet régime at the moment depended for its survival on its own wretched resources.

The first overt reaction to this consciousness of isolation and weakness was a recognition of the need to organize military defence. It was essential to Marxist teaching that the revolution would destroy the army, together with the other public institutions of the bourgeois state, and create its own armed forces on a different pattern : the condition of any popular revolution in Europe, wrote Marx at the time of the Paris commune, was " not to transfer the bureaucratic-military machine from one group to another, as has been done hitherto, but to destroy this machine ".[1] Both the

---

[1] Marx i Engels, *Sochineniya*, xxvi, 105. Lenin in *The Proletarian Revolution and Renegade Kautsky*, written in the autumn of 1918, declared that " the first principle of every victorious revolution ", as propounded by Marx and Engels, was " to smash the old army, to dissolve it and to replace it by a new

First and the Second Internationals passed resolutions demanding the abolition of standing armies and their replacement by what was variously described as a " people's militia " or " the nation in arms ". Lenin in his *Letters from Afar*, written in Switzerland in March 1917, wanted to " fuse the police, the army and the bureaucracy with the *universally armed people* " and to " create a really all-popular, general, universal militia under the leadership of the proletariat ". He disclaimed having any " plan " for such a militia, but thought that it would " really arm the whole people universally and instruct it in the art of war ", thus providing a guarantee " against all attempts to restore reaction, against all intrigues of Tsarist agents ".[1] In *State and Revolution* he once more coupled the bureaucracy and the army as " the two most characteristic institutions " of the bourgeois state machine, which the revolution would have, not to take over, but to destroy.[2] When, therefore, Bolshevik propagandists helped in the process of disintegrating and dissolving the Russian army in 1917, they were acting consciously or unconsciously in accordance with established party doctrine. Almost the only large units which retained their cohesion throughout the period of disorder and passed over more or less intact from the old army to the new were the Lettish regiments, which thus secured for themselves a certain notoriety in the early days of the revolution.

The Red Guard which was the forerunner of the Red Army was conceived as a different kind of institution from the old army, resting on a different class structure and a different outlook and purpose. It came into existence in Petrograd, in the form of factory guards of workers, during the summer of 1917, and was recognized by the Petrograd Soviet during the Kornilov affair as a " workers' militia ". It was in the main a creation of the Bolsheviks and its ultimate loyalty was to the party. It was the Bolshevik delegation at the " democratic conference " in Moscow in September 1917 which demanded " the general arming of the workers and the organization of a Red Guard ".[3] On the other

one " (*Sochineniya*, xxiii, 378-379) ; but neither Marx nor Lenin himself before 1917 ever seems to have referred to the prospective revolutionary levies as an " army ". The word " army ", like " bureaucracy " and like " state " itself, had an unfriendly connotation.
  [1] Lenin, *Sochineniya*, xx, 35-37.   [2] *Ibid.* xxi, 388.
  [3] *Protokoly Tsentral'nogo Komiteta RSDRP* (1929), p. 63.

hand, the Red Guard had no serious military training, and conformed to the pattern laid down by Lenin in the previous March of
a militia to defend the revolution against counter-revolutionary
plots and intrigues rather than of an army equipped to fight in the
field. The numbers of the Red Guard in Petrograd in October
were officially estimated at no more than 10,000 to 12,000.[1] In
the well-organized coup which secured the victory of the October
revolution it had no real military opposition to face. During the
first weeks of the Soviet régime the main function of the Red
Guard was to seize or protect public buildings, to ensure essential
services and to guard the persons of the Soviet leaders.

As the moment for the seizure of power approached, however,
the ambiguities of the situation had already begun to preoccupy
some of the Bolshevik leaders. Long ago, under the immediate
impulse of the experiences of 1905, Trotsky had written that the
first task of a provisional revolutionary government would be " a
radical reorganization of the army ".[2] In June 1917 a conference
of Bolshevik military organizations spoke cautiously of the need
" to create material armed support for the revolution out of
revolutionary-democratic elements in the army who join and follow
the social-democrats ".[3] But the predominant assumption was
still that the torch of revolution, once successfully kindled in
Petrograd and Moscow, would quickly carry the conflagration
throughout the rest of Russia and throughout Europe, so that
military operations in defence of the revolution against organized
armies scarcely entered into the picture. The primary function
of the three members of the first Sovnarkom who formed a joint
" committee for military and naval affairs " was to complete the
liquidation and demobilization of the old army. It was the formation of organized armies by the " white " generals, and the beginnings of something like regular warfare in the Ukraine, which
forced on the new régime the task of building up a military force
capable of taking the field against them. The decision to create a
Red Army is said to have been taken at a meeting of party leaders

---

[1] *Bol'shaya Sovetskaya Entsiklopediya*, xxxiv (1937), 579, art. Krasnaya
Gvardiya ; Trotsky mentions a contemporary estimate of 40,000, and considers
it " probably exaggerated " (L. Trotsky, *Istoriya Russkoi Revolyutsii* (Berlin),
ii, ii (1933), 207).

[2] Trotsky, *Sochineniya*, ii, i, 62.

[3] *VKP(B) v Rezolyutsiyakh* (1941), i, 248.

on December 19, 1917/January 1, 1918; the title " Workers' and Peasants' Red Army " was chosen at this time.[1]

When this decision was taken, the peace negotiations at Brest-Litovsk had been adjourned for the first time and Trotsky was about to take his place at the head of the Soviet delegation. But the military danger was not yet fully realized and progress was slow. The Declaration of Rights of the Toiling and Exploited People originally adopted by VTsIK on January 3/16, 1918, announced the principle of " the arming of the toilers, the formation of a socialist Red Army of workers and peasants and the complete disarming of the propertied classes ".[2] Then, on January 15/28, 1918, the day on which Trotsky returned to Brest-Litovsk with the mandate of the party central committee for the last stage of the negotiations, Sovnarkom issued a decree for the establishment of a " Workers' and Peasants' Red Army " to be composed of volunteers drawn from " the more class-conscious and organized elements of the toiling masses ". This decree was followed a fortnight later by another creating a " Socialist Workers' and Peasants' Red Fleet ".[3] But how much these decrees meant in practice is another matter. It was afterwards recorded that in Petrograd, where the impulse to defend the revolution may be supposed to have been at its strongest, only 5500 volunteers enlisted in the first month after the publication of the decree.[4] But on February 22, 1918, when the German advance had been resumed, and Hoffmann's final terms were on their way, a proclamation of Sovnarkom was published in *Pravda* under the heading " The Socialist Fatherland is in Danger ". It proclaimed that " all the forces and resources of the country shall be devoted wholly to revolutionary defence; that workers and peasants along the line of the new front should mobilize battalions to dig trenches; and that all able-bodied persons of the bourgeoisie should be included in these battalions, working under the eyes of the Red Guard; and it concluded with the three-fold slogan :

[1] Unpublished archives of the Red Army quoted in *Voprosy Istorii*, No. 2, 1948, p. 50. Lenin, Stalin and Podvoisky (the senior member of the collegium on military affairs) are named as present at the meeting; but the mention of Stalin and omission of Trotsky are conventional for an article published in 1948, and not necessarily authentic.

[2] *Sobranie Uzakonenii, 1917–1918*, No. 15, art. 215.

[3] *Ibid.* No. 17, art. 245 ; No. 23, art. 325.

[4] G. S. Pukhov, *Kak Vooruzhalsya Petrograd* (1933), p. 12.

The socialist fatherland is in danger !
Long live the socialist fatherland !
Long live the international socialist revolution ! [1]

This proclamation was the starting-point of the first real recruiting drive for the Red Army. The following day, February 23, afterwards came to be celebrated as " Red Army Day " ; [2] and Trotsky, in half-jesting defence of his Brest-Litovsk policy, declared that " General Hoffmann's offensive helped us to begin serious work in creating the Red Army ".[3] According to the records the number of recruits in Petrograd, which stood at a total of only 5500 on February 25, had risen by March 1 to 15,300.[4] On March 4, 1918, the day after the signature of the Brest-Litovsk treaty, came the announcement of Trotsky's resignation of his post as People's Commissar for Foreign Affairs and appointment as president of a Supreme War Council.[5]

From this time emphasis on national defence became the constant theme of the Soviet leaders. At the seventh party congress which debated the ratification of Brest-Litovsk Lenin dwelt on the military plight of the country with unusual bitterness :

[1] According to Trotsky, the phrase " the socialist fatherland " was his suggestion, and, when the Left SRs protested, Lenin replied : " It shows at once the change of 180 degrees in our attitude to the defence of the fatherland ; it is exactly what we need " (L. Trotsky, *O Lenine* (n.d. [1924]), p. 104).

[2] How February 23 came to be accepted as " Red Army Day " is difficult to discover. The first " Red Army Day " to stimulate recruiting was proclaimed on January 28/February 10, 1918 (*Rabochaya i Krest'yanskaya Krasnaya Armiya i Flot*, No. 10 (55) of that date). A further " Red Army Day " was proclaimed for the same purpose on March 22, 1918, and was the occasion of a speech by Trotsky (see p. 65 below). For some time authoritative Soviet writers (e.g. Antonov-Ovseenko in *Za Pyat' Let* (1922), p. 155) were in the habit of explaining that the decree of January 15/28, 1918, for the creation of the Red Army was first issued on February 23 ; this is, however, incorrect. The current official party history, first published in 1938, refers to a repulse of the German invaders at Narva and Pskov by the " new army " and adds : " February 23 — the day on which the forces of German imperialism were repulsed — is regarded as the birthday of the Red Army " (*History of the Communist Party of the Soviet Union (Bolsheviks) : Short Course* (Engl. transl. 1939), p. 217).

[3] L. Trotsky, *Kak Vooruzhalas' Revolyutsiya*, i (1923), 14.

[4] G. S. Pukhov, *Kak Vooruzhalsya Petrograd* (1933), p. 13.

[5] R. H. Bruce Lockhart, *Memoirs of a British Agent* (1932), p. 242. In the first Sovnarkom the control of military affairs had been entrusted to a committee of three commissars, Antonov-Ovseenko, Krylenko and Dybenko : this was presently expanded into an " all-Russian collegium " of which Trotsky was a member (L. Trotsky, *Kak Vooruzhalas' Revolyutsiya*, i (1923), 101-102). The Supreme War Council was a new creation.

A country of small peasants, disorganized by war, reduced by it to unheard of misery, is placed in an exceptionally difficult position : we have no army and we have to go on living side by side with a bandit armed to the teeth.

And again :

It is the fault of the army that we are making peace with imperialism.[1]

The resolution of the congress in favour of ratification, since it was not to be published, was limited by no diplomatic restraints :

The congress recognizes it as indispensable to ratify the burdensome and humiliating treaty with Germany signed by the Soviet power, in view of the fact that we have no army, in view of the extremely sick condition of the demoralized front line units, in view of the necessity of taking advantage of any, even of the smallest, breathing-space before the imperialist attack on the Soviet Socialist Republic. . . .
Therefore the congress declares that it recognizes as the first and fundamental task of our party, of the whole vanguard of the conscious proletariat and of the Soviet power, to take the most energetic, ruthlessly decisive, draconian measures to raise the self-discipline and discipline of the workers and peasants of Russia, to explain the inevitability of Russia's historical approach to a patriotic socialist [2] war of liberation, to create everywhere and on all sides mass organizations sternly linked and welded together by a single iron will . . ., and, finally, to provide for the universal, systematic, general training of the adult population without distinction of sex, in military skills and military operations.[3]

And the resolution of VTsIK which approved ratification two days later went out of its way to affirm " the right and obligation to defend the socialist fatherland ".[4]   In the second half of March 1918, with the treaty officially ratified and the Soviet Government established in its new capital, the task of organizing the Red Army began to assume paramount importance.   A speech by Trotsky

[1] Lenin, Sochineniya, xxii, 318-319, 325.
[2] The word " socialist " was added to the familiar phrase used by all traditional Russian historians of the " patriotic " war of 1812 : the echo was intentional and could be missed by no Russian.
[3] VKP(B) v Rezolyutsiyakh (1941), i, 278.
[4] Lenin, Sochineniya, xxii, 410.

at the Moscow Soviet on March 19 was followed two days later by a proclamation in Trotsky's best rhetorical style on the needs of the new army; and the next day, March 22, 1918, was proclaimed as " Red Army Day " to stimulate the recruiting campaign.[1] Early in April a new post was created: Trotsky became People's Commissar for War.[2] Hitherto the old Ministry of War, renamed the Commisariat of War, had continued to deal with questions relating to the disbandment of the old army and stood in an uncertain relation to the Soviet organs concerned with the creation of the Red Army. The death of the old order and the birth of the new were treated as totally independent processes. When Trotsky added the title of People's Commissar for War to that of president of the Supreme War Council, he brought all military organizations in the Soviet republic under a single control. The principle of unity and continuity was for the first time tentatively asserted. It became clear that to organize the Red Army from scratch, without taking advantage either of the accumulated experience or of the surviving machinery of the old Russian army, was a task of herculean proportions. As time went on, more and more of the bricks and foundation-stones of the old dilapidated edifice were used in the construction of the new. The effect of the new policy was reciprocal. Radek relates that before the end of the proceedings at Brest-Litovsk, Altvater, the admiral assigned to the Soviet delegation, came to him and said :

> I came here because I was forced to. I did not trust you. But now I shall do my duty as never before; for I sincerely believe that I shall be serving my country in so doing.[3]

It was perhaps at this time that Lenin and Trotsky had conversations with Altvater and Behrens, another high naval officer, on the reorganization of the armed forces — apparently the first direct contacts with officers of the former régime.[4] Trotsky at the

---

[1] L. Trotsky, *Kak Vooruzhalas' Revolyutsiya*, i (1923), 25-30, 99-100.
[2] The appointment was confirmed by VTsIK on April 8, 1918 (*Protokoly Zasedanii VTsIK 4ᵒᵒ Sozyva* (1920), p. 73 ; the date April 28 (*ibid.* p. 4) is a misprint) ; by a coincidence it was the same session which decided by acclamation to make the red flag the " national flag " of the RSFSR (*ibid.* p. 74).
[3] Quoted in E. Wollenberg, *The Red Army* (2nd ed., 1940), p. 63.
[4] D. F. White, *The Growth of the Red Army* (Princeton, 1944), p. 28.

People's Commissariat of War soon perceived that an efficient Red Army would depend on the possibility of taking over not only much of the old machinery, but a stiffening of the old officer corps, and he set to work to break down the barriers of mutual suspicion which stood in the way.

A few weeks later another significant step was taken. Voluntary recruitment, however agreeable to revolutionary ideology, proved a failure as a means of bringing adequate man-power into the ranks of the Red Army. On April 22, 1918, after a speech by Trotsky at VTsIK, a decree was passed making the whole adult population liable to be called on either for military or for labour service. The decree maintained the hitherto accepted doctrine of the class character of the Red Army by reserving military training and military service in the strict sense of the term for the workers and peasants ; the others were destined for the less honourable service of the labour battalions.[1] On the same occasion VTsIK approved the terms of a new military oath under which the member of the Red Army, as " a son of the toiling people and a citizen of the Soviet Republic ", made his vow " before the working classes of Russia and of the whole world " to devote all his " activities and thoughts to the great goal of the liberation of all the workers ", and to fight " for the Soviet Republic, for the cause of socialism and for the brotherhood of the peoples." [2] A month later a fresh decree proclaimed the " transition from a volunteer army to a general mobilization of workers and poorest peasants " ; and calling up decrees for specific classes followed immediately.[3] The civil war acted as a forcing-house for many developments of which the seeds had been sown after Brest-Litovsk, or even before it. The condemnation of Shchastny [4] was an advertisement to serving

---

[1] *Sobranie Uzakonenii, 1917-1918*, No. 33, art. 443 ; the principle that " the honourable right of defending the revolution arms in hand is granted only to the toilers " was reaffirmed in article 10 of the constitution of the RSFSR. The " Left communists " of the period (see vol. 1, pp. 188-189) protested against the enrolment of the bourgeoisie as well as the employment of specialists (see the manifesto in *Kommunist*, No. 1, April 20, 1918, reprinted in Lenin, *Sochineniya*, xxii, 561-571) ; Radek developed the argument against it in *Kommunist*, No. 2, April 27, 1918, pp. 14-16.

[2] *Protokoly Zasedanii VTsIK 4ᵍᵒ Sozvya* (1920), pp. 176-177 ; *Sobranie Uzakonenii, 1917-1918*, No. 33, art. 446.

[3] *Ibid.* No. 41, art. 518 ; No. 43, art. 528 ; No. 44, art. 534.

[4] See Vol. 1, p. 163.

officers that they had the option of loyal service to the new régime or of going over openly to the " whites " : by no means all were prepared for the second alternative. Foreign intervention in the civil war gave the Soviet cause a flavour of Russian patriotism which later became an important factor. Meanwhile the civil war imposed on the Red Army the task of setting up an efficient central administration and command ; and central organization gradually replaced local initiative taking the form of voluntary recruitment of local levies.[1] In May 1918 the Red Army obtained a general staff and a commander-in-chief in the person of Vatsetis, a Lett, who was replaced two months later by Sergei Kamenev, a former Tsarist staff colonel. Trotsky's speech at the fifth All-Russian Congress of Soviets in July 1918 when the civil war was just beginning in earnest, was devoted to a general exposition of military policy. Temporary resort to the principle of voluntary recruitment was excused on the ground that the machinery for full conscription had not been ready in time ; and the employment of Tsarist officers as " military specialists " was stoutly defended. The resolution of the Congress swept away the distinction between workers and peasants and the former bourgeoisie or ruling class by applying the compulsory principle to " every honest and healthy citizen of from 18 to 40 ". It declared for " a centralized, well-trained and equipped army " and approved the employment of " military specialists ".[2] But the Red Army which conquered in the civil war was the logical outcome of steps initiated and foundations laid before the war began. It was in the aftermath of the Brest-Litovsk crisis that the initial decisions were taken which made it possible to turn the inchoate and unorganized revolutionary Red Guard into a national army.

---

[1] An account of what happened at Nizhny-Novgorod is probably typical of the period. The Nizhny-Novgorod Soviet did nothing about the organization of the Red Army till members of the soldiers' committee of the old Third Army appeared there at the end of February. With their help, a provincial " military section " was founded on March 14, 1918. But between that date and April 23rd only 1680 volunteers were recruited — many of them undesirables ; and a mutiny occurred among these on April 23rd. After this the enrolment and training of recruits was first seriously taken in hand. But the general mobilization decree was not applied till the end of August (*God Proletarskoi Diktatury : Yubiliinyi Sbornik* (Nizhny-Novgorod, 1918), pp 54-57).

[2] *Pyatyi Vserossiiskii S"ezd Sovetov* (1918), pp. 167-174 ; *S"ezdy Sovetov RSFSR v Postanovleniyakh* (1939), pp. 88-91.

The changed outlook on national defence seemed to imply a changed outlook on foreign relations, which found symbolical expression when, on the conclusion of the Brest-Litovsk treaty, Trotsky resigned his post as People's Commissar for Foreign Affairs. The fiery revolutionary agitator was succeeded by a scion of the old diplomacy whose early conversion to Bolshevism had not effaced a certain ingrained respect for traditional forms. Georgy Chicherin had resigned his post in the Tsarist Ministry of Foreign Affairs in 1904, left Russia, and joined the Russian Social-Democratic Party, apparently fluctuating in his allegiance between Bolshevik and Menshevik factions. His most important party assignment at this time was characteristic. At the end of 1907, during the period of reunion between the factions, the central committee set up a special commission to investigate the " expropriations " conducted by the militant organization of the party ; and Chicherin, as a person of independent standing in the party, was made president of the commission. The investigation was hushed up, and produced no result. This episode must have helped to account for subsequent animosities between Chicherin and Stalin and Chicherin and Litvinov. In the years after 1907 Chicherin was a Menshevik, and did not rejoin the Bolsheviks till 1917. Chicherin was, in virtue of his character and background, a singular figure in the Soviet constellation — a cultivated man of fastidious personal tastes, something of an aesthete, something of a hypochondriac, whose attachment to Marxism was rooted in his subtle and highly trained intellect rather than in his emotions. After Trotsky's whirlwind career at Narkomindel, Chicherin sat down to a patient and less spectacular task of organization. On March 25, 1918, Narkomindel was established in its new premises in Moscow, with Karakhan as deputy commissar and Radek as head of the western division. Litvinov became a member of the collegium of the commissariat a few weeks later.[1] By slow degrees a departmental and diplomatic staff was built up ;[2] and a decree of June 4, 1918, which, recognizing the " complete equality of great and small nations ", abolished

[1] *Desyat' Let Sovetskoi Diplomatii* (1927), pp. 7-10.

[2] The process was naturally slow ; as late as June 1918, a German observer noticed that " Chicherin himself undertakes the signing of passes, the reservation of compartments for our couriers and such trivialities " (K. von Bothmer, *Mit Graf Mirbach in Moskau* (Tübingen, 1922), p. 59).

the titles and ranks of ambassador and minister and substituted " plenipotentiary representative " (*polpred* for short), was, in spite of a certain ostentatious flouting of tradition, the beginning of the organization of a regular Soviet diplomatic service.[1]

While, however, Brest-Litovsk threw into relief some of the embarrassments and contradictions of the dual policy, it did not affect its essence. On March 14, 1918, the fourth All-Russian Congress of Soviets replied to Wilson's ambiguous greetings with a message addressed " to the people and, first and foremost, to the toiling and exploited classes of the United States of North America ", expressing confidence that " the happy time is not far distant when the toiling masses of all bourgeois countries will throw off the yoke of capital and establish the socialist organization of society which alone can ensure a lasting and just peace ".[2] It was in the best style of foreign policy by revolutionary proclamation, and constituted, as Zinoviev is said to have boasted, a " slap in the face " for the American President.[3] But on the following day, while the congress was still debating the ratification of the Brest-Litovsk treaty, *Izvestiya* carried a leading article by its editor Steklov, which, while mentioning the reply and not criticizing it, adopted a quite different approach. It pictured Soviet Russia as confronted by " two imperialisms, of which one has taken us by the throat (Germany) or is preparing to take us by the throat (Japan), while the other — in its own interests, of course — is ready to hold out to us a helping hand ". The " other " was the United States. The only question was: " Which imperialism is more dangerous for us — the German and Japanese, or the American ? " What was at stake, added the writer in a revealing phrase, was " the state significance of the Russian revolution ". Then, after a hint that the United States, " in view of its rivalry with Germany and Japan, could not allow Russia to fall under the domination of either of these Powers ", and that the Americans might one day " give us money, arms, engines, machinery, instructors, engineers, etc. to help us to overcome economic disorder and create a new and strong army ", the article ended with a firm declaration of principle :

[1] *Sobranie Uzakonenii, 1917–1918*, No. 39, art. 505.
[2] Klyuchnikov i Sabanin, *Mezhdunarodnaya Politika*, ii (1926), 135.
[3] D. F. Francis, *Russia from the American Embassy* (N.Y., 1921), p. 230.

We are convinced that the most consistent socialist policy can be reconciled with the sternest realism and most level-headed practicality.

An out-and-out revolutionary foreign policy thus continued to be practised side by side with a foreign policy which took account of " the state significance of the revolution ". Brest-Litovsk was the first occasion on which the new régime had been compelled to conform to the customary usages of international relations and to assume obligations in its capacity as a territorial state. Chicherin's appointment no doubt ushered in the reign of a " passive " policy, when " the period of a revolutionary offensive policy was replaced by a period of retreats and manœuvres ".[1] But this change fitted in perfectly with the needs of a desperate situation ; and it was noteworthy that, when Lenin, in a confidential memorandum written in May 1918 and not published in his lifetime, set out to define the policy of " retreats and manœuvres " of which Brest-Litovsk was itself the prototype, he spoke in terms not of change but of continuity :

The foreign policy of the Soviet power must not be changed in any respect. Our military preparation is still not completed, and therefore our general maxim remains as before — to tack, to retreat, to wait while continuing this preparation with all our might.

Lenin did not exclude " military agreements " with one or another of the " imperialist coalitions ". Weighing against one another the threat from Germany and the threat from Japan, he considered that for the moment " the danger of an occupation by the Germans of Petrograd, Moscow and the greater part of European Russia" was the more serious. But it was most important at present to avoid any " hasty or ill-considered step " which might " help the extreme elements in the war parties " of either country ; and this precluded any agreement with the Anglo-French coalition.[2] For the purists who assumed that foreign policy could be deduced from revolutionary first principles without regard to the circumstances of the moment, and that one of these principles was the maintenance of an equal and unqualified hostility to all the

[1] G. Chicherin, *Vneshnyaya Politika Sovetskoi Rossii za Dva Goda* (1920), p. 7.
[2] Lenin, *Sochineniya*, xxx, 384.

capitalist Powers, such calculation was a descent into " opportunism ", or a reversion to the diplomacy of the old régime; Martov bitterly denounced it as " a retreat to the policy of Milyukov ".[1] But the charge in the form in which it was usually made, namely, that after Brest-Litovsk the Soviet Government embraced a narrow policy of national interest and " decided to renounce the policy of the attack on imperialism ",[2] was false. The new insistence — in so far as it was new — on the " state significance " of the revolution implied no abandonment of earlier revolutionary positions. The dual policy had come into being from the first moment of the victory of the revolution. Brest-Litovsk and what came after it did not create it. But they did throw into relief and bring to the consciousness of friends and foes alike the complementary and the contradictory character of its two facets. This was already clearly apparent in the summer of 1918 in Soviet policy both towards Germany and towards the western allies.

Relations between Soviet Russia and Germany were formally governed by the Brest-Litovsk treaty; and those who afterwards reproached the Soviet Government with the abandonment of its revolutionary principles generally cited article 2 of the treaty, by which each party had undertaken " to refrain from all agitation and propaganda against the government or the state or military institutions of the other party ". In practice this famous article was of little or no account. There is no record of any discussion of it either at Brest-Litovsk or in Moscow before the signature of the treaty, or of any objections raised to it. It seems to have been accepted by the Soviet delegation in the same light-hearted spirit in which the German delegation accepted the prohibition in the armistice on the removal of troops to Germany's western front, and with as little belief that compliance with it was seriously expected by the other party. " I hope we may be able to start a revolution in your country also ", Joffe had remarked amiably to Czernin at Brest-Litovsk.[3] In signing the Brest-Litovsk treaty Sokolnikov, the head of the Soviet delegation in its last phase, had

---

[1] *Chetvertyi Chrezvychainyi S"ezd Sovetov* (1920), p. 32.
[2] This charge was made by Radek in an article signed " Viator " in *Kommunist*, No. 2, April 27, 1918.
[3] O. Czernin, *Im Weltkriege* (1919), p. 305.

expressed Soviet confidence that " this triumph of imperialism and militarism over the international proletarian revolution will prove only temporary and transitory ".[1] In public it was necessary to maintain throughout 1918 the fiction of faithfully carrying out article 2 of the treaty.

> This article we really observe [said Chicherin at a session of VTsIK], and if it is violated by any of our official organs the Soviet Government takes measures against it.[2]

But at the seventh party congress which met in private to debate the ratification of the treaty no such discretion was required. " Yes, of course, we have violated the treaty ", exclaimed Lenin in advocating ratification ; " we have already violated it thirty or forty times." [3] And Sverdlov at the same congress explained the situation in his more laboured style :

> It results from the treaty which we have signed and which we shall shortly have to ratify at the [All-Russian] Congress [of Soviets], it results inevitably that we shall no longer be able in our capacity as a government, as the Soviet power, to carry on that widespread international agitation which we have hitherto conducted. This does not mean that we shall engage in such agitation one single jot less. But we shall now have regularly to carry on this agitation not in the name of Sovnarkom, but in the name of the central committee of our party.[4]

Steps were at once taken to apply the new principle. The principal instrument of the Soviet Government for organized revolutionary propaganda had hitherto been the international section under Radek, attached first to Narkomindel and, since the beginning of 1918, to VTsIK, and composed mainly of national groups of prisoners of war.[5] This section was now abolished. The national groups were, in the words of a later report, " put on a strictly party footing ", being transformed into foreign sections attached to the central committee of the Russian Bolshevik party : these were later organized into a " federation of foreign groups of

[1] *Mirnye Peregovory v Brest-Litovske*, i (1920), 231.
[2] *Pyatyi Sozyv Vserossiiskogo Tsentral'nogo Ispolnitel'nogo Komiteta* (1919), p. 90.
[3] Lenin, *Sochineniya*, xxii, 327.
[4] *Sed'moi S"ezd Rossiiskoi Kommunisticheskoi Partii* (1923), p. 195.
[5] See p. 18 above.

the Russian Communist Party ".[1] Thus there were formed in Moscow during April 1918 German, Magyar, Austrian and Yugoslav groups of the Russian party, each under its national head, Thomas for the Germans, Bela Kun for the Magyars, Ebengolz for the Austrians and Mikhailov for the Slavs. Each of these groups issued its own periodical and other propagandist literature. Each carried on work among prisoners of war of its nationality, pressing some to join the Red Army and training others as propagandists and agitators to work behind the enemy lines or to be sent back, when opportunity offered, as missionaries to their own countries. The central groups were quite small. The German group started in April 1918 with eleven members, but increased during the year to some hundreds; the Magyar group started with four or five and rose to ninety by the end of the year.[2] All accounts pay tribute to the success of their work among prisoners of war :

> In every camp prisoners were divided into two camps — the grey mass of the rank and file (cannon fodder) on the one side, the gentry and officer class on the other. The first was drawn towards the Soviets, the second towards the representatives of the different legations of the so-called neutral states, and the embassies and consulates of their enemies of yesterday, the allies of the former Russia.[3]

The disintegrated armies of the central Powers herded in prison camps proved as fruitful a field as the defeated Russian army for a revolutionary propaganda which relied largely on class discrimination. Work among prisoners of war at this time was, as Lenin said

---

[1] *Vos'moi S"ezd RKP(B)* (1933), p. 435 ; John Reed in *The Liberator* (N.Y.), January 1919, p. 24 : according to this source the new "unofficial" organization received a subvention of 20,000,000 rubles.

[2] *Vos'moi S"ezd RKP(B)* (1933), pp. 436-439. The Czechoslovaks were favoured by being allowed to form in May 1918 an independent communist party of their own with nearly a thousand members (*ibid.* p. 438) ; its founding congress, held in Moscow from May 25 to 27, 1918, is described in P. Reimann, *Geschichte der Kommunistischen Partei der Tschechoslowakei* (1931), pp. 68-77. It did not survive, and the subsequent Czechoslovak Communist Party represented a fresh start. Reference is made to a "Hungarian party school" in Moscow in November 1918 (*Krasnaya Nov'*, No. 10 (1926), p. 140).

[3] *Proletarskaya Revolyutsiya*, No. 7 (90), 1929, p. 97 : according to one source, the work was much more successful among the Austrians than among the Germans, who, "even the social-democrats, displayed a disappointing hostility " (J. Sadoul, *Notes sur la Révolution Bolchevique* (1919), p. 325).

later, " the real foundation of what has been done to create a Third International ".[1] Nor were the eastern peoples immune from the same process. Suphi, a Turkish socialist who had fled to Russia in 1914 and been interned, was the principal agitator among Turkish prisoners of war; at the end of 1918 he was able to claim that " Turkish military-revolutionary organizations already exist in Russia " and — no doubt with considerable exaggeration — that " thousands of Turkish Red Army men are serving at present in the ranks of the Red Army on different fronts of the Soviet republic ".[2] Chinese coolies imported into Russia for labour during the war were similarly organized into a " union of Chinese workers in Russia ".[3]

The elaborate attempt to place the prisoners of war propaganda organization on an unofficial and party basis did not prevent the holding in Moscow in the middle of April 1918 of a series of organized demonstrations. On April 14 Bela Kun addressed a mass meeting of prisoners of war :

> Sweep from the path all obstacles to the liberation of the enslaved, turn into ashes all castles, all palaces into which your wealth flows and from which poverty and hunger are spread all over the country. . . . Turn your weapons against your officers and generals and against the palaces. Let every one of you be a teacher of revolution in his regiment.[4]

Three days later saw the opening of an All-Russian Congress of Internationalist Prisoners of War with 400 delegates. It issued a manifesto appealing to prisoners of war to join the Red Army or to return home and become " pioneers of the international socialist revolution of proletarians "; and among its slogans was an anticipatory " Long Live the Third International ".[5] The con-

[1] Lenin, Sochineniya, xxiv, 128.

[2] Sowjet-Russland und die Völker der Welt (Petrograd, 1920), p. 33.

[3] Foreign Relations of the United States, 1919: Russia (1937), pp. 190-194 ; early in 1919 the United States Government objected to a British proposal to arrange for their repatriation on the ground that it was undesirable to bring back to China " workmen and coolies who have been under the influence of Bolshevik rule in Russia ".

[4] Izvestiya, April 17, 1918.

[5] Ibid. April 19, April 21, 1918 ; Proletarskaya Revolyutsiya, No. 7 (90), 1929, pp. 102-103 ; J. Sadoul, Notes sur la Révolution Bolchevique (1919), pp. 313-314. The scanty and rather inconspicuous reports of the congress in Izvestiya suggest a certain anxiety about the consequences of too much publicity. Congresses of prisoners of war were held about the same time in other centres.

gress set up a central executive committee which, in a half-hearted attempt at camouflage, called itself the " executive committee of foreign workers and peasants ".[1]

These proceedings were watched with growing indignation by the victors of Brest-Litovsk. On the eve of the Moscow congress a strong protest was received from the German Government; it declared among other things that Ebengolz and Mikhailov had been compelling prisoners in camps visited by them to join the Red Army, and demanded the arrest of both.[2] The reply was cautious and evasive. Soviet nationality was hastily conferred on those who might be exposed to reprisals. On April 20, 1918, Trotsky in his capacity of People's Commissar for War issued an order enjoining on all military institutions strict observance of the Brest-Litovsk prohibition on propaganda, especially in relation to prisoners; this was followed by similar warnings from Narkomindel and from the People's Commissariat of Internal Affairs addressed to " all Soviets of Workers', Peasants' and Soldiers' Deputies "; and a week later, the " executive committee of foreign workers and peasants " was replaced by a " central collegium for prisoners of war and refugees " attached to the People's Commissariat of War and presided over by Unshlikht, the deputy commissar.[3] But this sharing between party and state of responsibility for prisoners of war did not herald any immediate change of policy. In the last days of April 1918 the first German Ambassador to the Soviet Government arrived in Moscow. One of his first official appearances was at the May Day parade; and among the military units which passed in procession was a detachment of German prisoners carrying a banner which exhorted their German comrades to throw off the yoke of the emperor. This episode led to a further stiff protest, and to a Soviet reply promising in future to enlist no foreign nationals in the Red Army — an undertaking which could at once be readily circumvented by conferring Soviet nationality on those incriminated.[4] Propaganda

[1] *Proletarskaya Revolyutsiya*, No. 7 (90), 1929, pp. 108-110.
[2] *Izvestiya*, April 16, 1918; *Proletarskaya Revolyutsiya*, No. 7 (90), 1929, p. 107.
[3] *Izvestiya*, April 21, 23, 1918; *Proletarskaya Revolyutsiya*, No. 7 (90), 1929, pp. 107-108; *Sobranie Uzakonenii, 1917-1918*, No. 34, art. 451.
[4] W. Hard, *Raymond Robins' Own Story* (N.Y., 1920), p. 182; *Papers Relating to the Foreign Relations of the United States, 1918: Russia*, ii (1932), 131. The

among prisoners of war by the national groups under party auspices, as well as the recruitment of prisoners for the Red Army,
continued unabated down to the armistice of November 1918,
though repetition of the open provocations of April and May seems
to have been avoided. After November 1918 German and Austrian
prisoners of war took over their respective embassy buildings in
Moscow,[1] and set up councils of workers' and soldiers' deputies
which organized the despatch of agitators to central Europe.[2]

The Brest-Litovsk treaty, while it did little or nothing to check
Bolshevik activity among prisoners of war, opened up a new and
hitherto untried channel of propaganda. The arrival of Joffe in
Berlin in April 1918 as the first Soviet representative to Germany
was the signal for an intensive revolutionary campaign. Joffe
refused to present his credentials to the Kaiser, and invited to his
first official banquet the leaders of the anti-war Independent
Social-Democratic Party, several of whom were in prison.[3] Many
years later Joffe gave an account of his mission to an American
writer who has put it on record :

> His embassy in Berlin [he said] served as staff headquarters
> for a German revolution. He bought secret information from
> German officials and passed it on to radical leaders for use in
> public speeches and in articles against the government. He
> bought arms for the revolutionaries and paid out 100,000 marks
> for them. Tons of anti-Kaiser literature were printed and
> distributed at the Soviet Embassy's expense. " We wanted to
> pull down the monarchist state and end the war ', Joffe said
> to me. " President Wilson tried to do the same in his own
> way." Almost every evening after dark, Left-wing independent

arming of German and Austrian prisoners of war also caused anxiety to the allies
and was one of their excuses for intervention. The idea that these prisoners
would fight again for the central Powers against the allies was, of course, far-
fetched ; but some of them participated in hostilities against the Czech legion
in Siberia.

[1] Radek records the good-humoured protest of the Austrian Ambassador,
who kept his room in the embassy ; on the other hand, " the German officials
behaved with unheard of cowardice " (*Krasnaya Nov'*, No. 10 (1926), p. 143).

[2] *Vos'moi S"ezd RKP(B)* (1933), p. 437 ; two delegates of a Petrograd
German Council of Workers' and Soldiers' Deputies were refused admission to
the second All-German Congress in Berlin in April 1919 (2[i] *Vsegermanskii
S"ezd Rabochikh i Soldatskikh Sovetov* (1935), pp. 325-326).

[3] John Reed in *The Liberator* (N.Y.), January 1919, p. 24 ; the same source
adds the picturesque detail that Joffe sent out ten " expert propagandists " to
tour Germany on bicycles.

socialist leaders slipped into the embassy building in Unter den Linden to consult Joffe on questions of tactics. He was an experienced conspirator. They wanted his advice, guidance and money. " In the end, however," Joffe commented ruefully, " they, we, accomplished little or nothing of permanent value. We were too weak to provoke a revolution." [1]

After the German collapse both sides had for different motives a certain interest in magnifying the part played in it by Bolshevik propaganda ; and some exaggerated statements of the scope of Joffe's activities were current.[2] But it is well established that he furnished money to Ernst Meyer, the editor of the *Spartakus Letters*, for the distribution of his pamphlets,[3] and that large sums passed through the hands of Oskar Cohn, a member of the USPD, who seems to have acted as legal adviser and business factotum for the Soviet Embassy.[4] The trade in arms can hardly have been

[1] L. Fischer, *Men and Politics* (1941), p. 31.

[2] Joffe, in reply to a German statement that he had spent 105,000 marks on arms for the revolutionaries, retorted that he had given " not 105,000 marks, but several hundred thousand marks " for the purpose to Barth, the independent social-democratic leader (*Izvestiya*, December 6, 1918) ; Chicherin, who had formerly asserted the complete fidelity of the Soviet Government to the Brest-Litovsk treaty, admitted in a note to the German Government that funds had been supplied to Joffe for propaganda (*ibid.* December 26, 1918). On the German side, Hoffmann repeats a report that Joffe had a balance of 22,000,000 marks at a Berlin bank (*Die Aufzeichnungen des Generalmajors Max Hoffmann* (1929), i, 223).

[3] The Spartakusbund was the name popularly applied to a revolutionary anti-war group composed mainly of intellectuals which arose on the extreme Left of the German Social-Democratic Party in 1916 : its outstanding figure was Rosa Luxemburg. The name was derived from the *Spartakusbriefe*, the title under which its illegal literature was circulated. In April 1917 a split occurred in the Social-Democratic Party (SPD), and its Left wing formed the Independent Social-Democratic Party (USPD) with a predominantly anti-war platform. The Spartakists joined the USPD, but remained an independent group within it, continuing to form an extreme revolutionary Left in the new party.

[4] According to Joffe's statement in *Izvestiya*, December 17, 1918, Cohn received from him 10,000,000 rubles " in the interests of the German revolution ", and a further 500,000 marks and 150,000 rubles were handed over to Cohn on the eve of Joffe's expulsion : of this, 350,000 marks and 50,000 rubles were earmarked " for the needs of Russian citizens remaining in Germany ". For information from the German side see R. H. Lutz, *The Causes of the German Collapse in 1918* (Stanford, 1934), pp. 108, 152 ; Cohn, who boasted in December 1918 that he had " gladly accepted the funds which our party friends placed at my disposal through comrade Joffe for the purpose of the German revolution ", tried later to pretend that most of the money had been intended for the relief of Russian prisoners of war in Germany.

large. But the flow of incendiary literature was copious and continuous.

These proceedings were a straightforward continuation of the policy of the period before Brest-Litovsk, and a logical deduction from the doctrine that the primary aim of that policy was to encourage revolution in the principal capitalist countries, especially in Germany. But, apart from these propaganda activities on the Soviet side, other causes contributed to the extreme tension which continued to mark Soviet-German relations during the two months after the conclusion of the Brest-Litovsk treaty. The German Government made haste to consolidate the advantages accruing to it from the treaty. On March 7, 1918, it signed a treaty of peace with the " white " government of Finland, then engaged in a bitter civil war against a Finnish Socialist Workers' government, which had concluded a treaty with the Soviet Government a week earlier,[1] and had for the past two months enjoyed the support of Russian units. At the beginning of April a German army under Von der Goltz landed in Finland ; and a month later the civil war was over — except for the " white terror " which followed it. In the Ukraine the German troops steadily advanced till they had occupied the whole country, ineffectively harried by SR and Bolshevik partisan detachments supported or encouraged from Moscow.[2] On April 22 Chicherin protested against a German advance into the Crimea beyond the frontiers of the Ukraine as laid down at Brest-Litovsk or as claimed by any Ukrainian Government.[3] The coolness of the official reception of the German Ambassador, Mirbach, when he presented his credentials to Sverdlov on April 26, 1918, was widely noted ; [4] and on the same day Chicherin despatched a further note protesting against the incursion of German forces into central Russia and the Crimea and demanding strict adherence to the terms laid down at Brest-Litovsk.[5] At the same moment the Russian Black Sea fleet

---

[1] See Vol. 1, p. 288.

[2] Voroshilov, later People's Commissar for War, rose to fame in these operations as a partisan leader ; a highly idealized account of them is given in a volume published in the second world war, *Razgrom Nemetskikh Zakhvatchikov v Ukraine 1918 g.* (1943).

[3] *Izvestiya*, April 23, 1918.

[4] *Foreign Relations of the United States : Russia*, i (1931), 506.

[5] *Ibid.* i, 512-513.

was withdrawn from Sebastopol to Novorossiisk to save it from falling into German hands, and, when the Germans demanded its return, secretly scuttled — much to the satisfaction of the western allies.[1] As late as May 5, 1918, Bruce Lockhart in a letter to Robins listed the steps taken by Trotsky to promote cooperation with the allies and concluded that " this does not look like the action of a pro-German agent ".[2] In that aspect of Soviet policy which consisted in manœuvring between the groups of capitalist Powers and seeking reinsurance against the hostility of one group by appeasement of the other, it seemed in the spring of 1918 as if Germany was the final and irreconcilable enemy.

The balance of Soviet policy was, however, rapidly reversed by the development of a new and direct threat from the opposite camp. Up to the middle of May 1918 the threat from Germany still appeared as the worst external danger confronting the régime. But about this time it became apparent that the Japanese landing at Vladivostok in April[3] was not an isolated incident, but the forerunner of allied intervention on a much larger scale. The revolt of the Czech legion actually occurred in the last days of May 1918 and the first British landing in force at Murmansk towards the end of June.[4] Thus, just as in the darkest days of January and February 1918, a desperate and abortive attempt had been made to woo allied support to ward off the imminent German peril, so now the threat of allied intervention almost automatically set in motion the manœuvre of seeking support on the other side and of reaching an accommodation with the German Government on a more solid basis of mutual advantage than the unilateral

[1] Official material relating to this affair is in *Arkhiv Russkoi Revolyutsii* (Berlin), xiv (1924), 153-221 ; see also R. H. Bruce Lockhart, *Memoirs of a British Agent* (1932), p. 279.

[2] *Russian-American Relations*, ed. C. K. Cummings and W. W. Pettit (N.Y., 1920), pp. 202-203.

[3] Japanese troops landed at Vladivostok on April 5, 1918, as an alleged reprisal for the murder of two Japanese on the previous day. On April 6 Chicherin addressed a note to the allied representatives asking to be informed of the attitude of their governments " to the events which have taken place in Vladivostok " (*Correspondance Diplomatique* (Moscow, 1918), p. 3) — a request to which no replies were received.

[4] There had been a small British detachment in Murmansk for the ostensible purpose of guarding stores and the railway against possible German attack since the beginning of March, when it had landed with the tacit consent of the Soviet authorities.

settlement of Brest-Litovsk. It was a desperate manœuvre, rendered still more desperate by the need to combine it with the revolutionary tactics pursued by Joffe in Berlin. But the peril from the allies was growing every day. What made the manœuvre possible — though this was not yet realized in Moscow — was the growing consciousness in German military circles of the same peril. As the great German offensive in France petered out in the summer of 1918, Germany was for the first time really hard pressed in the west : it became a peremptory German interest to improve on the state of armed truce which was all that the Brest-Litovsk treaty had left behind it on the eastern front.

The change-over was signalled by the long and rather rambling speech on foreign policy delivered by Lenin to a joint meeting of VTsIK and the Moscow Soviet on May 14, 1918. He was clearly seeking to sound a note of caution. He described Soviet Russia, now restricted to the limits of " Great Russia ", as " for the time being an oasis in a raging sea of imperialist banditry " ; he repeated the warning of his confidential memorandum of a few days earlier [1] against any rash step which might " help the extreme parties of the imperialist Powers of west or east " ; and he ended by reading a soothing telegram just received from Joffe, who reported the willingness of the German Government to negotiate on all out-standing issues.[2] Even this hint of the need to improve relations with Germany was, however, greeted with a degree of hostility which explains Lenin's cautious approach. Strong opposition was encountered from the Right SRs who frankly wanted a pro-Entente orientation, from the Left SRs who believed that the revolution was " sufficiently strong to have its own orientation ", and from the Mensheviks who still regarded the Germans as " leaders of all counter-revolutionary forces " and proposed to recall the Constituent Assembly.[3]

But allied plans of intervention and allied support for counter-revolutionary conspiracy were now maturing fast and could no longer be concealed. The session of May 14, 1918, which ended in a formal vote of confidence for the Soviet Government, marked a turning-point. A Soviet-German commission on the repatria-

[1] See p. 70 above.   [2] Lenin, *Sochineniya*, xxiii, 3-16.
[3] *Protokoly Zasedanii VTsIK 4ᵍᵒ Sozyva* (1920), pp. 277-278, 281-282, 290-291.

tion of prisoners of war was already working in a leisurely but not unfriendly way in Moscow.[1] On May 15, 1918, Soviet-German negotiations for a renewal of commercial relations opened in Berlin : it was explained from the Soviet side that a loan would be necessary to enable Soviet Russia to discharge her financial obligations to the central Powers, the question of payment in gold or in goods was discussed, and concessions in Russia were tentatively offered.[2] The principal negotiators on the Soviet side, besides Joffe, were Larin, Sokolnikov, Krasin and Menzhinsky,[3] who was at this time Soviet consul-general in Berlin ; on the German side, Nadolny and Kriege,[4] two officials of the Ministry of Foreign Affairs who had also taken part in the Brest-Litovsk negotiations, and Stresemann as a member of the Reichstag speaking for German industry.[5] No details of these negotiations were divulged ; but already before the end of May there was talk in

---

[1] Many details will be found in K. von Bothmer, *Mit Graf Mirbach in Moskau* (Tübingen), 1922 ; the author, an officer on Mirbach's staff, worked on this commission. The Germans were evidently in no hurry to complete the negotiations, since they did not wish to lose the labour of the 1,500,000 Russian prisoners held by them.

[2] Statement by Bronsky, head of the Soviet trade delegation in Berlin, in *Izvestiya*, July 4, 1918.

[3] These are named in an interview by Joffe in *Izvestiya*, August 16, 1918. Krasin, who played a rôle in the early history of the party (see Vol. 1, pp. 45-46), left it about 1908 and devoted himself exclusively to his professional work as an engineer : he became manager in Petrograd of the German firm of Siemens-Schuckert. He was in Petrograd in November 1917, but played no part in the revolution and left for Sweden early in 1918. In May 1918 he came to Berlin at Joffe's invitation to assist in the Soviet-German negotiations. In August 1918 he returned to Moscow, became a member of the presidium of the Supreme Council of National Economy and took charge of foreign trade.

[4] Kriege, who was head of the legal department, is named both by Hoffmann (*Die Aufzeichnungen des Generalmajors Max Hoffmann* (1929), ii, 218) and by Ludendorff (*My War Memories* (Engl. transl., n.d.), ii, 657) as the evil genius who foisted a pro-Russian policy on the German Government. The same view is expressed by K. von Bothmer (*Mit Graf Mirbach in Moskau* (Tübingen, 1922), pp. 91, 105), who also reflects military opinion. That the anti-Soviet view had its representatives in Mirbach's mission is suggested by W. von Blücher, *Deutschlands Weg nach Rapallo* (Wiesbaden, 1951), p. 15, which speaks of the secret relations of the mission with " the opposition ", and adds that " they never, so far as I know, came to the knowledge of the Bolsheviks ".

[5] H. Kessler, *Walther Rathenau : His Life and Work* (Engl. transl., 1929), pp. 291-292 ; according to this source " negotiations were prolonged by the fantastic demands of Ludendorff and his staff ", who demanded " a Cossack republic on the Don under a German protectorate ".

Moscow of a " German orientation ".[1] Krasin's German contacts, which were influential and extensive, were probably more important at this time than the official activities of Joffe. Early in June Krasin travelled to the western front for an interview with Ludendorff, which seems, however, to have gone no further than a fairly amicable exchange of recriminations about breaches of the Brest-Litovsk treaty by both sides. He met leading German official personalities, including Brockdorff-Rantzau, now German Minister in Copenhagen and a recent candidate for the chancellorship. In the German business world he was thoroughly at home. The directors of Siemens-Schuckert, whose manager in Petrograd Krasin had formerly been, were anxious only to wind up their Russian commitments. But Krasin was able to discuss with the rival AEG the supply of electrical equipment to Russia, and arranged for immediate shipments of coal " to save Petrograd from succumbing to the cold ".[2] Meanwhile negotiations were proceeding in Kiev for the making of peace between the Soviet Government and the German-sponsored government of the Ukraine ; and every attempt of the Left SRs to involve Moscow in revolts against German authority in the Ukraine was sternly repressed. The decision of the Left SRs to assassinate several leading Germans was a deliberate attempt to destroy this incipient Soviet-German *rapprochement*. The assassination of the German Ambassador, Mirbach, was carried out on July 6, 1918, during the session of the fifth All-Russian Congress of Soviets, at a moment when counter-revolutionary risings against the Soviet Government were timed to begin in several centres.[3]

[1] J. Sadoul, *Notes sur la Révolution Bolchevique* (1919), p. 354 ; the letter in which this is reported is a well-balanced description of policy and opinion in Moscow at this period. Rumours of an impending " Russo-German alliance " were sufficiently current in Germany in the summer of 1918 to reach Rosa Luxemburg in prison (P. Fröhlich, *Rosa Luxemburg : Her Life and Work* (1940), pp. 268-269).

[2] The only sources for Krasin's stay in Germany are unfortunately his non-political letters to his wife, of which extracts are printed in English translation in L. Krasin, *Leonid Krasin : His Life and Work* (n.d. [1929]), pp. 79-95. From these nearly everything of political interest is omitted ; for example, the record of the conversation with Brockdorff-Rantzau runs : " We talked about all sorts of things, and he offered his help in case you should decide to go and live in Denmark ".

[3] See Vol. 1, pp. 164-165 ; a graphic eye-witness account of the assassination is in K. von Bothmer, *Mit Graf Mirbach in Moskau* (Tübingen, 1922), pp. 71-79.

It was not an unreasonable calculation of the Left SRs that the murder of Mirbach would lead to a worsening of Soviet-German relations, if not to an open breach. The precedent of the murder of the German Minister in Peking by Chinese Boxers, and the military reprisals which followed this act, was freely quoted. This time, however, to the astonishment of many, there was no such sequel to record. The Soviet Government, at a moment when it was meeting both internal conspiracy fostered by the western allies and the external threat of allied intervention in the north as well as in Siberia, had to seek at almost any cost to avoid a breach of its relations with the other imperialist camp. But Germany, faced with a rapidly deteriorating military situation, equally wished above all to avoid a recrudescence of trouble on its eastern front. Hence the Mirbach murder was handled on both sides in a spirit of unlooked-for caution and conciliation. An initial demand from the German Government to send a battalion of German troops to Moscow was whittled down to an agreement for an unarmed guard of 300 men on the premises of the embassy.[1] The German Government continued to protest, now and later,[2] that it had not received full satisfaction. Nevertheless, three weeks after the murder, on July 28, 1918, the new German Ambassador, Helfferich, was installed in Moscow. His brief stay was marked by a significant episode. On August 1, 1918, Chicherin visited him at the German embassy[3] — it was apparently their only meeting — and informed him that, owing to the British landing in Murmansk, the Soviet Government had no further interest in " postponing " a German-Finnish intervention in Karelia which had already been mooted in Berlin. He added that " an open military alliance was impossible in the state of public opinion, but parallel action in fact was possible ".[4] This

---

[1] *Pyatyi Sozyv Vserossiiskogo Tsentral'nogo Ispolnitel'nogo Komiteta* (1919), p. 89 ; G. Chicherin, *Vneshnyaya Politika Sovetskoi Rossii za Dva Goda* (1920), pp. 14-15.

[2] See pp. 94, 325 below.

[3] For security reasons Helfferich did not leave the embassy building except for one short walk during his ten days in Moscow (K. von Bothmer, *Mit Graf Mirbach in Moskau*, pp. 120-121). Eichhorn, the German commander in the Ukraine, was assassinated two days after Helfferich's arrival.

[4] K. Helfferich, *Der Weltkrieg* (1919), iii, 466. Chicherin recorded the same conversation in a commemorative article published after Lenin's death : " When in August the Entente was already virtually waging war against us, occupying Archangel and pressing southward from there, advancing in the east

virtual invitation to German troops, with Finnish support, to march through Soviet territory against the allied invaders at Murmansk and Archangel was a precise counterpart of Trotsky's attempts of the previous February to enlist allied aid against the advancing Germans. But Germany, like the allies, hesitated to embark on so hazardous an adventure. Ten days after his arrival, having given instructions to move the embassy to Petrograd, Helfferich left Moscow to attend a German crown council at Spa. Here on August 8, 1918, the German high command first faced the danger of impending defeat and decided on the urgent need to curtail military commitments. Thereafter there could be no question of eastern adventures. Helfferich did not return to his post, and a few days later the German embassy moved to Pskov in German-occupied territory.[1]

Meanwhile the Soviet-German negotiations were proceeding smoothly in Berlin, where the Soviet negotiators were more pliant than they would have been if they had realized the full extent of German military weakness.[2] At the end of June the German

with the help of the Czechoslovaks and directing the " volunteer " army of Alexeev in the south, Vladimir Ilich made the attempt to utilize the antagonism of the two warring imperialist coalitions in order to weaken the attack of the Entente. After detailed discussion with Vladimir Ilich, I visited personally the new German Ambassador Helfferich in order to negotiate with him about common action against Alexeev in the south and about the possibility of sending a German detachment against the Entente troops on the White Sea. The further development of this plan was interrupted by the sudden departure of Helfferich " (*Lenin : Sein Leben und Werk* (Vienna, 1924), p. 93). The state- ment in L. Fischer, *The Soviets in World Affairs* (1930), i, 129 that Helfferich " in his extreme Moscowphobia never even submitted Chicherin's offer to his Government " is an instructive example of Soviet suspiciousness, and certainly untrue. K. von Bothmer, *Mit Graf Mirbach in Moskau* (Tübingen, 1922), p. 117, explicitly records that " the question of an alliance with Germany against the Entente in order to march against the Murman territory with our Finnish and Baltic troops is being seriously considered ".

[1] G. Chicherin, *Vneshnyaya Politika Sovetskoi Rossii za Dva Goda* (1920), p. 15.

[2] According to Chicherin (*ibid.* p. 15), it was not till August 1918 that the Soviet Government had an inkling of German weakness : " In the summer we were still afraid that harvest time might be the moment when German troops would advance into the heart of Russia to carry off the grain. But, when harvest time came, it appeared that the appetite of the German imperialist monster had become less rapacious." According to a private letter of Krasin of September 7, 1918, it was still feared in Moscow at that time that, " if the Czechoslovaks take Nizhny, the Germans will occupy Petrograd and Moscow " (L. Krasin, *Leonid Krasin : His Life and Work* (n.d. [1929]), p. 90).

general staff had forced the resignation of Kühlmann. He was succeeded at the Ministry of Foreign Affairs by Hintze, a retired admiral, who had once been German naval attaché at Petersburg. But the German military machine was running down fast, and the exaggerated military ambitions and pretensions which had at first delayed the course of the negotiations were now a thing of the past. In the middle of August 1918 Joffe informed *Izvestiya* that " more than ever public and official circles in Germany recognize the necessity of maintaining peaceful relations with Russia ", and that the economic negotiations " had ended very satisfactorily for us ".[1] On August 27, three agreements supplementary to the Brest-Litovsk treaty were quietly signed in Berlin — a political agreement, a financial agreement and a confidential exchange of notes, this last representing the first recourse of the Soviet Government to secret diplomacy. In return for the evacuation of White Russia by the Germans, the RSFSR formally renounced all rights of sovereignty over Estonia and Latvia (subject to " access to the sea " through Tallinn, Riga and Windau), recognized the independence of Georgia (now under German protection), and undertook to pay partly in gold and partly in bonds an indemnity of six billion marks. Germany undertook to lend no support to forces, Russian or other, operating against the Soviet Government in Russian territory. Soviet Russia undertook to " employ all means at her disposal to expel the Entente forces from north Russian territory in observance of her neutrality "; if she failed to do so, then Germany — this was one of the provisions relegated to the secret exchange of notes — " would find herself obliged to take this action, if necessary with the help of Finnish troops ", and Russia " would not regard such intervention as an unfriendly act ". The project discussed between Chicherin and Helfferich in Moscow thus found its way into the Berlin agreement, but at a moment when Germany was no longer in a military situation to give effect to it.[2]

---

[1] *Izvestiya*, August 16, 1918.

[2] The two agreements appear in an abbreviated form in Klyuchnikov i Sabanin, *Mezhdunarodnaya Politika*, ii (1926), 163-166 ; the secret exchange of notes was published from the German archives in *Europäische Gespräche*, iv (1926), 148-153 ; no Russian text has ever been officially published. Translations of all these documents are in J. Wheeler-Bennett, *Brest-Litovsk: the Forgotten Peace* (1939), pp. 427-446.

If the original Brest-Litovsk treaty had been a unilateral act of force imposed on a prostrate and passive victim, the supplementary instruments of August 27, 1918, partook of the ordinary diplomatic character of a bargain between two partners each actively bent on securing certain advantages for itself, each prepared to pay a certain price in order to secure at any rate the passive good-will of the other. It was thus a stage in the normalization of Soviet foreign relations. Chicherin, in presenting the two agreements to VTsIK for ratification, once more stressed the importance of " peaceful relations " between imperialist Germany and the " workers' and peasants' state " :

> In spite of the great difference between the régimes of Russia and Germany and the fundamental tendencies of both governments, the peaceful cohabitation of the two peoples, which has always been the object of our workers' and peasants' state, is at present equally desirable to the German ruling class. . . . Precisely in the interests of peaceful relations with Germany we signed those agreements which are today submitted to VTsIK for ratification.[1]

Soviet policy had already moved far from the conception of the preaching of world revolution as its primary function. Chicherin at Narkomindel was deeply committed to the policy of balancing against one another the two groups of hostile Powers, and of appeasing political enemies who were amenable to pacific gestures ; and this policy, plainly recognized as a policy of weakness, was endorsed by Lenin. That it was possible for several months to combine this policy with the revolutionary activities of Joffe in Berlin was due mainly to the growing paralysis of the German Government as the catastrophe drew nearer.

Improved Soviet relations with Germany were the counterpart of deteriorating relations with the allies, which followed an inverse variation of the same pattern. In the Soviet attitude to Germany, the *leitmotif* of conciliation and accommodation gained ground throughout the summer of 1918. In the Soviet attitude to the allies, the abortive movement towards accommodation in Feb-

[1] *Pyatyi Sozyv Vserossiiskogo Tsentral'nogo Ispolnitel'nogo Komiteta* (1919), pp. 95-96.

ruary and March faded away in face of the uncompromising character of allied hostility and the imminent threat of allied intervention. After the summer of 1918 no serious doubt could be entertained of allied determination to destroy the régime and to give assistance to any who sought to destroy it. The British landing at Murmansk at the end of June was followed by a British and French landing at Archangel at the beginning of August; during August American troops joined the British and French in north Russia and the Japanese in Vladivostok; in south Russia the " white " forces coalesced under the leadership of Denikin with allied encouragement, and, a little later, active allied support. The counter-revolutionary conspiracies of July and August in central Russia were organized and financed from abroad. On August 31 the official British agent, Lockhart, was arrested on the charge of complicity in them, and two days later a detailed Soviet statement denounced " the conspiracy organized by Anglo-French diplomats ".[1] The last bridge had been broken. No form of appeasement or conciliation was any longer open to the Soviet Government.

This conclusion, while accepted without qualification in regard to Great Britain, France and Japan, was applied with the utmost reluctance to the United States. From the first days of the revolution the impression had prevailed that sentiment in the United States was more sympathetic to the Bolsheviks than in any other capitalist country. In November 1917 Trotsky had speculated that " American diplomats understand that they cannot defeat the Russian revolution and therefore want to enter into friendly relations with us, calculating that this will be an excellent means of competing with German and, in particular, with British capitalists after the war ".[2] Now Soviet policy, relying on the unconcealed American antipathy to Japan[3] and on Wilson's obvious reluctance to participate in intervention, endeavoured to drive a wedge between the allied governments by ostentatious gestures of friendliness to the United States. When Robins returned to Washington in May 1918, he carried with him detailed offers of concessions in

[1] See Vol. 1, p. 167 ; the statement appeared in *Izvestiya* of September 3, 1918. [2] Trotsky, *Sochineniya*, iii, ii, 179.
[3] Lenin, in his speech of May 14, 1918, put the American-Japanese conflict side by side with the British-German conflict as the two fundamental divisions among the imperialist Powers (*Sochineniya*, xxiii, 5).

Soviet Russia for American capitalists.[1] As late as August 4, 1918, a naïvely worded note was addressed to Poole, the American consul in Moscow, as " the representative of a nation which, to use your own words, will take no action against the Soviets ", protesting against the intervention of " Anglo-French armed forces " in Soviet territory, and conveying assurances of unalterable friendship for the American people.[2] A month later Chicherin, in a speech to VTsIK, explained that American citizens were not being interned with those of the other allied powers " because, although the United States Government was compelled by its allies to agree to participation in intervention, so far only formally, its decision is not regarded by us as irrevocable ".[3] But within a few weeks this agreeable fiction of American friendship had become untenable. Two American regiments had landed at Vladivostok ; others were soon to join the allied forces on other fronts ; and the RSFSR was faced with a solid phalanx of interventionist powers. At the beginning of October 1918 a resolution of VTsIK on the international situation grouped together " the Anglo-French, American and Japanese imperialist robbers " under a single rubric.[4] The circle had been closed.

These catastrophic developments left a lasting mark on Soviet thought. The action of the allies confirmed and intensified the ideological aspect of Soviet foreign policy and made international revolution once more its principal plank, if only in the interest of national self-preservation. The vital question whether the co-existence of capitalist and socialist states was possible had at any rate been left open by the first pronouncements of the Soviet Government, and notably by the decree on peace ; in some, at any rate, of the pronouncements of the spring and summer of 1918 it had been answered in the affirmative. Now it seemed irrefutably clear that this coexistence was impossible, at any rate with the countries of the Entente, and that revolutionary pro-paganda directed to the workers of these countries was the most

---

[1] See p. 280 below ; according to L. Fischer, *The Soviets in World Affairs* (1930), i, 300, the properties of the American International Harvester Corporation, Westinghouse Brake Co. and Singer Sewing Machine Co. were exempted from nationalization owing to the intervention of Robins.

[2] Klyuchnikov i Sabanin, *Mezhdunarodnaya Politika*, ii (1926), 162-163.

[3] *Pyatyi Sozyv Vserossiiskogo Tsentral'nogo Ispolnitel'nogo Komiteta* (1919), p. 95.   [4] *Izvestiya*, October 4, 1918.

effective, and indeed the only effective, weapon in the hands of a government whose military resources were still negligible. Soviet foreign policy from the autumn of 1918 to the end of 1920 was in all probability more specifically and exclusively coloured by international and revolutionary aims than at any other time. World revolution was in a certain sense the counterpart in Soviet foreign policy of war communism in economic policy. In form a logical, though extreme, development of communist doctrine, it was in fact imposed on the régime, not so much by doctrinal orthodoxy, as by the desperate plight of the civil war.

The undeclared war which began with the allied military landings in the summer of 1918 meant a rupture of such quasi-diplomatic relations as had been established in the preceding winter and spring. At the end of July 1918 the allied representatives, who had retired from Petrograd to Vologda five months earlier, left Russia altogether or withdrew to occupied territory, taking with them the military missions through which some contact with the Soviet authorities had been maintained. After the assassination of Mirbach and the risings against the Soviet Government in July 1918, the few allied representatives, civil and military, left in Moscow were regarded as agents of counter-revolutionary conspiracy. Lockhart, after four weeks of confinement, was released and allowed to leave the country, and Litvinov was expelled from Great Britain as a reprisal for the expulsion of Lockhart. The closing of the channels of normal intercourse with the outside world stimulated the use of the weapons of " open diplomacy "; as Chicherin afterwards put it, " we write fewer notes to governments and more appeals to the working classes ".[1] On August 1, 1918, Sovnarkom issued an appeal to " the labouring masses of France, England, America, Italy and Japan ", concluding with the words :

> Compelled to struggle against allied capital, which to the chains imposed on us by German imperialism seeks to add new chains, we turn to you with the call :
> Long live the solidarity of the workers of the whole world !
> Long live the solidarity of the French, English, American, Italian proletariat with the Russian !

[1] G. Chicherin, *Vneshnyaya Politika Sovetskoi Rossii za Dva Goda* (1920), p. 31.

Down with the gangsters of international imperialism!
Long live the international revolution!
Long live peace among the nations![1]

A few days later Chicherin commented in an official note to the American consul :

> At this very moment we are speaking to the countries whose armies are taking the field against us with open violence, and we turn to their peoples with the call : " Peace to the cottages!"[2]

Towards the end of August *Pravda* published an open letter from Lenin himself to the American workers :

> The American millionaires, those modern slave-owners, have opened a particularly tragic page in the bloody history of bloody imperialism by giving their consent . . . to the armed campaign of the Anglo-Japanese beasts for the purpose of crushing the first socialist republic. . . . We are in the position of a beleaguered fortress until other detachments of the international socialist revolution come to our aid. Such detachments exist, they are more numerous than ours. . . .We are unconquerable because the world proletarian revolution is unconquerable.[3]

Meanwhile the part played a year earlier by *Die Fackel* and *Der Völkerfriede* among the German invaders was now taken over by the innumerable pamphlets and broadsheets in English and French distributed to the allied troops landed on Russian soil. The tale was still the same :

> You will be fighting not against enemies [ran a sheet addressed to British and American troops in Archangel] but against working people like yourselves. We ask you, are you going to crush us? . . . Be loyal to your class and refuse to do the dirty work of your masters. . . . Go home and establish industrial republics in your own countries, and together we shall form a world-wide cooperative commonwealth.[4]

[1] Klyuchnikov i Sabanin, *Mezhdunarodnaya Politika*, ii (1926), 161.

[2] *Ibid.* ii, 163 ; the concluding phrase is taken from the slogan of the armies of the French revolution : " War on the great houses! Peace to the cottages!"

[3] Lenin, *Sochineniya*, xxiii, 176-189.

[4] M. Fainsod, *International Socialism and the World War* (Harvard, 1935), p. 184 : the titles of several other pamphlets are listed in A. L. P. Dennis, *The Foreign Policies of Soviet Russia* (1924), p. 488. The texts of similar pamphlets distributed to the French forces in south Russia are in A. Marty, *La Révolte de la Mer Noire*, i (n.d. [1927]), 149-166 ; Lenin, *Sochineniya*, xxv, 600, note 49, mentions two papers, *The Call* and *La Lanterne*, issued for the British and French troops respectively.

Tracts and journals prepared in the propaganda department of Narkomindel were dropped by aeroplane over the enemy lines.[1] The work of propaganda and indoctrination which had proved successful with German and Austrian prisoners of war was now undertaken among prisoners captured on the allied fronts. The number of prisoners was small, and the men had not experienced months or years of captivity, so that successes were relatively few. But they occurred, and were heralded as triumphs.[2] This reversion to propaganda for world revolution in its crudest and most outspoken form was, however, part of a desperate defensive action by the forces of revolution against the embattled onslaught of the western capitalist world. It was the action of the western Powers, quite as much as of the Soviet Government, which had forced the international situation into a revolutionary setting.

The German collapse in the autumn of 1918 put the prospects of world revolution in an altogether different light. Soviet propaganda suddenly became the instrument, no longer of a desperate defensive action against allied intervention, but of a victorious offensive which promised to sweep over central Europe. The Bulgarian surrender and the German request for an armistice at the end of September 1918 showed that the central Powers were at the end of their tether. Already on October 1, 1918, Lenin was sending to Sverdlov and Trotsky impatient notes on " the beginnings of the revolution in Germany " and laying down tactics :

No relations with the government of Wilhelm, nor with a government of Wilhelm II + Ebert and other scoundrels.

But for the German working masses, for the German toiling millions, once they have made a start with the spirit of revolt (for the moment it is *only* spirit), we begin to propose brotherly union, *bread*, military help.

And he demanded " by the spring " an army of 3,000,000 " to help the international workers' revolution ".[3] Two days later he had regained all his faith in imminent world revolution :

Now even the blindest of the workers of the different countries will see how right the Bolsheviks were in basing all

[1] *Kommunisticheskii Internatsional*, No. 9-10 (187-188), 1929, p. 189.
[2] For examples see p. 118 below.
[3] *Leninskii Sbornik*, xxi (1933), 252-253.

their tactics on support of a world-wide workers' revolution and in not fearing to make various most heavy sacrifices. . . . The Russian proletariat will understand that in the near future the greatest sacrifices will be required for the sake of internationalism. The time is approaching when circumstances may demand from us help for the German people to liberate itself from its own imperialism against Anglo-French imperialism. . . . World history in the last few days has remarkably speeded up the course towards a world-wide workers' revolution.[1]

A fortnight later, with open contempt for diplomatic proprieties, Lenin wrote to Joffe in Berlin :

We ought to play the rôle of a bureau of ideas of international scope, and we are doing nothing ! ! We must publish 100 times more. There is money. Hire translators.

A short staccato letter ended with a request to forward it to Vorovsky in Stockholm for similar action.[2] At the same moment he sent a letter of greeting to the Spartakusbund, whose work had " saved the honour of German socialism and of the German proletariat ", and expressed his " unshakeable hope that in the near future it will be possible to hail the victory of the proletarian revolution in Germany " ; and, a few weeks later, when the news arrived of Karl Liebknecht's release from prison, a message was sent to him in the name of the central committee of the party, signed by Lenin, Sverdlov and Stalin, welcoming his release as " the token of a new era, the era of victorious socialism which is now opening for Germany and for the whole world ".[3]

The concluding words were significant. Though Germany was in the centre of the picture, the view of the Bolsheviks was not limited by it. Six months ago, it was pointed out in a resolution of VTsIK, Germany had seemed as all-powerful as the other " imperialist robbers " seemed today. But their doom also was at hand.

The profound internal struggles among those taking part in the universal robbery, and the still more profound upheavals

[1] Lenin, *Sochineniya*, xxiii, 215-217.
[2] *Leninskii Sbornik*, xxi (1933), 253.
[3] Lenin, *Sochineniya*, xxix, 514-515.

among the deceived and exhausted masses, are leading the capitalist world into the era of social revolution.

Now, as in October of last year and as at the time of the Brest-Litovsk negotiations, the Soviet Government builds its entire policy on the prospect of social revolution in both imperialist camps. . . .

VTsIK declares in the face of the whole world that in this struggle Soviet Russia with all its forces and resources will support the revolutionary power in Germany against its imperialist enemies. It does not doubt that the revolutionary proletariat of France, England, Italy, America and Japan will find itself in the same camp as Soviet Russia and revolutionary Germany.[1]

Events moved with breathless rapidity through October. At a meeting in Moscow on October 22, 1918, when Germany was already on the point of collapse and demonstrations in favour of the Bolsheviks had occurred in Berlin, in Paris, in Italy and in Scotland, Lenin allowed himself a note of triumphant confidence :

Bolshevism has become the world-wide theory and tactics of the international proletariat ! It is due to Bolshevism that a sturdy socialist revolution has been staged in the face of the whole world, that disputes have broken out among all the peoples on the question for or against the Bolsheviks. It is due to Bolshevism that the programme of the creation of a proletarian state is on the agenda. . . . Never have we been so near to world revolution, never has it been so evident that the Russian proletariat has established its might, so clear that millions and tens of millions of the world proletariat will follow us.[2]

The same note of confidence was transposed into diplomatic terms. Two days later Chicherin broadcast a long and defiant note to President Wilson, who was ironically addressed in almost every paragraph as " Mr. President ". Recalling the pious professions of the fourteen points and the assurance of American sympathy in Wilson's telegram to the fourth All-Russian Congress of Soviets in March 1918,[3] the note contrasted the ideals of Wilson's project for a League of Nations with the realities of allied and American armed intervention on Soviet territory, and compared

[1] *Pyatyi Sozyv Vserossiiskogo Tsentral'nogo Ispolnitel'nogo Komiteta* (1919), p. 252.
[2] Lenin, *Sochineniya*, xxiii, 230.   [3] See pp. 48-49 above.

the allied governments with "the imperialist government of Germany, headed by Wilhelm II, to whom you, Mr. President, behave no better than we, the workers' and peasants' revolutionary government, behave to you ".[1] And Lenin in his main theoretical work of the period, *The Proletarian Revolution and Renegade Kautsky*, which he completed on the eve of the German surrender, returned to the international argument which he had so steadily sustained up to the moment of the October revolution :

> My task, the task of a representative of the revolutionary proletariat, is to prepare the *world proletarian revolution* as the *only* salvation from the horrors of world war. I have to reason not from the point of view of " my " country . . ., but from the point of view of my participation in preparing, preaching and hastening the world proletarian revolution.[2]

During the first week of November 1918, with the Habsburg empire already dissolving into its component parts,[3] with the German armies in headlong retreat, and soldiers' and workers' councils springing up in many German cities, the German Government indulged in a last defiant gesture of protest against Joffe's notorious activities. On November 2, 1918, reviving the now half-forgotten memory of Mirbach's murder four months earlier, it addressed a note to the Soviet Government declaring that it " cannot tolerate the crime against the ambassador remaining unexpiated "[4] Two days later the police arranged that a piece of diplomatic baggage consigned to Joffe should break open in transport at the Berlin railway station ; and a flood of revolutionary proclamations emerged.[5] Next day, Solf, the newly appointed

---

[1] Klyuchnikov i Sabanin, *Mezhdunarodnaya Politika*, ii (1926), 181-188.

[2] Lenin, *Sochineniya*, xxiii, 381.

[3] On November 3 a message was broadcast in the name of " the workers, peasants and soldiers of Russia " to the " comrade workers, peasants and soldiers of the former Austro-Hungarian Empire " (*Izvestiya*, November 3, 1918).

[4] This note has not been published.

[5] *The Memoirs of Prince Max of Baden* (Engl. transl., 1928), ii, 289, and P. Scheidemann, *Memoirs of a Social-Democrat* (Engl. transl., 1929), ii, 534-536, admit that the breakage was deliberate ; according to W. von Blücher, *Deutschlands Weg nach Rapallo* (Wiesbaden, 1951), p. 34, the suggestion came from Nadolny. The refinement that the documents themselves were planted by the police comes from a much later account in the Austrian press (quoted in J. W. Wheeler-Bennett, *Brest-Litovsk: The Forgotten Peace* (1939), p. 359).

Secretary of State for Foreign Affairs in Max von Baden's government, sent for Joffe and informed him that " the behaviour of the Russian embassy in violation of international law, as well as the fact that no adequate satisfaction has ever yet been given for the murder of the imperial ambassador, makes necessary a temporary withdrawal of representatives on both sides, which, however, does not constitute a formal breach ".[1] On the following morning, November 6, 1918, Joffe and his staff were hustled into a special train and despatched to the frontier.[2] On November 9, 1918, the day on which Joffe reached the frontier, the Kaiser abdicated ; and on November 10, while the German delegation was on its way to Compiègne to sign the armistice, the Berlin workers' and soldiers' council unanimously appointed a " council of people's representatives " to act as a provisional German Government. It was composed of three members of the SPD, Ebert, Scheidemann and Landsberg, and three of the USPD, Haase, Dittmann and Barth : Ebert acted as president of the council, and Haase had charge of foreign relations, though without replacing Solf at the Ministry of Foreign Affairs. In Moscow the proceedings of the concluding session of the sixth All-Russian Congress of Soviets were twice interrupted to allow the president to read the latest telegrams from Germany. In the evening there was a celebration in the Kremlin ; and next morning Lenin left the Kremlin for the first time since the attempt on his life at the end of August and addressed the crowds from a balcony. Radek describes the scene on his appearance :

> Tens of thousands of workers burst into wild cheering. Never have I seen anything like it again. Until late in the evening workers and Red Army soldiers were filing past. The world

---

[1] This declaration has not been published. On the same day the German consulate in Moscow handed a note to Narkomindel couched in similar terms, but at greater length, and omitting the final clause about the formal breach ; this was read *in extenso* by Lenin to the sixth All-Russian Congress of Soviets on November 8, 1918 (Lenin, *Sochineniya*, xxiii, 257-258).

[2] The occurrence was described two days later by Radek, amid cries of " Shame ", to the sixth All-Russian Congress of Soviets (*Shestoi Vserossiiskii Chrezvychainyi S"ezd Sovetov* (1919), pp. 52-53) ; the circumstances and the sequel lent some point to Bolshevik suspicions expressed by Lenin at the time (*Sochineniya*, xxiii, 259) that Joffe was expelled in the hope of propitiating the victorious western Powers.

revolution had come. The mass of the people heard its iron tramp. Our isolation was over.[1] The revolution in Germany seemed not only to bring welcome relief from immediate military dangers and break the ring of armies that encircled the Soviet republic, but to be the long-expected second and greater wave of the world revolution. The Bolshevik leaders from Lenin downwards were imbued with the unanimous and unquestioning conviction that it would quickly deepen and develop and, assuming a proletarian and socialist character, spread over western Europe. On November 13, 1918, VTsIK formally annulled the Brest-Litovsk treaty, and added to the declaration of annulment an appeal " to the toilers of Germany and Austria-Hungary " for a new kind of settlement to take its place :

The right of self-determination in full measure will be recognized for the toilers of all nations. Those really guilty of the war, the bourgeois classes, will be made to bear all the losses. The revolutionary soldiers of Germany and Austria, who are forming in the occupied territories councils of soldiers' deputies, and entering into contact with the local workers' and peasants' councils, will become the collaborators and allies of the toilers in the fulfilment of those tasks. By a fraternal union with the workers and peasants of Russia they will redeem the wounds inflicted on the population of the occupied regions by the German and Austrian generals who defended the interests of counter-revolution. . . . The toiling masses of Russia in the person of the Soviet Government offer such a union to the peoples of Germany and Austria-Hungary. They hope that this mighty union of the liberated peoples will be joined by the peoples of all other countries which have not yet thrown off the yoke of the imperialists.[2]

[1] *Krasnaya Nov'*, No. 10, 1926, p. 140. M. Philips Price, *My Reminiscences of the Russian Revolution* (1921), pp. 349-350, gives an eye-witness account of the Kremlin celebration, and attributes to Lenin even at this time a note of caution : " I fear that the social revolution in central Europe is developing too slowly to provide us with any assistance from that quarter " (*ibid.* p. 345) ; according to Radek (*Krasnaya Nov'*, No. 10, 1926, p. 139) Sverdlov remarked on this occasion : " Be on your guard ! Autumn flies bite hard." Radek's description of the scene next morning also mentions Lenin's " excited but profoundly anxious look ".

[2] *Sobranie Uzakonenii, 1917-1918*, No. 95, art. 947 ; the Brest-Litovsk treaty, so far as it concerned Turkey, had already been denounced by the Soviet Government on September 20, 1918 (G. Chicherin, *Vneshnyaya Politika Sovetskoi Rossii za Dva Goda* (1920), p. 21).

Nor was this vision of the rapid spread of a fraternal community of revolution as fantastic as it may appear to later generations which know that it was belied by the event. Never had the call to world revolution as the staple of Soviet foreign policy seemed more clearly justified by its fruits. While the final blow that laid Germany low had been struck by others, there was evidence — which no Bolshevik was likely to overlook or underestimate — of the part played by Bolshevik propaganda in demoralizing the German armies. The civil population was in revolt against the horrors and privations of the war; the monarchy had fallen without a blow amid general execration; workers' and soldiers' councils on the Soviet pattern had been formed all over Germany, and the Berlin council had created the counterpart of a Council of People's Commissars; Germany had entered its " Kerensky period "; it seemed inconceivable that, under the stimulus of Russian example and Russian encouragement, the parallel of the Russian revolution would not be followed to the end. When Radek reached Berlin in December 1918 he had the impression that " nine-tenths of the workers were taking part in the struggle against the government "; [1] other observers took much the same view. Even today it is not quite clear why the German revolution proved a fiasco — whether because the German masses did not want revolution, or because the revolutionary movement was disunited and poorly led, or because the allied governments, fearing revolution in Germany, gave just sufficient backing to the counter-revolutionary social-democrat elements in Germany to scotch it. The most plausible explanation appears to be that a revolt of the German masses against the war, and against a régime which was held responsible for it, was almost everywhere mistaken for a mass demand for social revolution.[2] The active demand for revolution, once the war was over and done with, was confined to a minority. The tradition of Lassalle had moulded a workers' movement which in its vast majority still pinned its faith to a policy of wringing concessions from the existing state, not of

---

[1] *Der Zweite Kongress der Kommunist. Internationale* (Hamburg, 1921), p. 256.

[2] The report of the subsequent Reichstag committee of enquiry into the causes of the German collapse drew attention to " the close connexion between the revolution and the question of peace in the minds of the German socialists " (R. H. Lutz, *The Causes of the German Collapse in 1918* (Stanford, 1934), p. 118).

destroying it. But this diagnosis could scarcely have been made in November 1918 ; and, both then and for more than two years after, the imminence of proletarian revolution in Germany continued to haunt many who feared it as well as the Bolsheviks who hoped for it.

Enthusiasm in Moscow was, however, quickly damped by the first episodes of direct contact with the new Germany. The first disconcerting experience arose out of the offer by the Soviet authorities of two trainloads of grain for the hungry German population. It was a symbolical gesture and, in view of desperate shortages in Russia itself, a generous one. Instead of the enthusiastic acceptance which had been expected from Berlin, nearly a week of silence followed. Then, on November 17, 1918, came Haase's answer. The offer was welcomed as a gesture of international solidarity. But Russia too was hungry ; and, so far as concerned Germany, America had already promised to deliver enough grain to maintain existing rations till the next harvest.[1] It was the first occasion on which Germany was called on to make the fateful choice between east and west. The paltry two trainloads from Moscow were weighed against the prospects of transatlantic abundance ; it would have been quixotic to accept the Soviet pittance at the risk of antagonizing Washington and the western allies. The reply was felt in Moscow as a slap in the face and as a proof that the so-called socialist leaders of Germany preferred the fleshpots of capitalism to the international solidarity of the socialist revolution. Radek, recalling the vote of the German social-democrats for war credits in the Reichstag of August 4, 1914, called it " a second August 4 ", and judged that " Judas Iscariot has completed his betrayal ".[2] The insult struck deep and rankled long. It was still a subject of bitter recrimination when the admission of the USPD to Comintern was debated eighteen months later.[3]

[1] The answer was conveyed in a teleprinter conversation between Haase and Chicherin, and no official text seems to exist : the contents were recorded by Radek in *Krasnaya Nov'*, No. 10, 1926, p. 142, and summarized by Haase's colleague Dittmann at the second congress of Comintern (*Der Zweite Kongress der Kommunist. Internationale* (Hamburg, 1921), pp. 322-324).

[2] *Krasnaya Nov'*, No. 10, 1926, p. 142.

[3] A still later echo of it can be found in an article by Stalin of November 1920, in which he proposed the creation of a " reserve of foodstuffs for the revolution in the west ". He wrote : " The fact is that the western states

The second episode concerned Joffe, the expelled Soviet representative in Berlin. When the German revolution broke out he was at Borisov on the Russian-German demarcation line. On November 10, 1918, the Berlin workers' and soldiers' council which appointed the Council of People's Representatives passed a resolution instructing the government to " resume relations with the Russian Government " and expressing eagerness for the arrival of the Russian representatives in Berlin; [1] and three days later VTsIK, in its decree proclaiming the annulment of Brest-Litovsk, observed that, whereas the last act of the Kaiser's government had been to expel Joffe, " the first act of the insurgent workers and soldiers of Germany who have overthrown the imperial régime was to recall the Soviet embassy ".[2] Meanwhile Joffe was hourly expecting the summons to return to Berlin. In the chaos of armistice Germany some delay in receiving instructions could be excused. But it soon transpired that the instructions would not be sent. Haase explained delicately to Chicherin that this was a matter for negotiation, and promised to submit it to his colleagues.[3] The USPD members of the Council of People's Representatives afterwards excused themselves (for this question too gave rise to prolonged recriminations) on the ground that the three SPD members were opposed to Joffe's recall, and that it was impossible to force a decision against them.[4] But this was not the whole truth. On November 19, 1918, two days after the rejection of the grain offer, the question of Joffe was at length discussed at the council; in addition to the six members, the meeting was attended by Kautsky, who now aspired to the position of elder statesman and impartial arbiter in the social-democratic movement and was known for his hostility to the Soviet régime, and by Solf, the former Minister for Foreign Affairs, who had retained direction of the ministry under Haase. Solf spoke strongly against the readmission of Joffe on the ground that he

(Germany, Italy, etc.) are completely dependent on America which supplies Europe with grain. The victory of revolution in these countries would face the proletariat with a food crisis on the morrow of the revolution if bourgeois America refused to supply them with grain, which is quite likely " (*Sochineniya*, iv, 380).

[1] *Der Zweite Kongress der Kommunist. Internationale* (Hamburg, 1921), p. 356.
[2] *Sobranie Uzakonenii, 1917–1918*, No. 95, art. 947.
[3] *Krasnaya Nov'*, No. 10, 1926, pp. 142-143.
[4] *Der Zweite Kongress der Kommunist. Internationale* (Hamburg, 1921), p. 324.

had abused his diplomatic privilege by intervention in internal affairs. Haase advised procrastination in this delicate issue ; and Kautsky supported him with the additional argument that the Soviet Government in Moscow would not last many weeks longer.[1] On November 23, the German consular party arrived on the frontier, and the exchange was effected.[2] Joffe returned disconsolately to Moscow. On December 1, 1918, Solf refused permission for Rakovsky to proceed via Berlin to Vienna as Soviet representative to Austria.[3]

The third episode threw still clearer light on the incompatibility of temper and purpose between the Bolshevik leaders in Moscow and the social-democratic leaders of both factions in Berlin. The first All-German Congress of Workers' and Soldiers' Councils was to be held on December 16, 1918. On an invitation from the executive committee which was organizing the congress, VTsIK appointed a strong Russian delegation to attend it, consisting of Bukharin, Joffe, Rakovsky, Ignatov and Radek.[4] This decision caused embarrassment in the Council of People's Representatives ; and the embarrassment turned to consternation when Radek, in a conversation with Haase by teleprinter open to interception by all the world, announced his intention of bringing with the delegation expert propagandists to work among the British and French prisoners of war still in German camps.[5] It seemed clear in Berlin that the Soviet authorities, recklessly or of set purpose, were doing their best to embroil Germany with the western Powers. Only an unquestioning revolutionary faith, such as the USPD leaders certainly did not possess, could have justified such a course. When the delegation reached the frontier, the Council of People's Representatives decided, by a vote of five to one,

---

[1] *Der Zweite Kongress der Kommunist. Internationale* (Hamburg, 1921), pp. 257, 356.

[2] The stay at Borisov is described by a member of Joffe's staff in M. K. Larsens, *An Expert in the Service of the Soviet* (1929), pp. 30-33.

[3] *Izvestiya*, December 3, 1918 ; according to *Diplomaticheskii Slovar*, ii (1950), 107, art. Markhlevsky, the German Government had already in October 1918 refused facilities for Markhlevsky to proceed to Vienna via Berlin as Soviet representative.

[4] *Otchet Narodnogo Komisariata po Inostrannym Delam Sed'momu S"ezdu Sovetov* (1919), p. 18.

[5] *Der Zweite Kongress der Kommunist. Internationale* (Hamburg, 1921), p. 326; according to another, more dubious, version Radek also offered Soviet help to resist the allied armies on the Rhine (*ibid.* p. 327).

" with regard to the situation in Germany " not to admit it.[1] According to a Russian official report, the German military authorities then " pointed a machine gun at our delegation, compelled it to turn back and in the most undignified conditions conducted it back across the demarcation line ".[2] The irrepressible Radek, undeterred by these indignities, and helped by his ability to vary his national status as required, disguised himself as an Austrian prisoner of war, and crossed the frontier in the company of Reuter-Friesland, a German prisoner of war, at that time a member of the USPD and later of the German Communist Party, and of two German communists whom he had picked up in Minsk.[3] He got through to Berlin, but just too late for the first All-German Congress of Workers' and Soldiers' Councils which had completed its session on December 21, 1918.

The conclusion drawn in Moscow from these episodes was the treachery of the German social-democratic leaders — of the USPD as well as of the SPD — to the revolutionary cause ; this was the first, but not the last, conspicuous occasion on which the Bolsheviks deceived themselves by believing, on the supposed analogy of their own Russian experience, in a conflict between revolutionary masses and counter-revolutionary leaders which would inevitably end in the revolt of the masses against the leaders. The realities of the German situation at the end of 1918 were far more complex. Germany was prostrate and helpless to do anything on her own account. Every decision about Soviet Russia was bound to present itself as a choice between leaning on Russia or leaning on the western allies. The mutual hostility between east and west made a choice unavoidable ; and, unless every apparent consideration of material advantage were ignored, the choice could not be in doubt. It was true that the German social-democratic leaders were particularly embittered against the Bolsheviks, who had been for four years past denouncing them as traitors and were already contesting with them the leadership of the masses, including the German masses. It was true that German social-democracy had been nourished for two or three decades

[1] *Ibid.* p. 357.
[2] G. Chicherin, *Vneshnyaya Politika Sovetskoi Rossii za Dva Goda* (1920), p. 23 ; Radek's own version is less dramatic and speaks only of " several soldiers with rifles " (*Krasnaya Nov'*, No. 10, 1926, p. 145).
[3] *Ibid.* No. 10, 1926, p. 146.

on contempt for semi-barbarian Russia, and that these sentiments had not vanished overnight with the change of régime.[1] It was also true that the prestige of western democracy and western liberalism exercised a strong pull on the social-democratic movement, especially in the form and in the conditions in which Woodrow Wilson was now preaching them to a world weary of " imperialism " and " militarism " These feelings were to make German social-democrats the strongest opponents of the eastern orientation in German policy advocated and supported by a majority of the German Right. But such considerations scarcely yet applied. At the end of 1918 the German masses were still dazed by defeat and dazzled by the sentimental glamour of the Russian revolution. But no serious body of German opinion, except for a small group of extremists on the Left, regarded an alliance with Soviet Russia, which would further inflame the hostility of the west, as practical politics for any German Government. The masses accepted the inevitable, and acquiesced without challenge in the caution of the leaders.

A new appointment marked the sharp revulsion in the Council of People's Representatives against Bolshevism and revolution. When, in the latter part of December, it became necessary to dispense with Solf, who was too much compromised with the allies by his record as Minister for the Colonies, the succession to Solf at the Ministry of Foreign Affairs was offered to Brockdorff-Rantzau. Brockdorff-Rantzau was an unusual figure in the diplomatic corps of the last days of imperial Germany. A keen intellectual interest in politics convinced him of the rising importance of the German Social-Democratic Party, and he made a point of keeping in touch with some of its leaders. It was through these connexions that, as German Minister in Copenhagen, he became the intermediary for the German Government in the negotiations that led to the passage of Lenin and his Bolshevik companions through Germany in the sealed train in April 1917. The same connexions brought him the appointment of German Minister for Foreign Affairs in December 1918. Before accepting it, he set forth his views in a memorandum to the Council of People's

---

[1] P. Scheidemann, *Memoirs of a Social-Democrat* (Engl. transl., 1929), ii, 533, contrasts " Germany, a land of education for centuries ", with " Russia, a land of millions of illiterates ".

Representatives, which unanimously endorsed them. Among his most important desiderata was the necessity of " taking the severest measures against Bolshevik propaganda and its leaders " and of " restricting the competence of the workers' and soldiers' councils ".[1] At the same moment the first All-German Congress of Workers' and Soldiers' Councils decided to hold elections for a German National Assembly on January 19, 1919, thus in effect decreeing its own demise as the sovereign organ of the German people. The hopes of Moscow in a German proletarian revolution on the Soviet model were ebbing fast.

On December 29, 1918, the three USPD members, conscious of the anomaly of their position, resigned from the Council of People's Representatives, which remained for the rest of its existence a one-party monopoly of the SPD. The same day was marked by a more significant event. The leaders of the Spartakusbund met in private and decided to secede from the USPD and form a separate party. It was to be called the German Communist Party (KPD), the word Spartakusbund being added to the title in brackets for old time's sake ; and on the following day the first congress of the KPD (Spartakusbund) duly assembled, 100 delegates being present. Radek, who had spent the days since his arrival in Berlin in discussions with the Spartakist leaders (he names Liebknecht, Rosa Luxemburg, Jogiches, Levi and Thalheimer),[2] represented the Russian party and delivered a massive oration on the Russian and the German revolutions. The comparisons which he made were flattering to his audience :

> When the news of the German revolution reached us, a veritable tumult of joy seized the working class of Russia. . . . The younger, organizationally much weaker, Russian working class knows well that without the socialist revolution in Germany the Russian workers' revolution, dependent on itself, would not have sufficient strength to build a new house on the ruins left behind by capitalism.

And again :

> What we are now carrying out in Russia is nothing but the great *unperverted teaching* of German communism, which Marx

---

[1] Brockdorff-Rantzau, *Dokumente* (1920), p. 11.
[2] *Krasnaya Nov'*, No. 10, 1926, p. 149.

represented for the working class of the whole world. . . . The international civil war will free us from the war of nations.[1]

The congress sent its greetings to the Russian Soviet republic. It condemned " the Ebert-Scheidemann government " as the " mortal enemy of the proletariat ", and protested against the use of German armed forces on British orders against Soviet troops in the Baltic. It called for the formation in all countries of workers' and soldiers' councils, and saw in this " the only effective way to the building of a new International in which the centre of gravity of the class organization of the proletariat must henceforth lie ". The only question on which an open difference of opinion was recorded was whether to participate in the elections to the National Assembly. It was argued that, since parliaments and Soviets were alternative forms of government representing respectively the supremacy of the bourgeoisie and the supremacy of the workers, and since the National Assembly was clearly designed to supplant the congress of Soviets, a vote to participate in the elections was a vote against the Soviets. Participation was eventually rejected by a majority of 62 votes to 23 : but most of the leaders, including Rosa Luxemburg, voted in the minority. Participation in the existing trade unions seems to have been unanimously rejected, though no formal vote was taken ; some delegates were in favour of forming separate communist unions, others, including Rosa Luxemburg, thought that trade unions would be altogether superseded by the workers' and soldiers' councils.[2]

Behind the formal proceedings of the congress lurked, however, unresolved difficulties and tensions. The reactions of the German Spartakist leaders to Russian Bolshevism were complex and not uniform. Karl Liebkneckt, who, though a brilliant and devoted revolutionary leader in action, had no solid Marxist background and no great intellectual acumen, might unreservedly welcome the Russian revolution and all its works, and be prepared

---

[1] K. Radek, *Die Russische und Deutsche Revolution und die Weltlage* (1919), pp. 15, 29-30.

[2] *Bericht über den Gründungsparteitag der Kommunistischen Partei Deutschlands (Spartakusbund)* (n.d. [1919]), pp. 13, 17-18. This illegally printed official record of the congress contains summaries of the speeches (only Rosa Luxemburg's appears to have been reported in full) and the programme : Radek's speech was not included on the ground that it had been published separately as a pamphlet (cited in note 1 above).

for uncritical imitation of it. But Rosa Luxemburg, the real genius of the Spartakusbund, had been ever since 1904 a stern assailant of Lenin's theory of party organization; [1] and, during the last months of the war which she spent in prison, she had written a long criticism of Lenin's interpretation of the dictatorship of the proletariat, which, though still unpublished, was certainly known to her immediate colleagues. [2] Rosa Luxemburg believed that a socialist revolution could be achieved only by a mass party, and that no such party yet existed or could exist in Germany. The time was ripe only for propaganda among the masses, such as the Spartakusbund had undertaken, but not for action. For these reasons Rosa Luxemburg and her close associate, Leo Jogiches, would have preferred in the first instance to postpone the creation of a German communist party; [3] and, though they allowed themselves to be overruled, Rosa Luxemburg's cautious views coloured more than one passage of the party programme which she drafted for the congress :

> The essence of socialist society consists in the fact that the great working mass ceases to be a regimented mass and itself lives and directs in free conscious self-determination the whole political and economic life. . . .
> The proletarian revolution needs for its purposes no terror, it hates and abominates murder. . . . It is no desperate attempt of a minority to fashion the world after its own ideal, but the action of the great mass of the millions of the people which is called to carry out the mission of history, to transform historical necessity into reality.

Nothing could have been cooler, or more unlike the enthusiasm for international revolutionary solidarity prevailing in Moscow, than the brief and conventional point in the programme devoted to " international tasks " (which at this point could have practical bearing only on relations with Russia) :

[1] See Vol. 1, p. 34.

[2] It was first published with some abbreviations in a pamphlet edited by Paul Levi (R. Luxemburg, *Die Russische Revolution* (1922)); the omitted passages were published in *Archiv für die Geschichte des Sozialismus und der Arbeiterbewegung* (Leipzig), xiii (1928), 285-298.

[3] This attitude, though not expressed publicly, was well known in party circles at the time, and was referred to in a statement by Klara Zetkin which was read at the third congress of Comintern (*Protokoll des III. Kongresses der Kommunistischen Internationale* (Hamburg, 1921), pp. 668-669).

The immediate taking up of relations with fraternal parties abroad, in order to put the socialist revolution on an international basis and to secure peace through international brotherhood and through the revolutionary rising of the world proletariat.[1]

The divergence of views between Rosa Luxemburg and Lenin which lurked behind the scenes at the founding congress of the KPD was a further stage in the long controversy which had opened with the publication of *What is to be Done?* It may have been rendered more acute on this occasion by personal antipathy between Rosa Luxemburg and Radek, arising out of the factional struggles of the Polish party in which they had both played leading parts. But it was a fundamental dispute which was to reappear again and again in relations between the Russian Communist Party and the communist parties of the west.

For the moment, these potential international embarrassments were less decisive than divisions of opinion on immediate policy within the party itself. Throughout the congress Liebkneckt, with no great encouragement from the other leaders, had been conducting negotiations to bring the shop stewards' movement into the newly founded party. The negotiations finally broke down on certain mainly formal conditions laid down by the shop stewards and judged unacceptable by the congress. But the real obstacle was the opposition of Rosa Luxemburg and her group. Rosa Luxemburg's scepticism on the prospects of a proletarian socialist revolution in Germany in the near future made her fear the admission to the party of a large majority of unschooled revolutionary hotheads who might force the party into revolutionary adventures for which neither it nor the political situation was ripe. Her practical insight was demonstrated by the immediate sequel. Within a few days of the congress an outbreak occurred in Berlin over the dismissal of a chief of police sympathetic to the Left. The shop stewards threw their forces whole-heartedly into the fray, and there was talk of proclaiming a revolutionary government. Officially, the newly constituted party held aloof; but some of its members, led by Liebkneckt, played conspicuous parts. Radek's rôle at this time is uncertain. But three months later he wrote from prison that he had been " against any attempt to seize power

[1] The programme is in *Bericht über den Gründungsparteitag der Kommunistischen Partei Deutschlands* (*Spartakusbund*) (n.d. [1919]), pp. 49-56.

in February " on the ground that " the seizure of political power can be effected only by a majority of the working class, which in January was certainly not on the side of the communist party ".[1] The rising was suppressed without much difficulty by the Reichswehr. In the reprisals which followed the new German Communist Party was declared illegal : and both Liebkneckt and Luxemburg were arrested and " shot while trying to escape " — apparently the first use of this consecrated formula for official assassination. A month later Radek was arrested and consigned to a cell in the Moabit prison, where he spent the first forty-eight hours in " heavy irons ".[2] In the vain hope of conferring on him the protection of diplomatic status the Soviet government of the Ukraine hastily appointed him its representative in Berlin ; it also arrested two or three prominent Germans in Soviet territory as hostages.[3]

The omens which attended the birth of the German Communist Party were on any sober view profoundly disquieting. Even the outward enthusiasm of the founding congress had not concealed two inherent weaknesses — lack of unity within the party itself and lack of unity between the party and the revolutionary elements in the German masses ; [4] and the congress had been followed by the prompt and crushing defeat of the first revolutionary movement with which the party — half-heartedly, it is true — had been associated, and by the killing of its two outstanding leaders. But the omens were not so read at the time, and least of all in Moscow. In a military situation dominated by the gathering strength of Denikin in the south and Kolchak in Siberia and the growing impact of allied intervention, the bare fact of the foundation of a communist party in the most revolutionary of all European countries was the single beacon of light on a dark horizon and sustained the prevailing mood of optimism. For Lenin, in particular, it had a symbolical significance. It was specifically the

---

[1] 2' *Vsegermanskii S"ezd Rabochikh i Soldatskikh Sovetov* (1935), p. 324.

[2] *Ibid.* p. 324.

[3] *Otchet Narodnogo Komissariata po Inostrannym Delam Sed'momu S"ezdu Sovetov* (1919), p. 22 ; one of the hostages afterwards wrote his memoirs (Heinz Stratz, *Drei Monate als Geisel für Radek* (1920)).

[4] " The congress ", wrote Radek some years later, " revealed very clearly the youth and inexperience of the party. The connexion with the masses was very weak. . . . I did not feel that this was yet a party " (*Krasnaya Nov'*. No. 10, 1926, p. 152).

treachery of the German social-democrats, whom he had hitherto regarded as the torch-bearers of the socialist revolution, which convinced Lenin in August 1914 of the bankruptcy of the Second International. Now it was the creation in Germany, in advance of any other great industrial country, of a party pledged to the destruction of capitalist governments and the building of a socialist world order, which retrieved the betrayal of 1914 and made possible the realization of Lenin's dream. In the first flush of enthusiasm he wrote in an open *Letter to the Workers of Europe and America* on January 12, 1919 :

> When the German Spartakusbund with its world-famous and world-renowned leaders, with such faithful champions of the working class as Liebknecht, Rosa Luxemburg, Klara Zetkin, Franz Mehring, finally broke its link with socialists of the type of Scheidemann and Südekum, with those social-chauvinists (socialists in word, chauvinists in deed) who for ever dishonoured themselves by their alliance with the imperialist robber bourgeoisie of Germany and with Wilhelm II, when the Spartakusbund called itself the " Communist Party of Germany ", then the *foundation* of a really proletarian, really international, really revolutionary Third International, a *Communist International*, became a *fact*. Formally this foundation has not yet been made secure, but in fact the Third International now already exists.[1]

Four days after these words were written, and before they appeared in print in the columns of *Pravda*, Liebknecht and Rosa Luxemburg were dead and the new party outlawed. These events did not suffice to destroy either the value of the symbol or Lenin's optimism. It remained to translate the " fact " of a Communist International into an institution.

[1] Lenin, *Sochineniya*, xxiii, 494-495.

CHAPTER 23

THE YEAR OF ISOLATION

THE year 1919 was the year of Soviet Russia's most complete isolation from the outside world. It was also the year in which Soviet foreign policy took on its most outspokenly revolutionary complexion. The two circumstances were interconnected, and it would be a mistake to attribute to premeditation the prominence assumed by the revolutionary aspect of Soviet policy at this time. Throughout 1919 the dominant factor in Soviet foreign policy, as in the Soviet economy, was the civil war, in which the enemies of the régime received the military, economic and moral support of Great Britain, France, Italy, Japan and the United States, as well as of some of the lesser allies. When the war against Germany ended in November 1918, there seemed to be a good chance that allied intervention in the Russian civil war would also come to an end : the invariable pretext for this intervention up to the date of the armistice had been the need to counteract German designs. So long as this possibility existed, the Soviet Government showed itself eager to seize any opportunity for conciliation and negotiation. On November 8, 1918, the sixth All-Russian Congress of Soviets proposed to the five principal allied governments " before the whole world " to enter into negotiations for peace.[1] Litvinov, recently expelled from Great Britain, was sent to Stockholm in the hope of establishing contact with the diplomats and journalists of western Europe ; and from Stockholm on December 24, 1918, Litvinov addressed to President Wilson an appeal for peace, whose mild and deprecatory language, innocent even of the faintest allusion to the goal of world revolution, contrasted notably with Chicherin's ironical note of two months earlier or even with the original peace decree of October 26/November 8, 1917.[2] The

[1] S"ezdy Sovetov RSFSR v Postanovleniyakh (1939), p. 116.
[2] Klyuchnikov i Sabanin, Mezhdunarodnaya Politika, ii (1926), 210-212.

109

immediate sequel to this appeal was encouraging. A State Department official named Buckler, then at the American embassy in London, was instructed to visit Copenhagen where, in the middle of January 1919, he had three long interviews with Litvinov. Litvinov was conciliatory about the possibility of recognizing foreign debts, though Soviet Russia would want " foreign machinery and manufactured imports as a *quid pro quo* ". He undertook that propaganda against the western countries would cease when peace was made, adding explicitly that " the war declared on Russia by the allies called forth that revolutionary propaganda as a measure of retaliation ", and that " Russians realize that in certain western countries conditions are not favourable for a revolution of the Russian type ".[1]

When, therefore, the peace conference assembled in Paris almost at the moment of the Litvinov-Buckler conversations, the prospects of an agreement seemed reasonably promising, especially as the Russian question was among the first to which the Council of Ten — the solemn conclave of the five principal allied Powers — devoted its attention. When on January 16, 1919, Lloyd George proposed to call for a " truce of God " between " all of the different governments now at war within what used to be the Russian Empire ", he encountered warm sympathy from Wilson and veiled opposition from the French and Italian delegates.[2] On January 21, when Wilson read to the council Buckler's report of his conversations with Litvinov, the proposal was approved in principle ;[3] and three days later the principal allied Powers issued an invitation by radio to " all organized groups exercising or attempting to exercise power in any part of former Russian territory " to attend a conference at Prinkipo.[4] The Soviet Government accepted with alacrity. Its reply of February 4, 1919, showed an anxious readiness to come to terms on disputed issues. It announced that the Soviet Government " does not refuse to recognize its financial obligations to creditors who are nationals

[1] *Foreign Relations of the United States, 1919 : Russia* (1937), pp. 15-17.

[2] *Foreign Relations of the United States : The Paris Peace Conference, 1919*, iii (1943), 581-584 ; these volumes provide the fullest and most convenient record of the proceedings of the conference, though many of the documents and reports had already been published elsewhere.   [3] *Ibid.* iii, 643-646.

[4] The text of the invitation is in *Foreign Relations of the United States, 1919 : Russia* (1937), pp. 30-31.

of the allied Powers "; that it " offers to guarantee the payment of interest on its loans by a certain quantity of raw materials "; and that it " is willing to grant to nationals of the allied Powers mining, timber and other concessions ".[1] It was, as Chicherin afterwards wrote, the first occasion of " an appeal to the Entente in the name of economic advantages " — an idea which became " one of the most outstanding in Lenin's foreign policy ".[2] The calculation was purely practical; the Soviet Government was prepared to pay a certain price in order to buy off the hostility of the capitalist world and obtain for itself a much-needed respite.

The Prinkipo proposal broke down owing to the refusal of " white " Russian groups, encouraged by covert French opposition; and this failure gave encouragement to the anti-Bolshevik wing of the British coalition, drawing its strength mainly from military and diplomatic circles which were most keenly conscious of the Russian defection in the war, and from financial and commercial circles which held assets and interests in Russia. Of both these groups Churchill became the outstanding spokesman. Lloyd George describes Curzon and Churchill at this time as the " two powerful men in the government who were zealous and untiring advocates of the policy of intervention ".[3] While Curzon remained in London, replacing Balfour at the Foreign Office, Churchill as Secretary of State for War made frequent journeys to Paris. On February 15, 1919, in the absence of Lloyd George and Wilson, Churchill made a strong appeal to the Council of Ten in favour of sending " volunteers, technical experts, arms, munitions, tanks, aeroplanes, etc." to Russia and " arming the anti-Bolshevik forces ", and repeated the plea at length at a further meeting on the same afternoon. Balfour extricated himself from an awkward situation by proposing that the question should be adjourned till the following week.[4] What exactly happened behind the scenes is unknown. But the discussion at the Council of Ten was never resumed. A week later the American delegation reported to Washington that " Churchill's project is

[1] Klyuchnikov i Sabanin, *Mezhdunarodnaya Politika*, ii (1926), 219-223.

[2] *Izvestiya*, January 30, 1924, quoted by L. Fischer, *The Soviets in World Affairs* (1930), i, 463.

[3] D. Lloyd George, *The Truth about the Treaties* (1938), i, 324.

[4] *Foreign Relations of the United States: The Peace Conference, 1919*, iii (1943), 1043-1044; iv (1943), 13-21.

dead and there is little danger that it will be revived again by the conference ".[1]

The defeat of the Churchill project balanced the failure of Prinkipo; and Lloyd George and Wilson, back in Paris, now initiated a further attempt at pacification. On March 8, 1919, William Bullitt, a junior official of the American delegation in Paris, arrived in Petrograd on a confidential mission with unofficial instructions from Lloyd George and Wilson to ascertain, without committing anyone, what peace terms would be accepted by the Soviet Government. Having conferred with Chicherin and Litvinov, he went on with them on March 10 to Moscow, where he had daily conversations with them as well as an interview with Lenin; and on March 14 he received from Chicherin a memorandum dated March 12, 1919, containing the text of proposals which, if made by the allied governments before April 10, the Soviet Government undertook to accept. The most important of the proposals were a cessation of all hostilities in Russia on lines of demarcation at present occupied by the contending armies, a withdrawal of all allied troops and cessation of allied assistance to anti-Soviet elements, a resumption of trade and official relations, and a recognition by Soviet Russia of financial obligations as offered in the note of February 4, 1919.[2] When, however, Bullitt returned to Paris with these proposals in the latter part of March, the climate of opinion had radically changed, and was veering towards the policy of Churchill and the French. Neither Wilson nor Lloyd George was prepared to submit the Soviet proposals to the conference. The utmost secrecy was maintained about them ; [3] and Lloyd George publicly disowned any responsibility

---

[1] *Foreign Relations of the United States, 1919 : Russia* (1937), p. 73.

[2] Bullitt's report is in *ibid.* pp. 76-77, the memorandum in telegraphic form, *ibid.* pp. 78-89 ; the original text of the memorandum was first published in *Hearings before the Senate Committee on Foreign Relations*, 66th Congress, 1st Session, pp. 1248- 1250, and is also in *Documents on British Foreign Policy : First Series*, iii (1949), 426-429. The memorandum was presented in English : the Russian version in Klyuchnikov i Sabanin, *Mezhdunarodnaya Politika*, ii (1926), 235-237, has minor variants.

[3] At the end of June 1919 the Foreign Office, having read a reference in the press to the Bullitt mission, asked the delegation in Paris for information " in regard to the alleged proposals " : in reply Lloyd George's secretary, Philip Kerr, forwarded the text of the proposals, together with a brief account of the episode, in which he himself had been closely concerned (*Documents on British Foreign Policy : First Series*, iii (1949), 425-426).

for Bullitt's mission.[1] The die was now cast. A compromise was reached in the allied camp between those who desired to give full military backing to the " white " Russians and those who desired to stand aloof. It was decided to send no more allied troops to Russia and gradually to withdraw those already there, but at the same time to supply the Russian anti-Bolshevik forces with military and other material on as generous a scale as possible.[2] The next three months were the period of Kolchak's most serious successes against the Red Army in Siberia and of the strongest and most enthusiastic allied support of his cause.

The Bullitt mission was the last attempt for more than six months to establish any kind of direct contact between Soviet Russia and the allies. The last allied diplomatic representatives had left Soviet territory in August 1918; unofficial or consular agents in Moscow had been expelled or withdrawn after the arrest of Lockhart in September. The neutral representatives had one by one followed the example of their allied colleagues. The German embassy retired to occupied territory in August 1918, and the consular staff remaining in Moscow returned to Germany when Joffe was expelled from Berlin in November 1918. After

[1] Lloyd George's disclaimers are in *House of Commons: 5th Series*, cxiv, 2945-2946 (April 16, 1919) ; cxxi, 719 (November 17, 1919).

[2] No formal decision was announced or can be traced in the records since published : the fullest public exposition of the policy was in a speech of Lloyd George in the House of Commons on April 16, 1919, in which he justified the sending of supplies, but not troops, and undertook to support " General Denikin, Admiral Kolchak and General Kharkoff ", as well as " the allied countries bordering on Bolshevik territory from the Baltic to the Black Sea — Poland, Czechoslovakia and Rumania " (*ibid.* cxiv, 2943). This was later referred to by Lloyd George as "the April policy" (*ibid.* cxxi, col. 720). His own conversion to it was apparently due to three factors : increasingly vocal opposition in the cabinet and in the House of Commons to conciliation of the Soviet régime; his desire to win over Clemenceau to a " moderate " peace with Germany by falling in with intransigent French views about Russia ; and Kolchak's first military successes. The last factor, which bred hopes that the Soviet régime could be overthrown without actually using allied troops, was probably the most important. Bullitt in his testimony before the Senate foreign relations committee thus described the prevailing mood at the Paris conference in April 1919 : " Kolchak made a 100-mile advance, and immediately the entire press of Paris was roaring and screaming on the subject, announcing that Kolchak would be in Moscow within two weeks ; and therefore everyone in Paris, including I regret to say members of the American commission, began to grow very lukewarm about peace in Russia, because they thought Kolchak would arrive in Moscow and wipe out the Soviet Government " (*The Bullitt Mission to Russia* (N.Y., n.d. [1919]), p. 90).

the expulsion of Litvinov from Great Britain in September 1918, the Soviet representatives who had attempted to establish themselves in neutral countries suffered the same fate.[1] In December 1918 a Russian Red Cross mission was expelled from Warsaw, and four out of its five members were assassinated on their way back to Moscow.[2] A Soviet delegation sent to France at the beginning of February 1919 for the ostensible purpose of arranging for the repatriation of Russian soldiers in France was refused admission and ignominiously confined on a small island off Saint-Malo pending expulsion.[3] In March 1919 Ludwig Martens, a Russian-born German resident in New York who had acquired Soviet citizenship, forwarded to the American State Department his credentials signed by Chicherin as Soviet representative in the United States. This communication, together with a memorandum containing proposals for Soviet-American trade, was ignored, and the only response was a search of his office by the police three months later for incriminating propaganda.[4] By the beginning of 1919, Moscow was cut off from all normal contacts with the outside world. For a long while the only foreigner remaining there in an official capacity was a representative of the Danish Red Cross, who had undertaken the protection of the interests of citizens of all the Scandinavian and other western European countries, and of the United States.[5] After the armistice of November 1918 and before the close of navigation, a few ships loaded with timber and flax had sailed from Petrograd in the

[1] Berzin, the Soviet representative in Switzerland, was expelled in October 1918 ; recognition was withdrawn from Vorovsky as Soviet representative in Sweden in December 1918 and he left in the following month (*Otchet Narodnogo Komissariata po Inostrannym Delam Sed'momu S"ezdu Sovetov* (1919), pp. 14-16).

[2] *Krasnaya Kniga: Sbornik Diplomaticheskikh Dokumentov o Russko-Pol'skikh Otnosheniyakh, 1918-1920* (1920), pp. 32, 35-36 ; more than a year later six men were charged before a Polish court with this crime, three receiving short prison sentences and three being acquitted (*ibid.* p. 94).

[3] *Otchet Narodnogo Komissariata po Inostrannym Delam Sed'momu S"ezdu Sovetov* (1919), p. 13. The delegates were Manuilsky, Davtyan and Inessa Armand ; an account of their experiences was given by Manuilsky in *Pravda*, May 20, 1919.

[4] *Foreign Relations of the United States, 1919: Russia* (1937), pp. 133-134, 140-141 ; *Soviet Russia* (N.Y.) January 31, 1920, p. 110 ; *Foreign Relations of the United States, 1920*, iii (1936), 456.

[5] *Otchet Narodnogo Komissariata po Inostrannym Delam Sed'momu S"ezdu Sovetov* (1919), p. 15.

endeavour to re-establish trade with Germany. These had been confiscated in Baltic ports; [1] and since then the blockade had been maintained in all its rigour.

These measures, tantamount to war in all but name, put an end to the first tentative efforts of Soviet diplomacy. The division of the world into two hostile camps, which had been a favourite theme of Bolshevik speakers and writers since before the Bolshevik revolution, was now an accomplished fact. In March 1919, at the eighth party congress, Lenin defended the régime against Kautsky's charge of " militarism ":

> We are living not merely in a state, but in *a system of states*; and it is inconceivable that the Soviet republic should continue to exist for a long period side by side with imperialist states. Ultimately one or the other must conquer. Until this end occurs a number of terrible clashes between the Soviet republic and bourgeois states is inevitable. [2]

What first appeared as a civil war waged on Russian territory between the Red Army and the armies of the " white " generals now took on the shape of a war between the revolutionary Soviet régime and the principal Powers of the capitalist world; and against these Powers " political warfare " in the form of propaganda for world revolution was the most effective weapon in the Soviet armoury. Though it fell short of its announced objective, its use was justified by the results which it achieved. But, just as it would be mistaken to suppose that the revolutionary element in Soviet policy was ever absent even when diplomacy appeared to have the upper hand, so it would be wrong to treat it, even in moments of greatest tension, as the exclusive factor. It is symbolical of the constant juxtaposition of the two elements that Soviet acceptance of the allied invitation to Prinkipo came only a few days after the issue of invitations from Moscow to a founding congress of a Communist International, and that Bullitt reached Russia two days after the congress had ended its sessions. The two elements could be kept in separate compartments without any sense of incongruity between them. Bullitt in his otherwise copious reports on his visit to Moscow does not mention the birth of the Communist International and may have been unaware of

---

[1] L. B. Krasin, *Voprosy Vneshnei Torgovli* (1928), p. 250.
[2] Lenin, *Sochineniya*, xxiv, 122.

it, though *Pravda* was still carrying reports of the congress during his stay. The occasion attracted little attention at the time outside — or even inside — Russia. Only in the light of later developments and achievements can it justly be described in retrospect as one of the outstanding events of the year.

The task of creating a new International had first been proclaimed by Lenin in the autumn of 1914, and was an item in his " April theses " of 1917. But the victory of the October coup left the Bolsheviks with little time for anything that did not immediately bear on the consolidation of the revolution at home ; the beginning of revolution elsewhere was disappointingly delayed ; and, so long as the war lasted, it was materially impossible to bring together anything like a representative international group. Progress was for all these reasons slow. Throughout the first winter of the revolution peace was still the predominant aim. It was VTsIK which, at its meeting on December 22, 1917/January 4, 1918, made a first move. It decided to send a delegation to Stockholm " in order to establish a close link with all working elements of western Europe " and to " prepare for convening a Zimmerwald-Kienthal conference ".[1] But this was governmental, not party, action (the delegation, reflecting the current composition of the coalition, was to contain Left SRs as well as Bolsheviks) ; the Zimmerwald organization was still recognized ;[2] and this implied that peace rather than world revolution was the overriding aim. The mood was still cast in the radical bourgeois mould of the peace decree : the net was being cast widely for as large a catch as possible. On January 24/February 6, 1918, the project was pursued at an " international socialist conference " convened on the premises of Narkomindel. The conference was attended by Bolsheviks (Stalin was the leading party representative) and Left SRs, by several representatives of the border countries and of Scandinavia, and by Petrov and Reinstein, representing the British Socialist Party and the American Socialist

---

[1] *Protokoly Zasedanii VTsIK 2 Sozyva* (1918), p. 179.
[2] For the Zimmerwald organization and the Bolshevik attitude to it, see Note F : " The Pre-History of the Communist International " (pp. 567-570 below).

Labor Party respectively,[1] and passed a general resolution advocating " a revolutionary struggle . . . for immediate peace " and support for " the Russian October revolution and the Soviet Government ".[2] A few days later a delegation was appointed to proceed to Stockholm consisting of two Bolsheviks, Kollontai and Berzin, and two Left SRs.[3] At the height of the Brest-Litovsk crisis the delegation set out on its mission, but was turned back in Finland; and the project fell to the ground.

The conclusion of the Brest-Litovsk treaty ruled out for some time any direct attempt to mobilize the international socialist movement in support of the Soviet Government, and communications with the outside world became increasingly precarious. It was only after the armistice of November 1918 that the obstacles seemed suddenly to melt away. Germany, far from being a barrier to the advance of revolution, was now a centre of the revolutionary ferment. The moment was ripe to raise high once more the banner of international socialism. On December 19, 1918, the Petrograd Soviet convened an " international meeting " which was presided over by Maxim Gorky. Gorky was an international figure of the Left, though at this time a strong anti-Bolshevik; and the company was doctrinally mixed.

> We have among us today [said Zinoviev in his opening speech] guests who are neither Marxists nor communists, but all of us here are agreed on one point, in our hatred of the bourgeoisie, in our hatred of a class guilty of the death of millions of men in the interests of a small group.

Reinstein spoke once more for the United States, and Fineberg, like him of Russian origin and recently returned to Russia, for Great Britain; Sadoul appeared for France; there were Serbian, Bulgarian, Turkish, Chinese, Hindu, Persian and Korean

---

[1] Petrov had been repatriated with Chicherin at the end of 1917, and does not seem to have held any credentials from the British Socialist Party. Reinstein who was head of the international propaganda section of Narkomindel (see p. 20 above), had come to Europe in the early summer of 1917 with a mandate from the American Socialist Labor Party to represent it at the abortive Stockholm conference (*Kommunisticheskii Internatsional*, No. 9-10 (187-188) 1929, p. 186); but he was later disowned by his party, and his appearance as its delegate at this conference, as well as at the first congress of Comintern, was unauthorized.

[2] *Pravda*, January 30/February 12, 1918.

[3] *Protokoly Tsentral'nogo Komiteta RSDRP* (1929), p. 219; Kollontai was nominated by the party central committee (*ibid.* p. 216).

representatives; and speeches were also delivered by Scottish, English and American prisoners of war captured on the Archangel front (the first was introduced as the " delegate for Scotland "), and by a member of the Petrograd German Soldiers' and Workers' Council. The meeting lacked nothing in fervour, and lived up to Zinoviev's description of it as " the modest precursor of a future grand assembly ".[1]

Shortly after this demonstration external events gave concrete form to these aspirations for the establishment of a new International. About the time of the international meeting it became known that a conference was being convened in the near future at Berne for the purpose of reviving the Second International; and on December 24, 1918, the central committee of the party issued a broadcast to the world denouncing this project.[2] At the end of December 1918 the foundation of a German Communist Party provided for the first time a respectable nucleus for an international communist organization. Early in January 1919 Lenin presided over a small meeting in the Kremlin, which decided without further delay to invite " all parties opposed to the Second International " to attend a congress in Moscow with a view to the creation of a Third International.[3] The invitation was broadcast to the world from Moscow on January 24, 1919, three days before the date set for the Berne conference.[4] It was

[1] The records of the meeting were published in German (*Sowjet-Russland und die Völker der Welt* (Petrograd, 1920) and in French (*La Russie des Soviets et les Peuples du Monde* (Petrograd, 1920), and presumably also in Russian and English; an earlier " international meeting " held in Moscow and presided over by Kamenev was reported in *Izvestiya*, December 7, 1918.

[2] *Ibid*. December 28, 1918.

[3] According to *Bol'shaya Sovetskaya Entsiklopediya*, xxxiii (1938), col. 737, art. Kommunisticheskii Internatsional, the final decision to convene the congress was taken " at the beginning of January 1919 at a meeting under the leadership of Lenin ". The only published account of the meeting seems to come from Fineberg, who, writing ten years later, could recollect only four persons as being present — Lenin, Chicherin, Sirola and himself (*Kommunisticheskii Internatsional*, No. 9-10 (187-188), 1929, cols. 201-202); he recalls that Lenin submitted to the meeting drafts of the invitation and of a " manifesto to the workers of the world ", which were approved. The invitation was drafted by Trotsky (see p. 119, note 2, below); if the manifesto referred to was the one eventually adopted by the congress, this also came from Trotsky's pen (see p. 123 below). But, even if Trotsky was present at the Kremlin meeting, it would have been inconvenient to remember the fact ten years later.

[4] The conference, having been originally convened for January 27, met on February 3, 1919.

signed in the names of the central committee of the Russian Communist Party (Lenin and Trotsky); of Polish, Hungarian, Austrian, Lettish and Finnish communist parties; of the Balkan
Revolutionary Social-Democratic Federation (Rakovsky); and of
the Socialist Labor Party of America (Reinstein). It was not
specifically addressed to anyone, but named 39 parties or groups
as eligible to attend the founding congress. Only one of these
(" socialist groups in Tokyo and Yokohama ") had its seat in
Asia.[1] Bolshevik thoughts of revolution were still confined mainly
to Europe ; and the principal appeal was to groups in revolt against
the Second International. The invitation set forth principles
purporting to be based on the programmes of the Spartakusbund
and the Russian Communist Party. The division of professed
socialists into Right, Centre and Left which had emerged during
the war was maintained. Of the three elements included in the
Second International, the " social-chauvinists " could be met only
by an " unsparing struggle "; for the Centre there must be a
" policy of splitting off its most revolutionary elements and of
unsparing criticism and exposure of its leaders "; the " Left
revolutionary wing " would, it was assumed, come over. The task
of the proletariat was now " the immediate seizure of state power ";
and the purpose of the congress was to create " a general fighting
organ for permanent coordination and systematic leadership of
the movement, the centre of a communist International, subordinating the interests of the movement in each particular country
to the interests of the revolution on its international scale ".[2]

At the beginning of March 1919 more than 50 delegates
assembled in Moscow, of whom 35, representing communist
parties or groups in 19 different countries, were recognized as full
delegates with voting rights, the others being admitted in a consultative capacity. A large majority of the delegates came from
Russia or from smaller countries within the Russian orbit, since
more distant countries were unable to fill the allotted quota of
five delegates for large nations, three for medium and one for
small. The Russian party was represented by Lenin (who was

---

[1] See p. 492 below.

[2] The invitation was originally published in *Pravda*, January 24, 1919. Its
inclusion in Trotsky, *Sochineniya*, xiii, 33-37, published in 1926, is sufficient
evidence of Trotsky's authorship ; an editorial note in Lenin, *Sochineniya*, xxiv,
724, published in 1935, attributes the authorship to Lenin and Bukharin.

elected to the presidium of the congress together with the German and Swiss delegates), Trotsky, Zinoviev, Stalin, Bukharin and Chicherin.[1] There were delegates representing communist parties of Poland, Finland, the Ukraine, Armenia, Latvia, Estonia, and White Russia and Lithuania ; and a " united group of the eastern peoples of Russia " had one full delegate. Turkestan, Azerbaijan and Georgia had " consultative " delegates. France and the United States had one full delegate each ; the one British delegate, Fineberg, had no formal mandate and had only " consultative " status. The Swiss Social-Democratic Party was represented by Platten, famous in history as the organizer of Lenin's journey to Russia in April 1917. " Consultative " delegates appeared from China, Persia and Korea. Most of these were resident in Moscow, and some of them purported to speak for countries where no communist organization as yet existed. The large Norwegian Labour Party, the main workers' party in Norway, sent a delegate ; and Dutch, Swedish, Hungarian and Austrian delegates represented tiny Left groups in their respective countries, not all of them unimpeachably communist in outlook. Rakovsky spoke for the Balkan Revolutionary Social-Democratic Federation.[2] The language of the congress was German.[3]

[1] Of these Stalin was the only one who, so far as the official record shows, played no part in the proceedings ; this was not unnatural, since he did not understand or speak German. He cannot be distinguished in the photograph of delegates published in *Kommunisticheskii Internatsional*, No. 2 (June 1919). He was not a delegate to the second, third or fourth congresses, but was a " candidate " delegate to the executive committee elected by the second congress.

[2] The only non-communist present as a spectator at the first congress appears to have been Arthur Ransome, whose report (*Six Weeks in Russia in 1919* (1919), pp. 140-147) adds disappointingly little to the official record.

[3] The proceedings of the congress were summarily recorded in German and were first published in that language (*Der I. Kongress der Kommunistischen Internationale* (Hamburg, 1921) : the Russian edition (*Pervyi Kongress Kommunisticheskogo Internatsionala* (1921)) was translated from the German (Lenin, *Sochineniya*, xxiv, 729-730). The linguistic pattern of the second congress was more variegated ; English, French and various eastern delegates spoke in their own languages (some of the eastern delegates in English). The Russian delegates continued to speak in German : Zinoviev and Bukharin apologized for their German (*Der Zweite Kongress der Kommunist. Internationale* (Hamburg, 1921), pp. 59, 404), which, though less perfect than that of Lenin and Trotsky, was fluent enough for all practical purposes. Inadequacy of translations was from time to time a subject of complaint by the English-speaking delegates. At the third congress the main speeches were delivered in German,

The attitude of the Germans was the crucial point for the future, as everyone knew. Of the two delegates chosen by the newly formed German Communist Party only one, Eberlein, had succeeded in eluding the German police : he appeared at the congress under the *nom de guerre* of Albert. He had, however, come with a mandate to oppose the creation of a new International as premature. The German communists, weak and persecuted at home, perceived clearly that an International founded in Moscow in.existing conditions must be almost exclusively Russian in character and leadership ; and they would have preferred to wait until communism had developed further in Germany and western Europe.[1] These objections first appeared at an informal preliminary discussion between a few of the principal delegates on March 1, 1919.[2] They were met to the extent that the delegates assembled on the following day not as a formal congress but as a " preparatory conference ". Zinoviev was elected president, not yet of the future International, but of the conference, with Angelica Balabanov and Vorovsky as secretaries.[3] Eberlein announced in the name of the KPD that he had " no objection of principle " to the creation of a Communist International, but asked that the present proceedings should be limited to a conference " to test

as occasional indications show (e.g. *Protokoll des III. Kongresses der Kommunistischen Internationale* (Hamburg, 1921), p. 49 (Trotsky), p. 626 (Zinoviev) ; but it was announced that there would be no translations except into Russian (*ibid.* p. 28). The situation appears to have been the same at the fourth congress of November 1922, the last attended by Lenin ; from the fifth congress of July 1924 onwards Russian began to compete with German and, finally, superseded it as the predominant language.

[1] According to an account given by Eberlein ten years later, Rosa Luxemburg, hearing a few days before her death of the intention to convene the congress (the formal invitation cannot have reached her), proposed to Eberlein that he should go to Moscow as delegate of the KPD with a mandate to propose a postponement (though only of a few months) in the foundation of the new International. This mandate was formally confirmed after her death by Jogiches, Levi, Pieck and the other party leaders (*Kommunisticheskii Internatsional*, No. 9-10 (187-188) 1929, p. 194). According to Ernst Meyer, Eberlein had instructions from Jogiches to leave the Congress if the decision were taken to proceed to the foundation of the new International (*Bericht über den 5. Parteitag der Kommunistischen Partei Deutschlands (Spartakusbund)* (1921), p. 27).

[2] Lenin, *Sochineniya*, xxiv, 724-725 ; *Kommunisticheskii Internatsional v Dokumentakh* (1933), p. 52.

[3] *Vos'moi S"ezd RKP(B)* (1933), p. 144 ; Balabanov had been secretary of the international socialist committee set up at Zimmerwald.

the available strength and review the political foundations on which we can unite ".[1] The resistance of the one serious communist party outside Soviet territory seemed at first decisive. The Bolshevik delegation saw nothing for it but to yield, and a long speech made on its behalf by Bukharin, implied willingness to defer the vital decision.[2] " The proposal to treat the meeting as the constituent assembly of a new International had ", in Balabanov's words, " been generally abandoned ", when the current of opinion was suddenly reversed by a fiery speech from the newly arrived Austrian delegate, Steinhardt, *alias* Gruber, which depicted the whole of central Europe as on the verge of revolution.[3] In the new mood further delay seemed pusillanimous, and Eberlein was completely isolated. When at the next meeting the formal constitution of a Communist International was proposed in the name of the delegates of Austria, Sweden, the Balkan federation and Hungary, Eberlein restated his objections :

> Real communist parties exist in only a few countries ; in most, they have been created only in the last few weeks ; in many countries where there are communists today they have as yet no organization. . . . What is missing is the whole of western Europe. Belgium, Italy are not represented ; the Swiss representative cannot speak in the name of the party ; France, England, Spain, Portugal are missing ; and America is equally not in a position to say what parties would support us.[4]

But he was induced to abstain from voting in order not to mar the harmony of the proceedings ; and on March 4, 1919, the conference by a unanimous resolution transformed itself into the first

[1] *Der I. Kongress der Kommunistischen Internationale* (Hamburg, 1921), p. 76.
[2] *Ibid.* pp. 84-95 ; the attitude of the Bolshevik delegation is confirmed by Zinoviev in *Vos'moi S"ezd RKP(B)* (1933), p. 137.
[3] Angelica Balabanov, *Erinnerungen und Erlebnisse* (1927), pp. 225-226 ; Reinstein in *Kommunisticheskii Internatsional*, No. 9-10. (187-188), 1929, pp. 191-192, also attributes the change in mood to Steinhardt's oratory. The speech is summarized (no stenographic record of this congress was taken) in *Der I. Kongress der Kommunistischen Internationale* (Hamburg, 1921), pp. 99-105.
[4] *Ibid.* p. 134. Writing ten years later, Eberlein complained that he had been misrepresented in the summary records of the congress, and had explained that, had his hands been free, he would have voted for the proposal, the reasons for his opposition being purely tactical (*Kommunisticheskii Internatsional*, No. 9-10 (187-188), 1929, pp. 195-196) ; but by this time Eberlein was eager to shed his reputation as the one man who had stood out in 1919 against the founding of Comintern.

congress of the Communist International.[1] The abstention of
Germany (though Eberlein signed the manifesto of the congress)
could do nothing to avert the danger which the German communists feared. Indeed whole-hearted cooperation from the
outset might at least have mitigated a Russian predominance
which resulted from lack of serious competition rather than from
any conscious Russian design.

The fact of the foundation of a Third or Communist International, henceforth familiarly known as Comintern, was more
important than anything done at its first congress. It adopted a
" platform " and a manifesto " To the Proletarians of the Whole
World ", which reviewed the rise and fall of capitalism and the
development of communism in the seventy-two (or more accurately seventy-one) years since Marx and Engels issued the
Communist Manifesto, and was afterwards described by Zinoviev
as " a second *Communist Manifesto* ".[2] The congress approved
a set of theses presented by Lenin in denunciation of bourgeois
democracy and parliamentarianism and in defence of the dictatorship of the proletariat (this was the theme of Lenin's main speech
at the congress) ; it derided the attempts of the Berne conference
to revive the " yellow " Second International, and attacked the
imperialism of the Entente Powers and the " white " terror.
Finally, it issued an appeal " To the Workers of All Countries ",
whose urgent tone and topical content distinguished it from the
other congress documents. This began by expressing the " gratitude and admiration " of the congress for " the Russian revolutionary proletariat and its directing party — the Communist
Party of the Bolsheviks ". The work of liberation and reform
pursued by the Soviet power had, however, been interrupted by
a civil war which was being waged with the aid of the Entente
countries and would collapse at once without that aid. Hence it
was the duty of the " working masses of all countries " to press
upon their governments by all available means (" including, if
necessary, revolutionary means ") demands for the cessation of
intervention, for the withdrawal of armies from Russia, for the

---

[1] *Kommunisticheskii Internatsional v Dokumentakh* (1933), p. 85. On the
following day, March 5, the first mention of the congress appeared in *Pravda* ;
for the next week *Pravda* carried retrospectively long reports of the proceedings.
[2] *Vos'moi S"ezd RKP(B)* (1933), p. 138 ; it was drafted by Trotsky and
appears in Trotsky, *Sochineniya*, xiii, 38-49.

recognition of the Soviet régime, for the establishment of diplomatic and commercial relations, and for the despatch to Russia of " some hundreds or even thousands " of engineers, instructors and skilled workers to assist in the restoration and reorganization of transport.[1] The congress elected an " executive committee of the Communist International " (IKKI or, by its English initials, ECCI) containing representatives of the communist parties of Russia, Germany, Austria, Hungary, the Balkan federation, Scandinavia and Switzerland, to act, like the central committee of the party, in the name of the institution in the intervals between congresses; other parties joining Comintern before the next congress were to receive a seat on IKKI.[2] Zinoviev became its president, and Radek its secretary. The appointment of Radek, who seemed likely to remain for an indefinite period in his Berlin prison, was an empty gesture of defiance to the capitalist world. As soon as the congress separated, Angelica Balabanov took over the functions of secretary of IKKI, but held the post only for a few weeks.[3] It was unthinkable for the present that IKKI should have its seat anywhere but in Moscow. But Zinoviev explained that this was temporary and that " we shall be glad if we can succeed in transferring the place of residence of the Third International and its executive committee as quickly as possible to another capital, for example, Paris ".[4]

---

[1] The principal resolutions of the congress are in *Kommunisticheskii Internatsional v Dokumentakh* (1933), pp. 53-88.

[2] *Der I. Kongress der Kommunistischen Internationale* (Hamburg, 1921), pp. 200-201. The resolution laid down that, pending the arrival in Moscow of its other members, the functions of IKKI should be discharged by the Russian delegation.

[3] Angelica Balabanov, *Erinnerungen und Erlebnisse* (1927), pp. 228-229, 239-241.

[4] This assurance did not appear in the record of the congress, but was reported by Zinoviev to the eighth party congress a few days later (*Vos'moi S"ezd RKP(B)* (1933), p. 139). This view was common to all the Bolshevik leaders. " If today ", wrote Trotsky in *Izvestiya* on May 1, 1919, " Moscow is the centre of the Third International, tomorrow — we are profoundly convinced — this centre will move to the west : to Berlin, Paris, London. However joyfully the Russian proletariat welcomed the representatives of the working class of the world in the walls of the Kremlin, it will with even greater joy send its representatives to the second congress of the Communist International in one of the western European centres. For an international communist congress in Berlin or Paris will mean the complete triumph of the proletarian revolution in Europe and, probably, in the whole world " (Trotsky, *Sochineniya*, xiii, 28).

The appeal " To the Workers of All Countries " to rally to the support of the Soviet régime in Russia was in some respects the most significant document of the first Congress of the Communist International. Beyond question the new organization had been conceived by its founders as in the fullest sense international — a successor of the defunct and discredited " Second International ". Lenin, in one of his rare flights of rhetoric, described it at the moment of its foundation as " the forerunner of the international republic of Soviets ".[1] But the conditions of its birth marked it out for a different destiny. The constant and ineradicable duality of purpose inherent in Lenin's outlook — the defence of the Soviet power in Russia and the furtherance of international revolution — coloured his view of the new instrument; and the partly unforeseen circumstances which put the effective control of it exclusively into Russian hands completed the organic link between Comintern and the Soviet régime. What had taken place in Moscow in March 1919 was not in fact the fusion of a number of national communist parties of approximately equal strength into an international organization, but the harnessing of a number of weak, in some cases embryonic and still unformed, groups to an organization whose main support and motive force was necessarily and inevitably the power of the Soviet state. It was Soviet power which created Comintern and gave it its influence and prestige; in return, it was natural to expect that international communist propaganda and action should help to defend that power at a moment when it was threatened by all the reactionary forces of the capitalist world. At this crucial moment of the civil war the supreme task naturally presented itself in Lenin's mind as " a struggle of the proletarian state surrounded by capitalist states ".[2] National and international aims, the security of the Soviet régime and the interests of the proletarian revolution, were once more inextricably blended. In an article contributed by Lenin to the first number of *Kommunisticheskii Internatsional*, the journal of the new organization, the simple truth was stated with the emphasis of italics :

The new third " International Workingmen's Association "[3]

---

[1] Lenin, *Sochineniya*, xxiv, 26.   [2] *Ibid.* xxiv, 56.
[3] This was the official title of the First International founded in London in 1864.

has *already begun to coincide* in a certain measure *with the Union of Soviet Socialist Republics*.[1]

The struggle was waged simultaneously on the two planes — the revolutionary plane and the plane of state action — without any sense of incompatibility between them. It would, therefore, be an error to suggest that the foundation of the Communist International marked any fresh departure in Soviet foreign policy, or had any immediate effect on its course. Once the civil war began, that policy was necessarily concerned to foster the disintegration of the enemy's power, both at home and in the field, through revolutionary propaganda. At the moment when Comintern came into being, the propaganda which had helped to destroy the war-weary German armies already threatened to have a similar effect on the victorious but equally war-weary forces of the allies. In January 1919 when the allied statesmen, assembled in Paris for the peace conference, discussed the occupation of Russia by allied troops, the British Prime Minister bluntly assured his colleagues that " if he now proposed to send a thousand British troops to Russia for that purpose, the armies would mutiny ", and that, " if a military enterprise were started against the Bolsheviki, that would make England Bolshevist and there would be a Soviet in London ".[2] Lloyd George was talking for effect, as was his manner. But his perceptive mind had correctly diagnosed the symptoms. Serious mutinies in the first months of 1919 in the French fleet and in French military units landed in Odessa and other Black Sea ports led to an enforced evacuation at the beginning of April. Of the troops of several nationalities under British command on the Archangel front the Director of Military Operations at the War Office reported in March 1919 that their morale was " so low as to render them a prey to the very active and insidious Bolshevik propaganda which the enemy are carrying out with increasing energy and skill ".[3] The details were disclosed much later through official American reports. On March 1, 1919, a mutiny occurred among French troops ordered to go up to the line ; several days earlier a British

[1] Lenin, *Sochineniya*, xxiv, 247.
[2] *Foreign Relations of the United States : The Paris Peace Conference, 1919*, iii (1943), 590-591.
[3] *The Evacuation of North Russia, 1919*, Cmd. 818 (1920), p. 25.

infantry company " refused to go to the front ", and shortly afterwards an American company " refused for a time to return to duty
at the front ".[1] It was in the light of such experience that the
British Government decided in March 1919 to evacuate north
Russia, though the evacuation was not in fact completed till six
months later.

Mutiny among the troops was matched by widespread dis-
affection in the industrial centres of Great Britain. At the time
of the armistice a report handed by the Foreign Office to the
American embassy in London expressed the belief that " apart
from certain centres, notably the Clyde and South Wales, Bolshevism as such is innocuous for the present ". Nevertheless no
chances were being taken :

> A careful watch is being maintained for such Bolshevik
> propaganda as may reach this country from abroad, in order
> that it may be intercepted and destroyed, and the same measures
> are being taken wherever possible in respect to inflammatory
> literature secretly printed at home. Counter-propaganda is
> meanwhile being conducted through the unostentatious dis-
> tribution of pamphlets designed to educate the people as to
> the true significance of Bolshevism, and appropriate articles
> appear in the Sunday papers customarily read by the working
> men.[2]

The first serious attempt to challenge public order by calling a
general strike was made in Glasgow at the end of January 1919;
and " Red Friday " was long remembered as the peak of the revolutionary movement on the Clyde. Political discontent was focused
on the government's Russian policy by a meeting at the Albert
Hall on February 9, 1919, which launched a " Hands off Russia "
campaign. At the founding congress of Comintern a month later
the British delegate, Fineberg, spoke in a language which seemed
to find support in the facts :

> The strike movement is spreading all over England and is
> affecting every branch of industry. In the army discipline is

---

[1] *Papers Relating to the Foreign Relations of the United States, 1919 : Russia*
(Washington, 1937), pp. 620-623 ; [J. Cudahy], *Archangel, the American War
with Russia* (1924), pp. 99, 126-127, and C. Maynard, *The Murmansk Venture*
(n.d. [1928]), p. 190, cite numerous instances of insubordination and petty
mutiny among allied forces in north Russia under the influence of Soviet
propaganda.

[2] *Foreign Relations of the United States, 1918 : Russia*, i (1931), pp. 727-72⁹

much weakened, which in other countries was the first symptom of revolution.[1]

" England may seem to you untouched," Lenin told a British correspondent at this time, " but the microbe is already there."[2] Meanwhile hunger was rife in central Europe, and disorganization was everywhere; strikes and disorders had occurred even in peaceful neutral countries like Holland and Switzerland. On March 21, 1919, just a fortnight after the founding congress of Comintern had dispersed, a Soviet republic was proclaimed in Budapest. On the next day House in Paris confided his apprehensions to his diary :

> Bolshevism is gaining ground everywhere. Hungary has just succumbed. We are sitting upon an open powder magazine and some day a spark may ignite it.[3]

Almost at the same moment Lloyd George dramatized the situation in a confidential memorandum designed to overcome Clemenceau's obstinacy at the peace conference :

> The whole of Europe is filled with the spirit of revolution. There is a deep sense not only of discontent but of anger and revolt amongst the workmen against pre-war conditions. The whole existing order in its political, social and economic aspects is questioned by the masses of the population from one end of Europe to the other.[4]

Early in April another Soviet republic was proclaimed in Munich. World revolution was on the march. Lenin, appealing to the central council of the trade unions in the same month to give their full support to the mobilization against Kolchak, referred

---

[1] *Der I. Kongress der Kommunistischen Internationale* (Hamburg, 1921), p. 70. In the United States, according to a highly coloured official intelligence report of June 1919, the office of Martens, the unrecognized Soviet representative in New York, was " the largest and most dangerous propaganda undertaking thus far started by Lenin's party in any country outside of Russia " (*Foreign Relations of the United States, 1919 : Russia*, (1937), p. 147). The demands of the " Hands off Russia " Committee included the withdrawal of British troops, the ending of support for the " whites " and of the blockade, and the establishment of diplomatic relations with the Soviet Government (W. P. and Z. K. Coates, *A History of Anglo-Soviet Relations* (1943), p. 141).

[2] A. Ransome, *Six Weeks in Russia in 1919* (1919), p. 149.

[3] *The Intimate Papers of Colonel House*, ed. C. Seymour, iv (1928), 405.

[4] *Papers Respecting Negotiations for an Anglo-French Pact*, Cmd. 2169 (1924), p. 78.

to the French mutinies at Odessa and to the Soviet republics in central Europe as proof that " our victory on an international scale is completely secure "; and his May Day speech on the Red Square ended with the slogans: " Long live the international republic of Soviets! Long live communism! " [1] Not only did Zinoviev in the first issue of the journal of Comintern make his famous prophecy that in a year's time one would begin to forget that there had ever been a struggle for communism in Europe, [2] but the far more sober Lenin was inspired by the Versailles treaty to discover " an immense revolutionary movement " in Germany and to predict that " this July will be our last difficult July, and next July we shall greet the victory of the international Soviet republic ". [3] Meanwhile the sapping of the hostile front by revolutionary action through every possible instrument — Comintern being merely the newest and most far-reaching — was the one effective foreign policy still open to the Soviet Government; and it seemed, in the summer of 1919, to be yielding excellent dividends.

It appeared, therefore, in no way anomalous that Chicherin, as head of Narkomindel, should at this time work hand in glove with Zinoviev, as head of Comintern, and that the language of the two organs should be scarcely distinguishable. When a Soviet government was set up in Munich in April 1919, Chicherin greeted it in a message which was published in *Izvestiya* :

> We may rest assured that the day is not far off when re-volutionary socialist allies will join forces with us and will give support to the Bavarian republic against any attack. Every blow aimed at you is aimed at us. In absolute unity we carry on our revolutionary struggle for the well-being of all workers and exploited peoples. [4]

And VTsIK, sending its greetings to the Soviet republics of Hungary and Bavaria, expressed the conviction that " the pro-letariat of the whole world, having before its eyes striking examples of the victorious insurrection of the workers in three countries of Europe, will follow them with complete faith in victory ". [5] Ten

---

[1] Lenin, *Sochineniya*, xxiv, 230, 269.
[2] *Kommunisticheskii Internatsional*, No. 1 (May 1919), col. 25.
[3] Lenin, *Sochineniya*, xxiv, 381.
[4] *Izvestiya*, April 9, 10, 1919, quoted in A. L. P. Dennis, *The Foreign Policies of Soviet Russia* (1924), p. 352.
[5] Klyuchnikov i Sabanin, *Mezhdunarodnaya Politika*, ii (1926), 237-238.

days later Chicherin signed an appeal to the workers of the allied countries protesting against the aid furnished by the allies to the " white " forces in the civil war and against the allied blockade.[1] A fresh opportunity was offered when the allied peace terms were first disclosed to Germany at Versailles. Zinoviev issued a proclamation on behalf of IKKI, which declared that " the proletarian revolution is the only salvation for the oppressed classes of the whole world " and concluded with the words :

Down with the Versailles peace, down with the new Brest! Down with the government of the social traitors! Long live the power of the Soviets in the whole world.[2]

At the same moment Chicherin issued a pamphlet, which was published in German and French by IKKI, *To the German Worker*, ending with the same revolutionary appeal :

In the ranks of the communist revolutionary fighters is your place ; there you will find salvation from your present calamity.[3]

In Germany, as in Russia, only revolutionary action now seemed relevant to the position. Chicherin analysed *The Foreign Policy of the Two Internationals* in an article which appeared in the journal of Comintern in October 1919. He described the whole activity of Comintern as constituting " a proletarian foreign policy — contact between workers' organizations and mutual help in all possible cases ". In the optimistic mood of the summer of 1919 he wrote throughout of " Soviet governments " in the plural :

Before the revolutionary proletarian parties and groups of all countries is set the task of struggling to guarantee and strengthen the international position of the revolutionary Soviet governments. Only in this way is a new programme of foreign policy open to those parties and groups which take their stand on revolutionary Soviet ground.

He admitted that those governments, " as governments existing *de facto* among other existing governments, are compelled to

[1] Klyuchnikov i Sabanin, *Mezhdunarodnaya Politika*, ii (1926) 238-242.
[2] *Kommunisticheskii Internatsional*, No. 2 (June 1919), cols. 149-150 : it was published in German in *Die Internationale*, i, No. 11-12 (August 18, 1919), pp. 244-48.
[3] G. Chicherin, *An den Deutschen Arbeiter* (Moscow, 1919).

place themselves in certain relations with the latter, and those relations impose on them obligations which have to be taken into account ". But, on the other hand, Soviet governments — here Chicherin was probably thinking of the League of Nations — " keep aloof from all participation in any kind of combination of imperialist governments ".[1] Mutual aid among workers and workers' governments seemed at this time to exhaust the content of a proletarian foreign policy. Nothing more was either necessary or practicable.

Yet the omens were by no means all propitious. On May 1, 1919, the ineffectual career of the Bavarian Soviet republic, left to its own devices and unsupported by any decisive action of the Prussian proletariat, had come to its inevitable end. In the middle of June an attempted communist rising in Vienna was ignominiously crushed. Early in August 1919 the slightly more substantial Hungarian Soviet régime succumbed to internal dissension and to the intervention of Rumanian troops, backed by the western allies. These defeats, and the delay in the time-table of world revolution, left the RSFSR cut off from all external aid in a hostile capitalist world. In the autumn of 1919 all the " white " forces arrayed against the Soviet power reached in turn the peak of their activity and of their success — Kolchak on the confines of Siberia, Yudenich in front of Petrograd, Denikin in the Ukraine and central Russia. The months of October and November marked the crucial point at which the continued existence of the régime hung by a thread.

In this bleak and hostile world the newly founded Communist International took its first steps. " White " Russian armies, actively supported by the Allies, had bitten deeply into Soviet territory; at all the main points on its periphery enemy forces were encamped. Everywhere frontiers were closed. The *cordon sanitaire* had become a reality. Even foreign newspapers reached Moscow irregularly or not at all; Lenin's writings of this year are full of complaints of the difficulty of obtaining accurate or up-to-date information of foreign happenings.[2] The journal of Comintern,

---

[1] *Kommunisticheskii Internatsional*, No. 6 (October 1919), cols. 817-828.
[2] Lenin, *Sochineniya*, xxiv, 27-29, 35, 317, 475.

Kommunisticheskii Internatsional, appeared regularly throughout the year under Zinoviev's editorship. But no more than the nucleus of a standing organization had been created; and in the desperate conditions of the summer of 1919 no steps could be taken to make it effective.[1] When Rutgers, who had been the Dutch delegate at the founding congress of Comintern, left Moscow for Holland in the middle of October 1919, he took with him a mandate from Lenin to set up a bureau of Comintern for western Europe in Holland and to summon an international conference there — a haphazard and rather desperate attempt to overcome the isolation of Moscow.[2] In spite of the most optimistic estimates of the prospects of world revolution, there was probably never a time when the Soviet leaders had less material possibility of promoting it than in the six months which followed the foundation of Comintern; there was certainly never a time after 1917 when the parties of the extreme Left abroad faced their problems with less aid or less interference from Moscow.

After the foundation of Comintern all contact with the German Communist Party seems to have been lost; and for a long period nothing was known of it in Moscow except that the *Rote Fahne* appeared illegally but regularly in Berlin, and that there were similar communist journals in other German cities.[3] The fortunes of the party, after the catastrophe of January 1919, were at a low ebb. Jogiches, since Rosa Luxemburg's death the recognized leader of what was left of the party, was murdered in precisely similar conditions on March 10, 1919. The succession now fell to Paul Levi, who had attended the Zimmerwald conference in 1915 and was, next to Luxemburg, the most distinguished intellectual in the Spartakusbund, but lacked the temperament of a leader or of a man of action. At the second and last All-German Congress

---

[1] Angelica Balabanov's account of the first months of Comintern is coloured by extreme hostility to Zinoviev, but the general picture of confusion and intrigue is plausible. She insists on the predominance of the Russians in IKKI; this could hardly be avoided, since the committee was composed, on the one hand, of " the most tried members of the Russian Communist Party " and, on the other, of " quite unknown and worthless elements . . . who had never before had anything to do with the International or even with the movement, ignoramuses who trembled before authority " (Angelica Balabanov, *Erinnerungen und Erlebnisse* (1927), pp. 239-240).

[2] *Istorik Marksist*, No. 2-3, 1935, pp. 90-91.

[3] Lenin, *Sochineniya*, xxiv, 476.

of Workers' and Soldiers' Councils, which took place in Berlin in April 1919, there was only one communist delegate. The proceedings resolved themselves into a struggle between the SPD majority and the USPD minority. But the struggle was completely unreal, since both sides accepted the authority of the National Assembly elected by universal suffrage, which had been in session at Weimar since February; and Lenin gibed from afar at the inconsistencies of the USPD leaders, who believed that parliamentary democracy was compatible with a régime of Soviets.[1] The speedy collapse of the Soviet republic in Bavaria, whatever its shortcomings of ideology or organization, was a further blow to the cause of the German revolution, whose supporters succumbed in the summer of 1919 to a universal mood of discouragement and retreat.[2] Under the " state of siege " proclaimed in January 1919 the KPD became an illegal organization and could operate only under cover. Even the Versailles treaty failed to dispel the prevailing apathy. The flaming denunciation of the treaty by IKKI found only a faint echo in the pronouncements of the KPD. The party's " Theses on the Peace ", which bore the mark of Levi's analytical and sceptical pen, argued that the military form of government which had ruled Germany before the war had now been restored, and that " under a bankrupt imperialism " acceptance or rejection of the terms of peace would be equally disastrous.[3] In a proclamation intended for general distribution, preference was given to rejection on the ground that, while the results of either course would be the same for the proletariat, acceptance would give " a breathing space to the counter-revolution ", whereas rejection would precipitate the German bourgeoisie " into its last crisis, in which it will finally perish ".[4]

In the late summer of 1919 the KPD did indeed acquire an important Russian contact. Radek, after his arrest in February 1919, was subjected to a prolonged process of interrogation and

[1] Ibid. xxiv, 317-319.
[2] Two years later the Bavarian communist Thomas declared at a party congress that " the overthrow of the premature Bavarian Soviet republic also meant the collapse of the German revolution " (Bericht über den 5. Parteitag der Kommunistischen Partei Deutschlands (Spartakusbund) (1921), p. 77).
[3] Die Internationale, i, No. 2-3 (May 30, 1919), pp. 28-32.
[4] Quoted in O. K. Flechtheim, Die Kommunistische Partei Deutschlands in der Weimarer Republik (Offenbach, 1948), p. 56.

held in strict confinement for six months. Then, on a decision which apparently emanated from the German Ministry of War, he was transferred to a privileged cell in the prison, where for some four months he held what he himself describes as a " political salon ". In December 1919 he was released from prison, and spent the last few weeks of his stay in Berlin under more or less nominal police supervision, in the apartment first of a sympathetic retired general, and then of a police commissioner, while awaiting the completion of arrangements for his journey to Moscow, on which he finally embarked in January 1920.[1] Between August 1919 and the end of the year, Radek was thus able to maintain ample and varied communications with the outside world, and soon acquired a position of unique prestige and influence in the KPD. According to his own account, he refused to allow its leaders to visit him in prison for fear of compromising them, though he maintained a regular correspondence with them and was impressed by their inability to lead : it was at this time that he acquired the sceptical view of the prospects of the party and of the German revolution which coloured all his later thought and action. After leaving the prison he saw Levi, Klara Zetkin and all the principal leaders.[2] But, at any rate till November 1919, when Kopp arrived in Berlin as semi-official Soviet delegate,[3] neither Radek nor anyone else in Berlin appears to have had regular means of communication

[1] Radek's reminiscences of this experience, written in a rather light-hearted vein, appeared seven years later in *Krasnaya Nov'*, No. 10, 1926, pp. 163-172. His first contact with the outside world was a veteran Swiss social-democrat of Austrian origin, passing under the name of Karl Moor, who " began to arrange interviews with me for many who without his cooperation would not have reached me " ; the only indication of the date of his transfer from strict confinement to the privileged cell is that it occurred when " the heroic Hungarian revolution had already been crushed ", i.e. after August 1, 1919 (*ibid.* p. 168). Ruth Fischer, who constantly visited him in prison, states that the necessary pass was obtained from the Ministry of War (*Stalin and German Communism* (Harvard, 1948), pp. 206-207) ; the reasons for the intervention of the Ministry of War on his behalf will appear later.

[2] *Krasnaya Nov'*, No. 10, 1926, pp. 166-167, 171 : the verdict on the leaders of KPD may reflect their subsequent failures. Radek's pessimism about revolution in Germany also led to pessimism about the survival of the revolution in Russia, since the two revolutions were still closely connected in all Bolshevik thinking. Ruth Fischer (*Stalin and German Communism* (Harvard, 1948), p. 93) describes Radek pacing his prison room at the time of the Yudenich offensive and hourly expecting news of disaster.

[3] For Kopp see p. 317 below.

with Moscow. Whatever he did was done on his own authority.[1] In the autumn of 1919, in an attempt to make up for these deficiencies in organization, a " western European secretariat " of Comintern was set up in Berlin. It can no longer be ascertained on whose initiative the step was taken, whether it preceded or followed the mandate given to Rutgers in Moscow in October to establish a " western European bureau " in Holland, or even whether the headquarters of Comintern in Moscow was consulted at all : that the danger of overlapping or conflict between the two institutions should apparently have occurred to nobody is symptomatic of the chaotic and unformed state of Comintern organization in the first year of its existence. Circumstantial evidence suggests that Radek was concerned in this new move. The chiefs of the secretariat were Thomas, a Bavarian communist, who had succeeded in creating an illegal Comintern press in Hamburg, and Bronsky, a communist of Polish origin, who in 1918 was Soviet trade delegate in Berlin under Joffe ; both had been among Radek's prison visitors.[2] The western European secretariat heralded its birth by a manifesto appealing to the workers of the world, on the occasion of the second anniversary of the October revolution, to oppose intervention in Russia. If the workers of Europe did not come to the assistance of the Russian revolution, then the workers of Russia would be entitled to say : " We have sacrificed everything for the liberation of the proletariat, you nothing. We die as free men, you will be condemned to live as slaves." [3] The main function of the secretariat was to publish

---

[1] Radek learned from *The Times* of his appointment as Ukrainian representative in Berlin (*Krasnaya Nov'*, No. 10, 1926, p. 162), and obtained documents of the eighth party congress held in Moscow in March 1919 only when Kopp brought them to Berlin eight months later (*ibid.* p. 169).

[2] *Ibid.* pp. 167-168 ; Bronsky agreed with Radek " that the first wave of the revolution had subsided, that the task consisted in organizing the masses for the next wave " (*ibid.* p. 167). When Levi and Zetkin visited Radek in his Berlin flat in November 1919, he helped them to draft " theses " for the western European secretariat (*ibid.* p. 171).

[3] *Kommunisticheskii Internatsional*, No. 7-8 (November-December 1919), cols. 1099-1102 ; this is one of the very few occasions on which the western European secretariat was mentioned in the official journal of Comintern. An odd feature of the manifesto was that it appeared to treat the Communist International as not yet in being : " The International of world reaction has risen anew. It is marching against the cradle of world revolution, against Soviet Russia. Therefore it is indispensable to found the International of world revolution."

information about the progress and achievements of the Soviet régime in Russia. But it seems to have had little contact with Moscow except for the receipt of official Comintern documents and to have enjoyed no political status or importance.[1] At the second congress of Comintern in July 1920 a speaker described it as " limited, narrow, and to a certain extent nationalist and not international ".[2]

Meanwhile a crisis had occurred in the affairs of the KPD. The views of the majority at the first congress of the KPD against participation in parliamentary elections and in the existing trade unions [3] were on the records. The first of these decisions had been carried out when the party refrained in January 1919 from participating in the elections to the National Assembly (though there were also special reasons for this abstention, since the assembly was the rival of the existing councils of workers' and soldiers' deputies). But no steps had been taken to withdraw from the trade unions ; nor were any likely to be taken under the existing leadership of the party. The whole question was reopened at a party conference held in August 1919, at which the leaders pressed for a reversal of the January decision, while an important opposition group led by two Hamburg communists, Laufenberg and Wolffheim, wished to withdraw all communists from the existing trade unions and form a single comprehensive communist trade union.[4] This was clearly marked out as the major issue at the second party congress, which was held secretly in the neighbourhood of Heidelberg in October 1919.

At this point Radek, now enjoying the facilities of the privileged cell, intervened.[5] Bolshevik doctrine in favour of participation in parliamentary elections and trade unions was clear and unequi-

---

[1] R. Fischer, *Stalin and German Communism* (Harvard, 1948), pp. 134-135 ; *Bericht über den 3. Parteitag der Kommunistischen Partei Deutschlands (Spartakusbund)* (n.d.), p. 77 (Klara Zetkin's remarks on it are quoted, p. 170, note 3 below).

[2] *Der Zweite Kongress der Kommunist. Internationale* (Hamburg, 1921), p. 590.

[3] See p. 104 above.

[4] O. K. Flechtheim, *Die Kommunistische Partei Deutschlands in der Weimarer Republik* (Offenbach, 1948), p. 59.

[5] According to Radek's statement seven years later his intervention was provoked by a letter from Levi showing that he had gone over to the standpoint of the Hamburg group (*Krasnaya Nov'*, No. 10, 1926, pp. 166-167) ; but this does not seem to be confirmed by any contemporary record.

vocal, and Radek wrote an address expounding it, which was read at the Heidelberg congress, and subsequently published by the KPD as a separate pamphlet.[1] But, shortly before the congress opened, Ruth Fischer visited Radek with a message from Bronsky to the effect that Levi intended to put before the congress a resolution which would not only endorse participation in elections and in the trade unions, but have the effect of expelling from the party those who voted against it. This information alarmed Radek, who was already preoccupied by the small numbers and by the isolation of the KPD,[2] and wholly opposed to a split which would reduce it still further to the position of an insignificant political sect. He hastily wrote a letter to Levi, begging him to make the issue one of persuasion rather than discipline, and not to split the party, and gave it to Ruth Fischer to take to Heidelberg.[3] The summons came at the last moment,[4] and was ignored by Levi, who presented his theses to the congress unchanged, with the

[1] K. Radek, *Zur Taktik des Kommunismus: Ein Schreiben an den Oktober-Parteitag der KPD* (Hamburg, 1919); Radek compared the view of the Hamburg group with Proudhonism, anarchism and the syndicalism of the American Industrial Workers of the World, and called it " the new Hamburg-Amerika line " (*ibid.* pp. 10-11).

[2] According to his own account, Radek at this time not only wanted to maintain contact with the Left of the USPD in order to encourage a split in that party (which occurred a year later at the Halle congress), but offered to Stampfer, the editor of *Vorwärts*, one of his few visitors from the SPD, a " temporary bloc " between the KPD and SPD to repel a prospective counter-revolutionary *putsch* on the condition of a revival of the Soviets — a condition which Stampfer rejected (*Krasnaya Nov'*, No. 10, 1926, pp. 167, 170). He apparently also received a visit from Laufenberg and Wolffheim (R. Fischer, *Stalin and German Communism* (Harvard, 1948), p. 92); writing seven years later, when orthodoxy had become more stringent, he did not record this contact with the leaders of a rebel group. Radek's description of his views at this time may have been influenced by hindsight; he probably did not anticipate anything like so explicitly as he pretends the later tactics of the " united front ". But what he records corresponds fairly well with what can be established by other evidence.

[3] *Krasnaya Nov'*, No. 10, 1926, p. 168; R. Fischer, *Stalin and German Communism* (Harvard, 1948), p. 207. The previous reference to this congress *ibid.* pp. 118-119 is misleading: the reason why the opposition received no notification of the last meeting of the congress was that it had already been expelled.

[4] According to P. Levi, *Was ist das Verbrechen? Die März-Aktion oder die Kritik daran?* (1921), p. 29, Radek's letter was received " half an hour before the opening of the congress ". This is denied by Radek (*Krasnaya Nov'*, No. 10, 1926, p. 168); but his statement that the letter was written " at the same time " as his address to the congress does not carry conviction.

final proviso that those who failed to accept the views set forth in them were excluded from the party.[1] After a bitterly contested struggle, with several close votes on specific issues, the resolution as a whole was voted by a majority of 31 votes to 18, and the minority left the congress.[2] The news of the split reached Moscow without warning through the official German radio. Lenin evidently knew nothing of the minority except that it was a " Left " opposition. Independently reaching the same conclusion as Radek, he thought it all-important at this time that the Left should be united against the " Kautskyites ", and wrote an anxious letter to the central committee of the German party suggesting that, if there were " agreement *on the fundamental issue* (for the power of the Soviets against bourgeois parliamentarianism) ", schism should be avoided by all possible means : " from the international point of view the re-establishment of the unity of the German Communist Party is both possible and essential ".[3] It was too late ; for the expelled opposition was already engaged in forming a separate German Communist Workers' Party (KAPD), which carried away from the KPD nearly half its total membership of 50,000, and almost all its members in North Germany and in Berlin itself. But it is of interest to record that the first instance after the formation of Comintern of the expulsion of a large dissident minority on grounds of party orthodoxy by party leaders occurred in the German Communist Party and against the views both of Lenin and of Radek.

The Heidelberg schism was the symptom rather than the cause of a fundamental weakness in the KPD which was still unsuspected in Moscow. In the summer and autumn of 1919 the revolutionary wave was ebbing fast throughout central Europe. The failures of Munich and Budapest sapped what was left of

---

[1] *Bericht über den 2. Parteitag der Kommunistischen Partei Deutschlands (Spartakusbund)* (n.d. [? 1919]), pp. 4-6.

[2] *Ibid.* p. 42. The records of the congress reveal the presence of an unnamed " representative of the Third International " who intervened to refute Wolffheim's argument that a federal structure for the party was justified by the precedent of the RSFSR (*ibid.* p. 35) but apparently took no other part in the proceedings. His identity is unknown, and he does not seem to have been in contact with Moscow.

[3] Lenin, *Sochineniya*, xxiv, 502-503 ; Lenin did not realize that the issue of German Soviets, which had been vital in the first weeks of the revolution, was already dead.

the revolutionary faith of the masses. It appeared that peace and bread rather than social or political revolution had been the overriding demands of those who had challenged the existing order in the grim winter of 1918-1919. In Germany the KPD found it easy, in face of these conditions, to revert from the conception of a mass party bent on immediate revolutionary action to the conception of a group of leaders concerned with the penetration and indoctrination of the still politically immature masses : it inherited the traditions and the name of the Spartakusbund which had been built on this second point of view. Thus, while Radek posed, and was accepted in Berlin, as the oracle of Moscow moulding the young KPD on Russian lines, the influence was not exercised only from one side, and there would be quite as much truth in a picture of the versatile Radek imperceptibly and unconsciously won over by familiarity with German conditions to the more cautious Spartakist tradition. The address to the Heidelberg congress was couched in a vein of conventional revolutionary enthusiasm ; but the words in which its author sought consolation for the downfall of the Soviet régime in Hungary were tinged with a note of profound pessimism :

> The world revolution is a very slow process in which more than one defeat must be expected. I have no doubt that in every country the proletariat will be forced to construct its dictatorship several times and will several times see the collapse of this dictatorship before it will finally win.[1]

This mood inspired the cautious tone of the " Theses on Communist Principles and Tactics " drafted by Levi and adopted by the congress :

> The revolution, which consists not of a single blow but of the long stubborn struggle of a class downtrodden for thousands of years and therefore naturally not yet fully conscious of its task and of its strength, is exposed to a process of rise and fall, of flow and ebb. . . . The notion that mass movements can be created on the strength of a particular form of organization, that the revolution is therefore a question of organizational form, is rejected as a relapse into petty-bourgeois utopianism.[2]

[1] K. Radek, *Zur Taktik des Kommunismus : Ein Schreiben an den Oktober-Parteitag der KPD* (1919), p. 5.
[2] *Bericht über den 2. Parteitag der Kommunistischen Partei Deutschlands (Spartakusbund)* (n.d. [? 1919]), p. 61.

Finally, when Radek in November 1919 helped Levi and Zetkin to draft theses for the western European secretariat of Comintern, the main point of emphasis in framing tactical directives was the assumption that " revolution, even on a European scale, will be a prolonged process "; and it was for this assumption, as Radek frankly confesses, that he was criticized by Bukharin after his return to Moscow.[1] The first symptoms can be traced at this time not only of divisions between the Bolshevik leaders about communist tactics in Europe, but also of a fundamental misunderstanding in Moscow of the scope and development of the European revolutionary movement. Radek, who had seen the German situation at close quarters, was less infected than any of the other Bolshevik leaders with this miscalculation.

In other leading countries developments were less advanced and hopes had not yet been exposed to the test of experience. In Italy the situation at the outset was dominated by the fact that the large Italian Socialist Party (PSI) had been consistently opposed to the war. Patriotism and socialism were in opposite camps; and socialists who, like Mussolini, rallied to the national cause were treated as renegades. The PSI greeted the Bolshevik revolution with fervent sympathy, as much on the ground of its peace appeal as of its social programme; Lazzari and Bombacci, the secretary and vice-secretary of the party, were arrested and sent to prison early in 1918 for demonstrating their enthusiasm. Though no Italian delegate could get to Moscow in March 1919 for the founding congress of Comintern, the PSI at once declared its adhesion to the new International. This adhesion was confirmed at a party congress at Bologna in October 1919, which, under the leadership and inspiration of Serrati, the editor of the party journal *Avanti*, adopted a programme bearing at any rate a close superficial affinity to that of the Bolsheviks — the forcible seizure of political and economic power by the proletariat — and hailed Comintern as " the organ of the world proletariat ". On the other hand, the congress revealed at least three minority groups — the " reformists " led by Turati, whose position was similar to that of the SPD in Germany; the " centrists " led by Lazzari, pacifist in general outlook and approximating roughly to the USPD; and the " Leftists " led by Bordiga, who were opposed

[1] *Krasnaya Nov'*, No. 10, 1926, pp. 171-172.

in principle to parliamentary action. There was also a Turin group named after its journal *Ordine Nuovo*, led by Gramsci, Tasca and Togliatti, which insisted on the importance of factory councils and, like the shop stewards' movement elsewhere, held vaguely syndicalist views. But nobody thought of expelling any of these groups from the party, which remained a body of frankly eclectic membership. The leaders of Comintern could, however, still not afford to be fastidious. Lenin welcomed this " brilliant victory of communism ", and hoped that the example would serve to eliminate the disagreements in the German party, though he added a warning against " open or secret opportunists " in the party. He regretted only that the party had retained its old name of " socialist ".[1]

In Great Britain a potential communist movement was developing in an irregular, unsystematic way ; and of this Lenin received a detailed and fairly accurate account in a letter from Sylvia Pankhurst written in the middle of July 1919 and received in Moscow at the end of August. The letter enumerated seven Left groups or parties in Great Britain : (1) trade unionists and Labour Party, who could not be counted as socialists at all ; (2) the Independent Labour Party (ILP), pacifist and often religious in outlook ; (3) the British Socialist Party (BSP), an offshoot from the old Social-Democratic Federation, having a revolutionary programme, but believing in parliamentary action ; (4) the shop stewards' organization, calling itself the Workers' Committee Movement, rejecting ordinary trade union and parliamentary methods as futile and believing in revolution by " direct action " of the workers ; (5) the Socialist Labour Party (SLP), flourishing mainly in Scotland, associated with the shop stewards' movement and sharing its belief in direct action, though it put forward a few parliamentary candidates in the general election of December 1918 ; (6) the Socialist Workers' Federation (Sylvia Pankhurst's own organization), originally an offshoot of the feminist movement, which now had some following in the east end of London, rejected parliamentary action and, at its congress at Whitsun 1919, claimed the title of the British Communist Party ; and (7) the South Wales Socialist Society, a local group holding similar views. Preliminary discussions between some of these groups on the possibility of

[1] Lenin, *Sochineniya*, xxiv, 475, 504.

union showed that the most serious bone of contention was the desirability of participation in parliamentary elections. Sylvia Pankhurst wrote to Lenin in the hope of obtaining from him an authoritative pronouncement in favour of direct as against parliamentary action. Lenin replied cautiously that he personally thought abstention from parliamentary elections a mistake. But a split between " sincere supporters of the Soviet power " on this secondary issue would be a still more grievous mistake. If unity was unattainable on this issue, then it would be " a step forward towards complete unity " to have " *two* communist parties, i.e. two parties standing for the transition from bourgeois parliamentarianism to Soviet power ", divided only by their differing attitude to an existing bourgeois parliament.[1] A circular letter was despatched from IKKI to all member parties of Comintern recognizing as permissible a divergence of opinions on this " second-rate " question.[2] This does not appear to have produced any effect, though the adhesion of the BSP to Comintern was announced in October.[3]

In France the situation was still less encouraging. The French Socialist Party, in which Marx's grandson Longuet was an outstanding figure, was still predominantly " reformist "; the Confédération Générale du Travail was syndicalist. The French Socialist Party had actively supported the war and shared the prestige of the victory; next to the British Labour Party, it was the strongest advocate of the resurrection of the Second International. A few French syndicalists opposed to the war had been represented at the Zimmerwald conference, and cautiously organized themselves as a " committee for the resumption of international relations ". In May 1919, after a wave of mass strikes had given new hopes to the Left, this body transformed itself under the leadership of Loriot and Rosmer into a " committee for adhesion to the Third International ".[4] But the group remained ineffective, and had little contact with Moscow. Of the Bolshevik leaders Trotsky, having spent nearly two years of the

[1] Sylvia Pankhurst's letter was published anonymously, together with Lenin's reply, in *Kommunisticheskii Internatsional*, No. 5 (September 1919), cols. 681-684 ; Lenin's reply is in *Sochineniya*, xxiv, 437-442.

[2] *Kommunisticheskii Internatsional*, No. 5 (September 1919), cols. 703-708.

[3] *Ibid.* No. 7-8 (November-December 1919), col. 1114.

[4] G. Walter, *Histoire du Parti Communiste Français* (1948), pp. 23-24.

war in Paris, had most personal knowledge of its principal members, and in September addressed an open letter to them in the journal of Comintern expressing confidence that " the cause of communism in France is in honest and firm hands ".[1] At the end of October Lenin received a letter of greetings from Loriot, and in his answer predicted a long struggle against " opportunists of the type of Longuet "; and this reply was printed in *La Vie Ouvrière*, the organ of the group, in January 1920.[2]

In the United States the three most important parties of the extreme Left before 1919 were the Industrial Workers of the World (IWW), a quasi-revolutionary syndicalist organization with a large following in the western states, but without any precise political programme, the Socialist Party of Eugene Debs, and the Socialist Labor Party founded by Daniel de Leon, who before his death in 1914 was the leading Marxist theorist in the United States; both the Socialist Party and the Socialist Labor Party had split after 1916 on the issue of the war. During the war Lenin made enquiries of Kollontai, who was in New York in 1916, about the Socialist Labor Party and its relations to the Socialist Party;[3] and after the February revolution, no doubt on the strength of information supplied by her, he had hopes of the Socialist Labor Party and of " internationalist elements in the opportunist Socialist Party ".[4] But the only Americans with whom Lenin was in touch for some time after the October revolution [5] were John Reed, a young intellectual without party affiliations, and Reinstein, who had been disowned by the Socialist Labor Party; and when, in August 1918, Michael Borodin, a

---

[1] Trotsky, *Sochineniya*, xiii, 123-126.

[2] Lenin, *Sochineniya*, xxiv, 501 ; Longuet at this time took up a " centrist " position.

[3] *Ibid.* xxix, 237, 290.

[4] *Ibid.* xx, 128. After the October revolution, Lenin read some writings of de Leon and " was amazed to see how far and how early de Leon had pursued the same train of thought as the Russians ", adding that " his theory that representation should be by industries, not by areas, was already the germ of the Soviet system " (A. Ransome, *Six Weeks in Russia in 1919* (1919), pp. 80-81) ; about the same time Lenin told an American correspondent, Robert Minor, that " the American Daniel de Leon first formulated the idea of a Soviet Government " (*The World* (N.Y.), February 8, 1919).

[5] Volodarsky, an old Bolshevik who had emigrated to the United States in 1913 and returned in 1917, scarcely counted as an " American " ; he was assassinated in Petrograd in June 1918.

Bolshevik who had emigrated to the United States after 1905, returned to Moscow and offered to transmit a letter to the American workers, the letter which Lenin wrote was a general propaganda appeal and tactfully ignored all issues of party.[1] It was the impetus given by the birth of Comintern rather than any domestic pressures which impelled a number of groups of the extreme Left to send delegates to a convention in Chicago on September 1, 1919, in order to found an American communist party. But optimists had underestimated the fissiparous tendencies in the American workers' movement produced by geographical dispersion, racial and linguistic diversities and by the presence of an unusually large stratum of prosperous and contented workers. The convention was by no means representative; and even the delegates who assembled in Chicago did not agree among themselves. Two separate parties finally emerged from the convention — a Communist Labor Party, in which the moving spirit was John Reed, and a Communist Party of America, led by Louis Fraina,[2] which made its principal appeal to recent immigrants from Europe. The resolution creating the Communist Labor Party and deciding on adhesion to Comintern was printed in the official journal of Comintern in the last issue of the year;[3] and it is doubtful whether much further information on the dispute was available in Moscow.[4]

[1] Lenin, *Sochineniya*, xxiii, 176-189. The letter has already been quoted on p. 90 above; at this time Lenin was more concerned with defence in the civil war than with the dissemination of communism. The most interesting comment on revolutionary prospects occurred towards the end : " We place our wager on the inevitability of international revolution, but this does not at all mean that we are so foolish as to place our wager on the inevitability of revolution within a *definite* short period. We have seen two great revolutions, 1905 and 1917, in our country, and know that revolutions are not made to order or by agreement." Even to Marxists revolution in the United States always seemed a far-off event. Lenin's so-called letter " to the American workers " of September 1919 was apparently an interview given to a correspondent of the *Christian Science Monitor (ibid.* xxiv, 465-466, 803, note 150), and did not touch on communism or revolution.

[2] Fraina, who was of Italian origin, had edited a selection of Lenin's and Trotsky's writings and speeches under the title *The Proletarian Revolution in Russia* (N.Y., 1918).

[3] *Kommunisticheskii Internatsional*, No. 7-8 (November-December 1919), cols. 1113-1114.

[4] Some account of these developments is contained in a report presented to the second congress of Comintern by the American Communist Labor Party in June 1920 (*Berichte zum Zweiten Kongress der Kommunistischen Internationale*

In the smaller countries the picture of the growth of communist parties in 1919 is equally confused. The Polish Communist Party had been formed in December 1918 by a fusion between the Social-Democracy of the Kingdom of Poland and Lithuania and the Left Polish Socialist Party (the PPS having split into Left and Right parties in 1905). For some weeks it controlled the Dombrowa coal basin where local Soviets seized power, and dominated the workers' movement in Warsaw and Lodz.[1] Early in 1919, however, the new Polish Government sponsored by the western allies successfully met the challenge of an insurgent communism, and established its authority throughout the country ; and when Markhlevsky (under the name of Karski) appeared at the founding congress of Comintern in March, the Polish Communist Party in whose name he spoke was already a persecuted and semi-illegal organization — a status which it retained for a quarter of a century. The Bulgarian Social-Democratic Party, captured by its Left wing (the so-called Tesnyaki, or " Narrows "), transformed itself in May 1919 without serious secessions into the Bulgarian Communist Party, thus bringing into the fold of Comintern its only mass party, other than the Russian, of indubitably Bolshevik complexion. The Norwegian Labour Party, which had a doctrinal flavour all its own, mingling Lutheran and anarchist strains with its professed Marxism, joined Comintern without changing its name. Its loose and variegated structure was not unlike that of the Italian Socialist Party ; and both these parties were to cause much the same difficulties to Moscow at a later date. Most of the other European parties which joined Comintern in the first year of its existence were small sectarian groups, composed mainly of intellectuals and exercising no influence on the political life of their respective countries. Of these, the Dutch party had the strongest indigenous roots and some support among the workers ; but it was also the least orthodox, having strong syndicalist leanings, and proved least amenable to Comintern discipline. Some of the

(Hamburg, 1921), pp. 367-368). Later American sources are numerous but contradictory and confused ; few authentic records seem to have survived.

[1] A detailed account of the origins of the Polish Communist Party is given in *The American Slavic and East European Review* (N.Y.), xi (1952), 106-122.

other parties, notably the Hungarian and Finnish parties, were composed mainly of exiles resident in Moscow.

Thus in the year of stress, 1919, when Moscow was almost completely isolated, even the indirect reinforcement which Soviet Russia might hope to draw from the foundation of Comintern was potential rather than actual. Chicherin in a pamphlet issued at this time called it " the greatest historical event which set its stamp on our whole foreign policy of the present year ", and declared that Soviet foreign policy was " ever more closely identified with the world struggle between the revolution and the old world ".[1] The seventh All-Russian Congress of Soviets, meeting in December 1919, proclaimed it " the greatest event in world history ", and concluded that " the closest link of the Soviets with the Communist International is dictated by the interests of the workers and toiling peasants of the whole world ".[2] But the new International possessed as yet none of the attributes of a working political organization — a representative membership, an efficient machine or a defined policy. A review of the parties belonging to it did indeed, even at this early stage, suggest an issue which would have to be faced in the immediate future. Was Comintern to aim at securing the adhesion of mass parties of the Left — like the Italian or Norwegian parties — at the cost of insistence on rigid doctrinal conformity ? Or was it to insist on strict ideological discipline at the cost of a numerically insignificant membership — the policy pursued by Levi at Heidelberg ? For the present, the attitude of Lenin and of the other Bolshevik leaders was one of studied moderation ; never again, in its eagerness for recruits, did Comintern show itself so tolerant of a diversity of opinions. But the limits of this toleration were none the less precise. Lenin was still obsessed with the treachery of the orthodox social-democrats in 1914 which had brought about the downfall of the Second International. The creation of the Third International was, first and foremost, an attempt to rally all sincerely international and Left-wing forces against the traitors. Subject to this overriding purpose a certain latitude could be tacitly conceded : Lenin showed comparative mildness at this

[1] G. Chicherin, *Vneshnyaya Politika Sovetskoi Rossii za Dva Goda* (1920), pp. 29, 32.
[2] *S"ezdy Sovetov v Postanovleniyakh* (1939), pp. 141-142.

time even to pacifists and syndicalists, since they were at least immune from the canker of state worship. Hence in Germany he deplored the splitting off of the KAPD from the KPD, and eagerly sought a *rapprochement* with the Left wing of the USPD ; in Great Britain he regarded with impatience divisions on such subsidiary issues (which in other times and circumstances he had treated as paramount) as participation in elections to parliament. But this did not mean any compromise at all with social-democratic or Labour parties of the old type, and still less with bourgeois parties. In spite of Lenin's obvious desire to open the gates as wide as possible, it would be an anachronism to read back into this initial period later conceptions of a " united front " with social-democratic or bourgeois parties, or to suppose that Lenin's apparent toleration of doctrinal diversity was prompted, even at this desperate moment, merely by thoughts of the security of the RSFSR.

CHAPTER 24

DIPLOMATIC FEELERS

THROUGHOUT the year 1919 the weakness of the Soviet Government, threatened by enemies on all sides, deprived it of any power of initiative in foreign policy, and made its course of action dependent on the successive moves of its adversaries. The direct cause of the complete rupture of relations between Soviet Russia and the outside world was the decision of the allied governments to give active support to the " whites " in the civil war, and to treat the Soviet Government as a rebel and hostile faction. It was the allied governments which deliberately and successfully sought to isolate Moscow, not Moscow which sought to isolate itself from the world. Thus a breaking down of the barriers had to await a change of mood and policy in the allied camp and particularly in Great Britain, whose attitude to the Russian question throughout the year continued to be marked by glaring fluctuations and inconsistencies. These reflected acute differences, not only in public opinion, but in government circles. The turn of policy in April 1919, when attempts to establish relations with Soviet Russia were abandoned and all-out aid, short of direct military action, extended to the " whites ", was never fully endorsed by Liberal and Labour opinion, which was in general anxious to cut commitments and to come to terms with the Soviet Government if this was in any way possible ; and this anxiety was shared by Lloyd George, in so far as he could indulge it without upsetting the uneasy balance of the coalition. Fear of the spread of Bolshevism in Europe, and hopes of the overthrow of the Soviet Government by the " whites ", had sufficed to give a fresh impetus in the summer of 1919 to anti-Bolshevik opinion. But this line, half-heartedly pursued in the face of growing public scepticism, failed in its purpose ; and, when it became clear in the late autumn of 1919 that the main effort of all the " white " generals — Kolchak, Denikin and Yudenich — had exhausted itself without forcing a decision, opinion began to set strongly against a policy which had been reluctantly accepted when it seemed successful, and was readily abandoned once its futility was revealed. The other factor which, combined with the patent failure of the " whites ", at last brought a return to conciliation was the growing consciousness of economic needs. As the world groped its way back to what it thought of as " normal ", recollections revived of Russia's former place in a now shattered world economy. It seemed increasingly difficult to maintain indefinitely a commercial boycott of one of the largest countries in the world merely because of objections to its form of government. On August 1, 1919, a letter in *The Times*, which at this period represented extreme anti-Bolshevik opinion, guardedly expressed anxiety about the future of British trade with Russia and stressed the need to consider " the new conditions which have been brought about by the war ". After the Bolshevik revolution the blockade applied to Germany by the allied Powers was extended to Russia, and was silently maintained even after the conclusion of hostilities with Germany. At the beginning of October 1919 an attempt was made by the Supreme Council to meet an obvious criticism by requesting the principal neutral governments to join in the existing blockade of Soviet Russia, which in order to appease American susceptibilities was referred to euphemistically as " economic pressure "; and a similar note, rather clumsily embodying the terms of the note to the neutral governments and requesting compliance with them, was addressed to the German Government.[1] The Soviet Government at once countered with a strong protest to the neutral governments and to the German Government, who were warned that compliance with the allied request would be regarded as a " consciously hostile act ".[2] The

---

[1] A first draft of these notes was considered by the Supreme Council on August 21, 1919, but referred back to the " blockade committee " in order to meet American objections (*Documents on British Foreign Policy, 1919-1939: First Series*, i (1947), 495, 501-502). The decision to despatch the note to the neutrals was taken on September 29, 1919 (*ibid.* i, 826 ; for the text of the note see *ibid.* i, 830). The decision to send the note to the German Government is not recorded, but it was sent and the text published in the press ; the text is in C. K. Cumming and W. W. Pettit, *Russian-American Relations* (N.Y., 1920), pp. 349-351.

[2] Klyuchnikov i Sabanin, *Mezhdunarodnaya Politika*, ii (1926), 398-399.

neutral answers to the allied request were evasive or frankly unfavourable. The German Government, while " fully conscious of the great danger threatening the culture and economic life of all peoples by the spread of Bolshevism ", thought that the blockade would not serve the purpose in view, and excused itself on the ground that it had now no common frontier with Russia. The note ended with the complaint that, " whilst the Allied and Associated Powers propose to Germany that she should participate in the blockade of Russia, they are actually applying the policy of blockade to the German coasts and German ships ".[1] No further attempt was made by the allies to press the demand. Blockade or no blockade, trade with Soviet Russia was for the present impracticable. But nobody was prepared to prejudice future prospects.

The failure to generalize the blockade, coming at a moment of disillusionment with the prospects of the " white " armies, prepared the way for a radical change of front. At the end of October Krasin, a shrewd observer who knew western Europe, accurately diagnosed the new mood in a private letter :

> The prospect of carrying on the war indefinitely will not appeal to the Powers, and if Denikin has not settled our hash by the beginning of winter, which is hardly likely, then England for one would deem it acceptable in her own interests to over-power the Bolsheviks in the domain of politics by coming to some agreement and entering into peaceful relations with Soviet Russia. Perhaps this plan of conquering Bolshevik Russia would have more chance of success than the fruitless military campaigns of the last two years.[2]

Lloyd George responded with his customary sensitiveness to the change of mood. In his Guildhall speech of November 8, 1919, he created something of a sensation by observing that " you cannot have peace unless you have peace in Russia ".[3] He spoke

[1] *The Times,* October 31, 1919 : the note does not appear in any collection of documents. For the debate on the question in the Reichstag, see p. 307, note 3 below.

[2] L. Krasin, *Leonid Krasin: His Life and Work* (n.d. [1929]), pp. 111-112 ; the originals of Krasin's letters quoted in translation in this volume have not been published.

[3] He had used almost the same words in a speech in the House of Commons on February 19, 1919 (*House of Commons: 5th Series,* cxii, 194) : but that was before the change of policy in April.

significantly of the cost of " intervention in an interminable civil
war ", referred to Russia as " a dangerous land to intervene in ",
and expressed the hope that " an opportunity may offer itself for
the great Powers of the world to promote peace and concord in
that great country ". Five days later in the House of Commons
he openly attacked the blockade, describing Russia as " one of
the great resources for the supply of food and raw material ".[1]
Then, on November 17, 1919, in response to a challenge by his
critics, he delivered a major speech which was evidently intended
to prepare the way for the winding up of the policy of intervention
and the substitution of a policy of commercial negotiations with
Soviet Russia. In a much-quoted passage he invoked the memory
of " Lord Beaconsfield, who regarded a great, gigantic, colossal,
growing Russia rolling onwards like a glacier towards Persia and
the borders of Afghanistan and India as the greatest menace the
British Empire could be confronted with ".[2] This argument
spoke strongly against the " whites ", who sought to reconstitute
the former Russian Empire, and in favour of the Bolsheviks who
were only too eager to promise self-determination to its constituent
parts.[3] Nor did these utterances pass unnoticed in Moscow,
where Chicherin, in a broadcast statement, propounded a new
and significant attitude to relations with the capitalist world :

> Relations with Russia are quite possible in spite of the
> profound differences between Britain's and Russia's régime. . . .
> The British customer and purveyor are as necessary to us as
> we are to them. Not only do we desire peace and the possibility

[1] *Ibid.* cxxi, 474. It was Russia as a supplier rather than Russia as a market
which preoccupied the British Government at this time. A confidential Board
of Trade memorandum of January 6, 1920, pointed out that Russia before 1914
had been the source of one-quarter of the world's wheat exports, and that Great
Britain had received from Russia one-third of her imports of flax : the memorandum ended with the recommendation " definitely to abandon the blockade
and to place no obstacles at all in the way of the restriction of commercial relations with the whole of Russia " (*Documents on British Foreign Policy, 1919–
1939: First Series*, ii (1948), 867-870). Lloyd George's much derided remark
that " the corn bins of Russia are bulging with grain " occurred in a speech in
the House of Commons on February 10, 1920 (*House of Commons: 5th Series*,
cxxv, 45).

[2] *Ibid.* cxxi, 723.

[3] It was a corollary of the new turn of policy when in January 1920 the
Supreme Council decided on a British initiative to extend *de facto* recognition
to the governments of Georgia, Armenia and Azerbaijan and of Latvia and
Estonia.

of internal development, but we also feel strongly the need of economic help from the more fully developed countries such as Great Britain. We are ready even to make sacrifices for the sake of a close economic connection with Britain. . . . I, therefore, gladly welcome the declaration of the British Premier as the first step towards such a sane and real policy corresponding to the interests of both countries.[1]

It was only eight months since Lenin had explained that it was " inconceivable that the Soviet republic should continue to exist for a long period side by side with imperialist states ", and that in the meanwhile " a number of terrible clashes between the Soviet republic and bourgeois states is inevitable ".[2] The doctrine was not abandoned. The Bolshevik leaders, from Lenin downwards, continued firmly to believe, not merely that revolution in Europe was necessary, but that it was imminent. But the change of mood in response to changing conditions was prompt and far-reaching.

With these new feelers put out from both sides, the situation was ripe for a renewal of contacts. The excuse was found in the need to negotiate an exchange of prisoners. Throughout the worst period, the British and Soviet Governments had managed to effect occasional exchanges of important agents captured by one side or the other — a curious instance of professional reciprocity ; and two British Red Cross representatives had continued to distribute relief to British prisoners in Soviet hands.[3] The peace proposals handed to Bullitt in March 1919 included one for the mutual repatriation of prisoners and other nationals. In May 1919 the British Government in a radio message had proposed a general exchange of prisoners, and on June 10, 1919, Chicherin replied through the same channel that this proposal was acceptable only " if the Russian Government is allowed to send to London, or alternatively to some neutral country, a commission enabled to get in touch with Russians in Great Britain ".[4] This condition caused prolonged embarrassment and procrastination, and it was not till the ice had begun to melt elsewhere that agreement was reached for a meeting between British and Soviet plenipoten-

[1] Moscow radio of November 20, 1919, quoted in A. L. P. Dennis, *The Foreign Policies of Soviet Russia* (1924), p. 380.
[2] See p. 115 above.
[3] *Documents on British Foreign Policy, 1919–1939 : First Series*, iii (1949), 418.
[4] *Ibid.* iii, 343-344, 360.

tiaries in Copenhagen, to be strictly confined to the discussion of questions relating to prisoners of war. The Soviet representative was Litvinov, the British representative a Labour M.P. named O'Grady; they met in Copenhagen on November 25, 1919 — the first formal quasi-diplomatic contact for more than a year with any of the allied Powers.[1]

The following month saw other significant developments. In September 1919 negotiations had been opened with the Estonian Government, which had, however, broken them off on the plea that it could not conclude peace with Soviet Russia except in conjunction with neighbouring states:[2] this refusal was the result of British pressure on the eve of the Yudenich venture.[3] The defeat of Yudenich in the second half of October threatened to produce a crisis in Soviet-Estonian relations. Trotsky voiced the desire of the Red Army to pursue Yudenich's beaten troops into Estonia, while Chicherin thought that the appearance of Soviet forces on Estonian soil would merely " antagonize English Liberals and moderate Conservatives " and " play Churchill's game ". Lenin supported Chicherin, and the Red Army was restrained, though a warning was issued to the Estonian Government insisting on the disarmament of Yudenich's troops which took refuge in Estonia.[4] These difficulties having been overcome, negotiations were opened at Dorpat on December 2, 1919, between

[1] *Ibid.* iii, 593, 643-644, 661.

[2] Klyuchnikov i Sabanin, *Mezhdunarodnaya Politika*, ii (1926), 344-346, 387-388.

[3] On September 16, 1919, the British Government made urgent representations to the Estonian and Latvian Governments to " take no action in the direction of peace " (*Documents on British Foreign Policy, 1919-1939: First Series*, iii (1949), 554). Two days later the Estonian Minister for Foreign Affairs informed the British representative in Tallinn that the Estonian cabinet had " decided not to make peace without the permission of Great Britain ", but " emphasized the necessity for entering into peace negotiations for internal reasons as a blind to satisfy public opinion " (*ibid.* iii, 558). Subsequent communications from both Latvian and Estonian Governments (*ibid.* iii, 562-564) showed, however, extreme restiveness on this point; and on September 25, 1919, the British Government made a formal communication to the Estonian, Latvian and Lithuanian Governments to the effect that it did not feel " entitled to exercise any pressure on the free initiative of the Baltic states ", and that " it is for them to determine with unfettered judgment whether they should make any arrangement, and if so of what nature, with the Soviet authorities " (*ibid.* iii, 570)

[4] This episode can be followed in documents in the Trotsky archives bearing dates from October 17 to October 27, 1919.

an Estonian delegation and a Soviet delegation headed by Krasin.[1]
Meanwhile negotiations had been proceeding in strict secrecy
in a railway coach at a desolate spot in the Pinsk marches between
Markhlevsky, the Polish communist who had appeared at the
founding congress of Comintern but now acted in the capacity
of a delegate of the Russian Red Cross, and Polish delegates
holding credentials from the Polish Red Cross. This picturesque
and little-known episode of Soviet diplomacy resulted in an agreement of November 2, 1919, for the release of Polish hostages held
by Soviet Russia and for the renunciation by both sides of the
practice of taking hostages, and in a second agreement a week
later for the release of civilian prisoners on both sides.[2] But these
practical arrangements also served as a screen for more delicate
discussions. When the negotiations began early in October 1919,
the Red Army was in a precarious plight on two fronts — against
Yudenich before Petrograd and against Denikin in central Russia ;
and it was necessary to buy off Polish intervention by a withdrawal
which ceded further territory to the Polish forces.[3] The success
of this plan was due not so much to the skill and flexibility of the
Soviet negotiators as to the unwillingness of Pilsudski to see the
overthrow of the Soviet régime by " white " generals who seemed
to represent in the long run a greater danger to Polish independence. On the other hand, not even the offer of much more extensive territorial concessions would induce Pilsudski to desert the
western allies and conclude a formal peace with the Soviet Government ; and in December, when the gravest danger for the Red
Army had passed, the negotiations ended with no result other
than the exchange of a few hundred Poles for a few hundred
Bolsheviks. Polish passivity had been temporarily secured, and

---

[1] Krasin's opening speech and proposals were published in *Pravda*, December 8 and 9, 1919, and reprinted in L. B. Krasin, *Voprosy Vneshnei Torgovli*
(1928), pp. 267-273.
[2] The documents are in *Krasnaya Kniga: Sbornik Diplomaticheskikh
Dokumentov o Russko-Pol'skikh Otnosheniyakh, 1918-1920* (1920), pp. 70-80.
[3] K. Radek, *Die Auswärtige Politik Sowjet-Russlands* (Hamburg, 1921),
p. 56, speaks of " a secret treaty with Pilsudski on the basis of which the Red
Army retreated to a given line ". The Trotsky archives contain the record of
a decision of the Politburo of November 14, 1919, when the campaign against
Denikin was still in a critical phase, to accept all Polish armistice demands
except the cessation of operations against Petlyura in the Ukraine : Petlyura
was at this moment seeking Polish aid (see Vol. 1, pp. 303-304).

beyond this Pilsudski would not go.[1] After the failure of these secret negotiations the Soviet Government, noting that the Polish Minister for Foreign Affairs had officially denied that any peace overtures had been received from Soviet Russia,[2] put forward a public proposal for peace negotiations which was ignored.[3]

The new year of 1920, which saw the capture and execution of Kolchak in Siberia and the final discomfiture of Denikin in South Russia, brought to a head these tentative moves to break through the wall of isolation which separated Soviet Russia not only from the western Powers themselves, but from her smaller western neighbours under their patronage. On January 14, 1920, the Supreme Council meeting in Paris gave audience to two representatives of the Paris office of the Russian cooperatives, which by some strange anomaly had continued to exist throughout the revolutionary period : these stated that " the cooperative society had no politics ", that it embraced 25,000,000 members, so that " practically the whole population of Russia was included ", and that south Russia had a surplus of 10,000,000 tons of wheat for export.[4] On the strength of these assurances, the Supreme Council announced two days later its decision to " permit the

[1] The negotiations are described in Y. Markhlevsky, *Voina i Mir mezhdu Burzhuaznoi Pol'shoi i Proletarskoi Rossiei* (Russian translation from Polish, 1921), pp. 12-15, 38. According to K. Radek, *Die Auswärtige Politik Sowjet-Russlands* (Hamburg, 1921), p. 56, which adds some further details, the offer to Pilsudski included the cession of " the whole of White Russia as far as the Beresina, Volhynia and Podolia " ; this is compatible with Markhlevsky's statement that Poland obtained at the armistice of October 1920 " far less than was offered to her in the autumn of 1919 ". The British Minister in Warsaw learned on November 3, 1919, that the " Bolshevist Red Cross Commissioner " had made " very attractive offers to the Poles ", covering " all White Russia including the eastern parts not yet occupied by the Polish forces ". This was characteristically diagnosed as an attempt " to entangle Poland in a second treaty of Brest-Litovsk " (*Documents on British Foreign Policy, 1919-1939 : First Series*, iii (1949), 630).

[2] On December 15, 1919, Pilsudski told the British representative in Warsaw that, " whilst the Bolsheviks would probably be prepared to make peace, they would never stick to any agreement they made, and he certainly would not enter into negotiations with them " (*ibid.* iii (1949), 787).

[3] Klyuchnikov i Sabanin, *Mezhdunarodnaya Politika*, ii (1926), 423-424 ; the British representative in Warsaw reported that the Polish Government found the proposal " rather embarrassing " (*Documents on British Foreign Policy, 1919-1939 : First Series*, iii (1949), 745).

[4] *Ibid.* ii (1948), 868-874.

exchange of goods on the basis of reciprocity between the Russian people and allied and neutral countries "; the purpose was to provide " for the import into Russia of clothing, medicines, agricultural machinery and the other necessaries of which the Russian people are in sore need, in exchange for grain, flax, etc. of which Russia has surplus supplies ". It was specifically added that " these arrangements imply no change in the policy of the allied governments towards the Soviet Government ".[1] This decision, which amounted to a concentration of Russian imports and exports in the hands of the All-Russian Central Union of Cooperatives (Tsentrosoyuz), presented no embarrassments to the Soviet Government. It was a convenient means of enforcing the monopoly of foreign trade, since Tsentrosoyuz was by this time fully under Soviet control.[2] On January 23, 1920, the president of Tsentrosoyuz telegraphed to the Paris office that this organ had been empowered by the Soviet authorities to enter into direct trade relations with the cooperatives, as well as with private firms, of western Europe, America and other countries.[3] The lifting of the blockade was an event of great symbolical importance : it was greeted in Soviet Russia as a declaration of the ending of the war with the western Powers. The practical difficulties in the way of a resumption of trade were to appear later.

This decision may well have hastened another. If Soviet Russia was to trade with western Europe, it was highly desirable to have a neutral, yet not unfriendly, port and clearing-house through which trade might pass. Tallinn, the Estonian capital, was well suited for the purpose. Soviet-Estonian negotiations proceeded rapidly and smoothly, and a treaty of peace was signed on February 2, 1920.[4] A few days earlier Lloyd George had given pointed advice to the Polish Prime Minister to make peace with the Soviet Government ;[5] and three weeks later the Supreme Council sitting in London issued a statement that, if the allied Powers were asked for advice by any of " the communities which border on the frontiers of Russia ", they would not be able " to

---

[1] *Documents on British Foreign Policy, 1919-1939 : First Series*, ii (1948), 912.
[2] See Vol. 2, p. 238.
[3] Klyuchnikov i Sabanin, *Mezhdunarodnaya Politika*, iii, i (1928), 2-3.
[4] See Vol. 1, p. 313.
[5] *Documents on British Foreign Policy, 1919-1939 : First Series*, iii (1949), 803-805.

take on themselves the responsibility of advising them to continue a war which may be injurious to their own interests ".[1] Meanwhile the negotiations in progress with Litvinov in Copenhagen since November 1919 had after many difficult passages resulted in an Anglo-Soviet agreement for the repatriation of prisoners ; this agreement was signed on February 12, 1920.[2] Lenin briefly and without emphasis pointed the moral of these events :

> We have shown that we know how to repel violence, but that we know, when victorious, how to renounce it.

And again :

> We have already opened a window on Europe which we shall try to utilize as extensively as possible.[3]

It seemed as if, after the alarms and excursions of the civil war and the allied intervention on the side of the " whites ", an interlude of peaceful cohabitation with the capitalist world was about to begin. The period of isolation was over.

The new attitude which began to develop in Soviet foreign policy in the first months of 1920 arose automatically out of the continued existence of Soviet Russia in a world of capitalist states. The Soviet Government found itself almost involuntarily in the posture of defending, not the interests of world revolution, but national interests which any government of Russia would be obliged to defend. Any direct admission of continuity was at first avoided. The protest made against the attempt of the allied Powers at the peace conference to settle the fate of the Åland Islands without consulting the " Russian Soviet Government " was not based on any formal invocation of the rights of former Russian governments. But the Soviet telegram of October 2, 1919, appealed both to the principle of national self-determination and to the military and political argument that " the very

---

[1] *Foreign Relations of the United States, 1920*, iii (1936), 647.

[2] *RSFSR : Sbornik Deistvuyushchikh Dogovorov*, i (1921), No. 20, pp. 120-124 ; *Agreement Between His Majesty's Government and the Soviet Government of Russia for the Exchange of Prisoners*, Cmd. 587 (1920).

[3] Lenin, *Sochineniya*, xxv, 21, 27 ; Krasin described Estonia as " the first window we managed to open " (*Voprosy Vneshnei Torgovli* (1928), p. 265).

geographical position of the Aland Islands at the entrance to the Gulf of Finland closely links the fate of these islands with the needs and requirements of the peoples inhabiting Russia ".[1] Four months later the Soviet Government specifically cited former Russian treaty rights in a protest against the treaty concluded at Paris on February 9, 1920, which assigned the island of Spitzbergen to Norway. The Soviet telegram of February 12, 1920, declared that " the international status of Spitzbergen has frequently been the subject of agreements between Russia, Sweden and Norway or between the governments of these countries and other governments ", and acts of 1872 and 1914 were cited in order to support the protest against the recognition of Norwegian sovereignty over Spitzbergen " without the participation of Russia " and " without even having informed the Russian Soviet Government ".[2] The mere existence of a government at Moscow exercising authority, in its own name and in that of other Soviet governments closely dependent on it, over approximately the same territory which was formerly ruled from Petrograd, made it the custodian of the same Russian national interests, and fastened on it a heritage of Russian national assets, claims and obligations of which it could not, in the long run, divest itself; and these conditions insensibly modified both the way in which the Soviet Government thought about itself and the way in which others thought about it.

The revival of hopes of world revolution and of a revolutionary policy under the impact of events of the summer of 1920 afterwards obscured much that was done in the first months of that year. The belief then current in Moscow that the civil war was over, and that a period of peaceful reconstruction was at hand, set in motion certain processes in Soviet foreign policy which were reversed or interrupted by the resumption of war in the summer of 1920, and came to fruition only with the introduction of NEP in the spring of 1921. Just as the main ideas which led to NEP itself had first been mooted a year before they were accepted and applied,[3] so the pronouncements of the first months of 1920 went far to anticipate foreign policies finally adopted only a year later. On January 22, 1920, Radek, then awaiting transport to Russia

---

[1] Klyuchnikov i Sabanin, *Mezhdunarodnaya Politika*, ii (1926), p. 391.
[2] *Ibid.* iii, i, 11-12.   [3] See Vol. 2, p. 280.

at " a small Polish station ", addressed a letter to the leaders of
the Polish Socialist Party appealing to them to resist Pilsudski's
designs for war against Soviet Russia, maintaining that " Soviet
Russia cherishes no plans for conquest with regard to Poland,
neither in the name of nationalism nor of communism ", and
particularly denouncing " militant communism ".[1] On January
28, 1920, Sovnarkom made a fresh appeal to the Polish Government to negotiate a line of demarcation between the Polish forces
and the Red Army. But the diplomatic phraseology of the note
was new and unfamiliar :

> The Council of People's Commissars declares that the
> Soviet Government has not concluded with Germany or with
> any other countries agreements or treaties directly or indirectly
> aimed against Poland, and that the character and meaning of the
> international policy of the Soviet power excludes the very
> possibility of such agreements, as well as of any attempts to
> utilize a possible clash between Poland and Germany or other
> states in order to infringe the independence of Poland or the
> inviolability of her territory.[2]

A few days later VTsIK issued a long and reasoned " Address to
the Polish People ", which combined the revolutionary appeal
with a careful attempt to reassure Polish national sentiment :

> *We, the representatives of the Russian working class and
> peasantry, have openly appeared and still appear before the whole
> world as champions of communist ideals : we are profoundly
> convinced that the working people of all countries will come out
> on the path which the Russian working people is already treading.*
> But our enemies and yours deceive you when they say that
> the Russian Soviet Government wishes to plant communism
> in Polish soil with the bayonets of Russian Red Army men. A
> communist order is possible only where the vast majority of
> the working people are penetrated with the idea of creating it
> by their own strength. Only then can it be solid ; for only then
> can communist policy strike deep roots in a country. The
> communists of Russia are at present striving only to defend their
> own soil, their own peaceful constructive work ; they are not

---

[1] The letter is said to have been published in the party journal *Robotnik* ;
a translation appeared in *Soviet Russia* (N.Y.), May 1, 1920, pp. 448-449.
[2] *Krasnaya Kniga : Sbornik Diplomaticheskikh Dokumentov o Russko-
Pol'skikh Otnosheniyakh, 1918-1920* (1920), pp. 84-85.

striving, and cannot strive, to plant communism by force in other countries.[1]

It remained to develop these vague hints into a policy. During February 1920 Lenin, Trotsky, Joffe and Litvinov all gave interviews to the foreign press on the opportunities of peace and commercial relations between Soviet Russia and the capitalist world.[2] On February 25 Chicherin sent out yet another appeal to the American and allied governments to enter into peace negotiations.[3] A few days later Radek embroidered the same theme with the greater bluntness which he always affected :

> If our capitalist partners abstain from counter-revolutionary activities in Russia, the Soviet Government will abstain from carrying on revolutionary activities in capitalist countries ; but we shall determine if they are carrying on counter-revolutionary agitation. There was a time when a feudal state existed alongside capitalist states. In those days liberal England did not fight continuously against serf-owning Russia. We think that now capitalist countries can exist alongside a proletarian state. We consider that the interests of both parties lie in concluding peace and in the establishment of an exchange of goods, and we are therefore ready to conclude peace with every country which up to the present has fought against us, but in future is prepared to give us, in exchange for our raw materials and grain, locomotives and machinery.[4]

At the ninth party congress in March 1920 Lenin spoke to a party audience in the traditional language of foreign policy all over the world :

> It behoves us most of all to manœuvre in our international policy, to stick firmly to the course we have adopted, and to be ready for everything. We have been carrying on the war for peace with extreme energy. This war is giving excellent results. . . . But our steps for peace must be accompanied by a tightening up of all our military preparedness.[5]

[1] *Krasnaya Kniga : Sbornik Diplomatischeskikh Dokumentov o Russko-Pol'skikh Otnosheniyakh, 1918–1920* (1920), p. 88.
[2] References to these interviews are in *Calendar of Soviet Documents on Foreign Policy*, ed. J. Degras (1948), p. 50.
[3] *Foreign Relations of the United States, 1920*, iii (1936), 447.
[4] Moscow radio of March 3, 1920, quoted in A. L. P. Dennis, *The Foreign Policies of Soviet Russia* (1924), pp. 358-359.
[5] Lenin, *Sochineniya*, xxv, 102.

And Chicherin continued to address the world on the theme of peaceful relations between Soviet Russia and the capitalist countries :

> There may be differences of opinion as to the duration of the capitalist system, but at present the capitalist system exists, so that a *modus vivendi* must be found in order that our socialist states and the capitalist states may coexist peacefully and in normal relations with one another. This is a necessity in the interest of all.[1]

An empirical appeal to the common interest of socialist and capitalist countries and to the possibility of " normal " relations between them may have seemed startling to some doctrinal purists. But the logic of the new approach was soon to earn its reward. After the January decision of the Supreme Council lifting the blockade in favour of trade conducted through the cooperatives, Tsentrosoyuz proposed to its Paris office to send a delegation abroad to negotiate on its behalf, and provisionally nominated Litvinov in Copenhagen as its delegate. Cautious negotiations failed to secure permission for the delegation to enter France or Great Britain. But it could at least operate in some neutral countries, and on February 25, 1920, its full composition was announced. It was headed by Krasin, and its other members were Litvinov, Nogin, Rozovsky and Khinchuk ;[2] of these only the two last were active members of the cooperative organization. The composition of the delegation was designed to efface as quickly as possible the formal distinction between representatives of Tsentrosoyuz and representatives of the Soviet Government ; in fact, the delegation was clearly empowered to speak with governmental authority. In the middle of March 1920 Krasin, accompanied by " fifteen experts representing various industries ", set out for Copenhagen and Stockholm.[3]

These promising developments, the product of the brief interval of peace which followed the defeat of Kolchak and Denikin, were once more cut short by an armed conflict with Poland which absorbed the resources and dictated the policies of

---

[1] Quoted in A. L. P. Dennis, *The Foreign Policies of Soviet Russia* (1924), p. 384.
[2] Klyuchnikov i Sabanin, *Mezhdunarodnaya Politika*, iii, i (1928), 3-4.
[3] L. Krasin, *Leonid Krasin : His Life and Work* (n.d. [1929]), p. 122.

the Soviet state. Throughout March and the first part of April 1920, increasingly eager efforts on the part of the Soviet Government to end the period of suspended hostilities and bring about peace negotiations with Poland met with an increasingly evasive response.[1] On April 28, 1920, Pilsudski issued a proclamation to the inhabitants of the Ukraine which announced a general offensive;[2] and by May 6, Kiev was in Polish hands. The immediate consequence was the issue in the name of VTsIK of an appeal to the " Polish workers, peasants and soldiers " to rise in revolt against their government and its aggressive action,[3] thus marking the prompt and unqualified re-emergence of the revolutionary element in Soviet policy under the impact of war. But relations with the rest of the capitalist world seemed at first unlikely to be affected, more especially as the Polish action had evoked little sympathy in any western country except France. At the moment of the attack Krasin was engaged in negotiations in Stockholm. The formal lifting of the allied blockade had failed to remove another obstacle to Soviet commerce — the so-called " gold blockade ". Soviet Russia enjoyed no credit ; nor were there in the shattered condition of the Soviet economy goods or materials in any substantial quantity available to export. The Soviet Government was prepared to pay for desperately needed imports in gold. None of the great banks of the world would, however, at this time accept Soviet gold, on the plea that it had been confiscated from former owners who might some day make good their claim to it ; and this was for some weeks an insuperable barrier to Soviet trade.

The first country which, under Krasin's persuasion, broke the gold blockade and took the risk of accepting Soviet gold was Sweden. The Swedish Government declined to negotiate with the Soviet delegation. But a group of fifteen Swedish firms accepted a Soviet order for goods to the value of 100,000,000 kroner, mainly agricultural implements and railway telegraph and telephone material, a quarter of which was to be paid for immediately in gold and the rest in short-term bills. This first unofficial

---

[1] The correspondence was published, after the outbreak of hostilities, in *Krasnaya Kniga : Sbornik Diplomaticheskikh Dokumentov o Russko-Pol'skikh Otnosheniyakh, 1918–1920* (1920), pp. 92-98.
[2] *Ibid.* pp. 104-105.   [3] *Ibid.* pp. 105-107.

Soviet trade agreement was signed on May 15, 1920.[1] The beginnings of the first post-war economic depression were already making themselves felt in Great Britain; and just about the time of the signing of the Swedish agreement, Krasin was invited by Lloyd George to come to London. He arrived on May 26, 1920, and was received by the Prime Minister on the last day of the month, Bonar Law, Horne and Curzon being also present. Negotiations for a trade agreement between the British and Soviet Governments were soon set on foot. At home, Krasin's position was strengthened by a decree of June 11, 1920, converting what was left of the People's Commissariat of Trade and Industry into a People's Commissariat of Foreign Trade (Vneshtorg) with Krasin at its head, all operations by government departments or state institutions in the field of foreign trade being brought under the control of the new commissariat.[2] In London, unofficial discussions seemed to show that no insurmountable difficulties stood in the way of an agreement. At a meeting on June 7, 1920, the British negotiators laid down three conditions for an agreement — the cessation of hostile acts and hostile propaganda, the return of all prisoners of war, and the recognition in principle of debts to private individuals. A long and argumentative note from Krasin of June 29, 1920, which was conciliatory in tone but evasive in substance, led to a reiteration of the three conditions in a British note of July 1, which demanded an affirmative answer within a week as a condition of continuing the negotiations. On the following day Krasin took this note back with him to Moscow, and the formal Soviet acceptance of the conditions followed on July 7.[3]

It was at this point that the Soviet-Polish war impinged

---

[1] L. B. Krasin, *Voprosy Vneshnei Torgovli* (1928), pp. 245-246.

[2] *Sobranie Uzakonenii, 1920*, No. 53, art. 235; failures to observe this decree on the part of some " central departments of the RSFSR " and of " government organs of the autonomous republics " called for a further reassertion of the powers of Vneshtorg in a decree of February 17, 1921 (*Sobranie Uzakonenii, 1921*, No. 14, art. 89).

[3] The best general sources for the negotiations are articles written by Krasin early in 1921 in *Narodnoe Khozyaistvo*, No. 1-2, 1921, pp. 3-12, and in *Ekonomicheskaya Zhizn'*, February 6, 1921 (the latter reprinted in L. B. Krasin, *Voprosy Vneshnei Torgovli* (1928), pp. 278-286); the three notes of June 30, July 1 and July 7, 1920, were published in *Soviet Russia* (N.Y.), August 14, 1920, pp. 149-151. The British documents on the negotiations are still unpublished.

decisively on the course of the negotiations. Even those western countries which had been shocked by Poland's assumption of an aggressive rôle against Soviet Russia were none the less perturbed when, in June 1920, the Polish forces were evicted from Kiev and the Ukraine, and the Red Army in its turn took the offensive. The threat to Poland threw the allied conference at Spa, which had assembled to consider German reparations, into a state of alarm ; and Curzon, who was present at the conference, addressed a communication to Chicherin on July 12, 1920, in which, after briefly noting the Soviet Government's acceptance of the three conditions, he formulated at length a new demand of a different character — the conclusion of an immediate armistice with Poland.[1] The tentative diplomatic contacts and compromises of the past six months were rudely interrupted, and both sides returned to the militant and intransigent mood of 1919.

[1] Klyuchnikov i Sabanin, *Mezhdunarodnaya Politika*, iii, i (1928), 34-35.

CHAPTER 25

REVOLUTION OVER EUROPE

THE outbreak of war with Poland in May 1920, bringing in its train a resumption of the civil war in the south against " white " forces led by Wrangel, reproduced on a smaller scale the situation of 1919. The Red Army was stronger, the military forces arrayed against it less imposing. But the country was exhausted, stocks were depleted and transport on the point of complete break-down, so that the threat of 1920 seemed scarcely less grave than in the previous year. The incipient *rapprochement* with the west which had begun in the first months of 1920 was nipped in the bud, with the same result of replacing diplomatic contacts by revolutionary propaganda as the staple of Soviet foreign policy. But here one striking difference became apparent. In 1919 the propaganda of the Bolsheviks, though often effective locally, had been a hand-to-mouth affair, and not organized on an international scale. In 1920 Comintern was already a going concern capable of playing a conspicuous part on the international stage and forming an effective focus for revolutionary propaganda in many countries. Whether it would in the long run achieve more than had been achieved by the comparatively unorganized and uncoordinated efforts of the Bolsheviks of 1919, remained to be seen. But the revolutionary propaganda which now emanated from Moscow was more confident, more bombastic and more coherent than anything that had been attempted before, and gave a clearer impression of organized power behind it. The summer and autumn of 1920 proved to be the high-water mark of the prestige of Comintern and of its hopes of promoting revolution throughout the world.

The gradual renewal of contacts between Soviet Russia and central Europe had helped to remedy the lack of organization which made Comintern, during the first year of its existence, a

negligible force.   In January 1920 Radek was released from his
Berlin exile and returned to Moscow; and in him Comintern
soon found a leader more energetic and flexible than Zinoviev,
and less preoccupied with party affairs.   Radek had claims to be
regarded as an international figure, and, enjoying no high party
status, could be employed in overtures or negotiations which
might afterwards have to be disowned.   In the person of Radek
Comintern at once resumed close and permanent contact with
the KPD and with other German parties; and Radek remained
for the next four years an active and conspicuous figure in the
politics of Comintern.   An institution where Radek was pro-
minently employed was unlikely to remain idle.   After the downfall of the communist régime in Hungary in August 1919 most of
its leaders fled to Vienna, where a new bureau of Comintern was
established under their auspices, and published from February
1920 onwards a journal under the title *Kommunismus*, to which
Bela Kun, Varga and Lukacs were prominent contributors.
In the summer of 1920 the Hungarian communists were expelled
from Vienna and took refuge in Moscow.   They could not be
absorbed into the Russian party or the Soviet administration.   But
it was natural and convenient to use them for building up the
international machinery of Comintern or for undertaking missions
to foreign communist parties which could be carried out less
invidiously by non-Russians.   Thus Bela Kun, Rakosi, Varga,
Rudnyansky and other Hungarian leaders formed the nucleus of
the new international bureaucracy of Comintern, and occupied
in the early years of that institution a place out of all proportion
to the importance of their country of origin.

The winter of 1919–1920 brought with it a new phase in
Comintern history.   The Second International seemed extinct.
Attempts to revive it at conferences at Berne in February and at
Lucerne in September 1919 had hopelessly broken down, and a
projected conference at Geneva in January 1920 was abandoned.
In the autumn of 1919 the Swiss Socialist Party, which represented the not very large Swiss proletariat employed in Swiss
heavy industry, won for itself a brief notoriety in socialist history
by putting forward, through its energetic leader Robert Grimm,
a project for a " reconstruction " of the International, which would
absorb the old Second and the new Third into a new comprehen-

sive organization. This was in effect a revival of the " centrist " position occupied during the war by the Zimmerwald majority. The project hung fire for some time. But, though not yet taken up officially, it appealed to the mood of Left parties in more than one country which were reluctant either to return to the old or to embrace the new, especially when it appeared in Russian guise, and hesitated between the two distasteful extremes. Among these intermediate parties the USPD occupied a crucial position. Its membership increased rapidly during 1919, reaching one million by the end of the year; and it seemed well on its way to become an important electoral rival of the SPD. But this numerical strength reflected in part what proved to be the fatal weakness of the USPD : an undefined political position. It had come into being as an anti-war party, and, once the war was over, found itself without any firm and coherent platform. It wavered between the revolutionary programme of the KPD and the reformist programme of the SPD ; between the demand for workers' and soldiers' councils and support for the National Assembly; between east and west ; between Third and Second Internationals. At its congress at Leipzig in December 1919, these issues were still glossed over. But the general movement was towards the Left. The poison distilled by Radek, during his sojourn in the Moabit prison, in the ear of some at least of the USPD leaders [1] had begun to work. On the immediate practical issue, the USPD unanimously decided not to join a revived Second International. It also decided by a majority not to join Comintern. But the compromise resolution adopted by the majority carried it far along that path. It declared that " an effective proletarian International should be formed by uniting our party with the Third International and with social-revolutionary parties of other countries ", and instructed the party central committee to enter into negotiations " to realize the union of the working class for revolutionary action in the Third International ". The phraseology was equivocal and manifestly designed to placate the minority. But the ultimate goal was clearly set.[2]

[1] *Krasnaya Nov'*, No. 10, 1926, p. 172.
[2] *Kommunisticheskii Internatsional*, No. 7-8 (November-December 1919), col. 1113 ; Lenin, *Sochineniya*, xxv, 598.

The official communication of the decision to Moscow raised a question of principle. The USPD was a mass party and would give Comintern what it lacked in Germany — the support of a large body of workers. The test was whether the USPD had in fact weaned itself from the errors of the SPD and could be trusted in the future to fight vigorously against it. On February 5, 1920, IKKI issued a general appeal " to all German workers, to the central committee of the German Communist Party, and to the central committee of the German Independent Social-Democratic Party ", in which, after drawing attention to past errors, it invited the party to send delegates to Moscow for negotiations. But the warning was given in advance that Comintern rejected all collaboration with the " Right-wing leaders . . . who are dragging back the movement into the bourgeois swamp of the yellow Second International ".[1] Two days later IKKI sent a letter to the dissident KAPD, expressing disapproval of its opposition to participation in the trade unions and in parliamentary elections, but inviting it to send delegates to Moscow for oral discussion.[2] Comintern was beginning to feel its strength and to take an active hand in the affairs of the German Left. Unity of all Left elements opposed to the social-democracy of the Second International, and conciliation and compromise on minor doctrinal differences between them, as laid down by Lenin in the autumn of 1919, was still the watchword. The significant new development was the summoning of candidates for favour to Moscow and the judging of doubtful cases by IKKI as a court of appeal.

Almost at the same moment the French Socialist Party, which had participated in the abortive attempts of 1919 to revive the Second International, rather unexpectedly followed the example of the USPD. Like the Italian party, it had always admitted a certain laxity of discipline and a wide diversity of opinion. Its Left wing had been strengthened by the aftermath of the war and the disappointments of the peace ; and at the party congress at Strasbourg in February 1920 the now familiar division of Right,

---

[1] *Kommunisticheskii Internatsional*, No. 9 (March 22, 1920), cols. 1381-1392.

[2] This letter does not seem to have been published in *Kommunisticheskii Internatsional*, but was referred to at the third congress of the KPD (*Bericht über den 3. Parteitag der Kommunistischen Partei Deutschlands (Spartakusbund)* (n.d.), p. 14).

Centre and Left was revealed. Renaudel, Albert Thomas and Sembat were the leaders of the Right, which had whole-heartedly supported the war, was faithful to the Second International, and supported or tolerated intervention in Russia. The small but well organized Left group, led by Loriot, Monatte and Souvarine, which had adhered to the Zimmerwald line during the war, now demanded adhesion to Comintern. Between the two extremes was a large central group of hesitating and undefined opinions. The congress, reflecting these divisions, voted by a large majority to leave the Second International. But an almost equally large majority rejected a proposal to join Comintern forthwith, and decided to send delegates to Moscow to investigate the credentials of the new organization.[1] Cachin and Frossard, both members of the Centre group, were selected for this mission. Before they left Paris, eighteen members of the Left group, including Loriot and Souvarine, had been arrested on charges of disturbing public security by the organization of mass strikes.

Another development of the first weeks of 1920 seemed to promise a rapid extension of Comintern's prestige and influence. Rutgers, with the assistance of a small but energetic group of Dutch communists, had carried out the instruction to establish a western European bureau of Comintern at Amsterdam. Its president, Wijnkoop, and its secretaries, Rutgers himself and Henriette Roland-Holst, were prominent Dutch Marxist intellectuals; and it set out to issue a bulletin in three languages.[2] Its first action was to convene an international conference of Left groups drawn mainly from western Europe for the beginning of February 1920 with the ostensible purpose of preparing the way for a second congress of Comintern in Moscow. It was attended, apart from the Dutch party, by three British delegates representing different groups, by French, Italian, Belgian, Scandinavian and American delegates, by three delegates of the KPD headed by Klara Zetkin (who arrived late and grudgingly, since their invitation had apparently been delayed), and, most important of all, by Michael Borodin, just back from the United States, as delegate of Comintern. The conference proved a fiasco, being broken up by the

[1] *Parti Socialiste: 17ᵉ Congrès National tenu à Strasbourg les 25, 26, 28 et 29 Février 1920* (n.d.).

[2] *Istorik Marksist*, No. 2-3 (1935), pp. 91-92.

police on the second day.[1] But the significant fact was that the communist movement in western Europe was beginning to take shape, and that it was taking shape under the auspices of an organization which, whatever the degree of its subordination to Moscow — and this, as the sequel showed, was slight — was plainly jealous and mistrustful of Berlin.

These proceedings were not at all to the taste of the KPD. Comintern had chosen to negotiate both with the USPD, which did not even profess to be a communist party, and with the KAPD, without regard to what claimed to be the one orthodox German Communist Party;[2] and the Amsterdam bureau, enjoying the patronage of Moscow, seemed to eclipse the western European secretariat in Berlin. The third congress of the KPD, meeting at Karlsruhe in February 1920, made some oblique references to the coquetting of Comintern with the USPD and the KAPD, and, after listening to a sour report from Klara Zetkin on the Amsterdam conference, passed a resolution demanding the retention of the Berlin secretariat and calling for a congress of Comintern in the near future to discuss these issues.[3] The political atmosphere was one of profound pessimism. The Saxon trade-union leader Brandler, one of the few workers in the active leadership of the party, exclaimed that " we still have no party ", and that in the Rhineland and Westphalia, which he had just visited, " what exists

---

[1] No official record of the conference exists ; it is described sympathetically in J. T. Murphy, *New Horizons* (1941), pp. 87-89, unsympathetically by Zetkin in *Bericht über den 3. Parteitag der Kommunistischen Partei Deutschlands (Spartakusbnnd)* (n.d.), pp. 79-84.

[2] The KPD was no doubt responsible for a statement on the USPD application issued by the " western European secretariat " on January 15, 1920, (reprinted in *Kommunisticheskii Internatsional*, No. 10 (May 11, 1920, cols. 1604-1620)) : this pointed out that " the question is not one of uniting different parties into a new revolutionary International, but simply whether the USPD wishes to enter the Third International or not ".

[3] *Bericht über den 3. Parteitag der Kommunistischen Partei Deutschlands (Spartakusbund)* (n.d.), pp. 84-85. According to Klara Zetkin's probably exaggerated statement at the congress, the western European secretariat had " developed beyond its function of information ", and become " a central point of communication and union for communists in western Europe ". Connexions had been made with Austria and Switzerland ; links had been sought with the " revolutionary-minded section of the French socialists " and with " serious communist-inclined organizations in England " ; feelers had been put out to " revolutionary socialists in the Balkans " (*ibid.* p. 77). If this was true, it would inevitably have been regarded in Moscow as a usurpation of the prerogatives of the central organization.

is worse than if we had nothing, so that it will not be possible in the near future to put the communist party on its feet ".[1] The extreme weakness of the KPD was sufficient by itself to explain the tactics of Comintern. The KPD leaders might consider that they were modelling themselves on the Bolsheviks, and Levi might justify the split at the Heidelberg congress by the example of Lenin, who throughout his exile in western Europe had preferred doctrinal purity to a mass following. But Germany was already in a revolutionary ferment, and possessed a large and politically conscious proletariat. At the beginning of 1920 it was unthinkable that Comintern should throw its mantle in Germany exclusively over a small sect composed mainly of intellectuals who, following Rosa Luxemburg, believed that the German masses were not ripe for the proletarian revolution. The belief may have been correct. But, in the first flush of revolutionary enthusiasm, it was bound to appear pusillanimous : something better had to be tried and hoped for. Lenin, at a moment when the civil war was moving towards a victorious end, would abate nothing of his confidence in the coming German and European revolution. If the capitalist governments had failed so abjectly in their nefarious design to destroy the Soviet power, this was because " the workers of the Entente proved to be nearer to us than to their own governments ".[2] In a speech in celebration of the first anniversary of Comintern Lenin boasted that " the defection of the German Independent Social-Democratic Party, and its recognition of the dictatorship of the proletariat and of the Soviet power, was the last decisive blow to the Second International ", that " the Second International is dead ", and that " masses of the workers in Germany, England and France are coming over to the side of the communists ".[3] In an article of the period he compared the USPD with its counterparts in France and England, the Longuet group of the French Socialist Party and the ILP, both of which had been opposed to the war, and hoped that they too would soon see the light.[4]

At this moment untoward events occurred in Germany. The weak and hesitant KPD had its hand forced — as had happened

[1] *Ibid.* p. 14.   [2] Lenin, *Sochineniya*, xxv, 50.
[3] *Ibid.* xxv, 75.   [4] *Ibid.* xxv, 32.

in January 1919, and as was to happen on more than one subsequent occasion — by a revolutionary situation which it had done
nothing to create and which its leaders secretly deplored. Two
generals led a revolt — the so-called " Kapp *putsch* " — against
the social-democratic government in Berlin. On March 13,
1920, the ministers fled to Stuttgart, and the generals installed a
Right nationalist government with a Prussian official named
Kapp as Chancellor in their place. The coup would probably
have succeeded but for a general strike called by the trade unions,
which prevented the new authority from establishing itself and
in the end forced a restoration of the old government. The KPD
Zentrale [1] in Berlin, in a leaflet issued on March 13, uncompromisingly refused " to lift a finger for the democratic republic ".[2]
The organizer of the strike, the trade union leader Legien, had
been more than once singled out for attack by Lenin as a typical
renegade ; and the struggle between the social-democrats and the
nationalists was treated as a matter of indifference to communists,
who were equally hostile to both. On the next day, however,
when the strike had proved a brilliant success, and when the rank
and file of the party were found to be following the lead of their
trade-union comrades, party headquarters hastily changed its
attitude to one of half-hearted support. The strike was approved ;
but local sections of the KPD were warned against " illusions
. . . about the value of bourgeois democracy " and instructed that
the only proper form of common action by the workers was the
institution of factory councils and workers' councils as political
organs.[3] The rather grudging recommendation to support the
strike was enthusiastically applied. In the Ruhr social-democrats,
independent social-democrats and communists issued a joint
appeal to the workers to strike against the " counter-revolution-

---

[1] The Zentrale was established by the statute of the KPD as an inner
group of seven members of the central committee residing permanently in
Berlin ; its position corresponded to that of the later Politburo (*Bericht über den
2. Parteitag der Kommunistischen Partei Deutschland (Spartakusbund)* (n.d.
[? 1919]), p. 68).

[2] The leaflet is quoted in M. J. Braun, *Die Lehren des Kapp-Putsches* (1920),
p. 8 ; this pamphlet is a German version of an article in defence of the attitude
of the Zentrale, signed " Spartak ", which appeared in *Kommunisticheskii Internatsional*, No. 10 (May 11, 1920), cols. 1581-1604.

[3] The instruction of March 14, 1920, is quoted in M. J. Braun, *Die Lehren
des Kapp-Putsches* (1920), pp. 28-29.

ary " Kapp government, and to fight for " the capture of political power through the dictatorship of the proletariat " and " the victory of socialism on the basis of the Soviet system ". In Chemnitz on March 15 Brandler and other communists actually joined the local social-democrats in proclaiming a Soviet government for common defence against the nationalists ; this lasted for some days and faded away only when the generals and their government had been ousted from Berlin. These first experiments in the history of Comintern in what were afterwards known as " united front " tactics against the Right were made in response, not to a.iy decision of policy in Moscow or Berlin, but to the hard logic of events.

Meanwhile in Berlin the *putsch* was over, and the victorious trade unions had made enquiries at KPD headquarters about the attitude of the KPD towards a social-democratic government. On March 21, 1920, the Zentrale issued a statement that, in the event of a workers' government being placed in power, the attitude of the KPD would be one of " loyal opposition ", i.e. of abstention from any attempt to overthrow it by force ; and this was taken as a further step by the KPD towards a policy of conciliation and a " united front " with the SPD and USPD.[1] The declaration, which was much criticized in party circles, lost its effect when the project of a workers' government fell through, and a coalition government, including both social-democrats and representatives of bourgeois parties, returned to power. This solution satisfied everyone except the extreme nationalists who had made the *putsch*. The Reichswehr had taken no part in the *putsch*. Though it had done nothing to suppress it (the Reichswehr did not fire on Germans, unless they were Germans of the Left), it had remained technically loyal to the constitutional order, and supported the restored constitutional government. As a reward it was now enabled to turn its arms, not against the nationalists who had been solely responsible for the *putsch*, but against the Ruhr workers who had taken up arms against it. The real victor in the Kapp *putsch* was Seeckt, who immediately afterwards received the new appointment of " chief of the army command ". By coming to terms with the Weimar republic, the Reichswehr

---

[1] The negotiations are described and the declaration of March 21, 1920, reprinted *ibid.* pp. 19-21.

became the strongest force within it, and Seeckt as head of the Reichswehr the strong man behind the scenes of German politics. Heavy industry, finding its spokesman in Stresemann, the leader of the German People's Party, also denounced the *putsch* and rallied to the restored government : the defeat of the *putsch* represented a blow to the *junker* interest in German politics, in so far as this was opposed to the interests of the industrialists. The trade unions had shown their power of resistance to attack, but also their lack of any constructive policy : they could not govern, but for the present nobody could govern against them. Only the KPD had given an unedifying display of blindness, vacillation and compromise. Levi, who was in prison when the *putsch* occurred, wrote on March 16 a long denunciation of the party's inaction.[1] The fourth congress of the KPD in the following month took the form of a post-mortem on the proceedings. The party central committee had meanwhile passed a resolution condemning the action of the Zentrale, and the congress endorsed this by a large majority.[2]

Events during the Kapp *putsch* had moved too rapidly for a pronouncement from Comintern or from any authority in Moscow.[3] The ninth congress of the Russian party, meeting immediately after the *putsch*, sent " warm greetings " to the German workers, and hopes for their success in " the heavy struggle " which they had undertaken.[4] But this was no more than a formality. Critical voices soon began to be heard. Bela Kun, writing in the communist journal in Vienna, correctly diagnosed the *putsch* as the first occasion on which " the democratic counter-revolution found in Germany an anti-democratic competitor " ; and he predicted that " the result will in any case be to sacrifice democracy ".[5] Three weeks later he attacked the

[1] The latter was published and appeared in *Kommunisticheskii Internatsional*, No. 12 (July 20, 1920), cols. 2077-2080.

[2] *Bericht über den 4. Parteitag der Kommunistischen Partei Deutschlands* (*Spartakusbund*) (n.d.), pp. 39, 53.

[3] A Berlin member of the KPD writes of this period : " It was only with difficulty that couriers could be sent to and fro. Important matters were arranged by letter or occasionally by telegraph ; between the Berlin group and the Moscow centre there was no direct telephone connexion. In this early period these technical difficulties made Russian opinion on German events in general available only after the critical moment had passed " (R. Fischer, *Stalin and German Communism* (Harvard, 1948), p. 235).

[4] *Devyatyi S"ezd RKP(B)* (1934), pp. 10-11.

[5] *Kommunismus* (Vienna), No. 11 (March 27, 1920), pp. 316, 322.

" loyal opposition " formula of the KPD declaration.[1] Radek also attacked the pusillanimous policy of the KPD throughout the *putsch* as well as its " loyal opposition " declaration.[2] Lenin, on the other hand, more cautiously wrote of the declaration that " the tactics were beyond doubt fundamentally correct ", though some of the phrases used were unfortunate.[3] This diversity of judgments was characteristic of a period when the Soviet leaders, gradually emerging from two years of almost complete isolation from the outside world, had still little attention to give to the problem of foreign communist movements, which they continued to judge from the standpoint of abstract theory rather than of objective observation.

Among the factors which explained both the supreme confidence of the Bolsheviks at this time in the imminent approach of the European revolution, and their increasingly didactic attitude towards western communist parties, the most important was perhaps the unquestioning acceptance, common to all the Bolshevik leaders, of the validity of precedents drawn from the Russian revolution. It was implicit in Marxism that revolution followed a scientifically charted course, obeying conditions which could be ascertained by observation and elucidated by theoretical analysis. While no serious Marxist pretended that these conditions were everywhere completely uniform or that any two revolutions would conform to an identical pattern, it was natural for the Bolsheviks to scan the course and prospects of other revolutions in the light of their own experience, to diagnose the same pitfalls and the same sources of strength ; and it was the German revolution, the farthest advanced, the most crucial and in every external aspect the most closely analogous to its Russian counterpart, which had from the first been constantly subjected to this process. The events of November 1918 were Germany's " February revolution " ; Ebert and Scheidemann were its Kerensky and its Tsereteli ; Liebknecht would be its Lenin. The first All-German Congress of Workers' and Soldiers' Councils in December 1918 seemed the plain counterpart of the first All-Russian Congress of Soviets in

---

[1] *Ibid.* No. 14 (April 17, 1920), pp. 403-411.

[2] *Kommunisticheskii Internatsional*, No. 12 (July 20, 1920), cols. 2087-2098 ; a year later he referred to the policy as " a castration of communism " (*Protokoll des III. Kongresses der Kommunistischen Internationale* (Hamburg, 1921), p. 45).

[3] Lenin, *Sochineniya*, xxv, 243.

July 1917, when a tiny Bolshevik minority had been far outnumbered by SRs and Mensheviks.[1] The clashes of January 1919 were Berlin's " July days ", less skilfully managed by the young and untried KPD than the Petrograd disturbances of July 1917 by the Bolsheviks, but representing the same step in the development of the revolution.[2] The road was so obviously the same that it could only lead to the same destination. Objectively considered, the Kapp *putsch* of March 1920 might have seemed a shocking revelation of the weakness of German communism — indeed of every group in Germany to the Left of the conservative trade unions. But Lenin, in the first flush of enthusiasm, had no hesitation in diagnosing it as " the German Kornilov affair ". The German workers, he told the ninth party congress, were " forming red armies " and " becoming more and more inflamed ".[3] Such had been the consequences of the Russian prototype, and how could those of the " German Kornilov affair " be any different? The German calendar had moved on as far as August 1917. The German October could not be delayed much longer. Similar analogies repeatedly occurred to Lenin elsewhere. At the end of January 1920 he justified the impending conclusion of a treaty of peace with a bourgeois Estonian government by the argument that Estonia was " passing through the Kerensky period ", and that the Estonian workers would " soon overthrow this power and create a Soviet Estonia which will conclude a new peace with us ".[4] In September 1920 he assumed that the " councils of action " set up in Great Britain to organize opposition to military action against Soviet Russia were Soviets under another name, that Britain had entered the February period of the " dual power ", and that the " British Mensheviks " were " clearing the road for the Bolshevik revolution ".[5] With this belief in the parallelism of revolutions so firmly rooted in his mind, it was difficult not to treat Bolshevik experience as the fundamental source of instruction for western communists.[6]

---

[1] This comparison was repeated by Stalin as late as January 1933 (*Sochineniya*, xiii, 226).
[2] These parallels were elaborated by Trotsky in an article of April 1919 (*Sochineniya*, xiii, pp. 97-98).   [3] Lenin, *Sochineniya*, xxv, 101.
[4] *Ibid.* xxv, 16.   [5] *Ibid.* xxv, 378-379, 403-404.
[6] The same revolutionary analogies were equally accepted by non-Russian communists. The comparison of the Kapp *putsch* with the Kornilov insurrection

In this mood of all-conquering hope and faith, the second
congress of Comintern was convened for the summer of 1920 and
Lenin wrote in April, by way of preparation for it, a pamphlet
entitled *The Infantile Disease of " Leftism " in Communism*. The
last of his major writings, it was among the most influential of
them; and it is therefore particularly important to recall the
circumstances which inspired it. It was written at a moment of
legitimate self-congratulation that the ordeal of the civil war had
ended in a victory surpassing all expectations; this triumphant
vindication of the theory and practice of Bolshevism gave point to
the theme, which ran through the pamphlet from the first sentence
to the last, that the Russian experience should serve as a beacon
and as an example to the revolutionary movements of other
countries. It was written at a moment when Russia's two-year
isolation from the outside world was only just beginning to be
broken, and when Lenin had few sources of information and
fewer direct contacts to bring home to him the realities of the
political situation, and especially of Left-wing movements, in the
west; European developments were seen by him in a distorting
mirror of all that happened in Russia since his dramatic return to
Petrograd in April 1917. Finally, it was written in the confident
belief that the proletarian revolution, having triumphed in Russia,
was about to sweep over western Europe. The arguments and
recommendations of the pamphlet were designed for the brief
interval necessary to bring about this consummation. It was
only later that what were conceived by Lenin as short-term
tactical expedients were invoked and applied over a far longer
period than Lenin had ever had in mind.

Starting from the premiss that some traits of the Russian
revolution were likely to be reproduced on an international scale,
Lenin sketched the history of Bolshevism in order to show how
the party had had to contend with two main enemies — social-
democratic opportunism on the Right, and petty bourgeois anarchism on the Left. The shafts of Lenin in opposition had been
directed mainly against the Right; those of Lenin in power were

was invoked at length in M. J. Braun, *Die Lehren des Kapp-Putsches* (1920),
pp. 14-19; and in the post-mortem at the KPD congress in April 1920 both
Pieck and Levi defended their positions by quoting Russian precedents (*Bericht
über den 4. Parteitag der Kommunistischen Partei Deutschlands (Spartakusbund)*
(n.d.), pp. 40, 50).

aimed in the opposite direction. Lenin believed that the danger
for the party from the Right, though graver than the danger from
the Left, had been substantially overcome; the Second International was at its last gasp. He therefore concentrated on the lesser,
but more topical, danger of " Leftism ". The two main instances
of " Leftism " in party history had been the opposition to participation in the Duma in 1908 and the opposition to Brest-
Litovsk in 1918; in both cases the opposition had based itself on
grounds of " principle " against " compromise ". Lenin went on
to attack the Left wing of the German (and also the English)
socialist movement for rejecting participation in parliamentary
elections and in the trade unions : the same " Leftist " errors
were exemplified in French and Italian and American syndicalism.
The lines of policy for the coming congress were clearly and precisely drawn, always with the proviso that the aim should be to
persuade the " Leftists " and not to break with them. The line
pursued throughout the past year of uncompromising hostility
to social-democrats of the Right, but tenderness towards deviations
on the Left among those who might yet be brought into a common
front against them, was not abandoned. In an appendix to the
pamphlet Lenin even admitted, with one eye on Germany, that
the Left communists were sometimes more successful than the
orthodox in winning mass support.[1] But the tone was noticeably
stiffer than in the previous summer and autumn, the insistence on
discipline and conformity more emphatic, the conditions of
acceptance more rigorously laid down. Participation in parliaments and in trade unions, which had been treated by Lenin
and by Comintern in the autumn of 1919 as a secondary question
not worth quarrelling about, now became an imperative obligation.

Lenin also attempted some broader generalizations. In a chapter headed *No Compromises?* he quoted a passage in which Engels
had declared that true communists must be prepared to pass
" through all the stages and compromises created not by them
but by the course of history " on the way to their goal. In reply
to the Leftists who claimed to stand on pure principle, he declared

[1] This might be true in Germany, where revolutionary feeling and a
potentially revolutionary situation still existed in 1920 ; here the extreme Left
could win mass support away from the official party. In most other countries,
where a revolutionary programme was an academic exercise, the extreme Left
remained a small doctrinaire sect with the masses far to the Right.

that " the whole history of Bolshevism, both before and after the October revolution, is *full* of cases of manœuvring, of conciliation, of compromises with other parties, including bourgeois parties ". But the most detailed example given in the pamphlet of the tactics of manœuvre and compromise revealed some of the practical difficulties. This was the famous passage which recommended British communists to " help the Hendersons and Snowdens to defeat Lloyd George and Churchill together ". A compromise was to be proposed to the " Hendersons and Snowdens " in the form of an " electoral agreement " for a common campaign against " Lloyd George and the Conservatives ", and for a division of seats won, on some principle which Lenin did not elaborate, between Labour and communists. All this was, however, to be achieved under conditions which allowed the communists " the most complete freedom to denounce the Hendersons and Snowdens " — just as the Bolsheviks had for a long time remained partners of the Mensheviks in a single party while continuing to denounce them without restraint. And lest this proposal for a compromise, even so limited, should seem to conflict with the line taken elsewhere in the pamphlet of unbending hostility to Right social-democrats, Lenin further advised the British communist to " explain in popular form " that he " would support Henderson with his vote as the rope supports the man who is being hanged ", since the nearer the Hendersons came to political power, the nearer they would be to " political death " through the revelation of their true political colour to the masses of the workers.[1] This cunningly contrived calculation for a temporary tactical alliance for specific limited objectives with forces which one was pledged to denounce and ultimately destroy might have sounded plausible to a leadership which had behind it a disciplined mass party willing to follow its prescriptions without criticism or discussion. But to recommend it as a form of political tactics in a British electoral campaign, where means and ends alike would be hotly debated both within and between parties, was to raise a smile among practical politicians.

The Infantile Disease of " Leftism " in Communism unconsciously revealed for the first time the weak link in the Bolshevik armoury — the embarrassment resulting from the assumption of

[1] Lenin, *Sochineniya*, xxv, 221-225.

a close and unassailable analogy between revolutionary processes
and revolutionary tactics in Russia, which had made an almost
direct transition from autocracy to the proletarian revolution, and
in countries where the proletariat had undergone a long period of
indoctrination in the theory and practice of bourgeois democracy.
When an anarchist deputy in a debate in VTsIK in 1918 pointed
out that, whereas the Russian proletariat was not " state-minded ",
the western proletariat " feels itself as the bearer of a fragment of
power and as a part of this same state which it is at present
defending ", Lenin retorted with unusual asperity that this view
of the western worker was " so stupid that I do not know how it
could be more so ".[1] The Bolsheviks, in their eagerness to deny
the existence of innate national differences, were sometimes
tempted to ignore the reality of national differences which had
profound social and economic roots. They consistently underestimated the proportion of the workers in western countries who
had derived benefits from resort to democratic procedures and
could not easily be weaned from belief in the validity of these
procedures. Lenin never really understood why " reformism ",
which meant nothing in Russia, was a persistent and successful
rival to the teaching of revolution in western Europe, why illegal
action, which was accepted as a matter of course by Russian
workers, aroused strong prejudices in the west, or why the dissolution of the Constituent Assembly, which raised no ripple of indignation among Russian workers, should have shocked large numbers
of western workers.

The embarrassment became particularly acute over the question
of the relation between party leadership and the masses, which
had recurred intermittently ever since the party controversy of
1903. Lenin was always keenly alive to the rôle of the masses in
the revolutionary movement. It was utopian socialism which
believed that the new society would be created by " specially
virtuous people bred in special frames and hot-houses ". Marxists
knew that it must be built out of " the mass of human material
twisted by centuries and millenniums of slavery, serfdom, capitalism, petty individual economies, and war of all against all for a
place on the market, for higher prices for goods or labour ".[2]

[1] *Protokoly Zasedanii VTsIK 4ᵍᵒ Sozvya* (1920), p. 231 ; Lenin, *Sochineniya*,
xxii, 493.   [2] *Ibid.* xxv, 458.

But this conception of the masses as the material of revolution entailed a particular view of the functions of leadership. If leadership was meaningless without a mass following, the masses were impotent without leadership. As Lenin vigorously protested in *The Infantile Disease of " Leftism " in Communism*, to raise the question of " the dictatorship of the leaders *or* the dictatorship of the masses " in that form was proof of " an incredible and inextricable confusion of thought ".[1] It merely meant to separate two things which were part of an indissoluble revolutionary whole. This conception had been born of a study of Russian conditions and brilliantly fitted them, as the success of Bolshevik policy showed. In Russia what was necessary was to create a revolutionary consciousness among masses of hitherto politically unconscious workers ; and for this purpose the imprint of a strong and disciplined revolutionary leadership was a paramount necessity. The very conception of " the masses " as a vast reservoir of oppressed and unorganized proletarians,[2] which acquired a growing importance in Bolshevik thought, reflected the backwardness of the typical Russian industrial worker. But the same conception was not applicable, or applicable only with far-reaching qualifications, to countries where the problem was not to imprint a revolutionary consciousness on the *tabula rasa* of politically unconscious masses, but to penetrate and transform a political consciousness already highly developed in the bourgeois democratic tradition. This task was different from anything that had confronted the Russian Bolsheviks, and far more subtle and complicated ; and the misunderstanding of this difference explains why the prescriptions offered to the west by the Bolsheviks, and afterwards by Comintern, so often seemed inadequate and inapplicable. It was many years before a situation was reached in which uniform decisions handed down from Moscow were automatically applied by docile communist parties with little or no regard for their validity in the light of local conditions and opinion. But the first insidious beginnings of the process must be traced back to the period of Lenin's *Infantile*

---

[1] *Ibid.* xxv, 187.

[2] The second congress defined " the masses " as " the totality of the workers and victims of capitalist exploitation, especially the least organized and least enlightened, the most oppressed and the least accessible to organization " (*Kommunisticheskii Internatsional v Dokumentakh* (1933), p. 95).

Disease of " Leftism " in Communism and the second congress of Comintern. Another constant element of Comintern doctrine made its first appearance at this time. As early as 1858 Engels, depressed by the complete bankruptcy of the Chartist movement, had thrown out in a letter to Marx the view that " the English proletariat is in reality becoming more and more bourgeois, so that this most bourgeois of all nations wants apparently in the end to have side by side with its bourgeoisie a bourgeois aristocracy and a bourgeois proletariat "; he added that " for a nation which exploits the whole world " this was " to some extent natural ".[1] The thesis was repeated in a letter to Kautsky of 1882 ; [2] and three years later, after Marx's death, Engels committed it to print in a retrospective article in an English periodical with a further elaboration which became highly important :

> So long as England's industrial monopoly was maintained, the English working class to a certain extent shared in the advantages of this monopoly. These advantages were distributed among the workers very unevenly ; the lion's share was snatched by a privileged minority, though something was left over from time to time for the broad masses.[3]

The implication here was no longer that the English proletariat had as such become " bourgeois ", but that a " privileged minority " within it had acquired this status at the expense of the rank and file. In *Imperialism as the Highest Stage of Capitalism*, Lenin, building on the foundations laid by Engels, repeated that a part of the English proletariat had become bourgeois, and added that " part of it allows itself to be led by men sold to, or at least paid by, the middle class ".[4] That monopoly capitalism, by its exploitation of colonial and semi-colonial markets, was able to benefit and thus corrupt a " privileged minority " of the working class, and that this minority played the rôle of leaders " paid by the

---

[1] Marx i Engels, *Sochineniya*, xxii, 360.   [2] *Ibid.* xxvii, 238.

[3] *Ibid.* xvi, i, 200 ; the passage was quoted by Engels *in extenso* in a new preface for the 1892 edition of *The Position of the Working Class in England* (*ibid.* xvi, ii, 275).

[4] Lenin, *Sochineniya*, xix, 157-158 ; the phrase " led by men sold to or at least paid by the middle class " was borrowed by Lenin from a letter of Engels to Marx of August 11, 1881, where it is used (in English) of " the very worst " of the trade unions (Marx i Engels, *Sochineniya*, xxiv, 529).

bourgeoisie ", now became a commonplace of Marxist doctrine. It seemed to be confirmed by the phenomenon of " revisionism " in the German Social-Democratic Party, which affected the leaders far more acutely than the rank and file, and by the experience of more than one socialist leader in France, who began by joining a bourgeois coalition government and ended by going over whole-heartedly to the bourgeoisie.

The Bolsheviks therefore inherited a well-established doctrine, which drew fresh strength from the collapse of the German revolution in the winter of 1918–1919, when leading social-democrats appeared as defenders of the bourgeois republic. In an article in celebration of the founding of Comintern, Lenin applied the argument to recent events in Germany. So long as Germany lagged economically behind Great Britain and France, German social-democracy had been pre-eminent and led the world.

> But when [Lenin went on] Germany had overtaken both these countries economically, i.e. in the second decade of the twentieth century, then at the head of this model German Marxist workers' party there appeared a gang of arrant scoundrels, the dirtiest rabble of capitalist hirelings, from Scheidemann and Noske to David and Legien, the most revolting working-class executioners in the service of the monarchy and the counter-revolutionary bourgeoisie.[1]

And two months later, in a further article on *The Tasks of the Third International*, he reverted to the theme of the conversion to the bourgeoisie of " the top levels of the working class in England ", and once more denounced the Second International as " the servant of imperialism, the agent of bourgeois influence, of bourgeois lies and of bourgeois corruption in the workers' movement ".[2] The argument led to a cogent and far-reaching conclusion which was accepted and applied without demur by the Bolshevik leaders in Comintern. Whenever obstruction or hesitation was experienced in workers' parties of western Europe, the diagnosis was obvious. The leaders of the movement in those countries — what came to be known invidiously as the " labour aristocracy " — were conscious or unconscious agents of the bourgeoisie and could be relied on in any crisis to rally to the support of bourgeois democracy and bourgeois capitalism. Thus

---

[1] Lenin, *Sochineniya*, xxiv, 249.   [2] *Ibid.* xxiv, 390.

formulated, the thesis of the " labour aristocracy " branded all reformists as heretics and traitors to their class, betrayers of the proletarian cause, who stood convicted not of intellectual error, but of moral ignominy. The task of the revolutionary was to enlighten the rank and file of the workers' parties on the true character of their unfaithful leaders and to split the parties against them. All the tactical prescriptions of *The Infantile Disease of " Leftism " in Communism* were deeply imbued with this idea.

Before Lenin's pamphlet was published, opportunities had already occurred of putting into effect the stiffening policy which it advocated. The western European bureau at Amsterdam, being under the control of the Dutch leaders, was convicted of Leftism in the form of advocating abstention from parliamentary and trade union action. By a decision of IKKI in April 1920 the bureau was dissolved, and its nebulous functions transferred to the western European secretariat in Berlin.[1] About the same time Lenin's expectation that the British ILP, like the French Socialist Party, would follow the example of the German USPD was in some part fulfilled. At its annual conference in April 1920,[2] the ILP decided by a large majority to withdraw from the Second International. But only a small minority voted for a proposal to join the Third International ; and the other decisions were exploratory and temporizing. The national administrative council of the party was instructed to enter into discussions with the Swiss Socialist Party, which had already taken the initiative in this sense,[3] on " the possibility of the re-establishment of one all-inclusive International ", but at the same time to enquire into the constitution of Comintern and the conditions of affiliation to it. This enquiry was entrusted to two ILP delegates, Wallhead and Clifford Allen, who travelled in the company of a large Labour Party delegation which was about to visit Soviet Russia. This also included a number of trade unionists, Labour M.P.s and Left intellectuals, among them Tom Shaw and Robert Williams, Bertrand Russell and Ethel Snowden, Haydn Guest and Roden Buxton. Three months earlier George Lansbury had visited

---

[1] *Kommunisticheskii Internatsional*, No. 10 (May 11, 1920), cols. 1659-1660 ; *Istorik Marksist*, No. 2-3 (1935), p. 92.
[2] *Independent Labour Party: Report of the Twenty-Eighth Annual Conference* (1920).   [3] See pp. 166-167 above.

Moscow and returned to Great Britain with an enthusiastic report on all he had seen. But the Labour delegation was the first large and influential group from the British Left to make the journey, and the occasion was therefore of some importance.

When the delegation reached Moscow in the middle of May 1920, Pilsudski's invasion of the Ukraine was in full swing and at the height of its success. It is scarcely surprising that Lenin, who received the delegates on May 26, should have been mainly concerned to impress on his visitors the Soviet desire for peace and the perversity of the British Government in giving aid to the " whites " and to Poland — more especially as some of them seemed sceptical of the reality of this aid. Some of the delegates asked the slightly disconcerting question which of two desiderata he thought more important : " the formation in England of a consistent revolutionary communist party or immediate help from the working masses for the cause of peace with Russia ". Lenin turned the question by calling it " a matter of conviction ". Those who wanted to liberate the workers could not be against the foundation of a communist party ; on the other hand nothing would be gained if people who continued to nourish illusions about bourgeois democracy and pacifism " had the idea of calling themselves communists and joining the Third International ". Such people would only pass " sugary resolutions against intervention ", though such resolutions would be useful in the end by making their authors appear ridiculous. This seems to have been the only mention of Comintern in the proceedings.[1] Lenin had other things to think about. The delegates dispersed into groups to visit various parts of Soviet Russia.

This could not, however, satisfy the two ILP delegates who had a special mandate to investigate the affairs of Comintern. Here they were less fortunate. Neither Lenin nor Trotsky had time to attend to them ; Zinoviev, who spoke little or no English, remained in the background ; and they were dealt with mainly by the ubiquitous Radek. The delegates, used to the formality of British institutions, were shocked to discover that Comintern after more than twelve months of existence was still " an entirely

---

[1] The record of the conversation was made by Lenin himself in the form of a *Letter to the English Workers* published a few days later in *Pravda* (*Sochineniya*, xxv, 262-265).

ad hoc body ", having " no formal constitution or rules ". Owing to " dilatory " methods at Comintern headquarters it proved difficult to obtain an official interview with IKKI as a corporate organ ; and, when one was at last arranged, the only spokesmen who took part in the proceedings were Bukharin and Radek, the foreign members being apparently of no account. A series of questions in writing were presented, and provoked a long answer from IKKI which was uncompromising in substance and unconciliatory in tone. Ramsay MacDonald and Snowden, the leaders of the ILP, were denounced as " centrists ", who had " protested in words against the war ", but " played the rôle of Pontius Pilate washing their hands of the guilt ". Progress would be made " only through the development of the revolution, through the growth of class consciousness, and not through conferences and compromises with the leaders ". IKKI knew well that the ILP was " made up of only one-fourth of consistent and sincere adherents to the Communist International ". These should join with other communist groups to form a single communist party ; and the note ended with the appeal : " Communists of Britain, unite ! " The attempt to split existing parties by bringing about a revolt of the rank and file against the leaders was openly proclaimed. The inflexible tone and mordant phraseology were certainly the product of Radek's indiscreet pen.[1] But the policy was perhaps a logical development of the line laid down in *The Infantile Disease of " Leftism " in Communism.* Comintern headquarters, undeterred by military reverses in the Ukraine, was in an intransigent mood. On May 27, 1920, simultaneously with the reply to the ILP delegation, a note was despatched to the central committee of the USPD complaining that it had not replied to the letter of February 5, 1920, and had not even communicated it to the members of the party.[2] It must not be thought that entry into Comintern would be made easy. " *It is necessary to put a lock on the doors of the Communist International,*" exclaimed Zinoviev in italics in the official journal, " *necessary to put a reliable*

[1] The reports of the delegates are in *Independent Labour Party : Report of the 29th Annual Conference* (1921), pp. 49-61, the questions and the reply from IKKI in *The ILP and the 3rd International* (1920) ; a Russian translation of the IKKI note was published in *Kommunisticheskii Internatsional*, No. 12 (July 20, 1920), cols. 2231-2256.

[2] *Kommunismus* (Vienna), No. 24 (June 26, 1920), pp. 833-834.

guard on the gate of the Communist International." [1]

The ILP delegates quickly had successors in the long-announced delegates of the French Socialist Party, Frossard and Cachin, who arrived in Moscow in the middle of June 1920, carrying instructions not only to ascertain the conditions of affiliation to Comintern, but to conduct a broad enquiry into social and political conditions in Soviet Russia.[2] On June 19, 1920, the delegates were summoned to a meeting of IKKI, more representative than that which had greeted the representatives of the ILP. Searching questions on the state of the French party were put to them by Radek, Zinoviev, Bukharin (who wounded their national pride by asking them to condemn the " treason " of the party during the war), Serrati, John Reed and, finally, Lenin. The points on which Lenin insisted were a clear party line, a disciplined press (*Humanité*, he observed, had only one socialist feature — its subscription list) and the expulsion of " reformists " from the party. The delegates, who had perhaps expected a more deferential wooing, could only argue and promise to report.[3] Great pressure was applied to persuade them to remain in Moscow for the impending congress, for which, since it had not been announced before their departure from Paris, they had no mandate from the party. After some hesitation, they agreed to remain.[4]

Before the second congress of Comintern assembled in the second half of July 1920, a dramatic reversal had occurred in the fortunes of war. The Polish invader had been driven back far beyond the boundaries of the Ukraine ; the Red Army was sweeping westward into Poland almost without opposition ; and the fall of Warsaw — and the outbreak of the Polish revolution —

---

[1] *Kommunisticheskii Internatsional*, No. 11 (June 14, 1920), col. 1730.

[2] The letter of instruction, dated April 23, 1920, is in L. O. Frossard, *De Jaurès à Lénine* (1930), pp. 235-244.

[3] The report of Frossard and Cachin on the meeting is *ibid.* pp. 245-269, a few personal comments by Frossard *ibid.* pp. 64-66 ; the caustic comments of IKKI were embodied in a letter of July 26, 1920, addressed " to all members of the French Socialist Party and all conscious French proletarians " (*ibid.* pp. 281-303).

[4] *Ibid.* pp. 105-110 ; Frossard portrays himself throughout as a weak man carried away against his better judgment by a more impetuous and enthusiastic colleague.

seemed all but certain. Zinoviev, who presided at the congress, afterwards described the scene :

> In the congress hall hung a great map on which was marked every day the movement of our armies. And the delegates every morning stood with breathless interest before this map. It was a sort of symbol : the best representatives of the international proletariat with breathless interest, with palpitating heart, followed every advance of our armies, and all perfectly realized that, if the military aim set by our army was achieved, it would mean an immense acceleration of the international proletarian revolution.[1]

Zinoviev himself, in opening the congress, had struck the same dramatic note :

> The second congress of the Communist International has passed into history at the moment of opening its sessions. Keep this day in mind. Know that this day is the recompense for all your privations and for your brave and steadfast struggle. Tell and explain to your children the significance of this day. Imprint on your hearts this solemn hour.[2]

The congress was attended by more than two hundred delegates from some thirty-five countries. The Russian delegation was once more outstanding. Zinoviev, speaking sometimes from the chair and sometimes as a Russian delegate, was the most prominent figure throughout the congress. Lenin spoke on all the main issues, and was ably seconded by Bukharin and Radek. Trotsky, occupied by the Polish campaign, made only fleeting appearances. Of the Germans, the KPD delegation was led by Paul Levi. The USPD sent four delegates, two in favour of affiliation to Comintern, two against ; but, since the adhesion of the party was still in question, they were admitted without voting rights. Two delegates of the KAPD were also admitted in a consultative capacity, but took no part in the proceedings.[3] The Italian

---

[1] *Desyatyi S"ezd Rossiiskoi Kommunisticheskoi Partii* (1921), p. 271.

[2] *Der Zweite Kongress der Kommunist. Internationale* (Hamburg, 1921), p. 14.

[3] Levi in the name of the KPD delegation apparently threatened to withdraw from the congress if representatives of the KAPD were admitted as voting delegates (*Bericht über den 5. Parteitag der Kommunistischen Partei Deutschlands (Spartakusbund)* (1921), pp. 27-29) ; according to a later statement of Zinoviev, Radek supported Levi (*Protokoll : Fünfter Kongress der Kommunistischen Internationale* (n.d.), i, 468).

delegation was led by Serrati but contained representatives of all groups of the Italian Socialist Party except the Right. The British delegation included representatives of the British Socialist Party, the Socialist Labour Party, the shop stewards' organization and several smaller groups. The two delegates of the French Socialist Party, like those of the USPD, had only consultative rights, since the party had not yet decided to join Comintern. But five other French delegates had full voting rights as representing the French " committee for the Third International ", some of them being at the same time members of the French Socialist Party. Delegates of the American Communist Party and the American Communist Workers' Party, regardless of the injunctions of Comintern to unite, contested the validity of one another's mandates.[1]

At its first session the congress adopted without discussion, on the proposal of the German delegate Levi, an appeal " to the working men and women of all countries " to prevent by strikes and demonstrations " any kind of help to white Poland, any kind of intervention against Soviet Russia ".[2] But, while the first congress had gathered under the shadow of the desperate stress of civil war, the second congress met at a moment of the military triumph of the Red Army ; and there was less emphasis than at the first congress — or at any later congress — on the need for direct assistance and support for the RSFSR. The weight of the proceedings rested on the broader task of hastening the world revolution which was now plainly in sight.

> The Communist International [ran one resolution] proclaims the cause of Soviet Russia as its own cause. The inter-

---

[1] *Der Zweite Kongress der Kommunist. Internationale* (Hamburg, 1921), pp. 607-610 ; according to official American sources a decision was reached in Moscow on January 12, 1920, to effect a unification of the two parties (*Russian Propaganda : Hearings before a Sub-Committee of the Committee on Foreign Relations, United States Senate* (66th Congress, 2nd Session, 1920), pp. 415-416), and communicated by a " Bolshevik courier " (*Foreign Relations of the United States, 1920*, iii (1936), 449-450), but failed to heal the rift.

[2] *Der Zweite Kongress der Kommunist. Internationale* (Hamburg, 1921), p. 56. In the German text the appeal ends with the sentence : " That is the action to which we call the proletarians of the world, and ' Russia expects that every man will do his duty ' " (the last words being in English). This sentence does not appear in the Russian edition : it apparently belonged to the speech of Levi, who liked to embroider his perorations with literary allusions, not to the text of the appeal.

national proletariat will not sheath the sword until Soviet
Russia becomes a link in a federation of Soviet republics of
the whole world.[1]

Confidence in the imminent approach of the *dénouement* of the
revolutionary drama was the constant theme of the congress,
colouring all its views both of the kind of organization required
and of the appropriate steps to create such an organization.
The supreme need now was to make Comintern the practical
instrument of revolution :

> What was the Third International at its foundation in
> March 1919 ? [asked Zinoviev]. Nothing more than a pro-
> paganda association ; and this it remained throughout its whole
> first year. . . . Now we want to be not a propaganda association,
> but a fighting organ of the international proletariat.[2]

This change of function implied a change of organization : instead
of a series of national parties, Comintern must become " a single
communist party having branches in different countries ".[3] More
than once a moral was drawn from the contrast between the First
and Second Internationals. The first had been " a strong centralized institution " ; Marx and Engels had recorded in its statute
the need of the workers for " international unity " and " strict
international organization ". The executive of the Second International was no more than " a letter-box ".[4] The Third International must not repeat the errors of the Second. At a moment
when the congress, as it sat and deliberated, could watch the
revolution spreading daily westwards with the advancing Red
Army, there was less reason than ever to question the validity of
Russian example for the rest of Europe. Unity of revolutionary
action and unity of party doctrine under the single and supreme
authority of a Communist International seemed to be established
beyond challenge. The minor deviations officially tolerated in
1919 were placed under a ban : no longer was it permissible to
differ on the question of participation in parliamentary elections
and in trade unions. Even in matters of detail a party line must
be clearly laid down and followed. When, on the admittedly
peculiar and esoteric question of the affiliation of the British

---

[1] *Kommunisticheskii Internatsional v Dokumentakh* (1933), p. 152.
[2] *Der Zweite Kongress der Kommunist. Internationale* (Hamburg, 1921),
pp. 193-194.   [3] *Ibid.* p. 102.   [4] *Ibid.* pp. 13, 238.

Communist Party to the Labour Party, a British delegate pleaded for some latitude, Lenin was emphatic in support of the principle of uniformity :

> Comrade Ramsay says : Let us English communists settle this question ourselves. What would become of the International if every small fraction came and said : Some of us are for, some against, let us decide for ourselves ? What need would there be for an International, a congress and all this discussion ?

Such laxity had been characteristic of the Second International and was " radically wrong ".[1]   In all issues of revolutionary strategy and tactics the right decisions were most likely to be reached by an institution which represented the whole revolutionary movement and generalized the whole body of revolutionary experience.

This end could be achieved only by rigid institutional discipline. The Second International, Zinoviev explained to the congress, had failed because it " tolerated in its midst parties whose practice and tactics were in flagrant opposition to the tactics of the revolutionary proletariat ".[2]   The revolution in Hungary last year had failed through making the same mistake.[3] Parties could assure their own orthodoxy only by rigorously excluding heretics from their ranks. " Schism, schism, schism ", Lenin had exclaimed in 1904, defending the split in the Russian Social-Democratic Party against his critics.[4]   Throughout the next ten years, in good and bad times, he had fought the Bolshevik battle of doctrinal purity against Menshevik eclecticism. To split the party, to reduce it to numerical insignificance, was a lesser evil than to dilute its doctrine or to weaken its discipline. In 1920 he applied the well-tried principle to Comintern. The essential condition of the admission of a party to Comintern was unqualified acceptance of the programme and rules of Comintern and exclusion of dissentients from the party. When an English delegate to

---

[1] Lenin, *Sochineniya*, xxv, 348, 365.

[2] *Der Zweite Kongress der Kommunist. Internationale* (Hamburg, 1921), p. 572 ; Zinoviev might have said the same of the First International — not, indeed, through the fault of Marx himself.

[3] *Ibid.* pp. 45, 241.   The preamble to the " 21 conditions " (see pp. 193-195 below) also referred to the " lessons " of the Hungarian failure : " The union of the Hungarian communists with the social-democrats cost the Hungarian proletariat dear ".   [4] See Vol. 1, p. 37.

the second congress complained that a majority of English communists would reject such terms, Lenin asked why it was necessary to agree with the majority : the faithful minority could be " organized separately ". Better a split than " to leave the question of the right tactics unanswered ".[1]   Zinoviev made a categorical declaration on this point in the name of the Russian party :

> Should it so happen that our Italian or other comrades were to tell us that they demanded to maintain the connexion with these Right elements, then our party is ready to remain quite alone rather than be connected with the elements which we regard as bourgeois.[2]

The principle of the split to exclude heretics, once adopted, was applied with a bitterness which was inevitable, so long as the heretical leaders were automatically regarded as traitors " sold to the bourgeoisie ". The implications of this doctrine quickly penetrated into the proceedings of Comintern.   Lenin in the *Letter to the English Workers*, in which he recounted his meeting with the British Labour delegation in Moscow, described " the passing over of a majority of the parliamentary and trade-union leaders of the workers to the side of the bourgeoisie " as a " longstanding abscess ".   It was not the avowed enemies of the workers whom it was most urgent to defeat, but the traitors from their own midst.   " The enemy is sitting in your own house ", exclaimed Zinoviev at the second congress.[3]   Lenin taunted Crispien, one of the USPD delegates, with having treated the split between the USPD and the SPD as a " bitter necessity " :

> The independents should not lament that, but should say : The international working class is still under the heel of the labour aristocracy and of the opportunists.

Crispien had said that the revolution could be carried out in Germany only on the condition that it did not impoverish the German workers " too much " :

> A labour aristocracy, which dreads sacrifices, which fears " too much " impoverishment at a time of revolutionary struggle, cannot belong to the party.[4]

[1] Lenin, *Sochineniya*, xxv, 350.
[2] *Der Zweite Kongress der Kommunist. Internationale* (Hamburg, 1921), p. 243.
[3] *Ibid.* p. 111.   [4] Lenin, *Sochineniya*, xxv, 357-358.

Those whom it was desired to cast out were not well-meaning men who took an erroneous view of the correct tactics of revolution; they were renegades and traitors to the proletarian cause. Such was the background of the most famous and important document which issued from the second congress — the " 21 conditions " determining the admission of parties to Comintern. The first congress had made no attempt to define the conditions of membership; nor had IKKI attempted the task. But it could no longer be ignored. Lenin prepared and circulated to the second congress a draft of 19 " conditions of admission to the Communist International ". The draft required each member party of Comintern to conduct propaganda in favour of the proletarian revolution and the dictatorship of the proletariat and be responsible for its party press and publications; to endeavour to fill all responsible posts in the workers' movement with its members, and to secure the removal of reformists and supporters of the Centre; to combine legal with illegal activities and to create an underground organization to prepare for the coming civil war; to conduct propaganda in the army and in the countryside; to denounce all social-patriots and social-pacifists, and to show that no expedients such as international arbitration or a reorganized League of Nations could avail to save humanity from imperialist wars; to break absolutely with all reformists, including well-known reformist leaders; to denounce colonial exploitation, especially by one's own government; to form communist cells, directly responsible to the party, in trade unions, cooperatives and other workers' organizations; to conduct a stubborn campaign against the " yellow " Amsterdam trade union International and to support the new International of the Red trade unions which was in course of formation; to supervise the activity of its representatives in parliament; to organize itself on the principle of democratic centralism with iron discipline and periodical purges; to support by all means every Soviet republic in its struggle against counter-revolutionary forces; to revise its party programme in accordance with the principles of Comintern and to submit it to the congress or to IKKI for confirmation; to accept as binding all decisions of Comintern; to take the name, if it had not already done so, of " communist "; and to call a party congress immediately to ratify its acceptance of the conditions.[1] The 19 draft conditions, though stiff, were a logical formulation of the conception of Comintern propounded during the previous months by Lenin and its other principal sponsors. They were submitted in the first instance to a commission of the congress, which made a few verbal amendments and added, on the motion of Lenin himself, a further " condition " requiring that, in every party now adhering to Comintern, the central committee and other central institutions should be composed, to the extent of at least two-thirds, of members who had previously declared themselves in favour of adhesion. By telescoping two of Lenin's original conditions, the total number of 19 was maintained. The new 19 conditions were then discussed by the plenary congress at three successive sittings. A substantial part of the time was occupied by the speeches of the four USPD delegates, two supporting and two rejecting the conditions, and by recriminations arising out of them. The USPD was the largest and most powerful mass party represented at the congress — a party whose fortunes were rising rapidly ;[2] the crucial question was whether or not it would accept the conditions and adhere to Comintern. The conditions themselves met with comparatively little opposition in the congress. Indeed they were tightened up at the last moment by two further conditions, raising the number to the final 21. One of these required all party organs to publish important documents and decisions of Comintern ; the other provided that members of any party who voted against acceptance of the conditions at the party congress should be expelled from the party. This twenty-first condition, in many ways the most drastic of them, was proposed by the Italian Bordiga and seconded by Humbert-Droz, a delegate from French Switzerland and a former Calvinist pastor, in the most uncompromising speech on the subject delivered at the congress :

> Bordiga's proposal to compel the parties to exclude those
> who vote against the programme of the Communist International

[1] Lenin's original draft of the 19 conditions, published in *Kommunisticheskii Internatsional* on the eve of the congress, is in *Sochineniya*, xxv, 280-284.

[2] In 1919 the SPD had outnumbered the USPD by five to one ; the KPD took no part in the 1919 elections. In the elections held in June 1920 the USPD had polled nearly 5,000,000 votes to the 5,600,000 of the SPD ; the KPD had polled 440,000.

is thoroughly useful in order to carry out a first purge of the extreme Rights. The word " split " frightens all opportunists who put unity before everything. This first purge will naturally be incomplete, but it is the first step to the creation of a genuinely communist party.[1]

The 21 conditions as a whole were then approved with only two dissentient votes.[2]

The 21 conditions were designed, not to complete the formal break with the Second International (this was regarded as already dead), but to destroy any possibility of compromise by excluding from the Third International those elements of the Centre which still had a lurking sympathy with the Second and were seeking a half-way house between them.[3] In Lenin's view these elements were confined mainly to the leaders. What therefore was required was to split the " centrist " parties — notably the USPD, the Italian Socialist Party and the British ILP — by discrediting and excommunicating their leaders, and drawing the loyal rank and file into the orbit of Comintern. The 21 conditions specifically named Turati and Modigliani, Kautsky and Hilferding, Mac-Donald, Longuet and the American Hilquit, as " notorious opportunists " who could in no circumstances be recognized as members of Comintern. On the other hand, in spite of their universality, these stern conditions were not designed in practice to exclude dissidents of the Left, towards whom a surprising tenderness continued to be shown. A resolution of the congress, while

[1] *Der Zweite Kongress der Kommunist. Internationale* (Hamburg, 1921), p. 365 ; Zinoviev afterwards made play at the Halle congress (see pp. 217-222 below) with the fact that this most severe of all the conditions had been proposed not by a Russian, but an Italian, delegate (*USPD: Protokoll über die Verhandlungen des Ausserordentlichen Parteitags zu Halle* (n.d.), p. 175). It seems clear that the Russians would not have proposed or demanded such a condition. It really superseded Lenin's proviso about the two-thirds membership of central committees and central institutions (which was, however, retained in the list of conditions) ; according to Zinoviev's statement at the time (*Der Zweite Kongress der Kommunist. Internationale* (Hamburg, 1921), pp. 235-236), the Russian delegation did not press even this as a " condition ", and would have been content to have the congress express a general wish in this sense.

[2] *Ibid.* p. 400 : the conditions as finally approved are in German, *ibid.* pp. 387-395, in Russian in *Kommunisticheskii Internatsional v Dokumentakh* (1933), pp. 100-104, and Lenin, *Sochineniya*, xxv, 575-579.

[3] Zinoviev much later described the 21 conditions as " a bulwark against centrism " (*Protokoll: Fünfter Kongress der Kommunistischen Internationale* (n.d.), i, 45).

condemning the views of such Left groups as the KAPD, the American IWW and the British shop stewards' committee, admitted that some of these represented " a profoundly proletarian and mass movement, which in its foundations stands on the ground of the root principles of the Communist International "; communists should therefore " not refrain from repeated attempts to unite with these organizations into a single communist party ".[1] Other resolutions of the congress reaffirmed the duty of communists to take part in the work of trade unions and bourgeois parliaments. A special commission wrestled with the vexed question whether the British Communist Party should seek affiliation to the British Labour Party, a loose federation which imposed no doctrinal loyalties on its constituent members; and on its report the congress answered the question by a majority of 58 to 24 in the affirmative.[2] There was a resolution on the agrarian question which has already been cited,[3] and an important debate and sets of theses on the national and colonial question which will be discussed in the next chapter. The second congress of Comintern made an ambitious attempt not only to establish a world-wide communist organization, but also to discuss and lay down the fundamental principles of communist policy in all major questions.

The second congress marked the crowning moment in the history of Comintern as an international force, the moment when the Russian revolution seemed most certainly on the point of transforming itself into the European revolution, with the destinies of the RSFSR merged in those of some broader European unit. No one was more interested in this consummation than the Russian Bolsheviks, who still implicitly believed that their own salvation depended on it. It was no doubt a part of the price of victory that the centre of gravity of the revolutionary movement would move westward across Europe; but this was a price at

[1] *Kommunisticheskii Internatsional v Dokumentakh* (1933), p. 99 ; Radek at the congress justified the " decision to admit syndicalist organizations to the International " on the ground that " we see in syndicalism only a malady of the transition period among revolutionary workers " (*Der Zweite Kongress der Kommunist. Internationale* (Hamburg, 1921), p. 496).
[2] *Ibid.* p. 654.   [3] See Vol. 2, p. 166, note 5.

which it would have been absurd to cavil. A deep paradox therefore underlay the proceedings of the second congress. The Russians were sincerely and eagerly seeking to destroy their own exclusive predominance in the revolutionary movement by spreading revolution all over Europe and the world. Yet, when they failed, when the revolution obstinately stood still at the Russian frontier, everything done at the second congress had the unlooked for consequence of confirming and codifying Russian predominance, so that many came to attribute to some sinister and deep-laid plan what was the inevitable result of the conditions in which the congress had to work. Nowhere was this process more apparent than in the framing of the statute of Comintern which was undertaken by the second congress. This followed closely the statute of the Russian Communist Party. The sovereign organ was the world congress which would in principle meet annually. The executive committee elected by it ruled in its stead in the intervals between its sessions and was " responsible only to the world congress ". The composition of IKKI was a delicate point. According to the decision reached at the second congress it was to be composed of from 15 to 18 members,[1] of whom five were to be provided by " the party of the country in which, by decision of the world congress, the executive committee has its seat ", and the remainder one each by " the other largest national parties ". In the desultory debate on the statute in the plenary session, a Dutch delegate tentatively suggested that IKKI might have its seat in Italy or Norway, and a German delegate half-heartedly proposed Berlin. But it was clear that in present conditions there could be no serious alternative to Moscow ; and, in default of the spread of revolution to the west, IKKI was fated to become, as the Dutch delegate correctly foresaw, " an enlarged Russian executive committee ".[2]

The historical rôle of the second congress, as distinct from its ostensible and even from its conscious purpose, was to establish Russian leadership of Comintern on an impregnable basis. Russian

---

[1] The number was raised immediately after the congress to 21.

[2] The relevant passages of the debate are in *Der Zweite Kongress der Kommunist. Internationale* (Hamburg, 1921), pp. 582-587, 594-597 ; the text of the statute, *ibid.* pp. 602-606 ; the vote for Russia as the seat of IKKI " for the immediate future " was unanimous (*ibid.* p. 659).

leadership throughout the congress was absolute and unchallenged. The Russians enjoyed the usual advantages accruing to the hosts at an international gathering : they could marshal their full available talent on any issue. The visitors were limited to the strength of the delegations actually in Moscow; many of the foreign delegates had made the journey with difficulty, and had been obliged to travel illicitly in order to avoid the ban imposed by their own governments. More important, the Russian delegation invariably spoke with a united voice ; the other principal delegations — German, British, French, Italian and American — were drawn from more than one national party or group and were divided among themselves on major issues, so that a situation automatically arose in which Russian leaders of Comintern played off dissentient foreign delegates against their own more amenable compatriots. Most important of all, leadership was the natural reward of revolutionary achievement. The Russians, and they alone, had proved that they knew how to make a successful revolution : thus and thus had victory been won in October 1917, and thus and thus would it be won elsewhere. One of the ILP delegates who negotiated with IKKI on the eve of the second congress has left a record of his impressions :

> It was very difficult to discuss matters with the leaders of the Third International owing to the strong nationalist direction they adopt. Every question is deeply coloured with ideas peculiarly Russian. I think it is understandable, but certainly the very pontifical attitude they adopt does not make discussion easy. They are quite prepared to admit that revolutions are not metaphysical in their origin ; are the outcome of historical development ; and that social revolution must develop in each country along different lines; but they always return to the point that their tactics are the model on which all socialist method must be based.[1]

It was the natural consequence of Russian prestige rather than of Russian design that the organization of Comintern reflected Russian experience and was framed on a Russian model. The Communist International which would make the world revolution

[1] *Independent Labour Party: Report of the 29th Annual Conference* (1921), pp. 53-54 ; the similar impression of Gorter, the Dutch Left communist, who visited Lenin at this time, is recorded in F. Borkenau, *The Communist International* (1938), p. 191.

was created in the image of the party which had made the Russian revolution.[1] Foreign delegates might cavil at this point or that, but nobody at the congress questioned — at any rate openly — the need for a new International; and nobody had any other prototype to put forward. The foreign parties and their representatives were all too conscious of their inferiority. Some of them made no bones about accepting it:

> What am I [exclaimed Serrati] compared with comrade Lenin? He is the leader of the Russian revolution. I represent a tiny communist socialist party.[2]

And the congress listened in patient docility while Zinoviev expatiated in turn on the defects of almost every communist or would-be communist party in Europe except the Russian.[3] Nor did lapse of time alter the position. The disappointment of the bright hopes entertained in the summer of 1920 merely widened the gap between the authority of those who had succeeded in making their revolution and those who had failed, and left the organization of Comintern firmly cast in a Russian mould.

Russian predominance in Comintern was further promoted by the procedure of " splitting " which was systematized by the second congress and became a regular instrument of Comintern policy. In most parties leaders soon began to arise who were known as the spokesmen and protégés of Comintern and were commonly referred to in Moscow as " the best representatives of the proletariat " — a phrase occurring for the first time in a resolution of the second congress and frequently on Zinoviev's lips. " In all countries of the world ", wrote Lenin, summing up the results of the congress, " the best representatives of the revolutionary workers have taken their stand on the side of communism." [4] But these leaders were not necessarily the best qualified to give an objective analysis of the situation in their respective countries, nor did they always enjoy the largest measure of support and

[1] Thus Hilferding, the Right USPD leader, was able to make an effective attack at the Halle congress on the organization of Comintern merely by quoting Rosa Luxemburg's strictures of 1904 on Lenin's organization of the Bolshevik group (*USPD : Protokoll über die Verhandlungen des Ausserordentlichen Parteitags zu Halle* (n.d.), pp. 194-196).

[2] *Der Zweite Kongress der Kommunist. Internationale* (Hamburg, 1921), p. 340.

[3] *Ibid.* pp. 243-255.   [4] Lenin, *Sochineniya*, xxv, 370.

confidence in their own parties. The charge was even heard that the main motive of the splitting policy was to destroy the independent power of the national parties and to make them subservient to Moscow.[1] The charge was certainly false, at least for this early period. But the temptation to rate docility in national leaders higher than independent judgment was inherent in a predominantly Russian organization; and such Comintern was bound to remain, so long as revolution had triumphed in Russia and in no other country.

While, however, the second congress seemed to have registered a sweeping victory for the principles of a highly disciplined organization and strict doctrinal orthodoxy, the old dilemma of reconciling these principles with the winning of mass support — the dilemma which had been so easily overcome in Russia and yet proved so insuperable in the west — recurred in a new form. Resolutions of the second congress enjoined communist parties in bourgeois democratic countries to participate in parliamentary elections by running candidates of their own, or, if this was impossible, by supporting candidates of other parties. The injunction was meaningless except on the assumption that the parties were to seek mass support, and to act in a way calculated to win such support. But this involved questions of tactics and of principle. The parliamentary game was played in every country under different and constantly changing national rules; it was not likely to be played with success by parties bound to follow uniform instructions issued in Moscow, where conceptions of parliamentary action were governed largely by recollections of the Tsarist Duma. But the obstacles were not merely tactical or formal. The injunction of the second congress to foreign communist parties to " utilize bourgeois state institutions in order to destroy them "[2] was the counterpart of Lenin's injunction to British communists to support British Labour leaders by way of

---

[1] It was made specifically against Zinoviev by Angelica Balabanov, a highly subjective witness, in *Erinnerungen und Erlebnisse* (1927), p. 257 ; Martov made it more generally at the Halle congress where he described the purpose of the splitting policy as being " to erect a solid wall against the invasion of elements capable of claiming a share in the taking of decisions for themselves and for their own parties " (*USPD : Protokoll über die Verhandlungen des Ausserordentlichen Parteitags zu Halle* (n.d.), pp. 210-211).

[2] *Kommunisticheskii Internatsional v Dokumentakh* (1933), p. 114.

hanging them. But these injunctions presupposed that the loyalty of the masses to state institutions and to Labour leaders could be effectively undermined. So long as this presupposition was not realized, communist parties in most western countries had the choice of two alternatives. They could retain the purity and rigidity of their doctrine at the cost of remaining small sects composed largely of intellectuals and without influence on the masses; or they could win influence in existing mass parties of the Left by compromises which involved acceptance of a temporary and conditional loyalty to existing institutions and existing leaders. It was this second course which was to expose them to charges of duplicity.

The issue of participation in the trade unions was analogous, but even more complicated. Theoretically, it was possible to argue that the trade unions were a by-product of bourgeois capitalism; that, like the political parties of the Second International, they had betrayed the cause of the workers in 1914 by supporting their respective national governments, and were by their nature incapable of a revolutionary rôle; and that communists should therefore boycott the existing unions and form new and separate associations of communist workers. This was the attitude adopted at the second congress, with some reservations, by most of the British, Italian and American delegates. Theoretically also it was possible to argue, though nobody now openly espoused this view, that the minor improvements in the lot of the worker which trade unions sought to achieve were not in themselves desirable, since they blunted the edge of the workers' discontent and thus tended to postpone the ultimate revolution. In opposition to both these views, the Bolsheviks maintained that the past defects of the trade unions had been due, in part to a corrupted leadership, in part to the fact that the unions in the advanced countries had hitherto contained a disproportionate number of highly skilled and privileged workers — the " labour aristocracy " — whose interests often ranged them with the bourgeoisie rather than with the less privileged members of their own class. The war had in all countries brought about a mass influx of workers into the trade unions and thus changed their character and potentialities. Far from splitting away from the existing unions and thus isolating themselves from the proletarian masses, communists must enter the unions and revolutionize them by working on the mass membership and raising it in revolt against leaders who no longer represented its true interests. The more firmly Comintern was wedded to a policy of restricting the size of communist parties by insistence on rigid discipline and doctrinal purity, the more essential it became to maintain contact with the masses of the workers through their trade unions.

But the decision to participate in the trade unions, like the decision to participate in parliamentary elections, was the beginning and not the end of embarrassment. In the first place, it appeared to commit communists to support existing unions, however reactionary, and to oppose break-away movements, however revolutionary in character and purpose. This issue was acute in the United States, where a minority of skilled workers were grouped in the American Federation of Labour, built on the craft union principle, and the only appeal to the mass of under-paid, largely immigrant, unskilled labour was made by the syndicalist and revolutionary IWW. In Germany the revolutionary shop stewards had attempted to organize the workers outside the trade unions; in Great Britain the shop stewards' movement, though not formally outside the trade unions, had arisen in face of their opposition, and had at the outset a syndicalist complexion. The attitude of communists to these dissident movements was difficult to define.

The second embarrassment of the Bolshevik attitude was graver still. The declared purpose of the Bolsheviks was to strengthen the cohesion, comprehensiveness and power of the trade unions by bringing them under communist leadership. But, except on the assumption that this could be achieved at a single stroke — or, in other words, that the proletarian revolution was imminent — the execution of this purpose was bound to require a long period of internecine warfare within the unions which would split and weaken them and all but destroy their existing power. Lenin, in a much-criticized passage of *The Infantile Disease of " Leftism " in Communism*, had foreseen the probability that " the leaders of opportunism " would use every device, fair or foul, to exclude or expel the communists from the trade unions :

One must know how to resist all this, to accept any and every sacrifice, even — in case of necessity — to resort to every kind of trick, cunning, illegal expedient, concealment, suppression of the truth, in order to penetrate into the trade unions, to remain in them, to conduct in them, at whatever cost, communist work.[1]

Radek, at the second congress of Comintern, came near to an open admission that communist policy meant the destruction of the existing unions as a preliminary to their transformation into the bigger and better unions of the future :

We shall attempt to transform the trade unions into fighting organizations. . . . We are going into the trade unions, not in order to preserve them, but in order to create that cohesion among the workers on which alone the great industrial unions of the social revolution can be built.[2]

Such a programme sounded agreeably enough in Bolshevik ears. In Russia the trade-union tradition was weak. Few trade unions had wielded any effective power or commanded any profound allegiance among their members ; and some of these few had been dominated by Mensheviks, who turned them into centres of resistance to the new régime. But in central and western Europe the trade unions were regarded by the mass of the workers as at any rate partial bulwarks against the otherwise untempered oppression of capitalist power. Any policy which promised even temporarily to split, weaken and perhaps destroy these bulwarks in the interest of a remote and uncertain future was bound to encounter deep suspicion and obstinate opposition, which was mistakenly attributed in Moscow to the machinations of a few leaders or of a " labour aristocracy ".

The leaders of Comintern at the second congress further complicated the difficult and delicate task that lay ahead by a step which revealed in a stark form all the incongruities of their trade union policy. A loosely organized International Federation of Trade Unions (IFTU) had existed before 1914, having no formal associations with the Second International, but akin to it in outlook. Since the Bolsheviks were firmly committed to the idea of creating a Third International to replace the defunct Second, it seemed in

[1] Lenin, *Sochineniya*, xxv, 198.
[2] *Der Zweite Kongress der Kommunist. Internationale* (Hamburg, 1921), p. 499.

the first days of the revolution a natural corollary to create a new trade union organization to replace the defunct IFTU. World revolution was at hand, and a resurrection of the international organs of the old order was unthinkable. The first All-Russian Congress of Trade Unions in January 1918 recorded its determination " to assist by all means the rebirth of the international trade union movement ", and convened an international trade union conference to meet in Petrograd in February 1918.[1] The invitation was broadcast to the world ; but in the conditions of the time it is not surprising that it provoked no response whatever. This did not, however, mean the abandonment of the project. The few communists who doubted its usefulness did so not because they feared a clash with IFTU (whose demise was taken for granted), but because they believed that trade unions belonged to the reactionary capitalist order, and had no part to play in the building of socialism. The official resuscitation of IFTU, shorn of its German membership, in July 1919, with a central office at Amsterdam (from which it came to be commonly known as the " Amsterdam International "), did not seriously affect this mood. The difficulties of reviving IFTU seemed at least as likely to prove fatal as those attending the rebirth of the Second International. Just as the Second International had " capitulated " before the Third, declared the president of the Petrograd trade union council at the end of 1919, so the time had come for all the trade unions of the world " to unite into a single powerful international organization ready to fight side by side with the Third International ".[2]

The establishment of relations with the trade unions of western Europe did not become practical politics till the spring of 1920, when the civil war seemed over, when the allied blockade had been lifted, and when the first tentative diplomatic contacts were being

[1] *Pervyi Vserossiiskii S"ezd Professional'nykh Soyuzov* (1918), p. 365. This decision was not taken in any spirit of hostility to the western trade unions, whose will to cooperate was naïvely assumed. The preface to the official record of the first All-Russian Congress of Trade Unions written by Tomsky and dated September 1918 is full of praise for the western trade-union movement (*ibid.* pp. i-xi). Lozovsky stated many years later that " there was no idea, even immediately after the October revolution, of establishing a revolutionary trade union International " (A. Lozovsky, *The World's Trade Union Movement* (1925), p. 126).
[2] *Kommunisticheskii Internatsional*, No. 7-8 (November-December 1919), cols. 983-988.

made.[1] Zinoviev now made a start by presenting to the ninth party congress in March 1920 a recommendation that " the Russian trade-union movement should take the initiative in forming a Red International of trade unions, just as the Russian Communist Party did in founding the Third International ".[2] The question did not, however, seem particularly urgent, and the congress did not discuss it. A month later, a decisive event made further inaction impossible. In April 1920 the western trade unions and IFTU took an active part in organizing the Washington conference at which the International Labour Organization (ILO) was founded. It was when, in Lozovsky's words, IFTU decided to " wed its fate to that of the League of Nations through the medium of the ILO ", that " the need made itself felt for a centre . . . for the concentration of the Left-wing trade-union movement of the whole world ".[3] The ILO was the embodiment of that notion of class collaboration which was the very antithesis of the class struggle and the dictatorship of the proletariat. At the third All-Russian Congress of Trade Unions in the same month Zinoviev launched a bitter denunciation of the " social traitors ", who, obeying the dictates of the capitalists, were attempting to rebuild the " yellow " Amsterdam International and thus to compensate for the collapse of the Second International. The time was ripe for " a really proletarian international union of Red trade unions standing for the dictatorship of the proletariat "; and he hoped that " the proletarian trade unions of the whole world " would attend the forthcoming congress of Comintern and constitute themselves a section of Comintern.[4] The congress resolution recorded the decision of the Russian trade unions to " enter the Third International " and to appeal to " the revolutionary trade unions of all countries " to follow their example; the central trade union council was to take steps in conjunction with IKKI to convene an international trade union congress.[5] It might have been argued that, if the policy of penetration into existing trade

[1] The delay in creating a trade union International after the successful foundation of Comintern is partly explicable by the fact that before 1920 Bolshevik control of the Russian trade-union movement was still precarious.

[2] G. Zinoviev, *Sochineniya*, vi (1929), 345.

[3] A. Lozovsky, *The World's Trade Union Movement* (1925), p. 127.

[4] *Tretii Vserossiiskii S"ezd Professional'nykh Soyuzov* (1920), i (Plenumy), 14-15.   [5] *Ibid.* i, 145.

unions, consistently preached by the Bolsheviks and recently confirmed by Lenin in *The Infantile Disease of " Leftism " in Communism*, were successful, it would slowly but surely change the leadership of the unions and therefore of IFTU, and transform the whole organization without destroying it. But this process seemed too pedestrian and too gradual for enthusiasts who believed that European revolution was now only a matter of weeks. It seemed essential to accelerate or anticipate the process by creating forthwith a new International, so that trade unions which were successfully penetrated and won over could at once disaffiliate from IFTU and join the new organization of " Red " trade unions. In pursuance of this idea, the matter was discussed with Williams and Purcell, two prominent British trade-unionists who were members of the visiting British Labour delegation ; both of them apparently expressed themselves in favour of a new trade union International.[1]

The ground had therefore been prepared when the second congress of Comintern met in the summer of 1920 under the revolutionary spell of the victorious march into Poland. Two of the 21 conditions of admission to Comintern adopted by the congress related to the trade unions. The ninth condition made it obligatory for party members to work actively in the trade unions and at the same time to " expose the treachery of the social-patriots and the vacillation of the centre " (the dual attitude laid down by Lenin in *The Infantile Disease of " Leftism " in Communism*) ; the tenth prescribed " an obstinate struggle against the Amsterdam ' International ' of the yellow trade union federations ". A long resolution on the trade unions followed the same line.[2] It was carried by a large majority, though it was opposed in a heated debate by most of the British and American delegates, who wished to reject existing trade unions and to found new revolutionary unions, and by a single Italian delegate who regarded trade unions as *per se* counter-revolutionary.[3] The congress

---

[1] B. Vinogradov, *Mirovoi Proletariat i SSSR* (1928), p. 72 ; Lenin mentioned to Murphy the approval of the project by Williams and Purcell (J. T. Murphy, *New Horizons* (1941), p. 157).

[2] *Kommunisticheskii Internatsional v Dokumentakh* (1933), pp. 120-126.

[3] *Der Zweite Kongress der Kommunist. Internationale* (Hamburg, 1921), pp. 510-526, 610-638 : Radek admitted in his report that " far-reaching differences of opinion " existed on the trade union issue, and that " many members in all communist parties " were in favour of forming new trade unions (*ibid.* pp. 622-623).

refrained from making any pronouncement on the creation of a trade union International — perhaps an indication that a majority could not easily have been obtained for it. But, while the congress was in session, a group representing the Russian, Italian and Bulgarian delegations, some members of the British delegation, and a single French delegate of the extreme Left, doubtfully claiming to speak for eight million organized workers, decided to create an International Trade Union Council (Mezhsovprof) whose principal function would be to organize " an international congress of Red trade unions ". Lozovsky became president of the new council, with Tom Mann and Rosmer as vice-presidents. The close dependence of Mezhsovprof on IKKI was shown by the proposal that IKKI should issue an appeal " to all trade unions of the world " exposing the " yellow Amsterdam International " and inviting them to join the new trade union International.[1]

This fateful decision was taken at a moment when the revolutionary tide was still in full flood, when the Second International was assumed to be dead, and when the minor success achieved in the revival of IFTU seemed to constitute the main obstacle to the capture of the international workers' movement by the communists.[2] The decision was the opening of a campaign to split the trade-union movement with the Moscow and Amsterdam Internationals as the rallying points for two warring and fratricidal factions. But a prolonged war of this kind was bound to bring to light the latent incompatibility between the duty imposed on communists of working within the existing trade unions and the duty of splitting the existing movement against Amsterdam and in favour of Moscow, between a policy of peaceful infiltration on the national plane and a policy of frontal attack on the international plane ; and this dilemma, which would not have arisen if world

---

[1] *Ibid.* pp. 622, 636-637.

[2] " The chief enemy is Amsterdam [i.e. IFTU], not Brussels [i.e. the Second International] ", exclaimed Zinoviev at the congress (*ibid.* p. 638). " Politically the Second International is smashed ", he repeated at Halle three months later, ". . . but the so-called trade union International is unfortunately still something, it is the bulwark of the international bourgeoisie " (*USPD: Protokoll über die Verhandlungen des Ausserordentlichen Parteitags zu Halle* (n.d.), p. 151) ; this accounted for the extreme bitterness of the attacks on IFTU.

revolution had in fact been just round the corner, was never faced by Lenin or by the other Bolshevik leaders in the new conditions. The proceedings by which Mezhsovprof was set up in July 1920 were enveloped in a haze of confusion on this very point. Only the Russians and their close allies the Bulgarians were whole-hearted advocates of the decision. The Italian party, like the Bulgarian party, was the heir of a socialist party which enjoyed trade union support in the past, and had not therefore to contend with divided loyalties in the Italian unions. But, even so, the Italian attitude was divided and equivocal.[1] Still greater confusion reigned in the British delegation. Murphy, who attended the meeting at which the decision to create Mezhsovprof was taken and became the British representative on it, afterwards recorded that, " had there been the slightest suggestion of splitting the trade unions ", the project would " of course " have had no British support.[2] Only Tanner, a leader of the shop stewards' movement and the one influential trade-unionist in the delegation, seems to have recognized the contradiction between the proposal to " remain in the unions at the national level " and the creation of an independent international organ ; and Zinoviev denied him the floor when he sought to expound this view in the plenary session of the congress.[3] The founding of Mezhsovprof thus carried Comintern a long step further on the ambiguous course on which it had been launched by *The Infantile Disease of " Leftism " in Communism*. It was a step taken in a moment of hot-headed enthusiasm and in the firm conviction of the imminence of the European revolution ; and a device designed to bridge a short transition and prepare the way for the great consummation had unexpected and fatal consequences when the interim period dragged on into months and years.

[1] Lozovsky records the " serious differences of opinion " which arose between himself and D'Aragona, the spokesman of the Italian delegation : " For several days I discussed with him the principles which divided us. Serrati then proposed a formula which sought to make a compromise, but was in my view not sufficiently clear. When I submitted Serrati's proposal to Lenin, Lenin said : ' It does, of course, contain unclear points, but that is not import-ant ; only create a centre, clarity will come later ' " (A. Lozovsky, *Lenin und die Gewerkschaftsbewegung* (Hamburg, 1924), p. 17).

[2] J. T. Murphy, *New Horizons* (1941), p. 158.

[3] *Der Zweite Kongress der Kommunist. Internationale* (Hamburg, 1921), pp. 637-638.

The period of the second congress of Comintern coincided with the rapid and continuous advance of the Red Army into Poland. Curzon's note to Chicherin from the Spa conference [1] had been despatched a few days before the congress opened. It proposed that armistice negotiations should be opened immediately between Soviet Russia and Poland on the basis of a line drawn up in the autumn of 1919, after a close study of ethnographical data, by the experts of the peace conference (afterwards known as the " Curzon line "), and significantly added that the British Government was " bound by the Covenant of the League of Nations to defend the integrity and independence of Poland within the limits of her legitimate ethnographical frontiers ". On July 17, 1920, Chicherin, while taunting the British Government on its belated interest in peace between Soviet Russia and Poland, agreed to open negotiations if the Polish Government requested it, and offered to Poland a frontier more favourable to her than the Curzon line.[2] On July 22 the Polish Government at length applied to Moscow for terms. But the Soviet Government was in no hurry. The opening of negotiations was delayed on various pretexts, and in the last days of July the Red Army crossed the Curzon line and entered what was undisputed Polish territory. After Brest-Litovsk fell on August 1, no serious resistance was to be expected till the outer defences of Warsaw were reached.

The decision to carry the war into Poland was preceded by controversy in the inner party counsels. Trotsky opposed the advance both on political and on military grounds. Lenin countered his objection with the specific argument that the Polish workers in Warsaw and other centres would rise on the approach of the Red Army and greet it as their deliverer. Radek, who knew Poland, warned Lenin against these hopes. But his views on Germany had earned him a reputation for pessimism, and Lenin called him a defeatist.[3] Stalin had sensibly pointed out, before the offensive began, that " the rear of the Polish armies is substantially different from the rear of Kolchak and Denikin ", being " homogeneous and *nationally* united ", so that, once Polish troops were

---

[1] See p. 164 above.
[2] Both notes are in Klyuchnikov i Sabanin, *Mezhdunarodnaya Politika*, iii, i (1928), 34-38.
[3] Klara Zetkin, *Erinnerungen an Lenin* (Vienna, 1929), pp. 20-21.

defending Polish soil, it would be " difficult to contend with them " ; and as late as the end of June he attacked " the bragga-docio and noxious self-complacency " of comrades who " call for a ' march on Warsaw ' " or " proudly declare that they will make peace only in ' Red Soviet Warsaw ' ".[1] But when the decisive moment came, Stalin did not make his voice heard. Trotsky was supported only by Rykov.[2] Lenin's view prevailed and the advance proceeded. Soviet troops had helped the Reds in Finland in the winter of 1917–1918 ; units of the Red Army had helped to establish Soviet republics in Estonia and Latvia at the end of 1918, and were to do the same in Georgia in 1921. But in all these cases local communists had provided a partial basis for the enterprise. The decision to march on Warsaw, coinciding with the second congress of Comintern, and taken at a moment when all caution had been swept aside by an enthusiastic faith in the imminence of the European revolution, imparted to the military campaign a distinctively revolutionary fervour which made it unlike any other war in Soviet history. That the Red Army was not a Russian, but an international, army, serving not the national interests of a country but the international interests of a class, had been accepted doctrine from the first ; the founding of Comintern seemed to provide the Red Army with a political counterpart. " I can assure you ", exclaimed Trotsky at the first congress of Comintern, " that the communist workers who form the real kernel of this army regard themselves not only as the forces defending the Russian socialist republic, but also as the Red Army of the Third Inter-national." [3] At the second congress the triumphant advance of the Red Army seemed the irrefutable demonstration of this prin-ciple. On the eve of the congress Tukhachevsky, the commander of the Red Army in its advance towards the west, wrote a letter to Zinoviev in which he argued that the proletariat must be prepared " for the forthcoming civil war, for the moment of a world attack

---

[1] Stalin, *Sochineniya*, iv, 323-324, 333.

[2] Trotsky twice mentions Rykov's support (*Moya Zhizn'* (Berlin, 1930), ii, 192 ; *Stalin* (N.Y., 1946), p. 328) ; on the first occasion he does not mention Stalin, on the second he names him among those who supported Lenin. Accord-ing to the chronology attached to Stalin's collected works (*Sochineniya*, iv, 474-475), Stalin was absent from Moscow at the front from July 12, 1920, till the middle of August.

[3] *Der I. Kongress der Kommunistischen Internationale* (Hamburg, 1921), p. 49.

by all the armed forces of the proletariat on armed world capitalism ", and proposed that, " considering the inevitability of world civil war in the near future ", Comintern should proceed to create a general staff.[1] This suggestion was not pursued. But at the opening session of the congress an address to the Red Army was proposed by the Italian delegate Serrati, who hoped that the day was near when " the proletarian Red Army will consist not only of Russian proletarians, but of proletarians of the whole world ", and greeted it as " one of the chief forces of world history ".[2]

Nevertheless, while everything that was done in the summer of 1920 was rooted in Bolshevik tradition, it represented one of those shifts of emphasis, one of those abrupt transitions of policy, which were tantamount to a radical change of front and exposed the Soviet Government to well-founded charges of bad faith. In the first months of 1920 unmistakable diplomatic feelers had been put out for a temporary accommodation with the capitalist world. Chicherin, Krasin and Radek seemed to occupy the centre of the stage as the artificers of the new policy of caution and compromise : Zinoviev and Bukharin were left to theorize about world revolution, but were relegated to the wings. At the end of January 1920 it had been vigorously denied that " the Russian Soviet Government wishes to plant communism in Polish soil with the bayonets of Red Army men ".[3] As late as July 20, 1920, while the delegates were assembling for the Comintern congress, Sovnarkom solemnly reaffirmed that " we are as far from any kind of attack on the independence of Poland or on the inviolability of her territory as in the days of our greatest military difficulties ".[4] But within a few days such assurances were forgotten or explained away. Military victories and the enthusiasm of the delegates revived a flagging faith in world revolution and in Zinoviev's waning star. With Lenin won over, caution was thrown to the winds and the revolutionary war begun in earnest. As soon as the Red Army crossed the frontier, a " provisional Polish revolutionary committee " was formed " in agreement with the Russian Communist Party and with its participation and that of the Red Army

[1] M. N. Tukhachevsky, *Voina Klassov* (1921), pp. 139-140.
[2] *Der Zweite Kongress der Kommunist. Internationale* (Hamburg, 1921), pp. 42-44.   [3] See p. 159 above.
[4] Klyuchnikov i Sabanin, *Mezhdunarodnaya Politika*, iii, i (1928), 43.

command ", and moved forward in the wake of the army. Its president was Markhlevsky, and among its members were Dzerzhinsky, Unshlikht and Kon — three veteran Polish Bolsheviks and a former leader of the Left Polish Socialist Party : it was to hand over its authority to the Polish Communist Party on arrival in Warsaw.[1] And Warsaw was only a beginning. " Near to it ", as Lenin said afterwards, " lies the centre of world imperialism which rests on the Versailles treaty " ; Poland was " the last bulwark against the Bolsheviks ".[2] How crucial it was, was shown by the eagerness with which the western Powers rushed munitions and military missions to Warsaw to stave off the threat. But most important of all, in Lenin's mind, was the appeal which the advance on Warsaw made to the workers of the capitalist world :

> Great are the military victories of the Soviet republic of workers and peasants over the landowners and capitalists, over the Yudeniches, the Kolchaks, the Denikins, the white Poles, and their backers — France, England, America, Japan.
> But greater still is our victory over the minds and hearts of the workers, of the toilers, of the masses oppressed by the capitalists, the victory of communist ideas and communist organizations throughout the world.
> The revolution of the proletariat, the downfall of the yoke of capitalism is on the march : it will come in all the countries of the earth.[3]

When German workers in Danzig went on strike rather than unload munitions for Poland, when British workers not only refused to load such cargoes but formed " councils of action " and threatened the British Prime Minister with revolution if help were sent to Poland,[4] then Bolsheviks could not help believing that the

[1] Y. Markhlevsky, *Voina i Mir mezhdu Burzhuaznoi Pol'shoi i Proletarskoi Rossiei* (Russian transl. from Polish, 1921), p. 22.
[2] Lenin, *Sochineniya*, xxv, 377.
[3] *Ibid.* xxv, 371.
[4] On August 10, 1920, a delegation from the central " council of action " was received by Lloyd George ; its spokesman was Ernest Bevin who *inter alia* said : " They had no hesitation in laying their cards on the table, and, if war were carried on directly in support of Poland or indirectly in support of General Wrangel, there would be a match set to explosive material, the result of which none of them could foresee " (*The Times*, August 11, 1920). On August 12 Wrangel, who had collected the remnants of Denikin's forces in the Crimea, and was advancing in South Russia, received the *de facto* recognition of the French, but not of the British, Government.

victory of communism " over the minds and hearts of the workers " had been won.

When the second congress of Comintern ended on August 7, 1920, the Soviet advance on Warsaw was proceeding rapidly and almost unopposed, and optimism and enthusiasm were unbounded. Arrangements were at last made for the Soviet and Polish peace delegations to meet at Minsk on August 11 ; and on the previous evening Kamenev in London communicated the Soviet peace terms to Lloyd George. They proposed, as had been promised, to rectify the Curzon line in favour of Poland in the regions of Belostok and Kholm. Poland was to limit her armed forces to 50,000 men, together with not more than 10,000 officers and administrative personnel ; in addition to this, a civilian militia was to be recruited for the maintenance of order. No reparations were demanded, but the Polish Government was to undertake to distribute land to the families of Polish citizens killed or disabled in the war. Lloyd George considered the terms reasonable, and advised the Polish Government to accept them. But when the terms were finally laid before the Polish delegation on August 17 (another unexplained delay had occurred), they were found to contain a proviso, not included in the summary communicated by Kamenev to Lloyd George, to the effect that the proposed civilian militia should be recruited exclusively from the workers.[1] This, and the provision for the distribution of the land, were clearly meant as attempts to alter the class structure of the Polish state in the interests of revolution : the first constitution of the Red Army confined it to workers and peasants.[2] Discussion of these terms did not, however, proceed far ; for the situation underwent a kaleidoscopic change. On August 16 a powerful Polish counter offensive had been launched. Within a few days the Red Army was retreating as rapidly as it had advanced.

Many explanations were afterwards offered of the Soviet defeat. Later Soviet military experts, enjoying the advantages of hindsight, tended to condemn the whole campaign as a military miscalculation : the Red Army was inadequately equipped and

[1] The full text of the terms is in Klyuchnikov i Sabanin, *Mezhdunarodnaya Politika*, iii, i (1928), 47-49 ; the summary presented by Kamenev to Lloyd George is in *The Times*, August 11, 1920. According to L. Fischer, *The Soviets in World Affairs* (1930), i, 269, the proviso about the civilian militia was deliberately omitted by Kamenev.   [2] See p. 62 above.

prepared, in everything except enthusiasm, for so serious an enterprise as the invasion of Poland.[1] Tukhachevsky, the commander of the forces advancing on Warsaw, was criticized for having devoted his main strength to an attempt to encircle Warsaw from the north, thus exposing his main front to a disastrous counterattack; this was regarded by some as a political manœuvre designed to cut off the Polish corridor and establish contact with the German Reichswehr. Finally, the southern army advancing on Lvov failed in the critical last days to respond promptly to an order from the commander-in-chief, Sergei Kamenev, to move north to the rescue of the troops in front of Warsaw, though it is not clear whether this was due to a failure in communications, to the impetuous obstinacy of Egorov its commander and of Budenny its cavalry leader, or to political jealousies.[2] Political as well as military blunders were made. The " provisional Polish revolutionary committee ", when it first set up its authority in Belostok, is said to have antagonized Polish communists by entrusting the administration to Russians and Jews.[3] But, whatever specific errors may have been committed, none of them was primarily responsible for the disaster. Nobody, except in the brief intoxication of unexpectedly easy military triumphs, had really believed that the Red Army could conquer Poland. Lenin and those who had voted with him for the advance had all counted on the Red

[1] An objective summary of the campaign, together with references to some of the military authorities, is in W. H. Chamberlin, *The Russian Revolution 1917-1921* (1935), ii, 311-314 ; Tukhachevsky's view, coinciding in the main with that of Trotsky, was expressed in lectures on the campaign delivered at the staff college in 1923, and reprinted *in extenso* in J. Pilsudski, *L'Année 1920* (French transl. from Polish, 1929), pp. 203-255.

[2] According to the case put forward in L. Trotsky, *Moya Zhizn'* (Berlin, 1930), ii, 192-193, and in more detail and with greater bitterness in L. Trotsky, *Stalin* (N.Y., 1946), pp. 328-332, Stalin, as representative of the military-revolutionary council with the southern army, induced Egorov and Budenny to persist in the advance on Lvov through jealousy of Smilga, his opposite number with the central army, who would share with Tukhachevsky the glory of the capture of Warsaw.

[3] Y. Markhlevsky, *Voina i Mir mezhdu Burzhuaznoi Pol'shoi i Proletarskoi Rossiei* (Russian transl. from Polish, 1921), p. 25. This blunder, and others like it, may have been due not so much to inadvertence or to chauvinism as to an inherent difficulty of the situation. Throughout the towns of eastern Poland the Polish element was confined mainly to the land-owning and official classes ; Jews formed a majority, or a large minority, of the urban population and supplied a majority of the local communists.

proletariat of Poland. The underground Polish Communist Party attempted, according to a subsequent statement, to call a general strike. But the response was limited to the miners in a few pits in the Dombrowa region in the extreme south-west, and the movement was easily suppressed.[1] When the Polish workers of Warsaw failed to rise, or even joined the national army to defend the capital,[2] the enterprise was doomed. It was not the Red Army, but the cause of world revolution, which suffered defeat in front of Warsaw in August 1920. The defeat was also significant in terms of the balance of forces in Soviet Russia itself. The peasant army had fought valiantly and successfully — and was to do so again — against the " white " invaders who challenged the survival of the Soviet régime. But the same peasant army now showed once more that it was formidable for defence and not for offence, and that, while it would fight obstinately on Russian soil, it had no stomach for the fight to carry the proletarian revolution into other lands. The Menshevik Dan put the point forcefully in a contemporary diagnosis of the event :

> The campaign against Warsaw irrefutably demonstrated the impossibility of an offensive " communist " war for the Red Army, and in this sense marked the real turning-point in the foreign policy of the Bolsheviks. . . . And after the shortest interval the same Red Army, which had proved impotent in attack against Poland, displayed prodigies of immortal valour and invincibility in the war with Wrangel, that epigone of Tsarist-feudal reaction. What could be clearer than this historical illustration ? And how could it be more strikingly emphasised that the real victor in all the civil wars of the Bolshevik period was the Russian *peasant* and nobody else ? [3]

---

[1] *Protokoll des III. Kongresses der Kommunistischen Internationale* (Hamburg, 1921), p. 581.

[2] The appearance of Polish workers as volunteers in the Polish forces confronting them is said to have had a discouraging effect on the morale of the Red Army (V. Putna, *K Visle i Obratno* (1927), pp. 137-138) ; an observer who was in Minsk during the campaign speaks of wholesale desertions (F. Dan, *Dva Goda Skitanii* (Berlin, 1922), pp. 73-74). Tukhachevsky, on the other hand, apparently refused to accept this diagnosis : " All the talk of the revival of national sentiment in the Polish working class in connexion with our offensive is simply the consequence of our defeat " (J. Pilsudski, *L'Année 1920* (French transl. from Polish, 1921), p. 231).

[3] F. Dan, *Dva Goda Skitanii* (Berlin, 1922), p. 74.

The fiasco of the advance into Poland may count as a first symptom of the reassertion of the power of the peasant to dictate Soviet policy which manifested itself in the following year in the introduction of NEP.

The completeness of the defeat soon became apparent. By the end of August the Red Army on the main front was back across the Curzon line, and during September the Polish forces established positions well in advance of the line held by them when hostilities began in April, though less favourable than the line which the Soviet Government had been prepared to concede in the previous winter.[1] Here a halt was called by both sides. If Lenin now recognized the folly of trying to revolutionize Poland at the point of the bayonet, Pilsudski had learned the hazards of attempting to penetrate too deeply into Soviet territory ; moreover, Wrangel, whom Pilsudski had no desire to assist, was scoring his first successes in southern Russia. Lenin found himself in the same position as at Brest-Litovsk of impressing on his colleagues and compatriots the need for an " unfavourable " peace.[2] But this time the opposition was slight. On October 12, 1920, Soviet and Polish delegates signed an armistice on the line then held by the opposing armies.[3] This line was confirmed by the treaty of peace which was signed five months later in Riga on March 18, 1921, and formed the basis of relations between Soviet Russia and Poland for nearly two decades. Besides ceding to Poland a large tract of predominantly White Russian territory, the new frontier allowed a broad wedge of Polish territory to be drawn between Lithuania and the RSFSR, thus isolating Lithuania and closing a potential channel of Soviet penetration towards the west.[4]

The Soviet-Polish war of 1920 had far-reaching repercussions on more than one aspect of Soviet foreign policy. But these repercussions were not immediately felt in anything like their full

---

[1] See p. 155, note 1 above.
[2] Klara Zetkin, *Erinneringen an Lenin* (Vienna, 1929), p. 21 ; the rather exaggerated comparison with Brest-Litovsk was made by Lenin himself. As late as September 22, Lenin was counting on the probability of a " winter campaign " (*Sochineniya*, xxv, 379-380).
[3] *RSFSR: Sbornik Deistvuyushchikh Dogovorov*, i (1921), No. 14, pp. 63-73.
[4] *Ibid.* ii (1921), No. 51, pp. 43-71.

force, nor were the broader lessons of the defeat digested at once. The military set-back was outweighed a few weeks later by the victory over Wrangel which finally ended the civil war with the rout of the last " white " invader ; and the temporary sacrifice of territory to Poland was still compensated by the thought that the birth of a Soviet Poland in the near future would make frontiers unimportant. The enthusiasm generated at the second congress of Comintern and the drives set in motion by it were not immediately relaxed. Like the policies of war-communism at home, the revolutionary offensive in Europe was continued throughout the winter of 1920–1921. From its second congress Comintern had emerged as the central directing staff of the forces of world revolution with national parties in the principal countries grouped around it. The headquarters of Comintern, where, beneath all international trappings, the voice of the Russian party was ultimately decisive, dealt separately with parties which normally had no dealings with one another except through the intermediary of Comintern. This was the essence of the relations set up by the 21 conditions. The submission of these conditions to the Left parties in the principal European countries in the autumn and winter of 1920–1921 was a turning point in the history of European socialism and of its attitude to Moscow. The same process can be traced in slightly differing forms in Germany, in France, in Italy and in Great Britain.

It was in Germany that the issue was fought out in the greatest detail and with the greatest asperity. Germany was the key-point of the European revolution ; Germany alone of the great European countries had a large workers' movement of a potentially revolutionary character ; and it was the determination to force the issue in the USPD which had led directly to the formulation of the 21 conditions. The first test came when the conditions were submitted in October 1920 to an extraordinary congress of the USPD at Halle. Three weeks before it was due to meet, IKKI addressed a long " open letter " to all members of the party containing a bitter attack on its Right-wing leaders who were opposed to affiliation.[1] Zinoviev in person attended the congress as delegate of Comintern, having received a *visa* from the German authorities

---

[1] *Kommunisticheskii Internatsional*, No. 14 (November 6, 1920), cols. 2901-2922.

for a stay of ten days ; his fellow delegate was Lozovsky, who had been in Germany for three weeks with a trade union delegation.[1] The opposition countered this Bolshevik invasion by inviting Martov, the former Menshevik leader, who had recently left Moscow to settle permanently in Berlin.

After almost a year of embittered argument in the ranks of the USPD, feelings ran high, and the proceedings were acrimonious. The four USPD delegates to the Moscow congress of the previous July spoke first ; two for, two against, affiliation. Then Zinoviev made a four-hour speech which was long remembered and, as a feat of oratory and endurance in a foreign language, impressed even those who were not convinced by his arguments. He was answered at almost equal length by Hilferding, the principal theorist of the party. Other noteworthy speeches were those of Lozovsky and Martov. The debate ranged far and wide. The Bolsheviks were attacked for their agrarian policy, which had distributed the land as small individual holdings to peasants instead of creating large state-owned units of cultivation, for their national policy, which had lent support to purely bourgeois national movements in Asia (the appearance of Enver Pasha at the recent congress of eastern peoples at Baku [2] was loudly criticized), and for the introduction of the terror. Denunciations by Zinoviev and Lozovsky of the " yellow " Amsterdam International provoked the stormiest scenes of the congress, Lozovsky at one point being howled down and prevented from continuing. It was an interesting symptom of the fact, already apparent at the time of the Kapp *putsch*, that the trade unions had a stronger hold on the loyalty of the German worker than any political party. The 21 conditions were assailed by the Right as constituting a " Moscow dictatorship ", and defended by the Left as the only safeguard against a return to the inefficiency and opportunism of

---

[1] According to a statement made by the German Minister for Foreign Affairs in the Reichstag, Lozovsky arrived on September 15, 1920, with a large Soviet trade union delegation to attend a congress of factory committees in Berlin (the speeches delivered by Lozovsky on this occasion are in A. Lozovsky, *Desyat' Let Bor'by za Profintern* (1930), pp. 102-123) ; only the seven for whom *visas* had been previously obtained were admitted. On October 4 Kopp asked for *visas* for Zinoviev and Bukharin to attend the Halle congress ; on the following day they were granted after consultation with the USPD (*Verhandlungen des Reichstags*, cccxlv (1921), 759-760). Bukharin did not make the journey.   [2] See pp. 264-266 below.

the Second International. But both sides showed a surprising eagerness to recognize that the 21 conditions were not the real stumbling-block. " We are splitting ", said Zinoviev, " not because you want not 21, but only 18, conditions, but because you do not agree on the question of world revolution, democracy and the dictatorship of the proletariat." [1] The issue turned primarily on a basic difference of opinion about the prospects of world revolution. True to the Bolshevik habit of interpreting European revolutionary problems in terms of Russian revolutionary experience, Zinoviev began his speech by comparing the congress with the Russian party congresses attended jointly by Bolsheviks and Mensheviks after 1906; and the presence of Zinoviev and Martov to support the Left and Right wings respectively of the USPD seemed to lend point to what was, historically speaking, a somewhat fanciful comparison.[2] The question which now divided the USPD could be summed up in the formula : 1847 or 1849 ? [3] Zinoviev quoted the statement of one of the Right leaders of the USPD that the world was " in a situation similar to that after the 1848 bourgeois revolution ". Zinoviev asked indignantly whether it was " really a fact that the whole policy of the working class must be governed by the assumption that world revolution will no longer occur in the near future ". Could this be said at a moment when the proletarian revolution was beginning in Italy, when England already had a council of action which was " the beginning of a Soviet, of a second government " and of the famous " dual power ", when revolution might break out at any day in Austria, and even the Balkans were " a ripe fruit for a proletarian revolution " ? [4]

[1] USPD : Protokoll über die Verhandlungen des Ausserordentlichen Parteitags zu Halle (n.d.), p. 156 ; this verbatim record of the proceedings was issued by the rump USPD after the majority had seceded to join the KPD.

[2] This motif ran through Zinoviev's speech : MacDonald and Henderson were described as Mensheviks (ibid. p. 154).

[3] The reference was to a well-known passage in Engels's introduction to Marx's pamphlet, The Class Struggles in France, summarizing Marx's con-clusions — " that it was really the world trade crisis of 1847 which generated the February and March revolutions, and that the industrial revival setting in little by little after the middle of 1848, and reaching its full development in 1849 and 1850, was the driving force of the renewal of strength of the European reaction " (Marx i Engels, Sochineniya, xvi, ii, 466).

[4] USPD : Protokoll über die Verhandlungen des Ausserordentlichen Parteitags zu Halle (n.d.), pp. 147-148, 153-154.

Zinoviev had not a moment's doubt that the Bolsheviks would be justified against the German Mensheviks today as they had been against the Russian Mensheviks after 1905. But his reference to the Balkans provoked cries of " Fantastic ! " from the Right wing of the congress ; and Hilferding in his reply, poking fun at Zinoviev's predictions, declared that a policy which counted on their fulfilment was " a game of *va-banque*, a gamble on which no party can build ".[1]

Behind this difference of opinion about the objective prospects of the revolution lay the old debate which haunted every controversy conducted in Marxist terms — the war between " consciousness " and " spontaneity " which Lenin had once waged against the " Economists ",[2] which was resumed under slightly altered slogans between Bolsheviks and Mensheviks, and which reappeared once more on the floor of the Halle congress. Was Zinoviev right in believing now that a conscious effort of will was all that was required to spread the revolution over Europe and Asia ?

Many tendencies making for a revolutionary development [replied Hilferding] are present in western Europe, and it is our duty to lead them and further them. But, comrades, the course of this revolutionary development cannot be determined from without, it depends on the relations of economic and social power between classes in individual countries, and it is utopian to suppose that it can be driven forward by any slogan, by any command from without.[3]

And, once more, behind this conflict between " voluntarist " and " determinist " interpretations of Marxist philosophy lay, as always, a hidden conflict of purpose. Zinoviev was wrong in his estimate of the revolutionary prospects. But he was perfectly right when, in face of shouts of protest, he accused his opponents of " fear of revolution, which runs like a red thread through your whole policy ". Moreover he correctly diagnosed the nature of the fear — fear of " dislocation ", of " hunger ", of " what we have in Russia ".[4]

[1] *USPD : Protokoll über die Verhandlungen des Ausserordentlichen Parteitags zu Halle* (n.d.), p. 184.   [2] See Vol. 1, p. 15.
[3] *USPD : Protokoll über die Verhandlungen des Ausserordentlichen Parteitags zu Halle* (n.d.), p. 188.   [4] *Ibid.* pp. 148-149.

But Zinoviev at Halle drew no conclusions from the diagnosis. The real conclusion was too damaging not merely to the case which he had to argue, but to the whole principle of argument by analogy from Russia to western Europe. The majority of Russian workers in 1917 had had nothing to lose but their chains ; standing at a level of subsistence not far removed from starvation, and maddened by the meaningless sacrifices of the war, they had neither hope nor belief in any existing institutions, and were desperate enough to accept with alacrity the revolutionary leadership of a small group of determined men bent on overthrowing them. The majority of the workers of western Europe — and not merely a privileged minority, as the Bolsheviks believed — had a standard of living which, poor as it may often have been, was still worth defending. At any rate they were unwilling to sacrifice it lightly in pursuit of the prospective benefits of revolution ; no propaganda damaged the Bolshevik revolution in western Europe so much as that which fastened on it the low standard of living of the Russian people and the privations of war and civil war. Thus the fear of revolution of which Zinoviev spoke was by no means confined in western Europe to a few leaders or to the privileged strata of workers. Too many had too much to lose to abandon lightly the legality of bourgeois democracy or to accept the discipline of revolutionary leaders. This was the fundamental difference which underlay disputes about bourgeois democracy and the dictatorship of the proletariat, about the splitting of the trade unions, about consciousness and spontaneity, and about the attitude of the masses to revolutionary leadership. After his return to Russia, Lozovsky drew a revealing picture of the mood which he had found among European workers in the autumn of 1920 :

> When a few months ago I talked to German workers in Germany, supporters of Scheidemann often appeared at meetings and said : " Yes, you Russians talk of revolution in Germany. Well, we will make a revolution in Germany, but what if there is no revolution in France ? " And at the same time a French colleague gets up and, beating his breast, also says : " And what if we make a revolution, and our comrades over there do not ? " Then the Italian opportunists, just as anxious as other opportunists and just as peevish, they too say : " It's easy for you to talk about revolution. Italy will make a revolution, but she gets coal from England. How can we exist

without coal ? "   So they will wait for one another till the second coming.[1]

And Lenin wrote a little later :

In western Europe there are hardly any people who have lived through at all serious revolutions ; the experience of the great revolutions is almost entirely forgotten there ; and the transition from the desire to be revolutionary· and from conversations (and resolutions) about revolution to real revolutionary work is a difficult, slow and painful transition.[2]

Some of the European workers wanted revolution ; most of them wanted first of all to make the world safe for revolution.[3]   In the Germany of 1920, however, many signs suggested that the masses were still in a revolutionary mood ; it was, Zinoviev remarked, " no accident " that there was a majority for the Bolsheviks at the Halle congress.[4]

The congress had been well canvassed and the result was known in advance within a few votes.   The motion to adhere to Comintern and to enter into negotiations for the creation of a united German communist party was carried by a majority of 237 to 156.   Zinoviev returned in triumph to Berlin to receive notice from the police of expulsion from Germany as an " undesirable alien ".[5]   While confined to his house awaiting the date of the

---

[1] *Chetvertyi Vserossiiskii S"ezd Professional'nykh Soyuzov* (1921), i (Plenumy), 61-62.   [2] Lenin, *Sochineniya*, xxvi, 487.

[3] A. Sturmthal, *The Tragedy of European Labour 1918-1939* (1944), is a sympathetically critical analysis of the political bankruptcy of European social-democratic parties between the two world wars ; the causes are found in the persistence of a " pressure group " mentality rather than a politically responsible attitude in these parties, which were unwilling to accept the responsibility of governing because they were unable to decide their fundamental attitude to the capitalist state.   This coincides with the famous aphorism of the social democratic leader Tarnow in 1931 : " We stand at the sick-bed of capitalism, no merely as a diagnostician, but also — what shall I say ? — as a doctor who seek to cure ? or as a joyful heir, who can scarcely wait for the end and would like best of all to help it along a little with poison ?   This picture expresses our whole situation " (*Sozial-Demokratischer Parteitag in Leipzig 1931* (1931), p. 45).

[4] *USPD : Protokoll über die Verhandlungen des Ausserordentlichen Parteitags zu Halle* (n.d.), p. 154.

[5] G. Zinoviev, *Zwölf Tage in Deutschland* (Hamburg, 1921), pp. 59-60. According to the German Minister for Foreign Affairs, orders were given to keep Zinoviev and Lozovsky on their return from Halle to Berlin under house arrest, since their *visas* expired on Sunday, October 15.   Zinoviev none the less attended a demonstration in Berlin on that day, though he was too hoarse to speak.   The two delegates then received notice to leave the country within a week, and permission to stay till November 1 was refused : Lozovsky (though not appar-

first sailing from Stettin, he saw representatives not only of the two parties about to join forces under the banner of Comintern, but also of the KAPD which he still hoped to bring into the combination.[1] This hope was frustrated. But in December 1920 the KPD and the majority of the USPD met in congress in Berlin to constitute a United German Communist Party.[2] The marriage between the intellectual leaders of the KPD and the proletarian rank and file of the USPD may have been a little uneasy at first.[3] But for the first time there was a mass communist party in Germany with a membership of some 350,000 [4] and a prospect of playing a rôle in German politics.

> The offensive of the Communist International in western Europe [Zinoviev wrote triumphantly on his return to Petrograd] has been completely successful. The battle between the representatives of communism and of reformism has ended in our favour.[5]

The example of the USPD proved decisive for the French and Italian parties. Frossard and Cachin had found themselves as firmly handled at the congress as at the preceding meeting of IKKI.[6] A mild declaration of sympathy read by Cachin was

ently Zinoviev) was accused of having violated the condition of his *visa* by delivering political speeches (*Verhandlungen des Reichstags*, cccxlv (1921), 759-760).

[1] G. Zinoviev, *Zwölf Tage in Deutschland* (Hamburg, 1921), pp. 78-80 ; a letter from Zinoviev to the forthcoming congress of the KPD begging it to " treat the KAPD with more tolerance than hitherto " is in *Bericht über den 5. Parteitag der Kommunistischen Partei Deutschlands (Spartakusbund)* (1921), pp. 62-63. A month later IKKI issued an ultimatum to the KAPD to join the enlarged KPD (*Kommunisticheskii Internatsional*, No. 15 (December 20, 1920), cols. 3367-3370), but once more failed to enforce it.

[2] *Bericht über die Verhandlungen des Vereinigungsparteitages der USPD (Linke) und der KPD (Spartakusbund)* (1921).

[3] Ruth Fischer's mordant description of the disgust of the USPD workers with Levi's polished speech at the congress (*Stalin and German Communism* (Harvard, 1948), p. 147) is certainly overdrawn, but contains an element of truth.

[4] Levi, *Unser Weg* (2nd ed., 1921), p. 3, claimed a membership of 500,000 in February 1921 on the eve of the " March action ". Radek at the third congress of Comintern stated that the KPD had " never had more than 350,000 members ", and that its claim to a membership of 500,000 had " not been verified " (*Protokoll des III. Kongresses der Kommunistischen Internationale* (Hamburg, 1921), p. 457) ; of the 350,000 about 300,000 came from the USPD. Sympathizers were far more numerous : over 1,100,000 votes were cast for communist candidates in the Prussian elections of February 1921.

[5] G. Zinoviev, *Zwölf Tage in Deutschland* (Hamburg, 1921), p. 90.

[6] See p. 187 above.

followed by the speech of another French delegate, Lefebvre, who demanded that the utmost rigour of discipline should be applied to the wavering French Socialist Party.[1] Zinoviev convicted the party of " Wilsonism ", " social-pacifism " and lack of discipline ; and Lozovsky declared that it suffered from the disease of " unity at any price ".[2] The two delegates proved, however, amenable to persuasion. They accepted the 21 conditions, and undertook to work for party approval of them. This task they discharged after their return to France.[3] The 21 conditions were submitted to a party congress which opened at Tours on December 25, 1920.[4] No Russian delegate had been able to obtain admission to France, though the proceedings were enlivened by a telegram from Zinoviev denouncing the leaders of the Centre, Longuet and Faure, as " agents of bourgeois influence on the proletariat ".[5] Klara Zetkin travelled illegally from Germany to plead the cause of Comintern. The opposition was stubborn, Léon Blum being among those who spoke bitterly against adhesion to Moscow. Nevertheless the situation proved somewhat easier than at Halle, partly because both the French delegates to the Moscow congress came out in favour of acceptance, and partly because the trade-union leadership, which in France as in Germany was hostile to Comintern,[6] had no influence in the French party. The motion of acceptance received 3247 mandates (the vote being taken on the card system) against 1308 for an alternative proposal to accept with substantial reservations, and some 150 abstentions by an irreconcilable Right wing. Thus the French Socialist Party became the French Communist Party, leaving the old name to

[1] Der Zweite Kongress der Kommunist. Internationale (Hamburg, 1921), pp. 261-270.   [2] Ibid. pp. 243-245, 307.

[3] Frossard seems from the first to have presented Comintern doctrine in a somewhat diluted form. " Workers," he is said to have told a mass meeting in Paris on August 13, 1920, " there is no question of asking you to make a revolution tomorrow, nor, if you make it, of slavishly copying the Russian Soviets. What is at stake is to affirm otherwise than by words our solidarity with the proletariat of Russia " (quoted in G. Walter, Histoire du Parti Communiste Français (1948), p. 31).

[4] The proceedings are fully recorded in Parti Socialiste: 18ᵉ Congrès National (1921).

[5] The receipt of this telegram is described in L. O. Frossard, De Jaurès à Lénine (1930), p. 176.

[6] Immediately after the Tours congress the Confédération Générale du Travail issued a warning to its members against the " new communist party " (G. Walther, Histoire du Parti Communiste Français (1948), pp. 44-45).

the dissident minority. Frossard was elected secretary-general of the party : Souvarine, released from prison, went to Moscow as French delegate to IKKI. The Italian Socialist Party represented an even more variegated medley of opinions than the French party. The dark days of 1919 when Lenin greeted its accession to Comintern with enthusiasm lay in the past; and its eclecticism was vigorously assailed by Zinoviev at the second congress.[1] Its delegates in Moscow had accepted the 21 conditions subject to confirmation by the party. But the issue was left in abeyance pending the party congress, which met at Leghorn in January 1921, and was attended by Rakosi, the Hungarian, and Kabakchiev, a Bulgarian, who had also been at Halle, as delegates of Comintern.[2] But the tide in the affairs of Comintern was by this time beginning to ebb. At Leghorn, Serrati, who had been the leader of the Italian delegation at the second congress of Comintern and a vice-president of the congress, appeared as the spokesman of a large Centre group nearly 100,000 strong, whose delegates commanded an absolute majority at the congress; Bordiga and the two other Italian delegates at Moscow represented a Left wing of some 50,000 which included anarcho-syndicalists as well as communists, and which alone unconditionally accepted the 21 conditions ; and there was a fiery Right wing of 14,000 uncompromising " reformists " who had not been represented at Moscow. The Centre group professed unswerving allegiance to the programme of Comintern, but refused to depart from the party tradition of tolerance for divergent opinions by expelling the reformist Right; this involved rejection of the last and most essential of the 21 conditions. Paul Levi, who was at the congress as delegate of the KPD, applauded Serrati's attitude. The result was that the Italian Socialist Party, by a majority vote, seceded

---

[1] *Der Zweite Kongress der Kommunist. Internationale* (Hamburg, 1921), pp. 250-252.

[2] No official record of the congress appears to have been published. The principal documents relating to the split were published in Russian in *Doklad Ispolkoma Kominterna o Raskole v Ital'yanskoi Sotsialisticheskoi Partii* (1921) and *Ital'yanskaya Sotsialisticheskaya Partiya i Kommunisticheskii Internatsional : Sbornik Dokumentov* (1921). Zinoviev and Bukharin were to have attended the Leghorn congress as delegates of the Russian party, but were refused *visas* by the Italian Government (*Protokoll des III. Kongresses der Kommunistischen Internationale* (Hamburg, 1921), p. 167).

from Comintern, leaving the Left wing of the congress under the leadership of Bordiga to form an Italian Communist Party on the basis of the 21 conditions. A small group, little larger than the KPD before its fusion with the USPD, replaced the mass Italian party which Lenin had welcomed into Comintern in the summer of 1919. At the Italian parliamentary elections of May 1921 it obtained 13 seats.

No other country was comparable as a field for the activities of Comintern with Germany, France and Italy. The first initiative in the attempt to combine the small British Left splinter parties into a single communist party seems to have been taken in April 1920. But jealousies were strong and progress slow ; and several groups and parties sent independent delegates to the second congress of Comintern. It was while this congress was still sitting that the Communist Party of Great Britain (CPGB) was actually founded at a congress in London on August 1, 1920. The only important issues which divided the congress were the questions of parliamentary action and of affiliation to the Labour Party. On the first, after confused voting on several resolutions, a formula was found which approved participation in parliamentary elections and was carried without a division ; on the second, the proposal to apply for affiliation was carried by a majority of 150 to 85,[1] though, when the application was made immediately after the congress, it was firmly and decisively rejected by the Labour Party.[2] The CPGB held a further congress in Leeds in January 1921 in order to complete its constitution and to record its acceptance of the 21 conditions. But, though it had been successful in rallying to its fold all the small groups of the extreme Left, it had little promise of becoming a mass party, its authentic membership not exceeding 2500 :[3] the ILP rejected the 21 conditions at

[1] *CPGB : Communist Unity Convention* (1920), pp. 29, 57. The account of the negotiations leading up to the foundation of the CPGB in T. Bell, *The British Communist Party* (1937), pp. 52-57, was criticized (*Labour Monthly*, xix, No. 6 (June 1937), p. 382) as overstating the rôle of the Socialist Labour Party of which Bell was a member ; more than half the delegates at the founding congress came from the British Socialist Party.

[2] The correspondence is in T. Bell, *The British Communist Party* (1937), pp. 63-67.

[3] T. Bell, *Pioneering Days* (1941), pp. 194-195 ; the writer admits that the number of 10,000 claimed at the third congress of Comintern (*Protokoll des III. Kongresses der Kommunistischen Internationale* (Hamburg, 1921), pp. 18-19) was fictitious.

its conference in Southport in March 1921 [1] by a five-to-one majority, leaving a dissentient minority to secede and join the CPGB. The large Bulgarian and Norwegian parties, and the tiny Dutch, Austrian and Hungarian parties (the last confined to exiles in Vienna and Moscow), accepted the 21 conditions without demur. In Czechoslovakia a split occurred on the same lines as in Germany and France, and a sizeable Czechoslovak Communist Party was the result. A Serb-Croat-Slovene Communist Party was formed, and secured nearly 200,000 votes and 58 seats in the Serb-Croat-Slovene parliamentary elections of November 1920, emerging as the third strongest party. Its success, which seemed likely to emulate that of the Bulgarian party, proved fatal to it. Police measures were brought into operation, and virtually destroyed it within a year of its birth. In most of the other smaller European countries a majority of the socialists rejected the 21 conditions, and tiny groups broke away to form communist parties which adhered to Comintern.but had neither numbers nor influence. Two reprimands from IKKI [2] failed to end the schism between the two American parties.

In the winter of 1920-1921, the success of the policy introduced at the second congress of Comintern seemed on paper complete and far-reaching. The Second International, after failures at Berne and Lucerne in 1919, had formally succeeded in reconstituting itself at a conference held at Geneva in July 1920 at the same time as the second congress of Comintern. The British Labour Party, together with the German Social-Democratic Party, had rallied round them the social-democratic parties of north-western Europe and one or two small groups from other countries. But this ghost of the past seemed no serious challenge to the rising power of the young Communist International. A revolutionary organization had been created with its headquarters in Moscow and its outposts in every European country. Faithful and devoted bands of communists pledged to the proletarian revolution had been extricated, with greater or less numerical loss, but with corresponding moral gain, from their entangling alliance

---

[1] Its proceedings were recorded in *Independent Labour Party: Report of the 29th Annual Conference* (1921).

[2] *Kommunisticheskii Internatsional*, No. 14 (November 6, 1920), col. 2944; No. 17 (June 7, 1921), cols. 4295-4296.

with other parties of the Left. The forces of revolution were in the ascendant and were marching on to an early victory. The capitalist world continued to show symptoms of alarm; one of them was the growth of extensive anti-Bolshevik propaganda organizations, which, not content with an abundance of authentic material, engaged in the dissemination of forged documents depicting the scope and purposes of Comintern in highly coloured terms.[1] But the mood of triumphant optimism in Moscow did not outlast the winter; and the unquestioning faith in European revolution which actuated the Bolshevik leaders at this time never returned. The spring of 1921 brought the end of a period. It was marked by three crucial events, one affecting the domestic policy of the RSFSR, the second its foreign policy, and the third the prospects of revolution in the country where they had hitherto appeared brightest and most certain. In March 1921, after the Kronstadt rising, Lenin introduced the New Economic Policy; a trade agreement was concluded between the RSFSR and Great Britain; and a communist rising in Germany was heavily and ignominiously defeated.

[1] A. L. P. Dennis, *The Foreign Policies of Soviet Russia* (1924), pp. 363-365, quotes references to several of these forgeries which kept the journalists and intelligence services of many countries occupied for some time : the main source of supply seems to have been an organization called *Ost-Information* in Berlin.

CHAPTER 26

REVOLUTION OVER ASIA

MARX gave little thought to colonial questions, since it did not occur to him that the colonial or backward regions of the world would be called on to play any part in the overthrow of capitalism. The First International ignored them. The Second International remained for a long time equally apathetic. At the Paris congress of 1901, under the influence of the South African war, Rosa Luxemburg, who was afterwards to give colonial exploitation a central place in her theory of the accumulation of capital, for the first time proposed a resolution deploring the twin evils of militarism and colonial policy. The Russian revolution of 1905 transferred the immediate centre of interest from Africa to Asia, where national revolutionary movements — the Persian revolution of 1906, the " young Turk " revolution of 1908, the Chinese revolution of 1912, and the beginnings of Indian nationalism — stirred in the wake of the Russian upheaval. In 1907 Kautsky wrote a pamphlet called *Socialism and Colonial Policy* in which he published for the first time a letter from Engels of 1882 prophesying a revolution in India and arguing that, once the proletariat had won its victory in Europe and North America, " this will give such a colossal impetus and such an example that the half-civilized countries will follow us of their own accord ".[1] In 1908 an article by Lenin entitled *Explosive Material in World Politics* found a new significance in the revolutionary movements in Persia, Turkey, India and China: " The conscious European worker now has Asiatic comrades, and the number of these comrades will grow from hour to hour ".[2] A few years later, when the Chinese revolution had been victorious, Lenin diagnosed more precisely the significance of the re-birth of Asia:

[1] Marx i Engels, *Sochineniya*, xxvii, 238-239.
[2] Lenin, *Sochineniya*, xii, 306.

This means that the east has finally taken the road of the west, that fresh *hundreds and hundreds of millions* of human beings will henceforth take part in the struggle for the ideals to which the west has attained by its labours. The western bourgeoisie is rotten, and is already confronted by its grave-digger — the proletariat. But in Asia there is *still* a bourgeoisie capable of standing for a sincere, energetic, consistent democracy, a worthy comrade of the great teachers and great revolutionaries of the end of the eighteenth century in France.[1]

It was a significant departure, which Lenin did not at this time stress, that the democratic revolutionary movement for the national liberation of the backward countries of Asia should be linked in potential alliance with the socialist revolutionary movement of the industrial countries of Europe.

The war of 1914 proved a forcing house for the national aspirations of the backward countries. Asiatic and African peoples were driven to play their part in a struggle which was no concern of theirs. Colonial and Indian troops fought for the first time on the battlefields of Europe. Allied designs to annex the German colonies began to excite opposition in radical circles even in the victorious European countries, and almost universally in the United States. It became increasingly difficult to exclude the dependent peoples from the scope of Wilson's doctrine of national self-determination which the allies had so warmly espoused in Europe. Lenin, building in part on the foundations laid by Rosa Luxemburg in her *Accumulation of Capital* five years earlier, published early in 1917 his *Imperialism as the Highest Stage of Capitalism*, depicting the acquisition and exploitation of colonies by process of profitable investment as the essence of capitalism in its final phase. The question appeared for the first time in a Bolshevik party document in a resolution of the April conference of 1917, which observed rather casually that " contemporary imperialism, by strengthening the urge to subjugate weak peoples, is a new factor in intensifying national oppression ".[2]

When therefore the Bolshevik revolution occurred in the fourth year of the first world war, the colonial question had inflammable qualities which no serious revolutionary could ignore. The failure of the Provisional Government to take up this issue was

[1] Lenin, *Sochineniya*, xvi, 28.   [2] *VKP(B) v Rezolyutsiyakh* (1941), i, 233.

treated as one of many proofs that it had no serious credentials as a revolutionary government. Those who sought to apply Marxist doctrine to the contemporary world were faced with the task of working out programmes and policies not only for the " advanced " peoples of western Europe and their overseas derivatives, but also for the " backward " peoples of Asia and Africa. This was all the more incumbent on revolutionaries who found themselves masters of a vast country stretched between two continents — a country whose government had always been compelled to dovetail together two divergent patterns of foreign policy applicable to the widely differing standards of life and civilization of Europe and Asia.[1] With the other continents Moscow had as yet no points of contact ; and this at least limited the scope of the problem. Proletarian socialism between the industrial west and the teeming earth-bound east, Russia between Europe and Asia [2] — these were the twin formulae, revolutionary and national, which once more imposed a dual outlook and dual policy on the Soviet Government.

The success of the Asiatic policies of the Soviet Government was due mainly to its skill in assimilating the " colonial " to the " national " issue. The readiness of the RSFSR to recognize the right of secession of the dependent peoples, whether European or Asiatic, of the former Tsarist empire attested its sincerity in proclaiming the same right for the subject peoples of other empires. This made colonial policy a logical corollary and a natural extension of national policy ; the theoretical foundations of both were the same. Colonial emancipation, like all forms of national

[1] Slavophils like Danilevsky attributed to Russia a spiritual kinship with the east and a mission to mediate to it what was acceptable in western culture ; Russia's economic penetration of the east with material resources derived from the west was the practical basis of these romantic visions. Trotsky described the Russian economy as embodying characteristics both of a colonial Power and of a colony : " We had in our midst at the same time both London and India " (Trotsky, *Sochineniya*, xiii, 104).

[2] Bukharin dilated on this theme at the twelfth party congress in 1923, attributing the analysis to Lenin : " *Soviet Russia lies geographically and politically between two giant worlds — the still strong and, unfortunately, capitalist imperialist world of the west and the colossal numbers of the population of the east which is now in process of growing revolutionary ferment.* And the Soviet republic balances between these two enormous forces, which to a significant degree equalize each other " (*Dvenadtsatyi S"ezd Rossiiskoi Kommunisticheskoi Partii (Bol'shevikov)* (1923), p. 240).

emancipation, belonged to the stage of the bourgeois revolution. It was no doubt ultimately significant as a necessary prelude to the socialist world revolution. But in this phase it remained bourgeois; and Soviet policy could express itself in the Wilsonian language of self-determination and democratic freedom, thereby appealing not only to the oppressed peoples themselves but to advanced opinion throughout the bourgeois world. Nor was it necessary to distinguish between the different peoples of Asia. All, whatever their formal political status, had been subjected to the intrusion and to the domination of bourgeois capitalism; as Lenin had noted in *Imperialism as the Highest Stage of Capitalism*, Persia, Turkey and China were already " semi-colonial peoples ".[1] Soviet policy appealed in one broad sweep to the peoples of Asia as a whole, to the former subjects of the Tsar, to the subjects of other empires and to the nominally independent dependencies of the capitalist world-market.

These principles found their first application in an appeal of Sovnarkom " To all Muslim Toilers of Russia and the East " issued on November 24/December 7, 1917. The Muslims of Russia were assured that their " beliefs and usages ", their "national and cultural institutions ", were henceforth free and inviolable. Those of the east — among whom Persians and Turks, Arabs and Hindus were specifically named — were encouraged to overthrow the imperialist " robbers and enslavers " of their countries. The secret treaties providing for the seizure of Constantinople by Russia had been " torn up and destroyed ": Constantinople " must remain in the hands of the Muslims ". The treaty for the partition of Persia had met the same fate: the troops would be withdrawn from Persia as soon as military operations were at an end.[2] The treaty for " the partition of Turkey and the taking

---

[1] Lenin, *Sochineniya*, xix, 135; Lenin applied the same description to the same three countries in his speech to the second congress of Comintern in 1920 (*ibid.* xxv, 351).

[2] " On the basis of the principle of the freedom, independence and territoria inviolability of the neutral Persian state ", the Brest-Litovsk armistice of December 2/15, 1917, provided for the evacuation of Persia by both Russian and Turkish troops. Trotsky's declaration of January ·14/27, 1918, to the Persian people, published in *Izvestiya* of that date, explicitly disowned " treaties between Russia and England or other Powers affecting Persia "; and under the Brest-Litovsk treaty of March 3, 1918, the Soviet Government undertook not to maintain " spheres of influence and exclusive interests in Persia ".

away from her of Armenia " was also annulled : the Armenians would be free to determine their political destiny.[1]

> We are marching firmly and resolutely [concluded the manifesto] towards an honourable, democratic peace. On our banners we bring liberation to the oppressed peoples of the world.[2]

The Declaration of Rights of the Toiling and Exploited People announced in more general terms " the complete repudiation of the barbarous policy of bourgeois civilization, which built up the prosperity of the exploiters in a few privileged nations on the enslavement of hundreds of millions of the toiling masses in Asia, in the colonies in general, and in the small countries ".

The period of extreme weakness through which the young RSFSR passed during the first year of its existence lent point to this policy of high-minded self-denial. Throughout the greater part of 1918 German troops occupied the Ukraine, effectively cutting off the RSFSR from the Black Sea. Turkey under the Brest-Litovsk treaty had secured in thinly disguised form the cession of the former Russian regions of Kars, Ardahan and Batum, and improved on this during the summer of 1918 by occupying Baku. After the defeat of the central Powers British forces appeared in Transcaucasia. Since March 1918, when British troops moved forward in Persia in pursuit of the retiring Turks, Persia had been wholly under British influence. Japan, and later Kolchak, cut off Moscow from access to the Far East. In such conditions it cost little to renounce rights of the former Tsarist government which its successor was in no position to assert.[3] The pronouncements of the Bolshevik leaders on policy in Asia at this time scarcely went beyond the assertion of the right of self-determination for oppressed peoples and the denunciation of

---

[1] According to B. Bor'yan, *Armeniya, Mezhdunarodnaya Diplomatiya i SSSR* (1929), ii, 260, this passage was inspired by Armenian Bolsheviks, notably Shaumyan.

[2] Klyuchnikov i Sabanin, *Mezhdunarodnaya Politika*, ii (1926), 94-96 ; see also Vol. 1, p. 318.

[3] An article in *Izvestiya*, December 19, 1917/January 1, 1918, quoted in A. L. P. Dennis, *Foreign Policies of Soviet Russia* (1924), p. 237, pointed out that Soviet renunciation of Tsarist rights was the best means of destroying British influence in Persia.

imperialism and of secret treaties — all of them favourite Wilsonian themes. Only Stalin, in his capacity as People's Commissar for Nationalities, was continuously preoccupied with the Asiatic scene. In an anniversary article in *Pravda* in November 1918 he developed the theme of the " world significance of the October revolution " :

> The October revolution is the first revolution in the history of the world to break the age-long sleep of the toiling masses of the oppressed peoples of the east and to draw them into the fight against world imperialism. . . .
> The great world significance of the October revolution is, primarily, that it has . . . *by this very fact built a bridge between the socialist west and the enslaved east*, creating a new revolutionary front, which runs from the proletarians of the west through the Russian revolution to the oppressed peoples of the east, *against* world imperialism.[1]

And he followed this up with two articles in the journal of Narkomnats, *Do Not Forget the East* and *Light from the East*.[2] There was nothing original about these articles except their timing. In the first weeks after the armistice, when every Soviet leader had his eyes fixed on Berlin and on the incipient German revolution, Stalin's voice cried almost alone in the wilderness. The first All-Russian Congress of Muslim Communist Organizations in November 1918 [3] attracted little attention, and confined its attention primarily to the Muslims of the former Russian Empire. At the international revolutionary gathering in Petrograd presided over by Zinoviev in December 1918, it was left to the Turkish delegate, Suphi, to declare that " the brain of Anglo-French capitalism is in Europe, but its body rests on the plains of Asia and Africa ".[4]

The year 1919, though it did little to enhance Soviet military power, saw a great forward move in Soviet eastern policy. Two new factors had made their appearance. In the first place the international balance of power had been completely changed by the downfall of the central Powers. The RSFSR had no longer anything to fear from Germany or Turkey ; on the other hand the

[1] Stalin, *Sochineniya*, iv, 164-166.
[2] *Ibid.* iv, 171-173, 177-182.   [3] See Vol. 1, p. 319.
[4] *Sowjet-Russland und die Völker der Welt* (Petrograd, 1920), p. 32.

victorious allies, and especially Great Britain, showed a disposition to divert a part of the vast resources released by the armistice to the waging of a campaign against Bolshevism. This meant a shift in the major field of activities from Europe to Asia. Apart from supplies furnished to " white " Russian armies, British contingents in the Caucasus and in central Asia made in the first months of 1919 several moves openly directed against Soviet forces. Through this British action, the Middle East became in 1919 the theatre of an all but declared war between Great Britain and the RSFSR; the Middle East was, moreover, as events were soon to show, the most vulnerable point of British power. In these circumstances the RSFSR soon found itself committed, in default of other means of defence, to a general diplomatic offensive against Great Britain in Asia.

The other new factor, which helped to determine the form of this offensive, was the birth of Comintern and the increased emphasis on world revolution as the *leitmotif* of Soviet foreign policy. The first congress of Comintern, meeting in March 1919, did not concern itself greatly with eastern questions, and the only Asiatic delegates appear to have been members of the People's Commissariat of Nationalities. But one section of its manifesto, after referring to a " series of open risings and revolutionary unrest in all colonies ", observed that " the purpose of Wilson's programme, on the most favourable interpretation, is merely to change the label of colonial slavery ", declared that " the liberation of the colonies is thinkable only in connexion with the liberation of the working class in the metropolitan countries ", and ended with the appeal :

> Colonial slaves of Africa and Asia ! The hour of the proletarian dictatorship in Europe will strike for you as the hour of your deliverance.[1]

Later in the same month at the eighth congress of the Russian Communist Party Bukharin expressed himself on the subject with a cynical frankness :

> If we propound the solution of the right of self-determination for the colonies, the Hottentots, the Negroes, the Indians, etc.,

[1] *Kommunisticheskii Internatsional v Dokumentakh* (1933), p. 57 ; Trotsky, *Sochineniya*, xiii, 43-44.

we lose nothing by it. On the contrary, we gain ; for the national gain as a whole will damage foreign imperialism. . . . The most outright nationalist movement, for example, that of the Hindus, is only water for our mill, since it contributes to the destruction of English imperialism.[1]

And the congress adopted a revised party programme which noted that the world-wide growth of imperialism had brought about " a coupling of civil war within particular countries with the revolutionary wars of attacked proletarian countries and of oppressed peoples against the yoke of the imperialist Powers ", and demanded " a policy of bringing together the proletarians and semi-proletarians of different nationalities for a common revolutionary struggle against landowners and bourgeoisie ".[2] Later still in the year, at a second All-Russian Congress of Muslim Communist Organizations, Lenin carried the doctrine a step further :

> The socialist revolution will not be only or chiefly a struggle of the revolutionary proletarians in each country against its bourgeoisie — no, it will be a struggle of all colonies and countries oppressed by imperialism, of all dependent countries, against international imperialism.

And he spoke openly of the need to " translate the true communist doctrine which was designed for the communists of more advanced countries into the language of each nation ".[3] A resolution of the Congress boldly declared " the problem of the international social revolution " insoluble " without the participation of the east ".[4] Soviet foreign policy in the Middle East thus began in 1919 to take its dual shape as a struggle for world revolution in forms adapted to eastern conditions and as a struggle against Great Britain, the spearhead of the attack on Soviet Russia and the leading imperialist Power in Asia. Here as elsewhere the national

---

[1] *Vos'moi S"ezd RKP(B)* (1933), p. 49 ; at the same congress Zinoviev, reporting the recent visit of two Indians who had made speeches in Moscow and Petrograd, added that the movement in India was " not a purely communist, but a nationalist movement, only touched up a little here and there in a communist hue " (*ibid.* p. 145).

[2] *VKP(B) v Rezolyutsiyakh* (1941), i, 283, 286.

[3] Lenin, *Sochineniya*, xxiv, 548, 551.

[4] *Zhizn' Natsional'nostei*, No. 47 (55), December 14, 1919.

and international aspects of policy shaded into each other, and the distinction between them became unreal and difficult to sustain.

The first manifestation of the new policy occurred in Afghanistan. In April 1919 Amanullah, the young and would-be progressive amir, who had come to the throne as the result of a palace revolution two months earlier, denounced the treaty obligation accepted by his predecessor to follow British advice in the conduct of his country's foreign relations, and launched a campaign against British India which came to be known as " the third Afghan war ". The Afghan national movement headed by Amanullah was comparable, though at a far more primitive level, with the Persian revolution of 1906 and the " young Turk " revolution of 1908, and owed its inspiration to the Bolshevik revolution in the same indirect way in which those movements had owed it to the Russian revolution of 1905.[1] It is not certain — and perhaps unlikely — that anyone in Moscow was cognizant of the impending outbreak of hostilities between Britain and Afghanistan.[2] But Amanullah, casting about for moral support at this critical juncture, addressed a letter of oriental greeting to Lenin, as the " High-Born President of the Great Russian Republic ", and to Chicherin, as Commissar for Foreign Affairs, proposing the establishment of diplomatic relations ;[3] and about the same time there arrived in Moscow from Kabul by way of Tashkent a well-known anti-British propagandist calling himself Professor Barkatullah,[4] and

[1] A. Gurevich, *Afganistan* (2nd. ed., 1930), pp. 43-45, calls Amanullah's régime an " enlightened absolutism ", and attempts a rather cursory survey of the social forces for and against him ; according to the verdict in *Pravda*, January 26, 1929 (quoted *ibid.* p. 56), his reforms " were marked by an extremely superficial character and gave nothing real to the Afghan peasantry ".

[2] An Indian army officer employed in central Asia assumed that " it was the Soviet who organized the third Afghan war " (L. V. S. Blacker, *On Secret Patrol in High Asia* (1922), p. 186). This may reflect the views of the government of India ; but such reports readily obtained currency at that period without serious evidence to support them.

[3] *Diplomaticheskii Slovar*, ii (1950), 694, art. Sovetsko-Afganskie Dogovory i Soglasheniya.

[4] A British intelligence officer, who records Barkatullah's presence in Tashkent in the spring of 1919, gives the following account of his career, presumably extracted from official files : " He was a native of Bhopal State in central India and had been a teacher of Hindustani at Tokyo until expelled from the country by the Japanese, when he moved to America, where he let no opportunity pass

now described as " head of the Afghan delegation in Moscow ".
In this capacity he made a statement which was published in
Izvestiya of May 6, 1919, and offered a realistic basis of collabora-
tion between Moscow and the oppressed eastern peoples :

> I am neither a communist nor a socialist, but my political
> programme entails the expulsion of the British from Asia. I
> am an implacable foe of the capitalization of Asia by Europe,
> the principal representatives of which are the British. In this
> I approximate to the communists, and in this respect we are
> natural allies.

It was not, however, clear how Moscow could help; and the
Afghan armies were already in the act of surrendering to British
military prowess when Lenin on May 27, 1919, replied to Amanullah's letter of greeting with a telegram congratulating the
Afghan people on their struggle against " foreign oppressors "
and suggesting mutual aid against future attacks.[1]

The Afghan surrender was rather surprisingly followed by a
British recognition of the formal independence which Amanullah
had claimed.[2] This did not, however, impede the further development of Soviet-Afghan relations. In the autumn of 1919 an
Afghan envoy, Mohammed Wali Khan, arrived in Moscow; and
a Soviet representative, a former Russian consul named Bravin,
seems to have reached Kabul about the same time.[3] In November
Lenin addressed a further letter to Amanullah in which he greeted
Afghanistan as being " the only independent Muslim state in the

of vilifying our rule in India. He claimed to be a German subject and even
stated that he was the German diplomatic agent in Kabul. He held a German
passport issued at Dar-es-Salaam in East Africa. . . . During the war an organization called the provisional government of India had been formed in Berlin.
The president was Mahendra Pratap . . . and this Barkatullah was the foreign
minister " (F. M. Bailey, *Mission to Tashkent* (1946), p. 143).

[1] Quoted by L. Fischer, *The Soviets in World Affairs* (1930), i, 285-286,
from the archives of Narkomindel : it has never been published in full.

[2] The documents relating to this " war " and the agreements which concluded it were published in *Papers Regarding Hostilities with Afghanistan 1919*,
Cmd. 324 (1919).

[3] F. M. Bailey, *Mission to Tashkent* (1946), pp. 174-176, describes the
simultaneous departure of Mohammed Wali and Bravin from Tashkent on
June 14, and the difficulties which they experienced before reaching their
respective destinations ; according to the same source Bravin reported unfavourably on the attitude of Amanullah and of the Afghan Government. He was
soon afterwards assassinated in Kabul.

world " (Persia and Turkey were presumably at this time not really independent, being partially occupied by British or allied forces), and destined for " the great historic task of uniting around itself all enslaved Muslim peoples and leading them on the road to freedom and independence ". This was the prelude to a declaration of readiness " to engage in discussions with the government of the Afghan people with a view to the conclusion of trade and other friendly agreements, the purpose of which is not only the buttressing of good neighbourly relations in the best interests of both nations, but the joint struggle together with Afghanistan against the most rapacious imperialist government on earth, Great Britain ".[1] Coming from a government involved in a desperate crisis of civil war and cut off from effective means of communication with central Asia, the letter was perhaps not very impressive. Amanullah had strong Muslim loyalties and was attracted by pan-Islamic ambitions. Pan-Islamic and pan-Turanian movements in central Asia were, however, two-edged weapons; for, while their edge could easily be turned against Great Britain, particularly while British policy was hostile to Turkey, their appeal to Muslim and Turki-speaking peoples within the Soviet orbit also carried dangers for Soviet authority. Among other things Amanullah claimed a special interest in the fate of his fellow-potentate, the amir of Bokhara, which was not likely to make for easy relations with Moscow.[2] But this did not prevent him from playing off Great Britain and Soviet Russia against one another. The tradition of the nineteenth century had made Afghanistan a neutral region in which British and Russian secret agents waged their underground war. The system survived with the same methods

---

[1] Quoted from the archives of Narkomindel in L. Fischer, *The Soviets in World Affairs* (1930), i, 286; there is no doubt of its authenticity, though it may not have been drafted by Lenin personally.

[2] A letter of February 1920 from Amanullah's mother to the amir of Bokhara, stating *inter alia* that Amanullah " makes the independence of Bokhara, our brother and co-religionist, the first condition of his friendship with the Russian Soviet republic ", is quoted in *Asie Française*, November 1921, p. 420; the letter is full of religious fervour and the writer may have been a centre of Islamic influence at Amanullah's court. I. Maisky, *Vneshnyaya Politika RSFSR, 1917–1922* (1922), p. 147, speaks of friction at this time between the RSFSR and Afghanistan. According to General Malleson, who commanded the British force in central Asia, the RSFSR was worried by Afghan designs on Turkestan : the Afghans seemed to be aiming at " a huge pan-Islamic rising throughout central Asia " (*Journal of the Central Asian Society*, ix (1922), ii, 103-104).

and, probably, much of the same *personnel*. In the mood of 1919 and the following years it was unlikely that either the British or the Soviet authorities would miss any minor opportunity to make things inconvenient for the other; and Afghanistan was a fruitful breeding ground of such minor opportunities.

The other victims of British imperialism were not neglected. In Persia, as in Afghanistan, the summer of 1919 saw a recrudescence of Russian interest after a long period of forced inaction. A young Bolshevik envoy named Kolomiitsev had got through to Teheran from the Caucasus in the summer of 1918. But the Persian Government had refused to receive him on the ground that he had no credentials from Moscow, but only from the Soviet government in Baku; and his mission is said to have been attacked and driven out by " Cossacks " — Persian levies under " white " Russian officers.[1] The British occupation of Persia, so long as it was incidental to the war against the central Powers, gave rise to no political difficulties. But when the war was over, the British Government was faced by a fatal division of counsel. On the one hand, the pressure for demobilization was strong, and military operations were subject to the keen scrutiny of parliament and of public opinion. The War Office was disinclined to accept lasting commitments in northern Persia, which lay beyond the traditional British sphere; and this reluctance fitted in with Lloyd George's desire to avoid any policy involving direct military action against the Bolsheviks. On the other hand, the Foreign Office, now controlled by Curzon, sought to profit by the impotence of Russia in order to establish a veiled form of British protectorate over the whole of Persia; and this ambition found expression in a treaty negotiated in London in the early summer of 1919. While paying tribute in its preamble to " the independence and integrity of Persia ", it provided for the acceptance by the Persian Government of British financial advisers, British officers to reorganize the army, and British engineers for railway construction, the whole being sweetened with a loan of £2,000,000. This was a reversal of the principle accepted in the Anglo-Russian convention of 1907 of the recognition of a Russian sphere of influence in northern Persia and of a British sphere in the south ; and, though the Soviet

---

[1] *Diplomaticheskii Slovar*, i (1948), 809, art. Kolomiitsev; for the short-lived Soviet government in Baku see Vol. 1, p. 342.

Government had deprived itself of any title under the convention
by its declaration of January 1918,[1] this encroachment by a nation
engaged in scarcely veiled hostile action against the Soviet power
in the Caucasus and central Asia can hardly have failed to excite
alarm in Moscow.[2]

When the scope of the projected treaty became known, the
Soviet Government retaliated by a note to the Persian Government of June 26, 1919, recapitulating all the concessions which
it, by way of contrast with imperialist Britain, had made : the
cancellation of Tsarist debts, the renunciation of Tsarist concessions in Persia, the abandonment of consular jurisdiction and the
handing over to the Persian Government of former Russian public
property in Russia and of the assets of the Russian Discount Bank.[3]
The signature of the Anglo-Persian treaty on August 9, 1919, was
followed three weeks later by a public declaration from Chicherin
to " the workers and peasants of Persia ". It reviewed the different
attitudes of the Soviet and British Governments over the past two
years towards Persian independence and Persian rights, described
" the shameful Anglo-Persian treaty " as " a scrap of paper whose
legal validity it will never recognize ", and ended with a passage
which contained both a threat and a promise :

> The time of your liberation is near. The hour of reckoning
> will soon strike for English capitalism, against which a broad
> revolutionary movement is spreading ever more threateningly
> among the toiling masses of England itself. . . .
> The working people of Russia stretch out to you, the
> oppressed masses of Persia, their fraternal hand. The hour is
> near when we shall be able in deed to carry out our task of a

[1] See p. 232, note 2 above.
[2] One of the British financial advisers to the Persian Government appointed
under the treaty describes it as an act of " provocation " and writes : " Had
we been content to rest satisfied with our position and prestige, it is improbable
that the Bolshevists would have been provoked to action as they were ; but
instead of this we deliberately chose to run the most serious risks when no
corresponding advantage was to be anticipated. . . . That the Foreign Office
should seize upon the moment when Russia was in the throes of revolution to
repudiate the convention [of 1907], and should enter upon a policy avowedly
aimed at supplanting Russian influence, could only be regarded from the
Bolshevist point of view as an act of deliberate aggression " (J. M. Balfour,
Recent Happenings in Persia (1922), pp. 120-121).
[3] This note has not been published ; quotations from it are in L. Fischer,
The Soviets in World Affairs (1930), i, 289, and its contents were recapitulated
in the declaration of August 30, 1919.

common struggle with you against the robbers and oppressors, great and small, who are the source of your countless sufferings.[1]

Thanks in part to these promptings, the Anglo-Persian treaty was ill-received in Persia; and the convocation of the Mejlis which would have to ratify it before it could take effect was deliberately delayed. With the civil war in a critical stage, and British military forces still active in the Caucasus and in central Asia, the establishment of Soviet influence in Persia was an uphill task. Kolomiitsev, the envoy who had been rejected in the previous year, was sent back to Teheran in the summer of 1919 with proper credentials from Moscow, but was captured while crossing the Caspian and shot by " white " Russian forces " with the support of the English occupying forces in Persia ".[2] By the beginning of 1920, however, Denikin and Kolchak had been decisively beaten, and British troops were being everywhere withdrawn. In April 1920 Soviet power was re-established throughout Azerbaijan; and the time had come for more effective action in Persia.

The situation was complicated by the presence in Gilan, the northernmost province of Persia adjoining Azerbaijan, of a virtually independent ruler, part adventurer and part fanatic, professing nationalist and revolutionary doctrines, Kuchik Khan, whose programme appears to have included the expulsion of the English, the overthrow of the Shah, and the distribution of land to the peasants.[3] He was strongly Turcophil, and is said to have received German subsidies during the war for his anti-British activities; this made it easy for him at a later date to substitute Bolshevik for German support.[4] In the spring of 1920, when

[1] Klyuchnikov i Sabanin, *Mezhdunarodnaya Politika*, ii (1926), 341-344.

[2] *Novyi Vostok*, viii-ix (1925), 151.

[3] The two best available sources on Kuchik appear to be a contemporary article by Martchenko, a former " white " Russian official in Persia (*Revue du Monde Musulman*, xl-xli (1920), 98-116), and the later reminiscences of Ekshanullah, one of Kuchik's lieutenants (*Novyi Vostok*, xxix (1932), 88-107). Each has its particular bias, which is obvious and can be easily discounted; Martchenko gives the more romantic picture of Kuchik, whom he describes as " a disinterested fanatic, a nationalist dreamer ".

[4] According to *Revue du Monde Musulman*, xl-xli (1920), 104, Kuchik fled from Gilan to Afghanistan after the allied victory at the end of 1918, and returned a year later with Bolshevik backing; this is partly confirmed in *Novyi Vostok*, xxix (1930), 92, which recounts his attempts to establish contact with the Bolsheviks in the Caucasus in the summer of 1919.

the Soviet Government was ready to strike, weak British forces still remained in north Persia; but they were, for political reasons, under orders to avoid any direct engagement with Soviet troops. On the night of May 18, 1920, a considerable Soviet force under the command of Raskolnikov landed from the Caspian at the port of Enzeli for the immediate purpose of taking over the Russian ships of the Caspian fleet which, with their crews, had been abandoned there by the defeated Denikin. The coup was completely successful. The British garrison withdrew from Enzeli, and from the neighbouring town of Resht which was also occupied by the Soviet troops. At the same time Azerbaijan Soviet forces (or units of the Red Army posing as such) entered Gilan. At a meeting between Kuchik and Soviet representatives in Resht on May 20, 1920, an agreement was struck, and an independent Soviet republic of Gilan was proclaimed. In order to establish Kuchik's revolutionary credentials, a letter was addressed by him to Lenin begging " you and all socialists who are members of the Third International to help to liberate us and all other weak and oppressed peoples from the evil yoke of Persian and English oppressors ".[1] Simultaneously with these developments, and by way of demonstrating that they indicated no hostility in Moscow to the national government in Teheran, an exchange of notes was published between the Soviet and Persian Governments, agreeing to a resumption of official relations and the despatch of a Persian delegation to Moscow.[2]

The immediate result of the coup at Enzeli was a decline in British prestige which was fatal to any chance that remained of the ratification of the Anglo-Persian treaty. The Persian Government protested to Moscow against Soviet action in Gilan; and Chicherin in a deprecatory reply spoke of the security of the Caspian and disavowed any aggressive intention.[3] This was followed by a protest to the League of Nations, then less than six months old; but the meeting of the League council was delayed till June 16, by which time the Persian delegate reported that negotiations were in progress with the Soviet Government, and

---

[1] *Ibid.* xxix, 106; I. Maisky, *Vneshnyaya Politika RSFSR, 1917-1922* (1922), p. 157.   [2] *Pravda*, May 21, 1920.
[3] *The Times*, May 21, June 3, 1920; the notes do not appear to have been published.

SOVIET RUSSIA AND THE WORLD   PT. V

gave the council a welcome opportunity to shelve the matter.[1]
Meanwhile the Persian Prime Minister resigned. Had the Soviet
Government been able to press home its advantage, it might have
established its authority in Teheran in the summer of 1920. But
its power was not yet great enough, especially with its current
preoccupations in Europe, for decisive action. Moreover it, too,
suffered from divided counsels. Was it to uphold the authority
of Kuchik Khan, who was no communist, but might be used
against the British or against a hostile Persian Government?
Was it to encourage the small Persian Communist Party which
held its first congress at Enzeli in July 1920, and proclaimed " a
struggle against British imperialism, against the Shah's government, and against all who support them "?[2] Or was it to woo the
Persian Government, which was equally resentful of support
given to separatist and to communist movements, in the hope of
making Soviet influence paramount in Teheran? All these
courses had their supporters, but they were incompatible with one
another, and the choice had to be made. In Persia, as throughout
the Middle East, the summer and autumn of 1920 were a period
of hesitation in Soviet policy.

In Turkey the course of events was notably similar. Here, too,
the miscalculations of British policy played into the hands of the
Soviet power. While Soviet Russia, in Turkey as in Persia, published the secret treaties and ostentatiously renounced the imperialist claims of the Tsarist government as embodied in the
secret treaties, Great Britain had abandoned her traditional
nineteenth-century rôle as the protector of Turkish independence
against Russia to become Turkey's most implacable enemy.
Nationalism in Turkey was therefore bound, as in Persia and
Afghanistan, to take the form, first and foremost, of a revolt
against British policy ; and it was equally bound to find a natural
ally in Soviet Russia, the other chief object of British animosity in
eastern Europe and the Middle East. On September 13, 1919,
following the precedent of the appeal to Persia a fortnight earlier,
Chicherin issued a broadcast declaration to " the workers and

---

[1] *League of Nations : Official Journal*, No. 5 (July-August 1920), pp. 216-218.
[2] *Kommunisticheskii Internatsional*, No. 13 (September 28, 1920), cols.
2551-2552 ; No. 14 (November 6, 1920), cols. 2889-2892 ; according to a
report by Sultan-Zade in *Pravda*, July 16, 1921 (quoted in *Revue du Monde
Musulman*, lii (1922), 147), the party at that time claimed 4500 members.

peasants of Turkey ". Having recalled the prompt renunciation by the Soviet Government of the claim put forward not only by successive Tsars, but by the Provisonal Government, to Constantinople and the Straits, and the support given by the Soviet régime to all oppressed peoples, it analysed the present situation :

The way is open for England to seize on the Muslim states, small and great, with a view to their enslavement. Already she is running things as she pleases in Persia, in Afghanistan, in the Caucasus and in your country. Since the day when your government surrendered the Straits to the disposal of England, there has been no independent Turkey, no historic Turkish city of Istanbul on the mainland of Europe, no independent Ottoman nation.

It was, Chicherin went on, a venal ruling class which had betrayed the Turkish workers, first to Germany, then to the victorious allies ; the destiny of the country should be in the hands of the people. The declaration ended with an appeal from " the workers' and peasants' government of Soviet Russia " to " the workers and peasants of Turkey " to " stretch out a brotherly hand in order to expel the European robbers by simultaneous and combined force, and to destroy and render powerless those within the country who have become accustomed to build their fortune on your misfortune ".[1]

Some weeks before the issue of this declaration an event had occurred in Turkey of which it took no apparent account. At a gathering in Erzerum in August 1919, Kemal, the commander of the Turkish army in Anatolia, had publicly renounced his allegiance to the subservient government in Constantinople and placed himself at the head of a nationalist movement of revolt against the victorious western allies. The movement quickly swept the whole country outside Constantinople and the few other points in allied occupation. Kemal, though he remained at odds with the former " young Turk " leaders who had brought the country to disaster in the war, carried on the tradition of the " young Turk " revolution. This gave his programme a broad similarity to that of the Bolsheviks in regard to some practical reforms, notably industrialization, general education, the emancipation of women and the

[1] Klyuchnikov i Sabanin, *Mezhdunarodnaya Politika*, ii (1926), 384-387.

adoption of a western calendar and western script. The programme also included a ştrong emphasis on national self-determination as applied to the non-Turkish populations of the former
Turkish Empire ; and this enabled Kemal to appear as a champion
of oppressed peoples, and especially Muslim peoples, under
western rule — another important point of contact with the
Bolsheviks. The Kemalist revolution was, however, essentially
a national, not a social, revolution. Chicherin's declaration of
September 13, 1919, with its appeal to " the workers and peasants
of Turkey " from a foreign Power, cannot have been wholly
agreeable to the aspiring Turkish national leader.[1] Attempts
actively promoted from Moscow to create a Turkist communist
party [2] were still less likely to be regarded with favour. Nevertheless Kemal at this time desperately needed help and support,
which he found nowhere but in Soviet Russia ; and traditional
Turkish mistrust and hostility towards Russia were outweighed
by the recognition of an overriding, though perhaps transient,
common interest.

Meanwhile, in default of official Soviet-Turkish relations,
some personal contacts of a highly unorthodox kind had been
made in Berlin. The two former young Turk leaders, Talaat and
Enver, having been responsible as Grand Vizir and Minister of War
respectively for the German alliance, fled from Turkey after the
armistice and took refuge in Berlin. There, in August or September 1919, they were among Radek's first prison visitors. The
meeting was not without its piquancy. Talaat, who had confronted Radek rather more than a year before across the conference
table at Brest-Litovsk, now assured him that " the Muslim east
can be freed from slavery only by relying on the popular masses
and on an alliance with Soviet Russia ". But Enver was the
younger and more energetic figure ; and it was to him that Radek
made the proposal to proceed to Moscow in order to pursue there
the audacious project of a Soviet-Muslim alliance — a pact
between Russian Bolshevism and Turkish nationalism — against

---

[1] A report written a year later by a Turkish director of education complained
that " the notorious letter written by Chicherin " had undermined discipline in
the army and encouraged the resistance of the Armenians (*A Speech Delivered
by Ghazi Mustapha Kemal, October 1927* (Engl. transl., Leipzig, 1929), pp. 414-
415).
[2] See pp. 298-299 below.

British imperialism.[1]   Through General Köstring, an officer on
Seeckt's staff,[2] arrangements were made for Enver to fly to Moscow
early in October in a new Junkers plane with a director of the firm
who was making the journey. He travelled with a Turkish companion, concealed under false names as delegates of the Turkish
Red Crescent. Unfortunately for Enver the plane made a forced
landing near Kovno, and, while his identity was not discovered, he
was arrested on suspicion of being a spy and detained for two
months.[3] After this false start, Enver returned towards the end
of the year to Berlin, where a second journey was planned. This
time Radek, just released from prison, was to accompany him,
but was unable to obtain a Polish permit in time.[4] Once more
ill luck dogged Enver. He was again arrested _en route_ — this
time at Riga — and imprisoned for some time at Wolmar, reaching
Moscow only in the spring or summer of 1920.[5]

By this time much had happened that was important for
Soviet-Turkish relations. While attempts to establish contacts
between Angora and Moscow across Denikin's front appear to
have been foiled,[6] events in Asia Minor now moved fast. In
January 1920 some former deputies of the Turkish parliament in
Constantinople constituted themselves as an independent assembly
at Angora under the presidency of Kemal, and drafted the
" national pact " which was to become the programme of the
Kemalist movement — a document which recognized the claims
to independence of the non-Turkish populations of the former

[1] _Krasnaya Nov'_, No. 10, 1926, p. 164; according to K. Okay, _Enver
Pascha: Der Grosse Freund Deutschlands_ (1935), p. 333, Radek told Enver that
" in Soviet Russia everyone was welcome who would support the offensive
against English imperialism ".

[2] For Köstring see p. 313, note 2, below.

[3] The identity of the plane carrying Enver with the one detained by the
British authorities at Kovno on October 15, 1919, is established with reasonable
certainty by a comparison of _Documents on British Foreign Policy: First Series_,
ii (1948), 44-47 with K. Okay, _Enver Pascha: Der Grosse Freund Deutschlands_
(1935), pp. 334-335; the latter work is journalistic in style, but the author has
evidently used authentic sources. F. Rabenau, _Seeckt: Aus Seinem Leben,
1918-1936_ (1940), p. 306, misdates Enver's departure April 1919.

[4] _Krasnaya Nov'_, No. 10, 1926, p. 172.

[5] K. Okay, _Enver Pascha: Der Grosse Freund Deutschlands_ (1935), p. 336.

[6] At the end of 1919 two Turkish officers — one described as a nephew of
Kemal and the other as an aide-de-camp of Enver — were captured by Denikin's
forces in the Crimea while attempting to reach Moscow (_Documents on British
Foreign Policy: First Series_, iii (1949), 784).

Ottoman Empire, but asserted the same rights against the foreign invader for its predominantly Turkish territories. On March 16, 1920, strong British forces occupied Constantinople itself in the vain hope of crushing the nationalist agitation. Kemal now formally disowned the authority of the Constantinople government, and issued a proclamation calling for elections to a Grand Turkish National Assembly. The assembly duly met in Angora on April 23, 1920, and conferred on Kemal the functions of head of government, the Constantinople government, now under foreign duress, being pronounced incompetent to act in the name of the Turkish people. Three days later Kemal sent a note to the Soviet Government expressing " the desire to enter into regular relations with it and to take part in the struggle against foreign imperialism which threatens both countries ".[1]

At the moment when this note was sent, a new and direct common interest was drawing the two countries together. The three quasi-independent states under the patronage of the western allies and forming a buffer between Soviet Russia and Turkey — Georgia, Armenia and Azerbaijan — received de facto recognition from the Supreme Council of the allies in January 1920. In the past they had been a bone of contention between their two greater neighbours; and this rivalry was still very much alive. But it was none the less an immediate common interest of both to eradicate these centres, or potential centres, of a foreign influence hostile to both. When in April 1920 Soviet authority replaced British influence in Azerbaijan through the creation of an Azerbaijanian Soviet Socialist Republic, this step appeared to have the connivance, if not the active support, of the Turkish forces.[2] Whether or not it had been preceded by any tacit understanding, it can hardly have appeared to Kemal in any other light than as a

[1] The note has not been published, but its substance is quoted in Chicherin's reply of June 2, 1920 (see below) ; the date is given in L. Fischer, The Soviets in World Affairs (1930), i, 390.

[2] See Vol. 1, pp. 345-346. According to Revue du Monde Musulman, lii (1922), 194, high Turkish officers, including Halil Pasha, the uncle of Enver, assisted in the Sovietization of Azerbaijan ; an article of Sultan-Galiev in Izvestiya of May 7, 1920, speaks of Turkish officers in command of Azerbaijani troops, who were hostile to the Entente and openly advocated alliance with Soviet Russia ; these officers may have been former prisoners of war. Numerous subsequent reports of secret agreements between Soviet Russia and Turkey at this time are unsubstantiated.

blow to the common enemy; and it was while these operations were in progress that Kemal made his overture to the Soviet Government. When the allied peace terms for Turkey were disclosed in May they provided fresh matter for common alarm. The demand for the unconditional opening of the Straits and the granting of free access to the Black Sea for the warships of all nations was as frankly menacing to Soviet Russia [1] as it was humiliating to Turkey; and the offer to Persia of a free port at Batum was construed as part of a far-fetched design to make Britain, the would-be patron and protector of Persia, a Black Sea power to the detriment of both. This moment was, perhaps, the high-water mark of Soviet-Turkish friendship. On May 9, 1920, a remarkable demonstration in favour of Soviet Russia occurred in the National Assembly, when the appeal of Sovnarkom of November 24/December 7, 1917, " To all Muslim Toilers of Russia and the East ", was publicly read; [2] and it was shortly afterwards that Bekir Sami set forth as Kemal's first envoy to Moscow.[3] Simultaneously, the first unofficial Soviet envoy, Manatov, a Bashkir evidently selected for his racial and linguistic qualifications, arrived in Angora.[4]

None the less, the path of Soviet-Turkish friendship proved far from smooth. It was not till June 2, 1920, that Chicherin sent a reply to Kemal's note of April 26. He expressed the warmest sympathy with Turkish policy and aspirations, and took note of " the decision of the Grand National Assembly to coordinate our labours and our military operations against the imperialist governments ". But the concrete proposals made were limited to an offer to mediate " at any moment " in frontier negotiations with Armenia or Persia and a proposal for the immediate resumption of diplomatic relations.[5] A reply of June 20, 1920, signed by

---

[1] In 1919 to 1920 allied command of the Straits had enabled the allies to come to the aid of Denikin by sending naval units and military supplies to Black Sea ports.

[2] The official journal *Hakimiyeti Milliye*, quoted in *Die Welt des Islams*, xvi (1934), 28.

[3] *Ibid.* xvi, 28.   [4] *Ibid.* xx (1938), 123.

[5] Klyuchnikov i Sabanin, *Mezhdunarodnaya Politika*, iii, i (1928), 26-27. According to *Diplomaticheskii Slovar*, i (1948), 566, art. Diplomaticheskie Otnosheniya, relations were established as from the date of Chicherin's note; an article by Tewfik in *Dictionnaire Diplomatique*, ii (1933), 985, mentions an agreement of May 16, 1920, for the establishment of relations.

Kemal himself, took up a somewhat ambiguous attitude to the offer of mediation :

> We gladly accept the mediation of the Russian Soviet Republic to fix our frontiers with Armenia and Persia, and prefer the method of a solution of existing difficulties by diplomatic negotiations.

The note added that the Turkish Government had postponed military operations in the provinces of Kars, Ardahan and Batum on receipt of Chicherin's note, but complained of Armenian provocations and attacks, and invited the Soviet Government to put an end to them. The proposal for the establishment of diplomatic relations was welcomed : the Turkish diplomatic mission to Moscow was on the way, but had been held up by the Armenian authorities at Erzerum.[1] When it reached Moscow on July 11, 1920 differences over Armenia were the main obstacle to cordial relations.[2] But part of the difficulty was perhaps doctrinal. In the summer of 1920 Soviet policy still halted before the fateful choice between universal support of communist parties in foreign countries for the furtherance of world-wide revolution[3] and cooperation with selected bourgeois governments, where national interests appeared to require it, even at the expense of the communist parties in the countries concerned. Optimism about the prospects of world revolution, which had seemed in partial eclipse during the winter of 1919–1920, was once more general; and powerful circles in the Kremlin still shrank from military or diplomatic alliances with non-communist powers, and continued to believe in propaganda against all capitalist governments as the most effective, and indeed the only proper, instrument of Soviet foreign policy.

---

[1] The note was published in the Turkish official journal, *Hakimiyeti Milliye*, of July 8, 1920, and is translated in *Mitteilungen des Seminars für Orientalische Sprachen zu Berlin*, xxxvii (1934), ii, 135-136 ; Klyuchnikov i Sabanin, *Mezhdunarodnaya Politika*, iii, i (1928), 27-28, is therefore wrong in treating Kemal's note of November 29, 1920, as the reply to Chicherin's note of June 2. The apparent ambiguity of the Turkish reply on mediation might disappear on examination of the Turkish original : it is clear that the intention was politely to reject the Soviet offer.

[2] I. Maisky, *Vneshnyaya Politika RSFSR, 1918–1922* (1922), p. 164 ; *Die Welt des Islams*, xvi (1934), 28.

[3] For support given at this time to communist movements in Turkey, see pp. 298-299 below.

Such were the conditions when in July 1920 the second congress of Comintern set out to formulate a policy on what was known as " the national and colonial question ". The task before the congress was to apply the principles of world revolution to the eastern peoples, to develop the doctrine of a common struggle in which all the workers of the world, west and east, had their part to play, and, in particular, to strengthen the revolt under the leadership of the RSFSR against British imperialism. The congress, unlike its predecessor, was attended by delegates not only from the non-Russian peoples of the former Tsarist empire, including Georgia, Armenia, Azerbaijan and Bokhara, but from India, Turkey, Persia, China and Korea. There were still many absentees, but some of these were vicariously represented. The newly founded communist party of the Netherlands Indies was represented by a Dutchman from Java, who had played a part in creating it, and appeared at the congress under the name of Maring ; [1] and the cause of the negro in the United States was eloquently pleaded by the American, John Reed. On July 24, 1920, at one of its first sessions, the congress appointed a commission to consider the national and colonial question and to draft a report : Maring was chosen as its secretary.[2] The commission worked with extreme rapidity and presented the results of its

[1] The history of the communist party of the Netherlands Indies has an interest exceeding its intrinsic importance. In 1912 a Muslim party (Sarekat Islam) was founded by Javanese leaders to promote the interests of the native population. It acquired a large native membership, and took on a mixed religious-nationalist complexion. In 1914 a group of Dutchmen in Java, of whom Sneevliet and Baars were the most important, formed a Social-Democratic Association of the Indies (ISDV) as the centre of a secular radical movement among native workers, and started a journal *Het Vrye Woord*. This movement gathered strength during the war and especially after the Russian revolution ; and in 1919 Sneevliet was expelled by the Dutch authorities. In May 1920 Baars brought about the transformation of the ISDV into the Communist Party of the Indies (PKI) under the leadership of two Javanese, Semaun and Darsono ; and Sneevliet, who had gone to Moscow, represented this party under the *alias* Maring (by which he was thereafter known in Comintern) at the second congress of Comintern. The PKI was formally affiliated to Comintern in December 1920. The fullest source of information on the PKI is J. T. P. Blumberger, *Le Communisme aux Indes Néerlandaises* (French transl. from Dutch, 1929) ; an account in *Revue du Monde Musulman*, lii (1922), pp. 55-83, also covers the early years but seems less well informed in detail. An account of Sarekat Islam is given in S. Dingley *The Peasants' Movement in Indonesia* (Berlin, n.d. [1926]), pp. 33-37, a publication of the " Farmers' and Peasants' International ".

[2] *Der Zweite Kongress der Kommunist. Internationale* (Hamburg, 1921), p. 101.

labours to the congress on July 26 ; two days were then devoted to a discussion in plenary session. It was the first time, the Indian delegate, M. N. Roy, remarked, that he had ever been able " to take part seriously in a discussion of the colonial question at a congress of the revolutionary proletariat ".[1] The commission had found itself confronted with two sets of theses on the national and colonial question presented respectively by Lenin and by Roy.[2] The general theme of the liberation of the oppressed peoples through a world-wide proletarian revolution was common to both. But two minor differences and one major difference appeared between them. First, Roy described the economic order prevailing in colonial and semi-colonial territories as " pre-capitalist ". The majority of the commission preferred to describe it as " dominated by capitalistic imperialism " ; and this amendment to Roy's theses was readily adopted.[3] Secondly, Roy developed the familiar thesis that the bourgeoisie in capitalist countries was able to stave off the proletarian revolution only by subsidizing the workers out of the proceeds of colonial exploitation, and carried the argument to the point of asserting that revolution in Europe was impossible until the Asiatic countries had thrown off the yoke of European imperialism. This seemed to the majority of the commission to put an unfair emphasis on the revolution in Asia, but called only for some tactful readjustments of phrase to bring Roy's theses into substantial agreement with those of Lenin.[4] The third and major difference turned on a

[1] *Der Zweite Kongress der Kommunist. Internationale* (Hamburg, 1921), p. 150.

[2] For Lenin's theses in their original form, see *Sochineniya*, xxv, 285-290 ; for Roy's, see *Vtoroi Kongress Kommunisticheskogo Internatsionala* (1921), pp. 122-126, apparently the only edition which preserves them in their original form.

[3] Roy's theses were drafted and amended in English ; the phrase as amended was carefully reproduced in *Theses and Statutes of the Third (Communist) International* (Moscow, 1920), p. 70, but mistranslated in the German version (*Der Zweite Kongress der Kommunist. Internationale* (Hamburg, 1921), p. 145) ; and this mistranslation was followed in all Russian versions before 1934, when the correct version was reinstated in *Vtoroi Kongress Kominterna* (1934), pp. 496-498.

[4] Here too differences occur between different versions : the German version (*Der Zweite Kongress der Kommunist. Internationale* (Hamburg, 1921), pp. 146-147) and all Russian versions before 1934 emphasize the dependence of the European on the Asiatic revolution more strongly than the amended English text, which is correctly translated in the Russian version of 1934 (see preceding note).

practical issue of tactics which, in one form or another, was destined to be a constant source of embarrassment both to the Soviet Government and to Comintern. This issue was debated, first in the commission, and then in the plenary sessions of the congress, in the form of a direct challenge to the theses put forward by Lenin.

The starting point of Lenin's theses was the need for " an alliance of the proletarians and of the toiling masses of all nations and countries in a simultaneous revolutionary struggle for the overthrow of the landowners and of the bourgeoisie ", i.e. of feudalism in the backward countries and of capitalism in the advanced countries. The advantage was mutual; for such an alliance would hasten the victory of the proletariat over capitalism, and without this victory oppression of the subject peoples by the capitalist nations could not be overcome. Account must, however, be taken of the world political situation :

> All the events of world politics are necessarily concentrated round one central point, the struggle of the world bourgeoisie against the Soviet Russian republic, which inevitably groups about itself, on the one hand, the Soviet movements of the advanced workers of all countries and, on the other hand, all national movements of liberation of the colonies and oppressed nationalities, which are convinced by bitter experience that there is no salvation for them except in the victory of the Soviet power over world imperialism.

What therefore was needed was " a close alliance of all national and colonial movements of liberation with Soviet Russia ". It was an open question whether the movements with which this alliance would be struck would be proletarian-communist or bourgeois-democratic. This must be decided by the degree of development of the country concerned. In backward countries communists must be prepared to assist " a bourgeois-democratic movement of liberation ", and especially to support the peasantry against the large landowner and " against all manifestations and relics of feudalism ". But, where this was necessary, there must be no ideological confusion :

> The Communist International must march in temporary alliance with the bourgeois democracy of the colonies and

backward countries, but must not fuse with it and must preserve absolutely the independence of the communist movement even in its most rudimentary form.[1]

Roy's theses, which had been prepared independently, did not contradict those of Lenin. But they were markedly different in emphasis and, on the vital issue of tactics, seemed to point to a different conclusion. Roy sharply distinguished two types of movements in the colonial countries — the first, a bourgeois-democratic nationalist movement which sought political independence within the capitalist order, the second, " a struggle of landless peasants against every form of exploitation ". It was the business of Comintern to resist all attempts to subordinate the second type of movement to the first. The urgent need was " the creation of communist organizations of workers and peasants ", who in the backward countries could be won for communism, " not through capitalist development, but through the development of class consciousness ". Thus " the real strength, the foundation, of the liberation movement cannot in the colonies be forced within the narrow frame of bourgeois-democratic nationalism ". While, however, communist parties of class-conscious workers must take the lead, " the revolution in the colonial countries will not at first be a communist revolution " ; for instance, the agrarian policy of Comintern in such countries must be framed not on communist but on petty bourgeois principles, i.e. it must aim at a division of the land among the peasants. This provisional acceptance of peasant ownership was an implied answer to the criticism of the SRs that they alone, and not the Bolsheviks, could carry the revolution to the peasant peoples of the east. It was, after all, the policy followed by the Bolsheviks themselves in Russia when they borrowed the agrarian policy of the SRs in October 1917.

Though the proceedings in the commission were not fully reported, it is clear that Roy's theses enjoyed at least as much sympathy as those of Lenin. Lenin's theses emerged from the commission with a number of amendments. The most important of these had the effect of blunting the sharp edge of Lenin's thought and of bridging disagreement by resort to a potential ambiguity : wherever Lenin's draft had recommended communists

[1] Lenin, *Sochineniya*, xxv, 285-290.

in colonial countries to support " bourgeois-democratic national
liberation movements ", the specific epithet " bourgeois-democratic " was replaced by the comprehensive " revolutionary ",
which could no doubt be applied to a bourgeois-democratic
revolutionary movement, but had a less compromising sound.
The other important additions insisted on " the struggle against
the reactionary and mediaeval influence of the priesthood, of
Christian missions and similar elements ", and " the struggle
against pan-Islamism and the pan-Asiatic movement and similar
tendencies " : these additions seem to have been made at the
instance of the Turkish delegate, who did not wish support for
the Turkish national revolt against western imperialism to
degenerate into general sympathy for pan-Islamic movements,
such as were being sponsored at this moment by the renegade
Enver.[1] Lenin's theses, thus amended, were unanimously approved by the commission and sent to the congress, together with
Roy's proposals, also suitably amended, as " supplementary
theses ".[2] In defending his carefully balanced theses at the
plenary session, Lenin argued that the fundamental division in
the world at the moment was between oppressing and oppressed
nations ; the course of events was being determined " by the
struggle of a small number of imperialist nations against the
Soviet movement and the Soviet states with Soviet Russia at their
head ".[3] Moreover, Lenin was prepared by way of exception to
admit for the backward countries the same possibility which Marx
had once allowed for Russia. If the " victorious revolutionary
proletariat " came to their aid, then it was not inevitable that these
countries should pass through " the capitalist stage of economic
development" : they might, with such aid, "make the transition to
the Soviet order, and thence through defined stages of development
to communism, avoiding the capitalist stage of development ".[4]

    Lenin's whole-hearted support of national liberation move-
ments even of a bourgeois character was enthusiastically endorsed

---

[1] See pp. 264-266 below.
[2] The amendments to Lenin's theses were detailed in Maring's report to
the congress (*Der Zweite Kongress der Kommunist. Internationale* (Hamburg,
1921), pp. 144-145) ; Roy's theses were merely read to the congress by himself
in their amended form (*ibid.* pp. 145-150). Both sets of theses are in *Kom-
misticheskii Internatsional v Dokumentakh* (1933), pp. 126-132 ; these versions of
Roy's theses both contain the mistranslations noted on p. 252 above.
[3] Lenin, *Sochineniya*, xxv, 352.   [4] *Ibid.* xxv, 354.

by the Irish delegate, Connolly, son of the nationalist leader who had been executed in Dublin in 1916,[1] and by one of the British delegates, MacLean, who thought that the strength of British capitalism could be destroyed only by ending colonial exploitation.[2] On the other hand, delegates from Persia and Korea, where, as in British India, foreign capital had planted the beginnings of industrialization and an industrial proletariat, strongly reiterated Roy's warnings against too close a commitment to bourgeois-democratic nationalism.[3] Maring praised the Muslim party, Sarekat Islam, in the Netherlands East Indies which, in spite of its religious name, was revolutionary in the nationalist sense and had even " acquired a class character ". But, having thus in essence ranged himself on the side of Lenin, Maring tactfully argued that no discrepancy existed between the theses of Lenin and of Roy ; and the congress, relieved to take this view, cheerfully adopted both. The only opposing voice was that of the Italian delegate Serrati, who regarded both Lenin's and Roy's theses as an unwarrantable compromise with expediency, maintaining to the last that " the true liberation of the oppressed peoples can be achieved only through a proletarian revolution and a Soviet order, not through a temporary and accidental union

[1] Negotiations had recently taken place between Soviet and Sinn Fein representatives in New York, and a " draft treaty between the RSFSR and the Republic of Ireland " was circulating in June 1920 in Dublin, where a copy fell into the hands of the British authorities : to judge from the documents officially published by the British Government (*Intercourse between Bolshevism and Sinn Fein*, Cmd. 1326 (1921)), the negotiations were not taken very seriously on either side. Early in 1921 the official journal of Comintern published a message of greetings from the Irish Red Army and workers' republic to the Russian Red Army and workers' republic (*Kommunisticheskii Internatsional*, No. 16 (March 31, 1921), cols. 3779-3782. The alliance between communism and Irish nationalism in the early 1920s gave some electoral advantages to the CPGB ; one of the two successful communist candidates in the general election of 1922 was returned for a Glasgow constituency where the Irish vote was important.

[2] The British delegates in the commission, Quelch and Ramsay, made an uncomfortable impression by confessing that a majority of English workers would " regard support of the revolutionary struggle of the colonies against British imperialism as treason " and would applaud the suppression of a rising in India ; these remarks were several times referred to in the plenary sessions, where they were evidently discredited as too bad to be true (*Der Zweite Kongress der Kommunist. Internationale* (Hamburg, 1921), pp. 160, 185, 193, 199).

[3] For Korea, see pp. 495-496 below ; the Korean delegate, Pak Din-Shun, had already stated his views in an article in *Pravda*, July 27, 1920, quoted in K. S. Weigh, *Russo-Chinese Diplomacy* (Shanghai, 1928), p. 326.

of communist parties with so-called revolutionary bourgeois parties ".[1] The theses of Lenin became henceforth the accepted basis of Bolshevik theory and practice in the national and colonial question; Roy's supplementary theses were forgotten.[2] The line now laid down introduced no new principle. In 1905 Lenin had worked out the programme of an alliance between the proletariat and the petty-bourgeois peasantry to achieve the first stage of the revolution and had carried out this programme with brilliant success in 1917. This precedent was certainly in the minds of many delegates at the second congress of Comintern; even Roy admitted that the agrarian programme of eastern communist parties must still be the petty-bourgeois programme of distribution of the land to the peasants. Lenin's theses followed precisely the doctrine expounded in the party programme of 1919, which recognized the unconditional right of secession for subject nations, but made the decision which class — the bourgeoisie or the workers — was the bearer of this right, and therefore deserving of the support of the party, conditional on the " class-historical viewpoint ", i.e. the degree of development attained by the nation concerned; [3] an attitude which had been formulated primarily with reference to the subject peoples of the former Tsarist empire proved equally applicable to other eastern peoples. Finally, the new line also corresponded with the conception " of manoeuvring, of conciliation, of compromises with other parties, including bourgeois parties ", which Lenin had propounded so trenchantly three months earlier in *The Infantile Disease of " Leftism " in Communism*; [4] tactical cooperation with social-democratic parties in western Europe, which were none the less denounced as essentially bourgeois, was matched by tactical cooperation with bourgeois-democratic movements seeking to achieve national liberation for the eastern peoples. Yet these precedents, while they might serve to explain and justify the adoption of Lenin's theses by Comintern, also suggested the

---

[1] The instructive debate in the two plenary sessions is in *Der Zweite Kongress der Kommunist. Internationale* (Hamburg, 1921), pp. 137-232.

[2] It is significant that glaring mistranslations in the current German and Russian versions of Roy's theses remained undetected for fourteen years.

[3] See Vol. 1, pp. 270-271.

[4] See p. 179 above.

danger latent in them.   These projected temporary alliances with
bourgeois groups were, one and all, combinations in which the
allies of today — the peasants, the bourgeois nationalists, the
social-democrats — were the enemies of tomorrow, and had to
be proclaimed as such at the very moment when their cooperation
was being wooed.   This was merely another aspect of the fundamental dilemma of a proletarian socialist revolution not resting
on the secure and established basis of a bourgeois democratic
revolution : once the proletariat — or the communist party acting
in its name — was compelled to take the lead in completing the
bourgeois revolution as a prelude to embarking on the proletarian
revolution, its reciprocal relations with the bourgeoisie became
incurably ambivalent.[1]   What was difficult about the policy of
cooperation with bourgeois democratic national movements was
not that it exposed the Bolshevik leaders to charges of opportunism
from Leftists or doctrinal purists in the party ranks, but that the
potential allies whom it was proposed to enlist were as well aware
as the communists of the short-term calculation which inspired
the alliance, and equally disinclined to make that alliance a mainstay of their policy.

In the summer of 1920 the dangers inherent in this situation
were not obvious.   In the first place, cooperation with bourgeois
national movements, like the expedients recommended by Lenin
in *The Infantile Disease of " Leftism " in Communism*, was conceived in terms of the brief period before the now imminent
European proletarian revolution, which would transform the
Asiatic scene and sweep away any embarrassments resulting from
these transitory alliances.   Secondly, existing national movements
in Asia, outside as well as inside the boundaries of the RSFSR,
were still weak enough to be almost entirely dependent on aid and
support from Moscow (Turkey was an as yet unrecognized exception to this rule)[2] ;   it was Moscow that decided the terms on
which support could be given.   So long as these two conditions
prevailed, the question of a potential incompatibility between the
interests of the Soviet Government and of communist parties in
the countries concerned did not seem to arise.   But, when the

---

[1] See Vol. 1, pp. 41-44.
[2] China was the most important exception of all, but scarcely came within
the orbit of Soviet or Comintern policy at this time.

policy enunciated in Lenin's theses was applied over a long period, and in situations where national governments were strong enough to lay down their own terms for alliance with Moscow, and where these terms included the unimpeded right to suppress national communist parties, difficulties emerged which could not have been foreseen in the enthusiastic atmosphere of the summer of 1920. The decisions of the second congress of Comintern in the national question, like most of its other decisions, were taken in an unquestioning faith in the imminence of a proletarian revolution which would sweep the world. Once this faith was disappointed, the decisions themselves, applied in conditions utterly different from those for which they had been designed, not only falsified the intentions of their authors, but were used to justify a series of compromises and retreats which, in the hour of faith and enthusiasm, would have been brushed aside as inconceivable.

The long discussion of the national and colonial question at the second congress was evidence of a new concentration of interest on eastern questions, which corresponded with the shift in Soviet policy at this time from west to east following the victories over Kolchak and Denikin in the civil war.[1] For the first time it became possible to interweave the national policy pursued by the RSFSR within its own borders with its foreign policy of support for national movements in revolt against imperialist Powers, and to contrast the autonomy or independence bestowed on national republics within the RSFSR with the fate of the Asiatic peoples directly or indirectly within the orbit of the western Powers. The first All-Kalmyk Congress of Soviets in July 1920 celebrated its birth by issuing an appeal " to the peoples of India, Tibet, Mongolia, China and Siam and all other peoples under the heel of world imperialism " ; the first All-Kirgiz (i.e. Kazakh) Congress of Soviets followed suit three months later.[2] But the first step was to carry the eastern question into a setting more appropriate to it than a universal congress of Comintern in Moscow. The issue of the official journal of Comintern which appeared on the

[1] See Vol. I, pp. 325-329.
[2] Both these proclamations are in *Zhizn' Natsional'nostei*, No. 34 (91), November 3, 1920.

opening day of the second congress carried an invitation " to the enslaved popular masses of Persia, Armenia and Turkey " to a congress which was to assemble at Baku on August 15, 1920. The summons to Baku, drafted in the headquarters of Comintern before the debates of the second congress in Moscow, betrayed none of that inclination to compromise with expediency, none of that readiness to seek the alliance of bourgeois nationalist movements which Lenin preached in his theses at the congress. In apostrophizing the " peasants and workers of Persia ", the invitation went out of its way to denounce " the lackeys of the Teheran government ", who " oppress you with taxes at will and, when they had reduced the land to such a condition that it no longer yielded them enough, sold Persia last year to English capitalists ". In addressing the " peasants of Anatolia ", it expressed satisfaction that, in spite of Kemal's insistent appeals calling them to the colours, they were " trying to organize a people's party of your own, your own peasant party, which will be capable of continuing the struggle even if the Pashas make peace with the Entente despoilers ". It exhorted the workers of the east generally to resist not only the " foreign capitalists ", but also " native profiteers ". The traditional Muslim pilgrimage to the holy places was to be transformed into a pilgrimage to the meeting-place of world revolution :

> Formerly you used to cross the desert to visit the sacred places : now cross deserts and mountains and rivers to meet together and discuss how to free yourselves from the chains of servitude, and join in brotherly union to live an equal, free and fraternal life.[1]

The " first congress of peoples of the east " (as it was officially called) met in Baku on September 1, 1920, under the presidency of Zinoviev who, together with Radek and Bela Kun, represented Comintern at the gathering and greeted the delegates in its name. Thanks to the preparatory work done by party organizations in the Caucasus and in Turkestan,[2] it was by far the largest gathering which Comintern had yet brought together. Among the 1891 delegates were 235 Turks, 192 " Persians and Parsees ", 8 Chinese,

---

[1] *Kommunisticheskii Internatsional*, No. 12 (July 20, 1920), cols. 2259-2264.
[2] *Izvestiya Tsentral'nogo Komiteta Rossiiskoi Kommunisticheskoi Partii (Bol'shevikov)*, No. 22, September 18, 1920, p. 2.

8 Kurds and 3 Arabs ; the rest, including 157 Armenians and 100 Georgians, came mainly from the Caucasian and central Asian peoples formerly belonging to the Russian Empire and now forming part of the RSFSR or in treaty relations with it. Rather more than two-thirds of the delegates professed themselves communists.[1] The invitation had proclaimed the doctrine of world revolution in its purest and most uncompromising form. Zinoviev's opening speech, influenced no doubt by the debates of the second congress in Moscow, by the changed military situation in the west, and by the character of his audience at Baku, struck a rather different note. Muslim beliefs and institutions were treated with veiled respect, and the cause of world revolution narrowed down to specific and more manageable dimensions. The Muslim tradition of the Jehad, or holy war against the infidel, was harnessed to a modern crusade of oppressed peoples against the imperialist oppressors, with Britain as the main target of attack. The speech created a sensation and whipped the audience into a mood of frenzied enthusiasm. The peroration and the scenes which accompanied it may be reported in the language of the official record ;

Comrades ! Brothers ! The time has come when you can start on the organization of a true and holy people's war against the robbers and oppressors. The Communist International turns today to the peoples of the east and says to them : " Brothers, we summon you to a holy war, in the first place against English imperialism ! " (Stormy applause. Prolonged hurrahs. The members of the congress rise from their seats and brandish their weapons. The orator is unable for a long time to continue his speech. The delegates stand and clap applause. The cry rings out : " We swear it ").
May today's declaration be heard in London, in Paris, in all cities where the capitalists are still in power ! May they heed the solemn oath, taken by the representatives of tens of millions of the toilers of the east, that in the east the might of the oppressors, of the English, the capitalist yoke which weighs on the toilers of the east shall be no more !
Long live the brotherly union of the peoples of the east with the Communist International !
Down with capital, long live the empire of labour ! (Stormy

[1] *1ᵛᵗ S"ezd Narodov Vostoka* (1920), p. 5 ; on the other hand, Zinoviev in *Kommunisticheskii Internatsional*, No. 14 (November 6, 1920), cols. 2941-2944, described a majority of the delegates as " non-party ".

applause. Voices : " Long live the resurrection of the east ! "
Shouts of " Hurrah ! " Applause. Voices ; " Long live the
Third Communist International ! " Shouts of " Hurrah ! "
Applause. Voices ; " Long live the uniters of the east, our
honoured leaders, our dear Red Army ! " Shouts of " Hurrah ! "
Applause).[1]

More than one later speaker recalled with enthusiasm this opening
scene of the congress at which swords, daggers and revolvers had
been " bared " for the fight against imperialism.[2]

It does not appear that the congress in its subsequent proceedings ever quite recaptured this first uncritical frenzy. A multi-
national assembly nearly 2000 strong is not a working body ; and
the real business was transacted behind closed doors by two
" fractions " or committees representing respectively the party and
non-party members of the congress. The mere task of translation
made the proceedings laborious. Russian, Azerbaijani-Turkish
and Persian were recognized as the official languages.[3] Standard
Turkish was apparently not understood by some of the Azerbaijani
and Uzbek delegates, who from time to time demanded translations in their own tongues ; and mention is made of translations
into Kalmyk, Chechen and other languages. In spite of these
handicaps, the congress heard speeches not only from Radek and
Bela Kun, but from the delegates of a score or more of eastern
peoples. Radek was clearly concerned to remove any suspicions
that the friendship of Moscow might prove fickle and short-lived :

A permanent peace between the country of the workers and
the exploiting countries is impossible. The eastern policy of
the Soviet Government is thus no diplomatic manœuvre, no
pushing forward of the peoples of the east into the firing-line

[1] *Iᵛⁱ S"ezd Narodov Vostoka* (1920), p. 48. A hostile German commen-
tator, whose information came mainly from Georgian Menshevik sources,
states that the official record of the Baku Congress has been " in part directly
falsified " by the omission of documents and by the abbreviation or distortion
of hostile speeches, and that this is proved by comparison with reports in the
contemporary Baku press (*Archiv für Sozialwissenschaft und Sozialpolitik*
(Leipzig), l (1922), 195-196). The Baku newspapers of 1920 are no longer
readily accessible ; nor does the writer appear to have consulted them himself.
The documents which he names were probably omitted for reasons of space,
as happened in the records of most party congresses : some of them were
printed after the congress in *Kommunisticheskii Internatsional*.
[2] *Iᵛⁱ S"ezd Narodov Vostoka* (1920), pp. 72, 82.
[3] *Ibid.* pp. 99-100.

in order, by betraying them, to win advantages for the Soviet republic. . . . We are bound to you by a common destiny: either we unite with the peoples of the east and hasten the victory of the western European proletariat, or we shall perish and you will be slaves.[1]

And later another delegate from Moscow, Pavlovich, repeated the significant admission made by Lenin at the second congress of Comintern, and explained that " with the help of the leading proletarian countries the backward peoples can pass over to the Soviet system and through a definite stage towards communism while avoiding the capitalist stage of development ".[2]

The congress was not, however, free from its embarrassments. The skilful joinery which Lenin had effected in Moscow between the destinies of the oppressed proletariat of Europe and of the oppressed peoples of Asia was less convincing in the variegated assembly at Baku. The awkward issue of religion was shelved.[3] But even so, it was difficult to establish, either in practice or in Marxist doctrine, a permanent equation between the revolutionary proletariat of the west and the peasantry of the east. The leaders of Comintern and the eastern peoples found common cause in a common hatred, based on different though not incompatible grounds, of " English imperialism ". What united them was, first and foremost, the prospect of a joint campaign against a common enemy. The Baku congress met at a moment when belief in imminent world revolution had been fanned to its highest point; the congress itself was a product of that belief. If that hope was realized, all would be well. Mutyshev, a delegate from the Caucasus, voiced it in regard to Turkey:

> Mustapha Kemal's movement is a national liberation movement. We support it but, as soon as the struggle with imperialism is finished, we believe that this movement will pass over to social revolution.[4]

[1] *Ibid.* p. 70.   [2] *Ibid.* p. 144.

[3] A body calling itself " the Indian revolutionary organization in Turkestan " sent a petition to the congress from Tashkent begging for help for " the oppressed 315 millions of the people of India ", but asking that " this help should be granted without any interference in the domestic or religious life of those who await liberation from the yoke of capitalism and imperialism " (*ibid.* p. 106); there is no trace of any discussion of this question at the congress.

[4] *Ibid.* p. 159.

No delegate to the congress was craven enough to ask what would
happen if this belief were not realized.

The potential contradiction between alternative policies of
support for bourgeois movements of national liberation seeking
the alliance of the RSFSR or of support for local communist
parties in revolt against a national bourgeoisie had not been
resolved in the discussion of Lenin's and Roy's theses at the
second congress of Comintern. The same contradiction, which
could easily be represented as a choice between revolutionary
expediency and a rigid revolutionary internationalism, was in no
way allayed at Baku. On the contrary an unforeseen and un-
rehearsed incident of the congress gave a foretaste of the practical
dilemma which was soon to confront Soviet policy in other
fields — the choice between neglecting an apparent national
interest and taking action difficult to reconcile with revolutionary
principle. The conversations between Radek and Enver in
Berlin in 1919 had planted in Enver's mind a firm determination to
utilize Soviet Russia as a spring-board for his own rehabilitation
and for revenge on his major enemy, Great Britain. When he
arrived in Moscow in the summer of 1920 to offer his services to
the Soviet Government, his credentials were his considerable
military and administrative talents and his firm undying hatred of
Great Britain, the conqueror of his country and the source of his
own misfortunes. What passed in the ensuing conversations is
unknown. But there is ample evidence of his friendly welcome in
Moscow, and the report that he was received by Lenin is plausible.[1]
He was regarded with sufficient favour as a potential ally in eastern
policy to be allowed to appear as a visitor at the Baku congress of
eastern peoples.[2]

Here, however, the difficulties began. The " young Turk "

[1] W. von Blücher, *Deutschlands Weg nach Rapallo* (Wiesbaden, 1951),
p. 132 ; the report evidently emanated from Enver himself.
[2] In a letter to Seeckt of August 26, 1920, Enver wrote : " The day before
yesterday we concluded a Turkish-Russian treaty of friendship : under this the
Russians will support us with gold and by all means " (F. von Rabenau, *Seeckt :
Aus Seinem Leben, 1918–1936* (1940), p. 307). According to L. Fischer, *The
Soviets in World Affairs* (1930), i, 386, Enver " tried to act,as an intermediary
in the Russo-Turkish pourparlers and to put himself in the position of the real
representative of Turkey " ; while the evidence is slender, the agreement
referred to seems more likely to have related to Enver's own activities than to
relations with Angora.

revolution of 1908 was primarily nationalist in character, and therefore " anti-imperialist ". It might by some stretching of language be called bourgeois. But it was in no obvious sense democratic; and it was not a revolution of the workers, whether proletarian or peasant. Nothing in Enver's flamboyant record suggested a champion either of the proletariat or of oppressed nationalities. He was one of the authors of the notorious Armenian massacres; and there was a large Armenian delegation at the congress. On the hypothesis that the congress was a meeting-ground for those who on whatever pretext hated British imperialism, Enver Pasha was an honoured guest. On any other hypothesis he was the declared opponent of almost everything the congress professed to stand for. Worse still, Enver was the sworn enemy of Kemal, and was not unjustly suspected of an ambition to dislodge him from the seat of authority in the new Turkey. The Turks at Baku detested British imperialism and were for the most part faithful to the national revolution which Kemal had carried out in Turkey (it is not clear that they were revolutionaries in any other sense); [1] but they wanted no truck with Enver. Hence the principal sponsor of Enver at Baku was Zinoviev himself. Nor was this as paradoxical as it might appear at first sight. Enver was a potential asset of Soviet policy; but he could not easily be regarded as a supporter either of national liberation or of world revolution, except in the sense in which Soviet policy could be automatically identified with these two causes.

A compromise was reached. Enver did not appear in person in the congress hall. But a declaration was read from the platform — not without " noise " and " protests " from the floor — in which he regretted having been " compelled to fight on the side of German imperialism ", argued that, " if present-day Russia had then existed and had been fighting for her present aims ", he would have been whole-heartedly on her side, and, finally, claimed to represent a " union of the revolutionary organizations of Morocco, Algiers, Tunis, Tripoli, Egypt, Arabia and Hindustan " (which seems to have been invented for the purpose). This was followed by the reading of a declaration of " the representative

---

[1] According to Zinoviev, one Turkish delegate, a professor, " said openly that Turkey wanted nothing from Russia but arms " (*Kommunicheskii Internatsional*, No. 14 (November 6, 1920), col. 2943).

of the Angora government ", who was also in Baku as an observer and tactfully stressed the close friendship between the new " national and revolutionary government " of Turkey and revolutionary Russia. Then Bela Kun presented a resolution on behalf of the presidium; and Zinoviev from the chair, ignoring loud requests for a discussion, hastily declared it carried. After some general reflections on the Turkish revolution, it issued a warning against " those leaders of the movement who in the past led the Turkish peasants and workers to the slaughter in the interests of an imperialist group " (which might be taken as a censure of Enver), and summoned such leaders to redeem their past errors by action in the service of the working population (which left the door open to his further employment in the future).[1] Exactly what impression these proceedings made on the congress can no longer be ascertained. But the story of Enver as a champion of world revolution at Baku went the rounds in socialist circles in Europe; and six weeks later Zinoviev, when challenged at the Halle congress, had some difficulty in defending even the slightly garbled version of the resolution which he read to the delegates.[2] It was only too easy for the critics to argue, on the one hand, that " the Turks, the Persians, the Koreans, the Hindus and the Chinese " were turning " not towards the communism of Moscow, but towards the political strength of Moscow ",[3] and, on the other hand, that Comintern was not immune from a temptation " to regard the peoples of the east as pieces on the chessboard of the diplomatic war with the Entente ".[4] All these elements were

---

[1] *I^vi S"ezd Narodov Vostoka* (1920), pp. 108-118.

[2] *USPD: Verhandlungen des Ausserordentlichen Parteitags zu Halle* (n.d.), pp. 159-161. Enver's career remained eventful to the close. After the fiasco of Baku he returned to Moscow, and then, after the conclusion of the Soviet-Turkish treaty of March 16, 1921, returned to the Caucasus to conduct anti-Kemalist intrigues; according to L. Fischer, *The Soviets in World Affairs* (1930), i, 387, Kemal protested to the Soviet Government which put a stop to Enver's activities. Enver obtained permission to go to Bokhara; for his subsequent adventures and death see Vol. 1, pp. 338-339.

[3] As Longuet suggested at the Tours congress (*Parti Socialiste: 18e Congrès National* (1921), p. 403).

[4] As Martov alleged at the Halle congress (*USPD: Verhandlungen des Ausserordentlichen Parteitags zu Halle* (n.d.), p. 214); Hilferding had already argued that the Baku congress had nothing to do with socialism, and was pure power politics (*ibid.* p. 189). Apart from the Enver episode, Zinoviev's defence at Halle of the necessity of running the western and eastern revolutions in double harness was not unsuccessful (*ibid.* pp. 161-163).

present in the situation at Baku, and were superimposed on the original strain of sincere revolutionary enthusiasm. This uncomfortable episode probably played a larger part in retrospective criticism than at the congress itself. The public proceedings ended in an atmosphere of successful achievement and mutual congratulation. The congress issued two manifestos — one " To the Peoples of the East ", the other " To the Workers of Europe, America and Japan " [1] — and passed several resolutions. The first of these invited the " oppressed peasantry of the east " to " count in its revolutionary struggle on the support of the revolutionary workers of the west, on the support of the Communist International and of the Soviet states, present and future, and to set up Soviet power in the east ".[2] The second recommended the seizure of the land by the peasants and the expulsion both of " foreign capitalist conquerors " and of " landowners, bourgeois and other oppressors at home ".[3] By a third resolution, the congress set up a " council of propaganda and action " to execute the policies it had adopted. The council, composed of 47 members of more than 20 nationalities, was to meet once in three months at Baku. During the intervals its affairs were to be managed by a presidium of seven including two representatives of Comintern, who were accorded a right of veto on its proceedings. The council was to have a branch in Tashkent " and in other centres where it may find it necessary ".[4] The last symbolic act of the congress was to attend a funeral ceremony of the 26 Bolshevik commissars of Baku who had met their death at the hands of the " whites ", allegedly with British connivance, in September 1918, and whose bodies had just been brought back to Baku.[5]

The Baku congress, though described in its records as the first congress of eastern peoples, had no successor, and left little behind it in the way of machinery. The council of propaganda and action was set up at Baku, and made its first report to IKKI in November

---

[1] These were approved in principle by the congress without seeing the proposed text (*I*[vi] *S"ezd Narodov Vostoka* (1920), pp. 118-119) ; they were not included in the records of the congress, but were published in *Kommunisticheskii Internatsional*, No. 14 (November 6, 1920), cols. 2941-2944.

[2] *I*[vi] *S"ezd Narodov Vostoka* (1920), pp. 183-186.

[3] *Ibid.* pp. 199-206.   [4] *Ibid.* pp. 211-212, 219-220.

[5] *Ibid.* pp. 223-224 ; for this occurrence see Vol. 1, p. 344, note 1.

1920.[1] In December it announced the first issue of a journal, *The Peoples of the East*, to appear in Russian, Turkish, Persian and Arabic.[2] There is little other record of its activities. The speedy disappearance of the council and its journal[3] may have been in part a consequence of the Anglo-Soviet trade agreement of March 1921 ; it also illustrated the difficulty of creating any effective political organ outside Moscow. Yet, though the Baku council of propaganda and action proved a failure, the intensification of interest in eastern questions in the latter part of 1920 was responsible for the birth of a significant institution. The debate at the second congress of Comintern had produced a fruitful suggestion from the delegate of the Netherlands East Indies that Comintern should bring communist leaders from eastern countries to Moscow for six months' training in order to fit them for communist work among their own peoples.

We must here in Russia give the eastern revolutionaries the opportunity to get a theoretical education in order that the Far East may become a living member of the Communist International.[4]

Even earlier a propaganda school had been established in Tashkent, where promising young members of eastern nations, whether within or beyond the confines of the RSFSR, were trained to become propagandists and revolutionary leaders in their respective countries.[5] In the autumn of 1920 a new Institute of Oriental Studies was created on the foundation of the former Lazarevsky Institute of Eastern Languages, and the function was assigned to it of providing instruction for " those preparing themselves for practical activity in the east or in connexion with the east ".[6] Then in April 1921, by decree of VTsIK, a Communist University

[1] *Kommunisticheskii Internatsional*, No. 15 (December 20, 1920), col. 3367.
[2] *Ibid.* cols. 3473-3474 ; no copies of this journal have been traced.
[3] According to a note in Stalin, *Sochineniya*, iv, 439, the council " continued to exist for about a year ".
[4] *Der Zweite Kongress der Kommunist. Internationale* (Hamburg, 1921), pp. 195-196.
[5] This school was a source of constant anxiety to the British Government as a nest of potential Indian revolutionaries ; the bland assurance of the Soviet Government in November 1921 that " no propaganda school exists in Tashkent for the preparation of emissaries for India " was certainly taken with a grain of salt (*Anglo-Sovetskie Otnosheniya, 1917-1927* (1927), p. 24). According to Castagné (*Revue du Monde Musulman*, li (1922), 48), it had — at what period is not stated — 300 pupils.   [6] *Novyi Vostok*, i (1922), 456.

of Toilers of the East was established, in which, in order to prepare persons " without mastery of the Russian language " for political work, instruction was to be given in the native languages of the students.[1] It was attached to Narkomnats; Broido, deputy People's Commissar for the Affairs of Nationalities, being its first head. Natives of eastern countries both within and outside the RSFSR were enrolled for courses intended to last for four or five years, the principle being that periods of eight or nine months' instruction in Moscow should alternate with shorter periods of practical propaganda work in the field. At the end of the first year the university was said to have 700 students of 57 different nationalities ; and branches were being set up in Turkestan, at Baku and at Irkutsk.[2] At the end of 1921 an attempt was made to mobilize existing expert knowledge in Russia on eastern questions (in which party resources were small) by creating a Scientific Society of Russian Orientalists with a solid and often learned journal, *Novyi Vostok*, under the editorship of Pavlovich, which successfully combined the revolutionary and traditional Russian attitudes to the Asiatic peoples, and remained for some years an authoritative organ of official opinion.[3]

Thus, while the simple faith in world revolution simultaneously embracing the western industrial nations and the eastern colonial peoples which had originally inspired the Baku congress soon faded, what was left was a stout conviction of the importance of Asia both in revolutionary and in national policy and of the need to draw strength from the east in order to confront the hostile world of western capitalism. The Baku congress played at least a symbolical part in restoring to Soviet policy the sense of Russia's twofold destiny, in the east as well as in the west, in Asia as well as in Europe. It was easy, without changing the substance of that destiny, to express it in revolutionary terms. Stalin did so in the unusually eloquent peroration of a speech delivered in Baku, two months after the congress, on the third anniversary of the revolution :

---

[1] *Sobranie Uzakonenii, 1921*, No. 26, art. 191.

[2] *Revue du Monde Musulman*, li (1922), 46-48 ; the information appears to have been derived from a pamphlet written by Broido on the first anniversary of the university. Its fourth anniversary in 1925 was celebrated by a speech from Stalin (*Sochineniya*, vii, 133-152).

[3] *Novyi Vostok*, i (1922), 454 ; *Revue du Monde Musulman*, li (1922), 49-53.

Paraphrasing the famous words of Luther, Russia might say : " Here I stand on the border-line between the old capitalist and the new socialist world ; here, on this line, I unite the efforts of the proletarians of the west with the efforts of the peasantry of the east in order to demolish the old world.   May the God of history help me." [1]

Moreover, as disappointment grew with the failing prospect of revolution in the west, ever stronger reliance was placed on the aid that would come from the east for the final overthrow of the capitalist Powers.   Lenin, in his last published article *Better Less, but Better*, noting the slowness with which the western countries were " completing their development towards socialism ", consoled himself with the consideration that " the east has finally entered the revolutionary movement " and reflected that " Russia, India, China, etc. constitute a gigantic majority of the population of the world ".[2]   The Baku congress may fairly be called the starting point of this process of calling in the east to redress the unfavourable balance of the west.   Whether Soviet foreign policy was to follow revolutionary lines or to shape itself in a traditional mould of national interests, full recognition of the importance of the rôle of the east in determining its course may be said to date from the winter of 1920–1921.

[1] Stalin, *Sochineniya*, iv, 393.
[2] Lenin, *Sochineniya*, xxvii, 415-417.

CHAPTER 27

NEP IN FOREIGN POLICY

T HE summer of 1920 was the last period during which belief in the imminence of the European revolution was a dominant factor in Soviet foreign policy. The war with Poland and the interruption which it entailed in the incipient *rapprochement* with western Europe provided a fresh stimulus to revolutionary propaganda; and the spectacular victories of the Red Army opened up, for the first time since the winter of 1918–1919, what seemed an immediate prospect of revolution in Europe. But, when this short-lived vision faded with the defeat of the Red Army before Warsaw and the armistice of October 12, 1920, which represented at worst a defeat for the Soviet power and at best a stalemate, world revolution was once more a dream of the future, and foreign policy once more became primarily a matter of diplomatic manœuvre and negotiations. By the end of October 1920 Great Britain, at this moment Soviet Russia's most important adversary in the diplomatic game, was also prepared to treat the events of the summer of 1920 as a passing episode, and to take up again the threads which had been temporarily dropped while that episode was in progress. Negotiations were resumed, and carried forward to their conclusion in the Anglo-Soviet trade agreement of March 1921.

The months from May to October 1920, while they represented in one sense a digression from a course started before these events began and resumed as soon as they were over, left none the less a profound mark on Soviet relations with the outside world. In the first months of 1920 a sense of relief at the supposed ending of the civil war and an eager desire for peace and reconstruction had brought the policy of conciliation into the ascendant. The autumn of 1920 brought a further strengthening of those forces in Soviet policy which made for a temporary accommodation with the capitalist world. The infliction on the RSFSR of a further period of hostilities had increased the already intolerable hardships of the population, and carried a stage further the collapse of the shattered economic machine. The peasant discontents and disorders, which first became menacing in the autumn of 1920, demanded a relaxation in the tension of economic policy at home and an alleviation in material co.'ditions which only agreement with foreign capitalists could bring in any near future. Faith in the revolutionary aid of the European proletariat had once more been disappointed. While the machinery of Comintern continued to operate the intransigent and uncompromising policies laid down by the second congress, the country was moving towards the mood which made NEP both possible and indispensable; and a foreign policy of conciliation and compromise with the capitalist world was a natural corollary of NEP.

At the same time the war with Poland and the last stages of the civil war had been accompanied by a change of sentiment in all sections of the population which is more difficult to analyse. Even before 1920 the hazards of the civil war, and the increasing prestige and power of a régime which had seemed at first to have no great chances of survival, created in the masses, if not a positive loyalty to the new order, at any rate a tolerant acceptance of it. No worker and no peasant seriously desired the return of the " whites "; and the foreign aid received by them imparted a flavour of national sentiment to the struggle waged against the intruders in defence of the young republic.[1] It was the Polish invasion of May 1920 which finally rekindled in the RSFSR the flame of Russian patriotism. Even Zinoviev was quick to recognize the significance of this new asset and the prospect of turning it to good account :

> The war is becoming national. Not only the advanced sections of the peasantry but even the wealthy peasants are

---

[1] The intervention of Japan was more efficacious than that of the western allies in evoking patriotic reactions, partly because it recalled memories of the Russo-Japanese war, partly because it was more obviously inspired by ambitions of national aggrandizement. For this reason the use of Japanese troops was deprecated by both British and American representatives in Moscow.

hostile to the designs of the Polish landowners. . . . . We communists must be at the head of this national movement which will gain the support of the entire population and daily grows stronger.[1]

In the heady atmosphere of the triumphant advance into Poland and of the second congress of Comintern, patriotic sentiment proved as intoxicating a stimulant as revolutionary fervour, and at least equally lasting in its consequences.

Not less significant was the impetus given by the Polish war to the gradual reconciliation with members of the former official and administrative classes who were being drawn back into the service of the Soviet Government in increasing numbers as technicians and bureaucrats — a reconciliation which betokened not only a qualified recognition of Soviet aims and policies by its former opponents, but a certain measure of assimilation of those aims and policies to once despised traditional Russian sentiment.[2] The Polish war was also an important landmark in the transformation of the revolutionary Red Army into a national army. The Red Army which won the civil war was built up round a cadre of former Tsarist officers of many different types, ranging from senior officers like Vatsetis and Sergei Kamenev, the first two commanders-in-chief of the Red Army, both of them former colonels of the imperial general staff, to junior subalterns like Tukhachevsky, who made a brilliant career in the new army and within a year was promoted general. Trotsky records Lenin's surprise on hearing from him early in 1919 that 30,000 such officers had already been recruited into the Red Army, and his judgment that " for every traitor there are a hundred who are dependable ".[3] The eighth party congress in March 1919 gave its cautious approval to the employment of these " military

[1] *Pravda*, May 18, 1920 ; the British Labour delegation visiting Russia at the time noted " the birth and growth of a new patriotism " (*British Labour Delegation to Russia, 1920 : Report* (1920), p. 122).

[2] See Vol. 1, pp. 371-372. In the first years of the régime the charge commonly brought against it by " white " *émigrés* was that of sacrificing Russian national interests to communist ideals : a typical expression of this reproach may be found, for example, in L. Pasvolsky, *Russia in the Far East* (N.Y., 1922), p. 140-141. The converse charge of sacrificing communism to Russian national interests came later.

[3] L. Trotsky, *Moya Zhizn'* (Berlin, 1930), ii, 180 ; Lenin referred to this conversation in a public speech (*Sochineniya*, xxiv, 65).

specialists ";[1] and once victory had been achieved, tributes
began to be paid to their share in it.   In March 1920 Trotsky
paid an eloquent tribute to a former Tsarist general, Nikolaev,
who had been captured by the " whites " in the campaign against
Yudenich while serving with the Red Army, and shot.[2] In May
1920, on the outbreak of the Polish war, Brusilov, the last Tsarist
commander-in-chief, offered his services to the Red Army, and
proposed to convene a conference of prominent officers of the old
Tsarist army to consider ways and means of assisting in its
organization.   The offer was accepted by the Soviet Government.[3]
It would be unprofitable to generalize on the varied complex of
the motives, conscious and unconscious, animating those former
Tsarist officers who took service in the Red Army.   But, by
the spring of 1920, national loyalty to what was after all the
established government of their country had come to play an
important part ; and this evolution was completed by the opportunity of participating actively in war against one of Russia's most
persistent traditional enemies and invaders — the Poles.   In a
eulogy of Sergei Kamenev written towards the end of 1920, Radek
noted that " in the three years of civil war an élite has crystallized
out of the old Tsarist officers which is inwardly united with the
Soviet Government ".[4]   But here, too, the influence was mutual.
By absorbing into itself the officers of former Russian armies, and
by winning their loyalties, the Red Army was hastening its own
evolution into the national army of the Soviet republic.   Here,
too, the war against Poland was a fertile breeding ground of traditional patriotism.

Thus, in the autumn of 1920, as the long period of civil and

[1] *VKP(B) v Rezolyutsiyakh* (1941), i, 302 ; Sokolnikov, who was *rapporteur*
to the congress on the military question in the absence of Trotsky at the front,
spoke of " tens of thousands of old specialists " in the Red Army (*Vos'moi
S"ezd RKP(B)* (1933), p. 148) ; the so-called " military opposition " at the
congress did not contest the employment of former officers, but sought to
strengthen the control over them by the political commissars.

[2] *Kommunisticheskii Internatsional*, No. 9 (March 22, 1920), cols. 1423-1424,
reprinted in L. Trotsky, *Kak Vooruzhalas' Revolyutsiya*, ii (1924), i, 100 ;
other similar tributes are recorded *ibid.* ii, i, 106-107.

[3] *Ibid.* ii, ii, 115 ; Brusilov's letter containing the offer was published in
Pravda, May 7, 1920.

[4] K. Radek, *Die Auswärtige Politik Sowjet-Russlands* (Hamburg, 1921),
pp. 67-68 ; in a Russian translation published two years later (*Vneshnyaya
Politika Sovetskoi Rossii* (1923)) this passage was omitted.

international war was drawing to a close, the way was being prepared for a new conception of foreign policy which would emphasize the defence of national interests and mark the retreat from a policy hostile in principle to all capitalist governments towards a policy which was prepared to bargain with capitalist governments individually or collectively on grounds of mutual expediency. It would, however, be an exaggeration to describe the shift in emphasis as a radical reversal of outlook. The pursuit of world revolution was not eliminated under the new dispensation, just as the pursuit of national interest had never been absent under the old. Indeed it was always possible to argue that both policies were means of defending the national interest, and that they were complementary rather than alternative. If the Soviet régime had been enabled to survive the ordeal of the civil war, partly through revolutionary propaganda directed to the masses in the capitalist countries, partly through the mutual jealousies and hostilities of the capitalist world, it was reasonable to deduce that its survival and well-being would continue to be promoted not only by maintaining the propaganda but also by fostering the jealousies and hostilities. Thus, at a moment when the growing opposition of the workers in the capitalist world to anti-Soviet action, and the onset of the economic crisis, were driving the western countries towards cooperation with Soviet Russia, different, though equally compelling, forces were dictating to the Soviet leaders a new policy of cooperation with the capitalist world. Lenin struck the new note in his address to a Moscow party conference in November 1920 :

> We have not only a breathing space, we have a new stage in which our fundamental position in the framework of the capitalist states has been won.

To pretend that the Bolsheviks had " promised, or dreamed of being able, to transform the whole world by the strength of Russia alone " was absurd :

> Of such madness we were never guilty : we always said that our revolution will conquer when it is supported by the workers of all countries. It turned out that they supported us by halves, since they weakened the arm that was raised against us, but all the same in this way they did help us.[1]

[1] Lenin, *Sochineniya*, xxv, 485-486.

The notion of a Soviet republic, or group of Soviet republics, standing alone on the territory of the former Tsarist empire as an island in a capitalist world — a notion which had in the early days of the revolution been dismissed as chimerical — was beginning to take shape. And twice in his speech Lenin returned to what was bound to become in these conditions a major preoccupation of Soviet diplomacy :

> So long as we remain, from the economic and military standpoint, weaker than the capitalist world, so long we must stick to the rule : we must be clever enough to utilize the contradictions and oppositions among the imperialists. . . . Politically we must utilize the conflicts among our adversaries which are explained by the most profound economic causes.[1]

As he had done before,[2] Lenin depicted this policy in terms not of change but of continuity. " To utilize the division between the capitalist countries so as to make agreement between them difficult or, so far as we can, make it temporarily impossible ", he added a month later, had been " the fundamental line of our policy for three years ".[3] Yet the anxious caution displayed by Lenin in November and December 1920 stood in striking contrast with the optimism of his pronouncements earlier in the year. Politically the revolution had consolidated itself, as the rallying of the officer class and the former bourgeoisie to the Bolshevik flag had shown. Economically it was in a more desperate quandary than ever, since the proletariat of the more advanced countries had failed to come to its aid. The dilemma which was creating the conditions for NEP at home was also almost insensibly re-shaping the relations of the Soviet Government with foreign countries.

When Lenin now contemplated the necessity of coming to terms with the capitalist states, he was thinking primarily and specifically of agreements calculated to relieve economic difficulties and uncertainties by encouraging a flow of foreign imports to meet desperate needs, locomotives and machinery being the most urgent items.

---

[1] Lenin, *Sochineniya*, xxv, 498, 501.
[2] See p. 70 above.   [3] Lenin, *Sochineniya*, xxvi, 8.

We must be clever enough [wrote Lenin at this time], by relying on the peculiarities of the capitalist world and exploiting the greed of the capitalists for raw materials, to extract from it such advantages as will strengthen our economic position — however strange this may appear — among the capitalists.[1]

So far as this end could be achieved by comprehensive negotiations with capitalist countries, the informal Swedish agreement of May 15, 1920,[2] remained the sole achievement up to date. In the later stages of the Polish war the treaty concluded with Estonia in the previous February was supplemented by treaties with Lithuania, Latvia and Finland;[3] but these opened channels for trade rather than provided the substance of it. In September 1920 Litvinov went to Oslo and conducted prolonged trade negotiations with the Norwegian Government, but without result.[4] Above all, the vital negotiations with Great Britain had been brought to a complete standstill by the Polish dispute. When Krasin after a month's absence returned to London early in August, this time accompanied by Kamenev, he found the atmosphere wholly changed. Lloyd George was interested only in the saving of Poland;[5] political circles hostile to Soviet Russia were once more in the ascendant. Prejudices irrelevant to the Polish issue were invoked to prevent a resumption of the trade negotiations; and on September 10, 1920, Kamenev was requested to leave the country, the charges against him being that he had been concerned in the sale of Russian crown jewels, that he had been the channel for passing subsidies to the *Daily Herald*, that he had had relations with the subversive " council of action ", and that he had misled Lloyd George a month earlier on the terms offered to Poland.[6] A week later, Krasin issued a statement disclaiming responsibility for " Kamenev's activities ". It was an unreal situation in which a delegate could disavow the alleged actions of a colleague and the disavowal be accepted as satisfactory. But by this time the Red

---

[1] *Leninskii Sbornik*, xx (1932), 169.   [2] See pp. 162-163 above.

[3] *SSSR: Sbornik Deistvuyushchikh Dogovorov*, i-ii(1924), No. 35, pp. 130-142.

[4] The correspondence as published by the Norwegian Government was reprinted in *Soviet Russia* (N.Y.), December 25, 1920, pp. 642-645.

[5] Lloyd George received Krasin and Kamenev on August 4, 1920, and pressed them to stop the advance of the Red Army.

[6] The request for Kamenev's expulsion was published in *The Times* of September 11, 1920, the charges against him three days later; for the councils of action and the incident of the terms to Poland see pp. 212-213 above.

Army was in full retreat, and Wrangel had opened his offensive in south Russia. For a brief moment the wishful thinking of the summer of 1919 once more took command of British policy. A few weeks earlier, fears of an overrunning of Europe by the Red Army fighting under the banner of world revolution had ruled out any possibility of resuming negotiations with Krasin. Now hopes that the Soviet régime was about to succumb to the combined assaults of Pilsudski and Wrangel had exactly the same result. In Krasin's words : " Lloyd George was waiting to see whether the Soviet power would not collapse under the blows of the Polish legions ".[1] The interruption of the summer of 1920 was prolonged well into the autumn.

It was in part the slow progress of negotiations with Great Britain which in the summer of 1920 turned back the attention of Soviet leaders, for the first time for nearly two years, to the United States ; and about the same time American official circles began to canvass the opportunities of trade with Soviet Russia. In December 1919 Lansing, the Secretary of State, wrote a confidential memorandum suggesting the creation of an institution with a capital of 100 million dollars to finance American trade with Russia ;[2] and in March 1920 the first reports of an impending invitation to Krasin to visit London provoked jealous enquiries from the American Government.[3] Throughout 1920, however, anti-Soviet forces continued to predominate. In December 1919, 249 known or suspected communists were deported from New York to Soviet Russia — an incident which created some stir in a country which had hitherto enjoyed an unbroken record of offering an unqualified right of asylum to political rebels. Pro-ceedings for the deportation of Martens were set on foot in March 1920[4] following a searching public investigation of his record and activities before the Senate foreign affairs committee.[5] American policy continued to wear, in Soviet eyes, its ambiguous and problem-atical character. The United States had intervened like the

---

[1] L. B. Krasin, *Voprosy Vneshnei Torgovli* (1928), p. 279.
[2] *Foreign Relations of the United States, 1920*, iii (1936), 443 ; nothing more was heard of this project.   [3] *Ibid.* iii, 706-707.
[4] *Ibid.* iii, 455-456.
[5] *Senate Foreign Relations Committee : Russian Propaganda, Hearing . . . to investigate Status and Activities of Ludwig C. A. K. Martens* (1920) ; Martens was eventually deported in January 1921.

other allies in the civil war against the Soviet régime, while protesting that its policy was non-intervention. It had denied that it was participating in a blockade of the RSFSR, but had taken as effective steps as anyone to prevent its citizens from trading with that country. On July 7, 1920, the United States Government removed all restrictions on trade with Soviet Russia, but at the same time instructed American diplomatic and consular officers to take no action which " officially or unofficially, directly or indirectly, assists or facilitates commercial or other dealings " between American citizens and that country.[1] Finally in August 1920, in response to an enquiry from the Italian Government, Colby, Wilson's last Secretary of State, defined the American attitude in a note which was published and long remained famous. " The present rulers of Russia " were described as not being " a government with which the relations common to friendly governments can be maintained." On the contrary, they had " frequently and openly boasted that they are willing to sign agreements and undertakings with foreign Powers while not having the slightest intention of observing such undertakings or carrying out such agreements ". Moreover, they had proclaimed the opinion that " the very existence of Bolshevism in Russia, the maintenance of their own rule, depends, and must continue to depend, upon the occurrence of revolutions in all other great civilized nations, and made it plain that they intend to use every means, including, of course, diplomatic agencies, to promote such revolutionary movements in other countries ". The note provoked a counter-statement from Chicherin which appeared in *Izvestiya* under the heading "Refutation of a Bourgeois Lie " and was officially communicated to the State Department by Martens. After the usual comments on the unreality of bourgeois democratic freedom, the statement boldly declared that Soviet Russia had always faithfully observed her engagements — " even the Brest-Litovsk treaty which was imposed upon Russia by violence " — and that, " if the Russian Government binds itself to abstain from spreading communist literature, all its representatives abroad are enjoined scrupulously to observe this pledge ". But, in spite of its controversial nature, the statement ended with the propitiatory hope that " in the near future normal relations will be established

---

[1] *Foreign Relations of the United States, 1920*, iii (1936), 717-719.

between Russia and the United States ".[1] A fortnight later
Trotsky, in an interview with John Reed, dropped a strong hint
of another ground of common interest between Soviet Russia
and the United States :

> Not only can we live with bourgeois governments, but we can
> work together with them within very broad limits. It is per-
> fectly clear that our attitude to the antagonism in the Pacific
> will be determined by the attitude of Japan and the United
> States to us.[2]

It was at this moment, when the civil war was almost over,
when the economic pressures of war communism were setting up
intolerable stresses on the home front, and when determined
attempts to open up trading relations with Great Britain and other
capitalist countries of the west seemed to have reached a dead
point, that a chain of accidents led to the active revival of a plan
which had first been mooted in 1918 [3] and never wholly forgotten
— the offer of concessions in Soviet Russia to foreign capitalists.
It was logical that, at a time when Soviet Russia desperately
needed capital equipment for her industrial development from
abroad and had nothing to offer in return but her largely undeveloped natural resources, the idea of attracting foreign capital
by the offer of concessions to exploit these resources should
constantly recur ; it was also logical that thoughts should constantly revert to the United States of America as the most promising source of capital investments, not only because America had
capital to invest, but because America was less suspect than other
leading capitalist countries of political designs against the Soviet
power.   The memorandum handed to Robins in May 1918
suggested that America might " participate actively in the exploitation of the marine riches of eastern Siberia, of coal and other mines,
as well as in railroad and marine transportation construction in
Siberia and north European Russia ".   The development of
inland waterways both in northern Russia and in the basin of the
Don was cited as a further opportunity for American capital ;

---

[1] The Colby note and Chicherin's reply are in *Foreign Relations of the
United States, 1920*, iii (1936), 463-468, 474-478 ; Chicherin's reply originally
appeared in *Izvestiya*, September 10, 1920.
[2] L. Trotsky, *Kak Vooruzhalas' Revolyutsiya*, ii (1924), ii, 283.
[3] See Vol. 2, pp. 130-131.

and it was suggested that " the United States could also participate on a large scale in the development of certain well-known extensive agricultural tracts by introducing modern methods, receiving in return a large proportion of the products ".[1] The whole subsequent concessions programme of the Soviet Government was already outlined in rudimentary form in this memorandum. For some time the project of foreign concessions was kept in the forefront of Soviet economic policy. In the summer of 1918 Sovnarkom appointed a commission to consider the conditions on which concessions might be granted to foreigners; and in September 1918 Lomov made a report to Vesenkha, arguing strongly against the view of the Left opposition that such concessions were " incompatible with the socialist constitution of Russia ". But the subject was not actual at the moment, since no prospective investors had presented themselves; and Vesenkha refrained from passing any resolution.[2] In the winter of 1918–19 ambitious negotiations were started with Norwegian and " white " Russian interests for the construction of a railway from Murmansk across northern Russia to the mouth of the Ob in Siberia, the *quid pro quo* being a timber concession of 48 years' duration over a vast area of northern Russia. Lomov was once more the champion of the proposal. It secured approval in principle from Sovnarkom. But the " white " affiliations of the project made it an easy target for the opposition. In March 1919 it was abandoned, and some Soviet citizens associated with it were arrested on a charge of consorting with enemies of the régime.[3] Thereafter, with the progress of the civil war and Soviet Russia's increasing isolation,

---

[1] *Russian-American Relations*, ed. C. K. Cummings and W. W. Pettit (1920), p. 211. Robins presented the memorandum to the State Department with a covering report dated July 1, 1918, in which he advocated the sending of an economic commission to Russia (*ibid.* pp. 212-219); the memorandum was forwarded by Lansing to Wilson, who annotated it: " I differ from them [i.e. the proposals] only in practical details "; but nothing further transpired (*Foreign Relations of the United States: The Lansing Papers, 1914-1920*, ii (1940), 365-372).

[2] R. Labry, *Une Législation Communiste* (1920), pp. 168-172, where Lomov's report is translated in full; *Narodnoe Khozyaistvo*, No. 12, 1918, p. 27. Willingness to grant concessions to foreigners, as well as willingness to recognize foreign debts, was announced in the note to the allied Powers of February 4, 1919, accepting the Prinkipo invitation (see pp.110-111 above).

[3] The sources for this episode, mainly the contemporary press, are cited in G. Gerschuni, *Die Konzessionspolitik Sowjetrusslands* (1927), pp. 33-37; it is not clear that the project ever had solid financial backing.

and with the growing antipathy of war communism to capitalist methods and procedure,[1] the offer of concessions, though never formally abandoned, was allowed to lapse. It reappeared only in the late summer of 1920 with an article by Lomov, which was significantly translated for the Soviet journal published in New York.[2]

This was the situation when, in the autumn of 1920, an American traveller named Vanderlip reached Moscow. He was a mining engineer by profession, and more than twenty years earlier had made a journey with a companion through northern Sakhalin and Kamchatka, prospecting without success for gold.[3] He was apparently taken, and allowed himself to be taken, for a well-known banker of the same name, with whom he in fact had no connexion whatever.[4] But Americans were rare in Moscow in 1920 ; all American business men were reputed to be millionaires ; and Vanderlip was at once accepted as a highly important and influential personage. His assumed wealth and status assured him an attentive ear for what he had to put forward. According to Lenin, Vanderlip arrived with a proposal, expressed with all " the frankness, cynicism and crudity of the American *kulak* ", for a lease of Kamchatka, the mineral resources of which, especially oil and naphtha, would be invaluable in the coming American war with Japan. He explained that " our party ", i.e. the Republicans, was expected to win the forthcoming presidential election ; and, if the lease of Kamchatka were granted, this would create such enthusiasm that the recognition of the Soviet Government was certain.[5]

---

[1] An article in *Narodnoe Khozyaistvo*, No. 7, 1919, p. 32, argued that concessions should be granted to foreigners only for constructional projects which were destined to be directly operated by state or municipal authorities (railways, canals, electrical installations, etc.), so that full public control was assured.

[2] *Soviet Russia* (N.Y.), September 11, 1920, pp. 254-358 ; the original source of the article is not stated, and has not been traced.

[3] W. B. Vanderlip and H. B. Hulbert, *In Search of a Siberian Klondyke* (N.Y., 1903), describes the journey.

[4] According to the report of a State Department official who interviewed Vanderlip before his departure for Moscow, he represented a business group in California, whose interest was, however, conditional on a " binding agreement " between the American and Soviet Governments (National Archives of the United States, Record Group 861.602, v, 28/4).

[5] Lenin, *Sochineniya*, xxv, 502-503 ; xxvi, 6 ; L. Fischer, who had access to Soviet official sources, puts the value of the proposed concession at $3,000,000,000 (*The Soviets in World Affairs* (1930), i, 300).

Kamchatka had hitherto been naturally regarded as part of the Far Eastern Republic. But fortunately the frontier had not yet been drawn; Kamchatka was hastily restored to the RSFSR.[1] So far as any real authority existed at this time in the remote peninsula, it was apparently being exercised in Japan. But this did not diminish the attraction of the proposal to the Soviet Government, which was unlikely to miss any chance, however remote, of enlisting American support against Japanese encroachments in Siberia. Before Vanderlip left Moscow he had an interview with Lenin and a contract was signed;[2] and this agreement was the immediate inspiration of an important decree on concessions adopted by Sovnarkom on November 23, 1920. The decree noted that the rate of recovery of the Russian economy could be " increased many times over " by bringing in foreign firms or institutions " for the exploitation and development of the natural riches of Russia ", and that, on the other hand, a shortage of raw materials and an excess of capital existed " in some European countries and especially in the United States ": this had led to concrete proposals having already been made to the Soviet Government for concessions for foreign capital. Such concessions could in principle be granted to solid and reliable foreign concerns, which would receive by way of remuneration a proportion of the products of the enterprise under concession with a right to export them. Concessions of sufficient duration would be granted to ensure an adequate return with a guarantee against nationalization or confiscation. Soviet workers could be employed under the conditions prescribed in the Soviet labour code. A list was appended to the decree of 72 items available for concessions to foreign capitalists : these comprised timber concessions in northern Russia and in Siberia, mining concessions in Siberia and agricultural concessions in south-eastern Russia.[3]

The decree, which was an anticipation of NEP in the field of foreign policy, and was regarded with mistrust by many party

[1] The treaty drawing the frontier was signed in Moscow on December 15, 1920 (RSFSR: Sbornik Deistvuyushchikh Dogovorov, ii (1921), No. 53, pp. 78-79).
[2] On the Soviet side, the contract was signed by Rykov as president of Vesenkha (Trudy IV Vserossiiskogo S"ezda Sovetov Narodnogo Khozyaistva (1921), p. 57); the text never appears to have been published.
[3] Sobranie Uzakonenii, 1920, No. 91, art. 481.

stalwarts,[1] bore no immediate fruit. Though the main condition laid down in the Vanderlip agreement — a Republican victory at the American presidential election — was quickly realized, the project went no further; and Lenin, who remained suspiciously convinced that " all this story played a certain rôle in the policy of the imperialists ", felt aggrieved when Harding, the newly elected president, issued a statement that he knew nothing of any Vanderlip concessions.[2] But for Lenin the Vanderlip agreement and the concessions decree meant more than a clever stroke to play off the United States against Japan, more even than the prospect of some alleviation of present economic distresses; it meant a recognized place for Soviet Russia in a capitalist world economy, a basis of future relations with capitalist Powers.

If you read and re-read attentively the decree of November 23 on concessions [he told a group of party workers], you will see that we underline the importance of world economy : we do this deliberately. This is an incontestably correct standpoint. For the restoration of world economy the utilization of Russian

---

[1] Opposition was particularly strong in the trade unions, and was expressed at the fourth All-Russian Congress of Trade Unions in May 1921, when not less than 150 enquiries on this subject were sent up to the platform (*Chetvertyi Vserossiiskii S"ezd Professional'nykh Soyuzov* (1921), i (Plenumy), 61). The equivocal situation which might arise from the employment of Soviet workers by foreign *concessionaires* had been apparent from the outset ; as Radek put it in May 1918, " there must not in future be two sets of laws in Russian territory, laws for free workers working in Soviet enterprises and laws for slaves working for foreign capital " (*Trudy I Vserossiiskogo S"ezda Sovetov Narodnogo Khozyaistva* (1918), p. 22). A long semi-official article by Stepanov in defence of the concessions policy which appeared in *Russische Korrespondenz*, ii, i, No. 1-2 (January-February 1921), pp. 68-87, opened with the admission that " the question of granting concessions to foreign capitalists is provoking disquiet in party circles " ; this was omitted from the version in *Kommunisticheskii Internatsional*, No. 16 (March 31, 1921), cols. 3515-3522, which referred only to the " excitement " of the bourgeoisie over the decree.

[2] Lenin, *Sochineniya*, xxv, 505. The legend of Vanderlip, Soviet Russia's first millionaire visitor, died hard : the biographical index to the second edition of Lenin's works continues to identify the visitor with F. A. Vanderlip, the banker and industrialist (*ibid.* xxv, 652 ; Lenin made the same mistake in referring to F. A. Vanderlip's book, *What Happened to Europe, ibid.* xxv, 502). An impressionistic sketch of the all-powerful American millionaire who begged Lenin for concessions and sustained a rebuff appeared in L. Reisner, *Sobranie, Sochinenii* (1928), i, 214-218, and later still in a German translation, *Oktober* (1930), pp. 287-293) ; according to this account, Vanderlip went on from Moscow to Afghanistan, where the author met him. He passed through Moscow on his return at the beginning of March 1921 (see p. 340 below).

raw material is essential. . . . He [Vanderlip] says that it is necessary to count on Russia. And now Russia comes forward in front of the whole world and declares : We take on ourselves the restoration of world economy — that is our plan.[1]

It was a long-term view, and Lenin was to use the same argument with effect at a later date. But for the present, and with war communism still dominating Soviet economic policy, the new approach was premature, and the concessions decree had been born out of due time. Six months later Lenin had to confess that not a single concession had yet been granted because no sufficiently serious proposals had been received from foreign capitalists.[2]

While the changing fortunes of the Soviet-Polish war and the campaign against Kamenev [3] prolonged the standstill in Anglo-Soviet trade negotiations in London well into the autumn of 1920, the period of political ostracism and official idleness had not been wholly wasted by Krasin. He quickly took his bearings in the industrial world of Great Britain, and could exploit his advantage as the only big business man who ever occupied a leading position in the Soviet hierarchy. During the dead period when official negotiations were in suspense, Krasin opened tentative discussions with a large number of British firms. He himself mentions three examples — discussions with the Slough engineering works for the supply of 500 automobiles, with the Marconi company for " the formation of a British-Russian company for trade with England ", and with Armstrongs of Newcastle for a regular contract for the repair of Russian locomotives. At a time of increasing slump and unemployment the offer of substantial orders was a powerful magnet. Krasin cast his net wide. He claimed that the result of his activities was " pressure from several industrial circles on the Foreign Office and on Lloyd George ", and that " when negotiations were resumed the Russian delegation

---

[1] Lenin, *Sochineniya*, xxv, 507. A few weeks later Lenin further elaborated this idea : " We have hundreds of thousands of excellent farms, which could be improved with tractors, you have tractors, you have petrol and you have trained mechanics ; and we offer to all peoples, including the peoples of capitalist countries, to make the corner-stone of our policy the restoration of our national economy and the saving of all peoples from hunger " (*ibid.* xxvi, 20). A year later Soviet Russia was in the throes of famine and was receiving relief from the United States.

[2] *Ibid.* xxvi, 390. [3] See p. 277 above.

had behind it a fairly strong group in the English ' City ' ".[1] Certainly the aggravation of the economic crisis during the past six months had strengthened the hand of those who argued that an expansion of trade with the RSFSR would help to relieve British economic difficulties. The emphasis, which a year earlier had been on Russian supplies, had now shifted to Russian markets ; and Krasin skilfully held out prospects of substantial Russian orders to influential British firms. In October 1920 a Soviet trading company was registered in London under the name of Arcos (All-Russian Cooperative Society). During the first three months of its existence it placed orders in Great Britain for goods to a total value of nearly £2,000,000.[2]

In November 1920 the way was once more clear for official negotiations. The Soviet armistice with Poland in October had been followed a few weeks later by a complete victory over Wrangel. British policy, though alarmed by the threat to Poland, had never looked with favour on Polish military adventures under French aegis in eastern Europe ; and the unimpressive Wrangel had failed to revive, even in British military and Conservative circles, the enthusiasm once felt for Denikin and Kolchak. The British Government refused to follow France in recognizing Wrangel's government in August ; and, when two months later his armies were already in retreat, the British forces still in the Black Sea refrained from assisting the French in the work of rescue.[3] The Lloyd George policy which had brought Krasin to London in the previous May now re-emerged. The ball was set rolling again by a note from Krasin to Curzon of November 6, 1920, protesting against the interminable delays.[4] On November 18, 1920, Lloyd George told the House of Commons that the Cabinet had worked out a draft which was about to be sent to the Soviet delegation ; it was handed to Krasin ten days later. From this moment discussions moved with reasonable rapidity, turning far more on the

[1] L. B. Krasin, *Voprosy Vneshnei Torgovli* (1928), pp. 279-280 ; this, together with Krasin's other contemporary article (see p. 163, note 3, above), remains the best source for the negotiations.

[2] *Russian Information and Review*, No. 1, October 1, 1921, p. 19.

[3] This detail was noted in the annual report of Narkomindel to the ninth All-Russian Congress of Soviets, and evidently made an impression in Moscow (*Godovoi Otchet NKID k IX S"ezdu Sovetov* (1921), p. 4).

[4] Klyuchnikov i Sabanin, *Mezhdunarodnaya Politika*, iii, i (1928), 70-72.

subsidiary condition of the agreement that the Soviet Government should refrain from propaganda against the British Empire, especially among the peoples of Asia, than on actual questions of trade. At one moment the British Government desired to include Asia Minor and the Caucasus among the regions in which the Soviet Government would undertake to refrain from anti-British propaganda, but eventually agreed to abandon any specific enumeration of " the peoples of Asia ", except for " India and the independent state of Afghanistan ". On the Soviet side, the two main difficulties were the danger of legal proceedings by former owners of Soviet merchandise imported into Great Britain and the so-called gold blockade. The Soviet delegation asked for legislation to protect Soviet property in Great Britain against claims by alleged former owners, but was assured that a statement from the British Government that the conclusion of the agreement constituted *de facto* recognition of the Soviet Government might be expected to constitute an effective bar to such claims ; should the courts rule otherwise, the British Government undertook to find other means of resolving the difficulty.[1] As regards the gold blockade, the British authorities agreed, subject to certain formalities, to accept Soviet gold at its full value.[2] In December 1920 Lenin attributed the delay in reaching an agreement to " the reactionary part of the English bourgeoisie and the official military clique ", and declared that Soviet policy " proceeds on the line of maximum concessions to England ".[3] These efforts were at last crowned with success. On March 16, 1921, the agreement was signed in London by Krasin and by Horne, the Chancellor of the Exchequer.[4] It contained in the form of a preliminary

---

[1] L. B. Krasin, *Voprosy Vneshnei Torgovli* (1928), pp. 280-281. After the conclusion of the agreement, Lloyd George stated in the House of Commons that the agreement recognized the Soviet Government " as the *de facto* government of Russia, which it undoubtedly is " (*House of Commons: 5th Series*, cxxxix, 2506); and the courts subsequently gave the necessary protection to Soviet property.

[2] The United States quickly followed suit by withdrawing on December 18, 1920, all restrictions on dealings in Russian gold (*Foreign Relations of the United States 1920*, iii (1936), 724).   [3] Lenin, *Sochineniya*, xxvi, 12-13.

[4] *RSFSR: Sbornik Deistvuyushchikh Dogovorov*, ii (1921), No. 45, pp. 18-23 ; *Trade Agreement between His Britannic Majesty's Government and the Government of the Russian Socialist Federal Soviet Republic*, Cmd. 1207 (1921): the treaty was signed in English only, but the Russian translation when made was to be treated as equally valid with the English text.

condition the most elaborate provision yet devised against hostile propaganda :

> That each party refrains from hostile action or undertakings against the other and from conducting outside of its own borders any official propaganda, direct or indirect, against the institutions of the British Empire or of the Russian Soviet Republic respectively, and more particularly that the Russian Soviet Government refrains from any attempt by military or diplomatic or any other form of action or propaganda to encourage any of the peoples of Asia in any form of hostile action against British interests or the British Empire, especially in India and in the independent state of Afghanistan. The British Government gives a similar particular undertaking to the Russian Soviet Government in respect of the countries which formed part of the former Russian Empire and which have now become independent.

Great Britain undertook not to attach or take possession of any gold, funds, securities or commodities exported from Russia : should any court make an order for such attachment, the Soviet Government could terminate the agreement forthwith. The Soviet Government recognized in principle its liability " to pay compensation to private firms who have supplied goods or services to Russia for which they have not been paid " ; the settlement of such claims was reserved for a future treaty. In default of regular diplomatic relations each party undertook to receive an official agent or agents of the other. Simultaneously with the signature of the agreement, a letter signed by Horne was handed to Krasin containing a series of elaborate and detailed reproaches against " activities on the part of the Soviet Government in the regions of India and Afghanistan which are incompatible with the stipulations in the agreement ". This served as a reminder of the principal *quid pro quo* which Great Britain hoped to gain from it.[1]

The Anglo-Soviet trade agreement was signed just a week after Lenin had announced to the tenth party congress the proposals for the tax in kind on agricultural products which was the basis of the New Economic Policy. Like NEP, it could be regarded from different points of view as a step in a process

---

[1] The letter appeared in *The Times* of March 17, 1921, but never seems to have been officially published : a Russian version is in *Anglo-Sovetskie Otnosheniya, 1917-1927* (1927), pp. 8-11.

either of stabilization or of retreat. A year later a resolution of
IKKI justified NEP as " the expression of the solution of the task
of incorporating the proletarian state in the chain of international
relations ".[1] The same words would have been more aptly used to
describe the purpose of the Anglo-Soviet agreement of March 16,
1921. The Anglo-Soviet trade agreement was what Chicherin
called it, " a turning-point in Soviet foreign policy ", in the same
way and for the same reasons as NEP was a turning-point in
domestic policy. The emergency of the civil war which dictated
a hand-to-mouth policy and left no time for long-term reflection
was over ; the country was in a desperate plight ; reconstruction
was needed and, even at the apparent sacrifice of revolutionary
principle, concessions must be made not only to the peasant, but
to the foreign capitalist world. A month after the signature of
the agreement Lenin returned to a metaphor he had used a year
earlier :

> It is important for us to open one window after another.
> . . . Thanks to this treaty we have opened a certain window.[2]

A beginning had been made in the necessary policy of the " breathing space " for economic reconstruction through peaceful cooperation with the capitalist countries.

The same consummation was reached at precisely the same
moment in the eastern policies of the Soviet Government. In
the east, as in the west, the autumn of 1920 had been a high-water
mark of world revolution as the driving force of Soviet foreign
policy, and of Comintern as its chief instrument, and was succeeded by a certain reaction. The idea of Moscow as the deliverer,
through the processes of national and socialist revolution, of the
oppressed masses of the east was not abandoned. But it began to
take second place to the idea of Moscow as the centre of a government which, while remaining the champion and the repository
of the revolutionary aspirations of mankind, was compelled in the

---

[1] *Kommunisticheskii Internatsional v Dokumentakh* (1933), p. 272.
[2] *Leninskii Sbornik*, xx (1932), 179 ; I. Maisky, *Vneshnyaya Politika
RSFSR, 1917-1922* (1922), p. 103, calls it " a door opening on to the arena of
world politics ".

meanwhile to take its place among the great Powers of the capitalist world. Symptoms of this impending change had not been wanting at the Baku congress, and it gathered force as revolutionary prospects faded in the winter of 1920–1921. The forces which led in internal affairs to the New Economic Policy and in European affairs to the Anglo-Soviet trade agreement culminated almost simultaneously in a series of agreements with eastern countries — with Persia on February 26, 1921, with Afghanistan on February 28, and with Turkey on March 16. It was a further stage in the process by which relations between Moscow and the outside world were placed predominantly on a governmental basis.

Soviet relations with Afghanistan were the least complicated, since no local communist movement existed or was likely to exist, and single-minded support could be given from Moscow to the national government. Early in 1920 Surits arrived in Kabul to succeed the murdered Bravin as Soviet representative. More important, Jemal Pasha, one of the young Turk leaders who, like Talaat and Enver, had taken refuge in Germany after the defeat in 1918 and subsequently found his way to Moscow, was invited to Kabul by King Amanullah as his political adviser — a step probably taken at Soviet instigation.[1] At any rate it fitted in well with the ambition of the Soviet Government to foster an anti-imperialist Muslim block in Asia; and Jemal seems to have played an important part in dispelling Afghan suspicions of Moscow.[2] British apprehensions of Soviet activities in Afghanistan and of threats to the vulnerable frontier of British India were at this time acute. On the other hand Soviet-Afghan relations were not without their embarrassments. Disquiet was inevitably felt in

[1] *Diplomaticheskii Slovar*, i (1948), 554, art. Dzhemal Pasha; L. Fischer, *The Soviets in World Affairs* (1930), i, 385, states that it was " Moscow " which " directed Jemal Pasha's attention towards Kabul ". His ceremonial arrival in October 1920 is described in *Novyi Vostok*, ii (1922), 292-294.

[2] A letter from Amanullah to Lenin of December 1920 is said to have contained the following passage : " His Highness Jemal Pasha has told us of all the noble ideas and intentions of the Soviet republic in regard to the liberation of the whole eastern world and of the fact that this government has concluded an alliance with the Turkish Government " (*Asie Française*, November 1921, p. 421); according to L. Fischer, *The Soviets in World Affairs* (1930), i, 385, " the constitution of Afghanistan was largely his work " and " he likewise assisted in the organization of the Afghan army ". A writer in *Novyi Vostok*, ii (1922), 294, notes that " the friendly relations between the RSFSR and Angora partly helped the success of the policy of the RSFSR in Kabul ".

Moscow when in September 1920 the dispossessed amir of Bokhara, driven from his capital by a Bolshevik-sponsored " young Bokhara " movement,[1] took refuge in Kabul as the guest of the Afghan Government.[2] Friction on this and perhaps other issues arising from supposed Afghan designs on Soviet territory in eastern Turkestan seems to have delayed the signature of a Soviet-Afghan treaty, which is said to have been accepted in draft as early as September 1920.[3] In January 1921 Jemal left Kabul on a visit to Berlin, never to return (he was assassinated by an Armenian in Tiflis on the journey back); and in the same month a new and active British minister arrived in Kabul. This may well have seemed to presage a revival of British pressure and to have convinced the Afghan Government of the urgency of seeking a counter-weight on the other side; and it coincided with the increasingly strong desire in Moscow to stabilize Soviet foreign relations, in Asia as well as in Europe. On February 28, 1921, the Soviet-Afghan treaty was signed in Moscow,[4] and was followed on the next day by the signature — also in Moscow — of a Turkish-Afghan treaty of alliance.[5]

The Soviet-Afghan treaty established formal diplomatic relations between the two countries, thus clearly establishing the status of Afghanistan as an independent state. Afghanistan was also to have seven consulates in the RSFSR, the RSFSR five in Afghanistan. The parties declared themselves in agreement on " the liberation of the peoples of the east "; and Soviet Russia undertook to return to Afghanistan, subject to plebiscites, territories ceded by Afghanistan under duress to Russia or to Bokhara in the nineteenth century. Promises of technical and financial

---

[1] See Vol. 1, pp. 335-336.

[2] *Revue du Monde Musulman*, li (1922), 221, 226.

[3] I. Maisky, *Vneshnyaya Politika RSFSR, 1917-1922* (1922), p. 145; *Diplomaticheskii Slovar*, ii (1950), 694, art. Sovetsko-Afganskie Dogovory i Soglasheniya.

[4] *RSFSR: Sbornik Deistvuyushchikh Dogovorov*, ii (1921), No. 44, pp. 15-17.

[5] The Turkish-Afghan treaty is a curious document. It refers to " the age-long moral unity and natural alliance " between the " two brother states and nations ", and in one place invokes the will of God, but is in essence a mutual assistance pact between the two countries in the event of attack on either by " any imperialistic state "; Turkey promises " to help Afghanistan militarily and to send teachers and officers ". Both parties " recognize the independence of the states of Khiva and Bokhara " (*British and Foreign State Papers*, cxviii (1926), 10-11).

assistance were also given. From the Afghan standpoint the treaty was a noteworthy advance towards formal independence in international relations, and was well calculated to strengthen the hands of the Afghan Government in future dealings with Great Britain. From the Soviet standpoint, it marked a further stage in the recognition of Soviet power and prestige in Central Asia, and provided fresh opportunities for offensive and defensive action against Great Britain. The British Government felt that the proposed Soviet consulates in eastern Afghanistan could have no other function than the conduct of anti-British propaganda; suspected that one of the unwritten clauses of the treaty was an undertaking to allow the transit of arms across Afghanistan to Indian tribesmen; and regarded the whole proceeding as an attempt " to secure facilities for attacks through Afghanistan against the peace of India ".[1] While some of these charges may have been inaccurate or exaggerated, and while no organized campaign against India was within the scope of Soviet policy, the essence of that policy was at this time to denounce British imperialism and to stir up trouble for British authority wherever it was asserted on Asiatic soil. What was significant in all this was not the extension of propaganda for world revolution but the succession of Soviet Russia to the traditional Russian rôle as Britain's chief rival in central Asia.

Events in Persia moved more slowly and haltingly along the same road of compromise and consolidation. The hesitation of Soviet policy in the summer of 1920 [2] was not immediately dissipated. The ambiguous Kuchik continued to enjoy Soviet support in Gilan. Nevertheless, in the autumn of 1920, the policy of *rapprochement* between Moscow and Teheran began to gain the upper hand.[3] A curb was put on the not very serious activities of the Persian Communist Party. The central committee of the party was induced on October 22, 1920, to declare that revolution in Persia would be possible only when the full bourgeois develop-

[1] Horne's letter to Krasin of March 16, 1921 (see p. 288 above); the text of the treaty was not yet known in London when the letter was written.
[2] See p. 240 above.
[3] Martchenko recorded in the autumn of 1920 that the Bolsheviks had " taken a line against Kuchik " and were " declaring war on him " (*Revue du Monde Musulman*, xl-xli (1920), 114-115): the diagnosis was broadly correct though somewhat premature (see p. 470 below).

ment had been completed; [1] and this paved the way for an alliance with the rising Persian bourgeoisie which might hope to oust and replace the foreign capitalist. A few days later the Persian delegate arrived in Moscow to open negotiations for a Soviet-Persian treaty. These continued throughout the winter. The question of Gilan proved the most serious stumbling block; and Karakhan made a declaration on January 22, 1921, that Soviet troops would be withdrawn when, but only when, British troops had left Persian soil. [2] In February 1921 a *coup d'état* in Teheran brought to power Riza Khan, the Persian counterpart of the Turkish Kemal and the Afghan Amanullah, who quickly revealed himself as a nationalist dictator applying radical principles against the survivors of the *ancien régime*, but unswervingly opposed to anything that smacked of socialism or communism, and a relentless persecutor of local communists. The *coup* did nothing to interfere with negotiations in Moscow which had at this moment reached their climax. The Soviet-Persian treaty was signed on February 26, 1921. [3]

The Soviet-Persian treaty was the most detailed of the three eastern treaties concluded at this time — a tribute to the vital place of Persia in the foreign concerns of Soviet Russia. Much of it was occupied with a recapitulation of former declarations. The Soviet Government declared void all previous treaties concluded " to the detriment of the rights of the Persian nation "; expressed its " disapproval and detestation " of " the former policy of the Tsarist government which consisted in making agreements with European Powers about Asiatic countries contrary to the desire of the interested nations, and, under pretext of guaranteeing their independence, ended by taking possession of the country which was the object of the agreement "; and repeated its renunciation of all privileges, concessions and property of the Tsarist government on Persian soil on the understanding that these should remain the possession of the Persian people and not be transferred

---

[1] This resolution was quoted by Chicherin in an article in *Izvestiya*, November 6, 1921 and, also without indication of source, in *Revue du Monde Musulman* lii (1922), 105.

[2] *Ibid.* lii (1922), 106; the Persian Government apparently refused to receive Rothstein, whose appointment as Soviet representative in Teheran was announced in November 1920, until this question was settled.

[3] *RSFSR: Sbornik Deistvuyushchikh Dogovorov*, ii (1921), No. 49, pp. 36-41.

to any other foreign Power. In return for the satisfaction thus accorded to Persian interests and Persian pride, only one special right was granted by the treaty to the Soviet Government. Should a third Power intervene with armed force on Persian territory, or attempt to create there a " centre of action for attacking Russia ", and should the Persian Government not be strong enough to repel the danger, then the Soviet Government would have the right to bring Soviet troops into Persia for this defensive purpose. The clause was perhaps not wholly distasteful to the Persian Government, being manifestly directed against Great Britain : it was in fact invoked twenty-two years later against Germany. The treaty of February 26, 1921, while it did not solve all difficulties, put Soviet-Persian relations on a new footing. In the following month the central committee of the Persian Communist Party, established safely in Baku, exhorted local party committees to struggle against both " English colonial imperialism " and the government of the Shah.[1] But the " experiments " of toying with indigenous Persian communism, or with such separatist movements as that of Kuchik, which had been " conducted without a plan and without any consideration of local conditions and possibilities ",[2] were now abandoned in favour of consolidation of relations with the Persian Government. In April 1921 the arrival of Rothstein in Teheran as Soviet representative [3] introduced a new and active period of Soviet diplomacy.

Developments in Turkey were more complex than in Afghanistan or Persia, but led up to the same climax of treaty-making at approximately the same moment. The incident with Enver at Baku, whatever its other implications, registered the decision of the Soviet Government to make friendship with Kemal rather than with Enver the keystone of its Turkish policy. But much had still to be done. The first condition of stable relations between Moscow and Angora was to end the indeterminate status of the small Transcaucasian republics — the unwanted outcrop of

[1] *Revue du Monde Musulman*, lii (1922), 144-156 ; the same aims were proclaimed by the Persian delegate at the third congress of Comintern three months later (*Protokoll des III. Kongresses der Kommunistischen Internationale* (Hamburg, 1921), p. 1003).

[2] *Novyi Vostok*, ii (1922), 261 ; this article represents the view officially adopted in 1921.

[3] I. Maisky, *Vneshnyaya Politika RSFSR, 1917-1922* (1922), p. 157.

western military intervention — that still lay across the path of direct land communications between them. The fate of Azerbaijan, which had already been sealed in April 1920,[1] served as a prototype. On September 26, 1920, the Turkish Government announced to the world that it was about to take " energetic measures " against the Armenian Government in order to put an end to the persecution of the Muslim population.[2] Kemal was beginning to feel his strength, and was determined to consolidate his authority in Asia Minor. It may have been a coincidence that the move against Armenia was made at a moment when the Red Army had its hands full with the Wrangel offensive in southern Russia. For the moment the Soviet Government found itself restricted to diplomatic action. Its newly appointed envoy to Kemal, Mdivani, a brother of the Georgian politician, halted on his way to Angora early in October 1920 in Tiflis, the capital of the then Menshevik Georgia, and made to the Armenian Minister there an offer of Soviet military aid to Armenia, provided the Armenian Government requested that aid and declared itself willing to accept Soviet arbitration to fix the frontiers between Armenia and Turkey. The offer was rejected; indeed according to Soviet sources, the Armenian Government was at that very moment inviting the Georgian Government to join it in common action against the Bolsheviks.[3] In these circumstances Turkish military operations encountered little effective opposition. The Armenian Government was already suing for an armistice, in negotiations which seem to have been deliberately protracted from the Turkish side,[4] when the Soviet mission proceeded from Tiflis to Erivan. The anxieties felt in Moscow at the turn of events were now evident; and a statement was issued dissociating the Soviet Government from the " Turkish attack " and proclaiming

---

[1] See pp. 248-249 above.
[2] Écho de l'Islam, No. 21, February 1, 1921 ; extracts in Mitteilungen des Seminars für Orientalische Sprachen zu Berlin, xxxvii (1934), ii, 137-138 ; another Turkish pronouncement a little later ascribed " the cause of the new Armenian war " to " British rapacity " (Écho de l'Islam, No. 20, January 20, 1921).
[3] The source for this episode consists of unpublished Soviet archives quoted in Voprosy Istorii, No. 9, 1951, pp. 144-145 ; extracts from the Soviet proposal to Armenia are given.
[4] Mitteilungen des Seminars für Orientalische Sprachen zu Berlin, xxxvii (1934), ii, 138-142.

its " friendly feelings for the Armenian people ".[1] Meanwhile, a Soviet mission had arrived in Angora ; and its acting head, Upmal by name, was received on November 9, 1920, as the first official Soviet representative to Kemalist Turkey.[2] The course of the discussions which must have followed his arrival is unknown, though Chicherin is said to have repeated his offer of mediation, this time to the Turkish Government, and to have begged for a cessation of the Turkish advance.[3] On November 20 Lenin anxiously contemplated the possibility that " war may be forced on us from one day to the next ".[4] But within a few days the die was cast for peace. On November 29, a fulsome telegram was addressed by Kemal to Chicherin, once more referring to Chicherin's note of June 2 and expressing admiration for " the magnitude of the sacrifices which the Russian nation has accepted for the salvation of the human race ". The telegram ended with a significant passage :

I am deeply convinced, and my conviction is shared by all my compatriots, that, on the day when the workers of the west on the one hand, and the enslaved peoples of Asia and Africa on the other, understand that at the present time international capital is using them to annihilate and enslave one another for the exclusive benefit of their masters, and on the day when consciousness of the wickedness of a colonial policy penetrates the hearts of the toiling masses of the world, the power of the bourgeoisie will end.

The high moral authority of the government of the RSFSR among the toilers of Europe and the love of the Muslim world for the Turkish nation give us the assurance that our close alliance will suffice to unite against the imperialists of the west all those who have hitherto upheld their power through a subservience based on inertia and ignorance.[5]

[1] *Voprosy Istorii*, No. 9, 1951, p. 145 ; the statement was issued in Tiflis, presumably because this was the source of the numerous reports current at the time of a secret Soviet-Turkish agreement directed against Dashnak Armenia and Menshevik Georgia.
[2] *Godovoi Otchet NKID k IX S"ezdu Sovetov* (1921), p. 42 ; *Izvestiya*, November 6, 1921. Açcording to *Die Welt des Islams*, xvi (1934), 30, Mdivani himself reached Angora only in February 1921.
[3] Unpublished Soviet archives quoted in *Voprosy Istorii*, No. 9, 1951, p. 146.
[4] Lenin, *Sochineniya*, xxv, 487 ; Lenin's obvious anxiety provides further evidence against the view that the Turkish advance against Armenia had been preceded by an understanding with Soviet Russia.
[5] Klyuchnikov i Sabanin, *Mezhdunarodnaya Politika*, iii, i (1928), 27-28.

This cunningly drafted outline of an alliance between Soviet Russia, as the champion of the workers of Europe, and Turkey, as leader of the oppressed Muslim peoples of Asia, contained the scarcely veiled implication of a bargain that neither ally would encroach on the preserve of the other. On this basis an agreement could easily be reached.

On the same day on which this communication was sent, and while Turkish-Armenian negotiations were actually in progress in Alexandropol, a successful *coup* was contrived in Erivan. On November 29, 1920, a revolutionary committee set up on the Soviet frontier under the aegis of a detachment of the Red Army proclaimed an independent Soviet Armenia. Under the pressure of this event, the Armenian Dashnak government was transformed by the appointment of Soviet sympathizers to leading posts; and a military dictatorship was proclaimed in Erivan. On December 2, 1920, two treaties were signed. The first, signed in Erivan by the reconstituted Armenian Government with the RSFSR, recognized Armenia as a socialist republic, and, pending the constitution of an Armenian congress of Soviets, entrusted all power to a military revolutionary committee composed of five communists and two Dashnaks: pending the formation of this committee, the military dictatorship would continue. The second treaty was a treaty of peace with Turkey signed in Alexandropol by the delegation of the former Armenian Government, and constituted a complete surrender to Turkish territorial and other demands.[1] This treaty was at the outset indignantly repudiated by the new régime in Erivan and by its Soviet patrons.[2] But the two treaties

---

[1] The declaration of the revolutionary committee of November 29, 1920, is in *ibid*. iii, i (1928), 73-75. The text of the treaty between the RSFSR and the Armenian Republic, *ibid*. iii, i, 75-76, is much abbreviated; the full text is in *RSFSR: Sbornik Deistvuyushchikh Dogovorov*, iii (1922), No. 79, pp. 14-15, but has the incorrect title " Treaty between the RSFSR and the Armenian SSR ". The abbreviated text of the agreement with Turkey signed at Alexandropol in Klyuchnikov i Sabanin, *Mezhdunarodnaya Politika*, iii, ii (1929), 71-73, does not correspond accurately with the text quoted from Armenian sources in F. Kazemzadeh, *The Struggle for Transcaucasia (1917-1921)* (N.Y., 1951), p. 289. Other main sources for these events are B. Bor'yan, *Armeniya, Mezhdunarodnaya Diplomatiya i SSSR* (1929), ii, 122-123; *Mitteilungen des Seminars für Orientalische Sprachen zu Berlin*, xxxvii (1934), ii, 142.

[2] Article by Chicherin in *Izvestiya*, November 6, 1921; the reference to this treaty in Vol. i, p. 348, is incorrect.

taken together formed the ultimate basis of a compromise which was to find expression in the Soviet-Turkish treaty of the following March. The result was a settlement which in its territorial aspects was highly favourable to Turkey, but secured Turkish approval for the existence of a small and compact Armenian SSR with its capital at Erivan.

The elimination of an independent Azerbaijan and an independent Armenia was a common interest of Soviet Russia and of Turkey, and paved the way to the much desired agreement between them. The cognate case of Georgia would be dealt with by the same methods. But an embarrassment of a different kind still lay across the path : the existence of a small but vigorous Turkish communist movement. The movement was made up of three different strands : a Turkish communist movement created and organized by Turkish prisoners of war in Russia, and operating in and from Soviet territory ; a Turkish communist movement which apparently owed its origin to returned exiles from Germany trained in the Spartakist movement, and comprised before the end of 1919 separate and independent groups in Constantinople and Angora ; and various indigenous movements throughout Asia Minor not strictly communist in doctrine or organization, but professing vague sympathy for communism and for the Soviet form of government. The first two categories were from the first regarded by Kemal with hostility, and suppressed or reluctantly tolerated as expediency demanded ; the third category was composed of ardent supporters of the national movement and for some time enjoyed Kemal's encouragement and support.

The most important figure in the Soviet-sponsored Turkish communist movement was Suphi, the Turkish socialist who, having fled from Turkey to Russia in 1914, spent the greater part of the war in internment in Russia and took part in the international revolutionary meeting in Petrograd in December 1918.[1] He performed the task of creating communist groups from Turkish prisoners of war in Russia and preparing them for work in their own country. These operations were under the control of the " central bureau of communist organizations of the eastern peoples " attached to Narkomnats. The claim made in the spring of 1920 that " partisan groups " numbering 8000 men in all had

[1] See p. 234 above.

been organized and despatched to Turkey[1] was no doubt exaggerated. But prospects appeared hopeful, especially in view of the marked pro-Soviet orientation of Kemal's policy at this time. In May 1920 Suphi transferred his headquarters, and the Turkish newspaper edited by him, *Yeni Dünya* (" The New Day "), from Moscow to Baku ;[2] and at the second congress of Comintern two months later the representative of the Turkish section of the " bureau of communist organizations " was Ismael Hakki, whose brief speech as reported in the records of the congress struck an exclusively nationalist note.[3] Suphi was a member of the presidium of the Baku congress of eastern peoples in September 1920,[4] and in the same month presided at a conference of Turkish communists, also at Baku, for the purpose of organizing party activities in Turkey itself.[5] This conference was attended by a group of Turkish " Spartakists " from Angora, where a Turkish communist party had been secretly founded in June 1920.[6] In November 1920, apparently counting on the comparative toleration recently shown by Kemal, Suphi entered Turkey openly with several comrades in the company of the official Soviet mission.

The indigenous Turkish movement of sympathy for communism which grew up in 1919 was mainly of peasant origin and was rooted in agrarian discontents. Its overt expression was the creation of a multitude of local Soviets which became for a time the effective organs of local government.[7] The movement was

---

[1] *Zhizn' Natsional'nostei*, No. 15 (72), May 23, 1920.

[2] *Yeni Dünya* had been originally started in the Crimea in February 1919 before the German occupation.

[3] *Der Zweite Kongress der Kommunist. Internationale* (Hamburg, 1921) pp. 187-188.   [4] *I^{vi} S"ezd Narodov Vostoka* (1920), p. 28.

[5] A main source for Suphi's activities is a memoir and collection of his articles published in Turkish in Moscow on the second anniversary of his assassination, and quoted in *Voprosy Istorii*, No. 9, 1951, p. 60 ; a microfilm of this pamphlet is in the Hoover Library, Stanford.

[6] *Novyi Vostok*, ii (1922), 258.

[7] Two years later a Turkish delegate at the fourth congress of Comintern recalled that, when the Turkish Government was " in process of establishing its first relations with the Soviet Government, its delegates sent to Moscow affirmed that there was a large communist party and even peasants' Soviets in some districts " (*Protokoll des Vierten Kongresses der Kommunistischen Internationale* (Hamburg, 1923), p. 527) ; the statement about peasant Soviets is confirmed in a note from the Turkish Government to Chicherin of November 1920 which refers to " little Soviet governments " in certain Turkish districts being overthrown by Armenian Dashnaks (*Mitteilungen des Seminars für Orientalische Sprachen zu Berlin*, xxxvii (1934), ii, 136).

fostered by Kemal, partly because its loyalty to the nationalist cause was fervent and unquestioned, and partly because an outlet was required for the real social and agrarian discontent represented by it. In the spring of 1920 it took organized shape in the creation of a Green Army which, recruited from the small and landless peasants, formed a major part of the national forces. The principal sponsors of the movement at this time, Hakki Behic and Hikmet, were " easterners " in respect of Turkish foreign policy and are both said to have been convinced Marxists.[1] A somewhat farcical sequel of these proceedings was an officially sponsored Turkish communist party bearing the name of the " Green Apple ". Hakki Behic was its leader ;[2] and according to a subsequent statement of a Turkish delegate to Comintern it was composed mainly of " high officials and intellectuals ".[3] Meanwhile the most successful leader of the Green Army was Edhem, a soldier of fortune who, while professing allegiance to Kemal, threatened to become a Turkish Makhno.[4] The Green Army

[1] Halidé Edib, *The Turkish Ordeal* (1928), pp. 171-174. An article in *Voprosy Istorii*, No. 9, 1951, pp. 65-66, quotes the programme of the Green Army, explaining that it " was not a consistent class organization of the Turkish toiling peasantry, and could not be, since it lacked proletarian leadership ", but that it " reflected the interests of the peasants " ; no mention is made of Hakki Behic or Hikmet. On the other hand, the article, which is extremely hostile to Kemal, ignores the support given by the Green Army to the nationalist movement and Kemal's initial patronage of it.

[2] Halidé Edib, *The Turkish Ordeal* (1928), p. 175.

[3] *Protokoll des Vierten Kongresses der Kommunistischen Internationale* (Hamburg, 1923), p. 527. The " Green Apple " accepted at any rate the outward forms of religion ; it believed that communism could be realized without " bloody revolutions " ; it admitted some rights of property ; and it held that communist doctrine must be adapted to the needs of particular countries, and that communism would not necessarily be victorious everywhere at the same time or even at any time (M. Pavlovich, *Revolyutsionnaya Turtsiya* (1921), pp. 110-116 ; documents of the movement are quoted in an article by the same author in *Kommunisticheskii Internatsional*, No. 17 (June 7, 1921), cols. 4227-4232). It survived, or existed intermittently, for three or four years ; a resolution of the fourth congress of Comintern in November 1922 described the " Green Apple " as " a party which painted over pan-Turanianism in Turkey in a communist hue " (*Kommunisticheskii Internatsional v Dokumentakh* (1933), p. 320).

[4] He is described as " of Circassian birth and nearly illiterate " (Halidé Edib, *The Turkish Ordeal* (1928), p. 152) ; he was none the less a mainstay of the nationalist movement at its moment of greatest weakness, and his enthusiastic reception by Kemal at Angora is described *ibid.* p. 167. In Moscow he was at first regarded as a Turkish communist, but later discovered to be only a " bandit " (*Zhizn' Natsional'nostei*, No. 5 (11), April 1, 1922).

reached the summit of its success in the summer of 1920. But in September 1920 — the same month in which action against Armenia was decided on — Kemal felt strong enough to put his house in order by removing a potential source of rivalry or insubordination, and issued a decree dissolving it. The order was not obeyed, and Kemal temporized. In November he appointed as Turkish representative in Moscow Ali Fuad, an army commander whom he wanted to get out of the way, and made an offer to Edhem to accompany the mission. Edhem refused; and in December, when the campaign against Armenia had been successfully concluded, Kemal finally decided to take action against the Green Army. On January 6, 1921, Edhem was routed and fled to the Greeks, and what was left of his movement was then quickly mopped up.

The suppression of Edhem was immediately followed by drastic steps against the Turkish communists. Suphi was seized by unknown agents at Erzerum, and on January 28, 1921, together with sixteen other leading Turkish communists, thrown into the sea off Trebizond — the traditional Turkish method of discreet execution. It was some time before their fate was discovered. Chicherin is said to have addressed enquiries about them to the Kemalist government and to have received the reply that they might have succumbed to an accident at sea.[2] But this unfortunate affair was not allowed to affect the broader considerations on which the growing amity between Kemal and Moscow was founded. For the first, though not for the last, time it was demonstrated that governments could deal drastically with their national communist parties without forfeiting the goodwill of the Soviet Government, if that were earned on other grounds.

During the winter of 1920-1921 opinion in Moscow was

[1] This account of the Green Army comes in the main from *A Speech Delivered by Ghazi Mustapha Kemal, October 1927* (Engl. transl., Leipzig, 1929), pp. 401-404, 436, 455-456, 467 ; Kemal claims that " the original founders of this society were well-known comrades of ours with whom we were in close touch ", and nowhere suggests any communist or Soviet affiliations.

[2] The authorities for this episode are M. Pavlovich, *Revolyutsionnaya Turtsiya* (Moscow, 1921), pp. 108-123 ; a note by the same author in *Kommunisticheskii Internatsional*, No. 17 (June 7, 1921), cols. 4427-4428 ; and an article signed " W." in *Revue du Monde Musulman*, lii (1922), 191-208. The writers were obviously in possession of the main facts, the one from the Soviet, the other from the Turkish, side ; and their accounts supplement, without contradicting, each other.

moving in favour of the projected deal with Kemal.[1] In December 1920 the official journal of Narkomnats argued that friendly relations with nationalist Turkey would make a good impression on the Muslims of the Caucasus.[2] At the eighth All-Russian Congress of Soviets in the same month Lenin, dwelling once more on " the coincidence of fundamental interests among all peoples suffering from the oppression of imperialism ", spoke of the impending treaty with Persia and the strengthening of relations with Afghanistan and " still more " with Turkey.[3] At the same congress Dan accused the Bolsheviks of pursuing in the Caucasus " a policy which calls for unity among the nationalists of one oppressed country, for example, Turkey, and for collaboration with the military enterprises of these nationalists against others who perhaps are also nationalists oppressed by the imperialism of other countries " ; and the Mensheviks submitted a resolution demanding a breach with Kemal.[4] But an attitude so plainly inspired by the desire to serve the cause of a Dashnak Armenia and a Menshevik Georgia was unlikely to make any impression on Soviet policy. On February 18, 1921, the Turkish delegation for the negotiation of a Soviet-Turkish treaty arrived in Moscow.[5] Thereafter events moved rapidly. Before agreement could be finally reached it was necessary to come to terms on the one outstanding territorial bone of contention — the last of the three Transcaucasian republics. Both sides proceeded to stake out their claims. On February 21, 1921, the Red Army and its Georgian Bolshevik *protégés* crossed the frontier into Georgia, and four days later proclaimed the Georgian SSR.[6] Turkey

---

[1] One of the few signs of divided counsels in the party on this issue is an interview with Stalin on his return from his Caucasian journey (see Vol. 1, pp. 328-329), which appeared in *Pravda* of November 30, 1920 ; Stalin detected " symptoms indicating a serious attempt of the Entente to play with the Kemalists and perhaps a certain shift of the Kemalists to the Right ", and speculated on the possibility that the Kemalists might " betray the cause of the liberation of the oppressed peoples " or even " appear in the camp of the Entente " (Stalin, *Sochineniya*, iv, 411-412). Stalin was one of those who opposed the policy of aid to Turkey a year later (see p. 474 below).

[2] *Zhizn' Natsional'nostei*, No. 40 (97), December 15, 1920.

[3] Lenin, *Sochineniya*, xxvi, 27.

[4] *Vos'moi Vserossiiskii S''ezd Sovetov* (1921), pp. 36, 52.

[5] N. Rubinstein, *Sovetskaya Rossiya i Kapitalisticheskie Strany, 1921-1922 gg.* (1948), p. 67.

[6] See Vol. 1, p. 349.

replied with an ultimatum demanding the cession of the two districts of Artvin and Ardahan — a claim which Moscow was prepared to concede; and on February 28, 1921, Turkish troops occupied the port of Batum — an implied claim which the Soviet Government strongly contested. None of these events was, however, allowed to disturb the harmony of the negotiations in Moscow, where the Soviet-Turkish treaty was signed on March 16, 1921 — the same day on which the Anglo-Soviet trade agreement was signed in London. In addition to the emphasis in the preamble on the solidarity between the two countries " in the struggle against imperialism ", a special article solemnly proclaimed " the mutual affinity between the national liberation movement of the peoples of the east and the struggle of the workers of Russia for a new social order ". The treaty repeated the Russian renunciation of capitulations in Turkey as " incompatible with the free national development of any country or with the full realization of its sovereign rights ". The frontier provisions included the handing over to the newly born Georgian SSR of the port of Batum. In order to guarantee " the opening of the Straits and free access through them for the commerce of all nations "— without, however, prejudicing the full sovereignty of Turkey or " the security of Turkey and of its capital, Constantinople " — an international statute was to be drawn up by a conference of Black Sea Powers. Russia undertook to arrange for the three Transcaucasian republics to conclude with Turkey the necessary treaties registering the obligations assumed for them under the present treaty — an implicit recognition by Turkey of a Russian tutelage or protectorate over these states.[1] For Turkey, the treaty meant the moral and material support of Soviet Russia in her continuing struggle with Great Britain; for Soviet Russia, the reassertion of her position as the great anti-imperialist Power of the Middle East; for both, the exclusion of foreign interlopers from Transcaucasia and from the shores of the Black Sea. These advantages outweighed for both parties any differences about the treatment of Turkish communists. The Turkish communist journal *Yeni Dünya* once more began to appear from Baku. It

---

[1] *RSFSR: Sbornik Deistvuyushchikh Dogovorov*, ii (1921), No. 52, pp. 72-77; for the supplementary treaty signed by the Transcaucasian republics see Vol. 1, pp. 391-392.

was not till May 1921 that the journal of Narkomnats published a circumstantial account in a letter from Baku of the *noyade* of Trebizond.[1] Some months later the Turkish Government decided, as it informed Moscow, to " liberate all the imprisoned Turkish communists and hand over to justice those guilty of the murder of the Turkish communist Mustafa Suphi".[2]

The change of front carried out by Moscow in March 1921 affected the climate in which Soviet foreign policy henceforth operated rather than the substance of that policy. It did not mean, in domestic affairs, the abandonment of the goal of socialism and communism or, in foreign affairs, of the goal of world revolution. But it meant a recognition of the necessity of a certain postponement in reaching these goals, and in the meanwhile of building up the economic and diplomatic strength of Soviet Russia by all practicable means, even if these means were in appearance a retreat from the direct path to socialism and world revolution. The new foreign policy had been adopted, in the words used by Lenin of NEP, " seriously and for a long time ".[3] It was the relative durability thus imparted to expedients hitherto invoked only as short-time practical manœuvres which, more than anything else, changed the character of Soviet foreign policy after 1921.

[1] *Zhizn' Natsional'nostei*, No. 10 (108), May 14, 1921 ; the same letter also appeared, in small type, in *Kommunisticheskii Internatsional*, No. 17 (June 7, 1921), cols. 4427-4428.
[2] I. Maisky, *Vneshnyaya Politika RSFSR, 1917–1922* (1922), p. 165 ; the writer had access to the files of Narkomindel, which were evidently the source of this information.
[3] See Vol. 2, p. 276.

CHAPTER 28

RUSSIA AND GERMANY

IN the foreign relations of Soviet Russia Germany occupied
a unique place. If the Soviet leaders in the first years after
the revolution had come to divide the world into two broad
categories — the hostile capitalist Powers of the west and the
potentially friendly peoples of the east, themselves also victims
of the western Powers — Germany fitted into neither category.
The defeat of November 1918 had brought her into the category
of victims of western imperialism which she now shared with
Soviet Russia and with the oppressed eastern peoples — this was
an important theme of Lenin's speech at the second congress of
Comintern. On the other hand, her advanced industrial development and social organization, as well as her geographical position,
ranged her emphatically with the west : in the Russian economy
Germany had always been the outstanding capitalist Power and
main supplier of industrial goods. But there was yet a third
category for which Germany was destined by the unanimous
consensus of Bolshevik opinion — the rôle of pioneer, together
with Soviet Russia, of the proletarian revolution. Soviet policy
was at first exclusively preoccupied with the task of inducing and
equipping Germany to assume this rôle; and it was only very
gradually and reluctantly that this task was relegated to a secondary
place, and finally abandoned as hopeless. If these complexities of
Soviet-German relations did not immediately become apparent,
this was because Soviet Russia was for a long time scarcely in a
position to conduct a foreign policy in regard to Germany. From
the moment of the German collapse down to the middle of 1920
Soviet Russia was as completely isolated from Germany as from
the western countries ; nor, had the isolation been less complete,
was there any single political authority in Germany possessing
sufficient power or initiative to maintain effective relations with

Soviet Russia. Nevertheless, much that happened in Germany at this time proved highly significant, and furnished a background for the subsequent development of Soviet-German relations. The choice between east and west, which was forced on the German Council of People's Representatives within a few hours of the armistice by the offer of two trainloads of Russian grain,[1] was a permanent dilemma of German foreign policy, especially when the choice had to be made from a position of weakness. Of the German political parties under the Weimar republic only the SPD had its roots in the west and was consistently western in outlook. It was linked with the other parties of the Second International, whose main strength was in western Europe; it was traditionally hostile to Russia, which was regarded not merely as reactionary, but as backward and barbarous; and, having — in fact, though not in theory — rid itself of the revolutionary purity and intransigence of Marxism, it had imbibed much of the bourgeois-democratic radicalism of the western European Left. Thus, almost alone among German parties, it turned a receptive ear to Wilson's democratic pacifism, embodied in conceptions such as national self-determination and the League of Nations. During the first period of the Weimar republic, when a western orientation was essential to Germany, the SPD held the reins of power; its importance declined as Germany became capable of pursuing an independent foreign policy. Of the other parties the Catholic Centre had western leanings. But, being based on confessional rather than on political loyalties, it rarely spoke with a firm or united voice on major issues, and could for the most part act only as a balancing force. None of the other forces in German political life looked primarily to the west. The extreme Left, comprising the KPD and a section of the USPD (which wavered, and ultimately split, between communists and social-democrats), stood for an alliance with Soviet Russia. The parties standing to the Right of the Centre were all in a greater or less degree hostile to the west. The nucleus of these parties was formed by the two powers which, behind the façade of the Weimar republic, continued to rule Germany as they had ruled it under Wilhelm II : the army and heavy industry. The officer class of the defeated army nourished almost to a man the long-term ambition of avenging

[1] See p. 98 above.

itself on the west; and for this an alliance with the east would be indispensable. Heavy industry, excluded from western and overseas markets, could find an outlet nowhere but in the east.[1] The forces favouring an eastern orientation were already powerful in the Germany of 1919, even though they had few means of giving effect to their views and their ambitions.[2] It is significant that the first occasion on which the Weimar republic openly defied the allies on an issue of foreign policy was the refusal to participate in the blockade of Soviet Russia, and that this decision was endorsed with varying degrees of warmth by every party in the Reichstag.[3]

While, however, future cooperation with Russia was the goal of all the most influential forces in Germany, the goal seemed in 1919 infinitely remote and difficult to attain, and opinion was hopelessly divided about the way by which it might ultimately be reached. Broadly speaking, ideological conceptions still dominated the issue. The Left was unable to imagine cooperation with Russia except through a communist revolution and the establishment of a communist régime in Germany; the Right was unable to imagine it except through the overthrow of the Bolsheviks and the restoration of monarchy in Russia. By the spring of 1919 the prospects of revolution in Germany were fading. But hopes of a

[1] Later, divisions appeared within industry itself: the chemical and electrical industries, and some of the lighter industries, retained western connexions, and became dependent on western capital. But the iron and steel industry, which could not exist without Russian markets (until Hitler started a rearmament programme), remained the dominant factor.

[2] The situation was ably summarized in a report of the British military mission in Berlin of August 1919: "All classes in Germany are looking towards Russia for one reason or another. The extremists of the Left look upon her as the realization of their own political ideals; the pan-Germans look upon her as providing the only possible outlet for surplus population and compensation for the loss of colonies. Officers think that she may provide employment, which is no longer possible in their own country. Industrialists think that she will provide employment for capital and ultimately be the means of paying off the war indemnity. The realization of these ideas, however, lies in the far future, and, for the present, communication is much too difficult to make any practical steps possible " (*Documents on British Foreign Policy, 1919–1939: First Series*, iii (1949), 511).

[3] The debate in the Reichstag on October 23, 1919, on the allied request for German participation in the blockade of Soviet Russia (see p. 150 above) revealed complete unanimity for rejecting the proposal; even Wels, the spokesman of the SPD, who thought that " the existence of the Soviet Government is a misfortune for socialism ", declared that " there can for us be only one answer: a round, clear, simple ' no ' " (*Verhandlungen des Reichstags*, cccxxx (1919), 3362).

Russian restoration were still widely entertained in many countries. In Germany these hopes took practical form in the continued presence in Russia's former Baltic provinces of substantial German forces — the last organized remnant of the imperial German army — under the command of General von der Goltz, who had triumphantly come to the aid of the " whites " in the Finnish civil war in the spring of 1918. This anomaly was a consequence of allied policy which, even at the moment of the armistice, tempered its hostility to German militarism with fear of Russian Bolshevism. By article 12 of the armistice of November 11, 1918, Germany was bound to evacuate all former Russian territories " as soon as the allies shall think the moment suitable, having regard to the internal situation of those territories ".[1] It was intimated that the moment for evacuation of the Baltic had not yet come. In the first months of 1919 Von der Goltz consolidated his position, recruited strong reinforcements from the German colonies in the Baltic countries and from " white " Russian refugees, as well as from demobilized Germans and Russian prisoners of war in Germany, and proclaimed himself the leader of an anti-Bolshevik crusade. These proceedings were little to the taste of the allied governments, which, having partially recovered from their fear of the spread of Bolshevism, began to be haunted by the bogy of an alliance between Germany and a Russian monarchy restored under the banner of von der Goltz : the policy of supporting the independence of the Baltic states to form a barrier, together with Poland, between Germany and Russia was taking shape. On May 3, 1919, an order was given by the allied armistice commission for the evacuation of the Baltic countries. The order was ignored. On June 18, 1919, it was repeated by the allied governments to the German Government.[2] It was still ignored ; and, though the social-democratic government in Berlin professed its anxiety to comply,[3] the social-democratic governor of East

---

[1] By an odd incongruity this provision was repeated textually in article 433 of the Versailles treaty, though, by the time the treaty was signed, the order to evacuate had already been given.

[2] Further reminders were sent on August 1 and 24 and September 16 (*Documents on British Foreign Policy 1919-1939 : First Series*, i (1947), 720-721 ; iii (1949), 40).

[3] According to F. von Rabenau, *Seeckt : Aus Seinem Leben, 1918-1936* (1940), p. 135, the German Government took the formal decision to withdraw on the receipt of the first allied request on May 9, 1919.

Prussia, Winnig by name, was working hand-in-glove with von der Goltz. The armies of von der Goltz stood their ground, fighting intermittently both against the Bolsheviks and against the Latvian and Estonian troops which were receiving allied support.[1]

Before long, however, other currents of opinion appeared in Germany itself. The allied governments, in insisting on the complete disbandment of the old imperial army, had sanctioned the creation of a new German army, of limited size and recruited on a voluntary basis, the Reichswehr. This had been brought into existence by a decree of March 15, 1919. The organization of the Reichswehr in the summer of 1919 was in the hands of an exceedingly shrewd group of former staff officers : the shrewdest of them was General von Seeckt, who had ended the war as German military adviser to the Turkish general staff. This group now attempted a cool appraisal of the situation both in Germany and in Russia ; and in both cases they reached conclusions diametrically opposed to those of the vast majority of German officers (including the oldest and most distinguished), who saw in von der Goltz a new national hero. In Germany, men like Ludendorff and von der Goltz were irreconcilably opposed to the Weimar republic, and sought a return to some kind of monarchical or authoritarian régime ; Seeckt was ready to accept the Weimar republic as the most practicable and convenient instrument of his policy, at any rate until such time as German military strength had been re-created. In Russia, Ludendorff and von der Goltz were unable to conceive of any policy except an out-and-out offensive against Bolshevism. Seeckt, noting that the Bolshevik régime was now nearly two years old and that confident predictions

---

[1] An extensive literature exists on the events of 1919 in the Baltic. The most important items are *Die Rückführung des Ostheeres* (1936), an official collection of documents ; R. von der Goltz, *Meine Sendung in Finland und im Baltikum* (Munich, 1920), *Als Politischer General im Osten* (1936) ; P. Avalov-Bermondt, *V Bor'be s Bolshevizmom* (Glückstadt, 1926) ; A. Winnig, *Heimkehr* (1935) ; J. Bisschof, *Die Letzte Front* (1935) ; *United States Commission of Inquiry in Finland and the Baltic States : Report* (1919) ; *Documents on British Foreign Policy 1919–1939 : First Series*, iii (1949), ch. 1. Nothing seems to have been published on the Soviet side except a brief summary of events in M. G. Bakh, *Politiko-Ekonomicheskie Vzaimootnosheniya mezhdu SSSR i Pribaltikoi za Desyat' Let, 1917–1927* (1928). An illuminating history of this episode could be written.

of its downfall had been continually disappointed, began to suspect that it had come to stay. But, if so, then von der Goltz's armies in the Baltic were building not, as was said, a " bridge " to Russia,[1] but a wall against her. If the allied governments were bent on making Soviet Russia their implacable enemy, Germany had nothing to gain by following their example. In August 1919 the Reichswehr decided that the allied demand for the withdrawal of von der Goltz should be complied with. The order was issued, and after some delay von der Goltz himself returned to Germany. The bulk of his army remained, and took service under a " white " Russian adventurer, said to be of Caucasian origin, called Avalov-Bermondt. Official sources of revenue having been cut off, the new venture was financed by German heavy industry, which still believed in the policy of overthrowing the Bolsheviks to open the Russian market, and was unconvinced by Seeckt's subtler reasoning.[2] With this support, Avalov-Bermondt held his ground through the winter. By the spring of 1920, thanks to failing finances or to allied hostility, most of his forces had melted away.

It is easy to see in retrospect how clearly and inevitably the argument of Seeckt and his colleagues in the Reichswehr pointed to an ultimate alliance between Bolshevik Russia and a Germany of the Right. Assuming that the Bolshevik régime survived, such an alliance would give the Reichswehr what it would one day need — a free hand against the west ; it would also give German heavy industry its indispensable market. By January 1920 Seeckt had accepted " a future political and economic agreement with Soviet Russia " as " an irreversible purpose of our policy ", while at the same time proclaiming that " we are ready to form a wall

---

[1] Von der Goltz wrote to Seeckt on November 2, 1919 : " our whole state policy stands or falls with the Russian-German bridge " (F. von Rabenau, *Seeckt : Aus Seinem Leben, 1918-1936* (1940), p. 204).

[2] Evidence on the sources of Bermondt's finances will be found in R. von der Goltz, *Meine Sendung in Finland und im Baltikum* (Munich, 1920), pp. 299-303 ; *Documents on British Foreign Policy, 1919-1939 : First Series*, iii (1949), 55, 97, 211-212, 225-227, 296-297. According to a German diplomatic source, unnamed " English representatives " in Berlin and " English emissaries " in the Baltic spread reports that " important Englishmen like Churchill were in favour of a continuation of the Bermondt undertaking within thè framework of the general intervention campaign ", and that it would " soon be decided whether this line would win the upper hand in the British Government " (W. von Blücher, *Deutschlands Weg nach Rapallo* (Wiesbaden, 1951), p. 82).

against Bolshevism " in Germany itself.[1] Seeckt was perhaps the
first German in high office to realize that there was nothing incompatible in these two policies. But few Germans in the winter of
1919–1920 were able to see the future in such stark, unshaded
colours. In the confused welter of opinion which had marked
German political thinking since the hour of defeat, the need was
felt to establish some ideological, as well as a political, link with
the great eastern neighbour. The Russian revolution exercised
a fascination on vanquished Germany which went far beyond the
narrow circles professing sympathy with Bolshevik doctrine, and
was felt on the nationalist Right as well as on the communist Left.
For many Germans whose tradition was wholly of the Right,
including German officers, it seemed in 1919 that the only path to
salvation for Germany lay through revolution. The mood of
sheer despair counted for much in this vision of destruction : the
German Samson in the hour of defeat and humiliation would call
the dark powers of Bolshevism to his aid to pull down the pillars
of the temple and cheat the Philistines of their triumph. But the
vision also had its positive sides, which would not necessarily clash
with the aims of the Russian revolution. The blow would be directed against the west and against liberal democracy ; it would be
authoritarian, but would recognize the new power of the urban
proletariat ; and its aim would be the revival of German national
military power. Thus an alliance between nationalist Germany
and Bolshevik Russia might be sealed by a common hatred of the
west, determined by ideological antipathies as well as by conflicts
of interest with the western Powers.

The idea was at first sight fantastic and might have passed for a
typical concoction of politically unschooled officers and hare-
brained young men.[2] But it had its counterpart on the extreme
Left. Laufenberg and Wolffheim, the leaders of the Left group
expelled from the KPD at the Heidelberg congress in October

---

[1] F. von Rabenau, Seeckt : Aus Seinem Leben, 1918–1936 (1940), p. 252 ;
in his memorandum of September 11, 1922 (see pp. 438-439 below) Seeckt
repeated the same conviction that " Germany will not be bolshevized, not even
by an understanding with Russia on foreign affairs " (ibid. p. 317).

[2] Hoffmann, who like Ludendorff, remained fanatically anti-Bolshevik,
noted that cooperation with the Bolsheviks found numerous adherents " especially among professors and in student circles and among young officers " (Die
Aufzeichnungen des Generalmajors Max Hoffmann (1929), ii, 324-325).

1919,[1] were sponsors of a doctrine which came to be called
" national Bolshevism ", and invited German communists to
proclaim a " revolutionary people's war " against the Versailles
treaty and thus win the support of German nationalists for the
proletarian revolution ; [2] Radek attacked them in his open letter to
the congress for wanting to start a war against the Entente and for
vainly seeking to make peace with the bourgeoisie, which would,
if faced with the choice, prefer a total foreign occupation to a
dictatorship of the proletariat.[3] About the same time an anarchist
intellectual, Eltzbacher, wrote a pamphlet entitled *Bolshevism and
the German Future*, in which he argued that Germany could obtain
deliverance from the slavery of the Versailles treaty only by accepting Bolshevism, which would then sweep over western Europe and
destroy it ; for this end he was prepared to reckon with disorder,
terror and hunger.   In a confused argument the themes of ideological and political union (*Anschluss*) with Russia became indistinguishable : " the broken link with Russia is automatically
restored as soon as Germany embraces Bolshevism ".[4]   From this
extreme of revolutionary intoxication to the opposite extreme,
represented by Seeckt and the Reichswehr generals, of hard
calculation of the value of a Russian alliance, the prism of German
opinion about the great neighbour in the east showed every variety
of hue.   What was common to all these groups was hatred of the
west, admiration — sometimes enthusiastic, more often grudging
and reluctant — of Russian power, and the hope and belief that
this power could somehow be enlisted in the struggle against the
victors of Versailles.

The bewildering confusion of opinion among those Germans
who, in the autumn of 1919, were looking towards Russia for a
clue to guide them out of the political, economic and ideological
predicament of defeat was strikingly illustrated by the conversations held by Radek at this time, in his privileged room in the
Moabit prison and in the apartments in which he stayed in Berlin

  [1] See p. 138 above.
  [2] The fullest exposition of this doctrine was H. Laufenberg and F. Wolffheim, *Revolutionärer Volkskrieg oder Konterrevolutionärer Bürgerkrieg ?* (Hamburg, 1920) ; the ambiguity of the word *Volk* lay at the root of this programme.
  [3] K. Radek, *Zur Taktik des Kommunismus : Ein Schreiben an den Oktober-
Parteitag der KPD* (Hamburg, 1919), pp. 11-12, 15-16.
  [4] P. Eltzbacher, *Der Bolschewismus und die Deutsche Zukunft* (Jena, 1919).

while awaiting repatriation to Moscow. The influences that intervened in his favour [1] can hardly have been unconnected with the
new trend of opinion among the Reichswehr generals. Somebody
in high office saw the advantage of not antagonizing the only
leading Bolshevik who had come to Berlin since Joffe's expulsion
in November 1918, and perhaps of establishing some informal
contact with him. Available information about those whom Radek
saw at this time comes almost exclusively from Radek himself,
and has no claim to be exhaustive. He records no contact, direct
or indirect, with any German official quarter; and it is perhaps
unlikely that important Reichswehr officers would in 1919 have
risked compromising themselves by any direct approach to
Radek.[2] But the bold ideas about Turkey mooted in Radek's
conversations with Talaat and Enver [3] also had their application
nearer home in Germany; and it is conceivable that Enver, who
had been closely associated with Seeckt in Turkey during the war,
may have passed on some of these ideas to his old comrade in
arms. Enver, wrote Radek, " was the first to explain to German
military men that Soviet Russia is a new and growing world
Power with which they must count if they really want to fight
against the Entente ".[4] The climate of Berlin in the autumn of
1919 was already propitious for the birth of this idea. It would be
difficult, and is comparatively unimportant, to establish in whose
fertile brain it was born.

[1] See p. 134, note 1, above.
[2] Radek's reminiscences in *Krasnaya Nov'*, No. 10, 1926 (see preceding note),
were published at a time when Soviet-German military cooperation was at its
height and was a closely guarded secret : if he had, in 1919, any direct or indirect
dealings with any official spokesman of the Reichswehr, he might have deemed
it imprudent to mention them. According to B. Nikolaevsky (*Novyi Zhurnal*
(N.Y.), No. 1, 1942, p. 244), Radek's reminiscences were reprinted in 1927 as a
pamphlet with the omission of his report of conversations with Germans ; this
would indicate that what Radek did record was thought indiscreet in some
quarters, especially after the revelations on the subject in the Reichstag
in December 1926. In an interview in *Svenska Dagbladet*, September 5, 1949,
General Köstring, German military attaché in Moscow in the nineteen-thirties,
referred to Radek's military contacts in 1919 and his share in arranging them
(he was at that time on Seeckt's staff) ; unfortunately his evidence is vague, and
he subsequently denied the statement attributed to him in the interview that
Radek had a secret meeting with Seeckt (A. Fredborg, *Storrbritannien och den
Ryska Frågan, 1918-1920* (1951), p. 196, note 52).
[3] See pp. 246-247 above.
[4] *Krasnaya Nov'*, No. 10, 1926, p. 164 ; for Enver's letter to Seeckt of
August 1920, see p. 328 below.

The first and most regular of Radek's recorded contacts with German military circles was with a retired general, Reibnitz by name,[1] a former intimate of Ludendorff, from whose rabid anti-Bolshevik views, however, he now emphatically dissented. He had read and been impressed by Lenin's *Current Tasks of the Soviet Power* written in April 1918 and recently published in a German translation; it was a pamphlet devoted to the urgent practical tasks of creating an efficient administration, and ended by declaring that what was now required was not " hysterical outbursts " but " the measured tread of the iron battalions of the proletariat ". The general assured Radek that he was preaching to his brother officers " not only alliance with Soviet Russia, but a so-called peaceful revolution ". Reibnitz was perhaps more enthusiastic than intelligent. But it was in his apartment that Radek lived during the first weeks after his release from prison ; [2] and here further contacts were made with other spokesmen of similar views. Among Radek's new visitors two were of special importance. Colonel Max Bauer,[3] Ludendorff's former chief of intelligence, a man " with the movements of a cat ", quite unlike a soldier, looked forward to the seizure of power in Germany by the Right, but not until " the workers are disillusioned with bourgeois democracy and come to the conclusion that a ' dictatorship of labour ' is possible in Germany only by agreement between the working class and the officer class ". Radek records : " He gave me to understand that on this basis the officers might strike a bargain with the communist party and with Soviet Russia ; they understand that we cannot be conquered and that we are Germany's allies in the struggle with the Entente ". Admiral Hintze, once German naval attaché in Petersburg and Minister for Foreign Affairs for a brief period in the summer of 1918, during which he signed the series of agreements with Russia supplementary to Brest-Litovsk, now " stood for a deal with Soviet Russia ", and asked Radek whether world revolution would come in the west

---

[1] Radek transliterates the name in one place as Raivnits, in another as Reignits.

[2] *Krasnaya Nov'*, No. 10, 1926, pp. 169-172.

[3] According to R. Fischer, *Stalin and German Communism* (Harvard, 1948), p. 207, Bauer " regularly " visited Radek in prison ; Radek (*Krasnaya Nov'*, No. 10, 1926, p. 169) states explicitly that he met Bauer for the first (and, it would seem, only) time in Reibnitz's flat.

" in time to prevent the Entente strangling Germany ". But
Hintze too had his views about revolution. From talking to the
workers on his Silesian estate, who were Catholics, he had been
convinced that " the revolution consisted in the refusal of the
workers to work any longer for the capitalist ", that " the bourgeoisie was hated ", and that " Germany will hardly be able to
rise again without a change of régime ".[1]

Radek's most distinguished German visitor was, however,
Walther Rathenau, son of the founder of the great German electrical combine, the AEG, and creator in the first world war of the
raw materials division of the German Ministry of War — the
counterpart and forerunner of the British and French ministries
of munitions. The impression was mixed. Radek not unfairly
detected in Rathenau " a great abstract intelligence, an absence of
any intuition, and a morbid vanity ". A Jew of keen and inquisitive
mind, but of strongly marked temperamental instability, Rathenau
was a perfect representative of that sector of German industry
which, having retained financial and commercial links with the
west, was unable to share the unqualified eastern orientation of the
great iron and steel magnates, and was condemned to a halting
and ambivalent attitude on major issues of policy. In an open
letter to the victorious allies in December 1918, Rathenau had
argued that, if vindictive terms were imposed on Germany, " one
of the formerly strongest props in the European structure will be
destroyed, and the boundary of Asia will advance to the Rhine ".
But Rathenau's emotional aversion from the east was matched by
a strong intellectual fascination. He was apparently the promoter
of an " industrial mission " which went to Moscow in the summer
of 1919 to " study industrial conditions " ; [2] and he was the prime
mover in setting up in Berlin early in 1920 a small group of
industrialists as a " study commission " on Russian affairs.[3] He
now came to Radek without any preliminaries, settled himself
comfortably, one leg crossed over the other, and for more than an

[1] *Ibid.* p. 171 ; Bauer was reported as saying in April 1920 that " complete Bolshevism must first come in order that Germany may learn to demand the strong man " (E. Troeltsch, *Spektator-Briefe* (Tübingen, 1924),
p. 139).
[2] *Documents on British Foreign Policy, 1919-1939 : First Series*, iii (1949),
511.
[3] Walther Rathenau, *Briefe* (1926), ii, 229-230.

hour " developed his view of the world situation ". Here too a solid political argument — the need for economic cooperation between the two countries — was set in an ideological and quasi-revolutionary context. Rathenau admitted that there could be no return to capitalism, and claimed to have propounded in his writings a " constructive socialism " — the first scientific step in advance of Marx, who had given only " a theory of destruction ". The workers might destroy ; but for construction the leadership of " the intellectual aristocracy " would be required. There would be no revolution in Germany for long years, since the German worker was " a philistine ". Reverting to Russia, Rathenau added : " Probably in a few years' time I shall come to you as a technician, and you will receive me in silken garments ". Radek deprecated the idea that Bolsheviks would ever wear silken garments. But the pregnant offer of the services of German technicians started new trains of thought. The habit of looking east had set in fast even among the most " western " of German industrialists.[1] Radek's only contribution to the conversation recorded by himself was to read to Rathenau Lenin's article on the achievement of the *Subbotniki* in Moscow which had reached him " via the Scandinavian countries " — a brave attempt to develop a philosophy of voluntary labour under socialism.[2] Rathenau paid Radek a second visit, this time no longer in the prison but in Reibnitz's apartment, bringing with him Felix Deutsch, the general manager of the AEG. But Deutsch was married to the daughter of an American banker, and represented those German financial circles which were most closely affiliated to the west ; in the following year one of the first American loans to Germany since the armistice was secured by Deutsch for the AEG. At this second interview discussion of the impending end of capitalism and of the need of an eastern outlook for Germany seems to have receded into the background. But even Deutsch

---

[1] It is significant that the only visitor whom Radek reports as advocating a western orientation was the social-democrat Heilmann, who argued that " a socialist revolution in Germany is impossible now, since German industry is without raw material and the country without bread ", and that " a restoration of the German economy is impossible without the enslavement of the country to American capital " (*Krasnaya Nov'*, No. 10, 1926, p. 170).

[2] K. Radek, *Portrety i Pamflety*, ii (1934), 74 : this seems to be the only reference in Radek's later writings to his Berlin conversations. For Lenin's article, see Vol. 2, p. 208.

was prepared to concede that the Russians could have what
régime they pleased "if only we trade with the AEG", and
wanted to visit Soviet Russia.[1]
Radek's own record certainly does not exhaust the list of
Germans who visited him in Berlin. He apparently saw Otto
Hoetzsch, a professor of Russian history, later a member of the
Reichstag and the expert of the German National Party on Russian
affairs.[2] What passed between him and Radek is unknown.
Hoetzsch later became a consistent advocate of a German-Russian
alliance based on grounds of pure power politics, irrespective of
ideology; if he spoke to Radek in this sense in the autumn of
1919, he was in advance of most of his contemporaries. Radek
himself mentions the visit of Maximilian Harden, the radical
journalist who had won fame both before 1914 and during the
war as an opponent of the imperial system of Wilhelm II and for
whose journal *Die Zukunft* he promised to write an article.[3] The
immense variety of professional and political affiliation among
Radek's visitors is evidence of an almost desperate eagerness in
Germany to find some kind of meeting-place with the rising power
in the east. It would be premature to infer at this time the immediate prospect of any change in German policy. The Versailles
treaty was not yet ratified; the Weimar republic could still scarcely
afford to have a foreign policy. But two significant events occurred
towards the end of Radek's stay in Berlin. In November 1919, at
about the time when Litvinov journeyed to Copenhagen to establish contact with Great Britain as a delegate to negotiate an
exchange of prisoners, the German Government agreed to receive
a Soviet representative in the same capacity; and Victor Kopp,
once a Menshevik and an associate of Trotsky in Vienna before
1914, arrived in Berlin to become, in Radek's words, a "semi-
legal *polpred*".[4] In the same month Seeckt was appointed head
of the vaguely named Truppenamt of the German Ministry of

[1] *Krasnaya Nov'*, No. 10, 1926, p. 171.
[2] R. Fischer, *Stalin and German Communism* (Harvard, 1948), p. 207.
[3] *Krasnaya Nov'*, No. 10, 1926, p. 166; the article appeared in *Die Zukunft* of February 1920 (see p. 320, note 2, below).
[4] *Krasnaya Nov'*, No. 10, 1926, p. 169; Kopp, however, apparently received no formal recognition from the German Government till February 1920, and then only for negotiations about prisoners of war (I. Maisky, *Vneshnyaya Politika RSFSR, 1917–1922* (1922), p. 106).

War, a camouflage for the general staff which Germany was forbidden, by the Versailles treaty, to maintain. For the next four years German policy towards Soviet Russia was the policy of Seeckt.

In January 1920, after some delay in making arrangements for Radek's transit through Poland, he was ceremoniously conducted to the frontier. The journey across Poland was slow, and it was nearly the end of January before he reached Moscow.[1] Radek had arrived in Berlin in December 1918, a firm believer, like all other Bolsheviks, in the imminence of the German revolution. At the founding congress of the KPD in December 1918 he had offered his German audience the hope of liberation from the consequences of defeat through a proletarian revolution :

> There is no other way of making Germany defensible and protecting her against the yoke which the Entente seeks to impose on her than to make the German workers masters of Germany. . . . The lords of the Entente fear nothing so much as letting their armies come into contact with workers who know what they want.[2]

But this was a mere repetition of the old illusions of Brest-Litovsk. Germany was as powerless against Foch in the first weeks of 1919 as Soviet Russia had been a year earlier against Hoffmann. Radek soon began, as has already been seen,[3] to take a pessimistic view of the immediate future of the German revolution, and even of the prospects of survival of the Russian revolution : some new means must be found both of saving Soviet Russia and of liberating Germany from the Entente. In this way Radek came to believe, in advance of any other leading Bolshevik, in the necessity of a period of manœuvres and compromises rather than in any early revolutionary achievement. The views on Soviet foreign policy which he brought back with him from Berlin may be gleaned from several articles written there in the last three moths of 1919. The earliest of them was the open letter to the Heidelberg congress of the KPD in October 1919 at the moment of the lowest ebb in Soviet fortunes.

---

[1] *Krasnaya Nov'*, No. 10, 1926, pp. 172-175 ; for the chronology of Radek's return, see *Soviet Studies*, iii, No. 4 (April 1952), pp. 411-412.

[2] K. Radek, *Die Russische und Deutsche Revolution und die Weltlage* (1919), p. 29.   [3] See pp. 139-140 above.

The problem of the foreign policy of Soviet Russia [he wrote in an italicized passage] *and, unless the world revolution announces itself more quickly than hitherto, of all other countries in which the working class is victorious, consists in arriving at a* modus vivendi *with the capitalist states.* . . . The possibility of peace between capitalist and proletarian states is no utopia.[1]

This policy seemed the very antithesis of the " national Bolshevism " (not yet known by that name) of Laufenberg and Wolffheim, which Radek had denounced as liable to embroil Germany, and by implication Russia, with the capitalist countries of the west.[2]

The case was driven home in three further articles written just before his departure from Berlin. The first was a direct attack on " national Bolshevism " — this time under that name. " The problem of the foreign policy of Soviet Russia ", repeated Radek, " . . . . consists in attaining a *modus vivendi* with the capitalist states." [3] In a second article, published almost simultaneously in the German edition of the official journal of Comintern, Radek developed the same thesis from the revolutionary standpoint. The " decomposition of capitalism ", wrote Radek, was a certainty. But it would be a " long process ", and Soviet Russia would unavoidably be obliged in the interval " to seek and to find a *modus vivendi* with the capitalist states ". Another argument pointed the same conclusion. " If Soviet Russia has to go on fighting, she cannot begin to restore her national economy." The alternatives before her therefore were : " socialist construction within the framework of a temporary compromise, or war without any kind of economic construction ". What Radek was seeking was, in effect, a " compromise with world capital " which would leave the dictatorship of the proletariat intact — a striking anticipation of the foreign aspect of NEP. But it was not for nothing that Radek had spent three months in intensive conversations

---

[1] K. Radek, *Zur Taktik des Kommunismus : Ein Schreiben an den Oktober-Parteitag der KPD* (Hamburg, 1919), pp. 9, 11-12.
[2] See p. 312 above.
[3] *Gegen den National-Bolschewismus* (Hamburg, 1920), p. 9 ; this pamphlet contains articles by Radek and Thalheimer, of which the former, entitled *Die Auswärtige Potilik des Kommunismus und der Hamburger National-Bolschewismus*, was originally published in *Die Internationale*, No. 17-18 (December 20, 1919), pp. 332-346 under the pen-name " Arnold Struthan ".

with German politicians, soldiers and industrialists; and from this point the argument passed to Germany:

> Germany has suffered defeat, but in spite of this her technical apparatus and technical possibilities are still great. The Anglo-Saxon countries are the victors, but in spite of this their economic disorder has gone so far that they are not in a position to supply sufficient aid to France and Italy. . . . In Germany, thanks to the destruction of her external relations and the collapse of her economy, there are thousands of unemployed and hungry engineers who could render Russia the greatest service in the restoration of her national economy.

Radek attempted to defend himself against the charge of seeking to " help the Germans to restore the power of German capitalism on Russian soil ", and proceeded to his major conclusion :

> Not the exchange of goods and not the employment of German capital in Russia, but working help — that is the *new foundation of German-Russian economic relations.*

And the last shaft of all was a warning to Germany of the isolation which awaited her if she ignored these opportunities.[1] The third article, being designed for the bourgeois reader (it was addressed to " right-minded bourgeois "), was more cautiously phrased. But it rested on the same argument that " Germany and Russia need economic relations with one another because neither country can hope to get from the Entente alone what it needs and because they can help one another in many ways "; and it suggested as " practical conclusions " the resumption of diplomatic relations and the sending of German economic experts to Russia to organize an exchange of goods, or, failing this, the sending to Russia of representatives of German economic concerns who could prepare the way for such an exchange, and " also organize an objective reporting service on Russia for Germany ".[2] Thus

---

[1] K. Radek, *Die Auswärtige Politik Sowjet-Russlands* (Hamburg, 1921), pp. 37-39, 44, 46-47 ; this chapter is a reprint of an article in *Die Kommunistiche Internationale* (the Berlin counterpart of *Kommunisticheskii Internatsional*), No. 3 (Decembe r1919), pp. 9-27, which also appeared under the name " Arnold Struthan ", and was written " in December 1919 in the Berlin prison " (K. Radek, *Wege der Russischen Revolution* (Hamburg, 1922), p. 28).

[2] *Deutschland und Russland : Ein in der Moabiter Schutzhaft geschriebener Artikel für richtiggehende Bourgeois* (1920), pp. 11-12 ; it was originally published in *Die Zukunft* in February 1920, and an English translation appeared in *Soviet Russia* (N.Y.), April 17, 1920, pp. 383-387.

from the Soviet as well as from the German side the call to Soviet-German friendship was being sounded. But while the German interest was from the outset largely political and military, the Soviet interest at this stage was exclusively economic.[1] In the chaotic conditions of 1919 conversations with Radek committed nobody : this was no doubt one of their attractions on the German side. On the Soviet side Radek was playing a lone hand ; in so far as it was possible to speak of any recognized Soviet foreign policy at this time, he was certainly not its authorized exponent. But his influence can hardly be excluded from the many factors which contributed to the change of course set at the beginning of 1920. The crucial argument for compromise in Soviet policy towards the capitalist world was the prospect of prolonged delay in the maturing of the European revolution ; and on this point Radek was an emphatic first-hand witness.[2] But, while the general view of Soviet foreign policy which Radek had imbibed in Berlin fitted in with this trend and reinforced it with powerful arguments, there is no evidence that even Radek yet seriously entertained any specific project of collaboration between Soviet Russia and those forces in Germany which were in revolt against Versailles ;[3] and if he did, he found no echo in Moscow. In his pamphlet *The Infantile Disease of " Leftism " in Communism*, written in April 1920 in preparation for the second congress of

---

[1] That Radek was not thinking in terms of an exclusive friendship with Germany was shown by a statement given by him on January 6, 1920, on the eve of his departure from Germany to a correspondent of the *Manchester Guardian* : " It is the standpoint of the Russian Government that normal and good relations are just as possible between socialist and capitalist states as they have been between capitalist and feudal states . . . I personally am convinced that communism can only be saved through good relations with the capitalist states " (*Manchester Guardian*, January 8, 1920). This may be compared with a similar statement in Moscow two months later (see p. 160 above).

[2] Radek told the first public meeting addressed by him after his return to Moscow that " the road to revolution is harder for the workers of Europe than for the Russians, because on the side of the Russian proletariat there was the army which wanted peace, the peasantry which strove to seize the land, whereas in Europe the masses are disarmed and the bourgeoisie form a white guard " (*Izvestiya*, January 29, 1920).

[3] In a speech to the ninth party congress on April 1, 1920, he argued that, owing to the Versailles treaty, " a united front of capitalists is impossible " and the allies had failed in the attempt to arm the Germans against Soviet Russia. What conclusions he drew from his thesis is not known, since the full text of his speech is not extant ; it was reported in a brief summary in *Pravda*, April 3, 1920.

Comintern, Lenin, like Radek, dealt severely with the German deviation of " national Bolshevism ", which was tantamount to proposing " a bloc with the German bourgeoisie for a war against the Entente ". Communists were not " bound at all costs to reject the Versailles peace, and that immediately ". This was a confusion about the real ends of Bolshevik policy.

The overthrow of the bourgeoisie in any of the great European countries, including Germany, is such a gain for the international revolution that for its sake we can and must accept — if it proves necessary — the continued existence of the Versailles peace. If Russia single-handed could, with benefit to the revolution, endure the Brest peace for several months, it is not in the least impossible that Soviet Germany in alliance with Soviet Russia should, with benefit to the revolution, endure the continued existence of the Versailles peace.[1]

Thus the alliance of the Soviet cause with a German nationalist revolt against the Versailles treaty was emphatically rejected ; and, if Radek during his involuntary sojourn in Berlin had toyed with this idea, it was promptly disowned. While the notion of a temporary compromise with the capitalist world had gained ground in Moscow in the first months of 1920, nobody there was yet thinking in terms of an accommodation with Germany establishing special relations between the two countries. Nevertheless it is difficult to deny that Radek's scepticism about the prospects of the revolution, combined with his knowledge of Germany, gave him at this time a clearer intuition than Lenin of some of the forces at work.

The forces which, in the face of every obstacle, were making for a *rapprochement* between Bolshevik Russia and nationalist Germany ripened slowly. The Kapp *putsch* of March 1920 was an important occasion in the history of the Weimar republic, and was ultimately to have a decisive influence in its relation with its eastern neighbour. The makers of the *putsch* belonged to the military tradition of the old army, of the Ludendorffs and the von der Goltzes ; many of the detachments which marched on

[1] Lenin, *Sochineniya*, xxv, 214-215.

Berlin had fought in the Baltic in the previous autumn and winter.   They were irreconcilable anti-Bolsheviks who still believed in a restoration in Russia as the necessary prelude to a reconstitution of the German-Russian alliance.   The attitude of the new Reichswehr was quite different.   Its clever leaders had not only come to accept the Weimar republic as a suitable facade behind which they could work for the recovery of German military power; they were also prepared to accept Bolshevism in Russia as a potential partner to promote this end.   The Kapp *putsch* ended in the relegation to the lunatic fringe of German politics of those who still believed in the crusade against Bolshevism, and the emergence of military leaders who were ready to do business with Soviet Russia as an equal Power.   But official relations moved slowly.   In April 1920 a prisoners-of-war agreement was signed in Berlin with the Soviet representative, Kopp, whose ostensible function of looking after the repatriation of prisoners of war probably did not preclude some political activity; and another agreement on the same subject followed three months later.[1]   In June 1920 Gustav Hilger, one of the last members of the German consular staff who had left Moscow in November 1918, returned to Moscow as the German counterpart of Kopp in Berlin, and received from Chicherin the assurance that Soviet Russia's attitude to Germany was " dictated by the sole wish to establish closer economic, political and cultural relations ".[2]

The Soviet-Polish war of the summer of 1920 ripened these hidden seeds and set in motion new and vital forces.   On the Soviet side, a striking revival of Russian patriotism linked itself with Bolshevism, inoculating Soviet foreign policy with a new national element.[3]   On the German side, the original Polish offensive of May 1920 did not kindle any very lively interest in the war.   But when the Red Army unexpectedly struck back, and in

[1] *RSFSR: Sbornik Deistvuyushchikh Dogovorov*, i (1921), No. 22, pp. 128-130; No. 24, pp. 133-134.   Rumours that Kopp " had detailed discussions with Kapp before the Kapp *putsch* " (E. Troeltsch, *Spektator-Briefe* (Tübingen, 1924), p. 271) cannot be disproved, but are perhaps unlikely; the associations of the Kapp *putsch* were all anti-Bolshevik, and direct contact with German nationalists was not yet part of Soviet policy.   It would be interesting to ascertain whether Kopp had any contact with the KPD at this time; if so, no hint of it emerged in subsequent party recriminations.

[2] *Soviet Russia* (N.Y.), August 14, 1920, p. 148.

[3] See pp. 272-273 above.

July began its triumphant march into Poland, a wave of excitement swept over Germany. Alarm was mingled with elation. Bolshevism threatened to sweep into central Europe. But, by the same stroke, Germany's principal enemy in the east was in mortal danger, and the eastern bastion of Versailles was tottering. The attitude of Germany in this contingency had been outlined six months earlier by the far-seeing Seeckt :

> I refuse to support Poland even in the face of the danger that she may be swallowed up. On the contrary, I count on that : and, even if we cannot at the moment help Russia to re-establish her former imperial frontiers, we certainly should not hinder her.[1]

Maltzan, head of the Russian department of the German Ministry of Foreign Affairs, entered into confidential conversations with Kopp, whose stature in Berlin swelled with every advance of the Red Army. The request for an assurance that the Red Army would not cross the existing German frontier was promptly met. But when Maltzan delicately raised the question of " a revision of the unnatural German frontiers imposed by the Versailles treaty ", Kopp hedged and suggested *de jure* recognition and the resumption of full diplomatic relations as a necessary preliminary to any negotiations.[2] Clearly the liberation of Poland from its capitalist rulers as conceived at this time in Moscow included former German Poland, and could not be halted at the old 1914 frontier.

---

[1] F. von Rabenau, *Seeckt : Aus Seinem Leben, 1918-1936* (1940), p. 252.

[2] W. von Blücher, *Deutschlands Weg nach Rapallo* (Wiesbaden, 1951), pp. 100-101. According to an unpublished memorandum of Reibnitz written about 1940, extracts from which have been communicated to me by Mr. Gustav Hilger, Reibnitz negotiated with Radek and Kopp at this time a plan under which, as soon as the Red Army entered Warsaw, German *Freikorps* detachments would advance in West Prussia, Posen and Upper Silesia as far as the old German frontier ; R. Fischer, *Stalin and German Communism* (Harvard, 1948), refers to conversations between Radek, Kopp and Reventlow. Stories of Radek's presence in Berlin at the critical period of the Red Army advance in Poland are, however, open to doubt ; he was in Moscow at the latest on July 24, 1920, when he spoke at the second congress of Comintern. Stories of negotiations for Soviet-German military collaboration at this time are in general vitiated by too much hindsight ; any discussions must have been highly tentative. According to Krestinsky's " confession " in the 1938 trial, Seeckt was in touch with Kopp in July 1920 ; Krestinsky insisted that this was an " official ", not a " criminal " (i.e. a specifically " Trotskyite ") contact (*Report of Court Proceedings in the Case of the Anti-Soviet " Bloc of Rights and Trotskyites "* (1938), pp. 269-270).

But Kopp's hint did not pass unnoticed in Berlin. On July 22, 1920, Simons, the German Minister for Foreign Affairs, handed to Kopp for transmission to Chicherin a letter proposing discussions with a view to the resumption of normal diplomatic relations between Germany and Soviet Russia. The only condition laid down was a ceremonial hoisting of the German flag at the German Embassy in Moscow in the presence of a company of the Red Army by way of a mark of contrition for the murder of Mirbach. The note ended with an expression of hope for a resumption of trade betweeen the two countries and a request that, when Soviet troops in their advance approached " the old German frontier ", a German military representative might be attached to the army group concerned in order to avoid " undesirable incidents ".[1] By this time the western allies, equally foreseeing disaster to Poland, had organized the despatch of aid in the form of military advisers and munitions. Germany replied with a declaration of neutrality which involved a ban on the transit of munitions through Germany to Poland. In announcing this decision to the Reichstag on July 26, 1920, Simons significantly added that the formal German recognition of the Soviet Government contained in the Brest-Litovsk treaty had never been withdrawn, but avoided any specific reference to diplomatic relations.[2] A week later, on August 2, 1920, Chicherin replied to Simons's proposal to discuss the renewal of diplomatic relations in a note which abounded in courtesies and hopes of friendly cooperation, but firmly rejected the requested ceremonial of expiation for Mirbach's murder as unnecessary and out of place.[3] At a moment when hopes of military victory and the spread of revolution to the west were at their highest, any compromise with a bourgeois German Government may well have seemed superfluous.

These cautious official exchanges, however, by no means exhausted the significance of the advance of the Red Army for

[1] The note has not been published ; Radek in an article in *Pravda*, October 15, 1921, stated that the German Ministry of Foreign Affairs had been prepared to reopen diplomatic relations at this time.

[2] *Verhandlungen des Reichstags*, cccxliv (1921), 263.

[3] This note has not been published. The question of expiation for Mirbach's murder was mentioned again two years later in the debate in the Reichstag on the Rapallo treaty, when Hoetzsch insisted that " after, as before, we demand adequate satisfaction for the murder of Count Mirbach " (*ibid.* ccclv 1922), 7711) ; thereafter it seems to have dropped.

Soviet-German relations. A wave of popular enthusiasm for Soviet Russia swept over Germany. In the Free City of Danzig, formerly German and now under allied administration, the German dockers went on strike and refused to handle munitions shipped to Poland through that port.[1] The German communist newspaper *Rote Fahne* adopted so militant an attitude in support of the party slogan, " alliance with Soviet Russia ", that it incurred the accusation from the other Left parties of trying to involve the German workers in a war with France.[2] German volunteers (Tukhachevsky, the Red Army commander, described them as " Spartakists and non-party workers " and spoke of " hundreds and thousands " of them)[3] flocked to join the Red Army — a curious reversal of the situation of the previous autumn, when German volunteers were flocking to the Baltic to fight the Bolsheviks. Nor was the enthusiasm for the Soviet cause the exclusive prerogative of the communists or of the workers. For the first time, under the stimulus of the threat to Poland and to the hated Versailles settlement, the yearnings of the Right for a Russian alliance openly found expression in sympathy for the Soviet cause. The link between German nationalism and Russian Bolshevism no longer seemed a frightening paradox.[4] Looking back on these events two and three months later, Lenin referred to the " unnatural *bloc* of ' black hundreds ' and Bolsheviks ", and recalled that " everyone in Germany, even the blackest reactionaries and monarchists, said that the Bolsheviks will save us, when they saw the Versailles peace splitting open at all its seams ".[5] Even the professional soldiers began to feel respect and admiration for the

---

[1] A full account of this episode is in I. F. D. Morrow, *The Peace Settlement in the German-Polish Borderlands* (1936), pp. 67-72.

[2] This charge, supported by quotations from *Die Rote Fahne*, was repeated several times at the Halle congress (USPD : *Protokoll über die Verhandlungen des Ausserordentlichen Parteitags zu Halle* (n.d.), pp. 178-179, 198, 213).

[3] J. Pilsudski, *L'Année 1920* (French transl. from Polish, 1929), p. 231.

[4] R. Fischer, *Stalin and German Communism* (Harvard, 1948), p. 197, quotes an article by Reventlow in the *Deutsche Tageszeitung*, the newspaper of the German National Party, demanding a campaign " against the real enemies of the working class, against the Entente, which has bound the proletariat in chains of slavery " ; Reventlow afterwards stated that he tried in vain at this time to win over " leading German politicians " to the idea of military cooperation with Soviet Russia against Poland (K. Radek, *Schlageter : Eine Auseinandersetzung* (1923), p. 19).

[5] Lenin, *Sochineniya*, xxv, 378, 418 ; for a further pronouncement by Lenin, see pp. 330-331 below.

prowess of the Red Army and to reflect on the military value of an alliance.   Max Bauer afterwards paid tribute to Trotsky as " a born military organizer and leader ", and added :

> How he set up a new army out of nothing in the midst of severe battles and then organized and trained this army is absolutely Napoleonic.[1]

And Hoffmann passed the same verdict :

> Even from a purely military standpoint one is astonished that it was possible for the newly recruited Red troops to crush the forces, at times still strong, of the white generals and to eliminate them entirely.[2]

According to another witness, Lebedev, the Soviet chief of staff, was " rated very high in German military circles ".[3]   On the other hand no chances were taken with the danger of Bolshevik infection.   Seeckt's biographer relates that when, after the retreat of the Red Army, 45,000 Russians were interned in East Prussia, the political commissars were carefully separated from the troops, though this did not prevent them from creating " a centre of communist agitation within the Reich ".[4]

Mixed feelings and hesitant attitudes in the German camp were reflected on the Soviet side.   There is what appears to be an authentic story of a meeting at Soldau, just inside the East Prussian frontier, between officers and commissars of the Red Army and " German nationalists ", at which the Russians boasted that the Red Army would liberate West Prussia, ceded to Poland by the Versailles treaty, and restore it to the German fatherland — in earnest of which intention they refrained from setting up local Soviets, as they had done in occupied Polish territory.[5]   The most direct evidence of the way in which opinion was shaping itself in

---

[1] Max Bauer, *Das Land der Roten Zaren* (Hamburg, 1925), p. 79.

[2] *Die Aufzeichnungen des Generalmajors Max Hoffmann* (1929), ii, 321.

[3] W. von Blücher, *Deutschlands Weg nach Rapallo* (Wiesbaden, 1951), p. 173.

[4] F. von Rabenau, *Seeckt: Aus Seinem Leben, 1918–1936* (1940), p. 253.

[5] The story was told without challenge by Martov at the Halle congress in October 1920 (*USPD : Protokoll über die Verhandlungen des Ausserordentlichen Parteitags zu Halle* (n.d.), pp. 212-213): it is repeated with slight variations in C. Smogorzewski, *La Pologne Restaurée* (1927), p. 152.   On the other hand a report carried in *The Times*, August 20, 1920, from its special correspondent in Danzig, that Trotsky had met German staff officers secretly in East Prussia was certainly false.

some Soviet circles at the height of the Polish war is contained in a letter written by Enver, then in Moscow, to Seeckt in Berlin in ungrammatical German on August 26, 1920. Enver reported that he had just seen " Trotsky's really important *aide* " (the official best answering to this description would be Sklyansky, deputy People's Commissar for War), and continued :

> There is a party here which has real power, and Trotsky also belongs to this party, which is for an agreement with Germany. This party would be ready to recognize the old German frontier of 1914. And they see only one way out of the present world chaos — that is, cooperation with Germany and Turkey. In order to strengthen the position of this party and to win the whole Soviet Government for the cause, would it not be possible to give unofficial help, and if possible sell arms ? . . . I think it important that you should come to an understanding with their representatives in order that Germany's position also should be clear and certain. To help the Russians one can, in the corridor or in some suitable place, bring into being a volunteer army or an insurrectionary movement.[1]

If these recommendations could not be put into execution, it may be surmised that the spirit in which they were offered, and Enver's report of opinion in influential circles in Moscow, helped to confirm designs that were already shaping themselves in Seeckt's mind. In the revolutionary mood of 1920, a diplomatic deal to " recognize the old German frontier of 1914 ", i.e. to support the return to Germany of German territory ceded to Poland under the Versailles treaty, might still have seemed too cynical a move to be seriously contemplated in Moscow. The time was not yet ripe to strike a bargain between Russian Bolshevism and German nationalism. But it was, from the outset, inherent in the situation that such a bargain could be struck, and could only be struck, at the expense of Poland.

On the German side the disastrous ending of the Soviet military campaign in Poland put an end to the fleeting vision of a German-

[1] F. von Rabenau, *Seeckt: Aus Seinem Leben, 1928-1936* (1940), p. 307 ; two months later Enver, who had meanwhile been at the Baku congress, returned to Berlin to purchase arms, on whose behalf, or for what purpose, does not transpire (W. von Blücher, *Deutschlands Weg nach Rapallo* (Wiesbaden, 1951), pp. 133-134).

Soviet *rapprochement* at Polish expense.   In the autumn of 1920 many Germans still hoped for the possibility of an accommodation with the west; the East and West Prussian plebiscites had ended favourably for Germany, and the Upper Silesian plebiscite was still pending; the final reparations bill had not yet been presented; and the inflation had been momentarily stayed.   The premature and exaggerated faith of the past summer in military salvation from the east was followed by a reaction in which even the survival of the Soviet régime seemed once more seriously in doubt.   A growing coolness spread over official relations between the two countries.   When Simons, the Minister of Foreign Affairs, in October 1920 defended the refusal of the government to extend the *visas* of Zinoviev and Lozovsky,[1] it was noticed that he ended his speech with expressions of friendship for the Russian people but not for the Soviet Government; and another deputy of the Centre, the future chancellor Fehrenbach, congratulated himself that Germany had not been " misled into intervening in the Russian-Polish war ".[2]   About the same time Maltzan, who had been an ardent advocate of recognition of the Soviet Government in the previous summer, was transferred from the Ministry of Foreign Affairs to a foreign post.   Even trade relations received little encouragement from a grudging statement by Simons in the Reichstag in January 1921 that diplomatic relations with Soviet Russia could not be resumed " so long as satisfaction had not been given for the murder of the representative of the Reich ", but that " communism as such is no reason why a republican and bourgeois government should not trade with the Soviet Government ".[3] Kopp, though still without official function or recognition except in regard to prisoners of war, was attempting to establish with German firms the same commercial relations which Krasin was building up with firms in Great Britain; and these activities were winked at by the authorities, " so long as the interests and security of the Reich were not affected ".[4]   Kopp, who went on leave to Moscow in January 1921, even told *Izvestiya* that there was a prospect of opening trade delegations in Berlin and Moscow

[1] See p. 222, note 5, above.
[2] *Verhandlungen des Reichstags*, cccxlv (1921), 762-763, 786-787.
[3] *Ibid.* cccxlvi (1921), 1990, 1994.
[4] A police order to this effect was quoted by Klara Zetkin in the Reichstag (*ibid.* cccxlvii (1921), 2060).

respectively in the near future.[1] But such hopes were premature. Extreme caution still governed German official policy, and it was not till the ice had been broken by the Anglo-Soviet trade agreement that the German Government decided to follow suit. Official lukewarmness did not, however, complete the picture. During the same period secret overtures were being made through military channels, though these remained totally unknown at the time, and cannot even now be fully documented.[2]

It was a coincidence that, at a time when German military and political circles were pursuing divergent, and even opposite, policies in relation to Soviet Russia, Soviet foreign policy was exhibiting its normal ambivalence in a particularly acute form in regard to Germany. The defeat in Poland ended abruptly any tentative gropings towards Soviet-German cooperation. The events of August 1920 appeared in retrospect like a flash of lightning that had momentarily lighted up a prospect now once more shrouded in darkness. But the forces which, in the bleak winter of 1920–1921, were impelling the Soviet leaders towards an accommodation with the capitalist world began to make themselves felt in Soviet policy towards Germany. A month after the concessions decree of November 1920,[3] Lenin, speaking at the eighth All-Russian Congress of Soviets and recalling the extraordinary happenings of the past summer, for the first time publicly discussed the question of Soviet-German relations in a context other than that of world revolution. Having called Germany " the most advanced country with the exception of America ", he went on :

> This country, bound by the Versailles treaty, finds itself in conditions which do not allow it to exist. And in this position Germany is naturally pushed into alliance with Russia. When the Russian armies were approaching Warsaw, all Germany was in a ferment. Alliance with Russia for this country which is strangled, which has the possibility of setting in motion gigantic productive forces — all this helped to create political confusion in Germany ; the German black hundreds were marching in sympathy with the Russian Bolsheviks and the Spartakists. . . .

[1] *Izvestiya*, February 1, 1921.
[2] For the beginning of the secret negotiations see pp. 361-364 below.
[3] See p. 283 above.

Our foreign policy, so long as we are alone and the capitalist world is strong . . . consists in our being obliged to utilize disagreements. . . . Our existence depends, first, on the existence of a radical split in the camp of the imperialist Powers, and, secondly, on the fact that the victory of the Entente and the Versailles peace have thrown the vast majority of the German nation into a position where it cannot live. . . . The German bourgeois government madly hates the Bolsheviks, but the interests of the international situation are pushing it towards peace with Soviet Russia against its own will.[1]

Thus, three months before the introduction of NEP and the conclusion of the Anglo-Soviet trade agreement, Lenin had hinted in no uncertain terms at the willingness of the Soviet Government to receive German overtures if such should be made. It is doubtful whether those who now cautiously canvassed the advantages of cooperation with the German Government measured the distance that had been traversed since the salvation of the Soviet régime had been regarded as dependent on an early revolution in Germany, or the transformation in thinking which the new policy required. At any rate, Zinoviev and the other leaders of Comintern, flushed with the triumphs of the second congress and the victories since won in Germany and in France, were in no mood to abandon the bright dream of world revolution ; and in this dream Germany necessarily occupied the central place. Thus, in the critical winter of 1920–1921, two contrary and irreconcilable ambitions in regard to Germany confronted each other in Moscow. If the clash between them was not obvious, this was because the day-to-day work of Comintern and the day-to-day work of the Soviet Government (and even of different commissariats) was still largely carried on in watertight compartments, and it was as a rule only when some highly critical situation arose that a decision of the leaders, binding on all concerned, was taken in the central committee of the party or in its Politburo. During the winter of 1920–1921 the attention of the leaders was absorbed by the menacing growth of opposition within the party, by the trade union controversy and, above all, by the economic plight of the country. Whatever other interpretation may be put on the events that followed, it is fairly clear that no general review of

[1] Lenin, *Sochineniya*, xxvi, 14-15.

policy in regard to Germany was undertaken throughout this time. Events within the KPD itself led up to the new crisis. The mass infusion of new members into a much enlarged KPD, through the accession to it of the USPD majority at the Halle congress, was to all appearance a major victory for Comintern and for the KPD. But it raised new problems. The KPD could no longer be content to play the rôle of a small sect, a revolutionary *élite*, the lineal descendant of the *Spartakusbund*. It had become a mass party composed predominantly of workers who were unconcerned with the refinements of theory. It was expected, by its members as well as by others, to have an active policy and to pull its weight in the German political arena. The Russians, the KPD was told by one of its leaders in November 1920, accused it of " too little contact with the mass of workers ", of lack of " skill in agitation ", and even of an " anti-*putsch* mentality ", though it was hoped that this would be remedied by accession of the USPD majority and eventually of the KAPD.[1] This feeling, the legacy of Zinoviev's triumph at Halle, expressed itself within the party in a Left movement which, following the tradition of Liebknecht rather than of Rosa Luxemburg, rated revolutionary action above revolutionary propaganda and called for a forward policy. The movement started in the Berlin section of the party, where it quickly secured a majority ; its most vocal leader was Ruth Fischer, who had been Radek's messenger to Levi in October 1919. The party leadership was not impressed. Levi had inherited Rosa Luxemburg's scepticism of the revolutionary maturity of the German masses, and had never altogether shed the sectarian mentality of the old Spartakusbund. Brandler, the most impressive spokesman of the workers in the central committee of the KPD, was steeped in the trade union tradition, thoroughly understood mass organization and mass demonstrations, but instinctively shrank from armed insurrection. Levi decided to meet the call for action by an experiment in the united front tactics which Brandler had tried in Saxony in the Kapp *putsch*.[2] On January 8, 1921, the party journal, the *Rote Fahne*, carried an open letter from the central committee of the KPD addressed by name to a large number of trade union and political organizations of the

---

[1] *Bericht über den 5. Parteitag der Kommunistischen Partei Deutschlands (Spartakusbund)* (1921), pp. 27-28.   [2] See p. 173 above.

Left, including the SPD, the rump of the USPD and the KAPD. The letter, referring to the " intolerable position " of the German workers in the current crisis, proposed a joint campaign to raise wages and unemployment allowances, to reduce the cost of living, to introduce workers' control over articles of prime necessity, to dissolve and disarm " bourgeois organizations of defence " and create " organizations of proletarian self-defence ", and to establish trade and diplomatic relations with Soviet Russia. The KPD recognized that " these measures cannot radically improve the wretched situation of the proletariat ", and did not " renounce for one moment the struggle for the dictatorship " ; but, after this ceremonial genuflexion to party doctrine, it renewed its appeal for a joint struggle " for the demands set out above ".[1] In the Reichstag Levi, who was one of a small handful of communist deputies, drew out the international implication of the doctrine of the united front :

> This is a turning-point in world history. The oppressed of the whole world stand against the oppressors of the whole world ; and the leader of the oppressed of the whole world, the Power which today gathers together and leads the oppressed of the whole world, is Soviet Russia.[2]

The moral was clear : as the communists would champion the oppressed workers of whatever party, so Soviet Russia was the champion of oppressed nations of whatever political complexion. No German in 1921 doubted that Germany was an oppressed nation.

Radek, ever since his sojourn in Berlin in 1919, had shared Levi's pessimistic estimate of the revolutionary potentialities of the KPD, and was an enthusiastic supporter of the new line, if not its original instigator : the " open letter " is said to have been drafted jointly by Levi and Radek. Zinoviev, on the other hand, still nourished the dreams of world revolution which had seemed so near to realization only six months before. As the hero of the Halle congress, he regarded himself as responsible for the victory which had transformed the KPD from a sect of intellectuals into a mass party equipped for revolutionary action, and his views corresponded with those of the Left group in the KPD. When therefore Radek first mooted in IKKI the project of the

---

[1] Extensive extracts from the letter are in Lenin, *Sochineniya*, xxvi, 679-680, note 200.　　[2] *Verhandlungen des Reichstags*, cccxlvii (1921), 2318.

open letter, Zinoviev vigorously opposed it and was joined by Bukharin, still the self-appointed custodian of revolutionary orthodoxy. Lenin, who had recently swung over to the policy of temporary accommodation with the capitalist world, intervened in favour of Radek, and the open letter was approved.[1] It fell completely flat, meeting with no response from any influential organization of the Left. It was emphatically rejected by the SPD and by the rump of the USPD, which would have no truck with the KPD, as well as by the KAPD, which denounced it as sheer opportunism. In Moscow, where the leaders had more serious problems nearer home, the rebuff was scarcely noticed. In the KPD it had the effect of discrediting Levi's leadership and strengthening the hand of the Left group in the party.

When, a month after the issue of the open letter, Levi left for Leghorn as delegate of the KPD to the crucial congress of the Italian Socialist Party,[2] he may well have supposed that the approval just given from Moscow implied a new mood of leniency towards other Left parties and groups which were not prepared to accept the full rigour of communist doctrine. It was true that a distinction could be drawn between cooperation with other parties of the Left in pursuit of specified common aims and cooperation with heretics within the ranks of a professedly communist party. But this distinction was less familiar at the beginning of 1921 than it afterwards became. At Leghorn Comintern policy was in the hands, not of Radek, but of Rakosi and Kabakchiev, who were nominees of Zinoviev, and were mindful of the distinction between a temporary tactical cooperation with other parties and the toleration of unorthodoxy within the party itself. When the full rigours of the 21 conditions were pressed against Serrati, Levi rallied to his support and encouraged his resistance. Levi's open opposition to the policy of the accredited delegates of Comintern clearly created an intolerable situation, and gave a handle to his enemies in the KPD. When therefore Rakosi and Kabakchiev came to Berlin on their way back to Moscow, and demanded a vote from the central committee condemning Levi's action, they

---

[1] The facts were stated by both Radek and Zinoviev at the fifth congress of Comintern in 1924 (*Protokoll: Fünfter Kongress der Kommunistischen Internationale* (n.d.), i, 165, 468); Lenin at the third congress in June 1921 defended the open letter as " a model political move " (*Sochineniya*, xxvi, 443).

[2] See p. 225 above.

found many supporters and the vote was carried by a rather narrow majority.[1] Levi, Klara Zetkin and three others resigned from the central committee. The deposition of Levi was regarded in the party as a victory for a forward policy. The men who succeeded to the leadership of the party, Ernst Meyer, Brandler, Thalheimer and Fröhlich, though they did not belong to the Left wing of the party, had been converted to the so-called " theory of the offensive " and agreed that the time had come to pass from revolutionary propaganda to revolutionary action.

It was at this moment that Bela Kun, together with another Hungarian named Pogany and a Pole Guralsky, arrived in Berlin from Moscow as emissaries of Comintern.[2] A year earlier Bela Kun had been among the first and strongest critics of the passivity of the KPD during the Kapp *putsch*. As a member of Zinoviev's immediate following in Comintern, he was probably opposed to the " open letter ", and believed that Levi's eviction from the leadership provided an opportunity for a more active policy. He may have had instructions from Zinoviev to that effect. The members of the new central committee afterwards kept their counsel. But Bela Kun also talked to Levi and Klara Zetkin, who, though no longer in the central committee, were still leading members of the party. According to Levi, Bela Kun in conversation with Klara Zetkin on March 10, and with himself four days later, insisted that the KPD must act, if necessary by creating provocation for action : thus " the first impulse to this action in

---

[1] According to Levi, who appealed to unpublished party records, Rakosi said at the meeting of the central committee that the KPD, like the Italian party, needed purging ; Rakosi afterwards denied the expression, but not apparently the substance of the remark (P. Levi, *Unser Weg* (2nd ed., 1921), p. 54). He spoke in a similar strain to Klara Zetkin (see p. 389 below).

[2] The precise date of their arrival has not been established, but falls at latest within the first days of March 1921 ; they can hardly have left Russia after March 1, and the commonly accepted theory (e.g. O. K. Flechtheim, *Die KPD in der Weimarer Republic* (Offenbach, 1948), p. 73) which connects their mission with the Kronstadt rising falls to the ground. On the other hand they may, once in Berlin, have used the Kronstadt rising as an argument to drive home the need for action. The claim that the German workers had sacrificed themselves in the " March action " for the Russian workers was made as early as May 1921 by Heckert, the German delegate at the All-Russian Congress of Trade Unions : " These German communists let themselves be shot and thrown into prison because they were conscious that, in raising the standard of revolt, they were rendering aid to the Russian proletariat " (*Chetvertyi Vserossiiskii S"ezd Professional'nykh Soyuzov* (1921), i (Plenumy), 13).

the form which it took did not come from the German side ".[1]
Zetkin, who remained in the party, said more cautiously at the
third congress of Comintern that " representatives of the executive
[i.e. IKKI] bear at any rate a great share of responsibility for the
fact that the March action was conducted in the way that it was
. . . and for the false slogans and false political attitude of the
party or, rather, of its central committee ".[2] The period was one
of general unrest in Germany. A struggle was in progress between
the Bavarian Government and the Reich Government over the
existence of private armies of the Right enjoying Bavarian patronage ; the French had just occupied Düsseldorf as a reprisal ;
the pending plebiscite in Upper Silesia had led to plentiful
disorders in the area. Riots occurred with or without specific
encouragement from Berlin, in the Mansfeld mines in central
Germany, a well-known communist stronghold ; and on March
16, 1921, the police and the Reichswehr decided to occupy the
area and disarm the workers. This provoked armed resistance,
which spread to other centres of central Germany. On the
following day the central committee of the KPD called the workers
to arms and proclaimed open insurrection against the government ;
and a communist deputy in the Reichstag announced defiantly
that the German proletariat would " fulfil its historical mission
and carry the proletarian revolution from east to west ".[3] Desultory clashes occurred in several places. Fighting was severe only
in the regions of central Germany where the trouble had begun.
A week later, when the rising had begun to fizzle out, the central
committee announced a general strike. But this only aggravated
the disaster, leading communist strikers into fights, not only with
the police, but with the mass of workers who preferred to stick to
their jobs. On March 31, when the defeat of the communists
was complete with many casualties and thousands of arrests, the
central committee called off the whole action.

The " March action " was in itself neither so extensive nor so
significant an event as the Kapp putsch. But the moment of its
occurrence and its conspicuous failure made it a turning-point in

[1] Paul Levi, Was ist das Verbrechen? Die Märzaktion oder die Kritik
daran? (1921), pp. 8-9 : this pamphlet was a speech delivered by Levi to the
central committee on May 4, 1921, on his expulsion from the party.
    [2] Protokoll des III. Kongresses der Kommunistischen Internationale (Hamburg,
1921), p. 297.   [3] Verhandlungen des Reichstags, cccxlviii (1921), 3108.

the history both of German communism and of Soviet policy. In the KPD it is said to have resulted in a decline in the party membership within three months from 450,000 (perhaps an overestimate) to 180,000,[1] and set in motion a wave of recriminations which continued for many years to split the party into Right and Left factions. The central committee issued a set of theses in which, while attributing the action to police provocation against the Mansfeld workers, it congratulated itself on its attempt to " seize the revolutionary initiative " and undertake a " revolutionary offensive ", implicitly abandoned the pursuit of the " united front ", and condemned " the passive and active opposition of individual comrades during the action ".[2] Levi, throwing off the restraints of party discipline, published a pamphlet entitled *Unser Weg* in which he denounced the March action as " the biggest Bakuninist *putsch* in the whole of history ".[3] For this act of insubordination he was expelled from the party, though not without delivering a long speech of protest to the central committee, which was published as another pamphlet, and provoked a further reply from the central committee.[4] In Moscow IKKI hastened to approve the expulsion of Levi;[5] but the domestic recriminations in the German party were carried three months later to the third congress of Comintern, which had the delicate task of passing judgment on them.[6]

From the standpoint of Soviet policy, the collapse of the March action represented the German angle of the broad change of front signalized by the other two major events of March 1921 — the introduction of NEP and the conclusion of the Anglo-Soviet trade agreement. The question of personal responsibilities in Moscow for the action has never been fully cleared up. It is certain that Bela Kun's prompting, though by no means the only factor (the time had not yet come when the KPD automatically and submissively accepted directions from Moscow), was one of the

---

[1] *Bericht über den III. (8) Parteitag der VKPD* (1923), p. 63.
[2] *Taktik und Organisation der Revolutionären Offensive: Die Lehren der Märzaktion* (1921), pp. 139-145.
[3] P. Levi, *Unser Weg* (2nd ed., 1921), p. 39.
[4] P. Levi, *Was ist das Verbrechen? Die Märzaktion oder die Kritik daran?* (1921); *Der Weg des Dr. Levi und der Weg der VKPD* (1921).
[5] *Kommunisticheskii Internatsional*, No. 17 (June 7, 1921), col. 4297.
[6] See pp. 386-387 below.

factors which impelled the central committee to attempt its ill-fated " offensive ". It may be assumed that Bela Kun acted on explicit or implicit instructions from Zinoviev. But it is doubtful whether these instructions were considered or endorsed by the Politburo or whether their import was known or understood outside Zinoviev's circle. Lenin, Trotsky and the other principal party figures were absorbed in the economic crisis, in the trade union and party controversies and in the preparations for NEP, and had no time for German affairs. Radek, who was thoroughly versed in German affairs, does not seem to have known what was on foot ; [1] and the same was almost certainly true of Chicherin and the staff of Narkomindel. When the action proved a fiasco, the obvious moral could hardly be gainsaid. The attempt of the KPD to carry the day by a frontal attack on the bourgeois German Government had ended in ignominious disaster. But, where a relatively large and powerful party in a highly industrialized country had failed, no communist party in any other country could hope to succeed for some time to come. A new and well-grounded pessimism about the prospects of the European revolution confirmed and reinforced the drive towards a temporary accommodation with the capitalist world.

[1] Radek is the only leading Bolshevik about whose attitude specific, though rather inconclusive, evidence is available. In September 1921, Levi published in his journal *Unser Weg* (a new title for the earlier *Sowjet* cited on p. 402, note 5 below) a letter written by Radek on March 14, 1921, from Moscow to the central committee of the KPD. Having briefly referred to the introduction of NEP, Radek turned to KPD affairs and attacked Levi : " He by his policy is dividing the party, whereas we can attract new masses by activizing our policy ". Levi should be allowed to go, but everything possible should be done to prevent Däumig and Zetkin going with him. " Nobody here is thinking of a mechanical splitting — or indeed of any kind of splitting — in Germany." Radek continued : " Everything depends on the world political situation. If the rift between the Entente and Germany grows wider, it may come to war with Poland, and then we shall speak. Just because these possibilities exist, you must do everything to mobilize the party. One cannot shoot any action out of a revolver. If you do not now do everything, through uninterrupted pressure for action by the communist masses, to create the feeling of need for such action, you will again fail at the great moment " (*Unser Weg*, iii, No. 8-9, August-September 1921, pp. 248-249). These rather cryptic phrases suggest that Radek, having broken with Levi, had moved, in terms of KPD politics, towards the Left, but not that he was carrying out a decision to galvanize the KPD into immediate action. According to Trotsky, he stood with Zinoviev and Bukharin on the Left on the eve of the third congress of Comintern (see p. 383 below) ; but Radek's opinions were notoriously volatile.

CHAPTER 29

TO GENOA AND RAPALLO

IF the Soviet Government assumed that the conclusion of the Anglo-Soviet Trade Agreement of March 16, 1921, completed by the treaties just concluded with the three eastern nations — Persia, Afghanistan and Turkey — and followed two days later by the final peace treaty with Poland, would at once break the ice and result in the establishment of normal relations with the outside world, this expectation took too little account of the persistence of hostile attitudes in the capitalist countries. The example set by Great Britain failed immediately to inspire any important number of imitators. Of European countries only Germany, like Russia an outcast from the European community, made haste to conclude a provisional trade agreement with the RSFSR.[1] This was signed on May 6, 1921; and it was probably no mere coincidence that it was signed on the day after an allied ultimatum to Germany threatening further sanctions (three towns in the Ruhr had already been occupied in March 1921) in the event of non-compliance with reparations and disarmament demands. The trade agreement settled some of the practical difficulties of trade between private firms and a state trading monopoly. But its most important provisions did not relate to trade at all. Both countries agreed to accord diplomatic privileges to the accredited representatives of the other; and the German Government undertook to recognize the Soviet mission as the sole representative of Russia in German territory. This meant a withdrawal of the informal recognition hitherto extended to " white " Russian organizations in Berlin, and was the official burial of the anti-Bolshevik crusade. Henceforth, whatever might be the Russian policy of the German Government, it would be directed to maintain relations with the Soviet Government, not to overthrow it. None the less, the

[1] *RSFSR : Sbornik Deistvuyushchikh Dogovorov,* ii (1921), No. 46, pp. 24-28.

persistence of an unfriendly atmosphere is indicated by Krasin's complaint that the German Government not only failed to carry out its obligation under the agreement to put suitable premises at the disposal of the trade delegation, but " did not give the trade delegation proper help in obtaining possession of the few houses which the delegation had acquired for this purpose ".[1] Of other European countries Italy agreed to receive a Soviet trade mission in March 1921. But its welcome was cool; and not till the end of the year did protracted negotiations lead to the signature of a trade agreement.[2] By this time Norway and Austria had concluded similar agreements.[3] An agreement with Sweden was signed at the beginning of 1922,[4] but not ratified by the Swedish Government. An agreement with Czechoslovakia followed a little later;[5] all these were based on the British model. The list of countries where Soviet trade delegations were established at the end of 1921 included Finland, Estonia, Latvia, Lithuania, Poland, Sweden, Norway, Germany, Czechoslovakia, Austria, Italy, Great Britain, Turkey (Angora and Constantinople) and Persia.[6]

On the other hand, two great nations remained implacably hostile. The Republican victory in the United States and the replacement of Wilson by Harding inspired vain hopes of a change in the American attitude. The indefatigable Raymond Robins had for some time been canvassing in the United States for recognition of Soviet Russia, and apparently believed himself to have obtained an election promise from Harding of his readiness to reopen the Russian question.[7] This may have been known in Moscow; and Vanderlip, passing through Moscow on his return journey in March 1921, spoke of Harding's " favourable views " on trade with Russia.[8] A note addressed in the name of VTsIK to the newly installed American Congress on March 20, 1921,

---

[1] L. B. Krasin, *Voprosy Vneshnei Torgovli* (1928), p. 254.

[2] *Izvestiya*, May 27, 1921; *RSFSR: Sbornik Deistvuyushchikh Dogovorov*, iii (1922), No. 86, pp. 39-45.

[3] *RSFSR: Sbornik Deistvuyushchikh Dogovorov*, ii (1921), No. 48, pp. 32-35; *SSSR: Sbornik Deistvuyushchikh Dogovorov*, i-ii (1924), No. 2, pp. 4-8.

[4] *Russian Information and Review*, May 1, 1922, pp. 355-356.

[5] *RSFSR: Sbornik Deistvuyushchikh Dogovorov*, iv (1923), No. 111, pp. 17-21.   [6] *Za Pyat' Let* (1922), p. 416.

[7] Information from the Gumberg papers in the University of Wisconsin, communicated by Mr. W. A. Williams.

[8] *Leninskii Sbornik*, xx (1932), 189; Lenin did not see Vanderlip again but referred him to Chicherin.

suggested negotiations for a trade agreement between the two countries, but met with the chilling response that any attempt to restore trade relations would be futile until Soviet Russia had laid a " solid economic foundation ", implying " safety of life, the recognition of firm guarantees of private property, the sanctity of contract and the rights of free labour ".[1] Unofficial attempts by the Far Eastern Republic to establish discreet contact with Washington were, on the other hand more successful, and American observers visited Chita in May 1921.[2] France was the other great Power which remained implacably hostile. She had concluded a treaty of alliance with Poland in February 1921, and was busy during this year consolidating the Little Entente under her aegis.[3] These political and military entanglements, as well as the claims of French holders of Russian bonds, dictated an attitude of no compromise with the defaulter. French acrimony on the subject of the Anglo-Soviet trade agreement, which found expression in the summer of 1921 in a series of official notes [4] as well as in the French press, contributed to the deterioration of Anglo-French relations at this time.

Within four months of the signing of the Anglo-Soviet agreement the situation in Russia itself was overshadowed by the impending disaster of famine. Reserves had been exhausted; transport was chaotic; and drought had seriously affected the new harvest. The appointment on July 21, 1921, of an All-Russian Committee for Aid to the Hungry [5] was followed a few

[1] Klyuchnikov i Sabanin, *Mezhdunarodnaya Politika*, iii, i (1928), 104-105 ; *Foreign Relations of the United States, 1921*, iii (1936), 768.

[2] *Ibid.* iii (1936), 732-744. Informed Soviet opinion was strongly impressed at this time by the rising power of the United States : Trotsky at the third congress of Comintern in June 1921 referred to " the elementary facts " that " Europe is ruined, that the productive capacity of Europe is far lower than before the war, that the economic centre has moved over to America " (*Protokoll des III. Kongresses der Kommunistischen Internationale* (Hamburg, 1921), p. 74).

[3] The delegation of the Far Eastern Republic at the Washington conference at the end of 1921 communicated to the press correspondence between the French and Japanese Governments from December 1920 onwards, culminating in an alleged secret agreement of March 12, 1921, for common action against Soviet Russia (summary in *Manchester Guardian*, January 2, 1922) ; but no full text has been published and its authenticity remains dubious.

[4] *Correspondence between His Majesty's Government and the French Government respecting the Anglo-Russian Trade Agreement*, Cmd. 1456 (1921).

[5] See Vol. I, p. 178.

days later by an appeal from IKKI to workers of all countries.[1] A prompt response came from Herbert Hoover, then at the height of his reputation as an organizer and dispenser of American aid ; and on August 20, 1921, an agreement was signed by Litvinov in Riga with a representative of the American Relief Administration (ARA).[2] A week later a similar agreement was signed in Moscow with Nansen, representing a Red Cross conference which had just met at Geneva.[3] The terms of these agreements, which involved the admission to Russia of large numbers of foreign agents to carry out the distribution of the supplies, were humiliating. But the need was dire, and the fact that they were made not with governments but with private organizations seemed a mitigating circumstance. A proposal of the allied Supreme Council to send a commission " for the study and investigation of means of rendering help to the Russian people " was rejected immediately afterwards in language of the greatest bitterness, the more so since the former French Ambassador in Russia, Noulens, who had distinguished himself by his hostile utterances at the outset of the revolution, had been designated as president of the commission.[4]

Throughout the winter of 1921-1922 the American and Red Cross relief missions were active in the Volga area, where starvation and disease reached catastrophic proportions.[5] In spite of the generosity of the help rendered, ARA was still regarded with intense suspicion, at any rate at party headquarters. Its desire to secure for itself a monopoly of relief, manifested in its attempt to exclude other American organizations from working in the same field and in its boycott of the Nansen mission,[6] was disliked ; and many members of its staff were suspected, at worst of direct espionage, at best of attempting to further their own or their country's commercial interests.[7] Most of all, the work of ARA

[1] *Kommunisticheskii Internatsional*, No. 18 (October 8, 1921), cols. 4758-4759.
[2] *RSFSR : Sbornik Deistvuyushchikh Dogovorov*, ii (1921), No. 73, pp. 152-155 ; *Foreign Relations of the United States, 1921*, ii (1936), 813-817.
[3] Klyuchnikov i Sabanin, *Mezhdunarodnaya Politika*, iii, i (1928), 109-112.
[4] *Ibid.* iii, i, 114-118.
[5] See Vol. 2, p. 285, for reports on the famine.
[6] *Foreign Relations of the United States, 1921*, ii (1936), 821.
[7] According to L. Fischer, *The Soviets in World Affairs* (1930), i, pp. 316-317, " the entire personnel of the ARA consisted of United States Army men, and the Bolsheviks suspected the type, especially since the relief association's native assistants were frequently recruited from elements in the populations not quite

was felt as a subtle form of foreign intervention.   Few of those
engaged in it professed anything but unqualified hostility to the
régime ; and Hoover and other western leaders often stressed the
part played by relief in combating Bolshevism in Europe in 1919.
The immense value of the practical aid furnished by ARA was
none the less fully recognized ; both Kamenev and Chicherin
emphatically stated that it far exceeded the help received from all
other sources.[1]   The ninth All-Russian Congress of Soviets,
meeting in December 1921, devoted a long resolution to the
famine.   It expressed " warm gratitude " to the workers of all
countries who had come to the help of their suffering comrades
(a reference to the International Workers' Aid [2]), adding that the
Russian toilers " especially value the fraternal support of the
horny hands of European and American workers ".   It noted that
a part of the bourgeois world looked on the famine as " a convenient opportunity for a new attempt to overthrow the Soviet
power " and another part as " a favourable chance to acquire
for itself in Russia an economically dominant position " ;   none
the less the congress expressed its gratitude to Nansen, to ARA,
and " to other countries which have rendered help to the hungry
in whatever form ".   Apart from the resolution, it voted a special
address of " profound gratitude " on behalf of " millions of the
toiling population of the RSFSR " to " the great scientific explorer
and citizen F. Nansen, who heroically forced his way through the
eternal ice of the frozen north, but was powerless to overcome the
boundless cruelty, greed and heartlessness of the ruling classes of
the capitalist countries ".[3]

sympathetic to the Red régime ".   The motive of obtaining commercial information was scarcely disguised : " full information will be obtained in this way
without the risk of complication through government action ", wrote Hughes
on September 2, 1921 (National Archives of the United States : Record Group
59 : 861. 48/1601).   But it is doubtful whether any other form of information
was seriously sought at this time.
    [1] For Kamenev's appreciation of the scope of American relief see Vol. 2,
p. 285 ; Chicherin's tribute is in *Materialy Genuezskoi Konferentsii* (1922),
p. 20.
    [2] See p. 404 below.
    [3] *S"ezdy Sovetov RSFSR v Postanovleniyakh* (1939), pp. 204-206 ; a dele-
gate at the congress repeated a comparison, said to have been made by a British
M.P., of the sums contributed by the allied countries to relief with the amounts
spent on supporting Denikin and Kolchak (*Devyatyi Vserossiiskii S"ezd Sovetov*
(1922), p. 35).

The disasters of the famine, the hostility of the capitalist world towards the Soviet régime and continued scepticism of its capacity to survive, the suspicion and sensitiveness bred by this attitude in Soviet minds — all these factors made the latter part of 1921 a troubled period in Soviet Russia's foreign relations. The results of the new foreign policy, like those of NEP at home, did not really mature till the following year. For a long time the Anglo-Soviet trade agreement did not appear to have done much to allay the friction endemic in relations between the two countries. A permanent British commercial mission, as provided for in the agreement, established itself in Moscow on July 31, 1921, but was soon plunged into political controversy. If counsels were divided in Moscow on the relative importance of concord between governments and propaganda for world revolution, British policy towards Soviet Russia was equally a battleground between warring factions. The Anglo-Soviet agreement had represented a victory for the Prime Minister and the Board of Trade; the letter simultaneously addressed to Krasin on Soviet activities in Afghanistan bore every stamp of a joint product of Foreign Office, War Office and India Office.[1] The underlying situation in Great Britain seemed for some time little changed by the agreement. Lloyd George had his way where he chose, or found time, to exercise his power. But, while he was occupied elsewhere, the daily course of Anglo-Soviet relations continued to be determined by these three influential departments; and, especially so long as Curzon ruled the Foreign Office, they were conducted in a spirit of profound mistrust of Soviet actions and intentions.

The first major diplomatic clash occurred less than six weeks after the arrival of the British mission in Moscow and at a moment when Soviet fortunes seemed at their lowest ebb. On September 7, 1921, Curzon despatched to the Soviet Government a long memorandum of protest against a series of utterances and activities of the Soviet Government and of Comintern which were declared to be contrary to the undertaking in the Anglo-Soviet agreement to refrain from propaganda " against the institutions of the British Empire ". The general charge that anti-British activities in Asia had not been abandoned was certainly true; such activities were cited in India, in Persia, in Turkey and in Afghanistan.

[1] See p. 288 above.

But the note appears to have been somewhat light-heartedly compiled from reports of secret agents which did not withstand scrutiny, and were easily refuted in detail.[1] On September 27 the Soviet Government replied in a skilful and disingenuous note signed by Litvinov; and a counter-reply from the British Government on November 12 closed the correspondence for the time being.[2] The correspondence throws a valuable light on the attitude and state of mind of both parties to the agreement. The Soviet authorities, who had been willing almost from the moment of the revolution to undertake to abstain from hostile propaganda against other states, interpreted that undertaking in a purely formal sense. It applied, so far as they were concerned, only to direct and avowed government policy and did not cover the action of agents in receipt of confidential instructions. Thus, they felt entitled to deny, in the face of well-known facts, that there was a propaganda school in Tashkent for Indian revolutionaries, or that Jemal had received support from the Soviet Government for his mission to Kabul; and the whole rejection of responsibility for the activities of Comintern and its agents rested on no more than a formal distinction. They would have been on stronger ground if they had been content to argue that the British, no more than they themselves, had allowed the conclusion of the agreement to interfere with the unfriendly behaviour of their agents. In fact, both sides, undeterred by the agreement, continued to regard the activities of their own agents as legitimate retaliation or legitimate self-defence and those of the other party as unprovoked aggression. The significant difference between them was that, while the British

[1] The note purported to quote reports made to the " central committee " of Comintern by Stalin, " the president of the eastern division of the Third International ", by Eliava, and by Nuerteva, described as " director of propaganda under the Third International ". The Soviet reply of September 27 stated that none of these persons had ever exercised any functions under Comintern ; to which the British counter-reply of November 12 bewilderingly retorted that " it was never said of any of these persons that they belonged to the Third International, though that is not a point of substance ". The British note of September 7, 1921, quoted a speech of Lenin of June 8. When it was pointed out that Lenin had made no speech on that day, the date was shifted in the British note of November 12 to July 5 ; but the official record of Lenin's speech at the third congress of Comintern on that date contains no passage resembling that quoted in the British note.

[2] The three notes were published in *A Selection of Papers dealing with the Relations between His Majesty's Government and the Soviet Government*, Cmd. 2895 (1927), pp. 14-30.

departments mainly responsible for the conduct of Anglo-Soviet relations at this time would willingly have seen the agreement break down, the corresponding Soviet authorities merely wanted to see how far they could go without causing a break. Nor were there any signs of improved relations between Soviet Russia and her immediate neighbours on the west. The conclusion of a treaty of alliance between Rumania and Poland in the spring of 1921 with evident French encouragement was calculated to complete the anti-Soviet triangle (France — Little Entente — Poland), and confirmed Soviet suspicions that Rumania, like Poland, had become a pawn in the French diplomatic and military game. On September 13, 1921, Narkomindel issued a *communiqué* quoting an alleged note to the Polish and Rumanian Governments in which the French Government had proposed a simultaneous ultimatum by all three countries to the Soviet Government, to be followed in case of non-compliance by a joint declaration of war, and offered in that event substantial military aid to its partners.[1] Friction with Rumania had been endemic ever since her annexation of Bessarabia in 1918. In October 1920 the allied governments concluded a treaty recognizing Rumanian sovereignty over Bessarabia;[2] and at this moment Frunze and Voroshilov, flushed with their easy victory over Wrangel, seem to have made a proposal for the military re-conquest of Bessarabia which was overruled by Lenin, acting on the advice of Rakovsky. After the new turn of March 1921, the opposite proposal — to wipe a troublesome question off the slate by recognizing the Rumanian annexation of Bessarabia — is said to have been made, somewhat surprisingly, by Trotsky, supported by Litvinov. But Chicherin and Rakovsky opposed this act of appeasement, and it, too, was vetoed.[3] The summer and autumn of 1921 saw a flood of joint protests, signed on behalf of the RSFSR and the Ukrainian SSR by Chicherin and Rakovsky, to

---

[1] *La Russie des Soviets et la Pologne* (Moscow, 1921), pp. 48-50 ; a few days later Trotsky made a speech to the Moscow Soviet on the same theme (*Izvestiya*, September 22, 1921).

[2] The treaty did not come into force owing to an unexplained failure by Japan to ratify it ; but this formal flaw did not affect the situation.

[3] Both these proposals were mentioned by Rakovsky in conversation with Louis Fischer in 1928 and are recorded in L. Fischer, *The Soviets in World Affairs* (2nd ed., 1951), i, xiv-xv : they are not improbable, but lack documentary authority.

the Rumanian Government against alleged frontier incidents, encouragement given to " white guards " and " Petlyura bands ", and failure to extradite the anarchist Makhno, who for some time found asylum in Rumanian territory with a remnant of his forces; and a joint note of November 11, 1921, recapitulated the whole Bessarabian controversy, and reiterated the refusal to recognize Bessarabia as Rumanian territory.[1] Alone of the border countries, Rumania still refused to maintain any relations, diplomatic or commercial, with the Soviet Government. But Soviet-Polish relations, though conducted with all the forms of diplomatic intercourse, were no better in substance. The peace treaty with Poland signed at Riga on March 18, 1921, favourable as it was to Polish aspirations, left behind it a persistent legacy of friction and mistrust. Between April and September a long and acrimonious correspondence turned on Soviet demands that the Polish Government should cease to tolerate and encourage " white " organizations on Polish territory, notably those of the SR conspirator Savinkov and the former Ukrainian dictator Petlyura, and Polish demands for the return of prisoners of war and Polish civilians still in Soviet territory.[2] It was not till August 1921 that diplomatic relations were established, Karakhan arriving as Soviet representative in Warsaw, and Filippovich as Polish chargé d'affaires in Moscow.[3]

Even in the Baltic, where the Soviet Government had achieved its first diplomatic break-through in 1920 with the treaties with Estonia and Latvia,[4] the tide in the latter half of 1921 seemed to set once more against Moscow. As early as October 1919 the Soviet Government had reasserted the traditional Russian interest in the destiny of the Åland Islands and protested against any attempt to regulate this question without its participation.[5] The protest was renewed when " a group of Powers calling itself the League of Nations " placed the question of the Åland Islands on its agenda in June 1920, and again in a separate note to Finland and Sweden in the following year.[6] These protests were ignored;

[1] These notes are collected in *L'Ukraine Soviétiste* (Berlin, 1922), pp. 78-106.
[2] *La Russie des Soviets et la Pologne* (Moscow, 1921), contains a collection of these documents.
[3] *Ibid.* p. 7.   [4] See pp. 156, 277 above.
[5] See pp. 157-158 above.
[6] Klyuchnikov i Sabanin, *Mezhdunarodnaya Politika*, iii, i (1928), 29-30, 108.

and on October 20, 1921, without any kind of intimation to the Soviet Government, a convention was signed at Geneva between the principal allied Powers, Finland and Sweden, recognizing Finnish sovereignty over the islands and prescribing a régime of demilitarization. On November 13, 1921, a Soviet note to all the governments concerned declared the convention " unconditionally non-existent for Russia " and protested once more against the violation of Russia's " substantial and elementary rights " : [1] the offence clearly consisted, not in the contents of the agreement, but in the continued intention of the western Powers, notwithstanding the events of March 1921, to exclude Soviet Russia from the comity of nations. In the same month a long-standing trouble with Finland over the Karelian Workers' Commune, which had the status of an autonomous republic within the RSFSR, came to a head. For some months past frontier incidents had been a cause of frequent complaint on both sides. In the autumn of 1921 serious disorders occurred in Soviet Karelia. According to Moscow, " bandit detachments under Finnish officers " organized in Finland had penetrated the territory ; according to Helsingfors, a popular rising against Soviet misgovernment had been put down with great cruelty to the local Finnish population. On November 27, 1921, Finland appealed to the League of Nations and invited it to send a commission of enquiry to investigate conditions on the spot. The appeal was denounced by Chicherin as " an attempt to introduce outside Powers into the internal affairs of the RSFSR and an attempt to settle questions relating to the Russo-Finnish treaty by way of the intervention of third Powers " ; and the result was to breed fresh suspicion between Soviet Russia and Finland.[2] In December 1921 the foreign ministers of Finland, Poland, Latvia and Estonia met in conference in Helsingfors and decided to negotiate a mutual assistance pact. Poland was the driving force in the alliance ; and behind Polish initiative the hand of France, then at the height of her post-war military power and prestige, was plainly seen. Little attempt was made to deny that

---

[1] Klyuchnikov i Sabanin, *Mezhdunarodnaya Politika*, iii, i (1928), 146-147.

[2] *Ibid.* iii, i (1928), 148-154 ; the course of this dispute may be followed in the current records of the League of Nations, and in volumes of official documents published by both disputants, *Livre Rouge : Documents et Correspondance Diplomatique Russo-Finlandaise concernant la Carélie Orientale* (Moscow, 1922), and *La Question de la Carélie Orientale*, 3 vols. (Helsinki, 1922-1924).

Soviet Russia was the potential enemy against whom protection was to be sought through common action.[1] Far from having succeeded in opening a window towards the west, the Soviet Government began to have visions of a revival of the *cordon sanitaire*. The pessimistic mood engendered in Moscow by the diplomatic situation in the latter part of 1921 is well illustrated by one of Stalin's, at this time rare, excursions into international affairs. Writing in *Pravda* in December 1921, he noted that " the period of open war has been replaced by a period of ' peaceful ' struggle ". His review opened with a noteworthy diagnosis :

> Gone on the wing is the " terror " or " horror " of the proletarian revolution which seized the bourgeoisie of the world, for example, in the days of the advance of the Red Army on Warsaw. And with it has passed the boundless enthusiasm with which the workers of Europe used to receive almost every piece of news about Soviet Russia.
>
> A period of sober calculation of forces has set in, a period of meticulous work in the preparation and accumulation of forces for the battles of the future.

Suspicion of foreign intentions held a conspicuous place in Stalin's estimate. Trade and other agreements were good in their way.

> But [he went on] we should not forget that commercial and all other sorts of missions and associations, now flooding Russia to trade with her and to aid her, are at the same time the best spies of the world bourgeoisie, and that now it, the world bourgeoisie, in virtue of these conditions knows Soviet Russia with its weak and strong sides better than ever before — circumstances fraught with serious dangers in the event of new interventionist actions.

Turkey, Persia, Afghanistan and the Far East were being " flooded by agents of imperialism with gold and other ' benefits ' in order to build round Soviet Russia an economic (and not only economic)

---

[1] The pact was signed in Warsaw on March 17, 1922 (*League of Nations: Treaty Series*, xi (1922), 168-171), but never came into force owing to the eventual failure of Finland to ratify it ; L. Fischer, *The Soviets in World Affairs* (1930), ii, 517, cites a collection of Polish documents published in 1924 which is said to make clear the anti-Soviet aims of the pact.

ring-fence ". In this process Poland, Rumania and Finland were also playing their part, arming themselves " at the expense of the Entente " and " hurling on to the territory of Russia (for purposes of espionage ?) the white-guard detachments of their Savinkovs and Petlyuras ". All these were " separate links in the general work of preparing a new offensive against Russia ".[1] The article, which bears marks of Stalin's long-standing antipathy to Chicherin, was significant, not because Stalin was at this time concerned in the framing of Soviet foreign policy, but because it appealed to prejudices and discouragements common in party circles about the policy of *rapprochement* with the western capitalist world which had been inaugurated in March 1921, and of which Chicherin and Krasin, with Lenin's support, were the most active exponents.

When a week later Lenin addressed the ninth All-Russian Congress of Soviets on the work of VTsIK and Sovnarkom during the past year, he too served notice on " the representatives of the military parties and aggressive cliques in Finland, Poland and Rumania " that the Soviet policy of " concessions and sacrifices " for the sake of peace was not unlimited in its scope.[2] But Lenin was more concerned to dwell on the positive achievements of the past nine months. Having noted the existence of " a certain equilibrium " in the international situation, he proceeded to draw a reassuring picture.

Is such a thing thinkable at all [he asked] as that a socialist republic could exist in a capitalist environment? This seemed impossible either in a political or in a military sense. That it is possible in a political and in a military sense has been proved; it is already a fact.

The past year had begun to prove that it was possible also in an economic sense : the capitalist world needed Soviet Russia as

[1] Stalin, *Sochineniya*, v, 117-120.
[2] Lenin, *Sochineniya*, xxvii, 117-118 ; on the eve of the congress Lenin telephoned to the Politburo suggesting that the congress should register a protest against the " adventurist policy " of Poland, Finland and Rumania, and adding : " about Japan better keep silent for a variety of reasons " (*Leninskii Sbornik*, xxxv (1945), 304) ; this was done (*S"ezdy Sovetov RSFSR v Postanovleniyakh* (1939), pp. 239-243).

much as Soviet Russia needed the capitalist world. Lenin quoted
figures to show that Soviet imports for 1921 were three times as
great as those for the three previous years taken together, and
exports for 1921 (though still totalling less than 25 per cent of the
imports) more than four times as great as the total of the three
previous years. The figures were miserably small, but it was a
beginning. Among particularly valuable imports were 13 locomotives from Sweden and 37 from Germany.[1]

The unemployment crisis in western Europe made the pressure
for export markets particularly acute; and Krasin and the other
Soviet negotiators were quick to profit by this fortunate circum-
stance — especially fortunate for a country which was eager to
import almost everything, and had hardly anything to export.
The de facto recognition of the Soviet Government by Great
Britain had validated Soviet nationalization laws in the eyes of the
British courts, so that the Soviet authorities no longer had to fear
action by alleged previous owners of cargoes exported by them to
Great Britain or of gold used in payment for imports; and the
British example was accepted as decisive by most other trading
countries. Boycotts of Soviet goods were still sometimes attempted
by private traders or trading organizations. But after 1921 direct
interference with Soviet trade by governments was as a rule no
longer practised. The forms of trade were more difficult to
establish, especially as merchants in capitalist countries retained
all their objections to dealing with a state monopoly. The precedent of Arcos, which was a Soviet-owned company registered in
London under British law,[2] was followed elsewhere, notably in
Amtorg, the corresponding organization set up in New York. The
year 1921 saw the birth of the fruitful experiment of " mixed
companies ". These were formed jointly by a foreign capitalist
group and a department of the Soviet state, and had the dual
advantage of helping to mask the governmental character of the
concern and of securing an investment of foreign capital in an
enterprise operating partly in Soviet Russia.[3] At the eleventh
party congress in March 1922, Lenin reported the existence of

[1] Lenin, *Sochineniya*, xxvii, 119-122; official statistics showed that the value
of imports calculated in pre-war rubles rose from 125·7 millions in 1920 to
922·9 millions in 1921, and exports from 6·1 millions to 88·5 millions.
[2] See p. 286 above.
[3] The earliest mixed companies were Soviet-German (see pp. 367-368 below).

17 mixed companies " with a capital of many millions " — nine sponsored by Vneshtorg, six by a newly created committee presided over by Sokolnikov and attached to STO, and two by Severoles (the northern timber trust); eight months later, at the fourth congress of Comintern, Lenin rather apologetically defended the system of mixed companies on the dual ground that " in this way we learn how to trade ", and that it was always possible for the Soviet partner to dissolve the company if it became dangerous.[1]

Whatever steps might, however, be taken to revive normal commercial relations between Soviet Russia and the capitalist world, the basic obstacle remained. Soviet Russia, as an importer, had an almost unlimited hunger for machinery, equipment of all kinds, and even (as a temporary result of the 1921 famine) foodstuffs; Soviet Russia, as an exporter, had little to offer by way of immediate return except unworked timber, hides and limited quantities of flax; her potentially rich resources were undeveloped and therefore inaccessible. If the aid of foreign capital and foreign technical skill, which had already played so large a part in the industrialization of Russia before the revolution, could once more be invoked, these unused resources could be developed in such a way as to enrich the country both directly and indirectly — directly by promoting fresh industrial expansion and indirectly by making raw materials available for export in exchange for foreign goods. This conception had underlain all Soviet thinking about foreign trade since the opening of 1918, and had been responsible for the vitality of the idea of foreign concessions. The purpose of concessions as contemplated in the decree of November 23, 1920, was to provide for the development of unused natural resources in order to make them available for industry and for export. In expounding the concessions policy to the tenth party congress in March 1921, Lenin justified it on the ground that " we cannot by our own strength restore our shattered economy without equipment and technical assistance from abroad ", and that " the mere import of this equipment is not enough ". In order to obtain the necessary assistance, he was ready to give extensive concessions " to the most powerful imperialist syndicates " — for example, " a quarter of Baku, a quarter of Grozny, a quarter of our best forests "; later he named

[1] Lenin, *Sochineniya*, xxvii, 240 (see also 531, note 100), 350.

timber and iron ore as typical products for concessions.[1] This was indeed the only type of concession which fitted in with the scheme of war communism, where the main industrial undertakings were owned and operated by organs of state. The introduction of NEP appeared to stimulate and broaden the whole conception, partly because comparatively free and unembarrassed contacts could now be established with the capitalist world, and partly because the recognition of the rôle of private capital in Soviet Russia itself, and all the consequences resulting from it, removed many of the obstacles, practical and psychological, which had stood in the way of the introduction of foreign capital in the era of war communism. If industrial enterprises were to be leased to entrepreneurs to be run on a profit-earning basis, there could be no objection of principle to similar leases being granted to suitable foreign capitalists, who might thus play their part in producing consumers goods for exchange with the peasant. In April 1921 Lenin already thought that it would not be dangerous " if we let concessionaires have a few factories "; to the third congress of Comintern two months later, he explained the dual purpose of the concessions policy — " to hasten the revival of our heavy industry and a serious improvement in the position of workers and peasants ".[2]

Nevertheless, the record of the first year of NEP in the field of foreign concessions was one of discussion (in the course of which the original idea was broadened out in several ways) rather than of realization. The first concession would appear to have been granted by the Far Eastern Republic on May 14, 1921, to the American Sinclair Exploration Company for the exploitation of the oil of northern Sakhalin;[3] since the whole island was in

---

[1] *Ibid.*, xxvi, 213, 255. A long discussion took place at this time on the desirability of opening the Grozny and Baku oilfields for concessions, which had been approved in principle by Sovnarkom on February 1, 1921 (*Leninskii Sbornik*, xx (1932), 126-159); at the same time Lenin suggested the opening of " Donbass (+ Krivoi Rog) ", i.e. the major coal and iron deposits, for concessions (*ibid.* xx, 151).   [2] *Ibid.* xxvi, 308, 433.

[3] L. Fischer, *Oil Imperialism* (n.d. [1927]), p. 181 ; *The Soviets in World Affairs* (1930), i, 302-303 ; the Soviet authorities appear to have believed, as in the case of Vanderlip, that the granting of the concession would lead to the recognition of the Soviet Government by the United States. Three years later, when northern Sakhalin had passed into Soviet possession, the Soviet Government took occasion to annul the concession which was never worked (L. Fischer, *Oil Imperialism* (n.d. [1927]), p. 249).

Japanese occupation this was a political gesture rather than an economic proposition. About the same time, it was stated in Moscow that negotiations were in progress with an Anglo-Canadian firm for a timber concession, with German firms for mining concessions, and with a Swedish firm for the construction of a turbine factory.[1] An experiment of a different kind was tried in the autumn of 1921, when a concession for a mining area in the Kuznetsk basin in western Siberia was given to a group of American engineers and workers, who had come to Soviet Russia not as investors of American capital but as enthusiasts eager to participate in the building of the workers' state. The concession agreement was signed with Rutgers, the Dutch communist engineer who had attended the founding congress of Comintern, and Bill Haywood of the American IWW, on November 26, 1921.[2] The resourceful Krasin in London set on foot two highly promising projects. At the beginning of June 1921 he was approached by Leslie Urquhart, a mining engineer who had spent many years in Russia and was now chairman of Russo-Asiatic Consolidated, a company which had owned and worked a large mining area in the Urals, the source, among other things, of 60 per cent of Russia's total production of lead. Krasin explained to Urquhart the Soviet policy of concessions; and preliminary discussions so far succeeded that in August 1921 Urquhart paid an exploratory visit to Moscow to discuss terms.[3] This project broke new ground by introducing the element of compensation, the concession being offered to the former owner of the property concerned in satisfaction of claims arising from the expropriation of the property. An agreement was drafted in 27 clauses, and prospects seemed favourable. But in October Urquhart, having consulted his

[1] *Trudy IV Vserossiiskogo S"ezda Sovetov Narodnogo Khozyaistva* (1921), pp. 111-112.

[2] *Leninskii Sbornik*, xxiii (1933), 37-46 ; *Istorik Marksist*, No. 2-3, 1935, pp. 94-98 ; *Devyatyi Vserossiiskii S"ezd Sovetov* (1922), p. 87, where the number of those engaged is put at 5000 ; according to *Russian Information and Review*, August 15, 1922, pp. 516-517, the entire output of the " autonomous industrial colony " belonged to the RSFSR, but all agricultural products were allocated to the colony together with 50 per cent of its industrial output above a minimum figure. A full account of this experiment, which dragged on in a desultory way for several years, has still to be written.

[3] *Russische Korrespondenz*, ii, ii (1921), No. 7-9, pp. 714-715 ; L. Krasin, *Leonid Krasin: His Life and Work* (n.d. [1929]), pp. 184-186.

board, called the deal off. The points on which the negotiations broke down — though the breach was not treated by either side as final — were the Soviet refusal to concede the principle of compensation or to grant a lease for so long a period as 99 years, and Soviet insistence that engagement of workers should be subject to Soviet labour legislation, and, in particular, that workers should be engaged or dismissed only through the trade union concerned and with its consent.[1] About the same time a representative of the Royal Dutch-Shell oil group, a Colonel Boyle, approached Krasin with the specific backing of the Foreign Office [2] to request a concession for the oil-bearing areas formerly owned by the group in south Russia and the Caucasus; and Boyle too made a pilgrimage to Moscow. These negotiations appear to have made a good start, and were brought to an end in the following year only by the intervention of other oil interests. The ice seemed to be melting rapidly.

Meanwhile a further initiative came from the Soviet side. The question of responsibility for the financial obligations of former Russian governments was clearly still the main psychological barrier to trade relations with the capitalist world. On October 2, 1921, Chicherin issued a further note to the western Powers. Having proclaimed the principle that " no people is bound to pay the cost of the chains which it has worn for centuries ", the Soviet Government none the less announced that it was " opening a possibility for private initiative and capital to cooperate with the power of the workers and peasants in exploiting the natural wealth of Russia "; that, in order to meet the wishes of the Powers and, in particular, to satisfy small investors, it was willing to assume responsibility for Tsarist loans before 1914; that it regarded this concession as conditional on the cessation of hostile acts by the Powers and on their willingness to recognize the Soviet Government; and that it proposed the summoning of an international

---

[1] L. B. Krasin, *Voprosy Vneshnei Torgovli* (1928), pp. 389-390; a letter from Urquhart to Krasin giving his reasons for not accepting the Soviet draft (which does not appear to have been published) is in *The Russian Economist*, ii (1921), No. 5, pp. 1691-1698. For the sensitiveness of Soviet opinion on the conditions of employment of Soviet workers by foreign *concessionnaires* see p. 284, note 1, above.

[2] The letter from the Foreign Office to Krasin is in L. Fischer, *The Soviets in World Affairs* (1930), i, 324-325.

conference to settle these questions and elaborate a " final peace treaty between Soviet Russia and the Powers ".[1] The idea of a " new world conference at which all peoples and Powers will be represented " was taken up by the Soviet press ;[2] and Krasin worked hard to instil it into the not unreceptive ears of Lloyd George and his immediate advisers.[3]

This initiative converged, almost by accident, with a very different project launched simultaneously from another quarter. The activities of Krasin in London, and the British response to them, had made a certain stir in other countries, notably France and the United States, which feared that Great Britain might steal a march on them in a lucrative market. Thus the rivalries between capitalist countries, which had been responsible for the formal lifting of the blockade in January 1920, now stimulated an active campaign for the opening up of relations with the RSFSR. After the end of 1921, the question was no longer whether the capitalist countries could or would do business with Soviet Russia, but what form that business should take. The United States was the one country where the impulse to trade with Soviet Russia was still curbed by official disapproval.[4] France was in a more vulnerable

[1] Klyuchnikov i Sabanin, *Mezhdunarodnaya Politika*, iii, i (1928), 140-142. Lenin's amendments to the original draft of this note are in *Leninskii Sbornik*, xxxv (1945), 284 ; it was evidently treated as a state paper of great importance. An English translation was published by the British Government in *Anglo-Russian Negotiations*, Cmd. 1546 (1921), together with an answer from the Foreign Office asking for a more precise definition of the loans and other obligations covered by it.

[2] Notably in an article by Radek in *Pravda*, November 30, 1921.

[3] L. Krasin, *Leonid Krasin: His Life and Work* (n.d. [1929]), p. 171.

[4] When in November 1921 a member of Krasin's delegation proposed to call on the American Consul in London, the latter was instructed to receive him, but to reaffirm the statement of the preceding March (see p. 341 above) ; a request by Krasin to visit the United States was politely ignored (*Foreign Relations of the United States, 1921*, iii (1936), 784-785, 788-789). The fullest exposition of the American attitude at this time is in an unpublished letter from Hoover to Hughes of December 6, 1921, rebutting a suggestion of the State Department that encouragement should be given to German firms to ship American goods to Russia. Hoover believed that " Americans are infinitely more popular in Russia and our government more deeply respected by even the Bolsheviks than any other ", and that " the relief measures will build a situation which, combined with the other factors, will enable the Americans to undertake the leadership in the reconstruction of Russia when the proper moment arrives ". For this reason he argued that " the hope of our commerce lies in the establishment of American firms abroad, distributing American goods under American direction, in the building of direct American financing

position. Knowing her weakness if the Powers engaged in a scramble for the Russian market, she sought to establish the principle of collective action. Loucheur, the ingenious and resourceful Minister of Finance, had successfully encouraged agreements between French and German industrialists, the purpose of which was to bring France much-needed reparations through a share in the output of an expanding German industry; the Wiesbaden agreements of October 1921 had been a first step along this path. He now conceived a still more ambitious plan. In December 1921 a group of industrialists and financiers of allied countries (although not of the United States) met in Paris, and proposed the establishment of an " international corporation " for the reconstruction of Europe. It was understood that large-scale investment in Soviet Russia would be one of the major functions of the corporation, since the exploitation of Russian resources was now recognized as a condition of European recovery. German industry, by playing its part in the development of Russia, would make Germany capable of paying reparations to the west. The presence of Worthington-Evans, the Secretary of State for War, in the British delegation, though theoretically explicable on the ground of his business experience and connexions, was a clear indication of official backing. Rathenau, the German Minister of Reconstruction, who had been initiated into the scheme by Lloyd George himself while on a visit to London in December 1921,[1] was also present in Paris during these discussions, though he took no overt part in them.

Such were the origins of the famous Genoa conference, the product, on the one side, of a Soviet project for a general conference to settle relations between Soviet Russia and the capitalist world, and, on the other side, of an allied project for the international development of Russia as the by-product of a plan of reparations. It required only the ingenuity of Lloyd George to marry these two projects. On his proposal, the Supreme Council in its session at Cannes decided on January 6, 1922, to convene " an economic and financial conference ", to which all European countries, including Soviet Russia and the ex-enemy countries, would be

and, above all, in the installation of American technology in Russian industries ". Such relations could, however, be established only after " fundamental changes " in Russia (National Archives of the United States, Record Group 661 : 6215/1).
    [1] H. Kessler, *Walther Rathenau: His Life and Work* (Engl. transl., 1929), p. 320.

invited. " A united effort by the stronger Powers ", declared the resolution, " is necessary to remedy the paralysis of the European system ". Certain principles were, however, laid down. On the one hand, " nations can claim no right to dictate to each other regarding the principles on which they are to regulate their system of ownership, internal economy and government " ; the possibility of the peaceful coexistence of socialist and capitalist countries was recognized. On the other hand, governments must recognize all public debts and obligations and compensate foreign interests for confiscated property : [1] it was specifically added that this was a condition of the " official recognition " of the " Russian Government " by the allied Powers. But the other project was not forgotten. On January 10, 1922, the Supreme Council approved " the establishment of an international corporation with affiliated national corporations for the purpose of the economic reconstruction of Europe " and decided to set up an organizing committee with £10,000 at its disposal to work out the scheme.[2] Two days later Rathenau, summoned to Cannes to undergo a further examination on German reparations policy, concluded his speech with a carefully drafted peroration on " the reconstruction of Europe ". Germany, though without capital to invest, was qualified for participation by her familiarity with the " technical and economic conditions and practices of the east ". Neither Russia nor Bolshevism was named. But the speaker noted that Germany, even in the midst of " defeat, collapse and revolution ", had " none the less resisted the disintegration of state and society ".[3] Not perhaps for the first time, the hint was heard on

---

[1] *Resolutions Adopted by the Supreme Council at Cannes, January 1922, as the Basis of the Genoa Conference*, Cmd. 1621 (1922), pp. 2-4. On the following day, January 7, the Italian Government (since the conference was to be held in Italy) communicated the decision to the Soviet Government, together with an intimation from the Italian and British Governments, of their hope that Lenin would attend the conference in person. Next day Chicherin hastened to accept the invitation (which had not yet, strictly speaking, been sent), while making reserves about the presence of Lenin. The formal invitation, enclosing the text of the Cannes resolution, was despatched and accepted a few days later (Klyuchnikov i Sabanin, *Mezhdunarodnaya Politika*, iii (1928), i, 160-161).

[2] *Resolutions Adopted by the Supreme Council at Cannes, January 1922, as the Basis of the Genoa Conference*, Cmd. 1621 (1922), pp. 5-6.

[3] W. Rathenau, *Cannes und Genua* (1922), pp. 17-18. This is a collection of Rathenau's speeches : the official minutes of the Supreme Council have not yet been published.

the lips of a German official spokesman of Germany's role as a bulwark of the west against Bolshevism.

While Rathenau was actually speaking, news arrived from Paris of the downfall of the government of Briand, the French Prime Minister and principal delegate at Cannes. This brought the Cannes meeting to a somewhat confused end. The replacement of Briand by Poincaré, who had bitterly attacked the projected conference in the press, had an important effect on its prospects. Poincaré insisted that it should refrain from any discussion of German reparations, so that Soviet Russia remained as the major, if not exclusive, item of the agenda. Moreover the change dealt a death-blow to the conception of the international corporation; for this turned for its realization not only on close Anglo-French cooperation, which was no longer available, but also on a policy of economic cooperation with Germany, which Poincaré was determined to reject in favour of a policy of coercion. This consequence of the change was not, however, realized at once. Experts in London continued to draw up conditions for the resumption of trading with Soviet Russia which soared into the realm of pure fantasy. Not only was the Soviet Government formally to recognize the obligations of former Russian governments, but a schedule of payments on the lines of German reparations plans was to be drawn up, and control established over Russian assets. A system of capitulations was envisaged under which courts in Soviet Russia would apply foreign law in cases affecting foreigners, and no foreigner resident there could be arrested " without the assistance or consent of his consul ", and no judgment against him carried out without " the consent of the consul concerned ".[1]

Limited knowledge in Moscow of what was on foot encouraged perhaps an unduly rosy view of the prospect. At a session of VTsIK on January 27, 1922, which was devoted to preparations for the conference, Chicherin spoke with unusual tolerance of " Lloyd George with his flexibility, his feeling for all environmental political and social forces, with his understanding of compromise ". Having made it clear that the Soviet Government

---

[1] The memorandum containing these proposals was first communicated to the Soviet delegates at the Genoa conference (*Papers Relating to the Economic Conference, Genoa*, Cmd. 1667 (1922), pp. 5-24).

would accept no form of cooperation which might " take the form of economic domination ", he went on :

> The prognosis of Lloyd George and our prognosis of historical development are diametrically opposed, but our practical policy coincides with the striving for the establishment of fully peaceful relations, for the creation of economic links and for common economic cooperation.[1]

At the end of the session the appointment was announced of an unusually large and influential delegation for the conference, with Lenin as president (it was never seriously intended that he should participate in person), Chicherin as his deputy, and a membership including Krasin, Litvinov, Joffe, Vorovsky and Rakovsky.[2] Postponements on the allied side delayed the meeting till April. Lenin in a speech of March 6, 1922, in welcoming the conference, declared that " we are going to it as merchants, because trade with the capitalist countries (so long as they have not completely collapsed) is absolutely necessary for us ", but added that any plans of imposing conditions on Soviet Russia as on a conquered country were " simple nonsense not worth while answering ".[3] A few days later Chicherin issued a warning to the allied governments reputed to be engaged in private discussions of such plans :

> If it is true that this group of governments intends, as their press has stated, to present proposals that are incompatible with the sovereign rights of the Russian Government and with the independence of the Russian state, it must be stated that disregard for the principles of equality and free exchange of views between all governments participating at the conference will inevitably result in its failure.

The note went on to explain that " the essential point in its [i.e. the Soviet Government's] policy is the desire to create in Russia conditions that will favour the development of private initiative in the fields of industry, agriculture, transport and commerce ", and ended with some highly reassuring, if questionable, statements about the legal guarantees available to foreigners trading in Soviet territory :

> The state cannot confiscate property except for the same reasons as are admitted under all civil codes. .·. . Special decrees

---

[1] *I i II Sessii Vserossiiskogo Tsentral'nogo Ispolnitel'nogo Komiteta IX Sozyva* (1922), pp. 8-9.
[2] *Ibid.* pp. 25-26.   [3] Lenin, *Sochineniya*, xxvii, 169, 173.

guarantee the freedom of trade within the country, while the monopoly of foreign trade is reserved for the state. But even in the latter field of enterprise special conventions authorize participation by private capital.[1]

This note represents, just a year after the introduction of NEP, the high-water mark in the application of NEP principles to the task of attracting foreign capital and foreign trade.

At this point, the road that led to Genoa — the uneasy road of *rapprochement* with the western Powers along which Soviet policy had travelled ever since the Anglo-Soviet trade agreement of March 1921 — was joined by another road which Soviet policy had been simultaneously following, the road that led to Rapallo. The road to Genoa with all its ups and downs had been throughout in the full public view. The road to Rapallo was a clandestine path carefully shaded on both sides from any form of publicity. In April 1922 this road suddenly emerged into the open, and the two roads converged to form a single coherent foreign policy in which *rapprochement* with Germany predominated over *rapprochement* with the western Powers. But the earlier stages of the road that led to Rapallo were not fully revealed, and much of it is even now shrouded in obscurity.

The possibility of a surreptitious trade with Russia in military material whose manufacture in Germany was prohibited by the Versailles treaty may have dawned on German minds very soon after the conclusion of the treaty itself. The flight, or attempted flight, to Moscow as early as October 1919 of a Junkers plane, carrying a representative of the firm,[2] is scarcely explicable on any other hypothesis. But for a long time these ideas remained in the air without awakening any visible response from Moscow. The secret department of the German Ministry of War known as Sondergruppe R is said to have been established in the winter of 1920–1921,[3] and may have been an obscure outcrop of German

---

[1] *Telegram from M. Chicherin, Moscow, to the Governments of Great Britain, France and Italy respecting the Genoa Conference*, Cmd. 1637 (1922), pp. 3-4.

[2] See p. 247 above.

[3] A memorandum of February 13, 1939, from Tschunke to Seeckt's biographer, Rabenau, published in *Der Monat*, No. 2 (November 1948), pp. 48-50, is an important first-hand source for these events.

interest in the Soviet-Polish war. The first occasion when these issues are known to have been seriously considered in Moscow was in January or February 1921, when Kopp, then on leave from Berlin, discussed them with Trotsky, the People's Commissar for War and president of the military-revolutionary council; Kopp evidently returned to Berlin with instructions to carry conversations further. The moment was propitious for overcoming any hesitations still felt in German military or industrial circles. The astronomical demands of the western Powers (the final reparations bill was presented in March 1921) and their increasingly menacing attitude (the first sanctions for non-fulfilment of reparations demands were applied in the same month) continued to drive Germany towards the east; and this quite effaced any adverse impression which might have been created by the " March action " of the KPD. The Reichswehr might indeed well draw from the rapid collapse of the rising a new assurance of its ability to deal with communism at home. In any event it is certain that, at the moment when the KPD was receiving more or less direct encouragement from Zinoviev to overthrow the German Government, the German military authorities and German industrialists were in secret negotiation with Kopp for the rebuilding of the Russian armaments industry under German technical management and control. On April 7, 1921, Kopp reported to Trotsky, sending copies of his report to Lenin and Chicherin, that a project had been worked out under which aeroplanes would be manufactured in Russia by the Albatrosswerke, submarines by Blöhm and Voss, and guns and shells by Krupps, and suggested that a mission of five or six German technicians, headed by " Neumann, who is known to you ", should proceed to Moscow for discussions of detail : strict secrecy was enjoined.[1] In May 1921 the British Ambassador in Berlin recorded without special comment a visit to Berlin by Krasin, who had " meetings and

[1] The original report is in the Trotsky archives, bearing manuscript notes by Lenin approving the project, and by Menzhinsky, deputy chief of the GPU, asking to be kept informed so that proper security measures could be taken. The report refers to " what we said in Moscow " : the approximate date of Kopp's visit to Moscow is fixed by his interview in *Izvestiya*, February 1, 1921 (see p. 330 above). F. von Rabenau, *Seeckt: Aus Seinem Leben, 1918–1936* (1940), p. 305, confirms that discussions took place in Berlin in the spring of 1921, but gives no details.

luncheons and dinners with various German industrials ".[1]
In the early summer of 1921 the proposed German mission of
experts visited Soviet Russia. It was headed by Colonel Oskar
von Niedermayer (the " Neumann " of Kopp's report), whose
exploits in Asia in the first world war earned him the name of
" the German Lawrence "; [2] other members of the mission were
Colonel Schubert, who had been German military attaché in
Moscow in 1918,[3] and Major Tschunke, an officer on Seeckt's
staff. Among the projects examined by the mission was the
rehabilitation under German management of the derelict armament factories in and around Petrograd. The mission inspected
the factories, escorted by Karakhan, then deputy Commissar for
Foreign Affairs, and Kopp ; but the technical report was unfavourable, and the plan was dropped.[4] The results of this first German
visit were inconclusive. But it was followed by the foundation in
Berlin of a company with the meaningless name of GEFU (Gesell-
schaft zur Förderung Gewerblicher Unternehmungen), which later
acted as cover on behalf of the Reichswehr and of German firms
for illicit arms transactions with Soviet Russia.[5] Meanwhile on
September 10, 1921, at a meeting of the Politburo, a despatch
was read from " one of the German negotiators " whose identity
cannot be established, but who was evidently favourable to the
Soviet cause. He reported hesitations in German business circles,
due to new moves in western Europe for intervention in Russia,[6]
and to hints from Loucheur to Rathenau of concessions in the
decision on the Upper Silesian plebiscite if Germany refrained
from a separate agreement with Russia. The informant thought
that it was necessary to enhance confidence in German business
circles in Soviet stability, and advised the Soviet negotiators to

[1] D'Abernon, *An Ambassador of Peace*, i (1929), 176.

[2] His activities in Persia and Afghanistan, investigating the possibilities of
an attack on India, are described in [W. Griesinger], *German Intrigues in Persia :
The Diary of a German Agent* (1918), the captured diary of a member of his
staff published in London for propaganda purposes.

[3] Radek singled him out as the only German official left in Moscow in
November 1918 who " showed in conversation some glimmers of understanding
of what was happening " ; he had read Lenin's *State and Revolution*, and came
to Radek to borrow the *Communist Manifesto* and Engels's " Anti-Dühring "
(*Krasnaya Nov'*, No. 10, 1926, p. 143).

[4] Information from Mr. Gustav Hilger, who was present on the occasion.

[5] *Der Monat*, No. 2, November 1948, p. 49.   [6] See pp. 346-349 above.

" play the Polish card ",[1] i.e. to harp on fears of Poland. " Con-crete positive conclusions " had already been reached on the military side, but difficulties were still to be expected from the politicians. Lenin observed that the " idea of combining military and economic negotiations is correct "; the establishment of German arms factories in Russia was to be camouflaged under the heading of " concessions ". A curious detail which emerges from the record is that Krasin was at this time purchasing muni-tions for Soviet Russia in the United States.[2] In the same month, Seeckt's biographer records the opening of the negotiations in Berlin. They took place for the most part in private apartments, generally in that of Major von Schleicher. The principal Soviet negotiator at this stage was Krasin. The principal German negotiators were General von Hasse who had succeeded Seeckt as head of the Truppenamt when Seeckt became commander-in-chief of the Reichswehr, General von Thomsen, an aeronautical expert, and Niedermayer; Seeckt, in accordance with his habit, remained in the background.[3] In the latter part of 1921 Hasse himself visited Moscow at the head of a mission which included an admiral, an official of the German Ministry of Foreign Affairs, and a director of Junkers, and is reported to have had discussions with Lebedev, the Soviet chief of staff, on action " in the event of a Polish war ".[4]

In the autumn of 1921 allied action removed the last serious hesitations on the German side and, by making it easy for the Soviet negotiators to " play the Polish card ", smoothed the path of Soviet-German relations in every sphere. The decision on the division of Upper Silesia following the plebiscite was more unfavourable to Germany than most Germans had expected, or had reason to expect; and a wave of indignation against the western Powers swept over the country. This particularly affected those diplomatic circles where hostility to Soviet Russia and hope

---

[1] In E. H. Carr, *German-Soviet Relations between the Two World Wars* (Baltimore, 1951), p. 60, this phrase was erroneously ascribed to Lenin : it belongs to the German informant.

[2] This record is in the Trotsky archives.

[3] F. von Rabenau, *Seeckt : Aus Seinem Leben, 1918–1936* (1940), pp. 308-309.

[4] *Der Monat*, No. 2, November 1948, p. 49 ; H. von Dirksen, *Moskau, Tokio, London* (Stuttgart, 1949), pp. 44-45 : information from Mr. Gustav Hilger.

of mollifying the western allies had been kept alive. The Upper Silesian decision was reflected in an important change at the Ministry of Foreign Affairs. Berendt, a former business man who had been since 1919 director of the eastern division,[1] and was strongly anti-Soviet, resigned ; and Maltzan was recalled from abroad to succeed him.[2] Another significant step was taken about the same time. It was characteristic of the relations between the Reichswehr and the German Government that the latter had been kept in complete ignorance of the Reichswehr's delicate negotiations with Soviet Russia. Seeckt now decided to inform the Chancellor, Wirth, who was also Minister of Finance, of what was on foot ; it might be necessary to have the support of the civil authorities, and more finance might be required than could conveniently be furnished out of secret military funds.[3] About the same time the secret was imparted to a small circle in the Ministry of Foreign Affairs — perhaps at first only to Maltzan.[4] Henceforth German policy towards Soviet Russia could be fully coordinated, and flowed simultaneously in three converging channels — military, economic and political. Economic relations now began to feel the stimulus which the trade agreement of May 6, 1921, had at first failed to give. Political negotiations seemed to arise naturally out of the economic negotiations,[5] and had an active promoter at the Ministry of Foreign Affairs in the person of Maltzan. Relations between the two countries were now put on a formal, though still not fully diplomatic, basis. In September Wiedenfeld arrived in Moscow as German trade representative ; and at the end of October Krestinsky was received in Berlin as Soviet representative in a capacity which does not seem

[1] W. von Blücher, *Deutschlands Weg nach Rapallo* (Wiesbaden, 1951), p. 94.
[2] Radek recorded this change in a leading article in *Pravda*, November 11, 921, and connected it with the Upper Silesian decision.
[3] F. von Rabenau, *Seeckt : Aus Seinem Leben, 1918–1936* (1940), p. 308. Rabenau is vague about the date of Wirth's initiation, but mentions his position as Minister of Finance ; Wirth relinquished this post, while retaining the chancellorship, on October 26, 1921.
[4] A junior official discovered the secret through a casual meeting with Niedermayer in the corridors of the ministry (W. von Blücher, *Deutschlands Weg nach Rapallo* (Wiesbaden, 1951), pp. 152-153).
[5] *The Times*, October 13, 1921, reported from Berlin that German-Soviet commercial negotiations were proceeding, and that " these preliminary commercial negotiations are intended to pave the way to a political understanding ".

to have been precisely defined.[1]   His status was marked by the
fact that his credentials were presented to Wirth as Chancellor,
not to the President of the Reich.[2]   Stomonyakov, a member of
Krasin's staff in the trade delegation in London, was transferred
to Berlin as head of the trade delegation there under Krestinsky,
but apparently continued to be directly responsible to Krasin.[3]

A long tradition built on a solid foundation of common interest
favoured the rapid development of commercial relations between
the two countries.   Germany had occupied a predominant place
in Russia's foreign trade before the first world war, taking, in
1913, 29·8 per cent of Russian exports and providing 47·5 per cent
of Russian imports ;   Germany was the only important country
(except the United States of America, whose trade with Russia
was not large) with which Russia's balance of trade was markedly
passive.   Krasin in an article of 1922 described the relation in
terms which underlined rather than concealed its " semi-colonial "
character :

> Russia and Germany, to judge by their former economic
> relations, were so to speak made for each other.   On the one
> side, an immense country with inexhaustible natural riches,
> contained in her soil, forests and mineral deposits, with a work-
> ing population of many millions which had proved its capacity
> to raise itself in any branch of productive activity to the levels
> attained by the advanced countries of the west ;   on the other
> side an industrial country with the most up-to-date technique,
> and with a surplus population for whose maintenance the
> development of export trade and transport is an indispensable
> condition.   None of the western European countries has such
> experience of working with Russia or such profound and exact
> knowledge of all the conditions in our country as Germany.
> Hundreds of thousands of Germans used to live in Russia
> before the war ;   many of them are complete masters of the
> Russian language, and have the most extensive personal con-
> nexions throughout the length and breadth of Russia.   Finally
> our whole civilization, in particular our technical development,

[1] I. Maisky, *Vneshnyaya Politika RSFSR, 1917–1922* (1922), pp. 106-107 ;
the German Ministry of Foreign Affairs rejected Joffe, who was Moscow's first
choice for the post, and for some weeks raised objections to Krestinsky as being
a prominent communist (W. von Blücher, *Deutschlands Weg nach Rapallo*
(Wiesbaden, 1951), p. 149.
[2] *Izvestiya*, November 27, 1921.
[3] V. N. Ipatieff, *The Life of a Chemist* (Stanford, 1946), pp. 327-330.

industry and trade, have been based for decades past mainly on work done in partnership with Germany, and it is easier for the Russian industrialist, merchant and even worker to get on with the German than with any other foreigner.[1]

Links so strong and so profitable to both parties were not easily broken. Refusal in the autumn of 1919 to participate in the blockade of Russia was the first independent act of German policy after the war. From 1920 onwards, with the Baltic ports reopened, Russian-German trade began to flow again in a steady and increasing trickle; the provisional trade agreement of May 6, 1921, was a formal recognition of its existence and an attempt to stimulate its expansion. Early in 1921 Lomonosov, the Russian railway engineer, came to Berlin to place extensive orders for locomotives.[2] On the other hand, Germany was in no position to undertake those capital investments in Russia which the Soviet Government was eager above all things to attract, and which were the main object of the concessions. For some time after the conclusion of the Anglo-Soviet trade agreement of March 16, 1921, Soviet hopes continued to be centred on Great Britain; and Great Britain remained Soviet Russia's largest supplier and most lucrative market during the greater part of that year. It was only in the autumn of 1921, when Anglo-Soviet political relations had failed to respond to the stimulus of the trade agreement, and when those groups in Germany which still looked to the west had been disillusioned by the decision on Upper Silesia, that both countries began to devote serious attention to the improvement of trade relations between them.

The shortage of capital in Germany made it easier to interest German concerns in trading companies which could operate with a small working capital than in industrial concessions requiring large-scale long-term investment. The autumn of 1921 saw the first development of the system of " mixed companies ", which for many years proved a popular instrument of Soviet foreign trade. The first of them appears to have been a shipping company formed by the Soviet Government and the Hamburg-Amerika Line under the name Derutra for the transport of cargoes between

[1] L. B. Krasin, *Voprosy Vneshnei Torgovli* (1928), p. 305.
[2] W. von Blücher, *Deutschlands Weg nach Rapallo* (Wiesbaden, 1951), p. 150.

Germany and Soviet Russia. This was followed by Deruluft, a corresponding company for handling air traffic between the two countries, and Derumetall, a company for trading in scrap metal.[1] Later came the foundation of Russgertorg, a general Soviet-German trading concern, of which half the capital was held by Vneshtorg and half by a German group headed by the iron and steel magnate Otto Wolff. Negotiations for concessions were reported to be in progress with several German firms;[2] and in January 1922 an agreement was signed with Krupps for a concession covering an extensive area in south Russia on the river Manych, a tributary of the Don, for the establishment of a factory and experimental station for tractors and agricultural machinery. Lenin particularly welcomed this concession and urged the importance of concluding such agreements " especially now before the Genoa conference and particularly with German firms ".[3]

The choice between west and east which now once again faced German statesmen was expressed in the indecisive and ambiguous personality of Rathenau, who became Minister for Foreign Affairs in Wirth's government on January 31, 1922. The project mooted by the western allies at the end of 1921 for an international consortium to develop and exploit Russian resources divided German economic interests into two factions — the interests centring mainly but not exclusively round light industry, which had close commercial and financial links with the west, and the heavy industrial interests which were primarily dependent on eastern connexions and markets. Rathenau's major economic interests, as well as his cultural and temperamental affinities, ranged him with the westerners, though he also, as his record and his conversations with Radek in 1919 showed, had an active consciousness of the opportunities open to German industry in the east. But, while Rathenau toyed in London, Paris and Cannes with the idea of cooperation in a western consortium for joint operations in Russia, the eastward-looking attitude of German

[1] L. B. Krasin, *Voprosy Vneshnei Torgovli* (1928), pp. 391-393 ; E. Fuckner, *Russlands Neue Wirtschaftspolitik* (Leipzig, 1922), pp. 25-26.

[2] I. Maisky, *Vneshnyaya Politika RSFSR, 1917-1922* (1922), p. 107 ; the writer reports " a gradual broadening of Russo-German trade during the whole winter of 1921-1922 ".

[3] Note to Politburo of January 23, 1922, in the Trotsky archives ; the Krupp agreement may have been a by-product of the military negotiations, but had in itself no military significance.

heavy industry was receiving strong reinforcements in Berlin from the secret military negotiations, which promised the armaments industry (the kernel of the iron and steel industry) a rich field for recovery and expansion in Soviet Russia. Of this tendency Stinnes, now the king of German heavy industry, was the chief industrial representative; [1] its political spokesman was Stresemann, leader of the German People's Party, the party of the great industrialists; [2] Wirth, the Chancellor, himself a member of the Centre, had been won over to it; and Maltzan was its influential champion in the Ministry of Foreign Affairs. Early in 1922, when the issue still seemed to hang in the balance, Maltzan told the British Ambassador that in his view trade with Russia should be organized by the Great Powers acting individually, and not through a consortium; [3] and shortly afterwards Wirth, echoing the very phraseology of Soviet protests against the consortium, explained to the Reichstag his objections to " any policy that wished to consider and treat Russia as a colony ".[4] The issue was first openly debated in the Reichstag on March 29, 1922, on the eve of the arrival of the Soviet delegation on its way to the Genoa conference. Stresemann attacked the treatment of Russia " as a colony for international capital to exploit ", and did not want Germany to become " a member of an international consortium economically hostile to her "; and Rathenau made a speech which was, in effect, a confession of his inability to face the dilemma :

> The path of syndicates is not decisive. Syndicates can be useful and we should not cut ourselves off from such syndicates. On the other hand, the essential part of the work of reconstruction will have to be discussed between us and Russia herself. Such discussions have taken place and are now taking place and I shall promote them by every means.[5]

The economic negotiations with Soviet Russia proceeded without concealment. The political and military negotiations

---

[1] The Spa reparations conference in July 1920 had already been the occasion of a public clash between Stinnes's uncompromising hostility to the west and Rathenau's inclination to seek an accommodation with the allies.

[2] For Stresemann's eulogy of Stinnes on his death in 1924, see *Gustav Stresemann : His Diaries, Letters and Papers* (Engl. transl.), i (1935), 311-313.

[3] D'Abernon, *An Ambassador of Peace*, i (1929), 238.

[4] *Verlandlungen des Reichstags*, ccclii (1922), 5562.

[5] *Ibid.* cccliv (1922), 6648, 6655-6656.

which were being conducted at the same time were shrouded in complete secrecy, and no full record of them can even now be given. The culminating period for both fell within the first months of 1922,[1] when the invitation extended to both countries to the forthcoming Genoa conference complicated the calculations of both. According to Hasse's diary the first conference between Seeckt and " the Russians " (presumably military experts) took place on December 8, 1921. On January 17, 1922, Radek arrived in Berlin from Moscow with Niedermayer,[2] and was observed by the British Ambassador to be " multiplying his interviews with German ministers, officials and party politicians " ; Rakovsky and Krasin joined him in February.[3] In view of Rath au's close association with the consortium proposal, his appointment as Minister of Foreign Affairs caused some trepidation in Moscow, but did not affect the military negotiations. On February 10, 1922, Radek, at his insistent request, had a personal meeting with Seeckt — apparently the first. He asked for German help in rebuilding Russia's armament industries and in the training of Soviet officers, and complained of the closeness of German relations with the west, especially with Great Britain — to which Seeckt replied that Germany needed to flirt with Britain as a counter-weight to France.[4] Radek in these talks is said to have made the offer that Soviet Russia, if equipped with German aid, would join Germany in an attack on Poland in the spring. If so,

---

[1] The German delegation, in an apologetic *communiqué* issued in Genoa on the day after the signature of the Rapallo treaty, stressed that the negotiations had been going on " for some months " and that " the date of the signature of this treaty could be foreseen for some time " (*Materialy Genuezskoi Konferentsii* (1922), pp. 305-306) ; the official German reply to the allied protest claimed that the treaty had been drafted " several weeks previously " (*Papers Relating to International Economic Conference, Genoa, April-May 1922*, Cmd. 1667 (1922), p. 55). These statements were made to exonerate Germany from the charge of deliberately wrecking the conference ; A. Joffe, *Ot Genui do Gaagi* (1923), p. 16, specifically states that the treaty was drafted during the talks in Berlin early in April 1922.

[2] *Journal of Modern History* (Chicago), xxii (1949), No. 1, p. 31.

[3] D'Abernon, *An Ambassador of Peace*, i (1929), 250-252, 261 ; Radek saw, among others, Maltzan, who arranged a meeting between him and Stinnes (W. von Blücher, *Deutschlands Weg nach Rapallo* (Wiesbaden, 1951), p. 155).

[4] *Journal of Modern History* (Chicago), xxii (1949), No. 1, p. 31 ; the slightly longer account in F. von Rabenau, *Seeckt : Aus Seinem Leben, 1918-1936* (1940), p. 309, corresponds closely, and is presumably also derived from Hasse's diary.

this scarcely represented a serious intention of the Soviet Government; Radek was applying with his customary irresponsibility the injunction to " play the Polish card ".[1] The new element in the negotiations at this time seems to have been the proposal that the Germans should not only organize and run factories for the forbidden weapons in Soviet Russia, but should train Red Army officers in the use of these weapons and at the same time set up training schools there for future German officers. The whole scheme broadened out into a project for a substantial German military establishment on Soviet soil, from which the Red Army would derive its share of advantage both in material and in training.[2]

Political negotiations meanwhile lagged. The need for a political agreement which would carry with it a resumption of full diplomatic relations was not seriously denied, but obstruction still came from certain quarters both in the German Ministry of Foreign Affairs and in the Social-Democratic Party, which were certainly unaware of the military negotiations. In February 1922 Radek had an interview with Rathenau. But there is no evidence of the extent of the progress made until, in the first days of April 1922, the Soviet delegation to the Genoa conference broke its journey in Berlin on the way to Genoa. What happened next is fairly well established. No confidence was felt in Moscow that any serious result would come out of the Genoa conference; the western Powers were attempting to impose unacceptable conditions on the establishment of economic relations with the RSFSR; a separate agreement with Berlin, which would prevent Germany from committing herself to the proposed international corporation, and facilitate independent trading between Germany and the RSFSR, would strengthen the Soviet position and break the threatened stranglehold of the western Powers. The Soviet delegation pressed, therefore, in Berlin for the immediate conclusion of a treaty. The rift between easterners and westerners in the German Ministry of Foreign Affairs was acute, with Rathenau himself now leaning to the west. The easterners were

[1] A year later, at the time of the Ruhr invasion, Trotsky told Nansen, who repeated it to the German chargé d'affaires in Moscow, that " the Red Army would not march if it came to a conflict between Germany and Poland " (W. von Blücher, *Deutschlands Weg nach Rapallo* (Wiesbaden, 1951), pp. 172-173).

[2] For the further history of these negotiations see pp. 435-437 below.

strong enough to secure approval for immediate negotiations; and in the next few days agreement was reached on the text of a treaty with only two minor points left in abeyance. When, however, the Soviet delegation pressed for immediate signature, Rathenau held back, still clinging to the hope of an agreement with the western Powers, and perceiving, perhaps more clearly than the Russians, that it might wreck the conference at the outset to present it with the *fait accompli* of a Soviet-German treaty. Both delegations therefore proceeded to Genoa with the treaty unsigned, with the draft still incomplete, and with its very existence unsuspected outside the inner circles of the German Foreign Office and the Soviet delegation.[1] It is unlikely that the political negotiators broached the questions of military collaboration which were being pursued through other channels. But it is on record that " Chicherin appealed to the Chancellor quite openly for the presence of German officers in Russia ".[2]

The opening of the Genoa conference on April 10, 1922,[3] found the Soviet delegation in a far more impressive position than there had been reason to expect a few weeks earlier. Poincaré, refusing himself to attend the conference, had sent Barthou with instructions to be intractable ; Lloyd George badly needed an agreement with Russia in order to revive his wilting prestige ; Anglo-French friction and Poincaré's attitude to Germany had virtually killed the menacing project of an international corpora-

---

[1] L. Fischer, *The Soviets in World Affairs* (1930), i, 333 ; according to Rathenau's biographer, the treaty " would have been signed had it not been for Rathenau's scruples about presenting the allies just before Genoa with a *fait accompli* which might have awakened their suspicions " (H. Kessler, *Walther Rathenau : His Life and Work* (Engl. transl., 1929), p. 329).

[2] F. von Rabenau, *Seeckt : Aus Seinem Leben, 1918–1936* (1940), pp. 309-310. According to statements made in the Reichstag in December 1926, the first agreement with Junkers for the manufacture of aircraft in Russia was concluded on March 15, 1922, after which a number of German officers proceeded to Russia with false passports (*Verhandlungen des Reichstags*, cccxci (1926), 8597) ; this matter was therefore probably under discussion at the time of the Rapallo negotiations.

[3] The proceedings of the conference were recorded in Soviet and British official publications : *Materialy Genuezskoi Konferentsii* (1922) and *Papers Relating to International Economic Conference, Genoa, April-May 1922*, Cmd. 1667 (1922). The only general non-official account of the conference is in J. Saxon Mills, *The Genoa Conference* (1922) : this is a detailed apologia for Lloyd George, and adds nothing substantially new.

tion ; and Soviet Russia had the prospect of a separate agreement with Germany to strengthen her hand against the western Powers. On the other hand, Soviet Russia desperately needed capital investments which could only come from the west. Chicherin's initial speech at the conference, delivered in French and inflated by journalistic curiosity into an international event, ranged far. He opened up visions of the vast potential contribution of Russia's untapped resources, developed and made available through the cooperation of western capitalists, to the cause of world-wide economic recovery. He observed that the measures introduced under NEP " go to meet the wishes contained in the Cannes resolution in regard to the juridical guarantees necessary for the economic cooperation with Soviet Russia of countries based on private property ". Noting that the restoration of the world economy would be impossible unless the threat of wars were removed, he announced that the Soviet delegation would at a later stage of the conference " propose a general reduction of armaments, and support all proposals aimed at lightening the burden of militarism ". Finally, he thought that the time had come for a world congress on the basis of equality between all nations " for the establishment of general peace " ; the Russian Government, for its part, was prepared to take existing international agreements as a starting point, while " introducing into these agreements necessary amendments ", and even to participate in a revision of the statute of the League of Nations " in order to convert it into a genuine alliance of peoples, excluding the domination of some by others and doing away with the present division into victors and vanquished ".[1] The seeming naïveté of these proposals masked a good deal of subtle calculation. The advocacy of a general reduction of armaments, the insistence on equality between victors and vanquished, and the bare hint of " necessary amendments " to the Versailles treaty, were designed to fall on the grateful ears of the German delegation and to remind it where the true friends of Germany were to be found. The raising of the issue of disarmament could also be counted on to deepen the rift between Great Britain and France, who had for some time

[1] *Materialy Genuezskoi Konferentsii* (1922), pp. 78-82 ; a memorandum was also handed in to the conference (*ibid.* pp. 42-47) on the juridical guarantees accorded to foreign commerce under NEP, including the projected legal codes and the abolition of the Cheka (see Vol. 1, p. 180).

been quarrelling on the subject at Geneva. When Barthou indignantly protested that a reduction of armaments did not figure on the agenda of the conference as drawn up at Cannes, and declared that the French delegation would participate in no such discussions, Lloyd George, while making it clear that his sympathies did not lie with Barthou, suavely begged Chicherin not to sink the ship by overloading it. Chicherin magnanimously waived the point. Next day it was agreed, against the sole vote of France, that the German and Soviet delegations, like those of the three principal allies, should automatically have a place in all commissions set up by the conference. This meant their formal promotion to the rank of Great Powers. The principle of equality had been recognized and accepted.

After this opening business, commissions were appointed to deal with political, financial, economic and transport questions ; and, while these indulged in meaningless generalities, the leaders of the allied delegations, meeting in Lloyd George's villa, entered into serious discussions with the Soviet delegation on the real issue of the conference, relations with Soviet Russia. Allied claims fell into three categories — Russian war debts, Russian pre-war public and private debts, and the nationalization of foreign enterprises by the Soviet Government. As regards the first, a proposal was mooted for the mutual cancellation of these claims and of Soviet claims for damages resulting from allied intervention in the civil war ; [1] and, though this was rejected by both sides, it was clear that a compromise would be reached on these lines if other issues proved susceptible of settlement.[2] As regards the second, the Soviet Government had formally recognized these claims ever since January 1919, but declared that it was materially incapable of meeting them at present unless the allied governments were prepared to make or guarantee a loan to it : [3] this was a

---

[1] These were set forth in detail in a volume issued by the Soviet delegation, *Les Réclamations de la Russie aux États Responsables de l'Intervention et du Blocus* (Genoa, 1922).

[2] This was clearly hinted at in a memorandum handed to the Soviet delegation on April 15 (*Papers Relating to International Economic Conference, Genoa, April-May 1922*, Cmd. 1667 (1922), p. 25).

[3] The Soviet delegation also sought to " make it clear, though it seems to be self-evident, that the Russian Government could not admit liability for the debts of its predecessors until it has been formally recognized *de jure* by the Powers concerned " (*ibid.* p. 26).

subject for hard bargaining, but no longer an issue of principle. The question of nationalization was the most stubborn. The Soviet delegation reiterated Soviet willingness to grant long-term concessions to former foreign owners of nationalized property; but, while the British delegation showed some inclination to close with this offer, the French and Belgian delegations insisted on the return of the properties or an adequate compensation for them.[1]

Germany, having under the Versailles treaty renounced all claims on Soviet Russia, had no part in these conversations; and Lloyd George rashly assumed that it was safe to let the German delegation kick its heels until he had finished with the Russians. This was a fatal error. Rumours reached the German delegation in its seclusion that the allies were about to clinch a bargain with the Soviet Government on terms which included a revival of Russian claims on Germany for reparations: these had been kept alive by article 116 of the Versailles treaty which cancelled the treaty of Brest-Litovsk. The suspicion was false. No such scheme seems to have been considered. But Radek had long ago taken pains to sow such fears in the German official mind;[2] and Maltzan, whether he shared these fears or not, played on them in the interests of his eastern policy, urging the importance of signing the treaty with the Soviet delegation before the latter had been further tempted to make terms with the allies at German expense. The German delegates were in a depressed state of mind when at one o'clock on the morning of Easter Sunday, April 16, 1922, Joffe telephoned to them to propose a meeting later in the day at the neighbouring resort of Rapallo to complete the unfinished treaty negotiated in Berlin. Rathenau's biographer has described how the principal members of the delegation assembled in their

---

[1] Chicherin's version of these discussions, which seems broadly accurate, is in L. Fischer, *The Soviets in World Affairs* (1930), i, 335-337; a memorandum of April 20, 1922, setting forth the official Soviet view is in *Materialy Genuezskoi Konferentsii* (1922), pp. 127-139.

[2] Radek is said to have told Maltzan at the end of January 1922 that France had offered *de jure* recognition and credits to the Soviet Government on condition that it asserted its claims against Germany under article 116 (W. von Blücher, *Deutschlands Weg nach Rapallo* (Wiesbaden, 1951), pp. 154-155). This was certainly untrue. But there is other, though slender, evidence of an attempt by Radek to make a deal with France at this time; according to L. O. Frossard, *De Jaurès à Lénine* (1930), p. 222, Cachin, on his instructions, offered Poincaré " the alliance of the Soviets ". Any such attempt, if made, was not taken very seriously.

pyjamas in Rathenau's bedroom, and debated the question to go or not to go to Rapallo. Hasse, Seeckt's representative in the secret military negotiations, was present at Genoa in the German delegation, but is not known to have participated in this famous bedroom scene. The reluctance of Rathenau was now finally overborne by Wirth and Maltzan.[1] The Soviet invitation was accepted. The day was spent in filling up the gaps in the draft, and at five o'clock the treaty of Rapallo was signed.

The fact of signature was more important than the formal contents of the treaty. It provided for the mutual renunciation of all financial claims, including German claims arising out of the Soviet nationalization decrees, " on the condition that the government of the RSFSR does not meet analogous claims of other states ". Diplomatic and consular relations were to be resumed ; and the most important article of the treaty dealt with economic relations :

> Both governments will mutually seek to meet the economic requirements of both countries in a spirit of good will. In the event of this question being settled in principle on an international basis, they will enter into a previous exchange of opinions with each other.

The effect of this clause was to ensure the exclusion of Germany from any international scheme for exploitation of Russian resources and the establishment of a common economic front between the two countries : this was its main immediate attraction for Soviet Russia. Another clause of the same article bound the German Government to support the creation of the mixed companies through which it was proposed to conduct Soviet-German trade.[2]

This major diplomatic event shattered the already creaking structure of the Genoa conference. The allied Powers had attempted to come to terms with Soviet Russia behind the back of Germany : Soviet Russia had come to terms with Germany behind their back. Their wrath fell primarily on the German delegation, and was expressed in a querulous joint note : had not " the German Chancellor himself declared at the opening session only a week

---

[1] The scene is described in H. Kessler, *Walther Rathenau : His Life and Work* (Engl. trans., 1929), pp. 320-321.

[2] *RSFSR : Sbornik Deistvuyushchikh Dogovorov*, iii (1922), No. 85, pp. 36-38 ; *League of Nations : Treaty Series*, xix (1923), 248-252.

ago that the German delegation would cooperate with the other Powers for the solution of these questions in a spirit of genuine loyalty and fellowship "? [1] Formally the proceedings of the conference were not affected. But the result of Rapallo had been to stiffen the attitude of the Soviet delegation, by improving its bargaining position, and of the French delegation, by providing it with at any rate a better pretext for its intransigence. The faint hope that Lloyd George's ingenuity might succeed in bridging the gap between them now vanished altogether. A restatement of the allied position in a memorandum to the Soviet delegation of May 2, 1922, while no longer sufficiently unyielding to secure French or Belgian approval, represented from the Soviet standpoint a long step back from the compromises discussed in Lloyd George's villa before Rapallo. [2] The week that followed was occupied by abortive private discussions between the British and Soviet delegations. [3] Then, on May 11, 1922, the Soviet delegation sent a long and argumentative reply which was clearly designed to bring the fruitless conference to an end. It abounded in historical precedents :

> Revolutionary France not only tore up the political treaties of the former régime with foreign countries, but also repudiated her national debt. She consented to pay only one-third of that debt, and that from motives of political expediency.

The United States had equally " repudiated the treaties of its predecessors, England and Spain ". The allied governments of 1919 had confiscated without compensation the property of nationals of the vanquished states. As regards Soviet claims arising

[1] *Papers Relating to International Economic Conference, Genoa, April-May 1922*, Cmd. 1667 (1922), pp. 53-54 ; a by-product of the allied protest was an acrimonious correspondence between Chicherin and Skirmunt, the Polish delegate, prompted by Polish participation in the protest (*Materialy Genuezskoi Konferentsii* (1922), pp. 314-322).

[2] *Papers Relating to International Economic Conference, Genoa, April-May 1922*, Cmd. 1667 (1922), pp. 28-36.

[3] According to a German source, members of the German delegation, now fully restored to favour with the British delegation, acted as intermediaries in these discussions — a first harvest of Rapallo : the only result was, however, that the Russians " realized at last that the sums they needed were not to be extracted from the allies except on terms which they could not grant " (H. Kessler, *Walther Rathenau : His Life and Work* (Engl. transl., 1929), pp. 355-356).

out of the civil war, the British Government had paid 15½ million dollars to the United States as compensation for damage caused by the *Alabama* in the American civil war. The allied proposal that compensation claims should be adjudicated by a mixed arbitral tribunal with a neutral president provoked an important declaration of principle :

> In the trial of disputes of this kind, the specific disagreements will inevitably end in opposing to one another two forms of property, whose antagonism assumes today for the first time in history a real and practical character. In such circumstances there can be no question of an impartial super-arbiter.

The memorandum closed by indicating once more that the Soviet Government was prepared to make " important concessions ", but only in return for equivalent concessions from the other side. If the Powers desired to pursue the question of " the financial disputes between themselves and Russia ", a " mixed commission of experts " might be convened at some other place and time ".[1]

Behind the scenes the Genoa conference had marked another stage in the struggle between British and American oil. Negotiations between the Royal Dutch-Shell group and the Soviet Government had reached a point where the former hoped to obtain an exclusive concession for the whole oil-bearing region of south-eastern Russia and the Caucasus : an agreement to this effect was said to be already in draft. This agreement no doubt inspired the British delegation, unlike the other allied delegations, to lend a ready ear to the Soviet proposal under which nationalized properties would be returned to their former owners, not in ownership, but as concessions for exploitation. The American Standard Oil Company had also acquired oil interests in the Caucasus, but only by purchase from a Russian owner since the nationalization decree of 1918 : these would not have been covered by the British-Soviet formula. The American counter-offensive opened with a statement made by a director of Standard Oil two days after the conference opened to *The Times* in London : this

---

[1] *Materialy Genuezskoi Konferentsii* (1922), pp. 230-241 ; *Papers Relating to International Economic Conference, Genoa, April-May 1922*, Cmd. 1667 (1922), pp. 38-47 ; there are minor discrepancies between Russian and English versions, but the latter appears to reproduce the French text officially presented to the conference.

expressed strong American opposition to any exclusive concession.[1]
During the course of the conference the terms of the draft agreement between the Royal Dutch-Shell group and the Soviet
Government were published in the American press as if the
agreement had actually been concluded.[2] This provoked a flood
of denials, including one from Austen Chamberlain in the House
of Commons.[3] The struggle was none the less acute, and French
and Belgian opposition to the British attitude was believed by
many to have been inspired from Washington. In the last stages
of the conference, on May 11, 1922, the American State Department itself intervened with an uncompromising pronouncement
issued in Genoa by the American Ambassador in Rome :

> The United States [ran the operative clause] will never
> consent that any scheme whatsoever, national or international,
> shall be applied unless it takes account of the principle of the
> open door for all and recognises equal rights for all.[4]

This statement, which finally dissolved the dream of an exclusive
British, or British-Dutch, oil concession in Soviet Russia, happened to coincide in date with the Soviet memorandum. Both
together signalled the end of the conference. The allies, rather
in order to wind up the conference with an agreed conclusion than
for any more practical purpose, seized on the Soviet proposal for
a commission of experts to pursue the study of outstanding
differences. It was decided that the experts should meet in The
Hague at the end of June 1922.[5] Thereupon the conference
dispersed.

The Genoa conference had ended in failure. It brought none
of the concrete results which the Soviet Government had sought
— de jure recognition, foreign capital investments, credits and a
settlement of claims. It had nevertheless given something, and

---

[1] The Times, April 12, 1922.
[2] This incident is described in The Autobiography of Lincoln Steffens (1931),
p. 810.
[3] House of Commons : 5th Series, cliii, cols. 1995-1996.
[4] A close similarity of language was noted between this statement and the
interview given to The Times a month earlier ; the request of the Standard Oil
Company to the State Department to intervene " for the protection of American
interests in Russia " is in Foreign Relations of the United States, 1922, ii (1938),
786-788.
[5] Papers Relating to International Economic Conference, Genoa, April-May
1922, Cmd. 1667 (1922), pp. 49-50.

more to Soviet Russia than to any other country. The Soviet Government, though not officially recognized, had been formally accepted at the conference table as an equal sovereign Power. Though no settlement had been reached, the bases of a settlement had clearly emerged : war debts and civil war claims would be mutually wiped out ; something would be paid on pre-war debts, provided the debtors advanced credits out of which to pay it ; expropriated foreign owners would get their properties back in the form of concessions, provided they were prepared to invest further capital. Above all, the Genoa conference had made possible the Rapallo treaty. The peculiar importance which the Soviet Government attached to this achievement was shown by the unprecedentedly warm and emphatic terms of a resolution recording its approval by VTsIK a month later. According to this resolution, VTsIK

Welcomes the Russian-German treaty concluded at Rapallo as the only correct way out from the difficulties, chaos and danger of wars,

Recognizes *only treaties of this type* as normal for the relations of the RSFSR with capitalist states,

Instructs the Council of People's Commissars and the People's Commissariat of Foreign Affairs to conduct its policy in the spirit indicated, and

Enjoins on the People's Commissariat of Foreign Affairs to admit departures from the type of the Rapallo treaty only in those exceptional cases where these departures are compensated by quite special advantages for the toiling masses of the RSFSR and of the Soviet republics allied with it.[1]

For the Soviet Government, as for the German Government, the Rapallo treaty had the rare and refreshing character of an equal bargain ; it was the first major diplomatic occasion on which either Soviet Russia or the Weimar republic had negotiated as an equal. The two outcasts of European society, overcoming the barrier of ideological differences, joined hands, and, in so doing, recovered their status and their self-esteem as independent members of the society. Confidence in the ability of the Soviet Government to

[1] *III Sessiya Vserossiisskogo Tsentral'nogo Ispolnitel'nogo Komiteta IX Sozyva No. 5* (May 19, 1922) ; p. 17 ; Klyuchnikov i Sabanin, *Mezhdunarodnaya Politika*, iii, i (1928), 192.

play a successful rôle in the game of diplomacy as a European Power began with the treaty of Rapallo.

The long-range implications of the change in Soviet policy and outlook of which the Rapallo treaty was the expression were not yet fully recognized. It had been a commonplace among Soviet leaders that the RSFSR had been enabled to survive in its critical first two years by the divisions and jealousies within the capitalist world. Crude attempts had been made in 1918 to play off the Germans against the western allies and the western allies against the Germans. Lenin on one occasion said that the whole foreign policy of the régime during its first three years had been to " utilize the division between the capitalist countries " ; [1] and at the time of the Washington conference American support had been an invaluable asset in hastening the evacuation of Siberia by Japan. But it was the Rapallo treaty which first made the balance of power a vital, though unavowed, principle of Soviet policy in Europe. The Genoa conference had confronted Soviet Russia with the danger, exaggerated by Soviet fears but not wholly lacking in substance, of a Europe united to exploit Russian resources and impose terms on Soviet Russia as an economically dependent " backward " country. This danger was conjured by wooing away one of the essential partners in such a project. The Rapallo treaty was not, strictly speaking, a treaty of alliance. It did not constitute on either side an exclusive association. Soviet Russia did not cease to be preoccupied with the improvement of her relations with the other European group, notably with Great Britain, or of her relations with the United States, still remote and still secure enough to adhere to neither European group. But Rapallo established the principle that the capitalist world must be prevented at all costs from uniting against the Soviet power and that this could be achieved by proffering the hand of friendship to one of the camps into which that world was divided ; and since, throughout the Weimar period, Germany was the weaker of the two groups, this established a special relation between Soviet Russia and Germany. A few months later Radek, who must be accounted one of the chief artificers of the Rapallo policy, defined this relation in terms of the eternal interests of Russia and the traditional arguments of the old diplomacy :

[1] See p. 276 above.

The policy of strangling Germany implied in fact the destruction of Russia as a great Power; for, no matter how Russia is governed, it is always to her interest that Germany should exist. . . . A Russia weakened to the utmost by the war could neither have remained a great Power nor acquired the economic and technical means for her industrial reconstruction, unless she had in the existence of Germany a counter-weight to the preponderance of the Allies.

It was perhaps odd that the occasion of this pronouncement should have been a report prepared for the fourth congress of Comintern.[1] But the changes which had come over the policies of that institution under the influence of NEP, Genoa and Rapallo will be examined in the next chapter.

[1] *Die Liquidation des Versailler Friedens: Bericht an den Vierten Kongress der Kommunistischen Internationale* (Hamburg, 1923), p. 22 ; Radek did not speak at the congress on this subject, and reports distributed to the congress were not included in the record of its proceedings. An English translation appeared under the title *The Winding-Up of the Versailles Treaty* (Hamburg 1922).

CHAPTER 30

RETREAT IN COMINTERN

THE predisposing cause of the " retreat " of March 1921, both on the domestic and on the diplomatic front, was the unexpected delay in the spread of revolution over Europe. The economic hazards of an indefinitely prolonged interim period required Soviet Russia to enter into amicable trading relations with the capitalist world ; the political hazards called for amicable political relations with some capitalist states as a reinsurance against the hostility of others — the policy of splitting the capitalist world. The cause which had produced these events — the long postponement of European revolution — was bound to affect even more directly the outlook and policies of Comintern, and required a corresponding readjustment in its activities. After the " March action " of 1921 in Germany this conclusion could not be evaded. The readjustment was duly made in the spring and summer of 1921, and recorded at the third congress of Comintern in June and July of that year. It was the natural counterpart of the change in Soviet policy, domestic and foreign, represented by NEP and the Anglo-Soviet trade agreement. The change of front in Comintern was, however, unlikely to be achieved without resistance, even within the Russian party ; and Trotsky's account of the discussions in the Politburo and in the central committee before the congress, with Lenin, Trotsky and Kamenev standing for retreat and compromise, and Zinoviev, Bukharin, Radek and Bela Kun continuing to preach the revolutionary offensive, may be accepted as broadly correct.[1] In any case, Lenin's firmness carried the day. At the congress the Russian delegates spoke with a single voice, though with varying degrees of emphasis.

[1] L. Trotsky, *The Real Situation in Russia* (1928), pp. 246-249. Zinoviev afterwards admitted that there had been differences of opinion on the March action at the time of the third congress " even in our Russian delegation " (*Protokoll des Vierten Kongresses der Kommunistischen Internationale* (Hamburg, 1923), p. 197).

The staging and organization of the third congress of Comintern, which assembled on June 22, 1921, were more grandiose than ever before; a larger number of delegates represented a larger number of parties and party members in Europe and beyond. During the interval between the second and third congresses Comintern began to organize itself as a large-scale institution, moving from the two or three rooms in the Kremlin where it had started work in 1919 to the imposing premises of the former German Embassy. It also acquired a hotel to house communist delegates from other countries, though this, according to an early British visitor, " was in a deplorable condition and was infested with rats ".[1] During the same period, as Zinoviev proudly reported to the third congress, IKKI had held 31 sessions; for the more expeditious transaction of business it had recently set up an inner bureau of seven members, which was specially concerned with the direction of secret and illegal activities.[2] But, in spite of these outward symptoms of progress, the note of sobriety and restraint contrasted strangely with the revolutionary optimism of 1920. An article entitled *Before the Third Congress of the Communist International*, written by Zinoviev when the summons to the congress was issued three months earlier, had admitted that " the tempo of the international proletarian revolution is, through a whole variety of circumstances, being somewhat slowed down ".[3] Trotsky, who made the first report of the congress on " The Economic Crisis and the New Tasks of the International ",[4] spoke of the recovery of self-confidence by the bourgeoisie since the threatening days of 1919, and the recession of the revolutionary wave. It was true that the apparent stabiliza-

---

[1] T. Bell, *Pioneering Days* (1941), p. 214.

[2] *Protokoll des III. Kongresses der Kommunistischen Internationale* (Hamburg, 1921), pp. 151, 1045.

[3] *Kommunisticheskii Internatsional*, No. 16 (March 31, 1921), col. 3481.

[4] The report exists in two forms — one in which it was delivered to the congress (*Protokoll des III. Kongresses der Kommunistischen Internationale* (Hamburg, 1921), pp. 48-90, the other in which Trotsky himself afterwards reprinted it (*Pyat' Let Kominterna* (n.d. [1925]), pp. 138-186). The second variant is fuller, but omits some passages, including the famous prediction of war between the United States and Great Britain " in the year 1923 or 1924 " (*Protokoll des III. Kongresses der Kommunistischen Internationale* (Hamburg, 1921), p. 86); even before the end of the congress Trotsky regretted this " accursed date ", which he had only " quoted by way of illustration " (*ibid.* p. 132).

tion of capitalism was illusory. Mindful of the old question
" 1847 or 1849 ? ", Trotsky was careful to explain there was no
real parallel with the situation after 1848, when bourgeois capitalism had entered on a fresh period of expansion. Capitalism had
received a mortal blow in the war of 1914–1918 ; the conflicts
between the capitalist Powers were increasing ; and the success
of the revolution was certain. Nevertheless the workers had
suffered a set-back and had been thrown on the defensive. Trotsky
concluded :

> The situation now at the time of the third congress of the
> Communist International is not the same as at the time of
> the first and second congresses. At that time we established the
> broad perspective and traced the general line and said : " On
> this line, under this sign, shalt thou win the proletariat and
> conquer in the world ". Is this still right ? Entirely. On this
> large scale it is still entirely right. Only we had not worked out
> the ups and downs of the line, and now we are aware of them.
> We are aware of them through our defeats and our disappoint-
> ments, and also through our sacrifices and through our mistaken
> actions, which have occurred in all countries — here in Russia
> in great quantity. Now for the first time we see and feel that
> we are not so immediately near to the goal, to the conquest of
> power, to the world revolution. At that time, in 1919, we said
> to ourselves : " It is a question of months ". Now we say :
> " It is perhaps a question of years ".[1]

At a later stage of the conference, Lenin registered his " final
conclusion " in the following terms :

> The development of the international revolution which we
> predicted makes progress. But this progress is not in the
> straight line which we expected. It is plain at a glance that
> after the conclusion of the peace, however bad that was, we did
> not succeed in provoking a revolution in the other capital-
> ist countries, though the revolutionary symptoms were, as we
> know, significant and abundant. . . . What is essential now
> is a fundamental preparation of the revolution and a pro-
> found study of its concrete development in the principal capitalist
> countries.[2]

And the resolution did its best to extract a grain of encouragement
from a drab diagnosis :

---

[1] *Ibid.* pp. 89-90.   [2] *Ibid.* p. 749 ; Lenin, *Sochineniya*, xxvi, 452.

Only petty bourgeois stupidity can read a collapse of the programme of the Communist International in the fact that the European proletariat has not overthrown the bourgeoisie during the war or immediately after its end. The setting of the course of the Communist International for the proletarian revolution does not mean the assignment of the revolution to fixed dates in the calendar, or the obligation to carry out the revolution mechanically in a certain time. Revolution always was, and still is, a struggle of living forms on given historical foundations. The destruction of capitalist equilibrium on a world scale by the war creates favourable conditions for the fundamental force of the revolution — the proletariat. All the efforts of the Communist International were and are directed to utilize this position to the full.[1]

The fiasco of the " March action " in Germany had played a prominent part in the new diagnosis, and the discussion of it occupied a large share of the time and attention of the congress. It dominated both the debate on the report of IKKI and the debate on " The Tactics of the Communist International ". The principal speakers from the Russian delegation were Radek and Trotsky ;[2] but nearly all the German delegates (as well as several from other countries) spoke, and contributed to the atmosphere of recrimination which commonly attends a political retreat. The debate presented two delicate issues for the leaders of Comintern. In the first place, it was necessary to dissociate IKKI from any share of blame for the March action. This proved relatively easy ; whatever the German delegates as a whole may have felt, only Klara Zetkin referred darkly to the responsibility of " representatives of the executive ".[3] Secondly, it was necessary, without condoning Levi's insubordination, to condemn the policy of the " revolutionary offensive ", whose sponsors had driven him out.

---

[1] *Kommunisticheskii Internatsional v Dokumentakh* (1933), p. 178 ; according to a later statement by Varga (*Protokoll : Fünfter Kongress der Kommunistischen Internationale* (n.d.), i, 108), the original draft of this resolution was more pessimistic in tone, but was modified in response to protests from " Leftists " in the German and Hungarian delegations.

[2] Zinoviev in his general report touched briefly on the subject, leaving it to be dealt with in Radek's report on tactics ; this was evidently the result of a party decision, and suggests that Zinoviev was personally too much implicated to be a suitable spokesman. Bela Kun spoke only once on a point of order, on which he ranged himself with the " so-called Left " (*Protokoll des III. Kongresses der Kommunistischen Internationale* (Hamburg, 1921), pp. 650-651).

[3] See p. 336 above.

This proved more difficult; for while nobody — not even Klara Zetkin who had resigned with him from the central committee — defended Levi's subsequent behaviour, or denied the justice of his expulsion from the party, it was widely felt that the policy now advocated by the leaders of Comintern was indistinguishable from the policy formerly advocated by Levi in the KPD.[1] The resolution unanimously adopted by the congress betrayed a keen consciousness of these embarrassments. It began with the categorical statement that the March action had been " forced on the KPD by the attack of the government on the proletariat of central Germany ". This dismissed as irrelevant anything that may have passed between Bela Kun and the central committee before March 17. It then referred to a " whole series of mistakes " committed by the party, the most important being " that the defensive character of the struggle was not sufficiently emphasized and that the call for an offensive gave an opportunity to the unscrupulous enemies of the proletariat to denounce the KPD to the proletariat for incitement to a *putsch* ". The March action represented a " step forward " — a rather hollow-sounding compliment. But for the future the KPD would " listen attentively to facts and opinions pointing to the difficulty of an offensive, and carefully test the validity of arguments against an offensive " before committing itself to action.[2]

The retreat sounded by the third congress was no less disconcertingly obvious in what had previously been known as " the national and colonial question ", but now became more specifically " the eastern question ". The eastern peoples evoked little interest in the rising communist parties of central and western Europe ; to the British, and to some extent also to the French, parties they were frankly a source of embarrassment. It was therefore not surprising that, in spite of Lenin's efforts at the second congress,

[1] After the congress Lenin admitted that it had been " necessary to defend Levi so long as his mistakes could be explained as a reaction to a series of mistakes made by the Left communists, especially in March 1921 in Germany " (Lenin, *Sochineniya*, xxvii, 8) ; at the next congress of Comintern Ruth Fischer plausibly complained that " the third world congress took up no clear position on the views of Paul Levi, and was unable to undertake its criticism of the March action without arousing the impression that Paul Levi had been excluded solely on disciplinary grounds " (*Protokoll des Vierten Kongresses der Kommunistischen Internationale* (Hamburg, 1923), p. 80).

[2] *Kommunisticheskii Internatsional v Dokumentakh* (1933), p. 194.

Comintern policy in regard to them continued to display a certain element of artificiality and outspoken pragmatism. The purpose of the first congress of eastern peoples at Baku in September 1920 had been to organize a campaign against British imperialism rather than against imperialism in general; the episode with Enver Pasha had shown how real the distinction was — at any rate in Zinoviev's mind. Only nine months passed between the Baku congress and the third congress of Comintern. But during this interval the signing of the Anglo-Soviet trade agreement had made open propaganda against British imperialism inopportune; and the treaties with Persia and Turkey equally discouraged communist propaganda which might threaten or offend the Persian and Turkish Governments. Nowhere in the east had communism made any appreciable advance. Zinoviev's immense report on the work of IKKI during the year, which occupied some sixty pages in the printed record, contained no more than three pregnant sentences on the subject:

> In the Near East the council of propaganda created by the Baku congress is working. From the point of view of organization, however, much remains to be done. In the Far East the situation is similar.[1]

The questions which had been debated with such ardour in the previous year were relegated to a hurried session on the last afternoon of the congress, when successive speakers from Asiatic countries made brief speeches, limited to five minutes each, expounding their aspirations. Delegates of the three newly formed Transcaucasian republics congratulated themselves on having achieved their destiny, not without some side glances at the menace of Turkish imperialism; and Kemal was openly attacked by the Turkish delegate. Delegates of China, Korea and Japan devoted themselves in the main to a denunciation of Japanese imperialism. British imperialism, deposed from the conspicuous position which it occupied in 1920, was the theme only of the delegates from Persia and Turkestan. None of the recognized leaders of Comintern, and not one Russian delegate, contributed to

---

[1] *Protokoll des III. Kongresses der Kommunistischen Internationale* (Hamburg, 1921), p. 211; the single reference to " the countries of the Near and Far East " in the resolutions of the congress was equally curt and formal (*Kommunisticheskii Internatsional v Dokumentakh* (1933), p. 165).

the discussion. Only the Indian Roy, mindful of the vigour and amplitude of last year's debate, had the boldness to describe this perfunctory performance as " pure opportunism " and " more suitable for a congress of the Second International ", and to protest against the patent lack of interest displayed by the European and American delegates.[1] Revolution among the peoples of Asia, it seemed clear, had never been regarded by Comintern as an end in itself. The third congress damped down its ardour and placed it in leading-strings.

The change of front at the third congress manifestly demanded a change of tactics. Since the second congress, the policy of Comintern had been to split parties remorselessly wherever doctrinal or party discipline was at stake ; this was, indeed, the essence of the 21 conditions. Thus Rakosi, having triumphantly split the Italian party at Leghorn, had insistently demanded Levi's head in Berlin ; according to Zetkin, he declared that it was " not a mass party that was valuable to Comintern, but a small, pure party ", and that the German party had " become far too big ".[2] Even Lenin repeated at the third congress the favourite remark that the Bolsheviks were a tiny party at the time of the February revolution.[3] But by this time the tide was setting strongly in the other direction. The Halle congress had been a brilliant success because it had produced a doctrinal split in the USPD and at the same time brought into being a mass communist party. But this success had not been repeated elsewhere, and there was little prospect of its repetition. In France, the new communist party was weaker in numbers than its socialist predecessor ; in Italy, it was a mere rump. In Germany a fresh split in the leadership already weakened the party on the eve of the March action. If the second congress had seemed to exalt quality over quantity, this was because it assumed that, quality once assured, quantity would follow : once parties had been split against unfaithful reformist leaders, the masses would flock to the new and purified leadership. This expectation had not been fulfilled. The third congress for the first time sounded a note of anxiety. Even Zinoviev seemed now converted :

[1] *Protokoll des III. Kongresses der Kommunistischen Internationale* (Hamburg, 1921), p. 1018.
[2] *Ibid.* p. 289.   [3] Lenin, *Sochineniya*, xxvi, 439.

In no case [he cried dramatically] can we have another split in the ranks of the German Communist Party. I really do not know whether our party can bear another split.[1]

The British and American parties were warned that it was a " matter of life and death not to remain a sect ". The British party, in particular, was reproved for its ineffectiveness during the miners' strike, and pointedly told that to be a small party was nothing to be proud of.[2] " The first of the tasks of the English communist party ", ran the congress resolution on the subject, " is to become a mass party." [3] Only the KAPD still openly denounced mass communist parties as a " gigantic bluff ", useless for serious revolutionary action and only " good for command demonstrations in favour of Soviet Russia on Sundays and holidays ".[4] The congress resolution on tactics emphatically pro-claimed the new standpoint in terms which, while not theoretically new, marked a noteworthy change of emphasis since the second congress :

The winning of exclusive influence over the majority of the working class, the drawing of its most active section into the immediate struggle, is at the present moment the most important task of the Communist International. . . . From the first day of its foundation the Communist International made it clearly and unequivocally its task not to create small communist sects which would strive to establish their influence over the working masses only through agitation and propaganda, but to participate directly in the struggle of the working masses, to establish communist leadership in this struggle, and to create in the process of struggle large, revolutionary, communist mass parties.

It was now the " social-democratic and centre parties " which sought to split the proletariat :

The communist parties have become the bearers of a process of unification of the proletariat on the ground of the struggle for its interests ; and from the consciousness of this rôle they will draw new strength.[5]

[1] *Protokoll des III. Kongresses der Kommunistischen Internationale* (Hamburg, 1921), p. 628.
[2] *Ibid.* pp. 208, 624, 654-655.
[3] *Kommunisticheskii Internatsional v Dokumentakh* (1933), p. 184.
[4] *Protokoll des III. Kongresses der Kommunistischen Internationale* (Hamburg, 1921), p. 223.
[5] *Kommunisticheskii Internatsional v Dokumentakh* (1933), pp. 183, 188-189.

Theoretically, the shift from the policy of splitting to a policy of unification was an application of the principle enunciated by Lenin twenty years before on the foundation of *Iskra* : " before uniting, and in order to unite, we must first decisively and definitely draw a line of separation ".[1] In practice, since splitting had not led to unification, it represented a transition from the tactics of the offensive to those of defence, a temporary retreat into the world of compromises and expedients which also marked Soviet policy under NEP.

So long, however, as the drawing of the working masses into communist parties remained almost everywhere a remote ideal, less direct ways of exercising influence must also be tried. If the hope of immediate revolution was abandoned and the main function of communist parties in the meanwhile was to put up a stubborn defence against " the offensive of capital ", cooperation with other workers' parties was required. While rigidity of discipline within communist parties was unabated, toleration of non-communist or unorthodox parties was continued and extended. Not only were delegates of the KAPD once more admitted to the congress (though without voting rights) in face of the protests of the KPD,[2] but the Italian Socialist Party also sent delegates, notwithstanding the fact that, as a delegate of the Italian Communist Party complained, " it includes in its membership out-and-out social-patriots not much better than a Thomas or a Scheidemann ".[3] But such concessions within the framework of Comintern were not enough, and indeed proved valueless. The mass of the workers in the most important industrial countries were organized in parties which still refused to have anything to do with Comintern ; to reach them, and to cooperate with them in repelling the " offensive of capital ", more extensive compromises would be required. Radek, co-author with Levi six months earlier of the " open letter " of the KPD, proposing joint action with all German Left parties, including the SPD and the

---

[1] See Vol. 1, p. 7.
[2] A protest of Levi against the continued tolerance shown to the KAPD had been rejected by IKKI in January 1921 (*Kommunisticheskii Internatsional;* No. 16 (March 31, 1921), cols. 3791-3792) ; the KAPD was finally excluded from membership of Comintern in September 1921.
[3] *Protokoll des III. Kongresses der Kommunistischen Internationale* (Hamburg, 1921), p. 356.

USPD, now proclaimed the watchword : " First and foremost, to the masses, by all means ".[1] It was not a novel injunction. The second congress a year earlier had proclaimed the slogans " Penetrate the masses " and " A closer link with the masses ".[2] But now the watchword was hailed as the keynote of the congress. It was perhaps only Levi's disgrace, and the impossibility of embracing too eagerly a policy associated with his now discredited name, which prevented the policy of the united front being openly proclaimed at the third congress. This was to come six months later.

That the leaders of Comintern at the third congress sincerely desired to modify their tactics in such a way as to win the allegiance of the masses is beyond dispute. But they did not understand the conditions which would have been necessary to make this policy a success ; nor perhaps would they have been willing to accept those conditions. Any serious attempt to build up mass communist parties in western Europe and in the English-speaking world, and to use these parties as a spearhead to penetrate other Left parties, would have required a willingness at Comintern headquarters to relax the rigidities not only of doctrine, but of discipline, and to concede to national parties and their leaders a far wider discretion in the framing of policies and tactics suited to local conditions, which could never be well enough or promptly enough appreciated in Moscow. Yet, at a moment when the congress was recommending policies of mass appeal which called imperatively for greater decentralization of authority, it was also strengthening bonds of organization and discipline which inevitably made for greater centralization. A monster resolution of the third congress on " The Organizational Structure of Communist Parties, the Methods and Content of their Work ", accompanied by a short resolution on " The Organization of the Communist International ",[3] attempted to define in the utmost detail the

[1] *Protokoll des III. Kongresses der Kommunistischen Internationale* (Hamburg, 1921), p. 480.
[2] *Kommunisticheskii Internatsional v Dokumentakh* (1933), p. 95.
[3] The main resolution is in *ibid.* pp. 201-225 ; the shorter resolution must be sought in *Protokoll des III. Kongresses der Kommunistischen Internationale* (Hamburg, 1921), pp. 986-989, 1043.

functions and obligations of Comintern and of member parties. The main resolution insisted on the disciplined subordination to the central authority of national parties, of their members and of their press, and on the duty of all party members to engage in active party work. Party members must " in their public appearances *always conduct themselves as members of a fighting organization* ". Fresh emphasis was laid on the importance of underground work by the parties ; for it was this argument which was principally used, as it had been used by Lenin in the early days of the party struggle, to justify a disciplined centralization of authority.[1] National party committees were made responsible not only to the national party congresses, but also to IKKI — the principle of " dual subordination " familiar in Soviet organization ;[2] and in this potential conflict of allegiance the authority of the closely knit central organ disposing of ample financial resources was likely to prevail in the long run over the dispersed and intermittent authority of an annual national congress. This was the resolution which Lenin attacked at the fourth congress more than a year later as " almost entirely Russian, i.e. everything taken from Russian conditions " : it had in fact remained " a dead letter ", since foreigners could not be expected to understand it or carry it out.[3] Nevertheless, the resolution as a whole was adopted unanimously by the third congress, and contrasted oddly with the desire to create mass communist parties in the western world.

Details of organization were dealt with in the subsidiary resolution. The membership of IKKI was enlarged ; the Russian party still had five delegates, other large parties two delegates each, smaller parties one delegate. This accretion in size of the parent body naturally increased the importance of the inner bureau of seven, which received for the first time formal recognition. A keen dispute arose on the question whether IKKI could appoint any member of the party to the inner bureau, or whether it was

---

[1] The original draft of the passage on "illegal " party activities was somewhat watered down in the final text of the resolution in order, as the spokesmen of IKKI explained to the congress, " that not too much should come out for the bourgeois governments " (*Protokoll des III. Kongresses der Kommunistischen Internationale* (Hamburg, 1921), p. 1042) ; it is doubtful, however, whether this was the sole ground of the opposition to its original form.

[2] See Vol. 1, pp. 217-218.

[3] Lenin, *Sochineniya*, xxvii, 354-355.

limited in its choice to its own members. A substantial majority voted for the unrestricted right; and the authority of the ruling group in IKKI was still further strengthened.[1] By way of carrying out the policy of a more active approach to the masses, it was announced that the official journal of Comintern, *Kommunisticheskii Internatsional*, appearing as an irregular periodical in four languages, would henceforth become a regular monthly — this ambition was in fact not realized till 1925 — and that a more popular weekly under the title *Internationale Presse-Korrespondenz* (*Inprekorr* for short) would be issued in German, English and French.[2] In February 1922 an innovation was made in the form of an " enlarged " session of IKKI, to which additional delegates from important parties were invited. This experiment was repeated in June 1922, and two months later Zinoviev announced that these " enlarged " sessions, which approximated to " small congresses ", would be held twice a year.[3] The change had two perhaps unintended consequences. Full congresses of Comintern ceased to be annual events and, after 1922, were held at irregular intervals; and ordinary sessions of IKKI seem to have fallen into disuse. The two active organs of Comintern were now the presidium and the enlarged IKKI.

The implications of the retreat for the outlook of Comintern, and especially of its Russian leaders, stretched, however, far beyond questions of structure and organization. It threw into relief the dilemma inherent from the outset in the dual policy, which sought at one and the same time to stimulate and support the hostility of the workers of the world to all capitalist governments and to exploit the divisions and rivalries of capitalist governments among themselves. Both these factors — the hostility of the workers to capitalism and the internal divisions in the capitalist world — had contributed to the survival of the Soviet régime in the civil war. Soviet policy could not afford to neglect either

---

[1] *Protokoll des III. Kongresses der Kommunistischen Internationale* (Hamburg, 1921), p. 1044. The inner bureau as constituted by IKKI after the third congress consisted of Zinoviev, Bukharin, Gennari, Heckert, Radek, Bela Kun and Souvarine (*Kommunisticheskii Internatsional*, No. 18 (October 8, 1921), col. 4756); by a decision of IKKI of August 26, 1921, it was renamed the " presidium " (*ibid.* col. 4758).

[2] *Ibid.* No. 18 (October 8, 1921), cols. 4756-4757.

[3] *Ibid.* No. 22 (September 13, 1922), col. 5689.

factor. Yet the courses of action which they dictated might at critical moments prove difficult to reconcile with one another. The first appeared to require unconditional support of workers against capitalists, the second the backing of one capitalist Power against another. But any plan to influence the attitude or action of capitalist governments by means other than attempting to overthrow them stood in potential contradiction to Bolshevik doctrine. At the Halle congress Martov had put the dilemma briefly and cogently :

> The Bolsheviks who see in the maintenance of their power the one guarantee for the success of world revolution are thus impelled to set in motion all means, even the most equivocal and dubious, in order to maintain their power, without regard to the effect of those means on the development of the international revolution.[1]

Twice during the third congress of Comintern was the ugly suggestion heard — only to be brushed hastily aside — of a latent contradiction between the immediate interests of the RSFSR and those of Comintern or of some of its member parties. An article by Serrati in the Italian socialist press, quoted by Zinoviev as proof of his hostility to Comintern, expressed regret that Comintern should have to meet under the aegis of " a great revolutionary government " which was obliged to " conduct its own policy of defence and offence against international and national capitalism ". Serrati had continued :

> A policy which, by helping the Soviet republic, must incontestably also help the whole proletariat may at the same time perhaps not correspond to the tactical needs of a state which finds itself at the critical stage of its still latent revolution.[2]

---

[1] *USPD : Protokoll über die Verhandlungen des Ausserordentlichen Parteitags zu Halle* (n.d.), p. 213. A different, but cognate, point was made by a critic at a party meeting in December 1920 when Lenin had congratulated his hearers on the increasing mutual hostility between capitalist Powers as a welcome guarantee of Soviet security ; the critic asked whether this was not a policy of inciting capitalist Powers to wars in which the workers and peasants of those countries would fight and suffer (Lenin, *Sochineniya*, xxvi, 11).

[2] *Protokoll des III. Kongresses der Kommunistischen Internationale* (Hamburg, 1921), p. 159 ; Trotsky quoted a statement by Turati, the leader of the Right wing at the Leghorn congress, to the effect that " the Russians invented the Soviets and the Communist International for their own advantage, in their own national interest " (*ibid.* p. 397).

The KAPD, whose delegates at the congress played the rôle of a despised and licensed opposition, went further, demanding "the political and organizational separation of the Third International from the system of Russian state policy" and making a formal declaration on this point :

> We do not for a moment forget the difficulties into which Russian Soviet power has fallen owing to the postponement of world revolution. But we also see the danger that out of these difficulties there may arise an apparent or real contradiction between the interests of the revolutionary world proletariat and the momentary interests of Soviet Russia.[1]

No serious answer to these charges was attempted at the congress ; and the impression remained on many minds, as a friendly Dutch delegate admitted, " as if Russia was rather putting the brake on the revolutionary process ".[2]

The persistence of the criticism evidently demanded a refutation ; and it was Trotsky, at this time the most active defender of the official policy, who undertook it. The occasion was a congress of the Communist Youth International which immediately followed the Comintern congress ;[3] and it fell to Trotsky to defend before this critical and impatient forum what he frankly called " the strategy of temporary retreat " prescribed by Comintern. He noted that " some extremely clever comrades have advanced a hypothesis according to which the Russians are chiefly to blame for the present ' Rightist tendency ', because the Russians have now entered into trade relations with a western state and are greatly concerned lest these relations be disrupted by the European revolution " ; and he ironically added that some of " these theoreticians of historical development " had even " extended their loyalty to the spirit of Marx so far as to seek economic foundations for this Rightist tendency as well ". Having thus stated the opposition argument in its most extreme form, Trotsky had no great difficulty in formally demolishing it. It could be played off against the parallel and seemingly contradictory accusation that the Russian party had, for reasons of Russian national policy, " insisted on artificially provoking a revolution in Ger-

---

[1] *Protokoll des III. Kongresses der Kommunistischen Internationale* (Hamburg, 1921), p. 224.
[2] *Ibid.* p. 799.   [3] See p. 403 below.

many " on the occasion of the March action. It remained true, as it always had been, that the " victorious socialist dictatorship " could not be stabilized in Russia except through " the world revolution of the international proletariat ". But Russia could, for this very reason, be interested only in " the internal logical development " of revolution, not in artificially hastening or retarding it.[1] This logical answer could have been strengthened by an appeal to current realities. The cautious and self-restrained note injected into Comintern policy at the third congress, while no doubt corresponding to an immediate interest of Soviet Russia, which required a respite from incessant and unmitigated strife with a capitalist environment, was equally justified on the ground of the ultimate interest of world revolution, which could not, as events had proved, be achieved by the hasty shock tactics contemplated at the second congress. The interdependence of the cause of world revolution and the cause of the Soviet power could once more be plausibly demonstrated. The delay in world revolution which had led to the retreat in the policy of the Soviet Government called for a corresponding retreat in the policy of Comintern. When the moment came, both could resume their advance together. But an argument that was theoretically impregnable was bound to seem tainted with self-interest when presented by the Russian leaders of Comintern to foreign communist parties which were required to subordinate their own tactics to a general and uniform line prescribed in Moscow.

Meanwhile the task was taken in hand of giving substance to the new slogan " To the Masses ". The attempt to hold out the hand of temporary cooperation to other Left parties was not abandoned : indeed, it was to be intensified in the coming year. But a new and apparently more promising expedient was now brought into play in the form of specialized international agencies possessing a potential mass appeal ; some that already existed could be brought under the general authority of Comintern, others could be created under its aegis. The conception in both cases was the same. The masses, which could or would not immediately enter communist parties or embrace the full rigour of communist

[1] L. Trotsky, *Pyat' Let Kominterna* (n.d. [1925]), pp. 254-255.

doctrine and discipline, might be drawn into subsidiary organizations of sympathizers, and thus make their indirect contribution to the cause of the proletarian revolution.

The most ambitious and most important of the subsidiary organizations now established under the auspices of Comintern was the Red International of Trade Unions, commonly called Profintern.[1] Since the time of the second congress of Comintern, Mezhsovprof[2] had been busily laying the foundations of a new International. Its first task had been to woo national trade unions away from their allegiance to IFTU, and to prepare them for affiliation to the forthcoming Red International. For this purpose it set up " bureaux of propaganda " in different countries. In general these do not seem to have been very effective organs. The British bureau[3] was active enough to incur the animosity of the most powerful trade union leaders. Inevitably an organ founded for the single purpose of preaching affiliation to Moscow rather than to Amsterdam tended to attract to itself the rebellious or dissentient elements in the unions ; and this by itself provoked the charge of trying to split the movement. In Germany the charge of splitting the trade unions was levelled at Zinoviev and Lozovsky with great bitterness at the Halle congress. Such charges made, however, little impression in Moscow, where it was still assumed that the winning over of the whole movement was only a matter of time. On January 9, 1921, IKKI decided to convene on May 1 an international conference for the foundation of a Red International of Trade Unions. The invitation was to be addressed to all unions opposed to Amsterdam (just as the invitation to the founding congress of Comintern had been addressed to all parties and groups opposed to the Second International) ; and it was issued jointly in the name of IKKI and of Mezhsovprof.[4] The meeting was later postponed till July 1921 in order to synchronize it with the third congress of Comintern.

---

[1] In German, it was generally known as " Die Rote Gewerkschaftsinternationale " ; in English, as " The Red International of Labour Unions (RILU) ".

[2] See p. 207 above.

[3] It apparently enjoyed the support of the national committee of shop stewards ; its chairman was Tom Mann (J. T. Murphy, *New Horizons* (1941), pp. 167-168).

[4] *Kommunisticheskii Internatsional*, No. 16 (March 31, 1921), cols. 3734-3740, 3787.

Meanwhile Lozovsky took advantage of the fourth All-Russian Congress of Trade Unions in May 1921 to deliver a long harangue in support of the projected trade union International, in the course of which he claimed that unions representing 14,000,000 workers had adhered to Mezhsovprof; and the congress passed an appropriate resolution. The theme of both was the struggle for mastery in the international workers movement under the watchword " Moscow or Amsterdam ".[1] The occasion marked perhaps the high-water mark of confidence in the project of harnessing the trade union movement of the world round a new centre in Moscow. During the congress it was announced amid general enthusiasm that a delegate had presented a gold ring " for the striking English workers " (it was the moment of the first major post-war British coal strike); and the congress voted to send " the striking English coal-miners " £20,000 from the funds of the All-Russian Central Council of Trade Unions.[2] At the third congress of Comintern a month later, Zinoviev once more attacked IFTU as " the last barricade of the international bourgeoisie ", and announced the tasks of the forthcoming first congress of Profintern : " to organize better the struggle against the yellow Amsterdam International ", " to define in a practical way the relations between the revolutionary trade unions and parties in each country ", and " to formulate precisely the relation between the Red trade union council and the Communist International ".[3]

The founding congress of Profintern, which opened on July 3, 1921, mustered 380 delegates (of whom 336 had voting rights) from 41 countries, claiming to represent 17 million out of a total of 40 million trade unionists all over the world.[4] But the proceedings soon revealed the dilemma that those who were most eager to establish the new International were the syndicalists who wanted to break away altogether from the existing unions, and demanded that the new International should be wholly independent of Comintern, the political organ : these views were expressed at

---

[1] *Chetvertyi Vserossiiskii S"ezd Professional'nykh Soyuzov* (1921), i (Plenumy), 80-94, 110-114.

[2] *Ibid.* i, 27, 194.

[3] *Protokoll des III. Kongresses der Kommunistischen Internationale* (Hamburg, 1921), pp. 672-673, 676.

[4] *Kommunisticheskii Internatsional*, No. 18 (October 8, 1921), col. 4508 ; J. T. Murphy, *New Horizons* (1941), pp. 174-175.

the congress by Bill Haywood in the name of the IWW and by French and Spanish delegates. Speeches from Zinoviev and Lozovsky, however, brought the congress to order, and Profintern was duly constituted on the lines laid down by Mezhsovprof. Its declared function was " to oppose to the equivocal bourgeois programme of the yellow Amsterdam International . . . a clear revolutionary platform of action " : the first condition of membership was " the carrying out and realization in practice of the principles of the revolutionary struggle ". Generally speaking, the rule was asserted that trade unions must disaffiliate from IFTU before affiliating to Profintern. But in certain countries where the major trade union organizations remained faithful to IFTU, it was permissible for individual trade unions to affiliate to Profintern without severing their connexion with the old organization.[1] This licence seems to have been widely used ; and Lozovsky boasted two years later, doubtless with much exaggeration, that a third of the workers affiliated to IFTU were also affiliated to Profintern.[2]

The most controversial debates of the congress turned on the question of the relation of Profintern to Comintern, the syndicalists standing out strongly for trade-union independence of any political organ. But here, too, the weight of authority proved too strong. A resolution sponsored by Rosmer and Tom Mann provided for " the closest possible link with the Third International ", to be secured by interchange of delegates between the council of Profintern and IKKI and by joint sessions between the two organs, and for a " real and intimate revolutionary unity " between the Red trade unions and communist parties in all countries.[3] The statute

---

[1] *Resolutionen, Statuten, Manifeste und Aufrufe der Ersten Internationalen Kongresses der Roten Fach- und Industrie-Verbände* (Bremen, n.d. [1921]), pp. 64-65.

[2] *Dvenadtsatyi S"ezd Rossiiskoi Kommunisticheskoi Partii (Bol'shevikov)* (1923), p. 280

[3] *Resolutionen, Statuten, Manifeste und Aufrufe der Ersten Internationalen Kongresses der Roten Fach- und Industrie-Verbände* (Bremen, n.d. [1921]), pp. 17-18. As an example of the translation of this into practice, the British bureau of Profintern prescribed that it " shall be independent of the British Communist Party, but shall work in accord and cooperation therewith, translating into the national arena the same relations as exist between the CEC of the RILU and the CI " (*Constitution of the Red International of Labour Unions* (n.d.), pp. 12-13) ; this was to be achieved through a mutual exchange of representatives.

adopted by the congress provided for the setting up of a central council consisting of four Russian delegates, two from each other major country, and one from each minor country, and of an executive bureau of seven, of whom two were to be drawn from " the country where the Red International of Trade Unions has its seat ".[1] The congress had delegates from Japan, China, Korea and Indonesia, and adopted a resolution urging " the workers of the Near and Far East " to " enter the ranks of the Red International of Trade Unions ".[2] The distinction between the Amsterdam International, which was almost exclusively confined to European workers, and Profintern, which offered a warm welcome to the workers of the " colonial " countries, became important later.

Another organization whose fate illustrated the dilemma which confronted the third congress of choice between international mass support and centralized control from Moscow was the Communist Youth International. This organization was not, like Profintern, a direct emanation of Comintern, and had a history of its own. A socialist youth international had existed before 1914, and at a conference in Berne in April 1915 adopted a pacifist and anti-war attitude. Eleven numbers of its journal were published intermittently in Zürich between September 1915 and May 1918, among its contributors being Lenin, Zinoviev, Trotsky, Kollontai, Radek, Angelica Balabanov, Liebknecht and other adherents of the Zimmerwald movement.[3] After the war the organization moved to Germany, and at a congress in Berlin, in November 1919, through the energy of its president, Willi Münzenberg, reconstituted itself as the Communist Youth International.[4] Its programme asserted its independence as an organization, while

---

[1] *Resolutionen, Statuten, Manifeste und Aufrufe der Ersten Internationalen Kongresses der Roten Fach- und Industrie-Verbände* (Bremen, n.d. [1921]), p. 73.

[2] *Ibid.* pp. 79-80.

[3] The eleven numbers were later reprinted by Comintern (*Jugend-Internationale: Kampf- und Propaganda-Organ der Internationalen Verbindung Sozialistischer Jugendorganizationen* (Moscow, n.d.) ; the eleventh number had the special title *Brot, Frieden und Freiheit*).

[4] In Soviet Russia, the Communist League of Youth or Komsomol (its later official title was " All-Union Leninist Communist League of Youth " or VLKSM) had been founded in October 1918 ; Zinoviev in the name of IKKI had issued in May 1919 an appeal for the constitution of an international communist youth organization (*Kommunisticheskii Internatsional*, No. 2 (June 1919), col. 241).

conforming its political activity to the programme of Comintern or of the respective national parties belonging to Comintern.[1] Münzenberg attended the second congress of Comintern, but failed to induce it to discuss the youth movement.[2] In spite of this rebuff, the Communist Youth International went on and prospered, claiming on its first birthday to represent 45 national youth organizations and 800,000 members;[3] and, when it convened its second congress to meet in Jena on April 7, 1921, IKKI suddenly awoke to the importance of this quasi-independent communist institution. The official journal of Comintern began by hailing the congress as an event of " great significance " and a " powerful demonstration of the communist movement ".[4] But on April 1, 1921, a letter was sent by IKKI to the secretariat of the Communist Youth International peremptorily instructing it to treat the forthcoming discussions at Jena as " not binding " and to transfer the congress to Moscow, where it would meet simultaneously with the third congress of Comintern in June.[5]

The executive bowed to the decision. Münzenberg received the honour of a seat on IKKI, and attended the third congress of Comintern in that capacity. The neglect shown by the second congress was not repeated. Tribute to the importance of the Communist Youth International was paid by Zinoviev in his general report, and half a session was devoted to a discussion of its affairs, in the course of which Münzenberg made an impas-

[1] The congress is described in Willi Münzenberg, *Die Dritte Front* (1930), pp. 293-302 ; the programme is *ibid.* pp. 375-380. This seems to be the best account of the early years of the Communist Youth International ; Russian accounts are purely propagandist. R. Schüller, *Geschichte der Kommunistischen Jugend-Internationale* (5 vols., 1931), has not been available. A monograph on the subject would be of interest. The documents of the first congress and an account of its proceedings appeared in *Kommunisticheskii Internatsional*, No. 9 (March 22, 1920), cols. 1411-1418, No. 11 (June 14, 1920), cols. 1895-1912.
[2] *Der Zweite Kongress der Kommunist. Internationale* (Hamburg, 1921), p. 640.
[3] W. Münzenberg, *Die Dritte Front* (1930), p. 331.
[4] *Kommunisticheskii Internatsional*, No. 16 (March 31, 1921), cols. 3943-3944.
[5] The letter is in *Sowjet*, May 15, 1921, pp. 49-50 : this was an independent Left journal of which Levi became editor on his expulsion from the KPD, and the publication of the letter was a calculated indiscretion. According to W. Münzenberg, *Die Dritte Front* (1930), pp. 343-344, the reason for the transfer of the congress to Moscow was fear of police interference following the March action ; but the text of the letter offers no such explanation.

sioned declaration of loyalty to the communist party, to Comintern and to Moscow ;[1] and the resolution of the congress on the status of the Communist Youth International was categorical on this point :

> Political influence and leadership must belong on an international scale only to the Communist International, in particular countries to the section of the Communist International in that country. The duty of the communist youth organization is to submit to this political leadership (programme, tactics, political directions) and to merge itself into the common revolutionary front. The Communist Youth International is part of the Communist International and as such is subject to all resolutions of the congress of the Communist International and of its executive committee.[2]

The second congress of the Communist Youth International assembled immediately after the congress of Comintern had adjourned. That resistance and criticism was experienced is suggested by the fact that Lenin intervened in person in order to reconcile divergent opinions,[3] and that Trotsky appeared at the congress to defend Comintern against the charge of subordinating the interests of world revolution to those of Soviet Russia.[4] But difficulties were overcome, compliance registered, and the headquarters of the Communist Youth International transferred to Moscow.[5] Subsequent congresses of the Communist Youth International were held in Moscow simultaneously with the congresses of Comintern. Once more, a step had been taken which favoured the centralized discipline of Comintern at the expense of that degree of independence which was necessary for the encouragement of mass movements. It may have been a coincidence

---

[1] *Protokoll des III. Kongresses der Kommunistischen Internationale* (Hamburg, 1921), pp. 220-221, 251-254, 887-905.

[2] *Kommunisticheskii Internatsional v Dokumentakh* (1933), pp. 256-259.

[3] W. Münzenberg, *Die Dritte Front* (1930), p. 346. According to *Bol'shaya Sovetskaya Entsiklopediya*, xxxiii (1938), 829, art. Kommunisticheskii Internatsional Molodezhi, the second congress was preceded by an " obstinate struggle ", and " the mistakes made by the first congress in the question of mutual relations with Comintern and communist parties were corrected ".

[4] See pp. 396-397 above.

[5] An account of the congress is in *Kommunisticheskii Internatsional*, No. 18 (October 8, 1921), cols. 4529-4532.

that Münzenberg was transferred after the congress to other work.[1] Both Profintern and the Communist Youth International were specifically communist organizations, and the drive to bring them within the all-embracing power of Comintern discipline proved irresistible. This demand had largely nullified the purpose which they had at first been intended to fulfil of providing a channel of approach to non-communist sympathisers. Some such approach was, however, necessary; and after the end of the third congress an attempt was made to effect it through a series of organizations loosely connected with the party by common aims, but free from the same commitments to revolutionary action and from the same stringent requirements of doctrine and discipline. The status of "fellow travellers", which had come to be recognized in the Soviet literary world after the introduction of NEP, was thus transferred to the field of international communism. The first impulse seems to have come, almost accidentally, from the emergency of the Russian famine. Under the leadership of the ingenious and ambitious Münzenberg, an International Workers' Aid Society (MRP) was founded in Berlin on September 12, 1921. Its initial function was to provide a Left-wing counter-weight to the generous relief supplies sent to Soviet Russia by ARA and other bourgeois agencies to mitigate the horrors of the famine. German workers undertook to work overtime and set aside their surplus production of machines or consumption goods for Soviet Russia; later, collections of money were made for Soviet workers and a loan was floated; and MRP began distributing popular literature and propaganda on behalf of Soviet Russia.[2] In a

[1] W. Münzenberg, *Die Dritte Front* (1930), p. 348. The spring of 1921 saw the creation of a Communist Women's International, which from April 1921 onwards published a few numbers of a monthly journal *Die Kommunistische Fraueninternationale*, held a conference simultaneously with the third congress of Comintern, and received the blessing of the congress (*Kommunisticheskii Internatsional v Dokumentakh* (1933), pp. 255-256); but this never seems to have achieved any vitality.

[2] Ruth Fischer gives a summary of the work of this organization in Germany in 1922: "27 municipalities gave important sums or sponsored children's homes in the Soviet Union. Tools and clothing valued at eight million marks were collected by young people and children. An issue of 'workers' bonds' raised two million marks. The organization had its own illustrated weekly, *Sichel und Hammer*, whose first edition was 130,000 copies. Russian films were shown and the proceeds went to Russia. A Russian violinist, Soermus, accompanied by a choral group that gave political recitations, toured the country" (*Stalin and German Communism* (Harvard, 1948), p. 220).

report to IKKI in March 1922 Münzenberg called MRP " the first practical attempt to set up the united front ". He claimed that up to the end of January 1922 a total of 200 million marks had been collected from workers or communist parties, mainly in Germany, Switzerland and Holland, and that 70,000 starving Russians had been cared for at the relief stations of MRP in Russia. Relief in the narrower sense was being supplemented by assistance in general economic reconstruction through the supply of machinery and tools and of foreign workers. " What we must today bring to the Russians is the intensive working capacity and form of organization of western European and American workers."[1] At a later period tractor stations and even Sovkhozy were operated under the control of MRP with foreign machines and foreign workers. The organization had the dual purpose, as a resolution of the fourth congress of Comintern clearly explained, of promoting sympathy for Soviet Russia among the workers and of achieving " real economic results ".[2] It continued to have its headquarters in Germany, but also enjoyed success in other European countries, including Great Britain, where it flourished for many years under the name of Workers' International Relief. In the United States, the " Friends of Soviet Russia " came into existence in the autumn of 1921 for the purpose of providing aid for the famine-stricken population. About the same time the foundation of the " Clarté " group in France by a number of prominent literary figures, including Anatole France, Romain Rolland and Henri Barbusse, served as a model for groups of intellectual fellow-travellers in other countries. Another creation of the period was the International Association for Aid to Revolutionaries, which was primarily designed to collect funds for victims of the " white terror ", and also received the blessing of the fourth congress of Comintern.[3]

In Great Britain a unique and promising experiment was attempted under the auspices of the CPGB. The unemployment

---

[1] *Die Taktik der Kommunistischen Internationale gegen die Offensive des Kapitals* (Hamburg, 1922), pp. 126-129.

[2] *Kommunisticheskii Internatsional v Dokumentakh* (1933), pp. 327-328 ; *Internationale Presse-Korrespondenz*, No. 95, June 6, 1923, was devoted to an account of the achievements of MRP in Soviet Russia.

[3] *Protokoll des Vierten Kongresses der Kommunistischen Internationale* (Hamburg, 1923), p. 837 ; in English it was commonly known as the " International Class War Prisoners' Aid " (ICWPA).

crisis of 1921 led to the formation of local committees, which combined to form a National Unemployed Workers' Movement (NUWM), the organizer and leading spirit being Wal Hannington, a prominent communist. On Armistice Day 1921, some 40,000 unemployed marched to the cenotaph in Whitehall carrying a wreath bearing the design of the hammer and sickle and the inscription :

> To the victims of capitalism who gave their lives on behalf of Rent, Interest and Profit ; from the survivors of the Peace who are suffering worse than death from the unholy trinity.[1]

The following year saw the birth within the trade unions of a " National Minority Movement " which performed among employed workers the same function of a communist-led and communist-inspired " ginger group " as was discharged among the unemployed by the NUWM.[2] These were only the first of several organizations through which the small British Communist Party sought, with a success which was soon nullified by political complications, to obtain a hold on the mass of the British workers.

These measures of cooperation and infiltration adopted in pursuance of the slogan of the third congress of Comintern " To the Masses " were sufficiently promising to call for a more precise definition of the new doctrine. The change of attitude was made explicit in December 1921, when IKKI issued a set of 25 theses on " The United Workers' Front ".[3] The theses purported to detect a movement to the Left, and growing confidence in the communists, among the masses of the workers, who were everywhere feeling " an unprecedented urge towards unity ". Thus the opportunity presented itself of " broader and fuller unity of practical action " : communist parties and Comintern as a whole were called on " *to support the slogan of a united workers' front* and take

[1] T. Bell, *The British Communist Party* (1937), p. 79 : the author adds that the party " was the main inspirer of the whole of this movement of the unemployed ".

[2] A delegate of the CPGB at the fourth congress of Comintern in November 1922 named both as " forms " which the movement took in Great Britain (*Protokoll des Vierten Kongresses der Kommunistischen Internationale* (Hamburg, 1923), p. 132).

[3] *Kommunisticheskii Internatsional v Dokumentakh* (1933), pp. 303-310, where they appear as an annex to the resolution of the fourth congress endorsing them ; they are also in *VKP(B) v Rezolyutsiyakh* (1941), i, 409-416.

the initiative in this question into their hands ". Certain qualifications had, however, to be recorded. Communist parties must preserve not only their complete independence of organization and doctrine, but also the right at all times " to express their opinions about the policy of all organizations of the working class without exception ". It was recalled that the Bolsheviks in their struggle against the Mensheviks — and such precedents were never far from Bolshevik minds — had once adopted the slogan " unity from below ". This left the way open for attacks on the leaders of other Labour and social-democratic parties : indeed it was noted that " the leaders of the Second, Two-and-a-half and Amsterdam Internationals have hitherto shown by their behaviour that, when it comes to *practical actions*, they *in fact* abandon their slogan of unity ". The proclamation of the " united workers' front " had in it, therefore, an equivocal element from the start. Other parties were to be summoned to join a united front. But the unity in question was confined to practical action in pursuit of defined common objectives. It did not mean a renunciation of those communist objectives which were not shared by non-communist parties, or of the attempt to split those parties against their leaders. So far as the leaders were concerned, Lenin's policy of supporting them " as the rope supports the man who is being hanged " still held good.

The pursuit of united front tactics led Comintern into a unique and unpromising experiment which was nothing less than an attempt to form a united front with the Second International. As long ago as April 1920 the British ILP had approached the Swiss Socialist Party on plans for the re-establishment of an all-inclusive International.[1] A year of consultations resulted not in the realization of this aim, but in the birth, at a conference held in Vienna in February 1921,[2] of yet another " International " equally boycotted by both the others. This was the International Working Union of Socialist Parties, popularly known as the " Vienna Union ", and dubbed by its enemies the " Two-and-a-half International " — the name which stuck. The

[1] See p. 184 above.
[2] A report of the proceedings is in *Independent Labour Party : Report of the 29th Annual Conference* (1921), pp. 33-47.

Two-and-a-half International was an attempt to resuscitate the
" Centre " group in the international movement, which had been
opposed to the war, but refused to accept the full implications
of national defeatism and social revolution, and which, as the
" Zimmerwald majority ", had been the target of Lenin's bitter
attacks.[1] The ending of the war had left it with no platform except
a well-meaning pacifism and an equally well-meaning desire to
find a half-way house between the two warring Internationals;
and it never acquired an independent policy or standing of its own.
But, when at the beginning of 1922 it proposed a general conference of all workers' organizations of the world, Comintern, then
in the first flush of its united front enthusiasm, accepted the
proposal with avidity. The enlarged session of IKKI in February
1922 welcomed the project on behalf of communist parties everywhere, suggested that the trade unions, whether affiliated to the
Amsterdam International or to Profintern, or non-affiliated syndicalist unions, should be invited to the conference, and emphatically declared that " unity of action of the working masses " could
be realized forthwith " in spite of differences of principle in
political opinions ".[2] The Second International was far more
cautious, and agreement could only be reached on a preliminary
meeting for discussion between delegates of the three Internationals.

On April 2, 1922, this strange gathering opened in the Reichstag building in Berlin. The delegation of the Second International was somewhat overweighted by a British group of six,
led by Ramsay MacDonald; next in prominence came the Belgian
group headed by Vandervelde. The delegation of the Two-and-a-
half International was led by the Austrians Adler and Bauer and
contained members from several countries, including Longuet
from France, two Russian Mensheviks, Martov and Abramovich,
and Wallhead of the British ILP.[3] The delegation of the Third

[1] See p. 564 above.
[2] *Kommunisticheskii Internatsional v Dokumentakh* (1933), p. 269.
[3] The ILP, though it had withdrawn from the Second International, was
still a constituent party of the British Labour Party; MacDonald, a member
of the ILP, could thus appear with a mandate from the Labour Party in the
Second International delegation, while the official ILP representative was a
member of the rival delegation. Radek did not fail to draw attention to this
puzzling intricacy of British organization (*The Second and Third Internationals
and the Vienna Union* (n.d.), p. 66).

International contained Bukharin and Radek from Soviet Russia, Klara Zetkin from Germany and several minor figures. Germany was the only country which had representatives in all three delegations. Serrati was also admitted to the conference as a delegate of the Italian Socialist Party which belonged to none of the three Internationals.

Few can have expected any substantial result from this ill-assorted gathering. What was achieved, little as it was, was due almost entirely to the eagerness of the Comintern delegation to record some agreement at almost any price. The proceedings opened with a cautiously worded statement by Klara Zetkin proposing a conference of representatives of all three Internationals and of all trade unions. The agenda was to include " assistance in the reconstruction of the Russian Soviet Republic " and " the treaty of Versailles and the reconstruction of the devastated regions ". Vandervelde replied with a highly provocative speech. After objecting to discussion of reparations or the Versailles treaty by the proposed conference, he raised three issues on which the Second International required guarantees before consenting to any conference : the forming of communist cells in workers' organizations, the overthrow of the Menshevik régime in Georgia by " Bolshevik imperialism " (Tsereteli, the Georgian Menshevik, was a member of the Second International delegation), and the impending trial of SR leaders in Moscow. Vandervelde, as a former socialist supporter of the war, and as a socialist minister in a bourgeois coalition government, was highly vulnerable; and Radek turned against him, as well as against Ramsay MacDonald, who intervened later in milder terms, some biting and effective sallies. But, rhetoric apart, " cell-building " (dignified by the invention of an ad hoc French word noyautage) was the real bone of contention. The old issue of temporary collaboration for defined purposes between sworn enemies was aired once again with no nearer approach to mutual understanding. Ramsay MacDonald complained that the Third International was trying " to use smooth words to bring us closer to it so that its knocks upon us may be all the more deadly ". Serrati, who rather surprisingly rallied to the defence of Comintern, subtly pointed out that the Second International had found no difficulty during the war in temporary collaboration with Clemenceau, and, as regards *noyautage*, thought that " a strong and healthy movement need not fear poison ". Radek's more direct approach dismissed the problem altogether :

> We have no confidence in the parties of the Second International ; we cannot feign this confidence. But in spite of this we say : " It is not a question whether we have confidence in one another ; the workers demand a common struggle, and we say : Let us begin it ! " [1]

In this uncompromising atmosphere nothing could have saved the gathering from shipwreck but Radek's unshakeable determination to avoid a final break. After Klara Zetkin's initial declaration, no other Comintern delegate took the floor except Radek, who spoke twice at length. But his public polemics were matched by extreme conciliatoriness behind the scenes. Radek may well have been the only man present who knew of the advanced state of the negotiations between the Soviet and German Governments which was to result, ten days after the Berlin meeting ended, in the Rapallo treaty, and was persistent in his demands for a joint denunciation of the Versailles treaty. But Vandervelde stubbornly defended the interest of his country in the treaty and in reparations ; and on this point, as on almost every other, Radek had to give way in order to stave off an imminent breakdown. Late on the evening of April 5, 1922, a joint resolution was achieved. It set up a joint organization committee of nine (three from each of the three Internationals) to prepare for " further conferences " and to bring about conversations between the " Amsterdam Trade Union International " and the " Red Trade Union International ". The conference noted a declaration made on behalf of Comintern that the SRs on trial in Moscow would be allowed to choose their own defenders ; that the trial would be public and representatives of all three Internationals allowed to attend it ; and that no death sentences would be inflicted. It authorized the organization committee to receive from the three executives " material . . . on the question of Georgia " and to report on it to a future conference. Finally, while agreeing in principle to the desirability of an early " general conference " of Left organizations, it noted the objection of the Second International to the summoning of such a conference

[1] *The Second and Third Internationals and the Vienna Union* (n.d.), pp. 47, 50, 53, 72.

" in April, that is to say, at the same time as the Genoa conference ". In the meanwhile, it called on the " workers of every country " to organize immediate demonstrations for certain specific ends :

For the eight-hour day ;
For the struggle against unemployment, which has increased immeasurably on account of the reparations policy of the capitalist Powers ;
For the united action of the proletariat against the capitalist offensive ;
For the Russian revolution, for starving Russia, for the resumption by all countries of political and economic relations with Russia ;
For the re-establishment of the proletarian united front in every country and in the International.

In a concluding statement on behalf of the delegates of Comintern, Radek declared that the joint resolution had been accepted by them " after much hesitation ", and that " their hesitation was due primarily to the fact that the Second International refused to adopt as the watchword for the workers' demonstrations the annulling of the Versailles treaty ".[1]

The acceptance by the Comintern delegation of this resolution provoked an immediate reaction in Moscow. On receiving the text Lenin published an article in *Pravda* of April 11, 1922, under the title *We Have Paid Too Dear*. The undertakings to admit representatives of all three Internationals to the trial of the SRs and to inflict no death sentences had been inadmissible ; besides, no concession had been obtained from the other side. The conclusion was, however, not that the tactics of the united front had failed, but simply that " the bourgeoisie in the person of its diplomats had once more proved cleverer than the representatives of the Communist International ". In order to support the proletariat against " the pressure of the capitalist offensive against it ", concluded Lenin, " we adopted the tactic of the united front and shall carry it through to the end ".[2] Ten days later, *Pravda* was still demanding united demonstrations in all countries by a " union of workers, communists, anarchists, social-democrats,

[1] *Ibid.* pp. 83-85, 88-89.   [2] Lenin, *Sochineniya*, xxvii, 277-280.

non-party workers, independents and Christian democrats against capital ".[1] On May 1, 1922, the customary May Day slogans issued by the Russian Communist Party for the first time made no mention of world revolution. But Lenin was right in the belief that Radek's concessions had availed nothing. Six weeks after the Berlin meeting the French, British and Belgian parties agreed to convene a conference to prepare the way for a reunion of the Second and the Two-and-a-half Internationals without the Third. When the Berlin organization committee met for the first time on May 23, 1922, the Comintern delegates announced their secession. This strange experiment in united front tactics was abandoned. Later in the year the rump of the USPD rejoined the SPD; and in the spring of 1923, as a natural corollary of this reunion, the Two-and-a-half International was peacefully absorbed into the Second.

The application of the united front policy to particular countries was subject not only to the weaknesses and inconsistencies inherent in the policy as such, but also to the embarrassments of fitting a professedly uniform policy to widely different national situations. The period after the third congress was one of general confusion and uncertainty in the national communist parties, which was an index of a decline in the prestige and influence of Comintern itself. What was uniform was the greater patience and tolerance shown by Comintern in handling the affairs of the national parties, the velvet glove donned by IKKI after the third congress contrasting with the bare iron hand of the previous period.

The " united workers' front " resolution, like so much else in Comintern policy, was directly inspired by German conditions and German precedents. United front tactics had first been successfully applied by Brandler in Saxony at the time of the Kapp *putsch*, and had been generalized in the open letter of January 1921. But this was a policy more likely to appeal to the Right than to the Left elements in the party. Levi's expulsion and the March action had crystallized the rift between Right and Left. The third congress of Comintern, while confirming Levi's expulsion, had in effect given its decision in favour of the Right :

[1] *Pravda*, April 22, 1922.

Ernst Meyer, the new leader, was an old member of the *Spartakus-bund* and in the Levi tradition.   The Left opposition in the KPD, which had begun to take shape at the third congress, found leaders in Maslow, a Berlin member of the central committee and by birth a Russian, and Ruth Fischer, his close associate, who had been one of Levi's keenest critics before his expulsion.[1]   Comintern was now above all anxious to forestall the danger of a further split. On the eve of the German party congress, which was to meet at Jena in August 1921, Lenin wrote a letter to the party in which he suggested that " Maslow and two or three of his sympathizers and collaborators " should be sent to Moscow " for a year or two " in order to be " digested " by the Russian party and kept out of the way of German mischief ; at all costs the " peace treaty " between the Right and Left wings of the KPD must be upheld and further splits avoided.[2]   But when the party failed to take the hint, the matter was dropped in Moscow.   The party congress at Jena in August 1921 marked, however, a strong movement towards the Right.   It not only endorsed the decisions of the third congress of Comintern, but issued a manifesto containing demands barely distinguishable from those of the SPD on such domestic questions as the confiscation of the property of the former ruling houses, the placing of reparations burdens on the rich, and the control of production by factory councils.   All this made up a radical, but not a revolutionary, programme.   The congress went still further along the lines laid down at the third congress of Comintern by openly advocating the policy of a " united workers' front ".[3] This represented a victory for the Right and, in particular, for Brandler ; and Ruth Fischer, in the name of a small Left minority, vainly attacked the Right as responsible for the failure of the

[1] See p. 332 above.
[2] Lenin, *Sochineniya*, xxvi, 490.   According to Ruth Fischer, *Stalin and German Communism* (Harvard, 1948), p. 182, Maslow and his friends had estab-lished contacts in Berlin with members of the Russian " workers' opposition " condemned at the tenth party congress in March 1921 (see Vol. 1, p. 200) ; if this was known, it must have confirmed the view taken of them in Moscow as troublemakers.
[3] *Bericht über die Verhandlungen des 2. Parteitags der Kommunistischen Partei Deutschlands* (1922), pp. 409-415.   After this congress the word " Vereinigte " added to the title of the KPD in December 1920 (see p. 223 above) was dropped ; a little later, continuous numbering of the congresses from December 1918 was resumed, so that the Jena congress became the seventh instead of the second.

March action and demanded a return to the " offensive ".[1] When, therefore, IKKI proclaimed the united front policy in December 1921, it was merely generalizing a decision already taken by the KPD for Germany; and the same resolution also endorsed the policy of a " united workers' government " for Germany (it was not mentioned for other countries).[2] The implications of these decisions slowly emerged. Cooperation with the SPD and with what was left of the USPD and even the formation of coalition governments might be practicable in local government and even in some of the German states, notably Saxony; but in the national politics of the Reich they were not a serious possibility. Behind this issue lay, however, the broader question of the relation of the KPD to the Reich itself and to the bourgeois governments which now normally ruled it. After the Jena congress the *Rote Fahne* proclaimed that " the workers have the right and the duty to undertake the defence of the republic against reaction " (a conspicuous reversal of the attitude taken up in the Kapp *putsch*), and that the Wirth government would have to decide " whether it wants to rule with the workers or against the workers ".[3] The conclusion that the workers, and the KPD speaking in their name, were not unconditionally hostile to a bourgeois German Government was a startling innovation on earlier doctrine.

Its full consequences were, however, revealed only with the signature of the Rapallo treaty in the following spring. This clearly took the KPD by surprise, though alliance with Soviet Russia had so long been a slogan accepted without question by all sections of the party that opposition to it would have been unthinkable. The embarrassment caused was indicated by the prolonged silence of the KPD on the subject and the colourless nature of its few pronouncements. The *Rote Fahne*, having hailed the Rapallo treaty two days after its signature as an outwitting of the French and British at Genoa, had no further comment for six weeks. On May 29, 1922, when the treaty was submitted to the Reichstag, Fröhlich, the spokesman of the KPD, gave it his support with the

[1] *Bericht über die Verhandlungen des 2. Parteitags der Kommunistischen Partei Deutschlands* (1922), p. 265.
[2] *Kommunisticheskii Internatsional v Dokumentakh* (1933), p. 305.
[3] *Die Rote Fahne*, August 31, 1921.

rather grudging observations that " the real content of this treaty
is nothing more than a record of facts which have already existed
for a long time " and that " what is included in this treaty of
Rapallo is up to the present no more than fine phrases ".[1] On the
next day the *Rote Fahne* went so far as to praise the treaty as " the
first independent act of foreign policy by the German bourgeoisie
since 1918 ". This scarcely hinted, however, at the real issue
involved. The notion that national communist parties could not
in all circumstances expect unqualified support from Moscow, and
that the short-term interests of the local party must sometimes be
sacrificed to the long-term advantage of the movement as a whole,
which was bound up with the defence and reinforcement of the
Soviet power, had already become familiar, especially in the Middle
East. But the principle of a European balance of power, consciously or unconsciously grafted on to Soviet policy by the
Rapallo treaty, meant that, among the most advanced communist
parties in the world, attitudes and policies would be different
according to whether the governments of their respective countries
were in hostile or friendly relations with the Soviet Government,
and would have to be modified from time to time to take account
of changes in those relations. These consequences took a long
time to develop fully, and were certainly not realized by those who
made the Rapallo treaty in the spring of 1922.[2]

Meanwhile the principal topic of controversy within the KPD
during the summer of 1922 was not the Rapallo treaty, but the
so-called " Rathenau campaign ". The assassination of Rathenau
on June 24, 1922, by members of a nationalist organization, following the similar murder of Erzberger in August 1921, seemed an
appropriate occasion for an application of united front tactics with
other Left parties under the banner of the defence of the republic
against reaction. But the SPD had no great eagerness for joint
action ; and the campaign fizzled out after a few rather ineffective
street demonstrations, leaving only a legacy of mutual recrimination

---

[1] *Verhandlungen des Reichstags*, ccclv (1922), 7738.
[2] According to Ruth Fischer, *Stalin and German Communism* (Harvard,
1948), p. 193, the KAPD " openly attacked this policy [i.e. Rapallo] as a Russian
capitulation to the German counter-revolution, and they found a ready response
among communist party members ". There is little or no contemporary
evidence of such response ; the party Left offered no open criticism of the
Rapallo policy.

between the Right and Left wings of the KPD, and bringing on the party the reproach of IKKI for having failed to understand that " a united front should never, never, never preclude the independence of our agitation " — yet another revelation of the ambiguity of this form of tactics.[1] About the same time an agreement signed by the KPD with the SPD and the trade unions undertaking to give support to the demands of the unions against the employers was extolled by the Right wing of the party as a means of reaching the masses and winning mass support, and attacked by the Left as a further deviation from the revolutionary path. Personal animosities increased the bitterness of the dissensions, which were carried at the end of the year to the fourth congress of Comintern in Moscow.[2]

The situation in the French party was more complex and the degree of independence greater. But, however severely the patience of Comintern might be tried, the new policy of avoiding a split was pursued at Moscow with stubborn determination. The shortcomings of the French party received little attention at the third congress itself, but were the subject of a long letter addressed by IKKI to the executive committee of the French party after the end of the congress. The weakness of the party's parliamentary work, its failure to infiltrate the trade unions, the lack of discipline shown by its press and the weakness of its central organization were all brought under fire ; and, above all, it was declared " unconditionally necessary " that communications between IKKI and the committee " should be conducted more regularly and at shorter intervals ".[3] The reproof was ill received. The inspiration of these attacks was traced to Souvarine, a member of the executive committee of the French party who had, however, resided in Moscow since the end of 1920 as French member of IKKI, and was thought to have been won over too easily to the view taken at headquarters : his own Russian origin added point

---

[1] The letter from IKKI was quoted by Zinoviev at the fourth congress (*Protokoll des Vierten Kongresses der Kommunistischen Internationale* (Hamburg, 1923), pp. 98-99) ; its correct date was presumably July (not June) 18, 1922.

[2] See pp. 452-454 below.

[3] *Zur Lage in der Kommunistischen Partei Frankreichs* (Hamburg, 1922), pp. 7-13. This collection of documents was published by IKKI after its session of June 1922 ; most of the documents appeared in *Kommunisticheskii International* and in the *Bulletin Communiste*, the organ of the French party, but the pamphlet has been traced only in its German edition.

and acrimony to this criticism.[1] On the eve of the French party congress, which met at Marseilles at the end of December 1921, a fresh letter of admonition and instruction, this time from Trotsky's mordant pen, arrived from IKKI. It conveyed the greetings of Comintern to " its French section ", but once more complained that " the French party has always stood too much outside the life of the International ", and protested against the indifference displayed to gross breaches of discipline by the party press.[2] This did not mollify the substantial body of opinion in the party which resented the interference of Moscow. The Marseilles congress passed off quietly enough so long as it debated abstract questions of doctrine. But, when it proceeded to the election of the executive committee, feeling ran high, and the unpopular Souvarine failed to obtain a place. This was rightly interpreted as a demonstration against IKKI and all its works. Four faithful members of the committee who had been re-elected resigned in protest ; and the congress ended in noise and confusion.[3] The situation was not improved when, after the ending of the congress, the executive committee received the IKKI resolution enjoining parties to adopt the policy of the united front. In France, where the communists now formed the largest political party of the Left, the call for a united front, whatever its utility elsewhere, made no sense ; and any hint of a united workers' government recalled the past scandal, always deeply resented by the French Left, of social-ists whose ambition had led them to ministerial posts in coalition governments. The new executive committee under the leadership of Frossard was therefore on popular ground when, not relishing the prospect of cooperation with those who had been defeated and expelled only a year earlier at Tours, it expressed the view that the new tactics were inapplicable to France. A special conference

[1] On December 8, 1921, IKKI explained to the French central committee that it had decided not to allow its correspondence with national parties to be dealt with by a national of the country concerned and had placed the French correspondence in the hands of Humbert-Droz, a Swiss, and begged the com-mittee to deal with the matter " independently of personal considerations " (*ibid.* pp. 13-15) ; but an independent party newspaper, the *Journal du Peuple*, continued to refer to the pronouncements of IKKI as " ukazes of Souvarine " (*ibid.* p. 21).   [2] *Ibid.* pp. 19-23.
[3] A full account of the congress derived from the reports in *Humanité*, December 26-31, 1921, is in G. Walter, *Histoire du Parti Communiste Français* (1948), pp. 65-75.

of party delegates was hastily summoned, and on January 22, 1922, endorsed the attitude of the committee by a handsome majority.[1] The situation was tense when the enlarged plenum of IKKI met in Moscow in February 1922. Four delegates appeared from the French party (though not Frossard himself) and recorded their votes against the united front. Trotsky in a reproachful speech complained that the old charge made against Comintern at the third congress of putting a brake on world revolution in order to " do business with the bourgeoisie of the west " was being " warmed up again in connexion with the united front ".[2] But neither side was prepared to carry the issue to an open break. The French delegates, having been outvoted (only the Italians[3] and Spaniards shared their objections), declared that they would accept the will of the majority ; and IKKI did not press for reprisals or sanctions. On March 4, 1922, a polite resolution of IKKI once more cautiously enumerated six principal shortcomings which were treated as " survivals of the past in certain groups of the party ". Note was taken of a declaration by the French delegation of its intention to restore discipline among its members and in the party press, and to reinstate the four who had resigned from the executive committee after the Marseilles congress ; and nothing was said of Souvarine.[4] By way of an example to the party

[1] G. Walter, *Histoire du Parti Communiste Français* (1948), pp. 82-83.

[2] L. Trotsky, *Die Fragen der Arbeiterbewegung in Frankreich und die Kommunistische Internationale* (Hamburg, 1922), p. 8. Lozovsky on the same occasion combated a French accusation that " the Russians . . . want to come to terms with the reformists in order to save the Soviet state " (*Die Taktik der Kommunistischen Internationale gegen die Offensive des Kapitals* (Hamburg, 1922), p. 85 ; the version of Trotsky's speech in this abbreviated record of the proceedings (pp. 78-83) does not contain the passage quoted above).

[3] The Italian Communist Party, encouraged by the French example, also rejected the united front policy at its congress in March 1922 : the practical result of this was that, up to the moment of Mussolini's *coup*, the Italian Communist Party continued, like the KPD on the outbreak of the Kapp *putsch*, to make no distinction between other Left or bourgeois parties and the Fascists.

[4] Trotsky's summing up and the resolution of IKKI are in *Die Taktik der Kommunistischen Internationale gegen die Offensive des Kapitals* (Hamburg, 1922), pp. 136-141 ; the resolution and the French declaration in *Zur Lage in der Kommunistischen Partei Frankreichs* (Hamburg, 1922), pp. 29-32. One unreconciled difference existed between the IKKI resolution and the party declaration : the former spoke of reinstatement of the four in the party leadership ; the latter merely undertook to propose to the next party congress to reinstate them.

press, Henri Fabre, the editor of the insubordinate *Journal du Peuple*, was expelled from the party.[1] But, apart from this single sanction, the decisions taken in Moscow remained without effect in France. The so-called party press remained as eclectic as ever in character and opinion ; and the united front policy was still vigorously attacked within the party on the heretical ground that it could not be regarded as binding until it had been endorsed by the next congress of Comintern. In May 1922 another anathema from IKKI descended on Paris,[2] and another session of the enlarged plenum was convened in Moscow in June. This time Frossard himself made the journey. Trotsky's introductory fulmination was fiercer, as was required by the lapse of time and by the presence in person of the chief culprit. But this only accentuated the element of comedy in the *dénouement* which did little more than repeat the admonitions, promises and mutual compliments of the February resolution.[3] The one new point which emerged in the Moscow discussions was the decision to hold a congress of the French party in October before the congress of Comintern in the following month.

The congress of the French Communist Party held in Paris in October 1922 provided an excellent illustration of the technique of Comintern in dealing with national parties and of the policy of conciliation and compromise pursued at this period. On September 13, in preparation for the congress, a letter of admonition and exhortation was sent by IKKI to the central committee of the French party.[4] Two delegates of Comintern, Humbert-Droz and Manuilsky, arrived in Paris well in advance of the congress to negotiate with the warring factions ; and at the congress itself delegates also appeared from the German and British Communist Parties to uphold the authority of the international body. The two representatives of Moscow, and especially the resourceful Manuilsky, abounded in projects of compromise between Right and Left factions, and were clearly more concerned to bring about an agreement than to produce a victory for the Left.

[1] *Ibid.* pp. 32-35.   [2] *Ibid.* pp. 35-43.
[3] *Kommunisticheskii Internatsional v Dokumentakh* (1933), pp. 284-289. There does not appear to be any official record of the proceedings of this session of IKKI ; Trotsky's speeches of June 8 and 10, 1922, are in *Kommunisticheskii Internatsional*, No. 21 (July 19, 1922), cols. 5405-5456.
[4] *Ibid.* No. 23 (November 4, 1922), cols. 6223-6246.

The final proposal made during the congress itself, when all else had failed, was for parity between Right and Left in all party organs with a casting vote for a delegate of IKKI in the event of dispute. This was not unnaturally accepted by the Left, but rejected by the Right in favour of a proposal to leave the composition of the party organs to a simple vote of the congress. The issue thus became one between the autonomy of the French party and the acceptance of arbitration by IKKI in its disputes. The decisive vote gave a narrow majority to the Right. Even now, however, the instructions of IKKI for conciliation at all costs held good. The Left received orders from Manuilsky to bow to the decision and to accept whatever posts the majority offered to it. But these orders showed a misunderstanding of the temper of the Right. Having won his victory by skilful handling of the congress, Frossard meant to exploit it to the full. All posts in all the party organs were filled by nominees of the Right. At the end of this congress the Left found itself excluded from everything but rank-and-file membership of the party. When the fourth congress of Comintern assembled in Moscow in November 1922, a breach between it and the French party seemed unavoidable and imminent. But the threat had come from the intransigence, not of IKKI, but of a bare majority of the party itself ; [1] and the issue was the desire of Comintern to adopt a less rigorous attitude than the national party approved.

In Great Britain the situation appeared peculiarly favourable for united front tactics. Nowhere in Europe had Marxism so signally failed to penetrate the labour movement ; nowhere was sympathy with Soviet Russia so keenly felt — a sympathy which had found expression not only in the nation-wide movement of protest against aid to the enemies of the régime, but in constant pressure from British trade unions for agreement with the Russian unions and with Profintern. The result was the coexistence of a tiny communist party and a vast army of sympathizers, whose support on concrete issues did not imply any inclination to embrace party doctrine or discipline. By cooperating with non-party

[1] The account of the Paris congress in G. Walter, *Histoire du Parti Communiste Français* (1948), pp. 101-111, overrates the standing and importance of Manuilsky at this time, which was mainly due to the accident that he was one of the few Bolsheviks speaking fluent French : in other respects it is excellent.

sympathizers the CPGB seemed able to exert an influence in British politics quite out of proportion to its insignificant numbers. Unfortunately other counsels had prevailed at its birth. Rejection of its demand for affiliation to the Labour Party had engendered great bitterness against the Labour leaders ; and when in March 1921 Ramsay MacDonald, whose pacifist record had kept him out of the House of Commons since 1918, stood at a by-election in Woolwich, the CPGB, full of the idea that MacDonald was the British Kautsky or the British Scheidemann, sent its best speakers into the constituency to attack him. There was no communist candidate. But the CPGB afterwards plausibly claimed that its campaign had cost MacDonald the seat by giving his Conservative opponent a small majority. At a further by-election in Caerphilly in August 1921 the CPGB for the first time put up its own candidate ; and though he came at the bottom of the poll the abuse of Labour leaders by communist speakers left an aftermath of still more intense animosity. When, therefore, the new line of conciliation was laid down by the third congress of Comintern in the summer of 1921 [1] and further defined by the united front resolution of IKKI in December, there was much lost ground to be made up, and many words to be eaten. Two successive numbers of the official journal of Comintern in the autumn of 1921 carried articles from the pen of Michael Borodin, the Russian-American communist who had become a worker in Comintern,[2] criticizing the CPGB for its failure to exercise any influence on the masses or in the trade unions.[3] During 1922 the CPGB, in an attempt at appeasement, withdrew all communist candidates from constituencies where Labour candidates had also been announced, even where the communist had been first in the field.[4] But this move had little effect ; the Labour Party at its annual conference

[1] In August 1921 Lenin, having heard that the South Wales Miners' Federation had voted by a majority in favour of joining Comintern, wrote a letter to Bell proposing the foundation of a workers' weekly in South Wales ; but he warned that it " should not at first be *too revolutionary* " and suggested that of three editors one should be a non-communist (Lenin, *Sochineniya*, xxvi, 482).   [2] See p. 169 above.

[3] *Kommunisticheskii Internatsional*, No. 18 (October 8, 1921), cols. 4661-4692 ; No. 19 (December 21, 1921), cols. 4943-4966.

[4] *Protokoll des Vierten Kongresses der Kommunistischen Internationale* (Hamburg, 1923), p. 131 ; *CPGB : Communist Policy in Great Britain* (1928), p. 115.

at Edinburgh in the summer of 1922 once more rejected by an overwhelming majority the communist request for affiliation. Meanwhile, in March 1922, a commission of three — Pollitt, a trade-unionist, Palme Dutt, a young party intellectual of Indian birth, and Harry Inkpin, brother of the secretary of the party — was appointed to report on the state of the party ; and Borodin was sent from Moscow to advise on the work of reorganization.[1] The problem was not, as in Germany, a party divided against itself, or, as in France, a party almost entirely united in opposition to the policy demanded by IKKI. The problem was a party, not divided by any serious dissensions and docile to directives from Moscow, but without serious influence in the political life of the country to which it belonged. The plan of reorganization evolved by the commission under Borodin's tutorship proposed to abolish the loose " federal " structure of the party constitution, and to re-organize it on what were now recognized as orthodox communist lines of centralization and strict discipline. At the end of August 1922 Borodin was arrested in Glasgow, sentenced to six months imprisonment for having entered the country illegally and deported.[2] The plan was carried at a party congress at Battersea in October 1922, not without further discussions and secessions.[3] But the forces that worked in Great Britain in favour of com-munism and in favour of Soviet Russia were to be found in organizations not specifically or professedly communist — the NUWM, the National Minority Movement in the trade unions, and even such quasi-philanthropic organizations as MRP,[4] rather than in the CPGB. It was through these organizations, if at all, that the tactics of the united front could be applied in Great Britain.

The adoption of united front tactics threw into relief the difficulty inherent in the conception of Comintern as an organiza-tion prescribing uniform policies and identical lines of action for communist parties all over the world. One of the corollaries of the united front was the increased importance attached to legal

[1] W. Gallacher, *The Rolling of the Thunder* (1947), pp. 38-39 : J. T. Murphy, *New Horizons* (1941), pp. 183-184.
[2] *The Times*, August 30, 1922.
[3] T. Bell, *The British Communist Party* (1937), pp. 83-84.
[4] See p. 404 above.

as opposed to underground activities : parties were to appear openly and woo the alliance of other parties for limited objectives, while at the same time proclaiming their own wider purposes. But such a policy could have no application in countries where communist parties were under a legal ban, and existed only as conspiratorial organizations ; and, during the seven years in which united front tactics were officially advocated, the number of these countries continually increased. In practice the only countries where serious attempts were made to apply the united front were Germany, Czechoslovakia and Great Britain. In the United States a highly anomalous situation arose. In May 1921 the scandal of rival communist parties was at last ended, and a single Communist Party of North America founded with the support of Comintern. But the founding congress was held in secret, and all the activities of the party were " completely underground ".[1] When, however, the united front decision was promulgated, it became necessary to found a new legal Workers' Party of America, of which members of the Communist Party became members ; this at first supplemented the activities of the illegal party and ultimately absorbed it, taking the name of the " Workers' (Communist) Party ".[2] But neither the legal nor the illegal party exercised any influence in American political life ; nor do they appear to have received any serious attention in Moscow, so that the rôle of the American party in the international communist movement remained unimportant as well as anomalous.

In an historical retrospect more than two years later Zinoviev enunciated with considerable frankness the motives which led to the adoption of united front tactics in the winter of 1921–1922 :

> The tactics of the united front were in reality at the beginning (i.e. in 1921–1922) an expression of our consciousness, first, that we have not yet a majority in the working class, secondly, that social democracy is still very strong, thirdly, that we occupy

---

[1] The report of an American delegate on this point is in *Die Taktik der Kommunistischen Internationale gegen die Offensive des Kapitals* (Hamburg, 1922), p. 23.

[2] The most satisfactory authority for the early history of American communism seems to be J. Oneal and G. A. Werner, *American Communism* (N.Y., 1947) ; but a special study would be required to unravel the conflicting and often highly tendentious evidence.

defensive positions and the enemy is attacking . . . , fourthly, that the decisive battles are still not yet on the immediate agenda. Hence we came to the slogan " To the Masses ", and to the tactics of the united front.[1]

This provided a reasonable defence of the tactics adopted by Comintern in terms of the prospects of the revolution. The retreat in Comintern could be justified by similar arguments to those used to justify NEP. The method of insisting on the rigorous and uncompromising pursuit by communist parties of immediate revolutionary objectives had proved disastrous in the same way as Soviet policies of " war communism " had proved disastrous. The argument in support of the united front tactics of Comintern was, indeed, independent of the current argument in support of NEP. As one of the British delegates to the congress records, " none of us drew any important conclusions concerning future policy from the introduction of NEP to which Lenin referred in his speech ".[2] But the two arguments were advanced simultaneously by the same people, and the cause ultimately responsible for both retreats was the same : the delay in the consummation of the European revolution. Hence the theoretical distinction between the two policies, and the two sets of arguments in support of them, became in practice increasingly difficult to maintain. Zinoviev established the equation in his speech to the enlarged session of IKKI in February 1922 :

> Had the Red Army of Soviet Russia in 1920 taken Warsaw, the tactics of the Communist International today would be other than they are. But that did not happen. The strategic set-back was followed by a political set-back for the whole workers' movement. The Russian proletarian party was compelled to make extensive concessions to the peasantry, and in part also to the bourgeoisie. That slowed down the tempo of the proletarian revolution, but the reverse is also true : the set-back which the proletarians of the western European countries suffered from 1919 to 1921 influenced the policy of the first proletarian state, and slowed down the tempo in Russia. It is therefore a double-sided process.[3]

[1] Protokoll : Fünfter Kongress der Kommunistischen Interhationale (n.d.), i, 77.
[2] J. T. Murphy, New Horizons (1941), p. 175.
[3] Die Taktik der Kommunistischen Internationale gegen die Offensive des Kapitals (Hamburg, 1922), p. 30.

From this time it became fashionable to refer to the united front tactics of Comintern as the counterpart of NEP ; and among foreign communist parties, which were directly concerned only with the first of the two policies, the impression that the actions of Comintern were being moulded in a pattern partly or mainly determined by the needs of the Russian Soviet republic received fresh confirmation. So long as the triumph of world revolution seemed imminent, the issue did not arise. But, once the retreat had set in, and compromise and manœuvre were the order of the day, the argument rolled on unceasingly and inconclusively between those who made a clear distinction between the aims and interests of Comintern and the aims and interests of Soviet Russia and those who regarded such a distinction as not merely invalid but inconceivable.

CHAPTER 31

CONSOLIDATION IN EUROPE

THE Genoa conference and the Rapallo treaty taken together gave Soviet Russia for the first time an assured status as a European Power. After the invitation to Genoa, the western Powers might quarrel with her, but could no longer ignore her. After Rapallo, she was the equal partner of another Great Power — another Power which had also been in temporary eclipse and also regarded the treaty as a way of escape from isolation and contempt. Broader opportunities of manœuvre entered into Soviet diplomacy. Hitherto the main choice open to the Soviet Government had been whether to pursue a policy of temporary appeasement of capitalist governments through diplomatic procedures or whether to seek to undermine and overthrow them through revolutionary propaganda. What was new in 1922 was the ability, within the limits of the first policy, to woo either one or the other of two capitalist groups which divided Europe between them — an option which the Soviet Government had tried in vain to exercise in 1918 in the days of its extreme weakness. The second half of 1922 was, in domestic policy, the culmination of the first period of NEP. The famine of 1921 had been outlived; the harvest of 1922 was excellent; and the stimulus administered by NEP was making itself felt throughout the economy. In these conditions it was natural that the compromise with capitalism should find expression in foreign, as well as in domestic, affairs. It was a time of consolidation and no fresh adventures. Another factor which contributed to this mood was the illness of Lenin, who succumbed to his first stroke at the moment of the ending of the Genoa conference and was totally incapacitated for four months. Few people knew the gravity of his condition, or suspected that his active life was virtually over (he was only in his fifty-second year). But what was thought of as the temporary removal from the scene of one who had so long had the last word on all major issues of policy encouraged an inclination to follow the steady and safe path which seemed to have been marked out in the spring of 1922, and to avoid radical decisions. The remainder of the year was a less adventurous period than any that Soviet Russia had yet known in her foreign relations. As a result of the Genoa conference, Soviet relations with the western Powers received something of a set-back. The obstruction of France and Belgium, now for the first time openly encouraged by the United States, had prevailed over the conciliatory intentions of the British Prime Minister, whose position in his own country had been correspondingly weakened. In France, Poincaré's uncompromising policy was in the ascendant. In Great Britain, the anti-Soviet wing of the coalition had regained its influence. On the Soviet side, the treaty of Rapallo made possible a more independent attitude towards the western Powers. To obtain capital from the west was still a major interest of the Soviet Government. Machinery was tightened up by creating a " chief concessions committee " attached to STO to centralize all decisions about concessions.[1] Two concessions were granted to American groups in the spring of 1922 — one for the Alapaev asbestos mines in the Urals and one for the Kemerov coal-mines in the Kuznetsk basin ; and Soviet-British and Soviet-Dutch mixed companies — Rusangloles and Rusgollandles — were formed to exploit timber concessions.[2] But capital was perhaps no longer so pressing and absolute a need as it had seemed in 1920 and 1921 ; and this allowed a greater freedom of bargaining. The summer of 1922 was thus a period of uncertainty. The process of *rapprochement* with Great Britain had come to a standstill ; would it be resumed, or would a recession set in ? The question was bound up in part with the position of Lloyd George in British politics. If he recovered his shaken power and prestige, the policy of *rapprochement* might be resumed ; if he fell, a deterioration in Anglo-Soviet relations could hardly be avoided.[3] The most

---

[1] *Sobranie Uzakonenii, 1922*, No. 28, art. 320 ; a year later the committee was transferred from STO to Sovnarkom (*ibid. 1923*, No. 20, art. 246).

[2] *Pyat' Let Vlasti Sovetov* (1922), p. 326 ; *Dvenadtsatyi S"ezd Rossiiskoi Kommunisticheskoi Partii (Bol'shevikov)* (1923), p. 353.

[3] Joffe, in reporting to VTsIK on the Genoa conference on May 19, 1922, explained that, if Lloyd George fell as a result of its failure, Great Britain

important landmark in these relations during the summer of 1922 was the Hague conference.

The Hague conference had been proposed and accepted at Genoa simply as a face-saving device and in order to gain time. No essential change had occurred when it met on June 26, 1922, and there was no better prospect of agreement than when the delegates separated at Genoa six weeks earlier. The situation had indeed worsened to the extent that the delegations at The Hague were led by secondary political figures. Litvinov, supported by Krasin and Krestinsky, took the place of Chicherin; the principal British delegate was Lloyd Graeme, head of the Department of Overseas Trade, whose affiliations were with big business and the Conservative Party. The conference abandoned any serious attempt to reach a result when the non-Russian delegations decided to form a separate commission of their own, with three sub-commissions to deal respectively with private property, debts and credits. Litvinov purported to make two advances on the attitude of the Soviet delegation at Genoa. He was prepared to concede the principle of compensation for nationalized property, provided always that credits were forthcoming; and he was prepared to admit that these credits might be forthcoming, not from governments, but from industrialists or financiers, provided that they were guaranteed by the governments. But the proviso seemed in each case to deprive the supposed concession of any real substance. The question of nationalized properties once more occupied the centre of the stage with the French and Belgian delegations again categorically demanding unconditional restitution or compensation, the British and Italian delegations toying with a lavish Soviet offer of concessions. Litvinov laid before the conference a long list of items available for concessions to foreign capitalists.[1] A comparison with the list attached to the original concessions decree of November 23, 1920,[2] revealed significant changes of outlook. Concessions were now no longer exclusively or mainly designed

---

would adopt a less favourable attitude to Soviet Russia, and would carry the weaker European countries with her (*III Sessiya Vserossiiskogo Tsentral'nogo Ispolnitel'nogo Komiteta IX Sozyva*, No. 5 (May 19, 1922), p. 14).

[1] *Gaagskaya Konferentsiya: Polnyi Stenograficheskii Otchet* (1922), pp. 218-248; the list as printed in this volume carries the note: " This document retains, of course, only an historical interest ".

[2] See p. 283 above.

for the development of hitherto unused natural resources. In addition to timber and mining concessions, concessions were offered for large numbers of existing factories and installations in the sugar, oil and electrical industries. The list included a large number of properties formerly in foreign ownership ; this followed the policy, inaugurated with the Urquhart project, of using the offer of concessions as a means of compensating former foreign owners and creditors.[1]

The battle for Russian oil was once more fought out behind the scenes. Here the attempt of the British-Dutch group to secure a concession for itself sustained a final and decisive defeat. The group associated itself with American, French and Belgian oil interests in a decision to refuse any offer short of full restitution, and in the meanwhile to institute a boycott of Soviet oil in all markets controlled by them.[2]   It may have been this defeat which finally inspired the British delegation to abandon its insistence on the concessions policy, and to accept in the concluding resolution of the conference the Franco-Belgian thesis of unconditional restitution, coupled with a recommendation to governments not to support their nationals in acquiring nationalized properties in Soviet Russia other than those which they themselves had owned. The resolution also laid down that no decision in regard to foreign property in Soviet Russia should be taken except jointly with governments not represented at the conference.[3]   The Belgian delegate who introduced the resolution pointedly added that he was authorized to state that it had the approval of the United States Government. The hidden American hand, which had appeared discreetly in the last stages of the Genoa conference, thus emerged openly at The Hague to defeat a policy of accommodation with the Soviet Government on a basis of concessions. No

---

[1] An interesting innovation among the conditions announced for concessions was that *concessionnaires* would be required to engage a certain proportion of Russian workers and employees in the enterprises under concession (*Gaagskaya Konferentsiya : Polnyi Stenograficheskii Otchet* (1922), p. 39) ; under NEP Soviet Russia had become a country with surplus labour and an unemployment problem (see Vol. 2, pp. 321-323).

[2] The agreement to boycott Soviet oil was reached at a meeting of oil companies in Paris on September 19, 1922 ; the text of the agreement is in L. Fischer, *Oil Imperialism* (n.d. [1927]), pp. 94-95.

[3] *Papers Relating to the Hague Conference, June–July 1922*, Cmd. 1724 (1922), p. 18.

attention was paid to a last-minute attempt by Litvinov to save the conference by an offer of fresh proposals. It dispersed on July 20, 1922, on the note of complete rupture. Litvinov returned crestfallen to Moscow.[1]

The emergence at the Genoa and Hague conferences of an anxious American concern in oil seemed to betoken the beginning of a more active, though still muted, interest in Soviet affairs. In July 1922, Hoover, the American Secretary of Commerce, initiated a proposal to send a " technical mission " to Russia to study economic openings; and on August 1 Houghton, the American Ambassador in Berlin, discussed the project there with Chicherin and Krasin, both of whom gave it a personal welcome.[2] But more cautious counsels prevailed in Moscow. Chicherin's official reply, dated August 28, 1922, while expressing readiness to receive any American business men or groups " for the purpose of conducting negotiations relative to concessions, trade or other economic questions ", made it clear that " a committee of experts or enquiry " would be welcome only on a basis of reciprocity — whereupon the matter was allowed to drop.[3] In the summer of 1922, the American Government at length recognized the independence of Estonia, Latvia and Lithuania (as the western allies had done eighteen months earlier), and wound up the old Russian embassy in Washington.[4] But the expectation widely aroused that these steps were a prelude to some form of accommodation with the Soviet Government was not fulfilled. Soviet-American relations settled down to a long period of uneventful indifference.

The breakdown at The Hague convinced the Soviet Government that " the system of conferences has failed for the time being."[5] The long-expected downfall of Lloyd George, which finally came in October 1922, and Poincaré's continued ascendancy in France, were symptoms of a more chilly attitude on the part of the western Powers, and ruled out the likelihood of any important

[1] Litvinov's final proposals are in *Gaagskaya Konferentsiya: Polnyi Stenograficheskii Otchet* (1922), pp. 188-192 ; the disappointment of the Soviet delegation is reflected in the number of different explanations given for the failure (L. Fischer, *The Soviets in World Affairs* (1930), i, 368-369).

[2] *Foreign Relations of the United States, 1922*, ii (1938), 825-826, 829-830.

[3] *Ibid.* ii, 830.

[4] *Ibid.* ii, 869-876.

[5] Interview by Chicherin in *The Observer*, August 20, 1922, quoted in *Soviet Documents on Foreign Policy*, ed. J. Degras, i (1951), 328.

decisions affecting Soviet Russia in the near future. The interest of Soviet diplomacy shifted mainly to the Middle East and the Far East, where the Lausanne conference and the Joffe mission were important landmarks.[1] The uncertainties of Soviet policy after the breakdown at The Hague were reflected in the treatment of the Urquhart concession. Urquhart had been present both at Genoa and at The Hague, and seems to have expected that the failure to reach an agreed settlement would make the Soviet Government all the more anxious to make a success of its concessions policy in one well-advertised case. This calculation came near to justifying itself. Two German concerns — Krupps and the Berlin bank of Mendelssohn — now acquired an interest in Russo-Asiatic Consolidated;[2] and it was in these conditions that Urquhart at length signed an agreement with Krasin in Berlin on September 9, 1922. The terms of the agreement[3] showed how much the introduction and development of NEP had done to remove the main obstacles : under the new conditions of labour, soon to be embodied in a revised labour code,[4] the employer had full freedom to engage and dismiss labour, subject to normal legal provisions for the protection of the workers. A percentage of the production of the enterprise was assigned to the Soviet Government. The right of compensation for loss of ownership was not formally admitted ; but the Soviet Government was to make to the company under the agreement an " advance " of £150,000 in cash and a further 20 million rubles in state bonds. This was compensation in a thin disguise. Lenin treated it as such, and reverted to the principle that the right of foreign creditors to

[1] These will be discussed in Chapters 32 and 34 respectively.

[2] The precise nature and extent of the German interest, and the circumstances in which it was acquired, do not appear to have been divulged : a German commercial intelligence agency report is quoted by G. Gerschuni, *Die Konzessionspolitik Sowjetrusslands* (1927), p. 112. According to M. Philips Price, *Germany in Transition* (1923), p. 77, Stinnes tried unsuccessfully to acquire an interest in Russo-Asiatic Consolidated during his visit to London in November 1921 ; Radek in an article in *Pravda*, November 11, 1921, alluded to attempts to make " an Anglo-German trust to do business with Russia ". D'Abernon, *An Ambassador of Peace*, i (1929), 232, recorded that Stinnes's proposals in London for " future cooperation in Russia " had been unfavourably received.

[3] The agreement never appears to have been published, but its terms are summarized in G. Gerschuni, *Die Konzessionspolitik Sowjetrusslands* (1927), pp. 112-113, from a contemporary report issued by the Soviet trade delegation in Berlin.   [4] See Vol. 2, pp. 330-331.

compensation could be recognized only in return for fresh foreign credits. While the negotiations were still in progress, he had written that the concession should be approved " only on condition that a big loan is granted to us ".[1]

The agreement was well received abroad. The British Labour leader, Clynes, was reported to have written a letter to someone in Moscow expressing the hope that the agreement would be quickly ratified in order to improve the chances of the Labour Party at the impending general election.[2] In Moscow it had strong support, especially among those who wanted to carry NEP to its logical conclusion. The agreement with Urquhart had been signed during Lenin's first illness. The decision on ratification was almost the last major political decision of Lenin's life. Finding himself alone in the Politburo in his opposition to ratification, he is said to have hesitated and changed his mind three times before finally deciding to impose his veto, which was, as a matter of course, accepted by his colleagues.[3] The decision was announced in the Soviet press on October 7, 1922. The motive of the rejection appears to have been primarily political. While Lenin's initial impulse had been to make ratification dependent on a foreign loan, he now told foreign journalists that the decision not to ratify was due to Great Britain's unfriendly attitude in the Turkish question, and could be reversed if that attitude changed.[4] Krasin declared that " the recent attitude of the British Government towards Russia " had been responsible for the rejection of the agreement " in spite of all the significance it bore for the economic development of Russia ".[5] Litvinov, on the other hand, took a low view of the economic merits of the agreement and thought that it would never even have been signed " if the economic advantages only had been considered ". He

---

[1] *Leninskii Sbornik*, xxxv (1945), 223.

[2] *Protokoll des Vierten Kongresses der Kommunistischen Internationale* (Hamburg, 1923), p. 30.

[3] L. Fischer, *The Soviets in World Affairs* (1930), i, 435-436, 464 ; the information probably came from Chicherin who, though not a member of the Politburo, would have known the position there in an issue of this kind.

[4] Lenin, *Sochineniya*, xxvii, 314-315, 330.

[5] *Russian Information and Review*, November 4, 1922, p. 73 ; according to L. Krasin, *Leonid Krasin : His Life and Work* (n.d. [1929]), p. 204, Krasin tendered his resignation on the non-ratification of the agreement, but was told by Lenin that party members were not allowed to resign.

attributed the refusal of the Soviet Government to ratify the agreement to the change of political forces in Great Britain, where the " predominating influence " now belonged to those who " do not sympathize with Mr. Lloyd George's endeavours to establish normal relations with Russia ".[1]   Finally, Lenin, in his last public speech in November 1922, spoke as if the main motive of the concessions policy were political, its purpose being " to give the capitalists such advantages as would compel any government, however hostile it might be to us, to enter into bargains and relations with us ".[2]

These explanations did not tell the whole story.   The rejection of the Urquhart concession, while it may have had immediate and specific political motives, was none the less significant of the lack of success of the concessions policy as a whole.   That policy had originally been conceived in 1918 as part of what Lenin called " state capitalism ", i.e. the system by which private capitalists would operate under the overriding safeguard of state control. Such a system fitted in perfectly with NEP ; and to bring in foreign capital, in particular, seemed a vital element in any attempt to redress the international balance of payments.   The rejection of the Urquhart concession in the autumn of 1922 was a symptom of inability to achieve this result on any terms acceptable to Moscow.   At the fourth congress of Comintern in November 1922 Trotsky correctly remarked that hitherto it had been a case of " big discussions, but small concessions " ;[3] and a few months later, when Zinoviev at the twelfth party congress gave a would-be optimistic review of the situation, he could claim no more than eight mixed companies with a total capital of £300,000 and 17 million German marks, and 26 concession agreements involving a total capital of 30 million gold rubles.[4]   The figures, even if they represented performance and not merely projects, were trivial ; and it was significant that the foreign country which held the first place in the list both of mixed companies and of concessions was impoverished Germany.   The failure of the concessions

---

[1] *Russian Information and Review*, October 21, 1922, pp. 43-44.

[2] Lenin, *Sochineniya*, xxvii, 365.

[3] *Protokoll des Vierten Kongresses der Kommunistischen Internationale* (Hamburg, 1923), p. 283.

[4] *Dvenadtsatyi S"ezd Rossiiskoi Kommunisticheskoi Partii (Bol'shevikov)* (1923), pp. 19, 22.

policy which became apparent in the winter of 1922–1923 [1] was coincident with a failure to establish friendly political relations with the English-speaking countries; [2] for these alone had significant reserves of capital available for investment. This failure had two results. Economically, it threw Soviet Russia on her own resources and left her to grapple alone with the problems of NEP as she had grappled with those of war communism : in this sense, it was a prelude to " socialism in one country ". Politically, it was an incident in the deterioration of relations between Soviet Russia and the western countries which set in at Genoa and Rapallo; in this sense it reflected the new policy of manœuvre which consisted in playing off Germany against the major capitalist Powers.

The coolness of relations between Soviet Russia and the western Powers in the latter part of 1922, matched by the increasing warmth of her relations with Germany, was the first symptom of a process familiar throughout the next two decade oy which deterioration of relations with one of the two main blocs of capitalist Powers led to a corresponding improvement of relations with the other. The months that followed Rapallo were the honeymoon period of Soviet-German friendship. The assassination of Rathenau in June 1922 was an exhibition of anti-Semitism rather than of anti-Soviet proclivities. The advocates of an anti-Soviet orientation had been virtually eliminated, and German industrialists set eagerly to work to avail themselves of the opportunities of a broadening Soviet market. Soviet trade was now expanding rapidly : imports increased from 922·9 million rubles in 1921 to 1181·7 million in 1922 and exports from 88·5 million to 357·4

---

[1] G. Gerschuni, *Die Konzessionspolitik Sowjetrusslands* (1927), is a general review of the concessions policy down to the end of 1925 ; the author records the conclusion for that date that " the significance of concessions in the whole economy of Soviet Russia is at present trivial " (p. 124). While details are often lacking, the predominant share of Germany in such success as was achieved clearly emerges.

[2] A passage in an authoritative British work written at this time recorded the view that " in November 1922 Russia was still largely in the position of an outcast among the nations " (*History of the Peace Conference*, ed. H. V. Temperley, vi (1923), 334).

million.[1] Not only did Soviet trade increase, but the German share in it increased.   In 1921, the year of the Anglo-Soviet trade agreement, Soviet Russia had taken 29 per cent of her imports from Great Britain and only 25 per cent from Germany (which before 1914 had supplied almost half of all Russian imports) ; in 1922, 32·7 per cent of Soviet imports came from Germany and only 18·8 per cent from Great Britain.   The same year saw the high-water mark of interest among German firms in concessions in Soviet Russia.   At a meeting of the Reichstag foreign affairs committee on December 9, 1922, Maltzan reported that some 20 German firms had signed concession agreements with the Soviet authorities.[2]

Side by side with these economic arrangements, and in part under cover of them, the secret military understandings which had been reached even in advance of the Rapallo treaty were carried into effect.   That some measures of military cooperation were on foot was widely known or suspected.   In the Reichstag, though Wirth emphatically affirmed that " the Rapallo treaty contains no secret political or military agreement ", the social-democratic deputy Müller continued to refer to current rumours of an agreement.[3]   The British Ambassador was " formally and deliberately assured that the subject of military preparations had never been mentioned between the Germans and the Russians ", and, though he was aware of the existence of " a number of alleged documents . . . including conventions, contracts for the sale of arms by Germany to Russia, etc., etc.", he convinced himself that " most of them are forgeries ".[4]   On May 25, 1922, negotiations opened between Hasse and Krestinsky for the participation of Ruhr industrialists in these transactions ; some of the industrialists were also prepared to provide funds to finance them.   What was,

---

[1] Even this, however, brought up the turnover of foreign trade in 1922 to only 14 per cent of its pre-war figure (*Dvenadtsatyi S"ezd Rossiiskoi Kommunisticheskoi Partii (Bol'shevikov)* (1923), p. 25.

[2] *The Times*, December 11, 1922.

[3] *Verhandlungen des Reichstags*, ccclv (1922), 7676, 7681.

[4] D'Abernon, *An Ambassador of Peace* (1929), i, 303-304, 311-312.   It was no doubt on the strength of D'Abernon's reports (which are still unpublished) that Lloyd George told the House of Commons on May 25, 1922 : " I am not going to dwell upon the silly forgeries of military conventions which take no one in " ; he added, however, with specific reference to armaments that " you have every natural resource in one country and every technical skill in the other " (*House of Commons: 5th Series*, cliv, 1455-1456).

so far as is known, the first general agreement was signed in great secrecy in Berlin on July 29, 1922 : its text has not yet come to light.[1] The despatch of German flying officers to Russia for training seems to have begun before the establishment of the factories. As early as September 1922, Krasin noted on passing through Smolensk that the aerodrome there was " full of German aviators ".[2] Niedermayer became head of the Moscow office of Sondergruppe R, in charge of all German military training schools and personnel in Russia.[3] Discussions continued actively in Berlin during the rest of the year. A second meeting between Seeckt and Radek took place in Schleicher's apartment on December 19, 1922.[4]

The scope of the arrangements, as they were established in the latter part of 1922 and in the following year, is known in broad outline. A contract between the Soviet Government and Junkers provided for the manufacture of aircraft and aircraft engines in a factory at Fili, near Moscow :[5] here and elsewhere German flying schools were established for both German and Soviet personnel. Shells were manufactured under the management of German technicians from Krupps at Zlatoust in the Urals, in Tula, in the former Putilov works in Petrograd and in Schlüsselberg : part of the output of these works was destined for the Red Army, part exported to Germany for the Reichswehr. A tank factory was established in Kazan, apparently also by Krupps, with training facilities in tank warfare for Germans and Russians. A mixed German-Soviet company was formed under the name

[1] Hasse's unpublished diary quoted in *Journal of Modern History* (Chicago), xxi (1949), No. 1, pp. 31-32. According to a statement made in the Reichstag in December 1926, the agreement was not ratified by the Soviet Government till February 1923 (*Verhandlungen des Reichstags*, cccxci (1926), 8584) ; this date received indirect confirmation in the Soviet state trial of 1938, when Rozengolts in evidence stated that the alleged treasonable agreement between Trotsky and the Reichswehr had been put into effect in 1923 (*Report of Court Proceedings in the Case of the Anti-Soviet " Bloc of Rights and Trotskyites "* (Moscow, 1938), pp. 259-260, 265).

[2] L. Krasin, *Leonid Krasin : His Life and Work* (n.d. [1929]), p. 201.

[3] *Der Monat*, No. 2, November 1948, p. 49.

[4] F. von Rabenau, *Seeckt : Aus Seinen Leben, 1918-1936* (1940), p. 319.

[5] The project of manufacturing aircraft engines at Fili broke down, and engines were imported from Germany (information from Mr. Gustav Hilger). This was probably one of the cases of unsatisfactory performance by German contractors referred to by Tschunke (*Der Monat*, No. 2, November 1948, p. 49) ; the other was Stolzenberg's failure over poison gas.

Bersol to put into operation a poison-gas factory thirty miles from Samara, partly built during the war but never used. But continuous efforts from 1923 onwards to bring the factory into production failed owing to the deficiencies of the process introduced by the German firm, Stolzenberg of Hamburg; and the project was ultimately abandoned.[1] Of the plans outlined in Kopp's memorandum of April 1921 [2] only one dropped out altogether. The German Ministry of Marine found a more efficient way of building submarines than could have been managed in derelict Russian shipyards. It set up a bogus company at The Hague which placed orders for the construction of submarines in Holland, Sweden, Finland and Spain : these were built under the supervision of German naval engineers and apparently tested by skeleton German crews. Some of them appear to have been delivered or promised to Soviet Russia.[3]

The consolidation of Soviet-German relations achieved by the Rapallo treaty, of which Soviet-German economic and military collaboration were the two main aspects, was symbolized by the arrival in November 1922 of the first German Ambassador in Moscow for more than four years. The Rapallo treaty had provided for a full resumption of diplomatic relations, and Krestinsky had presented his credentials to Ebert as first Soviet Ambassador in Berlin since Joffe in August 1922. The corresponding appointment in Moscow was held up by difficulties over the choice of the candidate.[4] It eventually fell on Brockdorff-Rantzau, who had been Minister for Foreign Affairs from December 1918 to May 1919. He had at that time been a declared enemy not only of the German workers' and soldiers' councils, but of the

---

[1] The main information comes from Tschunke in *ibid.* p. 49, and from notes from the German military archives published in an article by G. W. F. Hallgarten in *Journal of Modern History* (Chicago), xxi (1949), No. 1, p. 30. The abortive attempts to produce poison gas are described in detail in V. N. Ipatieff, *The Life of a Chemist* (Stanford, 1946), pp. 373, 381-386 : this is the only Russian source for any of the enterprises.

[2] See p. 362 above.

[3] This information comes from a confidential volume printed by the Oberkommando der Kriegsmarine, *Der Kampf der Marine gegen Versailles, 1919-1935* (1935), pp. 26-28.

[4] According to W. von Blücher, *Deutschlands Weg nach Rapallo* (Wiesbaden, 1951), pp. 166-167, Hintze and Nadolny were also considered ; the former was unacceptable to the Left parties in the Reichstag, the latter, who was known as an opponent of Rapallo (*ibid.* pp. 163-164), to the Russians.

Russian Bolsheviks, whom he denounced in a speech in the Weimar National Assembly on February 14, 1919, specifically arguing that, so long as Germany was weak, she should remain neutral in all international issues and attempt no " policy of alliances ".[1] He headed the German delegation to Versailles and on May 7, 1919, made his famous speech of protest against the terms presented by the allies. He then resigned his office, conducted a campaign against acceptance of the Versailles terms and, on its failure, retired into private life.

When, three years later, Brockdorff-Rantzau was proposed for the appointment of German Ambassador in Moscow, his views had undergone remarkably little change since 1919. The proposal to send him to Moscow provoked a memorandum to the President and the Chancellor dated July 15, 1922, in which he set forth his position. " The grave disadvantage of the Rapallo treaty ", he wrote, " lies in the military fears bound up with it." A German alliance with Russia would excite English suspicions and drive England into the arms of France. " A German policy directed exclusively to the east would at the present moment be not only premature and dangerous, but without prospects and therefore a failure." Participation in a Soviet war against Poland would expose Germany to French reprisals and make Germany once more a battlefield. The memorandum ended with a warning " not now to tie ourselves militarily to the Russians ". It is not surprising that the man holding these views should have been regarded by German military circles, and notably by Seeckt himself, as an unsuitable occupant of the German embassy in Moscow at this juncture. Seeckt, who apparently did not receive a copy of Brockdorff-Rantzau's memorandum till September 9, 1922, wrote two days later a long counter-blast. Starting from the proposition that " Germany must conduct an active policy ", he vigorously defended the eastern orientation :

A German link with Russia is the first and hitherto almost the only accession of strength we have achieved since the conclusion of peace. That the beginning of this link lies in the economic field, is in the nature of the whole situation ; but the strength lies in the fact that this economic rapprochement

---

[1] Brockdorff-Rantzau, *Dokumente* (1920), pp. 55, 81-82.

prepares the *possibility* of a political and therefore also military link.

He cautiously defended the secret military arrangements, the purpose of which was " to help to build up an armaments industry in Russia which would be serviceable to us in case of need " ; and Russian wishes for further technical assistance " in respect of material and personnel " should be met. For the rest, " the existence of Poland is intolerable ", and any policy must reckon with the possibilities of war.[1] The further course of the controversy cannot be traced. Brockdorff-Rantzau's appointment was announced at the end of September ; he left Berlin a month later, and presented his credentials in Moscow on November 6, 1922. Seeckt's fears proved groundless. Nothing was known in Moscow of the new ambassador's views apart from his hostility to the western Powers ; and Chicherin is said to have greeted him as " the man of Versailles ".[2] A firm friendship sprang up between the two men based, like the friendship between their two countries, on common mistrust of the west. Brockdorff-Rantzau quickly became converted to the eastern orientation of German policy ; and, while personal animosities persisted between him and Seeckt, their views on the essentials of German policy became undistinguishable. During the next five years, in spite of intermittent alarms and excursions on both sides, collaboration with Germany remained the stabilizing factor in Soviet policy in Europe.

A symptom of growing strength and confidence in Soviet policy at this time was the attempt to establish a rôle of leadership among the smaller states of eastern Europe. On March 30, 1922,

[1] The memoranda of Brockdorff-Rantzau and Seeckt are published in full in *Der Monat*, No. 2, November 1948, pp. 43-47 ; extensive extracts from Seeckt's memorandum had already appeared in F. von Rabenau, *Seeckt: Aus Seinem Leben, 1918-1936* (1940), pp. 315-318.

[2] E. Stern-Rubarth, *Graf Brockdorff-Rantzau* (1929), p. 124. Kopp had expressed to Maltzan in the previous year Soviet preference for a professional diplomat of the Right as the future German Ambassador in Moscow. He is said to have demonstrated his point with a flexible ruler : the extremes could be made to meet, but the extreme Left could not be brought into contact with the moderate Left or the Centre (W. von Blücher, *Deutschlands Weg nach Rapallo* (Wiesbaden, 1951), p. 149). After Rapallo, Radek asked for a member of " the high nobility " to be sent to Moscow as German Ambassador (*Journal of Modern History* (Chicago), xxi (1949), No. 1, p. 32).

on the initiative of the Soviet Government, delegates of Estonia, Latvia, Poland and the RSFSR met at Riga, the Latvian capital, to decide on a common line of action at the Genoa conference to which all had been invited. Having agreed on certain general and uncontroversial principles of economic policy, the delegates turned to questions of peace and disarmament and, taking their cue from the proceedings of the League of Nations at Geneva, recorded their support of " the principle of limitation of armaments in all countries ".[1] The conference at Riga had no concrete results at Genoa or elsewhere. But it helped to set, as was intended, a precedent. On June 12, 1922, the Soviet Government, complaining that the Genoa conference had " devoted practically all its attention to defending the material interests of a comparatively insignificant group of persons ", and had neglected both " the economic crisis through which Europe is now passing " and " the danger of new wars ", addressed a note to the same Powers proposing a conference to discuss " a proportional reduction of their respective armaments ". This time the invitation was extended to Finland. Litvinov, through the Rumanian delegate at the Hague conference, also invited the Rumanian Government ; and at the last moment Lithuania was included. The first date proposed by the Soviet Government was September 5, 1922, which coincided, doubtless not without design, with that fixed for the Assembly of the League of Nations. After much argument, the conference finally met in Moscow on December 2, 1922. Of those invited only Rumania, having made her acceptance dependent on Soviet recognition of the annexation of Bessarabia, failed to send delegates.[2]

The conference was in itself totally unproductive. It mirrored the contemporary discussions on disarmament at Geneva. Litvinov, imitating the rôle of British delegates of the period, proposed a specific reduction in land forces. The Soviet Government undertook to reduce the Red Army in the course of the two following years to one-quarter of its existing strength (from 800,000 to 200,000), provided the neighbouring countries would do likewise ; and, since the Red Army was one, the RSFSR could speak on this

---

[1] *Conférence de Moscou pour la Limitation des Armements* (Moscow, 1923), p. 241.
[2] The preliminary correspondence was published *ibid.* pp. 5-32.

matter in the name of all the Soviet republics.[1] The Polish delegate led a covert opposition, which followed French tactics at Geneva. He questioned the relevance of the initial totals on which the proposed percentage reduction was based, and argued that, before armaments were reduced, confidence must be created by agreements on non-aggression and arbitration ; the Soviet delegate in his turn did not reject such agreements, provided disarmament was not side-tracked. The lesser delegations manœuvred with some embarrassment between the positions of the two chief performers. On December 12, 1922, Litvinov accepted the fact that none of the other delegates was prepared to accept the Soviet proposal, and wound up the conference.[2] Its result was to advertise once more the advanced position of the Soviet Government on issues of peace and disarmament, and to offer to Soviet Russia's smaller neighbours an alternative leadership which might help them to resist the sometimes excessive pretensions of Poland. The difference in atmosphere from the Helsingfors conference exactly a year earlier, when Soviet Russia had been still an absentee and the predominant influence of Poland uncontested,[3] was remarkable and significant. The emergence of Litvinov on this occasion (Chicherin was away at the Lausanne conference) was also a landmark. It was his first major attempt to win a position for Soviet Russia in European diplomacy by appealing to advanced bourgeois opinion in the western countries and by outbidding the governments of these countries at their own game. A fortnight after the close of the conference, the tenth All-Russian Congress of Soviets made yet another appeal " to all nations of the world " reaffirming its " will to peace and peaceful labour ". It reiterated the disarmament proposals rejected at the Genoa conference, and now once more frustrated " by the unwillingness of the neighbours of Russia to proceed to a real reduction of their armies ". To clinch the matter it announced that, in spite of these rebuffs, the strength of the Red Army would be reduced forthwith from 800,000 to 600,000.[4]

The fourth congress of Comintern in November 1922 — the last held in Lenin's lifetime — marked an important point in the

---

[1] *Ibid.* pp. 46-51, 64.   [2] *Ibid.* p. 233.   [3] See pp. 348-349 above.
[4] *S"ezdy Sovetov RSFSR v Postanovleniyakh* (1939), pp. 273-274.

transformation and consolidation of Soviet policy. It was the end of the dramatic period of the Communist International; what was to come after was a long and sometimes embarrassing epilogue. The main acts were symbolized by its first four congresses. The first in March 1919 brought the institution into being, and issued its prospectus. The second meeting in July 1920, while the Red Army was marching on Warsaw, coincided with the high tide of power and self-confidence in its leaders, the belief that Comintern was about to fulfil its function as the directing staff of a victorious world revolution; this congress was succeeded by the congress of eastern peoples at Baku in September and by the creation in western Europe of communist parties submissive to the discipline of the central organization. Then in March 1921 came NEP, followed immediately by the disastrous failure of a communist rising in Germany; and the third congress of Comintern in June-July 1921, though organized on a more grandiose scale than ever, sounded a note of compromise and consolidation. The fourth congress in November-December 1922 was driven still further along the road of retreat. During the past year the Soviet régime in Russia seemed to have made giant strides. The famine had been stayed; the revival of prosperity engendered by NEP was well under way; the Genoa conference, the treaty of Rapallo, and the invitation to participate in the projected treaty on the régime of the Straits had registered the return of Soviet Russia to the ranks of the European Powers; a few days before the congress met the last Japanese soldier had left Soviet territory at Vladivostok; the solemn merging of the Soviet republics into a grand Union of Soviet Socialist Republics was in active preparation. Only the affairs of Comintern had conspicuously failed to prosper. The world revolution, the European revolution, the German revolution still tarried, and seemed more remote than in 1921 — not to speak of the great days of 1920. This diagnosis, however, implied a startling reversal of positions. So long as it could be assumed — as it was assumed by all concerned down to the end of 1920 — that the Russian revolution was a first and comparatively minor chapter in a story of world revolution, the prestige and authority of the Communist International necessarily overtopped those of any national government, not excluding the Soviet Government itself, whose main function, in its own interests as well as in those of others, was to serve the revolutionary cause.   But when Soviet Russia, having, contrary to all expectation, beaten back all her enemies unaided, was driven by the continued delay in the spread of the revolution into the compromises and accommodations of NEP, the whole balance of authority and prestige between Comintern and the Soviet Government was radically altered.   Nothing remained for Comintern but to take refuge in the defensive until the time was once more ripe for an advance ; and this meant to fortify Soviet Russia as the one present mainstay and future hope of the proletarian revolution.   Revolutionary fire and enthusiasm had been quenched by successive failures.   The strengthening of the Soviet power became the keynote of the fourth congress.

The cautious note which had been heard in the undertones of the third congress now became the dominant.   Zinoviev's opening address was cast in a minor key :

> It goes without saying that the victory of the Communist International in the historical sense of the word is assured. Even if our fighting organization were to be swept from the earth by the fire of reaction, as happened to the Paris *communards* and the First International, the Communist International would be born again and finally lead the proletariat to victory.   But what we are now concerned with is the question whether the Communist International in its present form, whether our own generation of fighters, will succeed in fulfilling the historical mission which the Communist International has undertaken. . . . We may now say without exaggeration that the Communist International has survived its most difficult time, and is so strengthened that it need fear no attack from world reaction.[1]

The policy exemplified in the " March action " of the previous year was now utterly and uncompromisingly condemned :

> The Communist International is against any precipitate action and against unprepared risings which would be stifled in the blood of the workers and might shatter the most precious possession of the proletariat — the organized international communist party.[2]

[1] *Protokoll des Vierten Kongresses der Kommunistischen Internationale* (Hamburg, 1923), pp. 3-4.
[2] *Ibid.* p. 11.

And in his report on the work of IKKI he almost nonchalantly repeated the same diagnosis :

> You know that we have spoken very much about the need to make the Communist International an International of deed, an International of action, a centralized international world communist party and much else. In principle this is absolutely right and we must insist on it. But in order really to carry it out we need years and years. It is pretty easy to adopt a resolution, and in this resolution to say that we must carry out international actions.[1]

The congress devoted three sittings to a discussion of " The Offensive of Capital " — the increasing unemployment, the lowering of the living standard of the workers, the shift away from the Left in the parliaments and governments of bourgeois countries, and the Fascist revolution in Italy, which was three weeks old when the congress met, and was described as " the last card in the game of the bourgeoisie ".[2] Radek who was the the *rapporteur* on this subject was more specific in his pessimism than Zinoviev :

> The characteristic of the time in which we are living is that, *although the crisis of world capital has not yet been overcome, although the question of power is still the centre of all questions, the broadest masses of the proletariat have lost belief in their ability to conquer power in any foreseeable time.* They are driven back to the defensive. . . .
> If that is the situation, . . . if the great majority of the working class feels itself powerless, *then the conquest of power as an immediate task of the day is not on the agenda.*

And later, in reply to the vague optimism of some speakers, he added with renewed emphasis that " *the retreat of the proletariat has not yet come to a stop* ".[3] The congress offered little scope for Zinoviev's fiery oratory. It was the occasion of Lenin's last public appearance but one.[4] He delivered a single speech which opened with an apology for his illness, and was devoted mainly to

[1] *Protokoll des Vierten Kongresses der Kommunistischen Internationale* (Hamburg, 1923), p. 33.
[2] *Kommunisticheskii Internatsional v Dokumentakh* (1933), p. 297.
[3] *Protokoll des Vierten Kongresses der Kommunistischen Internationale* (Hamburg, 1923), pp. 317-318, 390.
[4] Lenin spoke at the congress on November 13 ; his last speech was made to the Moscow Soviet exactly a week later.

an exposition and defence of NEP. In revolutionary times it was often necessary to be prepared to retreat in order to advance ; and NEP had illustrated and justified this maxim. The moral was allowed to appear, though it was not very clearly drawn (this was the speech of a tired and sick man),[1] that a measure of retreat was equally necessary for Comintern, and would prove equally salutary. Then, after censuring last year's resolution on organization as too exclusively Russian,[2] Lenin stumbled on to his peroration :

> I think that the most important thing for us all, Russian and foreign comrades alike, is that after five years of the Russian revolution we must study. Only now have we secured the possibility to study. . . . I am convinced that we must say in this matter not only to our Russian but to our foreign comrades that the most important task in the period now beginning is to study. We are learning in a general sense. They must learn in a special sense in order really to achieve organization, structure, method and content of revolutionary work. If this is done, then I am convinced that the prospects of world revolution will be not only good, but excellent.[3]

It was an odd last injunction from the man who had founded Comintern as a great fighting organization only three and a half years ago.

The prevailing pessimism about the affairs of Comintern set the stage for a corresponding mood of confidence in the Soviet power and eulogy of its achievements. Soviet Russia had brilliantly served the cause of the proletarian revolution, had discharged her last obligation to it. Already at the third congress Radek had put the point with brutal frankness :

> If we are today the great Communist International, this is not because we, the International, have been good propagandists, but because *the Russian proletariat and the Russian Red Army with their blood and their hunger have been good propagandists, and because this struggle*, the Russian revolution, was the great clarion of the Communist International.[4]

[1] Zinoviev later recalled Lenin's exhaustion after delivering this speech : he " could scarcely stand ", and was " dripping with sweat " (*Kommunisticheskii Internatsional*, No. 1, 1924, col. 29).
[2] See p. 393 above.
[3] Lenin, *Sochineniya*, xxvii, 354-355.
[4] *Protokoll des III. Kongresses der Kommunistischen Internationale* (Hamburg, 1921), p. 480.

At the fourth congress the argument was carried a step further. Soviet Russia had nobly fulfilled her task; it was the workers of the world, through their failure to consummate the world revolution promptly, who had let Soviet Russia down. The compromise of NEP would never have been necessary, Klara Zetkin explained, in a fiery speech which followed immediately on Lenin's sober exposition, " if the proletariat of new Soviet states with the highest economic development . . . had been able in fraternal solidarity to broaden and reinforce the expansion of the narrow foundation on which Soviet Russia rested ". But this had not happened. No fraternal Soviet states had come into being; and the Russian revolution had been driven to " a *modus vivendi* with the peasantry, a *modus vivendi* with foreign and Russian capitalists ".[1] The congress gave whole-hearted expression to these sentiments in a resolution " On the Russian Revolution ". It opened in terms of adulation :

> The fourth congress of the Communist International expresses its profound gratitude to the creative force of Soviet Russia, and its boundless admiration of the strength which was able, not only to seize state power and establish the dictatorship of the proletariat in the revolutionary struggle, but to continue victoriously to defend the achievements of the revolution against all enemies at home and abroad.

But the practical point was reserved for the final paragraph :

> The fourth world congress reminds the proletarians of all countries that the proletarian revolution can never triumph within the limits of a single state, that it can triumph only on an international scale by merging itself in a world revolution. All the activity of Soviet Russia, her struggle for her own existence and for the achievements of the revolution, is a struggle for the liberation of the oppressed and exploited proletarians of the whole world from the chains of slavery. The Russian proletarians have fully discharged their duty to the world proletariat as the protagonists of revolution. The world proletariat must at length in its turn discharge its duty. In all countries the impoverished and enslaved workers must proclaim their moral, economic and political solidarity with Soviet Russia.[2]

---

[1] *Protokoll des Vierten Kongresses der Kommunistischen Internationale* (Hamburg, 1923), p. 247.
[2] *Kommunisticheskii Internatsional v Dokumentakh* (1933), pp. 325-326.

Some of the consequences of this injunction to the workers of the world were clear and unequivocal. The congress, having heard a report from Münzenberg on the achievements of MRP, passed without discussion a strongly worded resolution on the duty of workers of all countries " to accord to Soviet Russia world-wide, real and practical aid, including economic aid ". Workers were to press on their governments " the demand for the recognition of the Soviet Government and the establishment of favourable trading relations with Soviet Russia ". Further, " the maximum economic as well as political power of the world proletariat must be mobilized in support of Soviet Russia "; and funds must be collected in order to produce " machinery, raw materials and implements " which Soviet Russia so sorely needed for " the restoration of her economy ".[1] Other implications of the same injunction were less specifically stated. Only Bukharin, in the course of a highly theoretical speech on the programme of Comintern (the drafting of which was postponed to the next congress), made what seemed to some a startling digression. Having insisted that the coming into existence of a proletarian state had fundamentally changed the attitude of communists to national defence, and that the proletarian state should be defended not only by its own proletariat but by the proletariat of all nations, he proceeded to ask the question " whether proletarian states, in accordance with the strategy of the proletariat as a whole, may make military blocs with bourgeois states ", and answered as follows :

> I assert that we are already great enough to conclude an alliance with a foreign bourgeoisie in order, by means of this bourgeois state, to be able to overthrow another bourgeoisie. . . . Supposing that a military alliance has been concluded with a bourgeois state, the duty of the comrades in each country consists in contributing to the victory of the two allies.[2]

The name " Rapallo " was not pronounced at the congress, and there was no return to the old charge that Comintern was being used as an instrument of Soviet national policy.[3] The obvious

---

[1] *Ibid.* pp. 327-328.

[2] *Protokoll des Vierten Kongresses der Kommunistischen Internationale* (Hamburg, 1923), p. 420.

[3] Zinoviev quoted a Polish delegate who had raised the question at a conference of the Polish party, but with surprising toleration treated him with ridicule rather than indignation (*ibid.* p. 210).

and inescapable dependence of the prospects of world revolution on Soviet prosperity and Soviet power made the dilemma seem illusory and unreal. " Whatever storms . . . may come ", wrote Trotsky shortly after the end of the congress, " the Soviet frontier is the trench line beyond which counter-revolution shall not pass, and on which we shall remain at our posts until the reserves arrive ".[1] In the new landscape, the prestige and authority of Soviet Russia overtopped every other prospect. In terms of Soviet policy, Narkomindel was in the ascendant at the expense of Comintern. In other countries, to support Soviet Russia became the paramount duty of the sincere revolutionary. From the fourth congress onwards this could be openly proclaimed. There had been a reversal in the balance of obligation, from which there would henceforth be no turning back.

The new prestige and predominance of Soviet power and of its creator, the Russian Communist Party, was reflected in the resolution of the congress " On the Reorganization of IKKI ". Lenin in his speech had condemned the organization set up by the third congress as too exclusively Russian in character. But hard facts were against him ; and his opinion was silently set aside. The fourth congress not only confirmed the decisions of the third, but tightened up several loose strands. The broad consequence of the 21 conditions had been to impose the view of Comintern taken from the outset by the Russian party as a single organization, a world party, of which the national communist parties were in effect local agencies or branches. Yet it is doubtful whether this view was ever really shared, even after acceptance of the conditions, by any other party than the Russian. At the fourth congress Bukharin still had to complain that, instead of dealing with the international situation as a whole, " almost every orator without exception has spoken exclusively about the position in his own party ".[2] Curiously enough — since the German party was the most recalcitrant to a preponderantly Russian control — the German party came nearest to accepting the centralized conception of a single world party. It was Eberlein, the German

---

[1] *Izvestiya*, December 29, 1922, quoted in A. L. P. Dennis, *The Foreign Policies of Soviet Russia* (1924), p. 370.
[2] *Protokoll des Vierten Kongresses der Kommunistischen Internationale* (Hamburg, 1923), p. 136.

rapporteur on the question of reorganization, who insisted on the need " to eliminate the federal spirit still, perhaps, present in the organization ", and to make IKKI the directing organ of " a really centralized world party ". The lessons of the last year had shown that resolutions of the world congresses had not always been punctually carried out by the national parties or even published in the party journals and that national party leaders had resigned or abandoned their posts rather than execute decisions from which they dissented.

We need international discipline [continued Eberlein] if we really wish to be a closed world party, a fighting organization of the proletariat, and in this fighting organization individual comrades must in all circumstances subordinate their personal wishes to the common interests of the International.[1]

This lesson was thoroughly taken to heart. The constitution of IKKI must be overhauled and put on a new basis. Hitherto its members had been delegates appointed by national communist parties to represent them on the central organ.[2] Henceforth its 25 members (with 10 candidates) were to be elected, not by the constituent parties, but by the world congress. In other respects the innovations introduced since the previous congress[3] were approved. The presidium of from 9 to 11 members was to act, in the words of the *rapporteur*, as " a sort of political bureau ". The presidium was to appoint an organizational bureau of seven members, two of whom were to be also members of the presidium ; and there was to be a secretary-general responsible to the presidium with two assistant secretaries. Thus, in defiance of Lenin's warning, the organization of the Russian party was precisely reproduced in the Communist International. Among the functions of the " organizational bureau " was the supervision of methods of appointment to important offices in the national parties (spontaneous resignations from party offices were henceforth to be prohibited and would involve expulsion from the party),

---

[1] *Ibid.* p. 805.

[2] The original plan in 1919 had been to follow the precedent of the First International, in which the members of a centrally nominated general council shared out among themselves the duties of acting as " correspondents " for the national parties (A. Balabanov, *Erinnerungen und Erlebnisse* (1927), p. 251) ; but this was abandoned in favour of the representative principle.

[3] See p. 394 above.

and the control of illegal work (the necessity for which had been fully demonstrated by recent events in Italy and Germany). The " enlarged executive ", consisting of the members of IKKI and of one or more members of each constituent party according to its size, was to meet twice a year in the intervals between congresses, occupying a corresponding place to the " party conference " in the organization of the Russian party. Finally, it was pronounced desirable that national parties should, as a rule, hold their congresses after, and not before, the world congresses of Comintern, the object being to avoid the arrival of delegates in Moscow with binding instruction on controversial issues from their national party congresses. This instruction, which was in line with the abolition of the " federal " character of IKKI, made it clear that Comintern was to be regarded not as a forum where delegates representing the views of the national party congresses reached collective decisions through processes of debate and compromise, but as a unitary directing organ whose decisions were handed down to be interpreted and applied by the national congresses.[1]

The frankness of the speech in which these far-reaching innovations were proposed suggests that the paramount need of centralized organization and discipline was accepted as a matter of course, at any rate by the German and Russian delegates. In the perfunctory debate which followed (the congress was in its concluding stage), the only point seriously challenged was the demand that national party congresses should follow and not precede the world congresses of Comintern ; and the resolution was carried without amendment.[2] Just as even important members of the Russian party had shown little appreciation of the political consequences of party decisions on organization and on the control of appointments,[3] so now vital decisions on the same questions were unanimously accepted almost without discussion, and apparently without serious misgiving, by the fourth congress of Comintern. The elections to IKKI held at the end of the congress bore

---

[1] *Protokoll des Vierten Kongresses der Kommunistischen Internationale* (Hamburg, 1923), pp. 803-813.
[2] The debate is *ibid.* pp. 814-823, the text of the resolution *ibid.* pp. 994-997 ; the resolution is not included in *Kommunisticheskii Internatsional v Dokumentakh* (1933).
[3] See Vol. 1, p. 204.

marks of the old system of national representation : " blocs of two or three nations wanted to have their representative on the executive, simply on national grounds ". But, as Zinoviev remarked in his closing speech, " it is to be hoped that we have seen such a spectacle today for the last time ". From now on it would be the task of Comintern " to combat everything federalist and introduce real discipline ".[1] What was still perhaps not yet fully understood or recognized, even by the Russian delegation, was that the centralization of the organization of Comintern, which was completed by the fourth congress, necessarily resulted in a still more exclusive concentration of power in the hands of the dominant Russian group : it thus corresponded to the increasing prestige and authority of Soviet Russia and the relative eclipse of the other member parties in Comintern. Henceforth the policy of Comintern would be fitted into a framework of Soviet foreign policy instead of Soviet foreign policy being fitted — as had once been the case, at any rate in form — into a framework of world revolution. It should be noted that this development, though not consciously planned by anyone, and in part consciously resisted by Lenin who alone saw something of its dangers, was virtually completed before Lenin disappeared from the scene, and before the emergence of Stalin, who played no important part in the affairs of Comintern till some time after the fourth congress.

The affairs of particular communist parties, which occupied a large part of the debates of the fourth congress, gave few occasions to strike a cheerful note. The numbers claimed by each were read out at the congress. The Russian party with 324,522 members (the parties of the Ukraine, White Russia and other still formally independent Soviet republics were counted separately, but were numerically small), the German party with 226,000 members and the Czech party with 170,000 members, could alone be regarded as mass communist parties, enrolling a substantial section of the workers in their respective countries. Elsewhere parties were still either small or of doubtful orthodoxy.[2] While

---

[1] *Protokoll des Vierten Kongresses der Kommunistischen Internationale* (Hamburg, 1923), pp. 977-978.
[2] *Ibid.* pp. 363-367.

the fourth congress passed no special resolution on the German question, it was still the German party which constituted the nerve-centre of Comintern and the focal point of all its controversies. " Unless all tokens deceive," repeated Zinoviev in his opening speech, " the path of the proletarian revolution leads from Russia through Germany ";[1] and, now that the Rapallo treaty had given Germany a recognized special position in Soviet foreign policy, the affairs of Germany had a still more weighty and delicate place in the preoccupations of Comintern. It was a symptom of their importance that, where the Bolshevik leaders differed on matters of Comintern policy, the difference always turned on the German issue. The leaders had been divided on the " open letter " policy in January 1921, and again after March 1921 on the moral to be drawn from the March action ;[2] in the summer of 1922, with Lenin withdrawn from the scene, strife broke out between Zinoviev and Radek on the interpretation of the policies of the " united front " and the " workers' government ", reflecting the divisions between Left and Right in the German party.[3] The fourth congress faced this issue in a major debate on tactics introduced by Zinoviev.

The protagonists of the German Right were Meyer and Thalheimer (Brandler was not present), of the Left Ruth Fischer, representing the Berlin group, and Urbahns, representing the Hamburg group ; these were left to make the running. Everyone accepted in principle the policy of the united front. But while Meyer argued that the united front meant primarily agreements reached with the leaders of socialist parties, Ruth Fischer spoke of " an exaggerated stressing and admiration of negotiations with leaders " and wanted the so-called " united front from below ", and Urbahns bluntly maintained that the record of the SPD and the USPD made cooperation with them impossible for communists. Meyer criticized Zinoviev's attempt to identify the " workers' government " of the IKKI resolution of December 1921 with the dictatorship of the proletariat or with a Soviet government, and thought that it obviously had a broader connota-

---

[1] *Protokoll des Vierten Kongresses der Kommunistischen Internationale* (Hamburg, 1923), pp. 36-37.   [2] See pp. 333-334 and 383 above.
[3] See pp. 413-414 above ; the clash between Zinoviev and Radek was not brought into the open till 1924 (*Protokoll : Fünfter Kongress der Kommunistischen Internationale* (n.d.), i, 493-496).

tion ; Ruth Fischer attacked as too vague and loose a phrase of
Radek to the effect that communists and socialists could collabo-
rate in policies designed to secure the worker's " slice of bread ".[1]
Behind these nuances of phrase lay fundamental differences of
policy about the attitude to be adopted to other Left parties. But
the leaders of Comintern were still less concerned (especially
when they were themselves divided) to settle issues of principle
than to compose disputes within the national parties, and thus
remove the danger of further secessions. Lenin, who presided
over the German commission of the congress, though he did not
speak on these issues at the congress itself, used his failing strength
to reconcile differences.[2] The resolution which emerged from
these discussions was a compromise : it repeated the catchwords
of both sides and settled nothing. In the pursuit of a united front
communists " are ready even to conduct negotiations with the
treacherous leaders of the social-democrats and the Amster-
damites "; on the other hand, " the true realization of the tactics
of the united front can come only ' from below ', by taking the
lead in factory committees, committees of action and such other
bodies in which members of other parties and non-party elements
would associate themselves with communists ". Five kinds of
" workers' governments " were distinguished, ranging from a
" liberal workers' government " such as had existed in Australia
and might soon arise in Great Britain, to a " genuine proletarian
workers' government " in the form of a full dictatorship of the
proletariat. But the conditions of communist participation in such
governments were laid down only in the vaguest and most general
terms. The only novelty was the recognition, as a legitimate
variant, of " a worker-peasant government "; this was a development which became significant later.[3] Within the German party,
the resolution left the Right in possession, but allowed the Left to
fight again another day on the same ground. Within the Russian

[1] *Protokoll des Vierten Kongresses der Kommunistischen Internationale* (Hamburg, 1923), pp. 76, 81.
[2] According to Ruth Fischer, *Stalin and German Communism* (Harvard, 1948),
pp. 183-186, Radek and Bukharin tried to persuade her to abandon her attitude,
and the expulsion of the German Left was thought likely : Lenin's attitude,
which " saved " the Left, came as a surprise to all. This account is, however,
coloured by later prejudices : to expel dissidents was quite contrary to Comintern policy at this time.
[3] *Kommunisticheskii Internatsional v Dokumentakh* (1933), pp. 299-302.

party, it upheld Radek — since Rapallo, at the summit of his
success — against the attacks of Zinoviev, whose exclusive identification of the " workers' government " with the dictatorship of
the proletariat was rejected, but not emphatically enough to
prevent a renewal of the same attack at a later date.[1]

The resolution " On the Versailles Peace Treaty " was non-
controversial, being equally accepted by the German Right and
by the German Left. It was none the less novel and significant.
The Bolsheviks had from time to time denounced the Versailles
treaty as a typical example of imperialist rapacity. Lenin had
once described it as " a thousand times more predatory " than
Brest-Litovsk.[2] But it had hitherto been only an incidental factor
in the Bolshevik analysis of the contradictions of the post-war
capitalist world. The main resolution of the third congress of
Comintern on " The World Situation and our Tasks " had dwelt
on the shifting of the centre of gravity of world economy from
Europe to America, on the rise of Japan and on the nascent
conflict between continents ; but, while casually remarking that
" the Germans are becoming the coolies of Europe ", it had placed
little emphasis on Versailles ; and the resolution of the same
congress on tactics, which issued detailed instructions to German
communists for an " unsparing struggle against the German
Government ", did not so much as mention it.[3] But a year later
the picture had changed. It was no longer lightly assumed that
nothing could be achieved without overthrowing the German
Government. The enlarged session of IKKI in March 1922, in
the course of a long resolution on " The Struggle against War and
the Danger of War ", demanded the abrogation of " all the treaties
concluded at the end of the imperialist war ".[4] The fourth congress, eight months later, under the joint influence of the Rapallo
treaty and the policy of penetrating the German masses, made the
Versailles peace treaty one of its principal themes, and, after listening to denunciations of the treaty from orators drawn from nearly
every European country, passed a special resolution, tactfully

---

[1] At the fifth congress of Comintern in 1924 Zinoviev tried to explain away
his acceptance of key passages in this resolution (*Protokoll: Fünfter Kongress
der Kommunistischen Internationale* (n.d.), i, 79-80, 81-82).

[2] Lenin, *Sochineniya*, xxiv, 545.

[3] *Kommunisticheskii Internatsional v Dokumentakh* (1933), pp. 163-180, 198.

[4] *Ibid.* p. 268.

proposed by the French delegate, Cachin, in which it became the pivot of a whole analysis of the international situation.[1] The treaty had turned central Europe, and Germany in particular, into " the new colony of the imperialist robbers ". The German bourgeoisie was seeking to ingratiate itself with the bourgeoisie of the victorious Powers and to shift the burden of reparations on to the shoulders of the proletariat. But, however deep the misery into which the German proletariat was plunged, the magnitude of the reparations claims made this policy unrealizable, and Germany " is being converted into a plaything in the hands of England and France ". After this bare hint of a common interest between German *bourgeoisie* and German proletariat in resisting Anglo-French pressure, the resolution returned to the tasks of the communist parties, which were to be coordinated in a general campaign against the treaty. The German party was to proclaim the willingness of the German proletariat to help in the restoration of northern France, but to oppose bargains between French and German industrialists to fulfil reparations obligations at the expense of the German proletariat by " turning Germany into a colony of the French bourgeoisie ". The French party was to protest against the " attempt to enrich the French bourgeoisie by further forced exploitation of the German proletariat ", to demand the withdrawal of French troops from the left bank of the Rhine and to struggle against the proposed occupation of the Ruhr. The Czech and Polish parties were to " unite the struggle against their own bourgeoisie with the struggle against French imperialism ". The resolution was perhaps the first instance in Europe (though Baku may have furnished an Asiatic precedent) of a conscious and calculated effort to coordinate Comintern action with the foreign policy of the Soviet Government. It also provided a foretaste of the embarrassments which might arise in this field in reconciling the rival susceptibilities of national communist parties.[2]

Paradoxically enough, Italy — with the Fascist *coup* still only six weeks old — was almost the only country where the fourth

---

[1] *Ibid.* pp. 339-343.

[2] Mention was made at the congress of an agreement recently reached between the German and French parties " especially in the question of the Versailles treaty " ; the German delegate complained that it was not being fully carried out (*Protokoll des Vierten Kongresses der Kommunistischen Internationale* (Hamburg, 1923), pp. 76-77).

congress had an encouraging development to record. The patience so long extended to the Italian Socialist Party (and even to the Italian Communist Party which had rejected the decision of IKKI on the united front [1]) had at length been justified. At its congress in Rome early in October 1922 the Italian Socialist Party had expelled the reformists, and decided to accept the 21 conditions and join Comintern; this would involve fusion with the Italian Communist Party. A long retrospective resolution on the Italian question adopted by the fourth congress of Comintern recalled that " the objective prerequisites of the victorious revolution " had been present in Italy in the autumn of 1920 when the workers occupied the factories; only a " genuinely communist party " had been lacking. This had been created by the split at Leghorn in February 1921, though the Italian Communist Party had remained small, and its leaders, while they had on paper renounced the errors of syndicalism, were still infected with its spirit. The resolution of the fourth congress, cheerfully citing " the victory of Fascist reaction " as a motive for " the most rapid union of all revolutionary forces of the proletariat ", provided for the creation of a committee consisting of two members of the Italian Communist Party, of Serrati and Maffi as representatives of the Italian Socialist Party, and of Zinoviev as chairman and arbiter, to work out the conditions of unity; and similar steps were to be taken in the local branches.[2] Negotiations were carried on in Moscow during the winter. But jealousies between communists and socialists delayed progress; and early in 1923 Mussolini pounced on both parties in Italy and put most of their leaders under arrest. Almost the only ray of hope which the fourth congress of Comintern had been able to register had been snuffed out.

The affairs of the British party, now in the throes of reorganization, were not discussed at the congress. But Zinoviev spoke of its progress in terms of unwontedly frank pessimism :

In England . . . the development of our party goes very, very slowly. Perhaps in no other country does the communist movement develop as slowly as in England. We must begin to study England ; we do not yet know the causes of this slow development. Considering the great unemployment and great

[1] See p. 418, note 3, above.
[2] *Kommunisticheskii Internatsional v Dokumentakh* (1933), pp. 356-360.

poverty of the proletariat the development of communism in England is remarkably slow.[1]

The crisis in the French party, on the other hand, received an inordinate amount of attention from the enlarged session of IKKI which preceded the congress, from a commission under the presidency of Trotsky appointed by the congress, and from the congress itself; no less than 24 French delegates from all sections of the party were in attendance, Frossard being the only noteworthy absentee.[2] Obstinately denying the facts, the congress once again ruled out " the very idea of a split, which is in no way called for by the position of affairs in the party ",[3] and continued its attempts to compel the Right and Left wings not only to settle down together, but to adopt the despised policy of the united front. In effect the Left emerged victorious through a roundabout device. In the Latin countries of Europe freemasonry had long been the uniform of anti-clerical radicalism, both bourgeois and socialist. In Italy, as long ago as 1914, the socialist party had excluded freemasons from its ranks. In France, freemasonry had continued to provide a link between bourgeois Left and socialists; and several of the French Right communist leaders, including Frossard himself, were freemasons. This fact came to light in the commission of the fourth congress — " for the first time, to our amazement ", as Trotsky afterwards declared.[4] This was too good a weapon for the Left. The congress issued the edict that all members of the French party who were freemasons must publicly declare before January 1, 1923, on pain of expulsion from the party, that they had ceased to be freemasons, and thereafter be ineligible for " responsible posts in the party " for a period of two years.[5] Frossard resigned from the party forthwith; others

---

[1] *Protokoll des Vierten Kongresses der Kommunistischen Internationale* (Hamburg, 1923), p. 50.

[2] These proceedings are fully described with references to the French sources in G. Walter, *Histoire du Parti Communiste Français* (1948), pp. 115-121.

[3] *Kommunisticheskii Internatsional v Dokumentakh* (1933), p. 344.

[4] *Protokoll des Vierten Kongresses der Kommunistischen Internationale* (Hamburg, 1923), p. 865. It was freely asserted by French dissidents that the discovery of freemasonry was merely a pretext for disciplinary action and that its existence in the French party had long been known: the question had in fact been raised by Serrati at a meeting of IKKI in 1920 (L. O. Frossard, *De Jaurès à Lénine* (1930), p. 266).

[5] *Kommunisticheskii Internatsional v Dokumentakh* (1933), p. 348.

severed their connexion with freemasonry. The two years' proscription does not seem to have been rigorously enforced. The affairs of the Norwegian Labour Party provided an equally disconcerting picture. It had from the first been a party of highly dubious orthodoxy.[1] It had accepted the 21 conditions with a single reservation : the party was built up on the collective membership of trade unions, and this made it difficult to apply the prescribed test of individual conformity.[2] But in practice the party went its own way, refusing even to exchange its old name for that of " Norwegian Communist Party " ; and, with the reaction against " splitting " tactics which set in after March 1921, Comintern did not venture to take action against it. At length in June 1922, Tranmael, the leader of the party, was induced to attend the enlarged session of IKKI ; but the result was a resolution which dealt only with party errors on particular questions and evaded the issue of principle.[3] But between this session and the fourth congress of Comintern in the following November, the split in the Norwegian party, as in the French party, had become an accomplished fact ; and Tranmael and the majority of the central committee, like Frossard and his associates, disobeyed the urgent summons of IKKI to attend the congress. Faced with this defiance, the congress appointed a commission under the tactful presidency of Bukharin, whose mandate clearly was to uphold discipline without pushing the issue to a break. The resolution once more demanded that the name of the party should be changed and dissident groups within it expelled, and proposed that " for the establishment of a better link between the party and IKKI " a delegate of IKKI should attend the next party congress.[4] But these soothing phrases meant nothing. It was clear that the mass Norwegian party was already lost to Comintern. Through delaying tactics the formal split was postponed till the

[1] See p. 145 above.

[2] *Der Zweite Kongress der Kommunist. Internationale* (Hamburg, 1921), p. 382.

[3] *Kommunisticheskii Internatsional v Dokumentakh* (1933), pp. 289-292 ; according to Zinoviev, Radek, who was sent at this time to discuss the question in Oslo, made a " rotten compromise " with Tranmael (*Protokoll: Fünfter Kongress der Kommunistischen Internationale* (n.d.), i, 469).

[4] Bukharin's report is in *Protokoll des Vierten Kongresses der Kommunistischen Internationale* (Hamburg, 1923), pp. 945-955 ; the resolution *ibid.* pp. 955-956.

autumn of 1923, when the party seceded from Comintern, and a small minority broke away from it to form a Norwegian Communist Party.

Simultaneously with the fourth congress of Comintern, Profintern held its second congress. The application of " united front " tactics to Profintern was direct and obvious, since this was an organization ostensibly formed to build up contacts with the masses of the workers. In December 1921, even before the promulgation of the new slogan by IKKI, a proposal was made to the Amsterdam International for joint action to avert a threatened split between syndicalists and socialists in the French trade-union movement;[1] in February 1922 a proposal of the Norwegian trade unions for a joint conference of the two trade union Internationals " to work out parallel forms and methods of struggle against the offensive of capitalism " was warmly endorsed by the council of Profintern.[2] Both these projects were ignored by Amsterdam. Undeterred by these rebuffs, Profintern took advantage of the Berlin conference of the Second, Third and Two-and-a half Internationals in April 1922 to issue a further appeal to the workers of all countries " to unite in resistance to the offensive of capital "; and Lozovsky once more proposed a conference between Profintern, the Amsterdam International and all independent unions.[3] These overtures served no purpose except to provide a spurious basis for the argument that it was Amsterdam, not Moscow, which was splitting the trade union movement and opposing the quest for unity. The year 1922 proved to be the high-water mark of Profintern's success in western and central Europe. In France the attempt of the leadership of the CGT to discipline and expel its syndicalists ended in a breakaway and in the formation of the Confédération Générale du Travail Unitaire (CGTU), which affiliated to Profintern and for some time

---

[1] *Desyat' Let Profinterna v Rezolyutsiyakh* (1930), pp. 89-90. During 1921 an active struggle was waged in the CGT to expel syndicalists (H. Marquand, etc., *Labour in Four Continents* (1939), pp. 14-15); since the syndicalists were the strongest supporters of Comintern and Profintern, the latter had an important interest in resisting their expulsion.

[2] *Desyat' Let Profinterna v Rezolyutsiyakh* (1930), pp. 83-84.

[3] *Krasnyi Internatsional Profsoyuzov*, No. 4 (15), April 1922, pp. 311-312, 313-316.

represented a majority of French trade-unionists ; and in Czecho-slovakia a majority of the unions also affiliated to Moscow   But elsewhere the big battalions of the western trade-union movement remained on the side of Amsterdam. At the German trade union congress in Leipzig in June 1922, there were 90 communist dele-gates out of a total of 700 ; and even this proportion was not maintained by the supporters of Moscow at later congresses.[1] In Great Britain Profintern never won the allegiance of more than a handful of unions. In these circumstances the charge that the Amsterdam International was responsible for splitting the move-ment lacked cogency, and — at any rate in Germany and Great Britain — recoiled on the heads of its authors.

The second congress of Profintern, which met in November 1922, attracted little limelight and was marked by the same mood of restraint and retreat as the meeting of the parent body. The report of the council was couched in intransigent terms, and recorded once more that " all attempts of Profintern to create a united front with the Amsterdam International met with obstinate sabotage from the latter ".[2] This made it all the more necessary for Profintern to come to terms with its own Left wing. As recently as July 1922 the official organ of Comintern had carried, in an article entitled *The Anarcho-Syndicalists and Profintern*, a bitter attack on French and Italian trade unions and on the IWW for demanding the independence of Profintern from Comintern.[3] But now conciliation was the order of the day. The delegation of the newly formed French CGTU came to the congress with a categorical demand for a withdrawal of the resolution of the first congress on the subordination of Profintern to Comintern, and — almost for the only time in the history of either of these institu-tions — the central authority yielded. A long resolution ended by recording the willingness of Profintern " to meet half-way the revolutionary workers of France, and to accept the proposal of the CGTU in order to strengthen at the congress the bloc of all sincerely revolutionary elements of the international trade-union movement who rally under the banner of the overthrow of

---

[1] O. K. Flechtheim, *Die KPD in der Weimarer Republik* (Offenbach, 1948), p. 91.

[2] *Desyat' Let Profinterna v Rezolyutsiyakh* (1930), p. 89.

[3] *Kommunisticheskii Internatsional*, No. 21 (July 19, 1922), cols. 5603-5628.

capitalism and the establishment of the dictatorship of the proletariat ": the resolution of the first congress was abrogated, and
no new definition of relations substituted.[1] This paper retreat
represented, as Zinoviev made clear in his speech at the congress,
only a tactical manœuvre : " what is happening here is that we
accept certain prejudices entertained by the revolutionary elements
in Latin countries ".[2] It is doubtful whether it changed anything
in practice. The two dilemmas which had confronted Profintern
from the moment of its foundation were still unresolved. The
only mass trade unions of western Europe which were eager to
break with Amsterdam were the syndicalists who stood for independent and non-political unions ; and elsewhere the campaign
against the Amsterdam International seemed irreconcilable with
the policy of peaceful penetration of the unions. A highly optimistic statement submitted by Lozovsky to the twelfth party
congress in April, 1923, claimed a total of 13 million adherents of
Profintern as against 14 or at most 15 million for Amsterdam.
But he admitted that in Germany Profintern had only 35 per cent
of the organized workers, in England 15 per cent and in Belgium
10 per cent ; and even these figures were probably exaggerated.[3]
The Bolshevik leaders never admitted defeat or publicly recognized that the foundation of Profintern had been a tactical miscalculation. It continued from time to time to have its value as
an instrument of propaganda ; and its embarrassments in Europe
were probably outweighed by its usefulness in Asia, where the
numerical strength claimed by Lozovsky principally resided. The
second congress improved on the first by passing a long resolution
" On Trade-Union Movements in Colonial and Semi-Colonial
Countries ". It recorded the growth in these countries of " a
numerous native industrial proletariat . . . working in undertakings
of the European and American type and concentrated in great
masses in large industrial centres " ; it looked forward to calling a
conference of " revolutionary trade unions " representing native
workers ; and in the meanwhile it decided to establish propaganda
bureaux in ports where seamen were likely to congregate.[4] The

---

[1] *Desyat' Let Profinterna v Rezolyutsiyakh* (1930), pp. 109-110.
[2] G. Zinoviev, *L'Internationale Communiste au Travail* (1923), pp. 176-177.
[3] *Dvenadtsatyi S"ezd Rossiiskoi Kommunisticheskoi Partii (Bol'shevikov)*
(1923), pp. 279-280.
[4] *Desyat' Let Profinterna v Rezolyutsiyakh* (1930), pp. 111-114.

activity thus set on foot was to prove of some importance in the Far East, and was a standing criticism of the geographical and racial limitations of IFTU and of the principal unions affiliated to it.

Another pendant to the fourth congress of Comintern was the attendance of a Soviet trade union delegation, consisting of Radek, Lozovsky and Rothstein, who had just returned from the post of Soviet representative in Teheran, at a peace congress convened by IFTU at the Hague in December 1922 and presided over by the British trade-union leader J. H. Thomas. The dual purpose of this move was to illustrate Bolshevik eagerness for a united front with other workers' parties and organizations and to proclaim Soviet interest in the cause of peace. The experience of the Berlin meeting of the three Internationals in the previous April with its mutual recriminations was reproduced with few variations, except that the Soviet delegation, mindful of Lenin's reproaches on that occasion, was now determined to make no concessions. Rothstein read to the congress a fourteen-point project of which the major proposal was to establish an international committee of action, and national committees of action, against war. This found no supporters, and Lozovsky's pleas for a united front were greeted with opprobrium and ridicule. The not very impressive resolutions in support of peace proposed by the bureau of the congress were eventually carried against the single dissentient vote of the Soviet delegation. Only at one point was Radek stung into an utterance which seemed out of tune with the obstinately conciliatory language otherwise held by the delegation :

We have an army. We will not demobilize our army. So you see we are not anxiously concerned about Russia. But we are now concerned with the danger to which the proletariat of western Europe is exposed. In order to avert that danger we now offer you, frankly and fearlessly the hand of friendship and cooperation. Reject that offer, and the outstretched hand of friendship will be turned against you.[1]

[1] *Report of the International Peace Congress held at the Hague, December 10-15, 1922* (Amsterdam, n.d.), pp. 102, 118, 143-145. *Internationale Presse-Korrespondenz*, No. 239 (December 18, 1922), is devoted to the congress ; it ends with a short article by Lozovsky describing the congress as a " zoological garden " in which " the flies almost die of boredom ". A further article on the congress by Lozovsky is in *Die Internationale*, vi, No. 1 (January 6, 1923), pp. 13-21.

The last episode of 1922, and an important factor in the consolidation of Soviet foreign policy, was a reaffirmation against strong party criticism of the monopoly of foreign trade. The authority and influence of Vneshtorg, which administered the monopoly, and of Krasin, as People's Commissar, had automatically grown with the revival of foreign trade, especially after the signature of the Anglo-Soviet trade agreement. On the other hand, the principle of the monopoly seemed to fit in better with the economic structure of war communism, under which it had begun to operate, than with the spirit of NEP. It was not surprising that demands began to be heard for a modification of the monopoly and the admission of private enterprise to the jealously guarded preserve of foreign trade. This view seems to have first found open expression at a conference on financial policy at Gosbank in November 1921;[1] and it came to be particularly associated with Sokolnikov, the People's Commissar for Finance.[2] A decree of March 13, 1922, while retaining the monopoly intact, evidently represented an attempt to mollify those who denounced its excessive rigidity. While authorizing Vneshtorg to acquire goods for export on a commission basis from state institutions or undertakings or from cooperatives, it also empowered these bodies to conclude contracts with foreign traders, though always subject to the approval of the commissariat; and a similar flexibility of procedure was applied to imports.[3] After this, criticism was concentrated on the bureaucratic methods of Vneshtorg; and it may be suspected that the commanding position held by Krasin in the Soviet economy inspired the jealousy of many whose party record was less chequered and present devotion to party orthodoxy less dubious. At a conference of departments concerned in foreign trade in June 1922, the commissariat was attacked by Bogdanov and Nogin on behalf of Vesenkha, and defended by Krasin; and a resolution of the conference, while upholding the principle of the foreign trade monopoly, demanded that its machinery should

---

[1] See Vol. 2, p. 352.

[2] In a pamphlet published in 1922 Sokolnikov argued that " the weakly organized and inadequately tested Soviet apparatus " was not equal to dealing with foreign capitalists, and supported the creation of mixed companies in which Vneshtorg would have only " a regulating rôle " (G. Y. Sokolnikov, *Gosudarstvennyi Kapitalizm i Novaya Ekonomicheskaya Politika* (1922), pp. 7-9).

[3] *Sobranie Uzakonenii, 1922*, No. 24, art. 266.

be made less bureaucratic.[1] Two months later Krasin was still
on the defensive, explaining that the monopoly was necessary
" until the recovery of the country, exhausted as the result of long
years of war, blockade and intervention, allows it to get on its feet
once more and become economically strong ".[2] Two decrees of
October 16, 1922, accorded to all State economic organs the right
to transact import and export business through their own representatives abroad, though without infringing the monopoly of
foreign trade, and under the supervision of Vreshtorg.[3] In the
same month Krasin repeated in a press interview that the foreign
trade monopoly " does not mean that all commercial operations are
carried out by organs of the People's Commissariat of Foreign
Trade " ; state undertakings, cooperatives, private concerns and
mixed companies all played their part, though under the authority
and supervision of the commissariat.[4]

Meanwhile the issue had been carried to the central committee
of the party, where on October 12, 1922, Sokolnikov proposed a
resolution demanding a relaxation of the foreign trade monopoly
in respect of certain categories of goods and over certain frontiers.
Bukharin, having sought to carry war communism to its logical
conclusion and stood at that time on the extreme Left, now
applied the same thirst for logical consistency to NEP and,
moving over to the extreme Right, supported Sokolnikov. In the
absence of Lenin (who had only just returned to work after his
first stroke) and of Trotsky, the resolution was carried. It could,
of course, have no formal effect until it was transferred to the
governmental machine ; and it was subject to appeal by any
member of the committee to the party congress. Lenin at once
protested, and demanded that the question should be brought up
again at the next session of the central committee in December.
On the following day, Krasin on behalf of Vneshtorg sent in a set
of theses opposing the decision ; and Bukharin in a letter of
October 15, 1922, to the central committee defended the resolution
against both Lenin and Krasin.[5] There the matter rested till the
middle of December 1922, when Lenin, whose health had again

---

[1] *Russian Information and Review*, July 15, 1922, pp. 470-471.
[2] L. B. Krasin, *Voprosy Vneshnei Torgovli* (1928), p. 306.
[3] *Sobranie Uzakonenii, 1922*, No. 65, art. 846 ; No. 66, art. 862.
[4] *Russian Information and Review*, November 4, 1922, pp. 72-73.
[5] Lenin, *Sochineniya*, xxvii, 558-559, note 177.

broken down, discovered that he would be unable to attend the central committee and became anxious about the coming discussion. On December 12, having learned that Trotsky was also opposed to the October resolution, Lenin wrote to him asking him " to take upon yourself at the coming plenum the defence of our common opinion on the unconditional necessity of preserving and reinforcing the monopoly of foreign trade ".[1] On the next day he dictated a long memorandum for the central committee which took the form of a refutation of Bukharin's letter and a defence of Krasin's theses :

> In practice Bukharin stands for the defence of the speculator, of the petty bourgeois, of the richest peasants, against the industrial proletariat, which is absolutely not in a condition to revive industry, and to make Russia an industrial country, without the protection, not of a customs policy, but only and exclusively of a monopoly of foreign trade. Any other kind of protectionism in the conditions of contemporary Russia is completely fictitious, paper protectionism which gives nothing to the proletariat.

The memorandum ended by supporting mixed companies as the best way " really to improve the bad apparatus of Vneshtorg ".[2] Two days later Lenin wrote again to Trotsky expressing hopes of victory, since " a part of those voting against us in October have now come over partially or completely to our side ".[3] Nothing is known of what passed at the central committee on December 18, 1922, except that the October resolution was unconditionally rescinded. Lenin was able to congratulate himself and Trotsky on having " captured the position without firing a shot ", and proposed that the matter should be clinched by a decision of the next party congress.[4] This proposal was carried into effect in April 1923, a month after Lenin's final incapacity, by an unusually emphatic resolution of the twelfth party congress :

> The congress categorically confirms the inviolability of the monopoly of foreign trade and the inadmissibility of any evasion of it and any weakness in its application, and instructs the new

[1] L. Trotsky, *The Real Situation in Russia* (n.d. [1928]), p. 287.
[2] Lenin, *Sochineniya*, xxvii, 379-382.
[3] L. Trotsky, *The Real Situation in Russia* (n.d. [1928]), pp. 288-289.
[4] *Ibid.* pp. 289-290.

central committee to take systematic measures to strengthen and develop the régime of the monopoly of foreign trade.[1]

A few days before the congress met, a decree of VTsIK had reaffirmed the authority of Vneshtorg and of its trade delegations abroad, and severely limited the rights of other state organs in the domain of foreign trade.[2] The foreign trade monopoly was thereafter impregnable.

[1] *VKP(B) v Rezolyutsiyakh* (1941), i, 472.
[2] *Sobranie Uzakonenii, 1923*, No. 31, art. 343.

CHAPTER 32

THE EASTERN QUESTION

THE retreat from the constant and active promotion of world
revolution, which characterized Soviet foreign policy after
March 1921, and had led by the end of 1922 to a marked
consolidation of Soviet interests in Europe, was equally conspicuous in eastern affairs. The transition in eastern policy was
in many respects less sharp and less difficult. While from 1920
onwards the emphasis on Soviet interest in Asia progressively
increased, there was no non-European country where the prospects
of proletarian revolution could be anything but remote, or where
any native communist party was more than a slavish imitation of
the Russian model or a direct emanation of Soviet influence. In
these circumstances, the question which for so long embarrassed
Soviet diplomacy in Europe — the question whether Moscow was
more directly interested in stimulating the downfall of capitalist
governments or in coming to terms with them — scarcely arose in
Asia, or arose only in minor and transient episodes like that of
Kuchik in Persia. In Asia such independent or semi-independent
national governments as existed constantly found themselves,
through the nature of their ambitions and aspirations, in a posture
of active or potential hostility to the western Powers. Soviet
Russia had every incentive, material and moral, to encourage their
aspirations and to fan the flame of their animosities against the
west ; the common position occupied by Soviet Russia and by the
Asiatic countries in relation to the imperialist Powers was an un-
ceasing theme of Soviet writers and politicians. If, in the period
after March 1921, some restraint entered into the pursuit of this
policy, this was due not to any inclination to support local communist elements in revolt against the national governments, but
to the peculiar obligations created by the Anglo-Soviet trade
agreement, which made it politic for the time being to avoid overt

demonstrations of support for anti-British elements in Asia. The substance of Soviet policy throughout the period after 1921 was to seek collaboration with national governments in Asia and to extend Soviet influence over those governments, but to pursue this policy as far as possible by gradual and unobtrusive methods which would not destroy or prejudice opportunities of profitable economic relations with the western capitalist world. Within the framework of the general policy, action in Asia in concrete cases responded sensitively to the barometer of those relations.

The comparatively restrained and diplomatic character of Soviet foreign policy in the period after March 1921 spread to Soviet relations with Afghanistan. Surits was succeeded as Soviet representative by Raskolnikov, the hero of the descent on Enzeli and the eviction of the British from northern Persia; and British agents continued to furnish lurid reports of his activities in Kabul. But Bolshevik propaganda in India, where it might have expected to find a fruitful soil, was strangely unsuccessful. The prospects of revolution there, which had never perhaps been treated very seriously in Moscow, faded ; and, with the signature of the Anglo-Soviet trade agreement, Soviet interest in them correspondingly declined. Afghanistan had settled down to a comfortable balance between the rival powers of Great Britain and Soviet Russia. The counterpart of the Soviet-Afghan treaty of February 28, 1921, was a new Anglo-Afghan treaty signed on November 22 of the same year : this provided for regular diplomatic and consular representation and removed the ban on the transit of arms and munitions via India to Afghanistan.[1] But, lest this should appear as too definite and uncompromising a turn towards the British side on the part of the Afghan Government, it was accompanied by a declaration condemning the unfriendly policy pursued by the British Government towards Turkey.[2] In the summer of 1922 Enver's last campaign against Soviet rule in eastern Turkestan is said to have excited Afghan sympathies and led to another bout of coolness in Soviet-Afghan relations.[3] On the whole, however, both Soviet Russia and Great Britain were moving at this time,

[1] *Treaty between the British and Afghan Governments, November 22, 1921,* Cmd. 1786 (1922).
[2] A. L. P. Dennis, *The Foreign Policies of Soviet Russia* (1924), p. 258 (where, however, the treaty is misdated 1922).
[3] L. Fischer, *The Soviets in World Affairs* (1930), i, 434.

slowly and haltingly enough, towards the recognition that an independent Afghanistan might serve as a barrier and a buffer, rather than as a bone of contention, between them. Fears of a serious Soviet threat to India became the personal prerogative of Curzon, and there was a faint note of condescension in the terms in which Chicherin addressed him at the Lausanne conference in December 1922 :

> You are uneasy because our horsemen have reappeared on the heights of the Pamirs, and because you have no longer to deal with the half-witted Tsar who ceded the ridge of the Hindu Kush to you in 1895. But it is not war that we offer you, it is peace, based on the principles of a partition wall between us.[1]

Consolidation rather than advance had become the key-note of Soviet policy in Central Asia.

In Persia, after the signature of the Soviet-Persian treaty of February 26, 1921, and Rothstein's arrival two months later as Soviet representative in Teheran, the struggle between Soviet and British influence was more actively and stubbornly pursued. But here, too, Soviet policy was quickly emptied of any revolutionary content. Correct relations were maintained with the Persian Government, and favour was shown to the rising star of Riza Khan, the military power behind the coup of February 1921. The strong hand of Riza, like that of Kemal in Turkey, seemed to Soviet observers to embody the forces of Persian nationalism, and to offer the best promise of an independent Persia capable of resisting British domination.

> Her [Soviet Russia's] direct interests [wrote a Soviet commentator at this time] are that Persia should be a strong centralized state capable of defending itself against any interference in its affairs by third parties and especially, of course, by England. Such a position would guarantee Soviet Russia against any utilization of Persian territory by English forces for an attack on Russia. In a strong central state power, resting on a single national army, will also be found a pledge of the commercial

---

[1] *The Lausanne Conference on Near Eastern Affairs, 1922–1923*, Cmd. 1814 (1923), p. 149 ; the mention of the Pamirs probably referred to an allegation in the Horne letter to Krasin of March 16, 1921 (see p. 288 above), that " an army order issued by the Soviet authorities has announced the unfurling of the red flag on the Pamirs as an indication to the people of India that their deliverance is at hand "

and cultural development of Persia and of her transition from feudal to modern forms of economic and political existence.[1]

It was an asset of Soviet policy in Asia at this time that it continued to regard the growth of strong national states as a Soviet interest, whereas British policy still lay under the imputation of favouring weak rulers and small semi-independent local chiefs dependent on British aid and British protection.

A serious crisis, however, occurred in Soviet counsels before the new policy was finally established, and provided a striking example of the lack of coordination which at this time still made it possible for different Soviet authorities to pursue independent and incompatible policies. The immediate ambition of the Persian Government was to complete the withdrawal of foreign troops from Persia; and the Soviet Government had made the withdrawal of Soviet forces conditional on that of the British. In May 1921 the last British troops left Persian soil. It was at this moment that the Soviet supporters of Kuchik and his independent republic in Gilan, who were radically opposed to the policy of appeasement of a national Persian Government, attempted their last throw. In the summer of 1921 Kuchik started to march on Teheran — a venture in which he received the support not only of his Soviet advisers, but of reinforcements sent across the Caspian Sea from the Azerbaijan SSR. The attempt proved a fiasco, and was disowned by Chicherin in Moscow and by Rothstein in Teheran, who is said to have made a personal protest to Lenin.[2] The policy of support for Kuchik was now finally abandoned. The withdrawal of Soviet forces proceeded according to plan, and was completed in September 1921. This paved the way for the final collapse of the Gilan republic, which came in October 1921 when Persian forces reoccupied Gilan with Soviet approval, and hanged Kuchik as a rebel.[3] Other movements by

[1] *Novyi Vostok*, iv (n.d. [1923]), 218-219.

[2] L. Fischer, *The Soviets in World Affairs* (1930), i, 288. This incident, which understandably " disturbed Soviet-Persian relations for a short period ", is glossed over by Soviet writers; according to further information (*ibid.* (2nd ed., 1951), i, xvi) Kuchik's army included not only levies from the Caucasus, but " Russian peasants from Tula ".

[3] *Novyi Vostok*, iv (n.d. [1923]), 217-218, which ignores the summer venture, records Kuchik's downfall in October and explains it in the following terms : " The revolutionary movement in Gilan, which flourished principally

semi-independent leaders in other frontier districts were mopped up shortly afterwards.

The period during which these events occurred was marked by a series of disputes about the application of the Soviet-Persian treaty, the ratification of which was delayed by the Mejlis till December 15, 1921.[1] It was not long before the perennial oil question once more raised its head. Under the treaty Soviet Russia had confirmed her renunciation of all concessions in Persia formerly granted to Russian governments or to Russian nationals, but on condition that the Persian Government did not transfer these concessions to any other foreign Power or to its nationals. In November 1921, in defiance of this provision, the Persian Government granted to the Standard Oil Company a concession in northern Persia which had formerly been held by a Georgian of Russian nationality, and the necessary authority was voted in surprising haste by the Mejlis. Vigorous protests were made by the Soviet Government.[2] Nor was the appearance of American capital in the Persian oil industry welcomed by the Anglo-Persian Oil Company, which was able to secure from the Standard Oil Company an agreement for the joint exploitation of the newly acquired concession,[3] and further strengthened its position by an issue of capital which made the British Government a majority shareholder. This combination was, however, little to the taste of the Persian Government, which in June 1922 cancelled its agreement with the Standard Oil Company and entered into fresh negotiations with the Sinclair Consolidated Oil Corporation.[4] In

on the slogan ' Down with the English ', went perceptibly downhill after the evacuation of Persia by the English forces. In view of the backwardness and inertia of the Persian peasantry, it found no support among the Persian peasantry ; the Persian traders and bourgeoisie in general connected the improvement of their position with an opening of commercial relations with Soviet Russia, and were not inclined at the moment to take up arms against the feudal central government."

[1] For an account of these items see *ibid.* iv, 210-215.

[2] *Ibid.* iv, 213-214 ; *Revue du Monde Musulman*, lii (1922), 167-168, cites a protest of Rothstein to the Persian Government of January 15, 1922.

[3] The Anglo-Persian Oil Company had already in 1920 purchased the same concession from its former Georgian holder ; but the Persian Government not unnaturally refused to recognize this transfer.

[4] A documented, though no doubt somewhat tendentious, account of these transactions appears in L. Fischer, *Oil Imperialism* (n.d. [1927]), pp. 210-232.

the end Soviet protests against the concession proved effective for a reason which was made clear in an uncompromising article in *Pravda* :

> These concessions are not utilizable without transit through Russia. The Russian Government cannot admit on the Russo-Persian frontier the organization of a capitalist centre capable at the right moment of transforming the concession into a purely military base which would be a menace for Russia.[1]

In November 1922 Rothstein returned to Moscow, and was succeeded as Soviet representative in Teheran by Shumyatsky. Rothstein had proved so powerful a defender of traditional Russian interests as sometimes to suggest that Soviet interference might be as distasteful to Persian pride as British interference, or as Russian interference in the past ; his withdrawal was said to be due to protests against his high-handed action in giving asylum in the Soviet mission to the editors of three Persian papers who were charged with having infringed the Persian press law by anti-British and pro-Soviet propaganda.[2]

The most important aim of Soviet policy in Persia in the period of more restrained diplomacy which followed Rothstein's departure was the conclusion of a trade agreement. The Persian Government, suspecting on the strength of past experience that close economic relations with a strong Power spelt political dependence, seems to have been obstructive from the start. A representative of Vneshtorg arrived in Teheran as early as August 1921 ; and in September and October Chicherin was pressing the Persian Government to send a delegation for trade negotiations to Moscow.[3] But it was not till June 1922 that negotiations began, and even then made little progress in face of Persian objections to the system of the monopoly of foreign trade. On November 9, 1922, the Soviet delegation made an important concession. This was a moment when the monopoly was under heavy attack in Soviet circles ;[4] and a certain licence for frontier traffic with Asiatic countries had long been conceded in practice, if not in

[1] *Pravda*, September 24, 1922.
[2] Rothstein's victory in this incident (the editors were apparently reinstated) is enthusiastically described in *Novyi Vostok*, iv (n.d. [1923]), 627-629.
[3] *Ibid.* iv, 216-217.
[4] See p. 464 above.

principle.[1] It was now announced that the Soviet Government was prepared to draw up lists of goods which could be imported into Persia from Soviet Russia and exported from Persia to Soviet Russia by processes of private trade and without passing through the hands of Vneshtorg; this concession was, however, made dependent on a change in the composition of the Persian Government which was accused (partly, no doubt, on account of the friction with Rothstein) of " feudal " and Anglophil propensities. In February 1923 a cabinet crisis occurred; the new government introduced a tariff more favourable to Soviet goods; and on February 27 lists of goods in which free trade with Persia would henceforth be permitted were approved by the Soviet Government.[2] This important concession was apparently intended to serve as a precedent. General regulations for trade with eastern countries, approved at a conference of representatives of Vneshtorg in the same year, laid down the principle that trade with eastern countries should be conducted on a more flexible basis, and on terms more favourable to the countries concerned, than trade with the capitalist west. The system of " licensed liberalism ", which permitted free trade in " Persian goods not competing with Russian goods ", was praised, and extended to trade with Turkey, Afghanistan and Outer Mongolia.[3] But this seems to have been the high point of NEP in its application to foreign trade; and the tendency thereafter was to restrict rather than extend these petty derogations from the foreign trade monopoly. Nor did the concession have the desired effect of smoothing the path of Soviet-Persian trade negotiations. A trade treaty was signed on July 3, 1924, but failed to secure ratification by the Mejlis.

It was, however, Turkey which continued during this period to provide the focal point of Soviet policy in the Near and Middle East. The conclusion of the Soviet-Turkish treaty of March 16,

---

[1] In 1921 a brisk private trade was in progress across the Black Sea between Turkey and the Crimea, to which it was considered " undesirable . . . to set up any hindrances " (L. B. Krasin, *Voprosy Vneshnei Torgovli* (1928), p. 338); the argument (*ibid.* pp. 333, 335) that Soviet trade with the eastern countries did not need the same rigid protection as trade with the " powerful commercial organizations " of western capitalism had some validity from the Soviet standpoint.

[2] *Novyi Vostok*, iv (n.d. [1923]), 224-226.

[3] *Entsiklopediya Sovetskogo Eksporta* (Berlin, 1924), i, 29; *ibid.* (Berlin, 1928), i, 34-36.

1921, and the simultaneous failure of the Turkish Government to come to terms with the western allies, was followed by the advance of the Greek army, supported and subsidized by the British Government, into Anatolia. Turkey, hard pressed, turned to Moscow for help, and faced the Soviet Government with a difficult decision. Help for a small nation struggling to assert its freedom against a flagrant act of imperialist aggression was a matter of principle for Bolsheviks ; and this principle had been frequently reaffirmed with specific reference to Turkey. On the other hand, the general desire of the Soviet Government at this time to play for safety and avoid rash adventures was reinforced by reluctance to endanger the commercial relations so recently established with Great Britain and by well-founded suspicions of Turkey's ambivalent attitude. Divided counsels [1] seem to have postponed a decision. Throughout the summer of 1921, while the Greeks were still advancing and the Anglo-Soviet trade agreement was in its honeymoon stage, Moscow held conspicuously aloof.[2] It was only in the autumn, when an acrimonious correspondence had begun with Great Britain and the Greek advance in Anatolia had been checked, that the Soviet Government began cautiously to give support to Turkey. A protest against alleged Greek atrocities appeared in *Izvestiya* on October 25, 1921. The decision to support Turkey with munitions and military advisers came shortly

[1] According to L. Fischer, *The Soviets in World Affairs* (2nd ed., 1951), i, xv, Lenin and Trotsky favoured support for Turkey, but " Stalin, Orjonikidze and other Georgian and Caucasian comrades advised moderation ", recalling Turkey's unfriendly attitude in seizing Batum in February 1921 and not wishing to see Turkey too strong. This information is stated to have come from Rakovsky, and is borne out by Stalin's interview of November 1920 (see p. 302, note 1, above). For evidence of divided counsels on the Turkish side see Halidé Edib, *The Turkish Ordeal* (1928), pp. 254-255. According to this source, Bekir Sami, who was a north Caucasian Turk, returned from Moscow at the end of 1920 highly disillusioned and became a convinced westerner. When as Commissar for Foreign Affairs he went to London in February 1921 as the head of the first delegation of Kemal's government to be received there, he made a proposal to Lloyd George for common action against Soviet Russia ; this came to the knowledge of Chicherin, and Sami was compelled to resign as the result of his protests. V. A. Gurko-Kryazhin, *Blizhnii Vostok i Derzhavy* (1925), p. 96, attributes Sami's resignation to an attempt to make a deal with France : it is at any rate clear that his orientation was western and anti-Soviet.

[2] During this period Enver was apparently still at Batum conducting propaganda against Kemal ; in the autumn of 1921, with the final decision in Moscow to support Kemal, Enver was despatched to central Asia to get him out of the way (*Revue du Monde Musulman*, lii (1922), 204-205).

afterwards, and resulted in the despatch to Angora in December 1921 of Frunze, the Soviet military expert, in the guise of a plenipotentiary of the Ukrainian SSR. The formal treaty signed between Turkey and the Ukraine on January 2, 1922, followed closely the Soviet-Turkish treaty of the previous March, and was merely a cover for the transaction of military business.[1] A little later the Soviet Government demonstrated its friendship for Turkey by espousing her claim to be invited to the Genoa conference.[2] Turkey reciprocated with a surprising concession. The ban was lifted on the Turkish Communist Party, which between March and October 1922, after fifteen months' intensive persecution, enjoyed " a second period of activity ".[3]

Strengthened by the material and moral support of Moscow, Kemal launched his attack against the Greek invaders in May 1922. It was a brilliant success. In three months the Greeks were routed; in September 1922 the last of them were driven into the sea, and Kemal's armies, flushed with victory, were making menacing gestures at the weak British garrison that still occupied Constantinople. But at this point caution prevailed. Strong pronouncements in London indicated a readiness to meet force by force. Kemal refrained from a direct challenge to British power; and Great Britain, falling in with the view long held by the other western Powers, recognized the necessity of withdrawing the forces of occupation from Constantinople and coming to terms with Kemal. A new peace treaty with Turkey and a new régime for the Straits would now have to be negotiated on equal terms.

[1] The treaty is in *British and Foreign State Papers*, cxx (1927), 953-957 ; L. Fischer (*The Soviets in World Affairs* (1930), i, 393) states categorically that Frunze's " short visit of twenty-three days was used to arrange for heavy shipments of Russian munitions and for the mapping out of a detailed plan of campaign against the Greeks in which, if need be, Red officers would participate ". This is a Soviet version ; it seems dubious whether Kemal would have welcomed the " participation " of officers of the Red Army, though he badly needed munitions. A telegram from Kemal expressing thanks for Frunze's mission and belief in the " profound mutual sympathies of our friendly nations " and in the " valuable solidarity of our two countries " was read at the ninth All-Russian Congress of Soviets in December 1921 (*Devyatyi Vserossiiskii S"ezd Sovetov* (1922), p. 213).

[2] *Materialy Genuezskoi Konferentsii* (1922), p. 33.

[3] *Protokoll des Vierten Kongresses der Kommunistischen Internationale* (Hamburg, 1923), p. 528 ; the first issue of *Yeni Hayat* (" New Life "), described as the journal of the People's Communist Party of Turkey, appeared on March 18, 1922 (*Novyi Vostok*, i (1922), 358).

This radical reversal of fortune led to far-reaching consequences. The immediate sequel of the Greek defeat was the downfall of Lloyd George.[1] But the incipient reconciliation of Kemal with the western Powers had another important result. Not only had Kemal, victory once achieved, no further need of Soviet support, but the chances of a favourable settlement by agreement with the west might even be prejudiced by too close an association with the Soviet Government, especially now that British domestic politics had taken a turn towards the Right. The first symptom of anxiety on the part of Kemal to demonstrate his ideological independence was a renewed persecution of Turkish communists which began in October. Communist groups which had recently enjoyed toleration in Angora and Constantinople were suppressed, and widespread arrests of communists occurred all over the country.[2]

Before these signs had become apparent or had been read in Moscow, the Soviet Government was already displaying its preoccupation with the future régime of the Straits. One of its first acts had been to renounce former Tsarist claims on Constantinople. But right of access to, and egress from, the Black Sea was a matter of concern to any Russian government; and an important clause in the Soviet-Turkish treaty of March 16, 1921, had proclaimed the freedom of the Straits under an international régime to be set up by agreement between the Black Sea Powers.[3] During the Greek-Turkish war constant protests had been registered against the unimpeded entry into the Black Sea of Greek warships under the protection of the allied forces in Constantinople.[4] On September 12, 1922, when the war was all but over, the Soviet Government hastened to inform the British Government that " Russia, Turkey, the Ukraine and Georgia, to whom belongs practically the whole Black Sea coast, cannot admit the right of any other government to interfere in the question of the settlement of the Straits ".[5] On September 24, 1922, when a British semi-official statement had

---

[1] See p. 430 above.
[2] *Protokoll des Vierten Kongresses der Kommunistischen Internationale* (Hamburg, 1923), pp. 528-530.
[3] See p. 303 above.
[4] Reference to these protests are collected in A. L. P. Dennis, *The Foreign Policies of Soviet Russia* (1924), p. 232, note 68.
[5] *Izvestiya*, September 14, 1922 ; the claim to speak in the name of Turkey could be justified by the Straits article of the Soviet-Turkish treaty of March 16, 1921, but was probably not particularly agreeable to the Turkish Government.

named Great Britain, France and Italy as the countries most interested in the question of the Straits,[1] Chicherin addressed a note on the question of the Straits to the governments of Great Britain, France, Italy, Yugoslavia, Rumania, Bulgaria, Greece and Egypt. Recalling the clause in the Soviet-Turkish treaty, Chicherin denounced the " usurpation " by the western Powers of the rights of " Russia and the allied republics ", and set forth in a few sentences the kernel of the Soviet case :

> No decision on the Straits taken without Russia will be final and lasting. It will merely sow the seeds of fresh conflicts. The freedom of the Straits which Great Britain has in mind means only the desire of a strong naval Power to control a route vitally necessary to other states in order thereby to keep them under a constant threat. This threat is directed primarily against Russia and Turkey.

The conclusion was a proposal for " the immediate convening of a conference of all the interested Powers and, first and foremost, of the Black Sea states ". Uncompromising in form, the proposal was in fact a retreat from the assertion of the exclusive interest of the Soviet republics and of Turkey, and an indication of willingness to negotiate.[2]

During October 1922 the Turkish question occupied the forefront of the diplomatic stage in Moscow. The western Powers went forward with preparations for a peace conference with Turkey at Lausanne, to which Soviet Russia, not being a belligerent, could not claim to be invited. The rejection of the Urquhart concession was moved and carried by Lenin on the publicly declared ground of Great Britain's opposition to Soviet participation in the conference.[3] In the middle of October a further note was sent, this time to Great Britain and Italy only, protesting against the exclusion of Soviet Russia.[4] Curzon reluctantly gave way, and a compromise was found. Soviet Russia could have no place at the negotiations of the peace treaty. But her delegates could be admitted to the Lausanne conference " in

---

[1] *The Times*, September 18, 1922.

[2] Klyuchnikov i Sabanin, *Mezhdunarodnaya Politika*, iii, i (1928), 201-202.

[3] See p. 432 above.

[4] *Pravda*, October 20, 1922 ; the omission of France was probably due to information that the French Government now favoured Soviet participation.

order to participate in the discussion of the question of the Straits ". On October 27, 1922, a formal invitation was handed to the Soviet Government in these terms. On November 2 Chicherin protested both against exclusion from the general conference and against the failure to extend the invitation to the Ukraine and Georgia, receiving on the second point the answer that Ukrainian and Georgian representatives could be included in the Soviet delegation.[1] In fact Moscow was well pleased to have won a partial victory ; and a full delegation headed by Chicherin set out for Lausanne.

Between the receipt of the invitation to Lausanne and the opening of the debates there on the question of the Straits, the fourth congress of Comintern was held in Moscow.[2] At the third congress in the summer of 1921, while the Anglo-Soviet trade agreement was a recent and notable achievement, the wrongs of the Asiatic peoples suffering under the imperialist yoke had been given short shrift.[3] At the fourth congress there was no longer the same reason to damp down anti-imperialist or anti-British fervour ; and while complaints were still heard of the curtailment of the time allowed to speakers and of poor attendance at discussions of the subject,[4] the spectacular neglect displayed at the previous congress was not repeated. Communist parties now existed bearing the names of most eastern countries. A few of them were legal ; most of them worked illegally, or were mainly or wholly confined to refugees residing in Moscow. Hardly any of them could boast more than a few hundred members. An Egyptian delegate appeared for the first time at the fourth congress ; but the record of the Egyptian Socialist Party which he represented was dubious, and he was admitted only in a consultative capacity.[5] It was, however, true that while capitalism in Europe

---

[1] This correspondence is in Klyuchnikov i Sabanin, *Mezhdunarodnaya Politika*, iii, i (1928), 203-205.

[2] The congress sat from November 5 to December 5, 1922 ; the Lausanne conference opened on November 20, but the discussion of the Straits to which alone the Soviet delegation was admitted did not begin till December 4.

[3] See pp. 387-389 above.

[4] *Protokoll des Vierten Kongresses der Kommunistischen Internationale* (Hamburg, 1923), pp. 609, 612.

[5] *Ibid.* pp. 615-617.

seemed to have made a recovery, unrest was still spreading in Asia; and Zinoviev relapsed into the facile optimism of earlier years when he prophesied that, by the tenth anniversary of the October revolution (the congress was just about to celebrate the fifth), " we shall see the world trembling with countless rebellions, as hundreds of millions of down-trodden human beings rise against imperialism ". The communists of the east might be few in number. But Zinoviev, and after him Safarov, repeated the classic consolation that the Russian Liberation of Labour group, which was the ancestor of the Russian Communist Party, had had only five members on its foundation in 1883.[1]

The imminent opening of the Lausanne conference brought Turkey into the forefront of the preoccupations of the congress and of the Soviet Government. At the session of November 20, 1922, the leading Turkish delegate, claiming to speak on behalf of the Angora and Constantinople sections of the Turkish Communist Party,[2] complained that, though the Turkish party had supported the government in accordance with the resolution of the second congress in its struggle against imperialism, the government had started a campaign of repression against the communists. He proposed a vote of protest which was unanimously adopted.[3] On the following day, *Izvestiya* took up the tale and accused the Turkish Government, by its persecution of communists, of " cutting off the branch on which it sits "; and this was followed by a whole series of articles on the theme that " the only country which could support the Turks at the Lausanne conference is Soviet Russia ".[4] It may be doubted whether it was yet realized in Moscow how little these admonitions and these effusive offers of support were relished by the Turkish delegation at Lausanne. A few days later, the fourth congress of Comintern took up the " eastern

[1] *Ibid.* pp. 11, 622.
[2] According to subsequent statements, the Turkish CP was created for the first time after the fourth congress " when all independent communist groups which formerly existed in Turkey were united ": this was the corollary of the unification of the country under Kemal. The Turkish Government, however, took action and " completely disorganized the activity of the party within a few months " (*From the Fourth to the Fifth World Congress: Report of the Executive Committee of the Communist International* (1924), p. 65); this is confirmed by protests in *Izvestiya*, February 14, 1923.
[3] *Protokoll des Vierten Kongresses der Kommunistischen Internationale* (Hamburg, 1923), pp. 526-532.
[4] *Izvestiya*, November 21, 22, 23, 1922.

question ". Two meetings were devoted to its discussion, and it was the subject of the longest and most detailed resolution of congress. The Dutch *rapporteur* took a broad sweep :

> The mightiest enemy of the proletariat as well as of the oriental peoples, and in particular of the Islamic peoples, is the British Empire, whose world-embracing imperialism also rests on dominion over the Indian world and on sea-power in the Mediterranean and in the Indian ocean. The Islamic peoples have it in their power to destroy the bridge which upholds British imperialism. If this bridge breaks, then this imperialism also collapses, and its collapse would have so mighty a repercussion in the whole Islamic world and the world of the east that French imperialism, too, could not survive the blow.[1]

But this singleness of purpose did not make it any easier to discover a single line of action. The experience of the past two years had made it no easier to provide a precise answer to the question stubbornly debated by Lenin and Roy at the second congress of the attitude to be taken up by national communist parties in " colonial and semi-colonial countries " to bourgeois and capitalist movements of national liberation. Roy, speaking from the standpoint of Hindu India and reverting to his argument at the second congress, thought that the policy of collaboration with bourgeois nationalism had gone too far. Two years' experience in " coordinating our strength with that of the bourgeois nationalist parties in these countries " had proved that this alliance was not always practicable. The leadership of the " anti-imperialist front " could not be left in the hands of the " timid and wavering bourgeoisie " ; the foundation of the whole movement must be its " most revolutionary social element ".[2] On the opposite side of the argument, Malaka, the Indonesian delegate, thought that collaboration had not been carried far enough. The Indonesian Communist Party had tried to work with the Muslim nationalist organization, Sarekat Islam, and had won over some of its followers. But harm had been done by the denunciation of pan-Islamism at the second congress of Comin-

---

[1] *Protokoll des Vierten Kongresses der Kommunistischen Internationale* (Hamburg, 1923), pp. 589-590 ; the reference to French imperialism derived special point from the current French colonial war in Morocco.

[2] *Ibid.* p. 598.

tern which had been used locally to discredit the communists. Did not the policy of the united anti-imperialist front imply support for " the war of liberation of the very aggressive, very active 250 millions of Muslims under the imperialist Powers ", in other words, for " pan-Islamism in this sense " ? [1] The question was not directly answered either by Zinoviev or Radek, to whom it was addressed, or by anyone else on the floor of the congress. The Turkish delegate, impatient of these refinements, brought back the issue nearer home by calling for " an anti-imperialist front " of the European nations, and demanded that the British Labour Party should bring pressure to bear on the British Government to conclude a peace treaty on the lines of the Turkish National Pact, to evacuate Constantinople and Thrace, and to settle the Straits question " in the sense of the Russian-Turkish treaty ".[2] Finally, Radek, applying to the east the tactics which he was busy commending to the German communists, repeated firmly the orders given to the Turkish party on its formation :

> Your first task, as soon as you have organized yourselves as a separate party, is to support the movement for national freedom in Turkey.[3]

The resolution on the eastern question adopted by the congress attempted to meet all these points of view. It introduced a new refinement into the Comintern doctrine of nationalism. In some

[1] *Ibid.* p. 189. In the interval between the third and fourth congresses Semaun, one of the leaders of the PKI, had spent some months in Moscow and attended sessions of IKKI in December 1921 and February 1922 ; here he is said to have received instructions not to press for the complete independence of Indonesia from Holland — an extreme example of the caution prevailing in the inner councils of Comintern at this time and reluctance to antagonize the western Powers (*Revue du Monde Musulman*, lii (1922), 75-80). An article in *Internationale Presse-Korrespondenz* (weekly edition), No. 18, May 5, 1923, pp. 425-426, admitted that Semaun on his return from Moscow had argued that Indonesia " still needs for the present the help of capitalist Holland ", but condemned this attitude as a symptom of " dissatisfaction with the Soviet régime ". This account receives partial confirmation from an Indonesian source (Sitorus, *Sedjarah Pergerakan Kebangsaan Indonesia* (1947)), which states that on his return he advised the party " not to act hotheadedly ", and that several members of the party " were not content with Semaun's explanations, and became disappointed with his turning to the Right ". Malaka appears to have been one of those who opposed him (*Revue du Monde Musulman*, lii (1922), 80-81).

[2] *Protokoll des Vierten Kongresses der Kommunistischen Internationale* (Hamburg, 1923), p. 624.   [3] *Ibid.* p. 630.

backward colonial and semi-colonial countries, where " feudal-patriarchal relations " had not yet been broken up, and a native feudal aristocracy was still in being, another hitherto unrecognized possibility existed : " the representatives of these upper strata may appear as active leaders in the struggle against the imperialist policy of violence ". Hence it was conceivable that the policy of the anti-imperialist front might call for temporary collaboration not only — as the second congress had proclaimed — with a national bourgeoisie, but even with a national feudal aristocracy. This covered the case put by the Indonesian delegate :

> In Muslim countries the national movement at first finds its ideology in the religious-political watchwords of pan-Islamism, and this gives the officials and diplomats of the great Powers the opportunity to exploit the prejudices and uncertainty of the broad masses in the struggle against the national move-ment. . . . Yet on the whole, as the growth of national liberation movements extends, the religious-political watchwords of pan-Islamism are replaced more and more by concrete political demands. The struggle recently carried on in Turkey for the separation of the secular power from the Khalifate confirms this.
>
> The chief task common to all national revolutionary move-ments consists in realizing national unity and achieving state independence.[1]

The pursuit of national unity through temporary support of pan-Islamism was thus endorsed on the comforting supposition that the religious aspect of the national movement would die away with the advance of the class struggle. The resolution compared the " united anti-imperialist front " now prescribed in eastern countries with the " united workers' front " advocated during the past year in Europe : both were policies called for by " the prospect of a prolonged and long drawn-out struggle " which demanded " the mobilization of all revolutionary elements ". But the anti-imperialist front must also be fitted into a world-wide picture :

> To explain to the broad masses of toilers the indispensability of an alliance with the international proletariat and with the Soviet republics is one of the most important tasks of the united anti-imperialist front. The colonial revolution can conquer, and defend its conquests, only side by side with the proletarian

[1] *Kommunisticheskii Internatsional v Dokumentakh* (1933), p. 318.

revolution in the leading countries. . . . The demand for a close alliance with the proletarian republic of Soviets is the banner of the united anti-imperialist front.[1]

A corresponding adjustment was made in the agrarian resolution. Varga explained that the assumption by the second congress of an identity between the national and the agrarian movements had been based on the experience of such countries as India; [2] there might be other countries — such as Turkey — where the landowners were themselves leaders of the national movement, and here different considerations would apply. The resolution, which took the form of a " Sketch of an Agrarian Programme ", made the point almost embarrassingly clear :

> In colonial countries with an enslaved native peasant population the national struggle for liberation will either be conducted by the whole population together, as for example in Turkey, and in this case the struggle of the enslaved peasantry against the landowners begins inevitably after victory in the struggle for liberation ; or else the feudal landowners are in alliance with the imperialist robbers, and in these lands, as for example in India, the social struggle of the enslaved peasants coincides with the national struggle for liberation.[3]

The theoretical dilemma of the relation of communist parties, and of oppressed workers and peasants, to national liberation movements in their own countries, far from being resolved, was intensified by the conclusions of the fourth congress. Proletariat and peasants were required to subordinate their social programme to the immediate needs of a common national struggle against foreign imperialism. It was assumed that a nationally minded bourgeoisie, or even a nationally-minded feudal aristocracy, would be ready to conduct a struggle for national liberation from the yoke of foreign imperialism in alliance with potentially revolutionary proletarians and peasants, who were only waiting for the moment of victory to turn against them and overthrow them. The practical lessons to be drawn from the debates and resolutions of the congress were, however, less obscure. Like the united front in

---

[1] *Ibid.* pp. 322-323.

[2] *Protokoll des Vierten Kongresses der Kommunistischen Internationale* (Hamburg, 1923), p. 830.

[3] *Ibid.* p. 833 ; *Kommunistischeskii Internatsional v Dokumentakh* (1933), pp. 329-330.

European countries, the united anti-imperialist front in Asia imparted the maximum of flexibility to the Comintern line, and made it readily adjustable to the changing needs of Soviet policy. It marked one further step in the identification of the ultimate interest of world revolution with the immediate national interest of the country which was alone equipped to act as the revolutionary standard-bearer. The application of the principle to Turkey at the present turning-point of her fortunes was also clear. After debating the eastern and agrarian questions, the congress adopted its resolution in condemnation of the Versailles treaty ; [1] and this resolution already established the implied parallel between the rôle of the Turkish and German parties by hailing Turkey as " the outpost of the revolutionary east ", and congratulating her on having " successfully resisted arms in hand the carrying out of the peace treaty ".[2] Radek, who played a particularly prominent rôle throughout this congress, may well have recalled the conversations with Enver in the Moabit prison more than three years before when he had first propounded the then novel idea of an alliance between Russian Bolshevism and a Turkish or a German nationalism in revolt against the peace terms imposed by western imperialist Powers. The idea had prospered and borne fruit both in Turkish and in German policy. In Germany it had been crowned by the Rapallo treaty ; six months later it seemed in Moscow as if the Lausanne conference was destined to put the coping-stone on an equally solid structure of Soviet-Turkish friendship. The persecution of Turkish communists did not appear any more significant than the repressive measures undertaken from time to time against German communists by Seeckt and the Reichswehr. As Bukharin consolingly observed at the twelfth party congress in April 1923, Turkey, " in spite of all persecutions of communists, plays a revolutionary rôle, since she is a destructive instrument in relation to the imperialist system as a whole ".[3]

The Lausanne conference of the winter of 1922–1923 marked the first appearance of the Soviet Government on an important

[1] See pp. 454-455 above.
[2] *Kommunisticheskii Internatsional v Dokumentakh* (1933), p. 339.
[3] *Dvenadtsatyi S"ezd Rossiiskoi Kommunisticheskoi Partii (Bol'shevikov)* (1923), p. 24.

international occasion as the champion, not of the interests of the
revolution of 1917, but of what were plainly and admittedly Russian
national and geopolitical interests.   A much-quoted article headed
Russia Comes Back, which appeared in *Izvestiya* of December 7,
1922, over the signature of its editor Steklov, showed that the
theme of continuity was not neglected in Moscow :

> As a result of the imperialist and civil wars, Russia tem-
> porarily disappeared from the horizon as a great Power.   The
> new Russia born during the revolution was still too weak to
> speak her word in international politics.   But the Soviet republic
> has been growing stronger every year, and has taken advantage
> of existing dissensions among the European Powers not less
> skilfully than the old Russia.   Aware of her ever-growing
> strength, Soviet Russia can never be discouraged by temporary
> diplomatic failure, since final victory is assured.   Russia is
> coming back to the international stage.   Let us hope that the
> day is at hand when this reappearance will be felt so strongly
> that no one will dare to contradict her voice.

The nature of the occasion was emphasized by the appearance,
as Chicherin's principal adversary at Lausanne, of the last authentic representative of the anti-Russian tradition of British foreign
policy in the later nineteenth century.   Curzon was concerned
not with the defence of the capitalist system, but with the defence
and expansion of British power, which he interpreted in military
and feudal terms.   Chicherin, a man of subtler intellectual percep-
tions, a sceptic in all, perhaps, save a profound conviction of the
bankruptcy of western imperialism and of its traditional diplomacy, combined the interests of Russian national policy with the
appeal to the national aspirations of weaker countries which had
been embodied from the outset in the revolutionary programme.
At Lausanne this seemed to be rendered easy for him by the
reversal of traditional national attitudes towards the question of
the Straits.   In the nineteenth century, Great Britain, eager to
confine the Russian fleet to the Black Sea, had always sought to
impose the most drastic restrictions on the passage of warships
through the Turkish waters of the Straits and to uphold unlimited
Turkish sovereignty over them ; Russia, on the other hand, had
sought to place on Turkey the obligation to afford freedom of passage in all conditions.   Now Great Britain, no longer apprehensive

of the Russian fleet and desiring freedom of access to the Black
Sea for her own warships, assumed the former Russian rôle of
seeking to limit Turkish sovereignty over the Straits in the interests
of unrestricted ingress and egress for warships of all nations;
Russia, having experienced the results of the unimpeded access
of foreign warships to the Black Sea during the civil war, reverted
to the former British championship of Turkish sovereignty over
the Straits. The equivocal element in the situation was the
attitude of Turkey, now somewhat recovered from her recent
buffetings at the hands of the western Powers, and apprehensive
of too close and exclusive association with her powerful neighbour.
Even the National Pact of January 1920, while insisting on the
security of Constantinople, had — unlike the Soviet-Turkish treaty
of March 16, 1921 — envisaged a fully international régime for
the Straits. The question of the Straits had thus become a secondary factor in Turkish calculations, and was examined in the light
of the broader issue of relations with the west and with the east.

When the Straits question was taken up by the Lausanne
conference for the first time on December 4, 1922, Ismet, the Turkish delegate, declined a pressing invitation from Curzon, as
president, to speak first; and it fell to the newly arrived Soviet
delegate to make the opening statement. Chicherin, who spoke
as head of a delegation representing " Russia, the Ukraine and
Georgia ",[1] gave an exhibition of polished diplomacy :

> There must be lasting guarantees for the maintenance of
> peace in the Black Sea, the safety of its shores, peace in the Near
> East and the security of Constantinople ; that is to say, the
> Dardanelles and the Bosphorus must be permanently closed
> both in peace and in war to warships, armed vessels and military
> aircraft of all countries except Turkey.
>   . . . The Russian Government and its allies, basing their
> argument on the fact that the Dardanelles and the Bosphorus
> belong to Turkey, and respecting as they do the sovereignty of
> each people, insist on the re-establishment and full maintenance
> of the rights of the Turkish people over Turkish territory and
> waters. . . . The closing of the Straits to warships is also in
> accordance with the principle of equality between all states,
> whereas the opening of the Straits to warships would confer a

---

[1] It was a composite delegation, but Vorovsky figured in it as delegate of the
Ukraine, and Mdivani of Georgia.

preponderant position on the strongest sea Power. . . . Soviet Russia has annulled without compensation all the agreements regarding the transfer of Constantinople to Russia; she has thereby enabled Turkey to defend her existence victoriously; she has liberated all the states of the Mediterranean from the threat of the century-old ambitions of Tsarism; but it was never her intention to acquiesce in a solution of the Straits problem aimed directly against her own safety.[1]

Chicherin was followed by the delegates of Rumania and Bulgaria, both Black Sea countries, and Greece, possessing direct local interests : all of these declared for the western view. Curzon then put to the obviously embarrassed Ismet the blunt question " whether he accepted the Russian case as the case of the Turkish Government ". Ismet replied that, while " among the various proposals submitted to the conference those of the Russo-Ukrainian-Georgian delegation seemed to him to correspond with the point of view of the Turkish delegation ", the latter was " obliged to examine " any other proposals which might be made.[2] The narrow wedge thus skilfully inserted between the Soviet and Turkish delegations widened as the conference proceeded.

This hint of a rebuff did not change Chicherin's tactics. Two days later, addressing himself to Curzon, he suggested that the " Russian advance in Asia " had been replaced by a " British advance in Europe " :

The Russian revolution has transformed the Russian people into a nation whose entire energy is concentrated in its government to a degree hitherto unknown in history ; if war is forced upon that nation, it will not capitulate. . . . But it is not war that we offer you ; it is peace, based on the principle of a partition wall between us and on the principle of the freedom and sovereignty of Turkey.[3]

The rights and interests of Turkey were espoused with ostentatious emphasis. The draft convention submitted by the western

---

[1] *Lausanne Conference on Near Eastern Affairs, 1922–1923*, Cmd. 1814 (1923), pp. 129-130.

[2] *Ibid.* pp. 131-135 : the scene is dramatically described by an eye-witness in H. Nicolson, *Curzon: The Last Phase* (1934), pp. 308-311.

[3] *Lausanne Conference on Near Eastern Affairs, 1922–1923*, Cmd. 1814 (1923), p. 149 ; the reference to the Pamirs, already quoted on p. 469 above, came in this passage.

Powers was "tantamount to depriving the Turkish people of control over transit and of effective sovereignty in the Straits" and "a flagrant violation of the sovereignty and independence of Turkey ".[1] Undeterred by its formal exclusion from the negotiations on the peace treaty, the Soviet delegation handed in a long memorandum dilating on the injustice to Turkey of the terms proposed by the western Allies.[2] It soon became clear, however, that the Turkish delegation at Lausanne was more embarrassed than flattered by Chicherin's eager championship. The Straits question was a matter of keener interest to Soviet Russia than to Turkey. Turkey did not particularly welcome the prospect of finding herself face to face with Soviet power in the Black Sea while warships of all other nations were excluded; and the delegation at Lausanne, having discovered that it could purchase other advantages by throwing over the Soviet alliance, prepared to do so without regard to the feelings or interests of the Soviet delegation. Chicherin thus found himself in the later stages of the conference both isolated and deprived of the main argument on which he had chosen to rely. The draft convention on the Straits, which was approved by the conference on February 1, 1923, was in its main outlines a victory for the British case. The only important limitation on freedom of access for foreign warships to the Black Sea was that no single Power might send in at any one time a naval force larger than the largest force of any one Black Sea country. The acceptance of these conditions provoked from the Soviet delegation a statement that "if certain Powers sign this convention without Russia, the Ukraine and Georgia, the Straits question remains and will remain open ".[3]

---

[1] *Lausanne Conference on Near Eastern Affairs, 1922–1923*, Cmd. 1814 (1923), p. 272.

[2] *Izvestiya*, January 11, 12, 1923 ; extracts in translation are in *Soviet Documents on Foreign Policy*, ed. J. Degras, i (1951), 359-366.

[3] *Lausanne Conference on Near Eastern Affairs, 1922–1923*, Cmd. 1814 (1923), p. 456. A minor incident of the conference was Chicherin's visit to Curzon — their one personal meeting. According to Chicherin's version (the only one hitherto available), the conversation turned mainly on the propaganda issue. Chicherin, while professing that the official prohibition on anti-British propaganda was strictly enforced, maintained that "we cannot compel a member of the communist party to cease to express himself as a communist " : to which Curzon replied that a mere "50 per cent reduction in propaganda" was unacceptable (*Tretii S"ezd Sovetov Sotsialisticheskikh Respublik* (1925), p. 93).

The accommodating attitude of the Turkish delegation on the question of the Straits, while enabling it to make its peace with the British delegation, did not save it from French and Italian intransigence on some of the peace terms. A few days after this agreement had been achieved, subject to Soviet dissent, on the question of the Straits, Curzon, in the name of the allied delegations, presented an ultimatum to Ismet on an issue relating to the legal status of foreigners in Turkey ; and on its rejection by the Turkish delegation — apparently with Chicherin's encouragement [1] — the conference broke down. It was resumed at the end of April 1923. This time, since the Straits question had been settled, no Soviet delegates were invited ; and Vorovsky, now Soviet representative in Rome, who was sent by the Soviet Government to Lausanne as an observer, was assassinated by a " white " fanatic. The Straits convention was eventually signed in Lausanne with the treaty of peace on July 24, 1923.[2] It was signed, under protest, three weeks later by Vorovsky's successor in Rome, but never ratified by the Soviet Government. For the Soviet Government it was an undisguised defeat. While the Lausanne conference represented a further step in bringing back Soviet Russia to the international stage, it had also proved that she was not yet strong enough to play a leading rôle there, or to attract weaker countries to her side, so long as she stood alone among the Great Powers. The partner in Europe, whose voice would henceforth make it increasingly difficult to ignore Soviet Russia in European affairs, was still lacking in Asia. What most of all had been demonstrated in Lausanne was the value of Rapallo.

[1] L. Fischer, *The Soviets in World Affairs* (1930), i, 409.
[2] *Treaty of Peace with Turkey, and other Instruments signed at Lausanne on July 24, 1923*, Cmd. 1929 (1923).

CHAPTER 33

THE FAR EAST : I — ECLIPSE

THE Far East entered the effective orbit of Soviet foreign policy later than the countries of the Middle East and of Europe. Both Japan and China were, formally speaking, among the belligerent nations to which the peace decree and other broadcast appeals of the first days of the régime were addressed. But they were scarcely present to the consciousness of those who drafted and publicized these documents ; the appeal of November 20/December 3, 1917, " To all Muslim Toilers of Russia and the East " was extended to the Hindus,[1] but not beyond the frontiers of India. Such early contacts as occurred were mainly hostile. The Russian-owned and Russian-managed Chinese Eastern Railway, established on Chinese soil under a protocol attached to the Russo-Chinese treaty of 1896, provided an immediate bone of contention. Within a few days of the revolution in Petrograd, a self-constituted Soviet of workers in Harbin, the headquarters of the railway administration, attempted to take over the railway from General Horvath, its Russian president. The attempt was resisted, and on the suggestion of the allied governments, 10,000 Chinese troops were sent to Harbin " to maintain order ".[2] On December 20, 1917/January 2, 1918 the Chinese Government virtually took over the railway by appointing a Chinese president in defiance of the treaty of 1896 ;[3] but at this time the substitution of Chinese for " white " Russian control was unlikely to cause any heart-burnings in Moscow. Two months later Chinese troops were in occupation of the whole railway up to the frontier station of Hailar, and were stopping all through traffic to or from Siberia.[4]

[1] See p. 232.
[2] *Foreign Policy of the United States, 1918 : Russia*, ii (1932), 3.
[3] *Millard's Review* (Shanghai), January 15, 1918, p. 169 ; *China Year Book, 1921* (Shanghai, 1922), p. 624.
[4] *Millard's Review* (Shanghai), March 16, p. 83.

In Petrograd the Japanese Ambassador followed the attitude of the other allied representatives, retiring with them to Vologda in February 1918 and studiously declining all relations with the new régime. The Soviet Government had at first better hopes of the Chinese Minister. It apparently repeated with specific application to China the general annulment of all treaties of the Tsarist régime, and suggested negotiations with the Chinese Government for the abrogation and replacement of former treaties affecting China. But in March 1918 the allies, in the words of a subsequent Soviet statement, " seized the Peking government by the throat " and compelled it " to abandon all relations with the Russian workers' and peasants' government ".[1] On April 5, 1918, the landing of a Japanese detachment at Vladivostok, which proved to be the first step towards allied military intervention on an extensive scale, provoked strong Soviet protests in the press and to the allied representatives in Moscow and in Vologda.[2] A few days later Yanson, a Soviet delegate of uncertain status in the Far East, had a meeting with a Chinese representative on the Manchurian frontier, at which he protested against incursions from Chinese into Soviet territory of the " white " Cossack general Semenov, enjoying allied support.[3] All these protests were wholly without effect. The Chinese Government formally associated itself with the allied intervention, even sending a token Chinese detachment to Vladivostok. From the summer of 1918 to the early months of 1920 Siberia was a main theatre of war against the Soviet Government. After the downfall of Kolchak came the formation of the buffer Far Eastern Republic and the gradual withdrawal of the remaining Japanese forces within the confines of the maritime province. But it was not till November 1922, four and a half years after their arrival, that the last Japanese troops left Vladivostok.[4] The wall of isolation which separated Soviet Russia from the outside world in 1919 was more impenetrable

---

[1] No documents relating to these transactions have been published : our knowledge of them is confined to two rather vague subsequent Soviet statements, the first in the Narkomindel report to the fifth All-Russian Congress of Soviets (see p. 503 below), the second in the Soviet declaration of July 25, 1919 (see pp. 504-505 below).

[2] See p. 79, note 3, above.

[3] *Izvestiya*, April 13, 1918.

[4] These events are described in outline in Vol. I, pp. 352-363.

on the side of the Far East than elsewhere, and afterwards took longer to break down. But a certain parallelism can be observed. The year 1920 brought the first signs, in the Far East as in Europe, that the period of eclipse and enforced exclusion was drawing to an end. The year 1921, in which Soviet diplomacy first began to consolidate its position in Europe and in the Middle East, was also the year of its first successes in the Far East.

Throughout the whole period from 1917 to 1921 no direct relations existed between Moscow and Tokyo. But Japan rather than China was at the outset the principal focus of Soviet concern and Soviet policy in the Far East, both because Japan was the principal enemy and the principal imperialist Power in eastern Asia, and because Japan, as a large industrial country with a growing and down-trodden proletariat, was potentially ripe for revolution and a promising field for revolutionary propaganda. From the Soviet point of view, therefore, Japan was both the Britain and the Germany of the Far East. The industrialization of Japan on western lines had been followed in the last two decades of the nineteenth century by a gradual infiltration into Japan of western political ideas. In 1901 a social-democratic party was founded by Katayama, later a leading Japanese communist, and Kotoku, later an anarcho-syndicalist, but was quickly disbanded by the authorities. During the Russo-Japanese war a radical journal published for the first time a Japanese translation of the *Communist Manifesto*. In August 1904 Katayama attended the congress of the Second International in Amsterdam; and his public handshake with Plekhanov was one of the high-lights of the congress. Throughout the ensuing period all Left movements and activities in Japan were subjected to systematic persecution and suppression. In 1911 Kotoku and other leading anarchists were executed on a charge of conspiring to kill the Emperor; and two years later Katayama emigrated to the United States.[1]

The first world war brought to Japan a period of inflated profits and prices which placed new strains on the underpaid and

---

[1] For a detailed account of this period see an article by Hyman Kublin in *Journal of Modern History* (Chicago), xxii, No. 4 (December 1950), pp. 322-339.

underfed worker. The so-called " rice riots " of August and September 1918 were the first overt appearance in Japan of anything like an organized labour movement caused by proletarian discontent. But the Russian Bolsheviks had at this time few resources to spare for anything so remote as the Far East from their own threatened vital centres, and few expert advisers on Far Eastern affairs. Clearly the field for revolutionary action in Japan was far more limited and less easily accessible than in western Europe. In the " international propaganda section " set up by the first congress of communist organizations of the east in November 1918 one of the twelve projected divisions was devoted to Japan.[1] But it is not known whether a Japanese division in fact ever came into existence. The summons from Moscow to the founding congress of Comintern sent out in January 1919 referred to " socialist groups in Tokyo and Yokohama ".[2] But no Japanese appeared at the congress ; and the fact that the occasion was taken to read a two-year-old declaration of a Tokyo group in honour of the February revolution,[3] which had been casually brought to Moscow by a Dutch communist, suggests both an eagerness to establish contact with Japan and a paucity of means for doing so. Under the impact partly of western radicalism and partly of the Bolshevik revolution, Japanese intellectuals began to form Left groups, which at this stage appear to have had little or no contact with the masses and no practical programme. A Japanese " socialist federation " is said to have been formed in October 1919 out of a coalition of an anarcho-syndicalist and a radical socialist group.[4] In April 1920 a " Japanese socialist group in the United States ", in which Katayama was a moving spirit, issued a protest against Japanese military reprisals in Vladivostok for the Nikolaevsk massacre ;[5] and Japanese in the United States appear

[1] *Zhizn' Natsional'nostei*, No. 5 (13), February 16, 1919.

[2] See p. 119 above. Their inclusion was apparently due to the accident of the arrival in Moscow at this moment of the Dutch Communist, Rutgers, who had travelled from the United States via Japan. He had taken with him from New York introductions from Katayama, the Japanese socialist, to socialist groups in Tokyo and Yokohama, and brought with him from Japan to Moscow a resolution of May 1, 1917 (see following note), welcoming the February revolution (*Istorik Marksist*, No. 2-3, 1935, pp. 86-88).

[3] *Der I. Kongress der Kommunistischen Internationale* (Hamburg, 1921), pp. 193-194.

[4] *Tikhii Okean*, No. 1, 1934, pp. 124-125.

[5] *Soviet Russia* (N.Y.), May 15, 1920, pp. 483-484.

to have inspired the foundation of a socialist league in Tokyo in December 1920.[1]

The first moves of Comintern in this field demonstrated little but the difficulties of the task. " Japan, torn by the contradictions of capitalism within its feudal framework ", declared the manifesto of the second congress of Comintern in August 1920, " stands on the eve of a profound revolutionary crisis ".[2] But the diagnosis was based on Marxist theory rather than on empirical evidence. In the autumn of 1920, Voitinsky, who had come to China as the representative of Comintern,[3] made a direct approach by inviting Osugi, a prominent Japanese Left-wing leader who was himself an anarchist, to visit him in Shanghai. As a result of this visit Osugi obtained funds to carry on activities in Japan, including the foundation of a Left journal in which communists were to cooperate. This journal was actually founded in January 1921 under the name of *Rodo Undo* (Labour Movement), with two communists on its editorial board, but was quickly suppressed by the police. In the spring of 1921 Kondo, one of the two communists, went to Shanghai. He was interviewed by a committee of twelve Chinese and Koreans presided over by Pak Din-shun as Comintern delegate, was given 6300 yen for work in Japan and was invited to attend the third congress of Comintern in Moscow in the summer of the same year as Japanese delegate. On his return to Japan, however, he too was arrested, though he appears to have been released soon after for lack of specific evidence.[4] In spite of this failure, a Japanese spokesman arrived in Moscow for the third congress, bringing " the revolutionary greetings of the communist party which has just been organized in Japan ".[5] But he had no credentials, and this enterprise was apparently still-born, since in the following winter the task of creating a Japanese party had to be taken up anew.

The impenetrability of Japan, whether to Soviet policy or to

---

[1] *Kommunisticheskii Internatsional*, No. 18 (October 8, 1921), cols. 4721-4722.

[2] *Kommunisticheskii Internatsional v Dokumentakh* (1933), p. 140.

[3] See pp. 507-508 below.

[4] Article by P. Langer and R. Swearingen in *Pacific Affairs* (N.Y.), xxiii (1950), No. 4, pp. 340-341 ; further information from Japanese sources communicated by Messrs. Langer and Swearingen.

[5] *Protokoll des III. Kongresses der Kommunistischen Internationale* (Hamburg, 1921), p. 1023.

Bolshevik propaganda, accounted for a considerable display of interest in Korea, the most conspicuous sore spot of Japanese imperialism. After the Russo-Japanese war large numbers of Korean refugees had settled in Siberia, and a few isolated Korean intellectuals had found their way to Petersburg.[1] Another handful of Korean exiles settled in the United States. The first world war, culminating in the February and October revolutions, naturally caused a certain ferment among these Korean groups. A Korean delegate spoke at the international meeting in Petrograd in December 1918 which preceded the foundation of the Communist International;[2] and another Korean appeared, though without credentials, at the founding congress of the International in March 1919. By this time two separate Korean national movements, both demanding the liberation of their country from Japan, had come into existence. One formed a Korean national council with a programme of independence for Korea framed on the basis of national self-determination and appealed for allied, or more specifically American, sympathy; its leader was Syngman Rhee, an American Korean and a former pupil of President Wilson. This group, which attempted to bring about a national rising in Korea in March 1919,[3] seems to have lost influence and faded away when the rising was easily suppressed by the Japanese, and the Paris peace conference refused to consider the Korean question. The other group sought collaboration with the Bolsheviks on a combined nationalist and revolutionary programme.[4] Under the name of the Korean Socialist Party, it held a " congress " at Vladivostok in April 1919, and sent Pak Din-shun and two other delegates to Moscow to make a report on its activities to IKKI.[5]

[1] The 1926 census showed some 85,000 Koreans of Soviet nationality, and about the same number of aliens of Japanese nationality, most of whom would be Koreans, residing in the USSR ; of the former group, only 10 per cent were urban and less than 40 per cent literate (F. Lorimer, *The Population of the Soviet Union* (Geneva, 1946), pp. 61-62).

[2] *Sowjet-Russland und die Völker der Welt* (Petrograd, 1920), pp. 36-38 ; for this meeting see pp. 117-118 above.

[3] *Tikhii Okean*, No. 1, 1934, p. 124 ; according to a Korean delegate at the seventh All-Russian Congress of Soviets in December 1919, 20,000 Koreans perished in the rising, which was organized by " Right groups " in the Korean proletariat (7^i *Vserossiiskii S"ezd Sovetov* (1920), p. 273).

[4] *Revolyutsiya na Dal'nem Vostoke* (1923), pp. 359-374.

[5] *Kommunisticheskii Internatsional*, No. 7-8 (November-December 1919), cols. 1171-1176 ; 7^i *Vserossiiskii S"ezd Sovetov* (1920), p. 274.

The official foundation of a Korean Communist Party took place in 1920.[1] Pak Din-shun was its delegate at the second and third congresses of Comintern, and became for a time the recognized spokesman on Korean affairs at Moscow. But the Korean movement, however sedulously fostered by Comintern, was no more than a minute pin-prick in the seemingly impenetrable armour of Japanese imperialism.

The situation in China as it presented itself at the outset to the framers of Soviet foreign policy was far more complicated than the situation in Japan, and at first sight equally unpromising. There were, however, two important differences which vitally affected Soviet policy, and in the long run offered it prospects of positive and successful action in China, which were not open to it in Japan.

In the first place, though the Chinese proletariat was far less numerous than the Japanese and the chances of a proletarian revolution therefore seemed far more remote, Chinese nationalism provided a source of revolutionary ferment which was wholly absent in Japan. Lenin had long ago included China with Persia and Turkey as " semi-colonial " countries exploited and oppressed by the imperialist Powers. The Chinese revolution of 1911 had given a strong impetus to national resentment against the " unequal " treaties imposed on China in the nineteenth century by the European Powers and by Japan ; the renunciation by the Soviet Government of Russia's share in these treaties and in the privileges conferred by them was a powerful asset of Soviet policy and Soviet propaganda. The growing rift between Soviet Russia and the western world almost automatically sealed an alliance between the Bolshevik revolution and Chinese nationalism. The association of Japan with the western Powers, both in their attitude to China and in their support of the " whites " in the Russian civil war, gave Soviet Russia and nationalist China a ground of common hostility to Japan. Moreover Chinese nationalism produced a split within China itself. At the time when Soviet policy first became concerned with Chinese affairs, the Chinese Government in Peking, working in more or less close conjunction with the

---

[1] *Kommunisticheskii Internatsional*, No. 12 (July 20, 1920), cols. 2157-2162 ; this article discusses on conventional lines the revolutionary importance of the Far East.

western Powers and with Japan, exercised a precarious and little more than nominal authority over the war-lords who dominated several of the most important provinces, and was actively opposed by a more or less organized nationalist government in Canton, whose moving spirit was Sun Yat-sen, the " father " of the 1911 revolution. Lenin in 1912 had compared the Chinese revolution with the Russian revolution, and, while denouncing as " reactionary " Sun Yat-sen's " dream " that it was possible in China to by-pass capitalism and make a direct transition to socialism, described Sun Yat-sen himself as "a revolutionary democrat, full of nobility and enthusiasm ".[1] Sun Yat-sen was no Marxist, and explicitly rejected class warfare. But his conception of democracy, like that of Rousseau, was direct and totalitarian ; and this made current forms of western democracy more alien to him than Bolshevism. He is said to have hailed the Bolshevik revolution as " a replica of its Chinese forerunner " ; [2] and there is evidence that he had learned from Lenin's conception of an organized and disciplined revolutionary party.[3] A certain natural sympathy therefore existed between the makers of the Chinese and of the Russian revolutions, long before it began to take political shape, and even before communications had been opened between them. In these conditions Soviet diplomacy, while maintaining formal recognition of the Peking government, retained a broad freedom of manœuvre, not substantially differing in this respect from the diplomacy of other Powers except in the ampler opportunities available to it.

Secondly, while direct territorial contact between Russia and Japan was limited to a small and specific area, Russia and China shared the longest land frontier in the world. Soviet-Chinese relations continued to be dominated, as Russian-Chinese relations had long been, by issues arising from traditional Russian pressure on those outer marches of the Chinese Empire whose populations were always more or less recalcitrant to the authority of a central Chinese Government. Three such areas sprawled along the frontier between Russia in Asia and China — Sinkiang (the so-

[1] Lenin, *Sochineniya*, xvi, 27-29.
[2] Sun Fo, *China Looks Forward* (1944), p. 10.
[3] B. I. Schwartz, *Chinese Communism and the Rise of Mao* (Harvard, 1951), p. 213, note 33.

called Chinese Turkestan), Outer Mongolia and Manchuria. The first two were sparsely inhabited by non-Chinese populations of Turki and Mongol speech respectively; [1] the third, Manchuria, alone possessed great natural wealth and a dense Chinese population, forming the only part of the Russian-Chinese frontier where Russians and Chinese were in direct territorial contact, and presenting a major bone of contention in the shape of the Chinese Eastern Railway. The situation was complicated by the interest shown in all these regions by Japan, passive throughout the nineteen-twenties in Sinkiang, intermittent in Outer Mongolia,[2] continuous and active in Manchuria.

Of these three regions, Sinkiang was at this period too isolated from the policy-making centres to play a vital rôle. On the Chinese side, a powerful and able governor, Yang Tseng-hsiu, had ruled the province since 1912 in virtually complete independence of Peking.[3] On the Soviet side, a complete interruption of communications between Moscow and Tashkent lasting for almost two years was the sequel of the Bolshevik revolution; the central authority did not begin to make itself felt before the spring of 1920, and was not effective throughout Turkestan till much later.[4] In the disturbed conditions on the Soviet side of the frontier, even local relations were established with difficulty, and these were confined to matters of local concern. Yang's principal anxiety at this period was to secure the repatriation to Russian territory of the many thousands of " white " refugees who had flooded into Sinkiang after the revolution,[5] and constituted a threat to security and order. The authorities of Soviet Turkestan urgently desired a re-establishment of trade across the frontier; imports from Sinkiang of livestock, hides and tea had played a substantial

---

[1] The most recent study of the complex ethnic structure of the population of Sinkiang is in O. Lattimore, *The Pivot of Asia* (Boston, 1950), pp. 103-151.

[2] For Japanese interest in Outer Mongolia before 1917 see G. M. Friters, *Outer Mongolia and its International Position* (Baltimore, 1949), pp. 217-226.

[3] An outline sketch of the period of Yang's rule, with references to sources, is in O. Lattimore, *The Pivot of Asia* (Boston, 1950), pp. 52-64.

[4] See Vol. 1, pp. 331, 335-336.

[5] Many Kazakhs had also fled to Sinkiang after the Kazakh rebellion of 1916, but these were easily absorbed into racially and economically cognate groups and presented no serious problem ; Kazakh migration into Sinkiang was a long-standing phenomenon (F. Lorimer, *The Population of the Soviet Union* (Geneva, 1946), p. 140).

CH. XXXIII THE FAR EAST: I — ECLIPSE

part in the economy of Russian Central Asia, though the exports of textiles and consumer goods which had been the counterpart of these imports were now scarcely available. On May 27, 1920, an agreement was concluded between the governor of Sinkiang and the Tashkent government. Each party was to have two " offices for commerce and foreign affairs " on the territory of the other. The Soviet offices were to be at I-li and I-ning, both on the northern frontier of Sinkiang; the Chinese offices were, somewhat mysteriously, to be not in Soviet Turkestan, but in Siberia, one in Semirechie at Semipalatinsk, the other at Verkhne-Udinsk on the Siberian-Mongolian border. Trade between Soviet Turkestan and Sinkiang was to be limited to a single route entering the northern, or I-li, province of Sinkiang. The Tashkent authorities promised an " inviolable amnesty " for all Russian civil and military refugees in Chinese territory who might be sent back by the Chinese authorities. Chinese property claims in Soviet Turkestan were reserved in vague terms for future "friendly and direct agreements ".[1]

This agreement represented a victory on almost all points for the Sinkiang authorities. The Sino-Russian treaty of 1881 had granted to Russia the right to establish seven consulates in Sinkiang enjoying extra-territorial rights; these were now reduced to two frontier offices, and trade was limited to a single route and subject in all respects to local law. The Tashkent authorities had agreed to take back the unwanted burden of " white " refugees. Such rights as the agreement conferred on Russian citizens to trade in Sinkiang were confined to the northern province; Soviet influence and infiltration were by implication strictly excluded from southern Sinkiang, where British power was still pre-

[1] Though the agreement was signed in Chinese and in Russian, no Russian text has ever been published, and the best available version is an English translation from the Chinese in. *Treaties and Agreements with and concerning China, 1919-1929* (Washington, 1929), pp. 24-25; the French translation in *Revue des Études Islamiques*, vii (Année 1933), 1937), pp. 158-159 (where the Chinese original is stated to have been officially published in the journal *Pei Kinh Je Pao* of September 13, 1920), is briefer and evidently less satisfactory. The name of the principal Russian signatory appears in Chinese form as Limaliehfu: he is described as " commissioner for foreign affairs of Russia with special authority ". While the text of the agreement commits only the Tashkent government, the agreement to the setting up of Chinese agencies outside the territory of Turkestan suggests that the Soviet negotiator had in fact some wider authority.

dominant.[1] The agreement of May 27, 1920, marked the lowest point of Soviet power and influence in Central Asia. Thereafter the resumption of regular communications with Moscow and the restoration of order in Turkestan, culminating in the establishment of the autonomous Turkestan SSR in April 1921,[2] enabled the Soviet power to reassert itself in its relations with Sinkiang as elsewhere. The disorders of the Chinese civil war and weakening of British authority and prestige in India and throughout the Middle East accentuated the essential dependence of Sinkiang, firmly established in the last period of the Tsarist régime, on trade with Russia. Neither China nor British India could offer Sinkiang such easy access either to markets or to sources of supply as could Soviet Turkestan ; and, once Soviet authority was firmly established there, no other power impinged so closely on Sinkiang. In these conditions, the story of the next decade is one of a gradual recovery of Russian influence. The process was at the outset extremely slow. But already in 1921 trade in livestock from Sinkiang on an extensive scale was being organized through a Soviet office in Semipalatinsk ; and the secretary of the Chinese consulate there was reported as stating that, once Sinkiang had been cut off from Chinese markets by the civil war, it had no option but to seek markets in Soviet Russia. In the following year, according to a Soviet writer, trade fell off owing to a change in the Soviet authority concerned and a failure to make prompt payment for consignments delivered.[3] The limiting factor in Soviet trade with Sinkiang at this time was clearly Soviet inability to deliver in sufficient quantities the consumer goods required by the customer. No formal change was made before 1924 in conditions of trade or in other relations between Soviet Russia and Sinkiang.

Outer Mongolia, the second of these frontier regions, was the larger but more sparsely populated of the two parts into which Mongol territory was traditionally divided, and had been, ever since the annexation of the Amur region to Russia in 1858, an outlying and loosely held bastion of the Chinese Empire abutting

---

[1] The British consul-general at Kashgar at this time records that the former large Russian colony in Kashgar had dwindled in the early nineteen-twenties to some twenty persons, and that no Soviet representative came to Kashgar till 1925 (C. P. Skrine, *Chinese Central Asia* (1932), p. 66).

[2] See Vol. 1, pp. 336-339.

[3] *Novyi Vostok*, viii-ix (1925), 26-39 ; *Pravda*, November 6, 1921.

on Russian territory for more than 1500 miles. Russian diplomacy gradually succeeded in making of Outer Mongolia a recognized no-man's-land between the two empires, and then, by the tripartite treaty of Kyakhta of 1915, in converting it into an autonomous region under formal Chinese suzerainty, but subject to what was virtually a Russian protectorate — a position comparable only with that of Tibet in relation to Great Britain.[1] The Mongols were in the position of a backward and not very numerous people caught between two powerful countries. But, since Russian immigration into Outer Mongolia (other than that of Buryat Mongols from Russian territory) was, and was likely to remain, insignificant, whereas Chinese immigration, which had already flowed extensively into Inner Mongolia, was a serious threat, it was at the outset possible for a certain number of politically conscious Mongols to regard Russian interference as an act of national liberation from China. Symptoms of national consciousness began to emerge quite strongly after 1911 when, as a result of the Chinese revolution, Outer Mongolia was able to assert her autonomous status and first acquired some of the rudimentary machinery of a modern state.

The February revolution of 1917 in Russia was followed by a rapid decline in Russian prestige and power in Outer Mongolia and elsewhere throughout the Far East; and this was soon reflected both in Japanese and in Chinese action to overthrow the régime established by the Kyakhta treaty. In the winter of 1918–1919 the Japanese authorities in Siberia, both directly and through their *protégé*, the " white " Russian general Semenov, were actively promoting a pan-Mongolian movement which was to embrace Inner and Outer Mongolia and the Buryats in Siberia. A pan-Mongolian congress assembled under Japanese auspices at Chita in Siberia on February 28, 1919, and proclaimed a provisional government for a vast Mongol state including all these regions and stretching to the confines of Tibet. These grandiose schemes were, however, even more distasteful to China than to Soviet Russia. The Peking government, formed from the pro-Japanese Anfu

[1] A convenient and documented account of Russian action and Russian-Chinese relations in regard to Outer Mongolia down to and including the treaty of Kyakhta is in G. M. Friters, *Outer Mongolia and its International Position* (Baltimore, 1949), pp. 44-112, 151-183.

group, successfully protested at Tokyo; and the pan-Mongol activities of Japanese agents were curbed.[1] The Soviet Government, having signalized its ascent to power by a denunciation of all treaties of the former Tsarist government, had no formal ground to protest; nor had it any longer any power in Asia to make the protest effective. In July 1919 it followed up its declaration surrendering former Russian concessions in China by a specific message to the Mongolian people. Mongolia was declared a " free country "; all " Russian advisers, Tsarist consuls, bankers and capitalists " should be driven out; no foreigner should be allowed to intervene in Mongolian affairs; and the Soviet Government offered to enter into diplomatic relations with Mongolia.[2] The last offer may have been intended as a reminder of traditional Russian support for the independence of Mongolia from China. But at the height of the civil war these sentiments had little practical application; and, once Japanese ambitions had been moderated, nothing stood in the way of a reassertion of Chinese authority over the territory. In October 1919 the Chinese Government determined to clinch the matter by sending General Hsü Shutseng,[3] a member of the ruling Anfu group, to Urga, the capital of Outer Mongolia. After a few weeks of bribery and intimidation a petition to the Chinese Government was signed by a number of Mongolian ministers and notabilities requesting the withdrawal of the country's autonomy; and on the strength of this a decree was issued in Peking on November 22, 1919, cancelling the autonomous status of Outer Mongolia and denouncing the treaty of Kyakhta.[4] It is reasonable to suppose that these proceedings had the tacit support and encouragement of Japan, now in course of consolidating her position throughout Siberia east of Lake Baikal. With the civil war in Russia at its height, Soviet power and Soviet diplomacy appeared to have been entirely excluded from this former Russian sphere of influence.

[1] A. Kallinnikov, *Revolyutsionnaya Mongoliya* (n.d. [1925]), pp. 68-69; further light is thrown on this episode in an article in *Novyi Vostok*, ii (1922), 591-603.

[2] *Tikhii Okean*, No. 3, 1936, p. 72.

[3] Commonly known as " little Hsü " by way of distinction from Hsü Shih-chang, the president of the Chinese republic.

[4] Chinese authorities for these events are cited in G. M. Friters, *Outer Mongolia and its International Position* (Baltimore, 1949), pp. 185-189; the decree is in *China Year Book, 1921* (Shanghai, 1922), p. 577.

The third frontier region, Manchuria, being traversed by the all-important Chinese Eastern Railway, figured far more conspicuously in the early pronouncements of Soviet policy; but these pronouncements had even less effect on the current situation. The momentary authority established by the Chinese Government in Manchuria in the first months of 1918 quickly evaporated. Throughout the civil war effective control was exercised by the allied military forces or by " white " generals operating under their patronage.   At the end of April 1918 the Russo-Asiatic Bank, in which the ownership of the Chinese Eastern Railway was formally vested, sought to avoid embarrassment by registering itself as a French company and transferring its seat to Paris;[1] and from January 1919 onwards the railway was managed, in the interests of military efficiency, by an allied board.   The Soviet Government, remote from the scene of events and from any vestige of influence over them, saw itself confined to propagandist gestures.   The report of Narkomindel to the fifth All-Russian Congress of Soviets of July 5, 1918, related that, in the negotiations with the Chinese minister earlier in the year, " we notified China that we renounce the conquests of the Tsarist government in Manchuria and we restore the sovereign rights of China in that territory, in which lies a main trade artery — the Chinese Eastern Railway, property of the Chinese and Russian people ", and went on to make a further and more specific statement of policy on the Chinese Eastern Railway and other Russian rights in China :

> We consider that, if part of the money invested in the construction of this railway by the Russian people were repaid by China, China might buy it back without waiting for the time-limit in the agreement imposed on her by force. . . . We agree to renounce all territorial rights of our citizens in China. We are ready to renounce all indemnities.[2]

On August 1, 1918, Chicherin wrote a letter to the Chinese nationalist leader Sun Yat-sen, the head of the dissident nationalist government in Canton, in which, though not specifically reverting

[1] *Millard's Review* (Shanghai), May 4, 1918, p. 354 ; *China Year Book, 1921* (Shanghai, 1922), pp. 650-652.

[2] *Izvestiya*, July 5, 1918 ; the report was not considered by the congress or included in the records of its proceedings. Under the protocol attached to the Russo-Chinese treaty of 1896 China could not buy out the Russian owners of the railway before 1932.

to the renunciation of Russian claims, he attacked the Peking government as " the puppet of foreign bankers ", and ended : " Long live the union of the Russian and Chinese proletariat ". The *leitmotif* of national liberation from imperialist oppression was thus subtly blended with the international solidarity of the proletariat. But this missive failed to reach its destination.[1] The creation at Moscow in January 1919 of a " Chinese Working Men's Association " as a centre for propaganda work in China was evidently part of the same campaign to woo Chinese support.[2]

In the summer of 1919, allied policy at the peace conference played into Soviet hands. The Chinese delegation in Paris protested in vain against the clauses in the Versailles treaty sanctioning the prolongation of the Japanese occupation of Shantung. On May 4, 1919, the treaty was the object of hostile demonstrations, especially from students, throughout China ; and the Chinese delegation in Paris was instructed not to sign the treaty.[3] The incident gave a great impetus to the nationalist cause, and offered the Bolsheviks their first real opportunity of contrasting Soviet sympathy for Chinese national aspirations and Soviet willingness to treat China as an equal with the unequal and oppressive policies of the other great powers. In July 1919 a successful offensive against Kolchak for the first time carried the Red Army across the Urals into Siberia. The occasion was seized to address a declaration on July 25, 1919, " to the Chinese people and the governments of south and north China ". It was signed by Karakhan, the deputy People's Commissar for Foreign Affairs. Having declared that the Red Army would " bring to the peoples liberation from the yoke of the foreign bayonet, from the yoke of foreign gold ", the Soviet Government renounced all territorial and other acquisitions of the Tsarist government on Chinese soil, including " Manchuria and other regions ", all extra-territorial rights and other privileges of Russian subjects,

---

[1] The letter was published in *Izvestiya*, March 9, 1919 (translation in *Soviet Documents on Foreign Policy*, ed. J. Degras, i (1951), 92-93) ; Sun Yat-sen in a letter to Chicherin of August 28, 1921 (see p. 511, note 1, below), stated that he had received no letter from Chicherin prior to one of October 31, 1920.

[2] A. L. P. Dennis, *The Foreign Policies of Soviet Russia* (1924), pp. 314-315 ; there was a Soviet of Chinese workers, said to number 1000, in Moscow (A. Ransome, *Six Weeks in Russia in 1919* (1919), p. 47).

[3] R. T. Pollard, *China's Foreign Relations, 1917-1931* (N.Y., 1933), pp. 79-82 ; this useful work is based mainly on the contemporary press.

and the outstanding instalments of the Boxer indemnity; all unequal treaties were in principle declared null and void as far as Soviet Russia was concerned. One sentence of the declaration specifically included the Chinese Eastern Railway in the act of renunciation :

> The Soviet Government restores to the Chinese people without compensation the Chinese Eastern Railway, the mining and forestry concessions and other privileges seized by the Tsar's government, by the Kerensky government, by Semenov, Kolchak and the Russian ex-generals, lawyers and capitalists.[1]

[1] No official text of the note was ever published by Narkomindel ; what was described as an English translation of the original French text was published in the authoritative *Millard's Review* (Shanghai), July 5, 1920, pp. 24-26, and subsequently in *China Year Book, 1924–5* (Shanghai, n.d.), pp. 868-870. A Russian version which appeared in *Izvestiya* on August 26, 1919, omitted the sentence quoted above (together with the last phrase of the preceding paragraph), and the authenticity of the sentence was afterwards strenuously and consistently denied by Soviet spokesmen, beginning with Joffe (see p. 540 below). Its authenticity has been established beyond question by A. S. Whiting in *The Far Eastern Quarterly* (N.Y.), x, No. 4 (August 1951), pp. 355-364. A Russian text containing the whole passage omitted by *Izvestiya*, and corresponding exactly to the English version published in China, appeared in a pamphlet by V. Vilensky, *Kitai i Sovetskaya Rossiya*, issued by the party central committee in 1919 (internal evidence suggests July or August as the time of publication). Vilensky was a party worker from Siberia, a former Menshevik, who in the summer of 1919 was serving in Moscow as member of a commission of Sovnarkom on Siberian affairs and wrote frequently for *Izvestiya* under the pen-name of Sibiryakov. He was probably concerned in the drafting of the declaration of July 25, 1919 ; on the following day he had an article in *Izvestiya* in which, recalling the demand for the return of the Chinese Eastern Railway among those made by China at the Paris peace conference, he concluded that " Soviet Russia might with a light heart resolve these questions in a sense favourable to China and thereby win an alliance with her ". A report of Narkomindel of December 1921 implies that the return of the Chinese Eastern Railway to China was one of the points covered by the declaration of July 25, 1919 (*Godovoi Otchet NKID k IX S"ezdu Sovetov* (1921), p. 54). The most plausible explanation of the facts seems to be that a change of heart occurred in Soviet circles between the despatch of the note on July 25, 1919, and its publication in *Izvestiya* a month later, and that the passage about the Chinese Eastern Railway was deliberately removed. But no attempt was apparently made to communicate the revised text to the Soviet representative in Siberia who, as the sequel showed, had only the original text as late as March 1920 ; nor is it clear why the harmless phrase at the end of the previous paragraph should have also been omitted (which would have been natural enough if the omission had been accidental). The episode is evidence of divided opinions in Soviet circles on the unconditional return of the Chinese Eastern Railway : this was already apparent in the Narkomindel report of July 1918 (see p. 503 above), which had referred to the railway as the " joint property of the Chinese and Russian people " and spoken of China being allowed to " buy it back " at a part of its cost and before the expiry of the time-limit.

In existing conditions in Asia, the declaration — by whatever channel it was despatched — failed to reach the Chinese Government until March 26, 1920,[1] when it was telegraphed to Peking from Irkutsk by Yanson, described as " representative for foreign affairs of the Council of People's Commissars of Siberia and the Far East " — evidently an embryonic form of the Far Eastern Republic which was officially proclaimed a fortnight later.[2] The declaration had an enthusiastic reception in Chinese circles, and strengthened the reaction against the western Powers and Japan which had been gathering force since the Versailles decision of the previous summer.[3] The civil war being over and allied forces, other than the Japanese, having been withdrawn, the Peking government had now issued a decree resuming full control of the Chinese Eastern Railway.[4] But this control was almost wholly fictitious. After the ending of the civil war, effective power in Manchuria was exercised by a vigorous Chinese war-lord, Chang Tso-lin, who, while not formally disowning the supremacy of the central Chinese Government, recognized the practical importance of keeping on good terms with the Japanese military authorities still active in Siberia, and was more likely to accept directions from Tokyo than from Peking.

In the spring and summer of 1920 the fortunes of Soviet Russia in the Far East touched their lowest point. Victory had been gained over Kolchak. But the newly created Far Eastern Republic had still to prove its diplomatic usefulness ; and relations with Japan were still further embittered by the Nikolaevsk massacre and the Japanese reprisals at Vladivostok.[5] It was at

---

[1] Its receipt was reported with special reference to the mention of the Chinese Eastern Railway in *Millard's Review* (Shanghai), March 27, 1920, p. 182.

[2] See Vol. 1, p. 356.

[3] Evidence of the impression made by it is quoted from Chinese sources in B. I. Schwartz, *Chinese Communism and the Rise of Mao* (Harvard, 1951), p. 214, note 44. The Chinese Government attempted to cast suspicion on the declaration by alleging, on supposed information obtained from Soviet sources inside Siberia, that it was a forgery (*Millard's Review* (Shanghai), June 5, 1920, p. 25) ; there is no other evidence that the authenticity of the text was challenged from either side before 1922.

[4] *Ibid.* March 27, 1920, p. 182.

[5] See Vol. 1, pp. 356-357.

this moment that the headquarters of Comintern decided to take a hand and despatched Voitinsky as its representative to China. In China, as in Japan, the result of the Bolshevik revolution had been to create for the first time a widespread interest in Marxism in intellectual circles; and a society for the study of Marxism was founded in Peking university in the spring of 1918. The leading figures of the movement were two professors of the university, Ch'en Tu-hsiu and Li Ta-chao, the former a professor of literature and the founder and editor of an advanced political review, the latter a professor of history whose main interest was in the philosophy of history.[1] The activities of the group, which was not committed to orthodox Marxism, remained academic until they became involved in the " May the Fourth Movement " — itself largely initiated and carried on by university students and teachers — against the terms of the Versailles treaty. The movement, though not inspired by the Russian revolution, had a natural affinity with it as being a movement of revolt against western imperialism. It found no specific inspiration or support in Marxist doctrine, and the connexion between it and the rise of Chinese Marxism was empirical and fortuitous. But in the China of 1919, resistance to the west, sympathy with the Russian revolution and the study of Marx were all expressions of " advanced " political opinion. A condition of political ferment, which had its focus in this revolt and stood, in some still undefined way, to the Left of the national and " democratic " revolution of 1911, had been created, but lacked any clear shape or concrete programme. There was still no serious labour movement; and agrarian discontent, a time-honoured phenomenon, was inarticulate and unorganized.

Such was the situation which confronted Voitinsky on his arrival in Peking as representative of Comintern in June 1920. He had conversations with Li Ta-chao, and went on to Shanghai where Ch'en Tu-hsiu was now established. Here the first steps were cautiously taken by Voitinsky towards the organization of a Chinese communist party. The first stage was the formation in August of a socialist youth group for which Voitinsky is said to have provided funds. But the constitution of this group tolerated a wide diversity of opinion; and when, in the following month, a

[1] B. I. Schwartz, *Chinese Communism and the Rise of Mao* (Harvard, 1951), pp. 7-16.

conference was held in Shanghai to discuss the founding of an orthodox communist party, the task proved too difficult.[1] The blessing given in the theses of the second congress of Comintern to the cooperation of communists in " colonial " countries with movements of national liberation [2] precisely fitted the Chinese situation. Nowhere were the opportunities of an alliance between communism and nationalism more promising ; and nowhere were they so fully exploited in the sequel. But the decisions of the second congress were taken without reference to China, and do not seem to have been known — or their implications understood — during Voitinsky's visit, which, while it prepared the ground by stimulating the formation of communist or quasi-communist groups in different parts of China,[3] yielded few concrete results.

It was about this time that the diplomatic situation began to show signs of improvement. As the results of the victory over Kolchak and the isolation of the Japanese forces in Siberia became gradually apparent, the balance of forces in the Far East also changed, and Soviet Russia could begin to recover lost ground. Anarchy was increasing in China, and the provincial war-lords fought and manœuvred against one another with less and less regard for a nominal central authority. In the late summer of 1920 the military backers of the Peking government were defeated by Wu Pei-fu, the war lord of Chili, and the government collapsed. Its successor noted that intervention in Russia had been abandoned by all the former allies except Japan ; and it could no longer afford to pursue a whole-heartedly Soviet policy which played into the hands of the southern nationalists. The first act of the new government was to admit Yurin, the delegate of the Far Eastern

[1] Information about the Voitinsky mission comes exclusively from Chinese sources which are quoted in B. I. Schwartz, *Chinese Communism and the Rise of Mao* (1951), pp. 32-33 ; the sources date from some years after the event, and should be treated with caution.

[2] See pp. 252-258 above : two Chinese delegates of uncertain credentials were admitted to the congress in a consultative capacity, but Chinese affairs do not seem to have been discussed.

[3] According to *Bol'shaya Sovetskaya Entsiklopediya*, xii (1928), 657-658, art. Voitinsky (Zarkhlin), Voitinsky " in the summer of 1920 took part in the organization of the first communist cells in Shanghai, Peking and Canton " ; a later Chinese account speaks of Chinese communist groups being established at this time in Peking, Canton and Hunan, as well as in Paris (*Kommunisticheskii Internatsional*, No. 9-10 (187-188), 1929, p. 181).

Republic, who had been waiting at Kalgan for some weeks.[1]
Next it formally ratified the agreement concluded in the previous
May between the Soviet authorities at Tashkent and the Chinese
governor of Sinkiang, which thus became the first officially recognized agreement between a Soviet and a Chinese authority.[2] Then
on September 23, 1920, recognition was formally withdrawn from
the former Russian minister and consuls;[3] and about the same
time a Chinese mission under General Chang Shi-lin arrived in
Moscow. Karakhan, who conducted the negotiations with the
mission on behalf of Narkomindel, handed to it on September 27,
1920, a note addressed to " the Ministry of Foreign Affairs of the
Chinese Republic " containing the heads of a proposed agreement
between the RSFSR and the Chinese Republic. The RSFSR
confirmed its renunciation of all annexations and concessions as
well as of the Boxer indemnity payments : full diplomatic, consular and commercial relations were to be established ; the Chinese
Government was to give no support or shelter to Russian counter-
revolutionary organizations ; and a subsequent treaty was to be
drawn up between the RSFSR, the Far Eastern Republic and
China to regulate the status of the Chinese Eastern Railway.[4]

Meanwhile the Soviet approach to China exhibited the same
careful blend of revolutionary appeal and hard-headed power
politics which was characteristic of Soviet foreign policy elsewhere.
In an article in *Izvestiya* on October 9, 1920, Vilensky noted that
" under the flag of Wu Pei-fu " policy in China had taken a more

[1] R. T. Pollard, *China's Foreign Relations, 1917–1931* (N.Y., 1933), pp. 133-134.

[2] *Izvestiya*, October 9, 1920 ; R. T. Pollard, *China's Foreign Relations, 1917–1931* (N.Y., 1933), p. 134. For the agreement see pp. 499-500 above.

[3] *China Year Book, 1921* (Shanghai, 1922), p. 626 ; on October 30, 1920, regulations were issued determining the legal status of Russian citizens in China (*ibid.* p. 644).

[4] No Russian text of Karakhan's note has been found. The English translation in the *China Year Book, 1924-5* (Shanghai, n.d.), pp. 870-872, is dated September 27, 1920 ; this date is quoted in the Joffe-Sun Yat-sen state-ment of January 1923, and is certainly correct. " An English translation made from a Russian text obtained at Narkomindel " is in V. A. Yakhontoff, *Russia and the Soviet Union in the Far East* (1932), pp. 384-387, and bears the date October 27, 1920 ; to add to the confusion, Joffe's note of September 2, 1922 (see p. 538 below) gives the date as September 27, 1921. R. T. Pollard, *China's Foreign Relations, 1917–1931* (N.Y., 1933), p. 135, without quoting any authority, says that it was received by the Chinese delegation on October 2, 1920.

friendly turn towards Soviet Russia. Nevertheless China " must choose between one ally and the other ". Though " good neighbourly relations between China and Soviet Russia may be as little to the liking of other allied robbers as of Japan ", the writer concluded that " for China herself, having begun the struggle for liberation from the rapacious grasp of Japanese imperialism, good neighbourly relations with Soviet Russia provide a practical chance of carrying on that struggle to a successful conclusion ". The appeal seemed at first to bear fruit ; three days later Chang Shi-lin told Narkomindel that " permanent representatives are being appointed by China to Russia ". But stronger pressures apparently prevailed in Peking. The Peking government chose the moment of Chang Shi-lin's mission in Moscow to reinsure itself with the financial authorities of the west by concluding, on October 2, 1920, a fresh agreement with the Russo-Asiatic Bank in its assumed capacity as legal owner of the Chinese Eastern Railway.[1] The agreement placed some Chinese officials in positions of prestige and profit on the board of the railway. In other respects it can have had little effect, since Chang Tso-lin, who was in control of Manchuria, was now less inclined than ever to listen to the behests of Peking. But it was none the less a demonstration of intention to exclude Soviet Russia from any share in the control of a vital artery of Russian communications with the Pacific. Then, on October 18, Krasin was requested by the Chinese Minister in London to inform Moscow that Chang Shi-lin's credentials had been withdrawn, and that a consul-general would be appointed to look after Chinese interests in the RSFSR.[2] A month later, in reply to further Soviet representations, the Chinese Government sent a polite but non-committal reply merely expressing a hope for negotiations in the future and protesting against the treatment of Chinese citizens in the RSFSR.[3]

The brief ray of hope which had dawned in the autumn of

[1] An English translation of the original French text is in *Treaties and Agreements with and concerning China* (Washington, 1929), pp. 29-31.

[2] *Godovoi Otchet NKID k IX S"ezdu Sovetov* (1921), p. 55. According to R. T. Pollard, *China's Foreign Relations, 1917-1931* (N.Y., 1933), p. 135, Chang Shi-lin had not been sent to Moscow by the Peking government, and was on a " private " mission ; but this was a fiction designed to propitiate western opinion by playing down any relations with Moscow.

[3] *Ibid.* p. 137.

1920, when the Anfu government fell in Peking and recognition was withdrawn from the former Tsarist representative, seemed therefore to have been once more extinguished. It may have been these rebuffs which caused the Soviet Government at this moment to recall that Soviet diplomacy in China also had two strings to its bow. On October 31, 1920, Chicherin wrote a personal letter to Sun Yat-sen in Canton and proposed trade negotiations; since the possibilities of trade between Soviet Russia and southern China scarcely existed, the letter was no doubt intended as a tentative political overture. But it was entrusted to an unnamed emissary, and failed to reach Sun Yat-sen till July of the following year.[1] Yurin remained in Peking as representative of the Far Eastern Republic throughout the winter of 1920-1921, engaged in intermittent negotiations for a commercial agreement. But, in spite of a number of conciliatory pronouncements, his conversations with the Chinese Ministry of Foreign Affairs led to no result. The failure was commonly attributed to pressure on the Chinese Government from allied sources, and particularly by the French Minister in Peking.[2] A Soviet delegate sent to negotiate with Chang Tso-lin at Mukden met with no better success.[3] Whatever avenue of approach was tried, China still seemed successfully sealed against any form of Soviet penetration.

Meanwhile startling events had happened in Outer Mongolia. Little Hsü's rule was sufficiently high-handed to provoke widespread discontent. Early in 1920[4] at least two revolutionary groups seem to have come into existence in Urga, led respectively by Sukhebator and Choibalsang; the second group is said to have

---

[1] The text of the letter has not been published: its tenor is known only from Sun Yat-sen's reply of August 28, 1921, published in *Bol'shevik*, No. 19, 1950, pp. 46-48.

[2] *Millard's Review* (Shanghai), December 11, 1920, p. 99; January 1, 1921, pp. 238-239; *Godovoi Otchet NKID k IX S"ezdu Sovetov* (1921), p. 53; many reports are quoted from the contemporary press in R. T. Pollard, *China's Foreign Relations, 1917-1931* (N.Y., 1933), pp. 137-139.

[3] *Millard's Review* (Shanghai), December 25, 1920, p. 213; April 9, 1921, p. 286.

[4] A. Kallinnikov, *Revolyutsionnaya Mongoliya* (n.d. [1925]), p. 73, says in general terms that a revolutionary movement " began to form itself " after the annulment of Mongolian autonomy by China in the autumn of 1919.

worked under the direction of two Soviet agents. In the spring
of 1920 a delegate of Comintern visited Urga, brought about a
union of the two groups under Sukhebator's leadership, and set on
foot a scheme for invoking Soviet aid against Little Hsü. The Bogda
Gegen, the "living Buddha" of Urga, and the highest ecclesiastical
and political authority in the country, who had already put out
feelers for American and Japanese help, had no objection to a similar
application to Russia : indeed, an application seems to have been
made, with a singular lack of realism, to Orlov, the former consul-
general of the Provisional Government who was still in Urga. But
now a direct approach was tried. On July 15, 1920, Sukhebator
with a party of five companions left Urga secretly for Irkutsk, being
joined later by Choibalsang. Here a petition for help was handed
to the " department for Far Eastern affairs " of the Far Eastern
Republic, while some of the delegates went on to Moscow. The
reply from Irkutsk was apparently non-commital, and laid down
two conditions representing a nice compromise between tradition
and progress — that the petition for aid should bear the seal of
the Bogda Gegen, and that a popular party should be founded to
provide support for a pro-Soviet policy. Both conditions were
complied with. The Bogda Gegen in Urga affixed his seal to a
document requesting aid ; and Sukhebator in Irkutsk drafted the
first manifesto of a Mongolian People's Party. A fresh petition
was handed in — this time to " the Far Eastern section of Comintern " and " the Soviet fifth army " — on November 2, 1920.[1]

While Sukhebator and Choibalsang were negotiating in
Irkutsk, the Anfu government fell in Peking and Little Hsü's rule
came to an unlamented end in Urga. During the autumn and
winter of 1920–1921 conditions approaching anarchy prevailed

---

[1] Two independent Mongolian sources exist for these events : a biography
of Sukhebator by Nachokdorgi published in 1943 (quoted by O. Lattimore
in his introduction to G. M. Friters, *Outer Mongolia and its International
Position* (Baltimore, 1949), pp. xxviii-xxxvi), and the unpublished political
memoirs of the Dilowa Hutuktu, one of the Mongolian " living Buddhas ".
The former is influenced by the patent desire to depict Sukhebator and Choibalsang (who was Prime Minister of the Mongolian People's Republic when the
work was published) as the Lenin and Stalin of Mongolia ; but the narrative
is credible, and the essential facts are confirmed by the Dilowa's memoirs,
which certainly have no communist or Soviet bias. By piecing together the
two sources, a fairly clear picture can be obtained of events not elsewhere
recorded. The most obscure point is how far the Bogda Gegen was cognizant
of Sukhebator's original mission.

in Outer Mongolia. With the end of the civil war in Siberia, the army of Semenov dissolved and dispersed; and out of its fragments one of Semenov's officers, Ungern-Sternberg, created a small force of miscellaneous composition enjoying Japanese patronage and in part apparently officered by Japanese.[1] In the autumn of 1920 this force attempted to force its way into Outer Mongolia. This was the occasion of the first overt entry of the Soviet Government upon the scene. It offered to the Peking government in a note of November 10, 1920, to send in Soviet troops to deal with the intruder; indeed it alleged, rightly or wrongly, that a request to do so had been received from the Chinese authorities in Urga, the Outer Mongolian capital. But the Peking government showed a natural reluctance to invoke the aid of the Soviet Government, whose patronage might be permanent; and the Soviet offer was declined.[2] For the moment the Chinese forces left in Urga proved adequate to repulse the attack which ended in failure. But during the winter conditions further deteriorated, the Bogda Gegen himself and many Mongolian notables being arrested by Chinese soldiers,[3] so that when Ungern-Sternberg returned in February 1921 he was greeted as a deliverer. Entering Urga at the head of his troops, he announced his intention of liquidating all those Mongols who had collaborated either with China or with Soviet Russia. The Bogda Gegen proclaimed himself emperor of an independent Mongolia (apparently including Inner as well as Outer Mongolia), and set up a so-called Mongolian Government with Ungern-Sternberg as its " military adviser ".[4] Yurin at once made an offer to the Peking

---

[1] I. Maisky, *Sovremennaya Mongoliya* (Irkutsk, 1921), p. 129, describes the force as consisting of 4000 Russians, 1500-2000 Tunguses and " some tens of Japanese officers " ; according to an independent eye-witness, Ungern-Sternberg entered Urga in the following year with a body-guard of 40 Japanese and mainly Japanese material (G. M. Friters, *Outer Mongolia and its International Position* (Baltimore, 1949), p. 230).

[2] *Izvestiya*, January 5, 1921 (quoted in L. Pasvolsky, *Russia in the Far East* (N.Y., 1922), pp. 115-116), printed the Chinese reply of December 31, 1920 : the Soviet note of November 10, 1920, has apparently not been published, but was summarized in the Chinese reply.

[3] These events are described in the Dilowa's memoirs.

[4] The fullest connected account of these events, based in part on Chinese sources, is in K. S. Weigh, *Russo-Chinese Diplomacy* (Shanghai, 1928), pp. 187-206 ; see also R. T. Pollard, *China's Foreign Relations, 1917-1931* (N.Y., 1933), pp. 161-162, and the Dilowa's memoirs.

government of the assistance of Soviet troops to repel the invader, but the offer was declined.[1] From this point dates the assumption by the Soviet Government of a forward policy in Outer Mongolia. After Ungern-Sternberg's first abortive incursion of November 1920, Sukhebator and his group, no doubt accompanied by their Russian advisers, left Irkutsk and established themselves on the frontier near Kyakhta. Here during the winter the process of organizing the Mongolian People's Party and a Mongolian government went on ; [2] and, when Ungern-Sternberg carried out his successful *coup* of February 1921, everything was ready. On March 1, 1921, what was afterwards described as the first party congress of the Mongolian People's Party took place under Sukhebator's leadership in Kyakhta, and decided to form a Mongolian People's Government and a national army to liberate the country from Chinese and from " white " Russian rule. On March 19 the new government was proclaimed with Sukhebator as Prime Minister and Minister for War, and Soviet aid invoked.[3] Ungern-Sternberg was not a man to await attack. In May 1921 he launched a full-scale offensive against Soviet territory.[4] This, however, was quickly repulsed by detachments of the Red Army which had been mustered near the frontier. Ungern-Sternberg, deserted

---

[1] R. T. Pollard, *China's Foreign Relations, 1917-1931* (N.Y., 1933), p. 163.

[2] According to Ma Ho-t'ien, *Chinese Agent in Mongolia* (Engl. transl., Baltimore, 1949), pp. 98-99, the party and the government were formed at Troitsko-Savsk : this may have been Sukhebator's otherwise unnamed head-quarters.

[3] The most detailed source of these events is Nachokdorgi's biography of Sukhebator : other accounts are in *Tikhii Okean*, No. 3 (9), 1936, p. 66, and in E. M. Murzaev, *Mongol'skaya Narodnaya Respublika* (1948), p. 18. All these accounts no doubt give the proceedings in retrospect a more formal character than they possessed at the time.

[4] Ungern-Sternberg's proclamation of May 21, 1921, to " Russian detachments on the territory of Soviet Siberia " on the launching of this offensive has been preserved. The general proclaimed the Grand-Duke Michael " All-Russian Emperor " ; announced the intention " to exterminate commissars, communists and Jews with their families " ; declared that " in this struggle with the criminal destroyers and defilers of Russia . . . the measure of punishment can only be one — the death penalty in various degrees " ; refused to rely on " former foreign allies who are experiencing the same revolutionary disease " ; and concluded with a quotation from the Book of Daniel predicting the appearance of " Michael the great prince " and ending with the words : " Blessed is he that waits and fulfils the 3330 days " (*Revolyutsiya na Dal'nem Vostoke* (1923), pp. 429-432).

by most of his army, was captured and shot; and on June 28 the decision was taken, in the name of the Mongolian People's Party and Mongolian People's Government, to march on Urga. The city was captured on July 6, and two days later a Mongolian Government was established. The Bogda Gegen remained as head of the state, though his functions were limited to religious matters. The new Prime Minister was Bodo, a lama, and said to have been a clerk in the former Russian consulate-general, and Sukhebator was Minister of War : these arrangements suggest a willingness to effect compromise between the old and the new order which was doubtless dictated in part by the almost complete absence of educated Mongols outside the lama class. The hard fact behind the régime was the presence of the Red Army and of Soviet advisers. Early in August 1921, when the new arrangements were complete, the Mongolian People's Revolutionary Government addressed a brief request to the RSFSR " not to withdraw Soviet troops from the territory of Mongolia pending the complete removal of the threat from the common enemy " : and Chicherin at once acceded to it in a long and somewhat fulsome reply, which contained an undertaking that the troops would be withdrawn as soon as " the threat to the free development of the Mongolian people and to the security of the Russian Republic and of the Far Eastern Republic shall have been removed ".[1]

The appearance of the Red Army in Urga, and the establishment there of a Mongolian Government under direct Soviet patronage, meant a reinstatement of the international situation of Outer Mongolia as it had existed before 1917 and had been registered in the treaty of Kyakhta. The easy success of Soviet arms and Soviet policy was a symptom of the changed attitude of Japan, whose hidden hand no longer afforded support to the " white " forces. In the summer of 1921, American pressure was being strongly exerted on Japan to withdraw her remaining troops from Siberia; and a conference between delegates of Japan and of the Far Eastern Republic was to meet at Dairen in August.[2] It was a dramatic reversal of the process of the extrusion of Russian

[1] This exchange of notes was published in *Izvestiya*, August 12, 1921 (Engl. transl. in L. Pasvolsky, *Russia in the Far East* (N.Y., 1922), pp. 176-179).
[2] See Vol. 1, p. 361.

power from the Far East which had been going on for four years : the period of eclipse was at an end. The portents were read in Peking; and when on June 15, 1921, Chicherin addressed a mild and deprecatory note to the Chinese Government explaining that the entry of Soviet troops into Outer Mongolia was a temporary measure dictated by the needs of security, and that they would be withdrawn as soon as Ungern-Sternberg was disposed of, a curt reply was sent that a mandate had been given to Chang Tso-lin to deal with Ungern-Sternberg, and that the forces available were sufficient for the purpose.[1] The reply was a confession of helplessness. Chang Tso-lin, himself dependent on Japanese favours, was most unlikely to move against Ungern-Sternberg, who was also a *protégé* of Japan. But this did not make Chinese resentment of the Soviet intrusion any less acute. Yurin, the delegate of the Far Eastern Republic, who had been absent on leave when the Red Army marched on Urga, reappeared in Peking on July 25, 1921, but left again within a week, nominally on a mission to Chang Tso-lin, never to return.[2]

In the spring or summer of 1921, while these events were in progress, a new step was taken which betokened the strengthening interest in Far Eastern affairs in Moscow ; Maring, the energetic Dutch delegate from Indonesia who had played an active part in the discussion of the national and colonial question at the second congress of Comintern,[3] was despatched on a mission to China. His mission, unlike that of Voitinsky in 1920, was evidently not confined to the formation and encouragement of local communist groups or parties. He was in search of an answer to the general question what was to be done about China ; and the question put in that way revealed the unreality of the distinction between the promotion of communism and the development of Soviet power and prestige in the Far East. Ignoring Peking, where Yurin represented the supposed interests of the Far Eastern Republic, Maring visited the two men who appeared to hold the greatest real power in China — Wu Pei-fu, the dominant war-lord of central China, and Sun Yat-sen, who had been installed by enthusi-

---

[1] R. T. Pollard, *China's Foreign Relations, 1917-1931* (N.Y., 1933), p. 162 ; the mandate to Chang Tso-lin had in fact been issued on May 30, 1921.

[2] *North China Herald* (Shanghai), July 30, 1921, p. 312 ; August 6, 1921, p. 386.

[3] See p. 251 above.

astic nationalists in Canton on May 7, 1921, as president of a still disunited Chinese Republic. The rise of Wu Pei-fu in the late summer of 1920 had resulted in the ousting of the Anfu government and had been noted in Moscow as inaugurating a turn of policy in Peking favourable, or at any rate less unfavourable, to Soviet Russia.[1] Whatever the general complexion of Wu Pei-fu's policy — and this had not yet been fully disclosed — he was hostile to Japan and to Chang Tso-lin, Japan's *protégé* in Manchuria; and it was natural that Soviet Russia should look on him at this time as a potential ally. On the other hand, Sun Yat-sen, as the leader of the Chinese democratic revolution and the accepted spokesman of Chinese radicalism, was *prima facie* a more sympathetic figure from the communist standpoint; and Maring at the second congress of Comintern had been one of those who helped to frame the policy of alliance between communism and bourgeois-democratic national movements. Little is known of what transpired in Maring's conversations either with Wu Pei-fu or with Sun Yat-sen, or of the nature of his report to Moscow. Seeds of future collaboration with Kuomintang were doubtless sown in the talk with Sun Yat-sen. But it is clear that no decisive choice was made in Moscow at this time.[2] An event which happened after Maring's arrival in China, but apparently without his participation, was the foundation of a Chinese Communist

[1] See pp. 509-510 above.

[2] The only source for Maring's visit to Wu Pei-fu is T'ang Leang-li, *The Inner History of the Chinese Revolution* (1930), p. 155; according to this source, Maring recommended the Soviet authorities to keep up relations both with Wu Pei-fu and with Sun Yat-sen, and relations with the former were broken off only in February 1923, when Wu Pei-fu turned his troops on strikers on the Peking-Hankow railway (and when the bargain with Sun Yat-sen had been finally struck). This source represents the later Left wing in Kuomintang, and is anti-communist, but appears to be generally reliable on facts. In an article written in August, 1922, Vilensky described Wu Pei-fu as first and foremost a nationalist, and praised him as " one of those Chinese public men who have avoided the alien influence of foreign capital " (*Kommunisticheskii Internatsional*, No. 23 (November 4, 1922), col. 6104); and Radek at the fourth congress of Comintern in November 1922 alluded to a period in which " the young Chinese Communist Party " gave support to Wu Pei-fu (*Protokoll des Vierten Kongresses der Kommunistischen Internationale* (Hamburg, 1923), p. 630). The other main source for Maring's journey in 1921 is H. Isaacs, *The Tragedy of the Chinese Revolution* (1938), p. 64, based on an interview with Maring in 1935. This does not mention the meeting with Wu Pei-fu; but it was natural in retrospect to overlook an event which had no sequel, and to concentrate on the meeting which ultimately bore fruit.

Party.   Delegates of various heterogeneous groups came together in July 1921 at a secret gathering in Shanghai.   But the record of those present does not suggest any uniformity of opinion, and the so-called first congress of the Chinese Communist Party left behind no statement of policy or written document of any kind.[1]   It played in Chinese party history the same rôle as was played in the history of the Russian Social-Democratic Party by its first congress at Minsk in 1898.

[1] B. I. Schwartz, *Chinese Communism and the Rise of Mao* (Harvard, 1951), p. 34.

CHAPTER 34

THE FAR EAST: II — RE-EMERGENCE

THE winter of 1921–1922 was a period of great activity in Soviet policy in the Far East, and marked the re-emergence of Soviet power on the Pacific. With the defeat of Ungern-Sternberg the last organized " white " force in Siberia had been destroyed; the Japanese occupation was being withdrawn step by step under American pressure; the Soviet Government had successfully reasserted the predominance of Russian interests and influence in Outer Mongolia. On the other hand no diplomatic relations had yet been established with China or Japan, and attempts to plant communist movements in these countries had all but failed. During this crucial winter the Washington conference further weakened and isolated Japan among the great Powers and hastened the final stages of the withdrawal; the Soviet position in Outer Mongolia was further consolidated to the detriment of Soviet relations with the Peking government, but without objection from any of the great Powers; and a conference of " toilers of the east " in Moscow was the signal for an intensive campaign to establish communist influence, and a foothold for organized communist parties, in the Far Eastern countries. In the summer of 1922, when the Genoa conference and the treaty of Rapallo were already conspicuous landmarks in the progress of Soviet diplomacy in Europe, Russia was once again a power to be reckoned with in the Far East.

The most important achievement of Soviet policy in the Far East in the winter of 1921–1922, though the least publicized, was the consolidation of Soviet power in Outer Mongolia. Delegates of the new Mongolian Government established in Urga by the efforts of the Red Army proceeded to Moscow, where the situation was quickly regularized by the signing of a treaty on November 5, 1921, on terms of strict formal equality, between the RSFSR and the Mongolian People's Republic. Each party recognized the other as the sole authority on their respective territories (Chinese sovereignty over Outer Mongolia, which had hitherto always been formally admitted, being thus implicitly abrogated) ; relations between them were to be conducted through diplomatic pleni-potentiaries of equal status on both sides ; extra-territorial and other rights and privileges reserved to Russia under Tsarist agree-ments were renounced ; each party undertook to prevent the establishment within its territory of any organization, group or " government " hostile to the other.[1] On one point Mongolian aspirations were left unsatisfied. A large but sparsely populated area to the west of Outer Mongolia, known as the Uryankhai territory, had been subject to long-standing ambiguities of status and allegiance, and to the same stubborn disputes between Russia and China as Outer Mongolia, from which Russian diplomacy was, however, always careful to distinguish it.[2] Its inhabitants were a Turki-speaking people (though there had been some Mongol infiltration in the south), partly pastoral nomads like their Mongol neighbours, partly, in the north and north-east, forest hunters and herders of reindeer. The Soviet authorities, following Tsarist precedent, intervened to prevent the incorporation of this region in the Mongolian People's Republic. Early in 1922, ostensibly on local initiative, it was reorganized as an independent republic under the name of the People's Republic of Tannu Tuva and entered into friendly relations with the RSFSR.[3]

The processes by which Soviet predominance was gradually established in Outer Mongolia can be followed in outline, though not in detail. Down to March 1921 Soviet Russia had been accepted by most politically conscious Mongols as an ally and liberator from Chinese and " white " Russians, the most recent intruders on the Mongolian scene. But when after 1921 the Chinese menace receded into the background and Soviet power

---

[1] *RSFSR: Sbornik Deistvuyushchikh Dogovorov*, ii (1921), No. 47, pp. 29-31 ; Engl. transl. in *Treaties and Agreements with and concerning China, 1919–1929* (Washington, 1929), pp. 53-54.

[2] G. M. Friters, *Outer Mongolia and its International Position* (Baltimore, 1949), pp. 102-106.

[3] *Godovoi Otchet NKID k IX S"ezdu Sovetov* (1922), p. 71.

began to consolidate itself in Outer Mongolia, the situation was reversed and friction arose between leading Mongols and the Soviet authorities. This seems to have taken several forms, social, religious and national issues being interwoven in a struggle which ranged Mongols against one another as well as Mongols against Russians. The régime established at Urga in the summer of 1921 was purely national, and had no explicit social programme : this was in Bolshevik terminology the stage of the bourgeois revolution. But after the conclusion of the Soviet-Mongolian treaty of November 5, 1921, the Soviet Government, adapting the policy which it had pursued in the Russian countryside, sought to win for itself a solid basis of support in Outer Mongolia by introducing far-reaching social and political reforms. According to one source, a set of demands was put forward, including the national-ization of lands, forests, mines and other natural resources, the distribution of land to poor workers, the abolition of the titles and prerogatives of the Living Buddha and the nobles, and the substitution of democratic elections, the introduction of Soviet engineers into the mines and of Soviet military advisers into the army, and the establishment of education and health services under Soviet control. These demands are said to have been opposed by the Mongolian Government and the Mongolian People's Party, but supported by the Revolutionary League of Youth, and accepted more or less under duress in January 1922.[1] Religious loyalties were also at stake since the reforms were clearly designed to secularize Mongolian life and break the authority of the lamas. In this policy the Russians appear to have counted on the assistance of considerable numbers of Buryat-Mongols from the other side of the frontier who, having been long exposed to the influences of a secular Russian civilization, were now introduced into Outer Mongolia in order to raise the cultural and political level of their hitherto priest-ridden kinsmen,

---

[1] Ma Ho-t'ien, *Chinese Agent in Mongolia* (Engl. transl., Baltimore, 1949), pp. 100-102. A later Soviet text-book gives the following list of "democratic reforms" introduced in 1922 : the government "abolished serfdom and the feudal obligations of the peasantry, declared the land state property, abolished feudal vocations and caste divisions, established election of local organs of government, introduced a system of progressive income-tax assessment, reorgan-ized the courts by introducing people's assessors, etc." (N. P. Farberov, *Gosudarstvennoe Pravo Stran Narodnoi Demokratii* (1949), p. 302).

among whom secular education had been virtually non-existent : this, too, evidently caused fresh resentment and bitterness in traditional circles.[1]

In these conditions conservative elements may well have looked to the days of Chinese supremacy with a certain regret, coupled perhaps with fear of the too exclusive predominance of a Power so deeply committed to revolutionary innovation. A request was made to Moscow for aid in improving relations with China, and received on September 14, 1921, the cautious reply that the Soviet Government fully endorsed this aim " provided the Mongolian people at the same time exercises its right of self-determination ".[2] A few weeks later Bodo, the Prime Minister, made a declaration in favour of friendly relations with China.[3] It was clear that opposition to Soviet policy was crystallizing round a conservative pro-Chinese group drawn from the old lama class. In March 1922 a significant step was taken in the setting up of an " internal security office ", about which the one recorded fact is that its heads were Mongols.[4] In the following month Bodo and ten other leading Mongols were arrested and executed on a charge of conspiring with China — presumably for the purpose of restoring Chinese suzerainty over Outer Mongolia.[5] The execution of Bodo and his accomplices was the beginning of something like a revolutionary reign of terror lasting for eighteen months, during which, according to a

[1] The scanty evidence on this point is collected and examined in G. M. Friters, *Outer Mongolia and its International Position* (Baltimore, 1949), pp. 125-126.   [2] *Izvestiya*, September 17, 1921.

[3] K. S. Weigh, *Russo-Chinese Diplomacy* (Shanghai, 1928), pp. 212-213.

[4] Unpublished memoirs of the Dilowa Hutuktu.

[5] G. M. Friters, *Outer Mongolia and its International Position* (Baltimore, 1949), p. 126, with the sources there quoted. According to the memoirs of the Dilowa Hutuktu the charge was one of conspiring with the " bandit " Dambidanzan — a former lama said to be of Kalmyk origin, a sort of Mongolian Makhno who controlled a tract of desolate country in western Mongolia, successively defied central authorities of whatever political or national complexion, and was finally liquidated as the result of a regular expedition organized by the internal security office shortly after this time. *Novyi Vostok*, iv (n.d. [1923]), 156-160, gives an account of the establishment of the authority of the Mongolian People's Republic over western Mongolia — a process which lasted from May to October 1921. According to *Sibir'skaya Sovetskaya Entsiklopediya*, iii (1932), 540, fighting with " white guards " continued till April 1922, and the territory was not finally pacified till the autumn of that year ; these disturbances produced a " wavering of the feudal landowners and lamas in accordance with the successes of one side or the other ".

Chinese source, " not a day passed without its clashes between the new and the old groups " in Mongolian life.[1] These events were accompanied by a regularization of the links between Outer Mongolia and Soviet Russia. On May 26, 1922, the arrival in Moscow of a permanent Mongolian representative is recorded.[2] Five days later a further Soviet-Mongolian treaty signed at Urga made still more apparent the resumption by the Soviet Government of the paramount rôle successfully asserted in Outer Mongolia by the last Tsarist government. All property in Outer Mongolia owned by former Russian governments or public institutions was to be handed over to the RSFSR ; former property of Russian firms and nationals was to be reserved for more detailed consideration.[3] The administration of Outer Mongolia was now effectively in the hands of Mongols sympathetic to Soviet aims and policies and of their Soviet advisers. If, as early as August 1922, the forces of the Red Army in Outer Mongolia were reduced to a single battalion " under the control of the Mongol War Office ",[4] this was a symptom not of a withdrawal of Soviet power, but of the ease and efficiency with which that power had been established and of the absence of any organized Mongol opposition to it.

While Soviet policy had been actively engaged throughout the winter of 1921-1922 in consolidating its influence over Outer Mongolia, the limelight of diplomacy had been focused on the decision of the Great Powers, announced in July 1921, to hold a conference on disarmament and on Pacific questions at Washington towards the end of the year. The occasion was not without its embarrassments for Soviet propaganda and Soviet foreign policy. Any agreement between the capitalist Powers, and especially between the two giants among them, the United States and Great Britain, not only ran counter to the accepted thesis of growing and inescapable contradictions within the capitalist world, but tended to strengthen the principal enemies of the RSFSR. On the other

[1] Ma Ho-t'ien, *Chinese Agent in Mongolia* (Engl. transl., Baltimore, 1949), p. 102. [2] *Izvestiya*, June 14, 1922.
 [3] *Treaties and Agreements with and concerning China, 1919-1929* (Washington, 1929), pp. 102-103.
 [4] *China Year Bock, 1923* (Shanghai, n.d.), p. 677 ; according to the same source (*ibid.* p. 678), " a section of the Soviet secret police made its appearance at Urga " in the same month.

hand, one of the specific aims of American policy which was
likely to be furthered at the conference was the eviction of Japan
from Siberia and a weakening of her hold on China. The first
reaction in Moscow was a formal protest to the inviting Powers
and to China, declaring that the Soviet Government would not
consider itself bound by any decisions taken by a conference in
which it had not been asked to participate.[1] A set of theses adopted
by IKKI a month later pronounced the object of the understanding
between the United States and Great Britain to be " the formation
of an Anglo-Saxon capitalist trust whose centre of gravity will be
in America " : the proposed Washington conference represented
" an attempt of the United States to snatch from Japan by diplomatic means the fruits of her victory ". The theses ended with a
general denunciation of imperialism, and a prediction that its
contradictions would not be relieved by the conference.[2] But this
intransigent attitude was soon mitigated by an element of calculation. Diplomatic necessities could be served by turning the edge
of the congress against Japan, whose delegates were at this very
moment proving intractable in the negotiations with the Far
Eastern Republic at Dairen.[3] The purpose of the conference, an
article in *Izvestiya* of September 30, 1921, explained, would be
" to disclose the schemes of Japanese imperialism, which is the
chief oppressor of the Far Eastern peoples, and to oppose to it
the organized will of the toiling masses of east Asia ". While all
moves to obtain an invitation to the conference either for the
Soviet Government or for the Far Eastern Republic failed, an
unofficial delegation of the Far Eastern Republic was despatched
to Washington with the acquiescence of the American Government[4] and appeared conspicuously in the corridors of the conference ; no opportunity was to be lost of such advantages as
might accrue from American hostility to Japan. Here, as else-

[1] *Sovetsko-Amerikanskie Otnosheniya, 1929-1933* (1934), pp. 47-48 : a
further protest followed in November (*ibid.* p. 51).

[2] *Kommunisticheskii Internatsional*, No. 18 (October 8, 1921), col. 4758 :
the theses originally appeared in *Pravda*, September 1, 1921.

[3] See Vol. 1, pp. 360-362, where the ambivalent attitude of Moscow towards
the Washington conference is also discussed.

[4] Unpublished official correspondence in National Archives of the United
States, Record Group 59 : 861 A 01, shows that *visas* were granted on October
4, 1921, ostensibly " for commercial purposes ", but really to counteract
Japanese pressure on the Far Eastern Republic.

where, the pursuit of world revolution was tempered by whatever expedients might be necessary in order to play off one capitalist Power against another. Soon after the conference had opened in Washington a leading article in *Izvestiya*, under the title " The Hegemon of the World ", described the United States as " the principal power in the world ", and argued that " all steps must be taken in one way or another to come to terms with the United States ".[1]

Exclusion from a major conference of Pacific Powers was, however, a blow to Soviet interests and Soviet prestige in the Far East ; and, if the blow could not be countered by diplomatic means, others must be tried. A year earlier, immediately after the congress of eastern peoples in Baku, IKKI had taken a decision to convene a similar congress for the Far East " in a town of Siberia ".[2] Japanese, Chinese and Korean comrades were said to have taken part in this decision, the importance of which was pointed by the claim that there were already 8,000,000 industrial workers in Japan. The practical difficulty of assembling a suitable gathering of delegates had hitherto prevented the fulfilment of this project. Successive attempts to found a communist party in Japan had hitherto been foiled ; and the Chinese Communist Party founded in June 1921 was no more than a heterogeneous group of Left intellectuals. The decision to convene a " congress of toilers of the Far East " for the following November [3] was taken at the same session of IKKI which adopted the theses on the Washington conference, and was evidently designed as a counterblast to the initiative of the western Powers. The initial intention was to hold the congress on the territory of the Far Eastern Republic at Irkutsk ; and the date was provisionally fixed for November 11, 1921.[4] Active preparations to recruit an impressive membership went on during the autumn. Chang T'ai-lei, the Chinese delegate to the third congress of Comintern,[5] visited Japan well supplied with funds and distributed invitations. Delegates were sent from the " Wednesday Society ", a group of

[1] *Izvestiya*, December 6, 1921 ; for the growing importance attached to the United States in Moscow at this time see p. 341, note 2, above.
[2] *Kommunisticheskii Internatsional*, No. 14 (November 6, 1920), col. 2947.
[3] *Ibid*. No. 18 (October 8, 1921), col. 4758.
[4] *Ibid*. No. 23 (November 4, 1922), col. 6070.
[5] See p. 388 above.

Marxist intellectuals including Tokuda, who was secretary-general of the Japanese Communist Party twenty-five years later, and from a student organization calling itself the " Dawn People's Communist Party "; Katayama was among a number of Japanese invited from the United States.[1] It is not known how the Chinese delegates to the congress were recruited. But most of them were not communists, and they did not include the leaders of the Chinese Communist Party as constituted in the preceding summer.

The reasons for the change in the meeting place of the congress are conjectural.[2] But, after a preliminary session at Irkutsk in December 1921,[3] the main congress assembled in Moscow on January 21, 1922. It continued for some ten days. Times had changed; and the congress could not match the Baku congress of eastern peoples sixteen months earlier either in size or in enthusiasm. Korea had 52 delegates, China 2 and Japan 16; and there was a handful of delegates from India, Mongolia and Indonesia, as well as Yakuts, Buryats and Kalmyks from regions of the RSFSR. Only about half the delegates were professed communists : Kuomintang figured among the " national-revolutionary " organizations represented at the congress. " Intellectuals and students " predominated. But there were also peasants from Korea, industrial workers from Japan, and both workers and peasants from China. Judging by the incomplete records published by Comintern,[4] the Far Eastern delegates confined themselves to conventional speeches on the hopes and prospects of revolution in their respective countries. As at Baku, the principal speech was entrusted to Zinoviev. Zinoviev adopted a rather chilly attitude towards the Chinese nationalists. He complained that

[1] Information from Japanese sources communicated by Messrs. Langer and Swearingen ; Katayama describes his arrival in Moscow from the United States in *Kommunisticheskii Internatsional*, No. 44-45 (118-119), 1927, col. 59.

[2] They may have been of a practical kind ; or it may have been felt that the Far Eastern Republic, whose delegates at Washington were at this moment protesting its democratic character and independent status, would be compromised by the holding of such a congress on its territory.

[3] *Tikhii Okean*, No. 1, 1934, p. 125.

[4] *The First Congress of Toilers of the Far East* (Hamburg, 1922) ; the German version, which is less full, but better arranged, has the title *Der Erste Kongress der Kommunistischen und Revolutionären Organizationen des Fernen Ostens* (Hamburg, 1922). These are not complete records, containing only a few main speeches together with the resolutions and manifesto of the congress. A Russian version presumably exists, but has not been traced.

some members of Kuomintang " are looking not unhopefully towards America, i.e. American capitalism, expecting that just from there the benefits of democracy and progress will be showered on revolutionary China "; [1] there were even doctrinaires among them who wanted to " put on the agenda the question of the return of Mongolia to China ". The main weight of Zinoviev's argument rested, however, on Japan : " the key to the solution of the Far Eastern question is in the hands of Japan ". Marx had said once that a European revolution without England would be a storm in a tea-cup ; the same was true in the Far East of Japan with her 3,000,000 industrial workers and 5,000,000 landless peasants. " Class-conscious communists " in Japan could still be " counted only in hundreds ". But Zinoviev confidently predicted that nothing could prevent war in the Far East except a proletarian revolution in Japan and the United States.[2] It was clear throughout the congress that the Russian communist leaders at this time, trusting to Marxist dogma rather than to the precedent of the Russian revolution, still believed that industrial and colonizing Japan was riper for revolution than agrarian and semi-colonial China.[3] Safarov, the chief Russian speaker after Zinoviev, cautiously assessed the outlook in China :

> These peasant masses must be won over to the side of the revolution. The Chinese labour movement is just learning to walk. We are not building any castles in the air for the near future, we do not expect the Chinese working class to take the commanding position which the Japanese are able to gain in the near future.

The policy must be to " support every national-revolutionary movement, but support it only in so far as it is not directed against

---

[1] The official Soviet view at this time emphasized the bourgeois character of Kuomintang ; the Chinese situation was summed up in *Izvestiya* on November 15, 1921 : " The Chinese bourgeoisie, struggling for power under the lead of Sun Yat-sen, defending the idea of a capitalist order slightly mitigated by a vague programme of the nationalization of separate branches of industry, is coming up against the armed resistance of the economically backward north supported by the foreign imperialists ".

[2] *The First Congress of Toilers of the Far East* (Hamburg, 1922), pp. 21-39.

[3] As late as November 1922 the second congress of Profintern noted in a resolution on the workers' movement in the east that " a specially important rôle is reserved for Japan, which is in close proximity to its colonies and semi-colonies (Korea, China, etc.) " (*Desyat' Let Profinterna v Rezolyutsiyakh* (1930), p. 114).

the proletarian movement ".[1] The main resolution of the congress, which described " the many-million-headed masses of the workers and peasants of the Far East " as " the last resources of mankind ", seemed less tolerant of a policy of supporting bourgeois national movements, since it called for " an alliance of the working masses of the peoples of the Far East with the proletariat of the advanced countries — and with it alone — for the struggle against all imperialists ".[2] But the main colour of the pronouncements of the congress — as could be expected from so mixed a gathering — was anti-imperialist rather than specifically communist. A final manifesto to the peoples of the Far East denounced " hypocritical and thievish American imperialism and the greedy British usurpers " in Zinoviev's best rhetorical vein.[3]

Particular attention was devoted to the Japanese delegates ; according to a Japanese source, they were received by Stalin,[4] presumably in his capacity as People's Commissar for Nationalities, since he was not otherwise associated with the congress or with the work of Comintern. Katayama remained at the headquarters of Comintern, being a member of IKKI and its leading Far Eastern expert during the next few years. Other members of the Japanese delegation entered the newly founded Communist University of Toilers of the East. Seven of them returned to Japan with funds and instructions for the foundation of a Japanese Communist Party. This was achieved at a meeting in Tokyo on July 5, 1922, which became the official birthday of the party ; and its first congress was held in great secrecy in a country guest-house a few weeks later. Its membership at the moment of its foundation was about forty, apparently all intellectuals ; and the congress appointed an executive committee of seven.[5] It received formal

---

[1] *The First Congress of Toilers of the Far East* (Hamburg, 1922), pp. 166-167.

[2] *Der Erste Kongress der Kommunistischen und Revolutionären Organizationen des Fernen Ostens* (Hamburg, 1922), p. 124 ; the version of this resolution in the English record (p. 215) has been garbled in translation.

[3] *The First Congress of Toilers of the Far East* (Hamburg, 1922), p. 234 ; the manifesto was published in *Pravda* on February 9, 1922, a week after the end of the congress.

[4] *Pacific Affairs* (N.Y.), xxiii (1950), No. 4, p. 341.

[5] Information from Japanese sources communicated by Messrs. Langer and Swearingen ; a statement to a Japanese court by the communist leader Itikawa in 1931 was deliberately vague on points of detail (*Tikhii Okean*, No. 1, 1934, pp. 122, 125-127).

recognition at the fourth congress of Comintern in November 1922, when it was announced that the party had 250 members and 800 candidates who, under the Japanese party's rules, were required to go through a probation period before they were received into the party.[1] All party activities in Japan were highly illegal.

The period of the foundation of the Japanese Communist Party was already the period of the " united front " slogan in Europe. Attempts were made to apply it in Japan. Japanese communists claimed to have been responsible for bringing together during this time " some thousands " of workers and members of Left wing organizations in a " league to oppose intervention in Russia ", to have headed a movement for " help to starving Russia " (presumably a Japanese section of MRP), and to have organized a mass protest against anti-labour legislation.[2] At the fourth congress of Comintern in November 1922, Katayama, who appeared as delegate of the Japanese Communist Party, declared that the Japanese, Chinese and Korean parties had formed a " united front against Japanese imperialism ", and proposed a resolution in the joint names of the Japanese and Chinese delegations denouncing the Japanese occupation " of the Russian island of Sakhalin ".[3] The resolution of the congress on the eastern question optimistically diagnosed " a rapid growth of elements of the bourgeois democratic revolution " in Japan, and " the passing over of the Japanese proletariat to an independent class struggle ".[4] The Korean movement, on the other hand, seems at this time to have passed into a complete eclipse. Four Korean delegates presented themselves at the congress. But the credentials committee reported that " since party strife in Korea is so great that it is impossible to decide who really represents the genuine communist party and what group he represents, two comrades were admitted as guests and two rejected ".[5]

[1] *Protokoll des Vierten Kongresses der Kommunistischen Internationale* (Hamburg, 1923), p. 364.

[2] *Kommunisticheskii Internatsional*, No. 23 (November 4, 1922), cols. 6063-6075 ; *Tikhii Okean*, No. 1, 1934, pp. 131-132.

[3] *Protokoll des Vierten Kongresses der Kommunistischen Internationale* (Hamburg, 1923), pp. 602-603.

[4] *Kommunisticheskii Internatsional v Dokumentakh* (1933), p. 317.

[5] *Protokoll des Vierten Kongresses der Kommunistischen Internationale* (Hamburg, 1923), p. 367.

In China, the situation which presented itself to Soviet observers in the new year of 1922 was almost infinitely complicated. The success of a forward Soviet policy in Outer Mongolia continued to hang heavily over relations with the still officially recognized Chinese Government. Yurin, whose hasty exit from Peking at the end of July 1921 [1] had apparently been due to this cause, was nominally a representative of the Far Eastern Republic. No direct relations between the Soviet and Chinese Governments had been established since Chang Shi-lin's abortive mission to Moscow in the autumn of 1920. [2] The Chinese consul whose appointment had been promised on that occasion arrived in Moscow on February 3, 1921, and apparently expressed the willingness of the Chinese Government " in principle " to receive the Soviet representative. Some time during the summer it was decided — following, no doubt, the precedent of the Anglo-Soviet trade agreement — that the Soviet mission should take the form of a trade delegation; [3] and on October 24, 1921, Alexander Paikes, an otherwise unknown figure in Soviet diplomacy, at length left Moscow with his staff for Peking. [4] On December 10 he was in Harbin and gave his first interview to the Chinese press. The Soviet-Mongolian treaty of November 5 was not yet known to the world, and Paikes repeated the soothing assurances given by Chicherin of the Soviet intention to withdraw from Outer Mongolia when the crisis provoked by " white " intervention was over. He also spoke of the return of the Chinese Eastern Railway to China " without compensation of any kind ", though with safeguards of the economic interests of the RSFSR and of the Far Eastern Republic. [5]

Paikes's short stay in Peking was wholly unproductive. It coincided with the duration of the Washington conference; and, since the Peking government still looked optimistically to the conference for relief from the financial bankruptcy and general political discredit which threatened it, no decisions of policy in regard to Soviet Russia were likely to be taken so long as it was in session. Paikes abounded in vague assurances which carried little

[1] See p. 516 above.   [2] See p. 510 above.
[3] This was announced by Chicherin to the Mongolian Government in his note of September 14, 1921 (see p. 522 above).
[4] *Izvestiya*, November 6, 1921.
[5] *Millard's Review* (Shanghai), December 24, 1921, p. 824.

conviction of the innocence of Soviet intentions, and " unofficial " conversations which were announced on the future of the Chinese Eastern Railway and the resumption of diplomatic relations between the two countries made no progress.[1] Finally, in April 1922 the publication of the Soviet-Mongolian treaty of November 5, 1921, fell like a bombshell on the Paikes mission. Chinese indignation at a document which repudiated Chinese sovereignty over Outer Mongolia, and transformed the region once more into a permanent and exclusive Russian sphere of influence, was aggravated by the manifest deception practised by the Soviet envoy over the past four months. On May 1, 1922, Paikes received an angry note in which the Chinese Government claimed that " Mongolia is a part of Chinese territory ", that " in secretly concluding a treaty with Mongolia, the Soviet Government has not only broken faith with its previous declarations, but also violated all principles of justice ", and that the Soviet action was " similar to the policy assumed by the former imperial Russian governments towards China ".[2] An intimation was given to Paikes that his presence in Peking was no longer welcome; and he returned crestfallen to Moscow.

The blow to Soviet hopes would have been more serious if the Peking government itself had not by this time lost any real claim to be regarded as a national government. But during the year 1922 a series of events drew the attention of the Soviet leaders more and more to the activities of the southern nationalists, and seemed to disprove the rather contemptuous views of Kuomintang expressed by Zinoviev at the congress of toilers of the Far East. The first months of 1922 saw the first successful mass strike in Chinese history — a strike of Chinese sailors and workers in Hong Kong which paralysed the trade of the port, and caused heavy losses to British merchants and to the whole colony. Kuomintang, from its headquarters in Canton, had played a part in organizing the strike and reaped a new prestige from it; for the first time the nationalists had shown an inclination and a capacity to place themselves at the head of the nascent labour movement. These developments made their impression on the Chinese

---

[1] Reports from the press are quoted in R. T. Pollard, *China's Foreign Relations, 1917–1931* (N.Y., 1933), pp. 165-166.

[2] *China Year Book, 1923* (Shanghai, n.d.), p. 680.

Communist Party ; and Moscow began to display an ideological sympathy for the aspirations of Kuomintang. The opportunity to enlist local revolutionary nationalism in the struggle against British imperialism, hitherto exploited only in the Middle East, now presented itself in the Far East as well. A fresh element of confusion was, however, introduced into the situation when in May 1922 the commander of the nationalist army of Kwantung (it was alleged that he had been subsidized by the British in order to break the Hong Kong strike) rebelled against Sun Yat-sen, and drove the nationalist leader from Canton. Sun Yat-sen took refuge in Shanghai.

It was at this moment that the embryonic Chinese Communist Party began to show signs of life. The theses of the second congress of Comintern on the national question had now been fully digested ; and the IKKI resolution of December 1921 on the united front found an obvious application in China. The first proposal for a " tactical agreement " between Chinese communists and Kuomintang is said to have been made at a trade union congress in Canton in May 1922, presumably before Sun Yat-sen's expulsion.[1] In the following month the Chinese Communist Party issued its " First Manifesto on the Current Situation ", which propounded a programme of practical reforms of a radical democratic character, and contained a specific proposal for a conference with other Left parties and groups with a view to common action.[2] The same line was pursued in a resolution adopted at the second congress of the party which met in July 1922 :

> The Chinese Communist Party is the party of the proletariat. Its aims are to organize the proletariat and to struggle for the dictatorship of the workers and peasants, the abolition of private property, and the gradual attainment of a communist society. At present the Chinese Communist Party must, in the interest of the workers and poor peasants, lead the workers to support the democratic revolution, and forge a democratic united front of workers, poor peasants and petty bourgeoisie.[3]

No representative of Comintern was apparently present at the congress ; and, though it was afterwards alleged that there had

[1] *Novyi Vostok*, ii (1922), 606.   [2] *Ibid.* ii, 606-612.
[3] C. Brandt, B. I. Schwartz and J. K. Fairbank, *A Documentary History of Chinese Communism* (1952), p. 64.

been opposition in the Chinese party to any compromise with bourgeois democracy,[1] the documents afford no evidence of precise directives from Moscow. Indeed the absence of any such inspiration might be suggested by the omission of any reference to Soviet Russia in the resolution, and by the inclusion in it of an unqualified demand for " the liberation of Mongolia, Tibet and Sinkiang ". Effect seems, however, to have been given to the decision by Dalin, a representative of the Communist Youth International, who submitted the proposal for a united front to Sun Yat-sen at an interview in Shanghai which followed the party congress.[2] Clearly an alliance between Kuomintang and the microscopic and exclusively intellectual Chinese Communist Party presented attractions for the communists. It would enhance their prestige ; it would give them a means of access to the workers which they at present lacked ; and it accorded perfectly with the policy of the united front and of support for the democratic revolution. It is not surprising that Sun Yat-sen found it less attractive. But he apparently suggested that members of the Chinese Communist Party could, if they liked, join Kuomintang. The party would thus retain its identity, but its members would also become individual members of the larger organization. Immediately after these events, and perhaps in consequence of them, Maring reappeared on the scene.[3] The policy which he was now seeking to promote was set forth in an article which appeared in the journal of Comintern in September 1922,[4] and represented a reversal of the policies of conciliation of the Peking government

[1] B. I. Schwartz, *Chinese Communism and the Rise of Mao* (Harvard, 1951), pp. 38-39.

[2] H. Isaacs, *The Tragedy of the Chinese Revolution* (1938), p. 61 ; the only other source for this meeting is an open letter of Ch'en Tu-hsiu of 1929 quoted by B. I. Schwartz, *Chinese Communism and the Rise of Mao* (Harvard, 1951), p. 40.

[3] There seems to be no evidence of Maring's whereabouts between the time of his interviews with Wu Pei-fu and Sun Yat-sen in 1921 (see pp. 516-517 above) and his reappearance in August 1922, except a mention in H. Isaacs, *The Tragedy of the Chinese Revolution* (1938), p. 64 of a visit to Canton in January 1922 ; that Dalin was entrusted with the important conversation with Sun Yat-sen after the second party congress in July 1922 suggests that Maring was not available at that time.

[4] *Kommunisticheskii Internatsional*, No. 22 (September 13, 1922), cols. 5803-5816. Most items appearing in this journal were written several weeks before publication ; and this article was probably written before, not after, Maring's second meeting with Sun Yat-sen. But the chronology of these events is still uncertain.

and support for Wu Pei-fu.[1] Now that the Peking government
was both impotent and unfriendly, and Wu Pei-fu had unequivocally gone over to the British and American camp, there was no
further thought of toying with the north. The Hong Kong strike
had revealed the strength of the labour movement in the south. The
theses of the second congress of the party clearly pointed the way :

> If we communists wish to work successfully in the southern
> Chinese trade unions . . . we must maintain the most friendly
> relations with the southern Chinese nationalists.

The line was to " support the revolutionary-nationalist elements
of the south " and " push the whole movement to the Left ".
This was all the more necessary owing to the weakness of the
party : the young intelligentsia, " even those who call themselves
Marxists ", were too much inclined to stand aside from the
workers' movement. In Shanghai Maring now had a second
interview with Sun Yat-sen, and came to the conclusion that
Sun Yat-sen's offer to the Chinese communists of individual
membership in Kuomintang should be accepted : he was doubtless
influenced in this view by the history of the Indonesian Social-
Democratic Party, whose members had operated successfully
within the Muslim organization Sarekat Islam.[2] The proposal
was put by Maring to the central committee of the Chinese
Communist Party at a special conference in Hangchow in August
1922, and more or less reluctantly accepted.[3] The decision is said

---

[1] These are the policies referred to in H. Isaacs, *The Tragedy of the Chinese
Revolution* (1938), p. 65 (probably following Maring) as " the Irkutsk line ",
i.e. the line supported by the Far Eastern bureau of Comintern ; the most
persistent advocate of " the Irkutsk line " would appear to have been Vilensky
(for whom see p. 505 above, and Whiting's article in *The Far Eastern Quarterly*
(N.Y.), x, No. 4 (August 1951), p. 363). Zinoviev's speech at the congress
of toilers of the Far East in January 1922 (see pp. 426-427 above) conformed to
this line.   [2] See p. 251 above.

[3] Two contrary versions of this meeting both date from a later period, when
the alliance with Kuomintang had ended in disaster and been thoroughly discredited.   According to Ch'en Tu-hsiu, who was president of the central
committee, the proposal was vigorously opposed by all the leading members of
the committee, and Maring forced it through by invoking party discipline and
the authority of Comintern (B. I. Schwartz, *Chinese Communism and the Rise
of Mao* (Harvard, 1951), p. 41) ; Maring stated that he had " no specific instructions from Comintern " and " no document ", and that his proposal was
accepted by the majority of the committee (H. Isaacs, *The Tragedy of the
Chinese Revolution* (1938), pp. 61-62). Maring's assertion that he had no

to have been formally communicated by Li Ta-chao to Sun Yat-sen and approved by him.[1] At the fourth congress of Comintern in November the Chinese delegate announced that the Chinese party had decided to form a united front with Kuomintang by entering it in the form of individual membership ; and he added, in words which can hardly have been heard gratefully if they were reported back to Canton, that the purpose of this procedure was to " gather the masses round us and split the Kuomintang party ".[2] Radek once more accused the members of the Chinese party of having " shut themselves up in their rooms and studied Marx and Lenin as they once studied Confucius ", and informed them that " neither socialism nor a Soviet republic is now on the agenda " : the task of the party was " to regulate its relations with the revolutionary bourgeois elements in order to organize the struggle against European and Asiatic imperialism ".[3] It was the same injunction which was being simultaneously given to the Turkish, and *mutatis mutandis* to the German, parties. The congress resolution gave its blessing to the united front and to " the struggle for national liberation ".[4] Neither Radek nor the resolution referred to the peculiar device of individual membership of Kuomintang by which the united front in China was to be achieved. The omission can hardly have been accidental, and suggests divided opinions at the headquarters of Comintern on the tactical or ideological propriety of the line proposed.[5]

specific instructions is almost certainly correct : it was contrary to the habit of Comintern at this time to bind its emissaries by rigid orders. On the other hand, his views were emphatic and well known, and it can only be guessed how much persuasion or pressure he used to secure their acceptance. Ch'en Tu-hsiu asserts that Maring justified his position at the conference by maintaining that Kuomintang was a multi-class party. It is unlikely that this argument, which became popular later, was anticipated by Maring in 1922. Bukharin in April 1923 described Kuomintang as a petty-bourgeois party, representing the poor peasant and the petty bourgeoisie of the towns (*Dvenadtsatyi S"ezd Rossiiskoi Kommunisticheskoi Partii (Bol'shevikov)* (1923), p. 244).

[1] T'ang Leang-li, *The Inner History of the Chinese Revolution* (1930), p. 156.
[2] *Protokoll des Vierten Kongresses der Kommunistischen Internationale* (Hamburg, 1923), p. 615.   [3] *Ibid.* p. 141.
[4] *Kommunisticheskii Internatsional v Dokumentakh* (1933), pp. 322-324.
[5] At the twelfth party congress in April 1923 Bukharin had still to defend the whole policy of cooperation with Kuomintang against " comrades " who saw in Sun Yat-sen only " just such another *tu-chun*, i.e. military governor, as the other generals " (*Dvenadtsatyi S"ezd Rossiiskoi Kommunisticheskoi Partii (Bol'shevikov)* (1923), p. 244).

The strengthening and consolidation of Soviet influence in the Far East in the summer and autumn of 1922 could be attributed to several causes. In part, it was a reflection of the more assured position which the Soviet Government could claim in world affairs generally after the Genoa conference and the Rapallo treaty. In part it resulted from the decay of any central authority in China, which relieved the Soviet Government of all anxiety over its forward policy in Outer Mongolia and substantially eased the tension in Manchuria. But, most of all, it was the indirect and uncovenanted result of the Washington conference of the preceding winter. Soviet Russia was in most respects the principal beneficiary of the Washington conference in the Far East. Pressure at the conference compelled Japan to complete her retirement from Siberia and to abandon her remaining outposts in Shantung, and terminated the Anglo-Japanese alliance. All these moves struck deep at Japanese prestige and power in the Far East. The United States enjoyed a corresponding accretion of prestige, but was notoriously unwilling to exercise its power on the Asiatic mainland; American policy remained essentially negative. China should have benefited most from the curbing of Japanese power at the Washington conference, but was a prey to ever-growing internal conflicts which reduced the country to anarchy and impotence. Thus the Soviet republic, which had extended its authority over Outer Mongolia in the summer and autumn of 1921, was able little more than a year later to advance to the Pacific on the final evacuation of Vladivostok by Japan, to reincorporate the Far Eastern Republic in the RSFSR (soon to be merged in the larger unit of the USSR), and to resume the position of the Tsarist empire as a major Far Eastern Power.

The process was far advanced when, in the late summer of 1922, about the time of Maring's bargain with Sun Yat-sen in Shanghai, the Soviet Government undertook its first major and comprehensive diplomatic action in the Far East — the Joffe mission; and the sequel suggested that Joffe had few preconceptions and no binding instructions. Three courses were open to the Soviet emissary, and could be pursued in such a way as to make them complementary rather than mutually exclusive. First, he could negotiate with the weak and distracted Peking government in a tone of greater firmness and authority than Soviet diplomacy had been hitherto in a position to use; the change was symbolized by the appointment of Joffe, a diplomat of the first rank, to take over the task previously assigned to a Yurin and a Paikes. Secondly, he could encourage and stimulate the revolutionary nationalists, whose following and influence had scarcely yet begun to penetrate north China, in their campaign against the Peking government and the foreign imperialists; this was the line suggested by Maring's activities in Shanghai and Hangchow. Thirdly, he could work to establish normal relations with Japan; the most concrete purpose of his mission to the Far East was to attend a conference with Japanese delegates at Changchun to discuss the completion of the Japanese evacuation and outstanding issues arising from it.[1]

When Joffe reached Peking on August 12, 1922, he found the Chinese Government in the throes of what was now almost a permanent crisis. Since the end of the Washington conference its position had gone from bad to worse. The authority of Wu Pei-fu, the most powerful war-lord in central China, was undisputed in Peking. He had, however, no constructive policy, and the impotence of the central government was only the more apparent. Shortly before Joffe's arrival, a new Chinese Government had been installed in Peking with Wellington Koo, one of the Chinese delegates to the Washington conference, as its Minister for Foreign Affairs. Since its writ scarcely ran outside the walls of Peking, it could have no real policy and no powers of negotiation. Its purpose, which was common to all groups in China, was to induce the Washington Powers to carry out as rapidly as possible the promises, financial and other, made to China at the conference. Its attitude towards its increasingly powerful continental neighbour showed little sense of reality or of its own precarious plight. Standing on its dignity, ideologically antipathetic to Bolshevism, smarting under the high-handedness of Soviet policy in Outer Mongolia and mistrustful of Soviet designs in Manchuria once Japanese power was withdrawn, it showed no alacrity to open discussions with the new Soviet envoy.

Joffe's first successes were won among the teachers and students of Peking university. In the words of a Chinese witness, he " was greeted with vociferous welcome by the Chinese intellectuals ".[1]   Much attention was attracted by a passage in the speech delivered by the chancellor of the university of Peking at a banquet in honour of the Soviet emissary :

> The Chinese revolution was a political one.   Now it is tending towards the direction of a social revolution.   Russia furnishes a good example to China, which thinks it advisable to learn the lessons of the Russian revolution, which started also as a political movement but later assumed the nature of a social revolution.   Please accept the hearty welcome of the pupil to the teachers.[2]

Joffe himself said nothing so compromising.   But his reputation as the ambassador who, in the Berlin of 1918, had successfully instigated revolution against the government to which he was accredited, was not forgotten in Peking ; and the press bureau which he hastened to set up was certainly not inactive.   Even his description of his function as " the establishing of good friendly relations between the Russian and Chinese peoples " sounded ominous to sensitive official ears.[3]   The reticence of the Chinese Government apparently obliged Joffe at length to take the initiative.   In a press interview he stressed that formal recognition and the establishment of normal relations were a *sine qua non* for any negotiations with the Soviet Government, which would no longer be " satisfied with compromissory treaties instead of usually and commonly accepted ones ".[4]   On September 2, 1922, he addressed an official note to the Chinese Minister for Foreign Affairs, Wellington Koo, referring to three " private conversations " of the past ten days, and proposing a Russo-Chinese conference to negotiate an agreement on the basis of the Soviet declaration of 1919 and Karakhan's note of September 27, 1920.   The Chinese reply of September 7 accepted the proposed conference.[5]   At this point negotiations were interrupted by Joffe's visit to Changchun, where the conference with Japan opened on September 4, 1922. It ended in complete deadlock,[6] leaving Joffe to make a leisurely return to Peking.

[1] K. S. Weigh, *Russo-Chinese Diplomacy* (Shanghai, 1928), p. 277 ; R. T. Pollard, *China's Foreign Relations, 1917–1931* (N.Y., 1933),] p. 169-170.
[2] K. S. Weigh, *Russo-Chinese Diplomacy* (Shanghai, 1928), p. 313.
[3] *China Year Book, 1924–5* (Shanghai, n.d.), p. 858.
[4] *Millard's Review* (Shanghai), September 9, 1922, p. 67.
[5] Both notes were published in *Pravda*, September 16, 1922.
[6] See Vol. 1, pp. 362-363.

Joffe was back in the Chinese capital on October 3, 1922, and settled down to a game of stone-walling diplomacy on both sides which lasted for three months. The three crucial points round which the discussions revolved were the establishment of formal diplomatic relations, the position in Outer Mongolia, and the question of the Chinese Eastern Railway. Wellington Koo's first counter-stroke was an attempt to make the evacuation of Outer Mongolia by Soviet forces a prior condition of any negotiations. Joffe replied in a memorandum of October 14, 1922, that this question could not be isolated from the rest, and that an immediate withdrawal from Outer Mongolia would be neither in Chinese nor in Soviet interests.[1] Meanwhile Joffe himself, in a note from Changchun on September 21, 1922, had reminded the Chinese Government of Soviet rights over the Chinese Eastern Railway.[2] This provoked an acrimonious correspondence, the tone of which on the Soviet side notably stiffened after the final Japanese departure from Vladivostok at the end of October. On November 3, 1922, Joffe declared that the Chinese Eastern Railway had been " built with the money of the Russian people ", and remained " Russian property so long as Russia does not voluntarily decide to transfer possession of it to anyone else " ; he protested against the attempt of the Washington conference to interfere in a matter which concerned Russia and China alone ; and finally he demanded the arrest of the present manager of the railway, a nominee of the Russo-Asiatic Bank, on the ground of financial misdemeanours. Three days later, he added that unless the Chinese Government discontinued its habit of ignoring Russian interests, Russia would perhaps after all be obliged to consider herself free from promises she had voluntarily given — promises conditional on an undertaking of the Chinese Government, which had notoriously not been fulfilled, to tolerate in Chinese territory no organizations conducting hostilities against the RSFSR.[3] Later, in a speech at the celebration of the fifth anniversary of the October revolution, read on his behalf owing to his absence through illness by a member of his staff, Joffe pointedly observed that, since the Soviet

[1] *China Year Book, 1924-5* (Shanghai, n.d.), pp. 859-860.
[2] *Pravda*, September 24, 1922.
[3] *Izvestiya*, November 11, 1922 ; *China Year Book, 1924-5* (Shanghai, n.d.), pp. 860-861.

Government lacked the means at present to build another railway, it must perforce retain this " heritage of the Tsar's régime ", and hoped that its interest would be " understood and satisfied by China ".[1] Later still, Joffe specifically denied the authenticity of the alleged undertaking in the declaration of 1919 to " restore without compensation to the Chinese people the Chinese Eastern Railway ".[2] Meanwhile the Peking government reverted to its grievances about Outer Mongolia. With these two burning questions unsettled, and neither side showing any inclination to budge, the negotiations had drifted before the end of the year into a complete deadlock. In a final note dated January 9, 1923, Joffe spoke of the Chinese Government's " downright and irreconcilable hostility " to Soviet Russia, and suggested that the time had come for it to " make its choice between ' reds ' and ' whites ' ".[3] It was the Soviet Government that could best afford to wait.

Whether on account of the intransigence of Peking, or in pursuance of a previous intention, Joffe now turned in the direction in which Soviet policy had been pointing throughout the latter part of 1922. Having announced his intention of moving south for the good of his health, he paused in Shanghai, and had a series of conversations with Sun Yat-sen. It was the first official contact between Chinese nationalism and an emissary of the Soviet Government, and was significant for both. Sun Yat-sen was smarting from the defeat of his eviction from Canton, which he attributed, in part to reactionaries in Kuomintang, and in part to the intrigues of British imperialism, anxious to be avenged for the Hong Kong strike. He was therefore well prepared both for a move to the Left in his own party and for an alliance against foreign imperialism. On the Soviet side, Soviet diplomacy had always been ready, as more than one communication from Narkomindel had shown, to flirt with Sun Yat-sen as a potential claimant to power in China. Such a policy was now rendered all the more attractive by the evident bankruptcy and decay of the Peking government; Joffe seems to have made the shrewd estimate, or lucky guess, that Sun Yat-sen, in spite of his temporary

---

[1] *The Living Age* (Boston), January 12, 1923, pp. 73-76.

[2] *China Year Book, 1924-5* (Shanghai, n.d.), pp. 860-864 ; R. T. Pollard, *China's Foreign Relations, 1918-1931* (N.Y., 1933), pp. 170-175, contains a general account of the negotiations based on the contemporary press.

[3] *Weekly Review* (Shanghai), January 27, 1923, pp. 340-341.

eclipse, was still a force to be reckoned with. The conversation between Sun Yat-sen and Maring in the previous summer had sealed the alliance between the nascent Chinese Communist Party and Kuomintang. It remained for Joffe to transfer the agreement to the diplomatic plane, and to offer to Sun Yat-sen the advantages of an alliance, not with the negligible Chinese Communist Party, but with the far from negligible power of the Soviet state against the common imperialist enemy. This meant a temporary renunciation or postponement by Moscow of communist aims in China. Joffe was prepared to make the sacrifice. Conversations on this basis quickly produced results ; and when the two men parted on January 26, 1923, a joint statement was issued to the press. The decisive paragraph ran as follows :

> Dr. Sun Yat-sen holds that neither the communistic order nor the Soviet system can actually be introduced into China, because there do not exist here the conditions necessary for the successful establishment of either communism or Sovietism. This view is entirely shared by Mr. Joffe, who is further of the opinion that China's paramount and most pressing problem is to achieve national unification and attain full national independence ; and, in connexion with this great task, he has assured Dr. Sun Yat-sen that China has the warmest sympathy of the Russian people and can count on the support of Russia.

The statement continued with a reaffirmation of the principles laid down in the Karakhan note of September 27, 1920 ; both sides agreed that the question of the Chinese Eastern Railway could be settled only by a Russo-Chinese conference ; and, while Joffe " categorically declared " that the Soviet Government had no intention of causing Outer Mongolia to " secede from China ", Sun Yat-sen did not " view an immediate evacuation of Russian troops from Outer Mongolia as either imperative or in the real interest of China ".[1]

---

[1] *China Year Book, 1924-5* (Shanghai, n.d.), p. 863 ; the version published in *Izvestiya*, February 1, 1923, significantly omitted Sun Yat-sen's statement that China was not ripe for communism or the Soviet system and Joffe's assent to it — a further symptom of divided counsels in Moscow. The authenticity of the passage is not in doubt : it appears in L. Fischer, *The Soviets in World Affairs* (1930), ii, 540, in a version re-translated from " the fortnightly bulletin of the Soviet political representation in Peking, February 1-15, 1923, now in the archives of the Commissariat of Foreign Affairs ".

The principles thus laid down required practical application; and, when Joffe a few days later left Shanghai for Japan, he was accompanied by a member of Sun Yat-sen's staff, Liao Chung-k'ai, in order to pursue the negotiations. The whole episode now suddenly assumed a new and enhanced importance. Within a fortnight of Joffe's conversations with Sun Yat-sen a turn of the wheel at Canton recalled the nationalist leader to power; and a bargain struck with an exile of uncertain status in Shanghai became an agreement with the head of the effective government of a large part of southern China. What passed between Joffe and Liao Chung-k'ai in Japan is not recorded, but was later summed up by a Chinese historian in a symbolical conversation between the Chinese and Soviet negotiators:

> Liao asked him whether communism could be realized in Russia in ten years' time. Joffe said "No". "In twenty years?" "No", was the answer again. "In a hundred years?" "Perhaps", said Joffe. "Well", said Liao, ". . . what is the use of dreaming about a utopia which might or might not be realized when we are all dead? Let us all be revolutionaries today and work for the accomplishment of the national revolution on the basis of the Three 'People's Principles'." These we can realize within our lifetime.[1]

The same argument from the delay in the spread of the revolution, and consequently in the full realization of socialism, which had justified the introduction of NEP, led by an irresistible logic, in the Far East as elsewhere, to compromises and alliances with revolutionary nationalism. When Liao Chung-k'ai rejoined Sun Yat-sen in Canton in March 1923, the path to cooperation seemed smooth and clear. The bargain struck between Russian communism and Kuomintang was to prove fruitful and fateful for both parties.

Joffe's departure for Japan early in February 1923 was the result of a "private" invitation [2] from Baron Goto, mayor of

---

[1] T'ang Leang-li, *The Inner History of the Chinese Revolution* (1930), p. 158.

[2] At a later stage of Joffe's visit, Goto stated in an interview to the press that before inviting Joffe he had made enquiries of the Prime Minister and been informed that Matsudaira, head of the bureau of European and American

Tokyo and president of a " Russo-Japanese society ". He spent six months in the country. His activities there, unlike those of his Chinese visit, were conducted in a diplomatic twilight; and no official information was ever divulged about this abortive episode in Soviet foreign relations. The minute but enthusiastic Japanese Communist Party founded in the previous summer had apparently endeavoured during the winter to establish contacts with the masses. According to Bukharin's report to the twelfth congress of the Russian Communist Party, a Japanese congress of small tenant farmers had passed at the beginning of 1923 a resolution in favour of cooperation between the peasantry and the urban working class for the remedy of their grievances, and a labour congress at the same time had voted for political action; and both these resolutions had been passed under communist influence. Some exaggeration of the rôle of the Japanese Communist Party may be suspected in these claims.[1] What is more certain is that communism aroused intense emotions of hatred and fear among the ruling classes of Japan, and that objections to recognition of the Soviet Government or to any dealings with the Soviet envoy were scarcely less strong in influential quarters. Adverse press comment followed the announcement of the invitation to Joffe; and a demonstration at the Tokyo railway station on his arrival, at which incendiary leaflets were said to have been distributed and several alleged socialists were arrested, was thought by some to have been arranged by the police in order to discredit the visitor.[2] Later in the month an attack was made

---

affairs in the Ministry of Foreign Affairs, would be allowed to see Joffe un-officially, " if circumstances made it seem desirable " (*Japan Chronicle* (Kobe), May 10, 1923, p. 654). According to the so-called " Tanaka memorial " of 1927 which, whether authentic or not, was the work of someone with inside knowledge, Japan's policy at this time was to " befriend Russia in order to hamper the growth of Chinese influence "; it was with this purpose that " Baron Goto of Kato's cabinet invited Joffe to our country and advocated the resumption of diplomatic relations with Russia " (*Japan and the Next World War* (Shanghai, 1931), p. 15).

[1] *Dvenadtsatyi S"ezd Rossiiskoi Kommunisticheskoi Partii (Bol'shevikov)* (1923), p. 246. Katayama and the recently arrived secretary of the Japanese Communist Party, Arahata, both spoke at the congress, but confined themselves to conventional phrases and made no specific claims (*ibid.* pp. 80, 609: Arahata spoke under the fictitious name Aote).

[2] This suspicion is apparent in the account of the incident in *Japan Chronicle* (Kobe), February 8, 1923, p. 166.

on Goto by a member of an " anti-Joffe league ", and in April six men were arrested for an alleged plot against Joffe.[1]

Whatever Joffe's personal reaction to these incidents, they played no overt part in his leisurely and tentative conversations with Japanese statesmen. These conversations passed through three stages. For the first three months they seem to have been limited to wholly unofficial and non-committal talks with Goto. Joffe's illness was not purely diplomatic. At the beginning of April, 1923, it was stated that he had been in bed ever since his arrival,[2] so that, when he told an anxious Chinese correspondent in Tokyo in 1923 that he " was conducting no negotiations with the Japanese Government and was merely on a health visit ",[3] he may not have diverged so far from the truth as most people supposed. The second stage began on April 24, 1923, when Goto informed Joffe that the Japanese Government was prepared for a further Japanese-Russian conference provided the questions of Sakhalin and of satisfaction for the Nikolaevsk incident were settled first : later, the recognition of obligations of former Russian governments was also demanded from the Japanese side.[4] Conversations between Joffe and Goto proceeded on this basis for some time. On May 3, 1923, it was announced that Joffe's health had improved, and that he had received permission to use code for his communications with Moscow.[5] A week later Joffe replied that the Soviet Government refused to recognize the debts and obligations of former Russian governments, but would sell northern Sakhalin to Japan at a high price and would express regrets for the Nikolaevsk incident, though only if Japan expressed regret for similar excesses committed by Japanese forces. Some concession was also offered on the vexed question of the rights of Japanese fishermen in Russian waters.[6]

---

[1] *Japan Chronicle* (Kobe), March 1, 1923, p. 304 ; April 5, p. 487. The phenomenon afterwards familiarly known in Europe as Fascism made an early appearance in Japan ; its origins are traced back to 1918 in an article *On Fascism in Japan*, in *Novyi Vostok*, iv (n.d. [1923]), 416-421.

[2] *Japan Chronicle* (Kobe), April 5, 1923, p. 487.

[3] *China Year Book, 1924-5* (Shanghai, n.d.), p. 865.

[4] L. Fischer, *The Soviets in World Affairs* (1930), ii, 553 ; Fischer had been given access to the records of these discussions, presumably by Joffe himself.

[5] *Japan Chronicle* (Kobe), May 3, 1923, pp. 610-611.

[6] L. Fischer, *The Soviets in World Affairs* (1930), ii, 553 ; *Japan Chronicle* (Kobe), May 17, 1923, p. 694. On March 2, 1923, a decree annulled all

At this point the question arose whether these private talks with Goto were to be put on a more official basis, and the decision appears to have become involved with events in the Japanese Communist Party. In February 1923 the party held its second congress, and in May 1923 a special conference was held to draft a party programme. This comprised demands for the abolition of the monarchy, the army and the secret police, the confiscation of estates of large landowners, of religious organizations and of the emperor, and the redistribution of confiscated land to the peasants ; the withdrawal of Japanese troops from China, Sakhalin, Korea and Formosa ; and the diplomatic recognition of Soviet Russia.[1] It is difficult to believe that Joffe, with his record as a diplomatic agent of revolution in Germany and with his recent successes among Chinese intellectuals, was not privy to these developments. However this may be, external decorum was preserved on both sides throughout his visit. He took no ostensible interest in the fortunes of the Japanese Communist Party, and no charge was made against him in Japanese official quarters of being concerned in them. On the other hand, the suspicion may be felt that the Japanese police authorities, in the action taken by them at this time, were influenced by a desire, not only to nip Japanese communism in the bud, but indirectly to discredit Joffe and rouse popular prejudice against the establishment of relations with Soviet Russia. In the middle of May, the police announced the confiscation of 100 copies of Bukharin's and Preobrazhensky's *ABC of Communism* which had arrived in a British ship.[2] On June 5, 1923, an extensive round-up of communists and communist sympathizers took place ; and on the following day it was stated that a communist plot had been discovered to assassinate the whole cabinet and set up a communist government.[3] The presumption is strong that the plot was an invention of the authorities.

In the middle of June it was announced that Kawakami, an

" treaties, concessions, contracts and other agreements " on fishing rights in the Far East before the fusion of the Far Eastern Republic with the RSFSR, and set out new regulations under which rights might be leased to citizens of the RSFSR or to foreigners (*Sobranie Uzakonenii, 1923*, No. 36, art. 378).

[1] *Tikhii Okean*, No. 1, 1934, pp. 128-134, 144 ; information from Japanese sources communicated by Messrs. Langer and Swearingen.

[2] *Japan Chronicle* (Kobe), May 24, 1923, p. 726.

[3] Information from Japanese sources communicated by Messrs. Langer and Swearingen.

official of the Ministry of Foreign Affairs who had been the first
Japanese Minister in Warsaw, had been authorized to conduct
negotiations with Joffe, who now received formal credentials from
Moscow for the purpose.[1]   At this moment Joffe had another heart
attack which caused a further postponement.   But on June 28,
1923 the negotiations were opened and continued for just over a
month, twelve meetings being held in all.   The major issue was
the fate of northern Sakhalin.   Joffe asked for its unconditional
evacuation ; the Japanese Government proposed to buy it outright
for 150,000,000 yen.   Between these two extreme points a number
of intermediate proposals were canvassed, the most promising
being a plan to accord to a Japanese company or companies long
leases over the oil, coal and timber resources of the area.   From
time to time Japanese demands for compensation for the Nikolaevsk massacre of 1920 were injected into the discussions.   But
this question was evidently used mainly as a barometer to register
the pressure of the argument about Sakhalin.   In the end negotiations appear to have broken down not on any specific point, but
on the resistance of the most powerful forces in the Japanese
Government to a resumption of relations with Soviet Russia.   On
July 24 Kawakami informed Joffe that the cabinet had rejected
the terms in which the Soviet Government had offered to express
its regrets for the Nikolaevsk affair.   On July 31 Joffe announced
that he had been instructed to discontinue unofficial negotiations,
and was authorised to continue them officially only if Japan undertook in advance to evacuate northern Sakhalin.[2]   On August 10
he left Japan for Moscow.[3]   He did not revisit China where,
during the summer of 1923, disorder and confusion reached their
highest point for many years, and the discredited Peking government seemed likely to lose its last vestige of authority.

When Joffe left the Far East after a stay of some ten months,
much had been done to clarify Soviet policy there and put it on a
firm footing.   If Japan still occupied northern Sakhalin and still
withheld formal recognition of the Soviet Government, the principle of direct discussion had been cautiously established.   In

---

[1] *Japan Chronicle* (Kobe), June 21, 1923, pp. 882-883.
[2] L. Fischer, *The Soviets in World Affairs* (1930), ii, 553-555 ; the course
of the negotiations may also be traced in *Japan Chronicle* (Kobe), July 12, 1923,
p. 62 ; July 19, p. 96 ; July 26, p. 132 ; August 2, p. 154 ; August 9, pp. 189,
200.   [3] *Ibid.* August 16, 1923, p. 237.

Japan, as in Turkey, the persecution of local communists was not a bar to friendly relations with the government concerned. In September 1923, within six weeks of Joffe's departure, the catastrophic earthquake in Tokyo and Yokohama was followed by a panic which led to the mass arrest of known communists; and a majority of the party central committee, afterwards denounced as " petty bourgeois elements " and " typical opportunists ", hastened to dissolve the party.[1] But for the Soviet Government the Japanese disaster was an unqualified gain; in the words of a report of IKKI a few months later, " Japan ceased to be a great Power, and her pressure on the Far Eastern part of our republic was considerably weakened ".[2] In China the situation was more complex. But here, too, progress had been made. About the time of Joffe's return to Moscow, the announcement was made of the appointment of a new Soviet representative to the Chinese Government in the person of Karakhan, who had for some time been in charge of eastern affairs in Narkomindel. Karakhan set out from Moscow at the end of August 1923; and his mission opened a new phase in relations with the Chinese Government. But the Soviet Government did not intend to commit itself to the dying central authority in Peking. Soviet relations with Sun Yat-sen, now firmly re-established in Canton, were cordial and far-reaching, and seemed to provide for the first time a solid basis for Soviet policy in China. In the same month of August 1923, Chiang Kai-shek, an able and ambitious lieutenant of Sun Yat-sen, known for his support of a Soviet orientation in Kuomintang,[3] proceeded on a mission to Moscow to obtain supplies of arms and to study questions of military organization.[4]

---

[1] *Tikhii Okean*, No. 1, 1934, pp. 133-134, 146 ; the party was not revived till 1927, after which the short-lived party of 1922-1923 was generally referred to as the " first " party.

[2] *From the Fourth to the Fifth World Congress* (1924), p. 12 ; Katayama, on the other hand, was credited with the view that the earthquake would not " seriously affect the economic and military power of Japan " (*Novyi Vostok*, iv (n.d. [1923]), xiii-xv).

[3] According to T'ang Leang-li, *The Inner History of the Chinese Revolution* (1930), p. 158, Chiang Kai-shek and Liao Chung-k'ai (see p. 542 above) were the strongest supporters of a Soviet orientation in Sun Yat-sen's entourage.

[4] H. Isaacs, *The Tragedy of the Chinese Revolution* (1938), p. 65 ; L. Fischer, *The Soviets in World Affairs* (1930), ii, 633 ; *ibid.* (2nd ed., 1951), i, viii-ix, quoting a " rigidly confidential " letter from Sun Yat-sen to Lenin, Trotsky and Chicherin requesting " arms for the Chinese revolution ".

In October 1923 Michael Borodin, the English-speaking communist who had already been actively employed in the affairs in Comintern,[1] arrived at Sun Yat-sen's invitation in Canton. Though he brought with him a letter of introduction from Karakhan, he appears to have been designated not by the Soviet Government or by Comintern, but by the Russian Communist Party. His function was that of political adviser to Sun Yat-sen.[2] Within six years of the Bolshevik revolution, Soviet Russia had emerged from the penumbra of confusion and helplessness, and was intervening decisively in the policies of a major Asiatic country.

[1] See pp. 143-144, 169, 421-422 above.
[2] T'ang Leang-li, *The Inner History of the Chinese Revolution* (1930), p. 159 ; L. Fischer, *The Soviets in World Affairs* (1930), ii, 634.

NOTE E

THE MARXIST ATTITUDE TO WAR

THE French revolutionaries established a clear distinction between wars of liberation to free peoples from the rule of oppressive monarchs and wars of conquest to bring peoples under monarchical rule ; and they approved the former as heartily as they condemned the latter. No objection was felt to war in itself, or even to " aggression " in the popular sense of being the first to start a war. The test was whether the war was being fought on behalf of " peoples " or " nations " or on behalf of autocrats.[1] The European democratic movements of the period from 1815 to 1848 were heirs to this tradition. At that time almost any war fought against the Austria of Metternich, then the main focus of autocracy and reaction in Europe, would have been regarded as worthy of democratic sympathy and support. Such was the attitude imbibed and whole-heartedly shared by Marx and Engels in their early years. After 1848, two minor readjustments were required in the doctrine. As social-democracy or socialism came to be distinguished from liberal democracy or democracy *tout court*, the wars worthy of support were those likely to further the socialist rather than the democratic cause ; and Russia replaced Austria as the principal enemy. Numerous passages can be quoted from the writings of Marx and Engels to show that one of the main criteria applied by them after 1848 to test the desirability of war was whether it was likely to weaken or destroy the Russian autocracy.[2]

There was, however, another and quite different strain in the socialist tradition. The early socialists, faithful to their utopian philosophy, stressed the universal brotherhood of men, and regarded war as monstrous and unnatural. The tradition which they inherited was

---

[1] A similar view of war was implicit in Clausewitz's definition of it as " a continuation of policy by other means " ; the same criteria of judgment were applicable to wars as to other acts of policy.

[2] The earliest of these passages occurs in an article in *Neue Rheinische Zeitung* in July 1848 : " Only *war with Russia* is a war of *revolutionary Germany*, a war in which Germany can redeem the sins of the past, acquire virility, conquer its own autocrats, in which it can, as befits a nation in process of shaking off the chains of a long, inert slavery, purchase the propaganda of civilization by the blood of its sons and liberate itself by liberating others " (*Karl Marx-Friedrich Engels : Historisch-Kritische Gesamtausgabe*, Ier Teil, vii, 181).

that of the eighteenth-century philosophers from Saint-Pierre and
Leibniz to Rousseau and Kant who had nourished visions of " perpetual
peace " ; their successors were the nineteenth-century liberal " pacifists " [1] whose opposition to war was based on humanitarian rather than
on political grounds. But when class consciousness was bred by the
class struggle, and socialism became proletarian, the opposition to war
also took on a proletarian colour which appeared to be reinforced by
the argument that war was the necessary consequence of capitalism.
National wars were waged at the behest of capitalists and for their
advantage. The coming of socialism would remove the fundamental
cause of war and its sole incentive. The workers, who bore the brunt
of the fighting and derived no profits from it, could have no interest
but in peace. The socialist tradition always embodied a strong element
of opposition to war, based on a specific interest of the workers in the
maintenance of peace ; it thus ran parallel to the liberal tradition of the
later nineteenth century which attributed war to autocratic government
and believed in democracy as a guarantee of peace. All these views
were potentially " pacifist ", in that war as such was condemned
irrespective of its motive or its object. Marx and Engels themselves
consistently denounced all forms of pacifism as implying belief in a
natural community of interests ; Marx was particularly contemptuous
of the opposition of Cobden and Bright to the Crimean War.[2] In
general, Marx and Engels were too fully conscious of the revolutionary
potentialities of war to regard it as an unconditional evil ; at the end
of 1848, having described England as " the rock on which the waves
of revolution break ", Marx concluded that " old England will be
destroyed only by a world war ".[3] In 1859 Engels welcomed the
" Franco-Russian alliance " on the ground that this would force
Prussia's entry into the Italian war on the side of Austria :

> We Germans must be in the water up to our neck before we can be
> transported in mass into the *furor teutonicus* ; and on this occasion
> the danger of drowning seems to have come sufficiently near. So
> much the better. . . . In such a struggle the moment must come when
> only the most resolute party, the party that shrinks from nothing,
> will be in a position to save the nation.[4]

[1] The best definition of pacifism in the Marxist sense is in Max Beer,
Krieg und Internationale (Vienna, 1924), p. 8 : " that political tendency which
regards war as an absolute evil, and which assumes that it is possible in bourgeois society to prevent war and establish eternal peace by leagues of nations,
arbitration courts, holy alliances, free trade, democracy, disarmament, etc.".
[2] *Karl Marx-Friedrich Engels : Historisch-Kritische Gesamtausgabe*, III^er
Teil, i, 385 ; ii, 84.   [3] Marx i Engels, *Sochineniya*, vii, 108-109.
[4] *Ibid.* xxv, 262 : the original text is in *Der Briefwechsel zwischen Lassalle
und Marx*, ed. G. Mayer, iii (1922), 184-185.

It was not easy to bring together these various strands into a consistent body of doctrine about war.

The comparatively few pronouncements of the First International on war and foreign policy reflected these contradictions and uncertainties. The Inaugural Address of 1864 drafted by Marx skilfully reminded the reader of the interest of the workers in preventing wars which squandered " the people's blood and treasure ", of the " criminal folly " of the ruling classes bent on the " perpetuation and propagation of slavery ", and of the wickedness of yielding to the " barbarous power " of St. Petersburg. But the argument was more eloquent than clear ; and the writer was perhaps more concerned to win the sympathy of muddle-headed English trade-unionists than to expound Marxist doctrine. Nor was any action proposed except to watch, and, if necessary, protest against, the diplomacy of governments. Concrete issues of war found the First International confused and divided.[1] On the eve of the Prussian-Austrian War of 1866 anti-war agitation began in Paris. In Marx's words, " the Proudhon clique among the students in Paris preaches peace, calls war obsolete and nationalities nonsense, and attacks Bismarck and Garibaldi ". Admittedly, " as a polemic against chauvinism ", this was " useful and explicable ". But none the less these disciples of Proudhon were " grotesque " ;[1] and when the General Council approved a sentimental appeal drafted by Lafargue to " students and young men of all countries " against war, it was contemptuously described by Marx, in whose absence it had been adopted, as " silly stuff ".[2] The outbreak of the war itself was followed by a series of inconclusive debates in the General Council, which at length agreed on a wholly non-committal resolution :

> The General Council of the International Workingmen's Association regards the present war on the continent as a war between governments, and advises the workers to remain neutral and unite among themselves for the purpose of winning power through their union, and using the power so won in order to achieve their social and political emancipation.[3]

Since the brief campaign that ended at Sadowa was over before this resolution was published, the advice to the workers had no practical consequences. But the Prussian victory, and the war scare between Prussia and France in the following spring, had a significant sequel. In

[1] *Karl Marx-Friedrich Engels : Historisch-Kritische Gesamtausgabe*, iii^{er} Teil, iii, 336.
[2] A translation of the appeal is in *Neue Zeit* (Vienna), xxxiii (1914–1915), ii, 440-441 ; for Marx's comment see *Karl Marx-Friedrich Engels : Historisch-Kritische Gesamtausgabe*, iii^{er} Teil, iii, 341.
[3] *Neue Zeit* (Vienna), xxxiii (1914–1915), ii, 442.

the summer of 1867 a committee of bourgeois democrats and progressives from the principal countries of western Europe convened a congress of supporters of peace which met at Geneva on September 9 of that year. This step aroused considerable sympathy in the working-class groups represented in the First International ; and Marx found it necessary to devote a half-hour speech in the General Council on August 13, 1867 to an attack on the " peace windbag ". He did not oppose individual delegates attending the congress, but argued against any kind of official participation by the International. The International was itself already a peace congress working for unity between the workers of different countries ; and, had the organizers of the Geneva congress understood what they were about, they would have joined the International. People who did not help to alter the relations between labour and capital were ignorant of the real pre-conditions of universal peace. Existing armies were mainly designed to keep the working class under, and international conflicts were favoured from time to time " in order to keep the soldiery in good shape ". Finally the peace at any price party would leave an unarmed Europe a prey to Russia ; it was necessary to maintain armies as a defence against Russia.[1]

Marx's proposals carried the day in the General Council. But at the Lausanne congress of the International which preceded the Geneva congress and at which Marx was not present, the divisions reopened in the ranks. A commission set up by the congress reported in enthusiastic terms in favour of " energetic support " for the Geneva project and " participation in all its undertakings ". After a strenuous debate in the full congress a French delegate named Tolain, who was a Proudhonist, proposed, and secured the adoption of, a compromise resolution declaring that, " in order to abolish war, it is not sufficient to disband armies, but also necessary to alter the social organization in the sense of an ever juster distribution of production ", and making participation in the Geneva congress dependent on its endorsement of that principle.[2] This enabled a representative of the General Council to appear at the Geneva congress and make, amid loud protests, a statement that " social revolution was the necessary pre-condition of a lasting peace ".[3]

[1] Marx's summary of his speech is in *Karl Marx-Friedrich Engels : Historisch-Kritische Gesamtausgabe*, III^{er} Teil, iii, 417. The best account of the attitude of the First International to the Geneva congress is by Ryazanov in *Neue Zeit* (Vienna), xxxiii (1914–1915), ii, 463–469 ; Ryazanov, writing in 1915, somewhat overstressed the pacifist element in Marx's attitude in order to invalidate the appeal of German social-democrats to his anti-Russian utterances as a justification for their action in 1914.

[2] *Ibid.* xxxiii, ii, 466–468.

[3] *Annales du Congrès de Genève* (Geneva, 1868), p. 172.

Marx was annoyed when an enthusiastic delegate named Borkheim delivered to the congress a speech advocating preventive war against Russia and thus caricatured (*verkladderadatscht*) Marx's own ideas.[1]

A further step was reached when the next annual congress of the International met at Brussels in the summer of 1868, once more in the absence of Marx and Engels. International tension was steadily mounting and the issue of war could no longer be evaded. A German-Swiss section of the International submitted to the congress a draft resolution inviting the workers of all countries to " refuse the service of murder and destruction, as well as all work of supply for the war armies ". The resolution finally adopted by the congress merely recommended " the cessation of all work " in the event of war — " a strike of the peoples against war ".[2] The " strike against war " was taken up by the dissident Bakuninist section of the International at its congress in Geneva in 1873, and became in later years an important tenet of French and other syndicalists, who accepted it as an alternative to political action. But for the moment the Brussels resolution had no effect and was quickly forgotten. It never received the approbation of Marx and Engels, who consistently opposed any formula banning war as such or directed indiscriminately against all wars.

The Franco-Prussian War exposed these conflicting views to a severe test. The mobilization on both sides and the outbreak of hostilities took place without any kind of representative pronouncement on behalf of the workers or of socialist parties or groups in either country. No question therefore arose of any practical opposition to the war ; and the campaign was so quickly decided that no kind of public opinion was likely to crystallize on either side with sufficient rapidity to affect its course. Such declarations of socialist policy as were made had their influence, not on immediate issues, but on the shaping of socialist attitudes to future wars. The German divisions of 1914 were already anticipated in 1870. While Bebel and Liebknecht came out in the Reichstag on July 21, 1870, with a protest against the war (which had then already been in progress for a week), the committee of the German Social-Democratic Party, in session at Brunswick, issued a statement condemning Napoleon III's " criminal aggression " and, by implication, giving support to the Prussian cause. The position of Marx and Engels was complicated. They condemned the war as a war of conquest equally on the part of Napoleon and of Bismarck. They were

---

[1] Marx i Engels, *Sochineniya*, xxv, 496.

[2] Ryazanov, who has reviewed the evidence on the discussions at Brussels (*Neue Zeit* (Vienna), xxxiii (1914–1915), ii, 509-518) has established that the original draft was abandoned because, being tantamount to an incitement to mutiny, it might have exposed its sponsors to the rigours of the law ; merely to recommend a strike, on the other hand, was nowhere illegal.

consistently opposed to the annexationist designs of both sides, including the annexation of Alsace-Lorraine. But, once war was in progress, a Prussian victory seemed to them, for a variety of reasons, the lesser evil. In the first place, they were bound to regard the downfall of Napoleon as a desideratum of the workers. Once that was achieved, the situation would change ; " as soon as a republican and not chauvinist government is at the helm in Paris ", wrote Engels to Marx on August 15, 1870, the task would be " to work with it for an honourable peace ".[1] Secondly, they favoured the unity of Germany, just as they favoured the unity of Italy, as a legitimate satisfaction of nationalist aspirations and an advance from reactionary *kleinstaaterei*. This gave rise to what seems in retrospect a somewhat exaggerated distinction between the aims of " Prussia " and the aims of " Germany ". Bismarck, thought Engels as early as July 22, 1870, had started with annexationist designs for Prussia ; but " the affair has already got out of his hands, and the gentlemen have evidently succeeded in bringing about in Germany a complete national war ".[2] Marx — under provocation, it is true, from a sentimental pro-French compatriot — went so far as to speak of " the defensive character of the war on the side of the Germans (I will not say, of Prussia) " ; [3] and Engels, summing up the position from the party standpoint, thought it important to " stress the difference between German-national and dynastic-Prussian interests ".[4]   Thirdly, they believed that in the event of the achievement of German unity, " the German workers can organize themselves on a much broader national basis than hitherto " with the beneficent consequence of " the shifting of the centre of gravity of the continental workers' movement from France to Germany ".[5]   Finally, a fresh blow would be struck at the traditional enemy, Russia : Marx hopefully conjectured that " a show-

[1] *Karl Marx-Friedrich Engels: Historisch-Kritische Gesamtausgabe*, III[er] Teil, iv, 366.
[2] Marx, a few days later, saw in the war a revival of the war of national liberation of 1812 and of the stifled aspirations of 1848 and was shocked only by its embodiment in Bismarck : " The German philistine seems absolutely enchanted that he can now give unlimited rein to his inborn servility. Who would have thought it possible that twenty-two years after 1848 a national war in Germany would possess *such* a theoretical expression ? " (*ibid*. iv, 346). Later still he noted that " all machinations since the Second Empire have finally led to the attainment of the aims of 1848 — Hungary, Italy, Germany " (*ibid*, iv, 358).
[3] *Ibid*. iv, 354.   [4] *Ibid*. iv, 366.
[5] *Ibid*. iv, 365, 382. The idea belongs to Marx's correspondent Kugelmann, who wrote to him on August 7, 1870 : " Through political unity (several centuries late) the whole bourgeois development will be accelerated, and the German proletariat will for the first time have ground on which it can organize itself on a national scale, and will certainly soon win an outstanding place in the general workers' movement " (*Neue Zeit* (Vienna), xxxiii (1914-1915), ii, 169).

down between Prussia and Russia " would be " by no means improbable ", and that Germany's " newly strengthened national feeling " would scarcely allow itself to be pressed into Russian service.[1]

The First International was now approaching its end ; and no further pronouncements were demanded from it on the question of war. But Marx himself, when he wrote in 1875 his famous criticism of the Gotha programme of the German Social-Democratic Party, allowed himself a last fling at the permeation of the party by pacifist illusions :

> And to what does the German workers' party reduce its internationalism ? To the consciousness that the result of its striving will be " the international brotherhood of the peoples " — a phrase borrowed from the bourgeois league of freedom and peace which has to do duty for the international brotherhood of the working class in its common struggle against the ruling class and its governments. Of the international functions of the working class not a word ![2]

The workers' movement remained, as the sequel showed, hopelessly divided on the issue of war. Marx and Engels, themselves not wholly free from inconsistencies on the subject, had failed to win over the workers to any clear-cut international standpoint.

The Second International found the dilemma harder to evade. The succession of minor wars in the two decades before 1914 gave no great trouble ; for these were colonial wars in which Marxists had so far taken little interest. But the prospect of an impending war between the European Powers soon began to loom darkly on the horizon. Engels raised the issue squarely in an article of 1891 :

> What " war " in our days means, everyone knows. It means France and Russia on one side, and Germany, Austria and perhaps Italy on the other. Socialists of all these countries, called to arms against their will, would be compelled to fight against one another. What would the German Social-Democratic Party do then ? What would become of it ?

Unfortunately Engels's answer, based on Marxist tradition of the past forty years, was one which could be, and was, used with effect in 1914. He blamed the German annexation of Alsace-Lorraine in 1871 for the present situation, and proudly quoted the prediction of the council of the First International in its proclamation of September 9, 1870, that Prussian greed would only " compel France to throw herself into the

---

[1] *Karl Marx-Friedrich Engels : Historisch-Kritische Gesamtausgabe*, III[er] Teil, iv, 358.
[2] Marx i Engels, *Sochineniya*, xv, 278.

arms of Russia ". As between France and Germany, France still represented revolution — " only the bourgeois revolution, it is true, but still revolution ". But France, once she allied herself with Russia, would " renounce her revolutionary rôle ", whereas " behind official Germany stands the German Social-Democratic Party, the party to which the future, the near future, of the country belongs ". Neither France nor Germany would start the war. Russia would move first ; then France would advance towards the Rhine ; and " then Germany will be fighting simply for her existence ".[1] And the article ended with a general prediction which, for all its aptness, offered little guidance to the Second International on the duty of socialists in the countries concerned in the event of war :

> No socialist of whatever nationality can wish the triumph of the present German Government in the war, nor that of the bourgeois French Republic, and least of all that of the Tsar, which would be equivalent to the subjection of Europe, and therefore socialists of all countries are for peace. But if it comes to war nevertheless, just one thing is certain : this war, in which fifteen or twenty million armed men will slaughter one another, and all Europe will be laid waste as never before — this war must either bring the immediate victory of socialism, or it must upset the old order of things from top to bottom and leave such heaps of ruins behind that the old capitalistic society will be more impossible than ever, and the social revolution, though put off until ten or fifteen years later, will surely conquer after that time all the more rapidly and all the more thoroughly.[2]

Engels's article was symptomatic of the dilemma of the Second International throughout the next two decades. On the one hand, the growing realization that war between the European Powers, if it occurred, would bring devastation and disaster on an unprecedented scale made it increasingly difficult to ignore the issue or to take refuge in vague declarations of protest. On the other hand, national recognition of trade unions and the gradual drawing of the workers into the framework of the nation were making it increasingly difficult to assert that the workers could remain indifferent to the victory or defeat of their country. It was Engels who, in the article already quoted, caused a rather uncomfortable sensation among German social-democrats by calculating that in 1900 socialists would probably form a majority of the German army.[3] But the Second International lacked even that degree of leadership which the outstanding figure of Marx had imparted to its predecessor. That war was the result of the economic contradictions of capitalism, and would vanish only when socialism replaced

---

[1] Marx i Engels, *Sochineniya*, xvi, ii, 245-247.
[2] *Ibid.* xvi, ii, 249-250.   [3] *Ibid.* xvi, ii 244.

capitalism as the form of social organization, was accepted doctrine which found its place in the resolutions of every congress. But no common conclusions were drawn from it. The Second International represented many shades of Left-wing opinion, from pacifists (mainly British) of every known variety and advocates (predominantly French) of the " general strike against war ",[1] to those whose policy was confined to peaceful agitation and those (mainly Germans) who desired to safeguard in one form or another the workers' right to participate in the defence of their country if it were attacked. It was left to the Russian social-democrats, Bolsheviks and Mensheviks alike, to inject a further strain of thought. The Russo-Japanese War and the fall of Port Arthur at the beginning of 1905 provoked an unequivocal pronouncement from Lenin's pen :

> The proletariat has cause to rejoice. The catastrophic defeat of our worst enemy does not only mean that Russian freedom has come nearer : it presages also a new revolutionary upheaval of the European proletariat. . . . Progressive, advanced Asia has dealt backward and reactionary Europe an irreparable blow.[2]

This diagnosis, which was shared by Bolsheviks and Mensheviks as well as by most SRs, seemed amply confirmed when, little more than a week later, " Bloody Sunday " signalled the beginning of the Russian revolution. Social-democrats elsewhere in Europe were not moved to dispute the view that national defeat might be an asset to the revolutionary cause so long as a Russian defeat was in question. But there was no eagerness to apply the same principle to other countries. Indeed, to make it the universal duty of socialist parties to oppose their national governments in time of war and thus to work for the defeat of their own nations would be to introduce an entirely new principle ; for Marx and Engels, and Marxists since their time, had always assumed that, when war occurred, one belligerent was more worthy of socialist support than the other. Even though the right criteria for making the choice were sometimes in doubt, it had always been taken for granted that a choice could and should be made.

---

[1] The policy of the general strike against war had been adopted by the French Socialist Party at its congress at Nantes in 1894. French delegations constantly advocated it at congresses of the Second International, but with little or no support (at the Copenhagen congress of 1910 it was supported by the British ILP) ; the French Socialist Party at its extraordinary congress on July 16, 1914, once more proposed, on the motion of Jaurès, " a general strike of workers simultaneously and internationally organized in the countries concerned " as a means " to hinder and prevent war and to impose on governments recourse to arbitration ".

[2] Lenin, *Sochineniya*, vii, 45.

Such were the current assumptions when the Second International, at its Stuttgart congress in 1907, found itself obliged to make a major pronouncement of policy on the issue of war. The Stuttgart congress was attended, on behalf of the Russian Social-Democratic Workers' Party, by Lenin, Martov and Rosa Luxemburg.[1] It proved a momentous occasion. The drift towards war in Europe was everywhere beginning to penetrate the consciousness of the masses and to provoke widespread pacifist reactions. The conception of war as something in itself basically inimical to the interests of the workers, and calling for condemnation and preventive action by the International, was in the ascendant. In its resolution on " militarism and international conflicts " the congress admitted that, in view of the wide prevailing differences of opinion, " the International is not in a position to establish in advance strictly defined forms for the struggle of the working classes against militarism ". But it made none the less some surprisingly definite pronouncements. The resolution declared it to be the duty of the working class and of the parliamentary representatives " to struggle with all their forces against armaments by sea and land and to refuse the means for them " — the famous pledge to vote against military credits. But its most sensational pronouncement was reserved for the last two paragraphs, which were originally proposed by the Russian delegation as an amendment to the draft put forward by the bureau, and were accepted after some opposition from Bebel and the German delegation. Here, for the first time in this context, the issues of the class struggle and the social revolution were specifically raised :

In the event of a threatened declaration of war the workers of the countries concerned and their representatives in parliament, supported by the unifying activity of the international bureau, must use all their exertions in order, by measures which seem to them most efficacious and will naturally vary with the exacerbation of the class struggle and of the general political situation, to prevent the outbreak of war.

Should war none the less be declared, their duty is to act in order to bring it to a speedy termination, and to strive with all their forces to utilize the economic and political crisis caused by the war in order to rouse the masses of the people and hasten the destruction of the class domination of the capitalist classes.[2]

[1] The composite character of the delegation was a sequel of the fourth party congress of 1906 where formal unity was re-established between Bolsheviks and Mensheviks (see Vol. 1, p. 49).

[2] The resolution is in *Internationaler Sozialisten-Kongress zu Stuttgart, 18 bis 24 August 1907* (1907) and in many translations, not all of them accurate. According to a subsequent statement of Lenin (*Sochineniya*, xii, 380), Bebel refused to accept a stronger wording originally proposed by the Russians on

These paragraphs, though nobody seems to have drawn attention to the point, abandoned the constant assumption of Marx and Engels that, in the event of war, social-democrats would have to make a choice, and would be able to make a choice in the light of the ultimate interest of socialism, between the opposed belligerents. In the historical period on which the world had now entered, social-democrats would be equally opposed to all belligerent capitalist governments. Two years later Kautsky, long recognized as the leading party theorist, not only accepted and elaborated the new thesis in his book *Der Weg zur Macht*, but provided it with a theoretical justification. International war was now diagnosed as a crisis in the capitalist system, thus offering to the workers the best opportunity of overthrowing capitalism. The formula achieved with so much difficulty at Stuttgart was repeated and endorsed by the Copenhagen congress of the Second International in 1910, and by a special conference convened at Basel in November 1912 to consider the issues raised by the Balkan War. This repetition appeared to lend a certain solemnity to the doctrine. Socialist and social-democratic deputies of all countries regularly carried out the gesture of voting against military budgets, though since they remained everywhere a comparatively small minority in their respective parliaments the gesture remained without practical effect.

In reality this picture of international social-democracy speaking through the Second International in the name of the united workers of the world remained an abstraction. In a world of uniform economic development and opportunities, national differences might, as the *Communist Manifesto* predicted, have progressively disappeared. But in a world where development had been highly unequal, wide divergences were bound to occur in the attitude of the workers of different countries. In the advanced countries, notably in Great Britain and in Germany, where the workers had attained a relatively high standard of living and a recognized place in the national polity, the pull of national allegiance was strong enough in the first decade of the twentieth century to challenge class allegiance. In all western European countries pronouncements of leaders of the workers against militarism and

the ground that it might expose the German Social-Democratic Party to legal reprisals. The fullest records of the congress are in the Russian volume, *Za Rubezhom: Mezhdunarodnyi Sotsialisticheskii Kongress v Shtuttgarte* (1907): Bebel's original draft is on pp. 68-69, the Russian draft of the last two paragraphs on pp. 81-82, and the final version on pp. 85-86, the last two paragraphs showing only minor variants from the Russian draft. When the last paragraph was quoted in a resolution of the first congress of Comintern in 1919, it was attributed to Lenin and Rosa Luxemburg, Martov not being mentioned — an early instance of falsification through the suppression of an unwelcome name (*Kommunisticheskii Internatsional v Dokumentakh* (1933), p. 73).

war were apt to carry an explicit or implied reservation of the right of
national self-defence ; and this meant not a return to the Marxist
criterion of supporting the side whose victory would further the
socialist cause, but tacit acceptance of the bourgeois liberal distinction
(which Marx had always derided as illusory) between aggressive and
defensive wars. Only in backward Russia, where the workers enjoyed
fewest advantages, was social-democracy largely impervious to the
claim of loyalty to a national government. Lenin in 1915 correctly
attributed this immunity of the Russian workers from " chauvinism "
and " opportunism " to the fact that " the stratum of privileged workers
and employees is with us very weak ".[1]

This, however, brought up in a new context the fundamental
dilemma of the Russian revolution. In the Marxist scheme of revolution, the difference between Russia and western Europe in economic
development was expressed in a difference between the stages reached
by them in the revolutionary process. The mandate of the Stuttgart
congress to utilize war " to hasten the destruction of the class domination
of the capitalist class " made sense, strictly speaking, only in countries
where a bourgeois revolution had been completed, and capitalism had
attained its maturity ; and this assumption stood out even more clearly
from Kautsky's interpretation of war in the contemporary period as a
crisis of capitalism. In Russia, as everyone agreed, the bourgeois
revolution had not yet been completed and capitalism had not yet
reached its maturity, so that the Stuttgart resolution made sense for
Russia only if the completion of the bourgeois revolution, which would
bring capitalism to its maturity, and the onset of the socialist revolution,
which would " hasten the destruction " of capitalism, were telescoped
into a single process. Nobody except Trotsky (who was not at Stuttgart) yet openly faced this contingency. But, whether or not one
plunged into the doctrinal refinements of " permanent revolution ", it
seemed clear enough as a practical proposition, especially after 1905,
that backward Russia, left to her own resources, was still far from
ripe for a proletarian revolution. While social-democrats in western
Europe might reasonably hope and work for the ultimate victory of
socialism in their own countries without much regard for what happened elsewhere, Russian social-democrats could hope for an early
victory of socialism in Russia only if it was also victorious in one or
more of the advanced European countries. The weaker brethren had
a greater practical interest than the stronger in the brotherhood of the
international proletariat. Russian social-democracy remained obstinately and outspokenly international in a sense which was no longer true
of social-democracy in western Europe.

[1] Lenin, *Sochineniya*, xviii, 209.

The outbreak of war in 1914 forced this latent divergence into the open. Western social-democrats, after some initial divisions and hesitations, rallied with few exceptions to the support of their national governments; the Stuttgart resolution was silently disobeyed and forgotten. The decision of the large German social-democratic group in the Reichstag on August 4, 1914, to vote for the war budget was a crucial moment. Kautsky in a series of articles afterwards collected under the title *Internationalismus und der Krieg* reverted to the standpoint of Marx and Engels that social-democrats should support the side whose victory would be more likely to help the socialist cause; and the conclusion that the victory of Germany and the defeat of Russia were preferable to the converse result followed without argument. In Russia, the initial impulse among social-democrats was to oppose the war by every means : the social-democrats in the Duma, Bolsheviks and Mensheviks alike, spoke and voted with a united voice against war credits.[1] But Plekhanov and some of the leading Mensheviks abroad followed the example of the western social-democrats and came out for national defence ; and a " patriotic " attitude was not uncommon in the small group of organized and relatively privileged workers in Russia, especially those whose party allegiance was predominantly Menshevik.[2] When pressure and persecution began, many Bolsheviks in Russia — Kamenev being notable among them — began to waver ;[3] and there was no unanimity even among the Bolsheviks abroad. From this welter of confusion a tripartite division soon emerged among Russian social-democrats. On the Right, a group of Mensheviks proclaimed the patriotic duty of national defence. On the Left, Lenin supported by a small group of Bolsheviks in Switzerland — at first by Zinoviev almost alone, later with some reservations by Bukharin, Sokolnikov, Pyatakov, Safarov and others — maintained the cause of national defeatism and civil war. Between these extremes a large miscellaneous group, composed of both Mensheviks and Bolsheviks, occupied a " centrist " position, denounced the war and demanded a " democratic " peace without annexations or indemnities, but refrained from preaching national defeatism or civil war ; this group, whose inclinations were pacifist rather than revolutionary, had its headquarters in Paris and was represented by a journal known successively (owing to periodical bans by the censorship) as *Golos, Nashe Slovo* and *Nachalo*, in which Martov

---

[1] See Vol. 1, p. 65.

[2] According to a Menshevik account of the demonstrations in Petersburg on the outbreak of the war, " the patriotic bacchanalia did not leave even the workers unaffected ; many of those who yesterday were on strike were found today in the ranks of the patriotic demonstrators " (Y. Martov, *Geschichte der Russischen Sozial-Demokratie* (1926), p. 274).

[3] See Vol. 1, p. 67.

and Trotsky were leading collaborators. It corresponded broadly to similar " centrist " groups which were beginning to emerge in other Left parties — notably a section of the German Social-Democratic Party headed by Kautsky, and an ILP group in Great Britain led by Ramsay MacDonald.

Lenin lost no time in defining his position. In a set of theses read to a tiny group of Bolsheviks in Berne in the first days of September 1914 he denounced " the treason to socialism of the majority of the Second International ", argued that " from the point of view of the working classes and of the toiling masses of all the peoples of Russia the least evil would be the defeat of the Russian monarchy and its armies ", and demanded the extension to all the warring armies of " propaganda for the social revolution, for the necessity of turning their arms, not against their brothers, the hired slaves of other countries, but against the reactionary and bourgeois governments and parties of all countries ".[1] The theses were embodied in a manifesto ₅ued two months later in the name of the central committee of the party, in which Lenin coined the slogan of " the transformation of the present imperialist war into a civil war ".[2] He became increasingly impatient of the " centrists ", who rejected national defence but refused to accept defeatism and civil war as a logical consequence, thus keeping one foot in the camp of " democratic " war aims and bourgeois pacifism. In March 1915 a conference of Bolshevik organizations abroad was held at Berne. Here Lenin temporarily settled his differences with the group which had gathered round Bukharin,[3] and produced a substantial declaration of Bolshevik policy. The war was described as an imperialist war, being a war for the division of colonies by Britain, France and Germany and the acquisition of similar territories (Persia, Mongolia, Turkey, etc.) by Russia: it was characteristic of an epoch " when capitalism has attained the highest phase of development . . . and when the objective conditions for the realization of socialism have completely ripened ". It was thus distinguished from the " nationalist " wars of

---

[1] Lenin, *Sochineniya*, xviii, 44-46.   [2] *Ibid.* xviii, 66.

[3] The principal difference between Lenin and the Bukharin group was that the latter, while accepting the transformation of the imperialist war into a civil war as the ultimate goal, wavered on the issue of defeatism, and did not wish altogether to discard or condemn bourgeois democratic peace slogans as instruments of propaganda : the document representing their views is in *Proletarskaya Revolyutsiya*, No. 5 (40), 1925, pp. 170-172. It is significant that, while many Bolsheviks still clung to the terra firma of bourgeois democracy and the bourgeois revolution, Lenin was moving rapidly forward, under the impetus of the war and the international situation, towards the position which he was to take up in the " April theses " of 1917. Bukharin and Pyatakov, however, again separated from Lenin in 1916 on the issue of national self-determination (see Vol. 1, p. 427).

the period 1789-1871 ; the national element in the struggle of Serbia against Austria was an exception which did not affect the general character of the war. The transformation of the imperialist war into civil war was therefore " the only correct proletarian slogan ". Peace propaganda not accompanied by this slogan was an illusion. " In particular, the idea that a democratic peace is possible without a number of revolutions is profoundly erroneous." [1]

Later in the year, Lenin for the first time contemplated the practical situation which would arise if a proletarian revolution occurred first of all in Russia during the war. He published in the party journal *Sotsial-Demokrat* a brief statement modestly entitled " Some Theses ", the last of which may be described by anticipation as the first foreign policy pronouncement of the future revolutionary government :

> To the question what the party of the proletariat would do if the revolution put it in power in the present war, we reply : we should propose peace to *all* the belligerents on condition of the liberation of colonies, and of all dependent and oppressed peoples not enjoying full rights. Neither Germany nor England nor France would under their present governments accept this condition. Then we should have to prepare and wage a revolutionary war, i.e. we should not only carry out in full by the most decisive measures our whole minimum programme, but should systematically incite to insurrection all the peoples now oppressed by the Great Russians, all colonies and dependent countries of Asia (India, China, Persia, etc.), and also — and first of all — incite the proletariat of Europe to insurrection against its governments and in defiance of its social-chauvinists. There is no doubt that the victory of the proletariat in Russia would create unusually favourable conditions for the development of revolution both in Asia and in Europe.[2]

---

[1] Lenin, *Sochineniya*, xviii, 124-128. The declaration also recommended for the first time " fraternization of soldiers of the warring nations in the trenches " ; Lenin had been attracted by reports in the press of cases of fraternization which had occurred at Christmas 1914 (*ibid.* xviii, 94, 136).

[2] *Ibid.* xviii, 313. A little earlier, in a famous passage in an article on " The United States of Europe Slogan ", which afterwards played its part in the controversy on " socialism in one country ", Lenin had anticipated in general terms the situation which might arise in the event of the proletarian revolution being successful in one capitalist country alone : " Inequality of economic and political development is an unconditional law of capitalism. Hence it follows that a victory of socialism is possible initially in a few capitalist countries, or even in one separate capitalist country. The victorious proletariat of this country, having expropriated its capitalists and organized its socialist production, would rise up *against* the rest of the capitalist world, attracting to itself the oppressed classes of other countries, provoking among them a revolt against the capitalists, appearing if necessary with armed force against the exploiting classes and their states " (*ibid.* xviii, 232-233).

The line was clear. The proletariat, having conquered power in Russia, would remain at first within the limits of the bourgeois revolution, making use of democratic slogans — in Europe, to discredit bourgeois governments which, owing to the now fully developed contradictions of capitalism, were unable any longer to realize even a bourgeois democratic peace ; in Asia, to raise the standard of bourgeois revolution among nations still lingering in the pre-capitalist stage and lead them to throw off the yoke of the European imperialist Powers. By both these procedures, reinforced if necessary by revolutionary war, the Russian proletariat would prepare the way for the triumph of the socialist revolution in Europe, and so in Russia itself.

Meanwhile, several attempts had been made by socialists opposed to the war to organize international conferences on Swiss soil. In March 1915 Klara Zetkin organized a conference of socialist women at Berne ; and in the following month Willi Münzenberg, secretary of the Socialist Youth International, convened, also at Berne, a conference of socialist youth. Bolsheviks drawn from Lenin's group attended both these conferences, but obtained no support when they put forward the slogan of " the transformation of the imperialist war into civil war ".[1] In September 1915 a general international conference of socialists opposed to the war met at Zimmerwald. The numerous but much-divided Russian delegation included Lenin and Zinoviev, Martov and Axelrod, Trotsky and the SR leader Chernov. Rakovsky represented the Rumanian social-democrats, Kolarov the Bulgarians. Most of the Germans were Left social-democrats who were prepared to abstain from voting on war credits, but not to break party discipline by voting against them. The rest of the participants were French, Italian, Swiss, Dutch, Scandinavian, Lettish and Polish (among these Radek).[2] Of the thirty or more delegates, nearly twenty formed the Right wing of the conference ; Lenin had the more or less qualified support of six or eight for his " civil war " policy ; the remaining delegates, of whom Trotsky was the most conspicuous, occupied a middle position and tried to mediate between the two extremes. The manifesto unanimously adopted by the conference was drafted by Trotsky, and was confined to general denunciation of the war. Six delegates — Lenin, Zinoviev and Radek together with a Swede, a Norwegian and a Lett — signed a declaration protesting against the inadequacy of the manifesto : this group formed what came to be known as the " Zimmer-

[1] Documents of the two congresses are translated, and the main sources cited, in O. H. Gankin and H. H. Fisher, *The Bolsheviks and the World War* (Stanford, 1940), pp. 280-308 ; both congresses are described by A. Balabanov, who was present, in *Erinnerungen und Erlebnisse* (1927), pp. 100-102.

[2] British delegates were nominated by the ILP and the British Socialist Party, but were refused passports.

wald Left ".[1] The conference decided to set up a standing international socialist committee and secretariat at Berne. These organs arranged a " second Zimmerwald conference ", which was held at Kienthal in April 1916 with a rather more numerous attendance of delegates. The most significant change since the previous autumn had occurred in the German movement. Not only had the Left wing of the German Social-Democratic Party gathered strength (it was to secede later in the year and form the German Independent Social-Democratic Party), but a group had appeared within it whose views approximated to those of Lenin : the so-called Spartakusbund. The appeal drafted and approved by the Kienthal conference marked a certain shift towards the Left since Zimmerwald, but still fell far short of the Bolshevik programme.[2] Throughout this period Lenin's supporters remained an insignificant minority in the anti-war wing of the international socialist movement, and on the vital issue of civil war and national defeatism could not count on the whole-hearted concurrence even of Bolsheviks in Russia or of other Bolsheviks groups abroad.

In the interval between the Kienthal conference and the February revolution in Russia no further attempt was made to hold an international socialist conference. Lenin's main efforts during this period were devoted to a controversy in the Bolshevik ranks on the issue of national self-determination ;[3] to an abortive attempt to wean the Swiss Socialist Party from its support of national defence ; and to the writing of *Imperialism as the Highest Stage of Capitalism*, which provided a theoretical basis for the transition from the original Marxist view that the workers should in the event of war support the side whose victory was most likely to advance the cause of socialism to Lenin's present position. Capitalism, in Lenin's analysis, had now reached its final, or imperialist, stage, in which war between the great European Powers was simply a struggle for colonial territory and markets. In such circumstances none of the belligerents could be deemed worthy of support by the workers ; and the fact that capitalism was now in its final phase proved that the moment was ripe for the transition to socialism and for action by the workers of all countries to hasten it. It was thus the supposed imminence of the socialist revolution which justified the abandonment of Marx's " opportunist " attitude towards wars between capitalist Powers in favour of a position

[1] For documents and sources, see O. H. Gankin and H. H. Fisher, *The Bolsheviks and the World War* (Stanford, 1940), pp. 320-356 ; the manifesto of the conference and a rejected Bolshevik draft are in Lenin, *Sochineniya*, xviii, 412-420.

[2] For documents and sources see O. H. Gankin and H. H. Fisher, *The Bolsheviks and the World War* (Stanford, 1940), pp. 407-438.

[3] See Vol. 1, pp. 424-428.

which regarded the defeat of all capitalist Powers as in principle equally desirable. Through moods of alternate optimism and pessimism as the war dragged on, Lenin never lost this guiding thread. When the February revolution broke out, he sounded a note of triumph in the *Farewell Letter to the Swiss Workers* written on the eve of his departure for Russia :

> The objective conditions of the imperialist war serve as a guarantee that the revolution will not stop at the *first stage* of the Russian revolution, that the revolution will *not* stop at Russia. *The German proletariat is the most faithful and reliable ally of the Russian and world-wide proletarian revolution.* . . . The transformation of the imperialist war into civil war *is becoming* a fact.
>
> Long live the proletarian revolution in Europe which is beginning.[1]

In this dual prediction of the rapid transition of the Russian revolution from its bourgeois-democratic into its proletarian-socialist phase and of the extension of the revolution to the other belligerent countries, Lenin looked forward to the coming realization of his slogan of the transformation of the imperialist war into the civil war of the proletariat against the bourgeoisie.

[1] Lenin, *Sochineniya,* xx, 70.

NOTE F

THE PRE-HISTORY OF THE COMMUNIST INTERNATIONAL

WHEN the principal constituent parties of the Second International betrayed the cause of international socialism on the outbreak of the war in 1914 by supporting their respective national governments, they seemed to Lenin to have signed the death-warrant of the International : its " political bankruptcy " was proclaimed by him in the Berne theses of September 1914.[1] For those who accepted this view the corollary — the creation of a new International — was obvious : it is not surprising that it should have occurred simultaneously to more than one revolutionary thinker. On October 31, 1914, Trotsky signed the preface to a pamphlet *The War and the International* which was published in Munich in the following month :

> The whole pamphlet from the first page to the last [he wrote] is written with the thought of the new International which must arise out of the present world cataclysm, of the International of the last struggles and of the final victory.[2]

On the following day, November 1, 1914, the *Sotsial-Demokrat* carried a manifesto from the party central committee which ended with the same thought :

> The proletarian International has not perished and shall not perish. The working masses in the face of all obstacles will create a new International. . . .
> Long live the international brotherhood of the workers against the chauvinism and patriotism of the bourgeoisie of all countries.
> Long live the proletarian International purged of opportunism.[3]

[1] See Vol. 1, p. 66 ; Lenin, *Sochineniya*, xviii, 44.

[2] L. Trotsky, *Der Krieg und die Internationale* (Munich, n.d. [1914]), p. 9. In a striking passage Trotsky recognized the danger that the war, if indefinitely prolonged, might destroy " the moral forces of the proletariat ", and that " the whole combative energy of the international proletariat, which imperialism has brought to the surface by its bloody conspiracy, may be entirely used up in the fearful work of mutual destruction " : then civilization might be set back " for several decades " (*ibid.* p. 83).

[3] Lenin, *Sochineniya*, xviii, 66.

The manifesto, of which Lenin was the author, was followed by an article in which Lenin embroidered the theme of the bankruptcy of the Second International, and made it clear that the new International as conceived by him was not the rival, but the successor, of the second — as the second had been of the first — the representative of a new stage in the historical process :

> The Second International performed its part of useful preparatory work on the preliminary organization of the proletarian masses in the long " peaceful " epoch of the most ruthless capitalist slavery and most rapid capitalist progress in the last third of the nineteenth, and beginning of the twentieth, century : the Third International is confronted with the task of organizing the forces of the proletariat for a revolutionary stranglehold on capitalist governments, for civil war against the bourgeoisie of all countries for political power, for the victory of socialism.[1]

In the three following years, these ideas were a constant theme of Lenin's thinking and writing. The issue of the Second or Third International became closely involved with the issue of the attitude of socialists to the war, and the same tripartite division emerged with the same leading personalities in each group. The Right which supported national war policies also remained faithful to the Second International and looked for its revival after the war. The extreme Left, composed at first mainly of Lenin's immediate supporters, rejected the Second International root and branch and called eagerly for the constitution of a new International after the war to take its place. The " centrists " hovered uneasily between the two extremes and thought of a reformed or reconstructed Second International rather than of a wholly new organization : this was the group which would one day, logically enough, create the Two-and-a-half International. In this question, as in the question of the war, Lenin denounced " social-patriots " and " centrists " alike. But the question remained academic, and he made little headway. The Zimmerwald manifesto of September 1915, representing the preponderance of " centrist " elements at the Zimmerwald conference, ignored the issue ; the draft manifesto of the Zimmerwald Left ended with the call for " a powerful International, the International which will put an end to all wars and to capitalism ".[2] At the Kienthal conference of April 1916, the " Zimmerwald Left " was strengthened by the appearance of representatives of the newly formed German Spartakus group ; the resolution submitted to the conference by this group proclaimed that " the new International

---

[1] Lenin, *Sochineniya*, xviii, 61-66, 71.
[2] *Ibid.* xviii, 420 ; for the conference see pp. 564-565 above.

which must rise again after the collapse of the old one on August 4, 1914,[1] can be born only of the revolutionary class struggle of the proletarian masses in the most important capitalist countries ", but hinted at a possible future divergence from Lenin's position when it added that this was " not a question of organization, not a question of agreement between a small group of persons acting as representatives of the opposition strata of the workers ", but " a question of a mass movement of the proletariat of all countries ".[2] Lenin, however, never wavered in his opinion. In the latter part of 1916, according to Krupskaya, he " thought that the time was ripe for a split on an international scale, that it was necessary to break with the Second International, with the international socialist bureau, to break for ever with Kautsky and Co., to begin with the forces of the Zimmerwald Lefts to build a Third International ".[3]

The February revolution and the return of all the leading Bolsheviks to Petrograd reopened the debate within the party. The tenth of Lenin's April theses ran :

> Renewal of the International.
> Initiative in founding a revolutionary International, an International against the *social-chauvinists* and against the " Centre ".[4]

In the pamphlet *Tasks of the Proletariat in Our Revolution* he elaborated the theme, and turned his heaviest guns against the Centre : " the whole Zimmerwald majority, composed primarily of ' centrists ' ", had taken the slippery path into " social pacifism ".[5] Meanwhile the standing international socialist committee set up at Zimmerwald had moved from Berne to Stockholm ; and throughout the summer of 1917 Lenin waged a single-handed fight against the general party view that the party should remain in the Zimmerwald organization and send delegates to a projected third Zimmerwald conference at Stockholm.[6] The April party conference adopted a long resolution which condemned the " centrists " and demanded the foundation of a Third

----

[1] This was the day on which the German Social-Democratic Party voted in the Reichstag in support of war credits.

[2] O. H. Gankin and H. H. Fisher, *The Bolsheviks and the World War* (Stanford, 1940), p. 435.

[3] N. K. Krupskaya, *Memories of Lenin*, ii (Engl. transl., 1932), 196.

[4] Lenin, *Sochineniya*, xx, 89 ; Lenin added in a footnote a definition of the " Centre " as " a tendency which fluctuates between the chauvinists (= " defencists ") and the internationalists — Kautsky and Co. in Germany, Longuet and Co. in France, Chkheidze and Co. in Russia, Turati and Co. in Italy, MacDonald and Co. in England, etc."   [5] *Ibid.* xx, 129.

[6] Not to be confused with the proposed international socialist peace conference which was also to be held at Stockholm but was finally abandoned (see pp. 5-6, 8, above).

International, but decided, against Lenin's opposition, to remain for the time being in the Zimmerwald organization.[1] At the end of May 1917 Lenin wrote impatiently to Radek in Stockholm that it was " imperative to sever connexions " with Zimmerwald :

> We must at all costs bury the rotten . . . Zimmerwald, and found a real Third International consisting only of Lefts. . . . If we could get quickly an international conference of Lefts, the Third International would be founded.[2]

But lack of interest in the party was once more shown at the sixth party congress, held in Petrograd in August 1917 while Lenin was in hiding in Finland, at which the question of a break with Zimmerwald was not raised at all ; and Lenin reiterated his views in a long letter to the central committee.[3] The third Zimmerwald conference finally met in Stockholm early in September 1918, the Bolshevik delegates being Vorovsky and Semashko. Its sole achievement was to draft a manifesto on the war which was to be submitted to the constituent parties for approval before publication : the most striking paragraph was one which called for " an international proletarian mass struggle for peace " which would " signify at the same time the rescue of the Russian revolution ".[4] On the eve of the conference Lenin wrote an angry note in which he complained that " we are taking part in a comedy " and demanded that " we should leave Zimmerwald at once ".[5] But very soon events nearer home absorbed his attention, and the October revolution relegated Zimmerwald to a backwater. The Bolsheviks never formally broke with it. The international socialist committee continued from time to time to issue pronouncements which attracted little or no notice, including one welcoming the Bolshevik revolution. In March 1919 the Communist International at its founding congress received a report from Angelica Balabanov as secretary of the Zimmerwald committee, and a statement signed by Rakovsky, Lenin, Zinoviev, Trotsky and Platten as former participants in the organization, expressing the view that it had " outlived itself ". On the strength of these documents the congress formally dissolved the Zimmerwald union, thus declaring itself the heir of any good will that Zimmerwald still possessed.[6]

[1] VKP(B) v Rezolyutsiyakh (1941), i, 235 ; Lenin's objections are recorded in Sochineniya, xx, 279.
[2] Leninskii Sbornik, xxi (1933), 57-58.   [3] Ibid. xiii (1930), 275-280.
[4] A mass of materials relating to the preparations for, and proceedings of, the third Zimmerwald conference are collected in O. H. Gankin and H. H. Fisher, The Bolsheviks and the World War (Stanford, 1940), pp. 582-683 ; the official report of the conference will be found ibid. pp. 669-675, the draft manifesto ibid. pp. 680-683.   [5] Lenin, Sochineniya, xxi, 129.
[6] Kommunisticheskii Internatsional v Dokumentakh (1933), p. 85.

LIST OF ABBREVIATIONS

BSP	= British Socialist Party.
CGT	= Confédération Générale du Travail.
CGTU	= Confédération Générale du Travail Unitaire.
Cheka	= Chrezvychainaya Komissiya (Extraordinary Commission).
Comintern	= Kommunisticheskii Internatsional (Communist International).
CPGB	= Communist Party of Great Britain.
Gosbank	= Gosudartsvennyi Bank (State Bank).
IFTU	= International Federation of Trade Unions.
IKKI	= Ispolnitel'nyi Komitet Kommunisticheskogo Internatsionala (Executive Committee of the Communist International).
ILO	= International Labour Organization.
ILP	= Independent Labour Party.
Inprekorr	= *Internationale Presse-Korrespondenz.*
IWW	= Industrial Workers of the World.
KAPD	= Kommunistische Arbeiter-Partei Deutschlands (German Communist Workers' Party).
KPD	= Kommunistische Partei Deutschlands (German Communist Party).
Mezhsovprof	= Mezhdunarodnyi Sovet Professional'nykh Soyuzov (International Council of Trade Unions).
MRP	= Mezhdunarodnaya Rabochaya Pomoshch' (International Workers' Aid).
Narkomindel (NKID)	= Narodnyi Komissariat Inostrannykh Del (People's Commissariat of Foreign Affairs).
Narkomnats	= Narodnyi Komissariat po Delam Natsional'nostei (People's Commissariat of Nationalities).
NEP	= Novaya Ekonomicheskaya Politika (New Economic Policy).
NUWM	= National Unemployed Workers' Movement.
Profintern	= Krasnyi Internatsional Professional'nykh Soyuzov (Red International of Trade Unions).
RILU	= Red International of Labour Unions (*see* Profintern).
RKP(B)	= Rossiiskaya Kommunisticheskaya Partiya (Bol'-

shevikov) (Russian Communist Party (Bolsheviks)).

RSFSR = Rossiiskaya Sotsialisticheskaya Federativnaya Sovetskaya Respublika (Russian Socialist Federal Soviet Republic).

SLP = Socialist Labour Party.

Sovnarkom = Sovet Narodnykh Komissarov (Council of People's Commissars).

SPD = Sozial-Demokratische Partei Deutschlands (German Social-Democratic Party).

SSR = Sotsialisticheskaya Sovetskaya Respublika (Socialist Soviet Republic).

SSSR = Soyuz Sovetskikh Sotsialisticheskikh Respublik (Union of Soviet Socialist Republics).

USPD = Unabhängige Sozial-Demokratische Partei Deutschlands (German Independent Social-Democratic Party).

Vesenkha = Vysshii Sovet Narodnogo Khozyaistva (Supreme Council of National Economy).

VKP(B) = Vsesoyuznaya Kommunisticheskaya Partiya (Bol'shevikov) (All-Union Communist Party (Bolsheviks)).

VKPD = Vereinigte Kommunistische Partei Deutschlands (United German Communist Party).

Vneshtorg = Narodnyi Komissariat Vneshnei Torgovli (People's Commissariat of Foreign Trade).

VTsIK = Vserossiiskii (Vsesoyuznyi) Tsentral'nyi Ispolnitel'nyi Komitet (All-Russian (All-Union) Central Executive Committee).

BIBLIOGRAPHY

To compile a comprehensive bibliography even of the principal source material for the history of Soviet Russia between 1917 and 1923 would be an immense undertaking, especially as much of it has appeared in several editions and some of it (notably the documents of Comintern) in several languages. The present bibliography has no claim to completeness. It does not include many occasional sources cited in the footnotes, or any secondary sources, and is confined to the principal primary sources on which I have relied. The editions which I have used are always listed first. Notes are added on other editions of the most important works, though my reason for using one edition rather than another has often been the fortuitous one of accessibility. It may be assumed that all the works listed in this bibliography are in the British Museum unless some other library is named in square brackets immediately after the title or volume number. Libraries in other countries are named only when the work in question is not known to be available in Great Britain. Libraries in the United States are named only when the title has not been traced in any library in western Europe; and, where it has been found in the Library of Congress, no other American library has been named. In one case I have had to record a work as being in private ownership, having failed to trace it in any library.

No systematic attempt has yet been made to compare texts of different editions of party or Soviet publications. While commentaries were progressively modified to meet the needs of current orthodoxy, and certain documents were withheld from publication from 1923 onwards for similar reasons, the actual text of documents published was rarely tampered with before 1936. Thereafter omissions began to occur frequently; these were at first confined to the omission of names of condemned party leaders, but afterwards became more extensive. In general, documents published from 1936 onwards require much more careful scrutiny than documents published before that date. Innumerable variants, great and small, occur between documents and records of Comintern in different languages; but these seem to be more often due to carelessness, or to discrepancies and misunderstandings originating at the congresses or conferences themselves, than to deliberate subsequent falsification.

I

THE RUSSIAN SOCIAL-DEMOCRATIC WORKERS' PARTY, LATER RUSSIAN [LATER ALL-UNION] COMMUNIST PARTY (BOLSHEVIKS)

(i) PROCEEDINGS OF CONGRESSES AND CONFERENCES

Vtoroi S"ezd RSDRP (Marx-Engels-Lenin Institute, 1932). The first edition is *Vtoroi Ocherednoi S"ezd Ross. Sots.-Dem. Rabochei Partii* (Geneva, 1904) [London School of Economics and Political Science; the British Museum copy is imperfect].

Tretii Ocherednoi S"ezd Sotsial-Demokraticheskoi Rabochei Partii 1905 Goda: Polnyi Tekst Protokolov (Istpart, 1924). The first edition is *Tretii Ocherednoi S"ezd Ross. Sots.-Dem. Rabochei Partii: Polnyi Tekst Protokolov* (Geneva, 1905).

Chetvertyi (Ob"edinitel'nyi) S"ezd RSDRP (Marx-Engels-Lenin Institute, 1934). The first edition is *Protokoly Ob"edinitel'nogo S"ezda Rossiiskoi Sotsial-Demokraticheskoi Rabochei Partii* (Moscow, 1907) [United States, Library of Congress]; a second edition is *Protokoly Ob"edinitel'nogo S"ezda RSDRP* (Istpart, 1926).

Pyatyi S"ezd RSDRP, Mai-Iyun' 1907 g. (Marx-Engels-Lenin Institute, 1935). The first edition is *Londonskii S"ezd Rossiiskoi Sotsial-Demokraticheskoi Rabochei Partii: Polnyi Tekst Protokolov* (Paris, 1909) [Hoover Library, Stanford].

Vserossiiskaya Konferentsiya Ross. Sots. Dem. Rab. Partii 1912 Goda (Paris, 1912). This is a brief account — not a stenographic record — of the Prague conference of January 1912, including the text of the resolution; a later edition *Prazhskaya Konferentsiya RSDRP 1912 Goda* (Marx-Engels-Lenin Institute, 1937) has much subsidiary matter, but some omissions.

Pervyi Legal'nyi Peterburgskii Komitet Bol'shevikov v 1917 g. (Istpart, 1927). Contains abbreviated records of proceedings from March 2 to December 28, 1917/January 10, 1918.

Sed'maya ("Aprel'skaya") Vserossiiskaya i Petrogradskaya Obshchegorodskaya Konferentsii RSDRP(B), Aprel' 1917 g. (Marx-Engels-Lenin Institute, 1934). The first edition is *Petrogradskaya Obshchegorodskaya i Vserossiiskaya Konferentsii RSDRP (Bol'shevikov) Aprel' 1917 g.* (Istpart, 1925).

Protokoly S"ezdov i Konferentsii VKP(B): Shestoi S"ezd (Istpart, 1927). The first edition is *Protokoly VI S"ezda RSDRP (Bol'shevikov)* (1919) [Hoover Library, Stanford]; there is also a later edition, *Shestoi S"ezd RSDRP* (Marx-Engels-Lenin Institute, 1934).

Sed'moi S"ezd Rossiiskoi Kommunisticheskoi Partii (Bol'shevikov) (1923) [London School of Economics and Political Science].

Vos'moi S"ezd RKP(B), 19-23 Marta, 1919 g. (Marx-Engels-Lenin Institute, 1933). The first edition is *VIII S"ezd Rossiiskoi Kom-*

munisticheskoi Partii (Bol'shevikov), 18-23 Marta, 1919 : Stenografi-cheskii Otchet (1919) [United States, Library of Congress].

Devyatyi S"ezd RKP(B), Mart-Aprel' 1920 g. (Marx-Engels-Lenin Institute, 1934). The first edition is *Devyatyi S"ezd Rossiiskoi Kommunisticheskoi Partii : Stenograficheskii Otchet* (1920) [Internationaal Instituut voor Sociale Geschiedenis, Amsterdam].

Desyatyi S"ezd Rossiiskoi Kommunisticheskoi Partii : Stenograficheskii Otchet, 8-16 Marta, 1921 g. (1921). A later edition with notes and additional material is *Desyatyi S"ezd RKP(B)* (Marx-Engels-Lenin Institute, 1933).

Vserossiiskaya Konferentsiya RKP(B) (Bol'shevikov) : Byulleten' (Nos. 1-5, December 19-29, 1921).

Odinnadtsatyi S"ezd RKP(B) (Bol'shevikov) (Marx-Engels-Lenin Institute, 1936). The first edition is *Odinnadtsatyi S"ezd Rossiiskoi Kommunisticheskoi Partii (Bol'shevikov) : Stenograficheskii Otchet, 27 marta-2 aprelya, 1922 g.* (1922).

Dvenadtsatyi S"ezd Rossiiskoi Kommunisticheskoi Partii (Bol'shevikov) : Stenograficheskii Otchet (17-25 Aprelya, 1923 g.) (1923) [School of Slavonic and East European Studies, University of London].

Trinadtsataya Konferentsiya Rossiiskoi Kommunisticheskoi Partii (Bol'-shevikov) (1924) [In private ownership].

(ii) Resolutions

Vsesoyuznaya Kommunisticheskaya Partiya (Bol'shevikov) v Rezolyutsiyakh i Resheniyakh S"ezdov, Konferentsii i Plenumov TsK (1941), i : 1898-1925 [United States, Library of Congress] ; ii : 1925-1939. This is the 6th and latest edition, no congress having been held between 1939 and 1952. The first edition under the title *Rossiiskaya Kommunisticheskaya Partiya (Bol'shevikov) v Postanovleniyakh ee S"ezdov 1903-1921 gg.* was published in 1921. The introductory notes to the resolutions of each congress or conference have been modified from edition to edition, but the text of the resolutions seems to have remained intact, except for the omission of the prefix *tov.* (comrade) before the names of condemned opposition leaders.

(iii) Party Histories

The following are selected from a large mass of literature in many languages :

G. Zinoviev, *Istoriya Rossiiskoi Kommunisticheskoi Partii (Bol'shevikov)* (1923). Contains 6 lectures delivered in March 1923 on the 25th anniversary of the foundation of the party and is translated into several languages.

Istoriya VKP(B), ed. E. Yaroslavsky, i (1926) (covers the period to 1904) ; ii (1930) (covers the period 1905-1907) ; iii (1929) (covers the period 1914-1917) ; iv (1929) (covers the period 1917-1920) [London School

of Economics and Political Science]. The preface to volume ii
announces two further volumes — iii, i (to cover the period 1907–
1914), and v in two parts (to cover the period after 1921). These I
have not traced, if they were ever published.
A. S. Bubnov, *VKP(B)* (1931). This is a reprint of the article under
this title in *Bol'shaya Sovetskaya Entsiklopediya*, xi (1930), 386-544,
and carries the history of the party as far as the 15th congress ; it
is chiefly valuable for statistical information.
N. N. Popov, *Outline History of the Communist Party of the Soviet Union*,
2 vols. (n.d. [?1934]). This is a translation of the 16th edition of
what was at that time the standard work on the subject and carries
the history of the party down to the eve of the 17th congress.
*History of the Communist Party of the Soviet Union (Bolsheviks): Short
Course* (1939). This is the English version of the standard history
published in Russian in 1938 and since translated into all languages.
The authorship of chapter 4, section 2, " Dialectical and Historical
Materialism ", was later attributed to Stalin ; later still Stalin was
referred to as the author of the whole work. It contains too many
misstatements to be regarded as evidence of anything but the official
view in 1938 and since that time.

II

PROCEEDINGS OF ALL-RUSSIAN CONGRESSES OF SOVIETS AND OF VTsIK

Pervyi Vserossiiskii S"ezd Sovetov R. i S.D., 2 vols. (1930-1931). Printed
from contemporary stenographic records.
Vtoroi Vserossiiskii S"ezd Sovetov R. i S.D. (1928). Printed from
contemporary press reports, no stenographic record having been
kept.
*Tretii Vserossiiskii S"ezd Sovetov Rabochikh, Soldatskikh, i Krest'yanskikh
Deputatov* (1918). A fairly full report in third person form, only
Lenin's main speech being reproduced textually.
*Chetvertyi Vserossiiskii S"ezd Sovetov Rabochikh, Krest'yanskikh, Soldat-
skikh, i Kazach'ikh Deputatov: Stenograficheskii Otchet* (1919)
[United States, Library of Congress].
*Pyatyi Vserossiiskii S"ezd Sovetov Rabochikh, Krest'yanskikh, Soldat-
skikh, i Kazach'ikh Deputatov: Stenograficheskii Otchet, 4-10
Iyulya, 1918 g.* (1918).
*Shestoi Vserossiiskii Chrezvychainyi S"ezd Sovetov Rab., Kr., Kaz., i
Krasnoarm. Deput.: Stenograficheskii Otchet, 6-9 Noyabrya, 1918 g.*
(1919).
*7ⁱ Vserossiiskii S"ezd Sovetov Rabochikh, Krest'yanskikh, Krasnoarmei-
skikh, i Kazach'ikh Deputatov: Stenograficheskii Otchet, 5-9 Dekabrya, 1919 goda* (1920).

Vos'moi Vserossiiskii S''ezd Sovetov Rabochikh, Krest'yanskikh, Kras-noarmeiskikh, i Kazach'ikh Deputatov : Stenograficheskii Otchet, 22-29 *Dekabrya,* 1920 *goda* (1921).

Devyatyi Vserossiiskii S''ezd Sovetov Rabochikh, Krest'yanskikh, Kras-noarmeiskikh, i Kazach'ikh Deputatov : Stenograficheskii Otchet, 22-27 *Dekabrya,* 1921 *goda* (1922).

Desyatyi Vserossiiskii S''ezd Sovetov Rabochikh, Krest'yanskikh, Krasno-armeiskikh, i Kazach'ikh Deputatov : Stenograficheskii Otchet, 23-27 *Dekabrya,* 1922 *g.* (1923).

I S''ezd Sovetov Soyuza Sovetskikh Sotsialisticheskikh Respublik : Stenograficheskii Otchet, 30 *Dekabrya,* 1922 *g.* (1923).

Vtoroi S''ezd Sovetov Soyuza Sovetskikh Sotsialisticheskikh Respublik : Stenograficheskii Otchet (1924).

Protokoly Zasedanii Vserossiiskogo Tsentral'nogo Ispolnitel'nogo Komiteta Sovetov R., S., Kr., i Kaz. Deputatov 2 *Sozyva* (1918).

Protokoly Zasedanii Vserossiiskogo Tsentral'nogo Ispolnitel'nogo Komiteta 4*go Sozyva* (1920).

Pyatyi Sozyv Vserossiiskogo Tsentral'nogo Ispolnitel'nogo Komiteta Sovetov Rabochikh, Krest'yanskikh, Kazach'ikh, i Krasnoarmeiskikh Deputa-tov : Stenograficheskii Otchet (1919).

I i II Sessii Vserossiiskogo Tsentral'nogo Ispolnitel'nogo Komiteta IX Sozyva (1923) [United States, Library of Congress].

III Sessiya Vserossiiskogo Tsentral'nogo Ispolnitel'nogo Komiteta IX Sozyva, 12-27 *Maya,* 1922 *g.: Byulleten'* (1922).

IV Sessiya Vserossiiskogo Tsentral'nogo Ispolnitel'nogo Komiteta IX Sozyva, 23-31 *Oktyabrya,* 1922 *g.: Byulleten'* (1922).

Iᵛᵃ Sessiya Tsentral'nogo Ispolnitel'nogo Komiteta Soyuza Sovetskikh Sotsialisticheskikh Respublik (1923).

Vtoraya Sessiya Tsentral'nogo Ispolnitel'nogo Komiteta Soyuza Sovetskikh Sotsialisticheskikh Respublik (1924).

III

PROCEEDINGS OF OTHER CONGRESSES AND CONFERENCES

Trudy I Vserossiiskogo S''ezda Sovetov Narodnogo Khozyaistva, 26 *Maya-4 Iyunya,* 1918 *g.: Stenograficheskii Otchet* (1918).

Trudy II Vserossiiskogo S''ezda Sovetov Narodnogo Khozyaistva, 19 *Dekabrya-27 Dekabrya,* 1918 *g.: Stenograficheskii Otchet* (n.d.) [London School of Economics and Political Science].

Rezolyutsii Tret'ego Vserossiiskogo S''ezda Sovetov Narodnogo Khozyaistva (1920). No other record of this congress appears to have been published.

Trudy IV Vserossiiskogo S''ezda Sovetov Narodnogo Khozyaistva, 18 *Maya-24 Maya,* 1921 *g.: Stenograficheskii Otchet* (1921) [London School of Economics and Political Science].

Trudy Konferentsii Sovnarkhozov Severnogo i Zapadnogo Raionov, 26-30 Augusta, 1921 g. (1921).

Trudy Vserossiiskogo S"ezda Zaveduyushchikh Finotdelami (1919) [London School of Economics and Political Science].

Vserossiiskoe Soveshchanie Predstavitelei Raspredelitel'nykh Prodorganov (1920) [London School of Economics and Political Science].

Oktyabr'skaya Revolyutsiya i Fabzavkomy, 2 vols. (1927).

Pervyi Vserossiiskii S"ezd Professional'nykh Soyuzov, 7-14 Yanvarya, 1918 g. (1918).

Vtoroi Vserossiiskii S"ezd Professional'nykh Soyuzov, i (Plenumy) (1921). No second volume appears to have been published.

N . . . skii, *Vtoroi Vserossiiskii S"ezd Professional'nykh Soyuzov* (1919) [International Labour Office, Geneva]. This much abbreviated record is useful as containing the proceedings of the sections as well as of plenary sessions.

Tretii Vserossiiskii S"ezd Professional'nykh Soyuzov, 6 Aprelya-13 Aprelya, 1920 g., i (Plenumy) (1920). No second volume appears to have been published.

Chetvertyi Vserossiiskii S"ezd Professional'nykh Soyuzov, 17-25 Maya, 1921 g., i (Plenumy), ii (Sektsii) (1920) [International Labour Office, Geneva].

Stenograficheskii Otchet Pyatogo Vserossiiskogo S"ezda Professional'nykh Soyuzov, 17-22 Sentyabrya, 1922 g. (1922) [International Labour Office, Geneva].

IV

COLLECTIONS OF LAWS, DECREES, ETC.

Sobranie Uzakonenii i Rasporyazhenii Rabochego i Krest'yanskogo Pravitel'-stva, 1917–1918 [the British Museum copy includes only Nos. 1-51 ; a complete copy is in the Foreign Office Library].

Collections under the same title for 1919, 1920, 1921, 1922, 1923 [London School of Economics and Political Science]. From 1922 onwards a " second section " (*Otdel Vtoroi*) of the *Sobranie* was also issued containing minor decrees and orders [Foreign Office Library]. Decrees in the *Sobranie* all bear the date of original publication ; in some cases this is preceded by the date of the adoption of the decree by the legislative body, generally VTsIK or Sovnarkom. Where this date is given, the decree is referred to in the text of the present work as being of this date ; where only the date of publication is given, this is quoted as the date of the decree. Unfortunately the practice of Soviet and other writers varies, so that the same decree is often referred to by different authorities under different dates.

Sbornik Dekretov i Postanovlenii po Narodnomu Khozyaistvu, 1917–1918 (1918).

Sbornik Dekretov i Postanovlenii po Narodnomu Khozyaistvu, ii (1920) ; iii (1921) [International Labour Office, Geneva].

Sbornik Dekretov, Postanovlenii, Rasporyazhenii i Prikazov po Narodnomu Khozyaistvu, No. 1, October 1922, and monthly thereafter [International Labour Office, Geneva].

Sbornik Dekretov i Rasporyazhenii po Finansam, 1917–1919 (1919) [London School of Economics and Political Science].

Sbornik Dekretov i Rasporyazhenii po Finansam, iv (1921).

Proizvodstvo, Uchet i Raspredelenie Produktov Narodnogo Khozyaistva (n.d. [? 1921]) [International Labour Office, Geneva].

Novaya Ekonomicheskaya Politika v Promyshlennosti : Sbornik Dekretov Postanovlenii i Instruktsii (1921) [London School of Economics and Political Science].

Novoe Zakonodatel'stvo v Oblasti Sel'skogo Khozyaistva : Sbornik Dekretov, Instruktsii i Postanovlenii (1923) [London School of Economics and Political Science].

Politika Sovetskoi Vlasti po Natsional'nomu Voprosu (1920).

Revolyutsiya i Natsional'nyi Vopros : Dokumenty i Materialy, ed. S. M. Dimanshstein, iii (1930) [International Labour Office, Geneva]. No other volumes of this collection appear to have been published.

Istoriya Sovetskoi Konstitutsii v Dekretakh (1936).

Konstitutsii i Konstitutsionnye Akty RSFSR, 1918–1937 (1940) [United States, Library of Congress].

S"ezdy Sovetov RSFSR v Postanovleniyakh i Rezolyutsiyakh (1939).

V

DOCUMENTS ON FOREIGN RELATIONS
(Published by Narkomindel unless otherwise stated)

(i) Treaties and Agreements

RSFSR : Sbornik Deistvuyushchikh Dogovorov, Soglashenii i Konventsii Zaklyuchennykh RSFSR s Inostrannymi Gosudarstvami, i (1921), ii (1921), iii (1922) [Royal Institute of International Affairs], iv (1923) [London Library], v (1923) [London Library].

SSSR : Sbornik Deistvuyushchikh Dogovorov, Soglashenii i Konventsii Zaklyuchennykh s Inostrannymi Gosudarstvami, i–ii (1924).

Klyuchnikov i Sabanin, *Mezhdunarodnaya Politika Noveishego Vremeni v Dogovorakh, Notakh i Deklaratsiyakh*, ii (1926) ; iii, i (1928), ii (1929).

Dokumenty i Materialy po Vneshnei Politike Zakavkaz'ya i Gruzii (published by the Georgian Government) (Tiflis, 1919).

(ii) PROCEEDINGS OF CONFERENCES

Mirnye Peregovory v Brest-Litovske, i (1920) [London Library]. Contains stenographic records of plenary sessions and meetings of the political commission.

Materialy Genuezskoi Konferentsii (1922) [Foreign Office Library].

Gaagskaya Konferentsiya : Polnyi Stenograficheskii Otchet (1922) [Foreign Office Library].

Conférence de Moscou pour la Limitation des Armements (1923).

(iii) DIPLOMATIC CORRESPONDENCE

Correspondance Diplomatique se rapportant aux Relations entre la République Russe et les Puissances de l'Entente, 1918 (1919) [Foreign Office Library].

Krasnaya Kniga : Sbornik Diplomaticheskikh Dokumentov o Russko-Pol'skikh Otnosheniyakh s 1918 po 1920 g. (1920).

La Russie des Soviets et la Pologne (1921). There is also a Russian edition *Sovetskaya Rossiya i Pol'sha* (1921).

L'Ukraine Soviétiste : Receuil des Documents Officiels d'après les Livres Rouges Ukrainiens (Berlin, 1922).

Anglo-Sovetskie Otnosheniya, 1917–1927 : Noty i Dokumenty (1927).

(iv) REPORTS OF NARKOMINDEL

G. Chicherin, *Vneshnyaya Politika Sovetskoi Rossii za dva Goda* (1919).

Otchet Narodnogo Komissariata po Inostrannym Delam Sed'momu S"ezdu Sovetov (1919).

Godovoi Otchet NKID k IX S"ezdu Sovetov (1921).

Desyat' Let Sovetskoi Diplomatii (1927).

VI

THE COMMUNIST INTERNATIONAL

(i) PROCEEDINGS OF CONGRESSES AND OF IKKI

Der I. Kongress der Kommunistischen Internationale : Protokoll der Verhandlungen in Moskau vom 2. bis zum 19. März, 1919 (Hamburg, 1921). The date March 19 appears to be a misprint, since the Congress ended on March 6; by another misprint the dates of the two last sessions (March 4, March 6) are reversed (*ibid.* pp. 148, 170).
      The Russian translation is *Pervyi Kongress Kommunisticheskogo Internatsionala : Protokoly Zasedanii v Moskve so 2 do 19 Marta, 1919* (1921) [United States, Library of Congress].

Der Zweite Kongress der Kommunist. Internationale : Protokoll der Verhandlungen vom 19. Juli in Petrograd und vom 23. Juli bis 7. August, 1920 in Moskau (Hamburg, 1921) [London School of Economics and Political Science].

The Russian translation is *2ᵒⁱ Kongress Kommunisticheskogo Internatsionala : Stenograficheskii Otchet* (1921) ; a later Russian edition, correcting some important errors, is *Vtoroi Kongress Kominterna* (Marx-Engels-Lenin Institute, 1934).

Protokoll des III. Kongresses der Kommunistischen Internationale (Moskau, 22. Juni bis 12. Juli, 1921) (Hamburg, 1921) [London School of Economics and Political Science].

The Russian translation is *Tretii Vsemirnyi Kongress Kommunisticheskogo Internatsionala : Stenograficheskii Otchet* (1922).

Protokoll des Vierten Kongresses der Kommunistischen Internationale Petrograd-Moskau vom 5. November bis 5. Dezember, 1922 (Hamburg, 1923) [Internationaal Instituut voor Sociale Geschiedenis, Amsterdam].

The Russian translation is *IV Kongress Kommunisticheskogo Internatsionala, 5 Noyabrya-5 Dekabrya, 1922 g.* (1923) [Hoover Library, Stanford].

Die Taktik der Kommunistischen Internationale gegen die Offensive des Kapitals : Bericht über die Konferenz der Erweiterten Exekutive der K.I. Feb. 24-März 2, 1922 (Hamburg, 1922) [London School of Economics and Political Science].

Sowjet-Russland und die Völker der Welt : Reden auf der Internationalen Versammlung in Petrograd am 19. Dezember, 1918 (1920).

Iᵛⁱ S"ezd Narodov Vostoka, Baku, 1-8 Sent., 1920 g. : Stenograficheskie Otchety (1920) [Hoover Library, Stanford].

The First Congress of Toilers of the Far East (Moscow, 1922) [London School of Economics and Political Science]. The German version has the title *Der Erste Kongress der Kommunistischen und Revolutionären Organizationen des Fernen Ostens* (1922) [Internationaal Instituut voor Sociale Geschiedenis, Amsterdam].

The Second and Third International and the Vienna Union (n.d.). A record of the meeting in Berlin of April 2-5, 1922, published by the Second International ; no record in Russian seems to have been published.

(ii) RESOLUTIONS AND OFFICIAL JOURNALS

Kommunisticheskii Internatsional v Dokumentakh (1919-1932) (1933).

Kommunisticheskii Internatsional (May 1919-   ) ; there were also German, English and French editions which appeared less regularly and omitted many items, but occasionally contained articles not found in the Russian edition.

Internationale Presse-Korrespondenz (September 1, 1921-   ) ; English and French editions also appeared, but were less full than the German edition. [The London School of Economics and Political Science has an almost complete file from September 1, 1922 ; the Marx Memorial Library has a complete file, lacking only No. 1, from September to December 1921.]

(iii) PROCEEDINGS OF PROFINTERN

*I*ʸⁱ *Mezhdunarodnyi Kongress Revolyutsionnykh Professional'nykh i Proizvodstvennykh Soyuzov : Stenograficheskii Otchet* (n.d.). Contains bulletins, separately paginated, of sessions from July 3 to 19, 1921, and of three meetings of the central council of Profintern, July 20-22, 1921.

Byulleten' II Kongressa Krasnogo Internatsionala Profsoyuzov (n.d.). A much abbreviated record of meetings from November 19-December 2, 1922.

A. Lozovsky, *Desyat' Let Profinterna v Rezolyutsiyakh* (1930).

VII

COLLECTED WORKS

Karl Marx-Friedrich Engels: Historisch-Kritische Gesamtausgabe, Iʳ Teil, i-v (1927–1931), vi-vii (Moscow, 1933–   ) ; IIIʳ Teil, i-iv (1929–1931). No further volumes of this edition have been published.

K. Marx i F. Engels, *Sochineniya,* 29 vols. (1928–   ). [The set in the British Museum has some gaps ; vols. 27-28 which are missing in the British Museum are in the Bodleian Library, Oxford.]

V. I. Lenin, *Sochineniya,* 2nd edition, 31 vols. (1930–1935. This is the most satisfactory edition for general use, containing far more items than the first edition ; the text does not appear to have been altered for ideological reasons. The notes are copious and valuable, though they have been modified to meet the needs of the orthodoxy of the period of publication and must sometimes therefore be treated with caution. This edition also contains valuable supplementary material in the form of party and Soviet documents not always readily available elsewhere.

The first edition in 19 volumes (1924–1925) was edited by Kamenev ; the works were arranged partly in chronological order and partly under subjects. Some of the notes in this edition, omitted or modified in the second edition, are still of value. The third edition was a reprint of the second edition without change.

The fourth edition in 35 volumes (1941–1950) contains many items not included in the second edition, but omits some items and passages for ideological reasons, and should not therefore be used by the serious student except for items not included in the second edition. This edition also omits the notes and other supplementary material contained in the second edition.

Leninskii Sbornik, 45 volumes (1924–   ). This collection, which is still in progress, contains drafts, notes and other material written by Lenin not published in the collected works.

L. Trotsky, *Sochineniya* (1925–1927). This edition was planned in six sections and twenty-one volumes, some of which were issued in two parts. The following volumes were published : i, parts i and ii, iii, parts i and ii, iv, vi, viii, ix, xii, xiii, xv, xx, xxi [School of Slavonic and East European Studies, University of London ; some of the volumes are also in the British Museum].

Of Trotsky's writings not included in this edition the most important for the period covered by the present work are :

Kak Vooruzhalas' Revolyutsiya, 3 vols. (1923–1925).

Istoriya Russkoi Revolyutsii (Berlin), i (1931), ii, parts i and ii (1933).

Moya Zhizn', 2 vols. (Berlin, 1930).

Permanentnaya Revolyutsiya (Berlin, 1930).

Stalinskaya Shkola Falsifikatsii (Berlin, 1932).

The Trotsky archives in the Widener Library at Harvard University contain important unpublished material. L. Trotsky, *The Real Situation in Russia* (n.d. [1928]), contains an English translation of the " opposition platform " submitted to the party central committee in September 1927 by Trotsky and twelve other members ; Trotsky's letter of October 21, 1927, to the bureau of party history ; and Trotsky's speech to the central committee of October 23, 1927. The Russian original of the letter of October 21, 1927 was published in L. Trotsky, *Stalinskaya Shkola Falsifikatsii* (Berlin, 1932), pp. 13-100.

G. Zinoviev, *Sochineniya* (1925–1927). This edition was planned in sixteen volumes of which i-viii, xv, xvi were published.

J. V. Stalin, *Sochineniya* (1946–   ). The thirteen volumes published up to 1952 cover the period down to January 1934. The edition contains all known writings and speeches of Stalin with some not very important exceptions ; short, but significant, omissions occur frequently in the text of items originally published between 1917 and 1927, which should therefore always be checked with the originals.

VIII

COLLECTIONS OF ARTICLES

O Zemle, i (Narkomzem, 1921) [London School of Economics and Political Science] ; ii (Narkomzem, 1922).

Chetyre Goda Prodovol'stvennoi Raboty (Narkomprod, 1922).

Za Pyat' Let (Tsentral'nyi Komitet Rossiiskoi Kommunisticheskoi Partii (Bol'shevikov), 1922) [London School of Economics and Political Science].

Pyat' Let Vlasti Sovetov (VTsIK, 1922) [London Library].
Na Novykh Putyakh, 5 vols. (STO, 1923) [International Labour Office, Geneva].

IX

NEWSPAPERS AND PERIODICALS

Files of all the newspapers and periodicals here listed, with the two exceptions noted, are in the British Museum. But the files of the newspapers are always incomplete, and sometimes only fragmentary, for the earlier years : they can occasionally be supplemented from other British libraries. The files in the United States Library of Congress, the New York Public Library and the Hoover Library, Stanford, are generally fuller, but also often defective for these years.

Pravda. The daily organ of the central committee of the Russian Communist Party, founded on April 22, 1912.
Izvestiya. Daily : founded on February 28, 1917, as *Izvestiya Petrogradskogo Soveta Rabochikh Deputatov* ; on March 2, 1917 the words *i Soldatskikh* were added after *Rabochikh*, and on August 1, 1917, it became *Izvestiya Tsentral'nogo Komiteta Sovetov i Petrogradskogo Soveta Rabochikh i Soldatskikh Deputatov* ; on September 29, 1917, the Petrograd Soviet was dropped from the title, but reappeared on October 27. Later changes followed the official nomenclature of the Soviets.
Ekonomicheskaya Zhizn'. Daily : founded in 1921 as the joint organ of Vesenkha and of the People's Commissariats for economic affairs,. later the organ of Narkomfin and Gosplan.
Trud. Daily : founded in 1921 as the organ of the All-Russian Central Council of Trade Unions [International Labour Office, Geneva].
Narodnoe Khozyaistvo. Fortnightly, then monthly, then irregular : founded in 1918 as the organ of Vesenkha.
Izvestiya Tsentral'nogo Komiteta Rossiiskoi Kommunisticheskoi Partii (Bol'shevikov). Irregular : founded in 1919 as the organ of the party central committee.
Zhizn' Natsional'nostei. Weekly, then irregular : founded in 1918 as the organ of Narkomnats.
Vestnik Truda. Monthly : founded in 1920 as the organ of the All-Russian Council of Trade Unions.
Sotsialisticheskii Vestnik (Berlin). Twice monthly ; founded in 1921 by a group of Menshevik émigrés [Bibliothèque de Documentation Internationale Contemporaine, Université de Paris].
Proletarskaya Revolyutsiya. Quarterly : founded in 1921 as the organ of Istpart, later incorporated in the Marx-Engels-Lenin Institute.

Novyi Vostok. Irregular : founded in 1922 as the organ of the All-Russian Scientific Association for Oriental Learning attached to Narkomnats.

Arkhiv Russkoi Revolyutsii (Berlin). Irregular : founded in 1922 by a group of Russian *émigrés.*

INDEX

(Capital roman numerals indicate volume numbers)

Abkhazia, I, 349-350, 394 n.
Abramovich, R., III, 408
Adler, V., III, 408
Adygeisk, I, 394 n.
Afghanistan, III, 237-240, 290-292, 468-469
Agrarian policy: party controversies on, II, 16-20, 147-148, 170-171 ; Tsarist, II, 20-23; and February revolution, II, 28-34, 115-116 ; and October revolution, II, 34-55 ; and " decree on land ", II, 39-41 ; and law on socialization of land, II, 45-46; and food supplies, II, 49-53; and " committees of poor peasants ", II, 53-55, 147, 154, 157-159, 160 n., 161; and beginning of war communism, II, 147; and food requisition, II, 148-150, 165, 167, 169, 227-228, 234, 249, 258 n., 271 ; and food detachments, II, 148-149; and taxation in kind, II, 150, 280-282, 286-287, 332, 334, 354-356; and collective cultivation, II, 151-156, 165-166, 168, 287, 289-290; decree of February 1919 on, II, 154-155 ; and Soviet farms, II, 155-156; and middle peasants, II, 161-165; and size of holdings, II, 167-169; and " sowing committees ", II, 171-172, 283; last phase of war communism in, II, 170-173 ; and beginning of NEP, II, 280 ; and freedom of trade, II, 282 ; institutions of, under NEP, II, 283; and 1921 famine, II, 284-286 ; and incentives, II, 286 ; and land tenure, II, 287-289; legislation relating to, under NEP, II, 288-289, 296 ; and law on exploitation of land, II, 289 ; criticism of, under NEP, II, 291-293 ; and effect of NEP, II, 294-295 ; and " Scissors crisis ", II,

297. *See also* Kulaks, Land tenure, Peasantry
Agrarian redistribution : methods of, II, 46-48 ; statistics of, II, 167-169
Ajaria, I, 350, 394 n.
Akimov, V., I, 26, 28, 30
Aland Islands, III, 157-158, 347-348
Albert, *pseud.*, *see* Eberlein, H.
Allen, Clifford, III, 184
All-German Congress of Workers' and Soldiers' Councils, III, 100-101, 103, 132-133
All-Russian Central Executive Committee of Soviets (VTsIK) : composition of, I, 90 ; changes in membership of, I, 111 ; and Constituent Assembly, I, 117, 120 ; and Constitution of RSFSR, I, 125-126, 132-134, 144, 146-148 ; powers of, I, 214-215 ; presidium of, I, 215-216, 221 n. ; and Sovnarkom, I, 215-216
All-Russian Committee for Aid to the Hungry, I, 178, II, 284, III, 341
All-Russian Congress of Muslim Communist Organizations, I, 317, 319, III, 234, 236, 493
All-Russian Congress of Peasants' Deputies, I, 110, 116, 143-144, II, 31, III, 11
All-Russian Congress of Soviets : first : and national self-determination, I, 71, 262 n. ; composition of, I, 89 ; second : and October revolution, I, 99-106 ; and abolition of death penalty, I, 153, 156, 163 ; and " workers' control ", II, 394-395 ; and decree on peace, III, 9 ; third : and Constituent Assembly, I, 116, 121 ; and local Soviets, I, 132 ; and constitution of RSFSR, I, 138, 140, 149; fourth : and economic policy, II, 85 ; and ratifica-

610 INDEX

Sverdlov, Y., I, 91, 96, 98, 118, 121, 125, 147 n., 163 n., 194, 215, II, 48, 164, III, 38, 40, 45, 72
Swiss Socialist Party, III, 166, 184, 565
Syndicalists, I, 238, III, 459-461

Tabouis, General, I, 296, 300
Tajikistan, Tajiks, I, 330
Talaat Pasha, III, 246, 313
Tanner, J., III, 208
Tannu Tuva, III, 520
Tarnow, F., III, 222 n.
Tasca, A., III, 141
Tatar-Bashkir republic, I, 320-321
Tatars, I, 311-322, 326, 393 n.
Taxation : early policy, II, 144-142 ; and system of " contributions ", II, 142-145 ; and central control, II, 142-144, 250-252, 347-348; and Left communists, II, 145-146 ; in kind, II, 150, 246-247, 249, 280-282, 286-287, 297, 332, 334, 354-356 ; " extraordinary revolutionary tax ", II, 246-248, 250 ; and middle peasants, II, 248-249 ; and kulaks, II, 249 ; and nationalized enterprises, II, 251 ; monetary, abolition of, II, 260, 347 ; of industry, II, 347 ; monetary, return to, II, 354-355 ; and poll-tax, II, 354 ; and income-tax, II, 354-355
Television, forecast, II, 378 n.
Teodorovich, I., II, 171
Terek region, I, 327-328
Thalheimer, A., III, 103, 335, 452
Thomas, Albert, III, 22, 169
Thornas, J. H., III, 462
Thomas (German communist), III, 73, 133 n., 135
Thomsen, General von, III, 364
Tikhon, V., I, 153 n.
Tkachev, P., II, 388
Togliatti, P., III, 141
Tokuda, K., III, 526
Tolain, H., III, 552
Tomsky, M., I, 195, 204 n., 338 n., 369, II, 104 n., 108, 114, 190, 194-195, 202, 209, 211, 212 n., 219, 221, 223-224, 324-327, 329-331, III, 204 n.
Trade, Foreign : interrupted by October revolution, II, 126 ; state monopoly of, II, 126-130, III, 463-466 ; and allied blockade, II, 126-

127, 244 ; III, 114-115, 149-151, 155-156, 279, 307 ; and Brest-Litovsk, II, 128-129 ; and foreign concessions, II, 130-131, 245 ; under war communism, II, 244-245, 257 ; and trade delegations, II, 245, III, 161-163, 351 ; and mixed companies, III, 351-352 ; and Genoa conference, III, 360-361 ; statistics of, III, 434-435 ; and NEP, III, 473. See also Concessions, Foreign ; RSFSR, relations with : Afghanistan, etc. ; RSFSR, treaties and agreements with : Afghanistan etc.
Trade, Internal see Distribution
Trade unions : and Rabkrin, I, 226 ; relation to party, I, 230, II, 323-328 ; centralizing influence of, I, 369-370 ; and workers' control, II, 62-64, 67-68, 73, 102-104, 106-107 ; First All-Russian Conference ot, II, 62 ; All-Russian Central Council of, II, 62 ; First All-Russian Congress of, II, 73, III, 204 ; and October revolution, II, 63, 104 ; before 1917, II, 100-104 ; and February revolution, II, 102 ; and Soviets, II, 102-103 ; and labour policy, II, 104, 108, 115, 204 ; and state, II, 105-107, 198, 200-202 ; and factory committees, II, 106-107, 115 ; and economic organization, II, 106-107, 114 ; and labour discipline, II, 110, 214-216, 226, 318 ; and productivity, II, 114-115, 329-330 ; organization and membership of, II, 180, 204-205, 325-326, 328 ; and one-man management, II, 190-191 ; and labour mobilization, II, 198, 206-207, 209, 213-214 ; and collective agreements, II, 198-199, 321, 327, 330 ; and People's Commissariat of Labour, II, 201, 225 ; and strikes, II, 202, 327-329 ; under war communism, II, 205-206, 219-227 ; and transport, II, 219-222 ; and bonus system, II, 226 ; and rural industries, II, 298 ; and heavy industry, II, 315-316, 319 ; under NEP, II, 323, 325-330 ; and social insurance, II, 328-329 ; and foreign concessions, III, 284 n. See also International Council of Trade Unions ; Labour policy ; Red International of Trade Unions